Over the centuries the Gregorian University Consortium has been a bulwark in the Church for learning and Catholic orthodoxy. We fully intend to carry on this role in support of the Holy Father, the magisterium and the bishops throughout the world in educating leaders for the Church. These volumes of *Vatican II: Assessment and Perspectives* are a gift from the Trustees of the Gregorian University Foundation to the American bishops in gratitude for their interest and support.

These volumes honor in a special way the memory of Albert and Anna Eckhardt.

The Gregorian University
Foundation
106 West 56th Street
New York, New York 10019

The Gregorian University
Foundation
3601 Lindell Boulevard
St. Louis, Missouri 63108

VATICAN II
Assessment
and Perspectives

VATICAN II
Assessment
and Perspectives

Twenty-five Years After
(1962–1987)

VOLUME THREE

Edited by RENÉ LATOURELLE

PAULIST PRESS/ NEW YORK/ MAHWAH

The publication of this project has been helped immensely by generous gifts from trustees of the Gregorian University Foundation and other friends. Specific contributions were made by Mr. John Brogan, Mr. and Mrs. Cyril Nigg, and Mr. and Mrs. John T. Ryan, Jr. To them and all others whose assistance made possible this publication—in French, German, and Italian as well as English—warmest thanks from the writer and editor.

Library of Congress Cataloging-in-Publication Data

Vatican II: Assessment and perspectives: twenty-five years after
      (1962–1987)/edited by René Latourelle.
          p.   cm.
      Contents: Chiefly English translations of works originally written
   in French, German, Italian, Latin, or Spanish.
      Includes bibliographies.
      1. Vatican Council (2nd: 1962–1965).   2. Catholic Church—
   Doctrines—History—20th century.   3. Catholic Church—
   History—20th century.   I. Latourelle, René.
   II. Vatican 2.
      BX830   1962.V322   1988   262'.52   87-35972
      ISBN 0-8091-0412-1 (v. 1)
      ISBN 0-8091-0413-x (v. 2)
      ISBN 0-8091-0414-8 (v. 3)

Published by Paulist Press
997 Macarthur Blvd.
Mahwah, NJ 07430

Printed and bound in the
United States of America

A Note on the English Translation

Except where the author of a given article is making his own translation (in which case the English translation is based on this), or in quotations found in already published English translations of works cited by the various authors, the translation of the Holy Scriptures used is *The Holy Bible,* Revised Standard Version, Catholic Edition (London: Catholic Truth Society, 1966). However, in some cases, the Jerusalem Bible and the New American Bible have been consulted.

Except where the author of a given article is making his own translation (in which case the English translation is based on this), the translation of the Council documents used is that found in A. Flannery (gen. ed.), *Vatican Council II: The Conciliar and Post Conciliar Documents* (Collegeville, MN: Liturgical Press, revised edition 1984). However, on some occasions, the translation found in W.M. Abbott (gen. ed.), *The Documents of Vatican II* (New York: Guild Press, 1966), has been consulted.

Except where the author of a given article is making his own translation (in which case the English translation is based on this), the translation of the 1983 Code of Canon Law used is that produced by the Canon Law Society of America (Washington, DC, 1983). However, on some occasions, the translation produced by the Canon Law Society of Great Britain and Ireland (London, 1983) has also been consulted.

Works quoted in the text of articles: If an already published English translation could be found, this has been used—as will be seen from the relative notes. However, if no English translation could be found, the present translators translated such quotations from the original-language version of the works in question—again, as will be seen from the relative notes.

Works quoted in notes: All such quotations have been left in the original language, and have not been translated into English.

Apart from the various people whose names appear at the end of the different articles as translators or cotranslators, the following have assisted with library research and/or advice: Philip Gillespie and Father Robert Hagan, S.J.

Leslie Wearne

Acknowledgments

The English edition of the present work has been made possible thanks to the generosity and large-scale contributions of a group of benefactors in the United States and Canada. We wish to express our deep gratitude to all these persons.

We should also like to address our sincere thanks to Miss Leslie Wearne, who is responsible for coordinating the English translation, and also to the whole team of translators.

René Latourelle, S.J.
Editor

Abbreviations

1. Abbreviations of the books of the Bible are those used in A. Flannery (gen. ed.), *Vatican Council II: The Conciliar and Post Conciliar Documents*.

2. *Abbreviations of Council Documents:*

AA   *Apostolicam actuositatem*, Decree on the Apostolate of the Laity

AG   *Ad gentes*, Decree on the Missionary Activity of the Church

CD   *Christus Dominus*, Decree on the Pastoral Office of Bishops in the Church

DH   *Dignitatis humanae*, Declaration on Religious Freedom

DV   *Dei Verbum*, Dogmatic Constitution on Divine Revelation

GE   *Gravissimum educationis*, Declaration on Christian Education

GS   *Gaudium et spes*, Pastoral Constitution on the Church in the Modern World

IM   *Inter mirifica*, Decree on the Means of Social Communication

LG   *Lumen gentium*, Dogmatic Constitution on the Church

NA   *Nostra aetate*, Declaration on the Relation of the Church to Nonchristian Religions

OE   *Orientalium Ecclesiarum*, Decree on the Catholic Eastern Churches

OT	*Optatam totius*, Decree on the Training of Priests
PC	*Perfectae caritatis*, Decree on the Up-to-Date Renewal of Religious Life
PO	*Presbyterorum ordinis*, Decree on the Ministry and Life of Priests
SC	*Sacrosanctam concilium*, Constitution on the Sacred Liturgy
UR	*Unitatis redintegratio*, Decree on Ecumenism

3. *Other abbreviations:*

AAS	*Acta Apostolicae Sedis* (Rome, 1909–)
AS	*Acta Synodalia S. Concilii Oecumenici Vaticani II*, 26 vols. (Vatican City, 1970–1980)
ASS	*Acta Sanctae Sedis* (Rome, 1865–1908)
CIC	*Codex Juris Canonici* (The Code of Canon Law)
DS	H. Denzinger and A. Schönmetzter, *Enchiridion Symbolorum, Definitionum et Declarationum de rebus fidei et morum* (Freiburg im Breisgau, 1965)
Mansi	J.D. Mansi, *Sacrorum Conciliorum nova et amplissima collectio* (Florence, 1759)
PG	*Patrologia Graeca*, ed. J.P. Migne (Paris, 1857–1866)
PL	*Patrologia Latina*, ed. J.P. Migne (Paris, 1844–1855)

Apart from this, the authors of certain articles use a system of abbreviations generally accepted in their specific fields of study when citing specialized publications dealing with their own disciplines.

Contents

PART VIII

PART IX

PART VII

THE CONSECRATED LIFE

CHAPTER 42

Consecrated Life and the Charisms of the Founders

Manuel Ruiz Jurado, S.J.

Summary

The title itself points to the development of teaching on the charisms of the founders, as put forward in Chapter VI of *Lumen gentium* and in the Decree *Perfectae caritatis*. The exemplary and normative role that the charismatic character of the founders has played in the Church seems to have been the kernel of the Council's teaching. In the ensuing years, it was developed in the official documents of the Church and in the writings of the theologians and canonists. These contributions revolve around three major questions: the relationship between the founders and their institutes, the meaning of the term "charism" when applied to consecrated life, and the meaning of the expression "charism of an institute." This chapter considers some general ideas on the grace of vocation and enumerates a few problems related to it.

———

———

Until now few themes of the Council have remained more topical than this one, which serves as an introduction to Part VII of the present work. Few theological texts of the Council have found such a strong reverberation in the Church. An abundant literature has emerged to nourish the seeds that the Council had sown in its teaching concerning the relationship of the charism of the founder and consecrated life.

At the start, it should be stated that one cannot find in the

official text of the declarations, decrees, or constitutions of the
Council the term "charism" as applied to the founders of institutes of consecrated life. Moreover, the expression "institutes of
consecrated life" is not used in these documents with reference to
our subject. This fact gives us some idea of the ground gained
between the publication of the texts of the Council and that of
the actual Code of Canon Law (1983) and the Apostolic Exhortation *Redemptionis donum* of 25 March 1984.

Book II of the new Code, dedicated to the people of God,
includes three parts: the first deals with the faithful, the second
with the hierarchical structure of the Church, and the third with
the institutes of consecrated life and the societies of apostolic
life. This structuring reflects the new perspective on the Church
that was clarified in the light of the teaching of *Lumen gentium*,
especially in the last paragraph of number 43 and in number 44.
In referring to the religious state, a distinction is made between
the laity and the clergy, so that all the faithful, whatever be the
state to which they belong, may be called to join those families
that form the religious state of life (No. 43), and that the latter
"although constituted by the profession of the evangelical counsels does not belong to the hierarchical structure of the Church,
nevertheless belongs inseparably to her life and holiness."

The new Code groups under the designation "institutes of
consecrated life" the religious and the secular institutes, since
both are committed to the practice of the evangelical counsels.
And in the third part of Book II, the Code treats the societies of
apostolic life, because it considers them to be similar to the
institutes of consecrated life (Canon 731).

Although in this chapter we are concerned with the whole
sphere of "consecrated life," which is characterized by the institutionalized practice of the evangelical counsels, special attention
is given to the institutes of religious life. With regard to the
charismatic character (*peculiari dono*: Canon 574) and its relationship to the founders, the teaching can be applied to all these
types of consecrated life, as is indicated in Title I of Section I:
"Norms common to all institutes of consecrated life," which
corresponds to the third part of Book II (Canons 573–606).

In *Redemptionis donum*, John Paul II speaks of the special gift of
religious life, which he calls a "charism," and places among "the
great universal community *of vocations and charisms* of all God's
people" (No. 15).

In Chapter VI, *De religiosis* of *Lumen gentium* (*LG*), religious are said to represent a state of life that essentially consists in the profession of the evangelical counsels. And it is declared that precisely by promising to practice them, the faithful "are more intimately consecrated to divine service" (No. 44).[1] In what follows, the terms employed by the Council are related to our subject, so as to help us to better understand the developments in the subsequent documents of the Church, and in the writings of the postconciliar theologians. In conclusion, I will provide my opinion on the present situation of the problematic and on certain points that remain open to theological debate.

The Problematic and Doctrine of the Council

Our subject concerns the teaching on religious life found both in the Dogmatic Constitution on the Church, *Lumen gentium* (*LG*), and in the Decree on the Up-to-Date Renewal of Religious Life, *Perfectae caritatis* (*PC*). Since our subject concentrates on the doctrinal principles that should direct the renewal of religious life, it is thus linked especially to Chapter VI of *Lumen gentium* and to the first three numbers of *Perfectae caritatis*.

An account of the finalizing of the two documents shows their mutual relationship within the Council itself. When they were drawn up during the preparatory stage, the titles of the two documents were rather theologico-canonical: *De statibus perfectionis acquirendae* (1962–1963), which later became *De accomodata renovatione vitae religiosae;* and *De statibus evangelicae acquirendae perfectionis* (1962), which became Chapter VI, *De religiosis*, of *Lumen gentium*. The second of these documents, after its rewriting in March 1963, was entitled *De iis qui consilia evangelica profitentur* and was presented as Chapter IV of the Dogmatic Constitution on the Church. These changes of title and positioning exert a great influence on the 1983 Code of Canon Law.

We know that in May 1963, it was decided not to dedicate a special chapter to religious, but to include them in the general chapter *De vocatione ad sanctitatem in Ecclesia*. The remarks about the project submitted by the Fathers of the Council in more than 500 pages and the documents signed by 679 Fathers and handed over to the doctrinal Commission by Paul VI himself launched a process that eventually divided the chapter on holiness into two parts, and definitively separated Chapter VI, *De religiosis*, from Chapter V, "The Call of the Whole Church to holiness."[2]

The Decree on the Up-to-Date Renewal of Religious Life went through a similar development. The constitutional outline *De statibus perfectionis acquirendae* became an outline of propositions *De religiosis*, when brought up for discussion in session 119 (1964). And it then became the decree *De accomodata renovatione vitae religiosae.*[3]

The changing of titles and the dividing of the chapters are indicative of the underlying problematic. According to many Fathers of the Council, the theoretical place that religious life enjoys within the Church became clear little by little. We must not forget that for the first time in history, the theme of religious life as a particular state in the Church was being systematically treated in a council.

Leaving aside other aspects that do not directly concern our subject, we can note that in the first attempts at systematizing the teaching, the prevailing *ecclesiological viewpoint* induces us to recognize in religious life, characterized by the profession of the evangelical counsels, an effect of the initiative of the Holy Spirit; divine Love allows men and women to feel called to consecrate themselves totally to evangelical perfection. Those who are called seem to gather into families due to the galvanizing power of these men and women, who are particularly endowed by the Spirit to propose new ways of life and service in the Church.[4]

Already in Chapter V of the first schema, *De Ecclesia et de Beata Maria Virgine* (1962), we can observe that the theme *De statibus evangelicae acquirendae perfectionis* has an ecclesiological structure. Two of its three numbers deal with "the importance" and "the place" of these states in the Church: ". . . ut eodem Spiritu Christi impellente, paulatim ex germine divinitus dato variae vivendi formae ad illam perfectionem assequendam exortae sint veluti arbor mirabiliter in vinea Domini ramificata."[5]

Nevertheless, in 1963, the conference of the Dutch bishops expressed the opinion that in Chapter V more importance was given to the practical organization of evangelical perfection in religious institutions than to their ecclesiological character; thus, they articulated the dual charismatic and institutional character that we must recognize in it. Otherwise, they said, "the charismatic character of evangelical perfection is less brought to light, and, on the other hand, the meaning of its institutional character for a given society is more enhanced."[6]

In the corresponding schema, reference to founders was explicit: the divine origin of religious life was attributed to the inspirations granted to founders by the Holy Spirit and recognized by the authority of the Church: "Provida Mater Ecclesia, motiones Sancti Spiritus assidue secundans, leges pro summa auctoritate ipsa tulit vel ab eminentibus viris ac feminis ipsa probavit, quarum sectatores statum perfectionis acquirendae constituerint."[7]

In the scheme of 22 April 1963, De statibus perfectionis acquirendae, it is stated that there are in the Church men and women who enter upon a life consonant with the evangelical counsels so as to follow Christ more closely, and that the Church constantly encouraged this life of evangelical perfection among those who seek it in its solitary form, as well as among those who have gathered into approved societies. After describing the place of religious life in the Church, Chapter I enunciates the basic criteria for its desired renewal: "Fundatorum propositum ac germanum spiritum, prout ab Ecclesia approbatum necnon venerabiles traditiones in singulis institutis receptas, ducente magisterio Sanctae Matris Ecclesiae" (No. 12).[8]

The theological and ecclesiological aspects of life in conformity with the evangelical counsels were more detailed in what was to become Chapter VI of the constitution De Ecclesia; these criteria were presented on 15 September 1964 at session 80 of the Council. This life was described as a "donum divinum quod Ecclesia a Domino suo accepit et gratia ejus semper conservat" (No. 43). Furthermore, the increase of charity to which the evangelical counsels lead was duly emphasized, and, consequently, the special union they create between the religious and the mystery of the Church, hence, the necessity of granting the spiritual life of religious as ecclesial orientation. According to their vocation, "sive oratione, sive actuosa quoque opera," they shall devote themselves to implanting the kingdom more and more in souls and to strengthening it throughout the world. Because of this intimate participation of religious in the mystery of the Church, it is an important concern "to defend and promote the distinctive character of the various religious institutions."[9]

The postulates presented by 679 Fathers proved to be effective, although the terms "charism" or "charismatic" did not appear in the definitive text approved in the public session of 21

November 1964. In the amended schema, it was declared more explicitly than before that the variety of religious families represents a *gift for the good of the Church:* "Quo factum est ut, quasi in arbore ex germine divinitus dato . . . variae formae vitae solitariae vel communis, variaeque familiae creverint, quae tum ad profectum sodalium, tum ad bonum totius Corporis Christi opes augent" (No. 43). It would be easy to point out the parallel between this text and the description of charisms we read in St Paul.[10]

During the discussion of the text *De accomodata renovatione vitae religiosae* on 11 November 1964, various interventions enhanced the *charismatic character* of religious life in the Church. Cardinal Doeffner affirmed that the epithet "charismatic" is proper to religious: "Etiam hodie Ecclesia opus habet impulsu et vigore religiosorum vere charismaticorum."[11] According to him, the Council had to deal not only with the adaptation of religious life to the needs of our time, but also with the renewal of religious. In connection with the latter, he noted in particular that in many institutes of women, attached to certain forms of piety of the last century, there was a need to return to basics: to Scripture, liturgy, and the great masters of spiritual life and genuine spiritual theology. This intervention afforded the Council Fathers the opportunity to speak of revitalizing contact with the founders.

Cardinal Bea did not miss the opportunity; his motion subsequently oriented the evolution of ideas, because he called for a new, more vital text. Religious life, he said, is the result of charismatic gifts that the Spirit has bestowed on founders. The use of these gifts has an ecclesial meaning: it aims to reflect the image of Christ more perfectly in the Church. Moreover, he did not fail to conjoin the charisms of the founders to those of their followers: "Fundatores sua dona charismatica habuerunt et assec-lis et filiis suis quodammodo transmittentes, ea perpetua in Ecclesia tradiderunt. . . ."[12] He added that each institute has to preserve faithfully gifts and reactivate them into life by putting them into practice, according to the possibilities and needs of the times, "non aspirantes ad alia, quae ab ipsorum proprio spiritu aliena sunt, neque iis qui aliam viam sequuntur invidentes aut detrahentes."[13]

Others also stressed the charismatic character of religious institutes: Cardinal Barros Camara, on behalf of the 103 bishops of

Brazil; Cardinal Silva Enriquez; Bishop Odo de Wilde; and the general of the Discalced Carmelites on behalf of 185 Fathers of the Council.

The latter pointed out that the spirit of the founders must also serve to maintain and renew the apostolate proper to each institute. Drawing attention to the respect that the Council had shown for the charisms of all the faithful, they claimed that the same respect should be extended to the charisms of religious that were recognized as authentic owing to both the saintliness of the founders and the repeated approval of the Church.[14]

Cardinal Silva Enriques encouraged a more profound treatment of the teaching by distinguishing two aspects of the charism of founders: the inner dynamism that "the spirit of the founder" comprises and the outward form that this dynamism assumes. Accordingly, preservation of the charism concerns faithfulness to the founder's spirit; and its renewal concerns turning aside from forms of the apostolate that are unfaithful to the founder's mission in the Church.[15]

In connection with our subject, the written communication of Monsignor Odo de Wilde, bishop of Niangara, is particularly significant, since it relates the charism itself to its institutionalization. The inspiration of the founders becomes established in the Church, as soon as it is approved. As long as their spirit perdures, the institutes readily distinguish the transitory from the permanent, and determine the activities consonant with the charism of the founder and are responsive to the needs of each epoch. Thus, the constitutions and rules of each institute must be institutionalized, so that its particular charism remains sound, efficacious, and vital.[16]

The Definitive Texts

The definitive text of Chapter VI, *De religiosis*, of *Lumen gentium* proclaimed the special consecration to Christ and the particular union with the life of the Church that religious express through the profession of the evangelical counsels; it also recognized the Spirit-inspired role in upbuilding the Body of Christ that both the rules (Nos. 43 and 45) and the apostolates "of all these saintly founders" have (No. 46).

The first number of the Decree *Perfectae caritatis* develops the same teaching by enriching it with biblical texts so that the profession of the evangelical counsels is shown to presuppose that Christ is being followed in a special way. Thus, not only the ecclesial fact of religious life, but also its charismatic-ecclesiological nature finds its root in the gospel, even though the term "charism" is not mentioned. The link with the founders is explicit, insofar as the various religious families existing in the Church find in them their charismatic origin. The normative role that the founders have is attributed to the example and the patrimony they bequeathed their followers and the distinctive spirit and goal they provided their institutes. The founders are sources of the sound traditions with which their patrimony was enriched after their ripetime. These traditions are constantly revitalized, if they are impregnated with the spirit of the founder who discerned a particular aspect of Christ, the supreme model on which we must always rely.

The seeds of the teaching concerning the charism of the founders were thus planted. The problematic had come to light in the interventions of some Fathers of the Council. By developing this teaching and illuminating, the problematic aspects were the tasks of the later documents of the magisterium and subsequent efforts of theologians.

Postconciliar Doctrine of the Magisterium

The motu proprio *Ecclesiae sanctae* of 1966 emphasized the distinctive character of each institute, so as to guide the renewal of consecrated life according to the intentions and principles set forth by the Council. Each general chapter was to revise the legislative texts of its institute, according to the spirit and intentions of the founder. Should the renewed texts not conform to the spirit of the founder, this would mean that the distinctive character of the institute has not been respected. God's design for an institute constitutes its own identity, or its vocation.[17] And God's design expressed itself both in the purpose given to it by the founder enlightened by the Spirit and in the ecclesial recognition granted to the institute. The Instruction *Renovationis causam* applies these principles especially to the spiritual formation characteristic of each institute, which must be guided by *the spirit and intentions of the founder* concerning it. Paul VI frequently repeats in his speeches to religious the theme that the loyalty of each institute to the Church presupposes loyalty to its founder. He told the Cistercians "that the required adaptation to the conditions of the times, in accordance with *Perfectae caritatis* cannot be achieved without rediscovering the original character-istic of the institute and putting them into practice."[18] Accord-ing to this guiding principle, once the original characteristics of an institute have been renewed, they should be further en-hanced. Those who are responsible for the renewal can resort to these historical and practical criteria.

From the doctrinal point of view, the Apostolic Exhortation *Evangelica testificatio* of 1971 implies that the concepts set out during the discussions of the Council are now integrated into the teaching of the magisterium. For the first time in a magisterial statement, the notion "charism of the founders" appears.[19] The Council had it in mind when, referring to founders, it said: "those whom God has raised up in his Church" (No. 11). And again, the Council considered the charisms of the founders when it indicated as a principle of renewal, *the spirit of the founders, their evangelical intentions, and their examples of saintliness* (LG 45, PC 2b).

It is precisely when the exhortation also employs the expres-sion "charisma vitae religiosae" that this phrase can be under-stood to mean "the charism of the founder of a peculiar form of religious life," since it is said regarding this gift: "Nedum impulsus quidam sit exortus *ex sanguinibus vel ex voluntate carnis* aut ex habitu mentis qui *huic saeculo conformatur*, fructus est Spiritus Sancti, in Ecclesia semper operantis."[20]

One can similarly interpret the expression used when allusion is later made to the various forms of life that were introduced "cha-rismatibus cujusque Instituti adhaerens"[21]; although the term "charism" here applies directly to the institute, I do not think that it was intended to settle the question whether the term "charism," which sometimes refers to the founder and sometimes to the insti-tute, is univocal or not.

In 1972, when Paul VI explained to the Salesians that the identity of their institute has its root in their founder, he re-minded them of the teaching and example of Don Bosco, and of the peculiar character he wanted to give to the Salesian Insti-tute.[22] And, in 1974, he explained to the Dominicans that the "carisma cujusvis Ordinis proprium," being a pact between God, the founder, and his followers, is a gift to which the institute must be loyal.[23]

Again, we confront the problem concerning the meaning of "charism," a term attributable both to the founder, and to the institute and its members. The problem is of consequence: if "charism" can be attributed to the founder in the same sense as to the institute and its members, this possibility would imply that the institute itself enjoys a permanent characteristic, almost a guarantee that it is inspired. Yet, it is clear that the institute and its members could wander from the way marked out by the founder. There is the danger that they would not have to turn their eyes toward their founder, but only toward themselves so as to determine the future. This problem concerns whether the character of the charism is more or less static or dynamic. However that may be, Paul VI, in presenting the charism as a divine pact, does not suppose that future loyalty is certain, but mentions the need always to remain loyal to the terms and clauses of the pact.

The official document that has provided a more detailed teaching on our topic is contained in the guiding notes *Mutuae relationes,* published in 1978 with the approval of Paul VI. Since then, it has been declared by John Paul II to be the magna carta of the relationship between bishops and religious in the Church.[24]

Interesting details of the Council's teaching on the consecrated life and on the charism of the founders can be found especially in Chapter 3. There it is stated that religious life, as a particular gift of the Spirit to the Church, enjoys a unique share in the sacramental nature of the Church. The consecration and testimony of religious tend to make visible certain aspects of the mystery of Christ (No. 10). And the variety that emerges from the distinctive character of each institute comprises a gift made to the Church through religious founders; and this gift is authenticated by the hierarchy of the Church (No. 11).

Mutuae relationes fully adopts the designation "charism of founders" from *Evangelica testificatio,* but it does not apply the term to the institute. To the latter are attributed "the identity," "the specific charismatic note" (12), "the peculiar feature" (13 and 14), the special "purpose" ("propositum," 13), "the particular spirit and special mission" (14), everything concerning "the loyalty to the charism of the founder," so that it retains its vitality, actuality, and authenticity. The charism of the founders is described as an "experience of the Spirit," passed on to their followers in order that they model their lives on it, preserve, deepen, and develop it, so as constantly to enlarge Christ's body (11).

This "experience of the Spirit," which is distinctive of the founders, produces a particular style of holiness and apostolate: it is handed down in their institute, represents their distinctive qualities, and can be identified by the objective elements that constitute it. The Church is interested in preserving the character or identity proper to each institute. For its part, an institute must insert itself into the Church through its vital activities, not in a vague, ambiguous, or undefined way, but in conformity with the distinctive character (11) handed down by its founder.

The *loyalty of the institute* to its distinctive character, according to *Mutuae relationes*, obliges it to prove itself consistent with it, even though attention must be paid to the particular gifts that some individuals in the institute might possess (12). To act differently would be to induce the Spirit to contradict himself. The recognition and good use of such personal charisms presuppose that they have been found to be in accord with the communal aspect of the institute, with legitimate authority, and with the needs of the Church.

The charism exempts neither the founder nor his followers from constantly reappraising their loyalty to God; on the contrary, it demands that they manifest docility to the Spirit. In other respects, the genuine nature of a special charism is usually revealed through the trials that the charismatic religious encounters, sometimes at the hands of the members of the institute or at those of the leaders of the Church, when they are confronted with the novelty of what he proposes. *Mutuae relationes* posits an historical link between the charism in question and the cross of Christ; the latter can detect the sincerity of the former through the practice of humility, obedience, and constant serenity amidst adversities (12).

It is further stated that formation in the spirit and mission proper to each institute demands that it be truly autonomous; yet, since the priestly offices of teaching, sanctifying, and guiding are dependent on the hierarchy of the Church and stipulated by the common law, the constitutions and rules proper to clerical institutes are to be duly adjusted. The new canon law has fully elaborated on this type of adjustment.[25]

In his Apostolic Exhortation *Redemptionis donum* (1984), John Paul II further clarified the connection between the various ways of serving the Church, proper to the particular apostolic mission of each institute, and the *particular gift of the founders*, "which received from God and approved by the Church, becomes a charism for the whole community" (15).[26] At every moment in history, this gift meets the needs of the Church and the world; but, in turn, it is prolonged and consolidated in the religious communities, "as one of the lasting elements of their life and apostolate in the Church" (15). The founders originally received the special gift; but this gift, destined to become a lasting good in the Church, endures through the faithfulness of their followers to their characteristic traits.

Moreover, we notice that John Paul II uses the word "charism" to designate this communal gift, although in the Code promulgated shortly beforehand, its use in the general sense has been systematically avoided.

Theological Speculation

The theological, spiritual, and canonical works concerning our subject have considerably grown in number in recent years,[27] but their teaching has not always been sound enough and their vocabulary precise enough.

These works could be grouped around three questions: (1) What kind of relationship exists between the founders and their institutes? (2) What do we mean when we say that in the Church consecrated life is a charism? (3) What meaning should we give to the expression "charism of an institute"?

The Founder and His Institute

As early as 1964, Gilmont published an article of importance because of the problem it poses and the method it employs: *Paternité et médiation du fondateur de l'Ordre*. His method combined theology and history, and his basic ideas are drawn from Jérôme Nadal, S.J. (1580), and thus revolve round the grace of vocation.[28] In relation to the grace of the institute he has founded, the grace of the founder has an *exemplary role*. The grace of the vocation of each person is marked by the power needed to carry out the ministries proper to each institute. Thus, with respect to his religious family, the founder is both a guide and an *intercessor*. In studying this question, Gilmont considers a whole series of classical cases drawn from history.

The thesis of F. Ciardi, *I fondatori uomini dello Spirito* (Rome, 1982), employed this same method, and broadened it by means of more varied cases and an updated technique. According to Ciardi, founders, guided by the Spirit, find a particular historical way of reflecting the mystery of Christ. An *intense spiritual experience* invites them to do so, and at the same time enables them to attract followers who *in a way, prolong their life and mission* as a kind of "small mystical body,"[29] behaving like them and responding to their presence among them.

But as early as 1967, Galot noticed that the Holy Spirit, the source of the spirituality and apostolic activity characteristic of an institute, creates molds of lasting existence through the formulation of the rule that serves to express the charism and guarantee its stability.[30]

Regamey, in the article "Carismi" in the *Dizionario degli Istituti di Perfezione* (1975), also declares that founders provide a kind of "form" for their followers, and that the religious charism includes institutional elements that cannot be separated from the whole body of the institute, just as the soul cannot be separated from the body.[31] Regamey admits that in some institutes, no one in particular can be pointed out as the founder, and that in others the founders are unimportant or eccentric persons.

In 1978, J.M. Lozano indicated that an essential element of the founder's charism is his *spiritual experience* that, at a certain point, he discerns as a call to give life to a religious family. This personal experience is handed on to others so as to fulfill the purpose of the institute and maintain the essential traits of its rule of life and constitutions.[32]

Great progress has been made since 1948, when Oesterle, O.S.B., wondering who could be considered a founder, answered: "Pro mea humili opinione fundator poterit definiri: auctor intellectualis aut immediatus executor alicujus specialis rationis pro agenda vita religiosa."[33] It is evident that he confined himself to canonical reality.

In 1968, X. Ochoa made a clear distinction between the charism of the founder and that of the institute.[34] He pointed out that the founder's charism sometimes goes beyond the bounds of an institute, since institutes with various orientations have the same founder. And, in other cases, the charism of the institute can be attributed to many founders. In fact, Ochoa claimed that each institute has at least two founders: the founder who presents it and the Church who approves it. Thus we can note that he did not identify the charism with the spiritual experience of the founder, and that he did not closely link the founder and the spiritual experience that induced him to found an institute.

Some have tried to distinguish the charism of the founder from that of the institute, by making a distinction between the charism of the origins of the institute and its present charism.[35] I do not think that such a distinction can soundly be based on the orientation of the magisterium. Without going so far, Lozano proposes that the original charism, which he acknowledges is important as the source of the religious institute, be redefined in contemporary terms.[36] Leaving aside the risks involved in such a suggestion, it seems best to maintain the original formulation, since it can always be used as a critical point of reference, to find out if any particular redefinition is true to it. In other respects, each redefinition should be submitted to the competent authority of the Church, in order to determine whether it is true to the original institute.

It seems obvious that we should make a distinction between the various charisms. More or less fame, complexity, scope, originality and transcendence[37] can be noted in the founders of the various institutes. Some of them provide merely a distinctive nuance within a spiritual trend already extant. For some institutes, it is difficult to isolate the precise charismatic element of their foundations, just as it is sometimes impossible to identify with certainty the person who founded them.

The Congregation of Religious and Secular Institutes periodically publishes a list of the institutes that have merged or regrouped into one.

A Charism of Consecrated Life?

In recent times, speculation has focused primarily on religious life as such. J. Galot finds in religious life the characteristic notes of a charism: a supernatural gift (inward or outward), although not always accompanied by extraordinary phenomena, which is efficient and contributes to the common good of the Church.[38]

Regamey thinks that the term "charism" applies to religious life only in a broad sense. In the strict and traditional meaning of the word, charisms are transitory and more or less spectacular experiences of the action of the Spirit, and not states of life or permanent offices. But we must admit, as does Regamey, that in the four lists of charisms drawn up by St. Paul (Rom. 12:6–8, 1 Cor. 12:7–11, 28–30, Eph. 4:11–12), there are some examples that indicate a certain character of stability as well as spontaneity; yet these lists are in no way systematic.

While admitting that a vocation to the religious life has the character of a charism, G. Lafont notices[39] that we cannot separate too rigidly the two aspects of grace: *gratis data* and *gratum faciens*. In the case of a vocation, it is question on the one hand of a gift that belongs to the order of grace and is given with the sanctification of the recipient in view, and on the other hand of a capacity to observe a certain style of life to the advantage of the Church. To describe the nature of this gift, Galot emphasizes *all* the aspects as well as the *depth* of the person who receives the charism of religious life so as to adopt a state of life and become inwardly disposed to remain in it forever. It is not a charism similar to those that orient one toward a limited ecclesial service or affect a single aspect of one's life. Galot explains the charism as orienting the person toward religious life as such.[40] M. Midali, on the other hand, is inclined not to recognize the existence of a proper charism of religious life, as distinct from the concrete reality of the founder or of the members of an institute. He views religious life simply as *a form of evangelical life,* with some essential components such as a ministry or a mission distinctive of it.[41]

We would agree, provided that one does not deny the existence of the essential elements, common to all institutes, of the state of religious life, as it is approved by the Church.

The Charism of an Institute?

Regamey accepts with some reservations the designation "charism of the founders"; for example, he notes that some institutes find their inspiration in individuals from the remote past, whereas others find it in the spirit of an epoch rather than in the intention of their own founder. Such seems to be the case of many institutes established during the ecclesial renewal experienced by the nineteenth century. Regamey also has reservations about the founder's charism, which he considers essentially to be intended for posterity: the Holy Spirit signifies his will by inspiring the religious families to adopt an orientation of their own choice.[42]

In general, theologians are inclined to maintain that charisms, as gifts of the Spirit, are given to particular individuals and not to institutions, although the founders, acting as benefactors, may pass on their charism to their followers. Thus, a distinction is to be made between the charism of the founder and that of his disciples.[43] This notion of charism seems to correspond better to the New-Testament teaching and to the nature of the "experience of the Spirit," as defined in *Mutuae relationes* with regard to the charism of the founders. It appears, therefore, that the experience of the Spirit should be attributed to individuals and not to institutions as such.

However, Lozano has come to the conclusion that charisms are transmitted from the founders to their followers. Thus, he attempts to describe the elements that form the communal charism of a religious family, while he admits that he goes beyond the teaching of the New Testament, without contradicting it.[44] He relies on the authority of Paul VI, who told the Passionists "that they had made theirs the charism of St Paul of the Cross"[45]; and to the Congregation of St. Joseph, founded by St. Leonardo Murialdo, that they "have inherited the charism"[46] of their holy founder.

The communal charism, inspired by that of the founders of the institute in the Church, would consist in (1) the vocation to a Christian way of life, dedicated to celibacy and brotherly love; (2) the ministry corresponding to the particular purpose of the institute; (3) the spirituality, rooted in what is common to all religious life, and yet adapted to the particular nature of the institute; and (4) the manner in which the founder has lived a particular aspect of the mystery of Christ, and which has been the germinal idea of his spiritual doctrine.[47]

We note that when it is time to define an institute, no one can refrain from referring explicitly to the charism of the founder. It seems that the texts of Paul VI, cited by Lozano, when taken within their context, only indicate the close relationship of filiation that exists between the religious and their founders who represent for them an inevitable point of reference. The citations do not directly specify in what sense the institute accepts as its own the founder's charism, or in what sense the religious can be considered to have inherited it. Is the charism handed down to them with a fully univocal or merely an analogous content? Can we say that the "founder's charism," or personal experience in itself, becomes the "community's charism"?

Final Assessment and Perspectives

1. To evaluate the present state of the question, we can first acknowledge the positive result that has emerged from the teaching of the Council: the theological fact of religious life in the Church is examined in relation not only to the evangelical counsels preached by Christ, but also to the charismatic inspiration given by the Holy Spirit. The pneumatic dimension reveals that the Holy Spirit guides the Church, in order to achieve through it his work of transforming humanity to Christ. By means of his inspirations and charisms, the Holy Spirit empowers the Church to carry out its mission of being an instrument of sanctification and of testifying to Christ throughout the whole world. The numerous vocations to various forms of consecrated life in the church are due to this activity of the Holy Spirit.

2. Each religious congregation refers to an origin which, in a more or less profound sense, we can qualify as *charismatic*. Even in those institutes having more than one founder, and in those whose inspiration was not very original, it is possible to detect one or more persons at their origins who, as a result of the influence of the Spirit (or "experience of the Spirit"), have induced others to live and act in ways approved by the Church as capable of leading to sanctity. In many cases, one discovers Spirit-filled persons who became creators and transmitters of new means of reflecting in the Church one of the aspects of the mystery of Christ.

3. The notion "charism," when applied to founders, captures quite well the transcendent character and the ecclesial nature of religious institutes. This charismatic character is especially evident in the founders, both because of the original way they were prompted by the Spirit, and because of their ability to attract and bring together followers, overcome obstacles, and embrace the cross as they founded their institutes.

The hierarchy of the Church is required to recognize the authentic-

ity of these charisms, protect them, and contribute to their development along the lines indicated by the Spirit in inspiring the
mission of the founders.[48] In a way, the institutes partake in the
charismatic character of their founders. They owe to them their
identity, particular character, and mission, once these have been
approved by the Church. The *members of the institute* also partake
in the charism of their founders, since they exist, due to the divine
call that binds them in filial devotion to "the experience of the
Spirit" proper to their founders. This call demands of them, as it
did of their founders, to remain faithful to Christ and docile to His
Spirit, when they are confronted with the hardships of life and
must make decisions consonant with their true vocation.

Obviously, the term "charism," when referring to the charism
of the founder, is used in a broader sense than that same term
when used to describe transitory yet extraordinary phenomena.
This broad sense is explained in *LG* 12, where reference is made
to charisms as gifts of the Holy Spirit, which along with the
sacraments celebrated by sacred ministers, guide and sanctify the
People of God. These gifts are valuable, no matter what their
nature: "sive clarissima, sive etiam simpliciora et latius diffusa."

4. Lafont's remark concerning the *compound nature of the grace
of vocation* to consecrated life seems to be appropriate.[49] In this
single grace, one can discern an element that accrues to the
personal sanctification of its recipient and another more specifically charismatic and directed to the common good of the
Church. In founders, the second element manifests a charismatic
character in a more literal sense, that is, one marked by originality, paternity, and instrumental mediation in relation to their
followers. In the latter, the second element shows itself in filial
reference to the exemplary and the normative character of the
founder's charism.

It would, therefore, seem to be particularly fruitful in developing our topic to integrate into it the depth and scope of Nadal's
theory,[50] already revived by Gilmont and Ciardi, on the grace of
vocation. The followers of a founder find in the grace of vocation
the help they need to embrace the founder's charism in their self-
awareness and activity, by remaining faithful to the patrimony of
their institute. The invigorating power of the founders' charisms
is linked by the divine Spirit to the well-being of their institutes,
to their preservation and development. That is why the Church
is interested in defending the originality of the founders and

promoting the work of the Spirit in their followers for the greater common good.

5. In connection with this theme, one can recall the intervention of Cardinal Bea, who explained this transmission of graces in some way ("quodammodo") to others by the founder of an institute[51] in terms of a *structure of loyalty.* We might say that this transmission resembles that operative in the covenants that God made with his people through a specially elected person. In 1974, Paul VI referred to vocations in much the same covenant terms.[52] The grace of vocation would imply an implicit covenant of loyalty to the founder's charism, and the evidence of the latter's efficiency in one's life would be linked to the existence of this covenant. Moreover, in this way, the laxity of an institute could be attributed to disloyalty to the charism of its founder. In such a case, some religious, anxious to show their loyalty to the original spirit, appeared in history so as to give a new vitality to their institutes; such was the case with the holy reformers of religious congregations.

Like any gift of the Spirit, the grace of vocation, according to Nadal, requires each individual to ask, accept, and cultivate it through prayer and mortification.[53] But the grace of vocation may also be betrayed or rejected; its addressee may let it grow weaker and lose its energy; or its vitality may be stifled by the worries of this world. And then, once its power to edify others decreases, its capacity to attract followers anxious to strive toward Christian perfection becomes exhausted. This is one of the main causes of the lack of vocations in some institutes. Other similar or less important causes could be pointed out. Be that as it may, it would be better for an institute to remain loyal to the charism of its founder, even if during a certain period it does not attract as many vocations, than to betray its graced heritage.

6. As happens to any living reality, the founder's charism lends the grace given to followers a *dynamic power of adaptation* in accord with the changes in human society.[54] Thus, No. 12 of *Mutuae relationes* states that the power to adopt the institute allows its leaders to discern the essential elements from the secondary ones, and to distinguish the true expressions of its spirituality, apostolate, and community life from those that have gradually become obsolete and must be adandoned. The motu propio *Ecclesiae Sanctae* defines the obsolete elements as those "not in conformity with the nature and aims of the institute, because

they have lost their power and meaning and are of no real help to religious life."[55]

7. General chapters, instituted to legislate regarding impera-tive adaptation, must make sure that "the charism proper to each order be preserved in its integrity and vitality."[56] They must give directives that are "nunquam contrarias, semper vero secundum ejus fundatoris spiritum."[57] The response to the "propensiones et postulationes" that are presented to the chapter must be found in the special organic structure of the institute, according to *Evan-gelical testificatio.*[58] No adaptation, Paul VI claimed, is acceptable "which does not tend to restore and put into practice the original characteristics of each institute."[59]

The magisterium has not encouraged religious to reformulate the charism of their institutes, and thus risk losing or abandoning the authentic formula of the founder, to which they might later resort so as to rediscover the pristine charism.

On the other hand, no one should take refuge in a vague permanent charism, or else, under the pretext of doing what the founder would do today, the institute does just the opposite. An effort at inner purification, study, and prayer is normally required in order to rediscover the founders' spirit and assimulate the principles and motives that guided them. These must direct their followers, if they intend to make decisions that conform to their spirit. *Evangelica testification* requires that every religious family, as it pursues the necessary adaptation, maintain a line of continu-ity: ". . . licet secundum mutabilia locorum ac temporum ad-juncta renovetur et distinguatur, semper tamen constantem cursum exposcit."[60] It is the grace of vocation, conjoined by God to the charism of the founders, that makes such historical conti-nuity possible.

There is certainly need to deepen and to refine the questions that have been examined here. For example, one could further develop the theological insights of Jérôme Nadal into the grace of vocation proper to each institute. With regard to whether reformers of religious institutes practically create a new entity, some terms would have to be clarified. While keeping in mind the ecclesiologico-pneumatic point of view of the Council, one should also enhance the theologico-christocentric aspect of reli-gious life. Yet one should acknowledge the theological progress that has been made during the last twenty-five years with regard to religious life. Studies on the charism of founders have proven fundamental means of appreciating the role of consecrated life in the Church.

Translated from the Spanish by Louis-Bertrand Raymond.

Notes

1. On the active and passive meaning of "consecrates himself" ("mancipatur . . . consecratur"), cf. P. Molinari and P. Gumpel, *Il Capitolo VI "De Religiosis" della Costituzione dogmatica sulla Chiesa* (Milan, 1985), 190–193; J. Galot, *Les Religieux dans l'Eglise* (Gembloux/ Paris, 1966), 79–81.

2. AS, I/IV, II/I, III/I and VIII; *Schemata Constitutionum et Decretorum de quibus disceptabitur in Concilii Sessionibus* (Vatican City, 1962); M.J. Schoenmackers, *Genèse du chapitre VI "De Religiosis" de la Constitution dogmatique sur l'Eglise "Lumen gentium"* (Rome, 1983); F. Sebastian, "Historia capitis VI Constitutionis 'Lumen gentium,' " *Commentarium pro Religiosis*, 45 (1966), 349–363; P. Molinari and P. Gumpel, *Il Capitolo VI "De Religiosis" della Costituzione dogmatica sulla Chiesa*, 7–83.

3. AS, III/VII, 85 and 138; IV/III.

4. *Schemata Constitutionum et Decretorum*, ser. sec., pp. 32–33; see ser. tert. p. 219.

5. *Ibid.*, ser. sec. p. 33.

6. AS, II/I, 593–594.

7. *Ibid.*, I/IV, 36.

8. *Ibid.*, III/VII, 761; see also IV/V, 584–585: ". . . Ideo fideliter agnoscantur et serventur Fundatorum spiritus propriaque proposita, necnon sanae traditiones, quae omnium cujusque instituti patrimonium constituunt."

9. *Ibid.*, III/I, 310–312.

10. Cor. 12:7: "Unicuique autem datur manifestatio Spiritus ad utilitatem"; Eph. 4:12: ". . . ad consumationem sanctorum in opus ministerii, in aedificationem Corporis Christi."

11. AS, III/VII, 431.

12. *Ibid.*, 443; the Cardinal relies especially on the texts of St. Paul: 1 Cor. 12:8–10, 25; 2 Tim. 3:17; Eph. 4:12. In these texts, charisms are considered manifestations of the Spirit (1 Cor. 12:4, 7).

13. *Ibid.*, 443.

14. *Ibid.*, 454.

15. *Ibid.*, 571–572 and 578–579. Obviously the preservation of the same spirit excludes certain forms that are not consonant with it.

16. *Ibid.*, 613.

17. *Ecclesiae Sanctae*, n. 25; cf. PC 25.

18. *AAS*, 60 (1968), 738.

19. *Evangelica testificatio*, n. 11.

20. *Ibid.*, n. 11.

21. *Ibid.*, n. 32.

22. *AAS*, 64 (1972), 29: "L'albero vive delle sue radici. E non vi è dubbio che la vostra più vitale radice sono gli esempi e gli insegnamenti di San Giovanni Bosco."

23. *AAS*, 66 (1974), 542: ". . . ita vos in Ecclesia vocati estis ad peculiare quoddam pactum servandum, quod Deus pro sua misericordia cum Conditore vestro ejusque progenie sanxit."

24. *Notae directivae pro mutuis relationibus inter Episcopos et Religiosos in Ecclesia* (Vatican City, 1978).

25. *CIC*, Canons *586, 578, 598, 646, 650, 652, 659, 662, 667, 674–678, 680–683.*

26. ". . . quod, *a Deo acceptum* et ab Ecclesia approbatum, totius communitatis carisma est factum." According to the context, this use of "communitatis" in the singular, accompanied by "totius," seems to refer to the universal community of the Church. Compare it with the plural "Conditorum," used in note 23, in reference to founders, and with the one still further above, "communitatum religiosarum vita," which refers to various institutes.

27. F. Viens, *Charismes et vie consacrée* (Rome, 1983), 112–192, presents them in great number.

28. *RAM*, 40 (1964), 393–426. The doctrines of Nadal, especially in *Epistolae et monumenta P. Hieroymi Nadal*, Vol. 5 (Rome, 1962), MHSI, 90; and in N. Nicolau, *Pláticas espirituales del P. Jerónimo Nadal en Coimbra* (Granada, 1965).

29. F. Ciardi, *I fondatori uomini dello Spirito*, 391.

30. J. Galot, *Porteurs du souffle d l'Esprit* (Gembloux/Paris, 1967), 32–35.

31. R. Regamey, "*Carismi*," DIP 2: 301–302.

32. J.M. Lozano, "Founder and Community: Inspiration and Charism," *Review for Religious*, 37 (1978), 226–228.

33. "Fundatores Ordinum et Congregationum Religiosarum quinam sint," *Commentarium pro Religiosis*, 27 (1948), 87. Ciardi, in the book already quoted, pp. 368–376, mentions that the special inspiration of the founder includes the spirit and the main norms of the institute that it strives to transmit in its rule. We should take into account the fact that sometimes the rule of the institute was not written by the founder, but has been accepted by him as his own, or as having inspired his own foundation.

34. "Modus determinandi patrimonium constitutionale cujusvis instituti perfectionis proprium," *Commentarium pro Religiosis*, 47 (1968), 98.

35. M. Midali, *Il carisma permanente di D. Bosco* (Turin/Laumann, 1970), 154.

36. J.M. Lozano, "Founder and Community," *Review for Religious*, 37 (1978), 214–236.

37. "Quae charismata sive clariora sive etiam simpliciora et latius diffusa, cum sint necessitatibus Ecclesiae apprime accomodata et utilia, cum gratiarum actione ac consolatione accipienda sunt," *LG* 12.

38. J. Galot, *Porteurs du souffle de l'Esprit*, 19–33 and 35–37.

39. G. Lafont, "L'Esprit-Saint et le droit dans l'institution religieuse," *Vie spirituelle, Supplément*, 20 (1967), 473–487.

40. J. Galot, *op. cit.*, 66–74.

41. M. Midali, "Il carisma della vita religiosa. Attuali correnti teologiche," *Vita consacrata*, 17 (1981), 386–387 and "La dimensione carismatica della vita religiosa," *ibid.*, 550–557.

42. R. Regamey, "*Carismi*," DIP II, 312.

43. J.M. Lozano, *El fundador y la familia religiosa* (Madrid, 1978), 86.

44. *Ibid.*, 88.

45. *Insegnamenti di Paolo VI*, Vol. IX (Vatican City, 1971), 1164–1165; Paul VI does not seem to intend any other meaning than that of referring to the original spirit, according to *PC* 2, quoted immediately above, so as to give an Exhortation: "Non temere l'affermazione del vostro severo stile di vita, che tanto vi distingue dallo stile del nostro secolo."

46. *Ibid.*, Vol. XI (Vatican City, 1973), 267, does not seem to intend to resolve the question concerning the nature of this heritage, but only to encourage them to remain loyal to the adage "facere et tacere," which they have inherited from their founder, and which he considers to be charismatic.

47. J.M. Lozano, *El fundador y la familia religiosa*, 90.

48. *LG* 45; *PC* 1.4; cf. note 25.

49. G. Lafont, "L'Esprit-Saint et le droit," *Vie Spirituelle*, supplément, 20 (1967), 486–487.

50. See note 28.

51. "Ordinum et Congregationum religiosarum fundatores propria sua dona charismatica habuerunt et, asseclis et filiis suis quodamodo transmittentes, ea perpetua in Ecclesia tradiderunt" (AS, III/VII, 443). We think that, in this respect, it would be beneficial to reflect about the bestowal of the Spirit on the seventy elders (Num. 11:10–30), the requirements of the covenant (Deut. 31—32:47), and David's speech to Salomon (1 Kings 2:1–4).

52. AAS, 66 (1974), 542 and 723–727.

53. N. Nicolau, *Pláticas espirituales del P. Jerónimo Nadal en Coimbra*, 57, 82, 85–88.

54. According to John Paul II: "Quod donum variis respondet Ecclesiae necessitatibus et singulis mundi historiae temporibus et vicissim continuatur firmaturque in communitatum religiosarum vita ut unum ex elementis mansuris vitae apostolatusque Ecclesiae," *Redemptionis donum,* n. 15: *AAS,* 76 (1984), 542.

55. *AAS,* 58 (1966), 778.

56. ". . . ut charisma, cujusvis Ordinis proprium, purum ac vitale permaneat," Paul VI to the Dominicans, *AAS* 66, (1974), 542.

57. To the Minors conventuals of the general Chapter: *AAS,* 61 (1969), 524.

58. *AAS,* 63 (1971), 523.

59. Speech to the Cistercians: *AAS,* 60 (1968), 738; cf. *PC* 2.

60. See n. 121, *AAS,* 63 (1971), 504.

CHAPTER 43

The Value of "Religious" Consecration According to Vatican II

Antonio Queralt, S.J.

Summary

After a brief introduction, which points out the importance of the concept "consecration," an analysis of all the texts of the Council containing this term reveals that: (1) the Council presents as "agents" of the consecration, on the one hand, various persons (God the Father, Christ, the Holy Spirit, the bishop, the priest, the religious, and the laypeople), and, on the other hand, certain sacraments (holy orders, marriage, confirmation, and baptism) and certain "nonsacramental" acts (vows, profession, and praise). The concept of "consecrating," as a whole, is not "univocal." The persons who receive the consecration are also different: Christ, the bishop, the priest, the baptized-confirmed, the husband and wife, the "religious," and even time itself. The same person may or may not receive more than one sacramental consecration. (2) The "nonsacramental" consecration bestows real graces comparable to those conferred by a "sacrament." Finally, (3) the characteristic note of "religious" consecration consists in participation in the salvific priesthood of Christ, as "victim" and in encouraging all Christians to be victims.

This chapter examines and evaluates the teachings of Vatican II dealing with "religious consecration."

The consecration mentioned by the Council in various passages is a central and essential theme in the attempt to understand correctly what religious life is.[1] Some have perceived the emphasis on consecration as a change of mentality. From now on, the concept of consecration is to qualify the vowed state of life, and not the concept "religious," as for centuries, and in part even at Vatican II, was customary.[2] This very fact clearly indicates how important it is properly to understand the meaning of the concept consecration.

Shortly after the closing session of the Council, various authors drew attention to the theological-spiritual importance of the concept of consecration.[3] We can maintain that since then this interest has not decreased. From various standpoints and with understandable intervals of silence, the theme has repeatedly been treated.[4] The interpretations given, even as far as the Council is concerned, are not always convergent.[5] Furthermore, attention was not given to all the texts containing the concept "consecrating," either as a verb or as a noun. Since I intend to do so, the results will provide an added dimension to our theme.[6]

Our study has but one objective, which we have pointed out, and readily understandable limits. Besides confining ourselves to Vatican II, the other limits we impose are the following: to use only the texts in which the word "consecrate–consecration" appears under one of its forms and to analyze only the final text, the history of which is presupposed, in order to bring out its value.

Above all, our presentation tries to provide a comprehensive framework and to accentuate those elements within it that concern religious consecration. Such a plan comes up against a diversity of texts and contexts, of persons forming the conciliar commissions and subcommissions, of interventions made during the discussion of the documents, and finally of conflicting opinion. As far as possible, we have taken all these factors into account in the analysis of the major texts,[7] yet such difficulties may still seem insuperable.

Nevertheless, our plan can be justified by one undeniable fact: the unity of the subject that promulgates the various documents, namely the Council itself. This is sufficient for us: we are more interested in observing and exposing what the Council teaches us by means of the authority proper to it.[8]

The material at our disposal is more than sufficient to provide an overall view. The word "consecrate" or "consecration" is found under one or the other of its various forms in ten different documents and is repeated forty-five times.[9] It takes on, as we shall see, different meanings.

Moreover, since the verb "consecrate" is an active verb,[10] we can ask four questions: Who or what is the "agent"? Who or what is the "patient" of the action? What "effect" does it produce? What is the "term" toward which the dynamism of the consecration tends?

The substantive "consecration," as an action or a state, complements the conclusions of the study of the verbal form. By determining "the agent," we specify the meaning of the word and the quality of its effect. By identifying "the patient," we can decide whether the same person can receive successive consecrations and if so which they can be. The "effect" indicates if there are "nonsacramental" means of grace of the same order as those of the sacraments. And the "term" that indicates the theological-salvific content of consecration reveals whether the Council uses this concept in an equivocal, or only univocal or analogous, sense. These are the problems we must clarify. The prospect of providing a solution to this multiple problematic appears to be positive: it could have an impact on the theological manner of conceiving the nature of consecrated life.

Our chapter contains three parts: the first two answer the four questions posed; the third points out the "characteristic" aspects of religious consecration. Finally, in a brief conclusion, we summarize the chapter as a whole.

The "Agent" and the "Patient" of Consecration

Before treating the texts of the Council, we have to indicate the meaning that the words "consecrate" and "consecration" have in the classical Latin literature.

The important dictionaries have led us to conclude that "consecrate" and "consecration" *separate* someone or something from the sphere of the profane.[11] We will explain the various aspects of this meaning by employing three of the questions already asked.

In this notion, the "agent" is an ordinary person or someone holding an office; the "patient" is a person or a thing, and also time itself; the "term" is the divinity or what is directly in touch with it; the "effect" is, in a sense double: (1) to "make" sacred, and consequently the verb "con-secrare" corresponds, in many respects, to the simple "sacrare" from which it derives (and "consecratio" to "sanctificatio"); and (2) to "put at the disposal" of the divinity, which is made explicit by the goal of consecration. [12] Note that in the classical notion, we can and must attribute a true effect to the "consecrare-consecratio," that is, a *consecrating* and a *divinizing*, because a real power was attached to "words," particularly to ritual ones, doubtlessly on account of the magical conception that was then widespread. The classical meaning of the verb "consecrare" and the noun "consecratio" provides the conceptual substratum used afterwards by the Christian liturgy and theology to express the reality of the mystery of salvation. [13] Moreover, the classical notion comprises "the shadowy figure" and "example" of what the Catholic Church teaches when it employs identical terminology.

In order to clarify the "agent" and "patient" of consecration in the texts of the Council, we are obliged to treat them together. Note first that we place the word "agent" in quotation marks so as to assure that its interpretation be based on a grammatical analysis of the texts. Yet, straightaway we can assert that the Council presents various "agents": persons, rites, and actions. We have to confirm this initial observation. Moreover, the category "agent" must be further specified: Is it the main cause of the action or, on the contrary, only an instrument or secondary cause? Thus, we leave open the possibility that various "agents" intervene in the same act of "consecration."

The "patient," the thing or the person that receives the action, is also variable and this fact may lead to a response to the question whether the Council always uses the concept in an univocal sense, or sometimes also in an "analogous," even an equivocal, sense. Determining the nature of the "patient" aids the comparison we intend to make between "nonsacramental" or religious consecration, and "sacramental" consecration arising from the liturgy of the Church.

It may seem superfluous, yet is quite useful for the overall view that we intend to provide, to point out that the texts vary a great deal in content, that the same concept is expressed by means of various phrases, [14] that our interest in this variety changes according to the particular angle from which we consider them,[15] and that some are clearer than others.

We begin by dealing with the "agent" and the "patient" of consecration. The texts that indicate the "agent" are divided into four groups. The first one deals with "persons," the second with "sacraments," the third with "nonsacramental" action, and the fourth with texts that do not explicitly identify the "agent." Note that the content of the four groups links them together: as we already mentioned, the various functions of the "agent," far from excluding the action of the others, actually requires it. To avoid repeating the references to the texts, we also mention the "patient" of the same action.

The "Person" Who Consecrates

The texts treating a "person" as agent are nine in number and can be found in the following documents: four in *Lumen gentium,* three in *Presbyterorum ordinis,* and one in *Perfectae caritatis* and *Optatam totius.* The persons are God, God the Father, the Holy Spirit, the bishops, and laypeople. Let us start with the most explicit texts.

The decree *Presbyterorum ordinis* leaves no doubt that God is an "agent," when it declares with all the necessary precision: ". . . through the ministry of the bishop, *God consecrates priests* so that. . ." (*PO* 5)[16]; in the same decree, it asserts the activity of the Father: "Christ, whom the Father sanctified and consecrated, and sent into the world, gave himself for us that he. . ." (*PO* 12).[17] The text of *Lumen gentium* is less explicit, but its content is the same: "Christ, whom the Father sanctified and sent into the world (Jn. 10:36) has, through His apostles, made their successors, the bishops, partakers of His consecration and His mission" (*LG* 28). We can observe that this text is less explicit concerning the consecration of Christ: it does not indicate, as does the text of *Presbyterorum ordinis* 12, that "consecrated" is synonymous with "sanctified." But it leaves no doubt that it is Christ whom he *consecrates,* by emphasizing that Christ transmits "his consecration," as *Presbyterorum ordinis* 12 states, to the world to which he was sent.[18]

Regarding the "agent," the text of *Optatam totius* 2 does not raise any difficulty: "the ministers of the Church exercise the further commission of *consecrating* to the worship of God and the service of the Church the candidates whose fitness has been acknowledged". The Constitution *Lumen gentium* declares as clearly that "laymen" *consecrate* the world itself to God, if they act as indicated in the text.[19]

The texts, therefore, consider the following as consecrated: Christ, the bishops, the priests, and the world itself.

We may not find the same clarity in the three texts still to be presented, of which two refer to the Holy Spirit, although grammatically speaking the direct "agent" is "the unction." And the third text, for the reason that we will explain, points out God as the agent.

In the first two texts, the grammatical phrase is not the same: in one, we find the preposition "per" with the accusative case, and, in the other, the ablative case without a preposition; the sacraments to which the consecration refers are also not the same: in the first text, it is a matter of baptism and confirmation, and in the second of holy orders.

In Chapter II, concerning the common priesthood, *LG* teaches that: "The baptized, by regeneration and the anointing of the Holy Spirit, are consecrated into a spiritual house and a holy priesthood" (*LG* 10).[20] The text from *Presbyterorum ordinis* 12, after asserting that Christ and his actions are consecrated, proceeds as follows: "Likewise, consecrated by the anointing of the Holy Spirit and sent by Christ. . . ."[21] I think that in both texts, the genitive "Spiritus Sancti" must be understood as being explicative, in the sense that the divine unction is the Holy Spirit himself who bestows the graces proper to the respective sacraments on their recipients through the sacramental unction used by the Church.

Finally, we have the text *Lumen gentium* 44, which would certainly require a detailed presentation,[22] since it is ambivalent.[23] The interpretation that should be given to "consecratur" in the phrase "he is consecrated to God" was a matter of considerable debate by the bishops at the Council.[24] The text regards the religious as one who obliges himself to observe the three evangelical counsels through the vows or equivalent sacred bonds:

> It is true that through baptism he has died to sin and has been consecrated to God. However, in order to derive more abundant fruit from this baptismal grace, he intends by the profession of the evangelical counsels in the Church, to free himself

from those obstacles which might draw him away from the fervor of charity and the perfection of divine worship. Thus he is more intimately *consecrated* to divine service (*LG* 44).[25]

The important conclusion to draw from the phrase "he is consecrated" (understood by God) is that it is God who consecrates, even by means of "nonsacramental" actions.

It can now be stated that a Trinitarian dimension pervades the whole teaching of the Council on "consecration," even if other "consecrators" are mentioned. This theme is evident in the treatment of the consecration given at holy orders: Christ himself anointed by the Spirit of the Father allows the apostles to partake in his own consecration, and through them the bishops, and the presbyters. This Trinitarian conception is also central in the texts regarding baptism: consecrated to Christ by the Spirit of the Father they "are assigned to the apostolate by the Lord Himself" (*AA* 3). And this Trinitarian conception does not diminish in the texts we examine concerning the "nonsacramental" consecration that is given through the religious vows.

On the basis of what has been discovered thus far, we can state that the conciliar concept of the personal "agent" is not "equivocal." But, at the same time, we must also admit that the Council does not always use it in an "univocal" sense. Confining ourselves to the texts already presented, we can maintain that Christ is consecrated by the Spirit of the Father, that Christians are consecrated by the Spirit of Christ, and that the "world" is consecrated by the activity of Christians. Clearly enough, the "patients" in these texts are Christ, the baptized, the priest, the religious, and the world.

A Sacrament as Consecrating "Agent"

Without intending in the slightest to contradict what has just been said, it is necessary to point out that in some passages the Council presents "a sacrament" as a consecrating "agent."

Yet, such an observation poses no particular problem. We only have to mention the texts on which our opinion is based, pointing out in passing that both the grammatical construction that indicates "the agent" and the word equivalent to sacrament are variable. We find what concerns baptism and confirmation in *Lumen gentium* 10 and *Apostolicam actuositatem* 3,[26] marriage in

Gaudium et spes 48,[27] and holy orders in *Lumen gentium* 28, *Presbyterorum ordinis* 3, and 12.[28] It should be stated, however, that in another section, we examine texts concerning the consecration of the bishop, because of the particular meaning that the substantive "consecration" has in them. Obviously, the baptized, the confirmed, and the ordained are those who receive the divine action. The prevailing meaning of "consecrate," as found in these texts, is that of receiving a grace, yet it is inseparably linked to that of being destined for worship and service.

An Action as "Agent" of Consecration

We call "action" a nonsacramental agent. This type of "agent" is of great significance to us, because the "consecration" brought about through the counsels belongs to it.

But before treating the counsels, we must present another significant text that illumines those on the religious life, and is, therefore, of greater interest to us. We mean the "action" that the recitation of the "Divine Office" entails. The Constitution *Sacrosanctum concilium* in the first two numbers (83 and 84) of Chapter IV, provides us the theological insight on which the prescriptions concerning the Breviary are based:

> By tradition going back to early Christian times, the Divine Office is arranged so that the whole course of the day and night is *made holy by the praises of God.*[29]

It appears that what is consecrated is "time," all the hours of the day; the "agent" is the "praise of God." The Church "consecrates" time through its prayer to the Father through Christ in the Holy Spirit. Therefore, the verb "consecrate" indicates that the Church is to "dedicate" time to the Triune God.

Four texts interest us more directly: three of them can be found in the Decree *Perfectae caritatis* and the fourth in *Presbyterorum ordinis*. We present them in this order.

The section of the Decree *Perfectae caritatis*, regarding members of secular institutes, presents their "profession" itself as an "agent." Concerning the three evangelical counsels, it does not use the verb, but the substantive "consecration":

> *This profession confers a consecration* on men and women, laity
> and clergy, who reside in the world. For this reason they
> should chiefly strive for *total self-dedication to God,* one inspired
> by perfect charity . . . (PC 11).[30]

Without doubt, the phrase "confers a consecration" is equivalent to "consecrate." If the "profession" is the grammatical
"agent," those who make it "consecrate themselves," whether
they be laymen or clerics.[31] Furthermore, the Council uses the
phrase "the total self-dedication" to mean "profession," and exhorts the members of secular institutes that "they strive (inten-
dant) to be inspired by *perfect charity.*" In the light of *Lumen
gentium* 44, it is clear that this consecration, like the religious
profession, "totally dedicates itself to God by an act of supreme
love," and that, therefore, grace is received so as to achieve this
goal. By describing this charity as perfect, its double orientation
is at least suggested: to honor God and serve him through love of
his people. The Council could not have declared this profession
a "true and total consecration" if it had not believed that it
contained these two elements. The "patients," or those who
receive the consecration, are those who pronounce it, even
though they are already clerics. Here, the term "consecration"
means "dedication" and reception of grace.

The second text we wish to present directly addresses the
"religious." It also deals with their "profession." Just as in the
preceding text, the substantive "consecration," and not the verb,
is used. Although it corresponds to No. 5 of the same decree, we
should note that the "agent" of the verb "constitutes" is not the
word "profession" but a phrase equivalent to it. Yet, this fact does
not diminish the clarity of the text.

The two first paragraphs of *Perfectae caritatis* 5 are of particular
relevance for our subject, and we will return to them when the
"effect" and the "term" of "consecration" are to be discussed:

> They have handed over their entire lives to God's service in
> an act of special *consecration* . . . (PC 5).[32]

Note that "the agent" consists in the act by which religious
"have handed over their entire lives to God's service." This is
equivalent to "the profession of the evangelical counsels." We
must emphasize that the "profession" entails "answering the divine

call" and that, at the same time, it is "a self-sacrifice" that, because
it is received by the Church, implies that "one is dedicated to its
service." By affirming that profession *constitutes a consecration* and
by employing the words "quidem" and "quamdam,"[33] the Council
teaches that religious have "consecrated themselves."

This text evidently possesses an inspiring tone, although it is
imbued with theological content: it centers precisely on the spiritual reality to be lived by religious and on the depth of consciousness that the Council wishes them to attain ("mente recolant").

The consecration made by religious involves putting themselves in God's hands and entering his service, as is clear from
the expressions: "soli Deo vivant," "ejus famulatui mancipa-
verunt," and "haec suiipsius donatio." But the text goes further
by explaining "the service of the Church": as an act of a member
of the Body of Christ, it is consequently of salvific order, and
under the influence of the Holy Spirit. This fact confirms what
we had mentioned at the beginning: religious consecration is not
a matter of personal initiative, but an answer to a "divine call."
The action of the Holy Spirit, the main consecrator is perhaps
only suggested, but no room for serious doubt is left. The professed are ministers of the Holy Spirit and their profession is the
instrument of their nonsacramental consecration.

Perfectae caritatis 1, which explains the objective of the decree,
indicates that the verb, the act of making profession of the counsels, is the agent of the consecration:

> A *life consecrated by a profession of the counsels* is of surpassing
> value. Such a life has a necessary role to play in the circum-
> stances of the present age. That this kind of life and its contem-
> porary role may achieve greater good for the Church, this
> sacred Synod issues the following decrees (PC 1).[34]

The words italicized are of special importance: the Council uses
them briefly to indicate that the "profession" is the cause or agent
of the religious consecration. Moreover, by use of the phrase
"munus necessarium," which we have translated as "necessary
role," the Council offers a developed conception of this consecration in terms of "worship" and "service." Therefore, the concept
of "consecration" used here includes its dual dimensions: to receive grace and to commit oneself.

In another text, "the agent" of the consecration is virginity or celibacy. We find this usage in *Presbyterorum ordinis*, which refers to Catholic priests of the Latin rite:

> Through *virginity or celibacy* observed for the sake of the kingdom of heaven, priests *are consecrated to Christ* in a new and distinguished way (*PO* 16).[35]

Here the Council teaches that one of the counsels is the instrumental "agent" of the consecration received by those who, for the motive mentioned, are called to practice it. Thus, "priests," consecrated by baptism, confirmation, and holy orders, are the "patients" who receive this consecration. By describing the latter as "new," the Council means that it is "different"; and by presenting it as "distinguished" (eximia), it means that it has no less value than those sacramental graces that the same person has received or can receive.

Obviously, the concept of "consecration" in these four texts is univocal: it refers to the same type of consecration and produces identical effects. But we still have to compare this consecration with the sacramental one. By examining the "effect" produced by both, we find it easier to make a sound comparison.

The Texts without an Explicit "Agent"

Many texts do not mention the "agent of the consecration: there are twenty-five in all. Several correspond to the sentences in which the substantive "consecration" and not the verb is used. Nevertheless, the vagueness of the "agent" is in fact corrected: one can differentiate between who receives the consecration in question (the bishop, the priest, the baptized, the religious) and who acts as "the agent" of such consecrations.

These texts are important to us, since in many the Council uses the word "consecration" as equivalent to "sacrament" or "profession." Thus, the content of these texts corresponds to that of the texts in which "the agent" was said to be a "sacrament." This fact indicates that "consecration" transmits gifts and graces; this affirmation allows us, from now on, to speak about "the effect" of the consecration.

One group of such texts uses the verb "consecrate": *Ad gentes* 38, dealing with bishops; *Ad gentes* 39, *Christus Dominus* 15 and 34, and *Presbyterorum ordinis* 12, concerning priests; and *Lumen gentium* 45, concerning religious. These texts can be interpreted as affirming a "divine passive," in that it is God who consecrates. The prevaling meaning of being "consecrated" is dedication. This is evident in *Ad gentes* 38: ". . . all bishops are consecrated not just for some one diocese, but for the salvation of the entire world" (AG 38).[36] The same meaning is evident in *Ad gentes* 39 intended for priests: ". . . they should fully understand that their life has also been consecrated to the service of the missions" (AG 39).[37]

Let us add two more texts, even if in doing so we anticipate the "term" of the consecration. In these texts, the "term" pointed to is God, and thus we find in them the most radical and all-embracing form of the art of being "consecrated." The Decree *Presbyterorum ordinis* urges priests to pursue perfection and provides as the reason: "(the fact that) they have been consecrated to God in a new way by the reception of orders" (PO 12).[38] The constitution *Lumen gentium*, speaking of the religious profession, also mentions God as the "term": "By her approval the Church not only raises the religious profession to the dignity of a canonical state. By the liturgical setting of that profession she also manifests that it is a *state consecrated to God*" (LG 45).[39]

The substantive "consecration" appears in a second group of texts in which the Council clearly refers to the sacraments of baptism or orders. For example, there is a "sacramental consecration," "by virtue of which" the bishops are constituted members of the episcopal college, and also brought into hierarchical communion with the visible head of the college, as mentioned in *Christus Dominus* 4 and *Lumen gentium* 22.[40] In its second paragraph, *Lumen gentium* 21 employs the noun "consecration" three times in this sense. Here is the sentence that summarizes all the preceding ones: "Episcopal consecration, together with the office of sanctifying, also confers the offices of teaching and of governing. These however, of their very nature . . ." (LG 21).[41] Furthermore, in *NP*, the words referring to bishops ("In the consecration, an ontological sharing in the sacred offices is given, as it appears without any doubt in the tradition in general, and also in the liturgical tradition" [NP 21][42]) are of importance to us since they point out that the grace conferred by episcopal consecration is of the ontological order. A grace of the same nature is conferred to priests; thus *Presbyterorum ordinis* underlines "the unity of the consecration" between them and the bishops (PO 7).[43]

Vatican II uses also the word "consecration" to indicate the sacrament of baptism. In *Presbyterorum ordinis,* priests are urged to strive for holiness, and, in connection with this, it is stated that: "Already indeed, in the consecration of baptism, like all Christians, they received the sign and the gift of so lofty a vocation and a grace that even despite human weakness they can and must pursue perfection according to the Lord's words: You therefore are to be perfect . . ." (PO 12).[44]

In all these passages, Vatican II emphasizes the effectiveness of being consecrated, but does not explain "the agent" because, without doubt, he can be identified as God, "who alone is holy and bestows holiness" (PO 5).

It appears that we can quote three passages from LG, in which the word "consecration" signifies "religious profession": one in number 44 and two in number 46.

We are already acquainted with the first passage, since we have pointed out that the "agent" of "being consecrated" is God. In the sentence that follows the one cited, it is said that: "this consecration gains in perfection since by virtue of firmer and steadier bonds it serves as a better symbol of the unbreakable link between Christ and his Spouse, the Church" (LG 44).[45] There is no doubt that here the word "consecration" replaces the word "vows," which are "sacred bonds" by which the faithful commit themselves to observe the evangelical counsels. This fact affirms that, without contradicting that God is the main agent, one can regard sacred profession at the same time as a nonsacramental means of consecration in which the one who makes it is also an agent. Indeed, the human "agent" is subordinate to the divine: the religious is an instrument collaborating with God who bestows the consecrating grace.

In the second and third paragraphs of *Lumen gentium* 46, the same conception is expressed as already noted. Having drawn attention to the meaning of the word "consecration," we are more aware of its evangelical character. Here we can briefly mention the normative words of PC: "Since it is a sign of a consecrated life, the religious habit should be simple and modest, at once poor and becoming" (PC 17).[46] The habit must reflect *what was professed* and not contradict the evangelical state in which one is set by the profession.

In all these texts concerning "consecration," Vatican II emphasizes that the origin of the term is the person of Jesus Christ, who was uniquely consecrated by the Spirit of the Father. Besides, we have considered texts in which the consecration of "time" and the "world" is affirmed. As we have seen, the Council does not mention the consecration of objects: to refer to things intended for worship or related to it, the adjective "sacred" is used.[47] But these extreme cases demonstrate that Vatican II does not in all cases use the concept "consecration" in a univocal sense.

From the point of view of the "patient," who receives the consecration, the texts confirm the possibility that the same person might undergo various successive consecrations, for example, that of baptism and confirmation, and that of orders and religious profession. Moreover, the one who has received priestly ordination can also receive episcopal ordination, which bestows the fullness of what a "consecration" is.

If in all these cases, the main "agent" is the Triune God; there is no reason to exclude that the concept "consecration" is univocal. In relation to the "patients" who receive the action, we come to the same conclusion: since the same persons are concerned, there is no question of changing the content of the consecration they receive.

If the concept "consecration" is *analogous*, this fact must be proved both by "the effect" produced by the "consecration" and by the differing nature of the "term" in which the grace bestowed is achieved. This is precisely what we must now clarify.

The "Effect" and "Term" of "Consecration"

Now that we know "the agent" and "the patient" of "consecration," we chiefly focus on the graces that it confers ("effect"), and on the purpose for which God gives these graces ("term").

Notice that these two concepts are correlative: any divine grace is granted with a "term" in view; and the nature of this term reveals the nature of the gift bestowed.

Moreover, in the texts we are examining, Vatican II often conjoins "consecration" and "mission." To show this, we confine ourselves to the texts that explicitly speak about Christ in whom one discovers the nature of all Christian consecration and mission (*LG* 28 and *PO* 2, 12).[48]

An example of the connection between consecration and mission is found in the sacerdotal ordination of the priest who is set

aside by celibacy[49] so as better to fulfill the baptismal mission
through service of all the baptized.

Keeping in mind that this person is doubly consecrated by
baptism and ordination,[50] we can understand why the Council
speaks, in *Presbyterorum ordinis* 16, about a "new and privileged
way" of consecrating oneself. Note that the Council teaches that
priests already possess the "effect" and "term" of their new consecration, because of the consecrations they have already received.
This affirmation brings out the richness of the new gift that
enables them to obtain "with greater facility" (facilius) the disposition of an undivided heart; "they possess a greater liberty"
(*liberius*) so that "in Christ and through Him" they might dedicate themselves "to the service of God and men" (liturgical dimension); they will thus "be more alert" (*expeditius*) to serve his
kindgom by working for the spiritual and temporal regeneration
of humanity (service dimension).[51] And through their consecration, priests are to make themselves "more capable" (*aptiores*) of
receiving "generously" (*latius*) a new type of paternity that is
achieved in Christ. These words mitigate the impression "of
infertility" which, in the eyes even of some Christians, characterizes celibacy.

Now let us turn to the comparison between baptismal consecration and that of the profession of the evangelical counsels. The
richness of baptismal consecration might at first seem to leave no
room for a new consecration, at least if it is not sacramental. On
the contrary, Vatican II clearly indicates that baptismal consecration is the indispensable condition of any subsequent Christian
consecration. Referring to the evangelical counsels of religions,
Vatican II explicitly states that "they are deeply rooted in their
baptismal consecration" (*PC* 5).

Supposing that baptism is the fertile soil from which the vivify-
ing sap of "religious" consecration must rise forth, let us first
notice that the two consecrations manifest in their "effect" and
in their "term" a very great convergence. After showing this, we
point out their differences due to the fact that one is sacramental
whereas the other is nonsacramental.

Bearing in mind the parallel teachings of *Perfectae caritatis* 5
and *Lumen gentium* 44, we can state that the two consecrations
share a common factor in that they both answer a "divine call"
(*PC* 5, dealing with the religious vocation, and *AA* 2, with the
Christian vocation in general); therefore, their "effect" is to ac-

cept this calling. Both must "die to sin" (in *PC* 5, by means of religious consecration; and in *LG* 44, by means of baptism) and "consecrate" themselves to God (*PC* 5 and *LG* 44). Notice that *Lumen gentium* 44 employs the simple word "sacratus" and not the compound "consecratus" when referring to baptism; yet the meaning remains the same. Likewise, the "term" of the two consecrations is basically the same. Hence, we can conclude that in both cases, God grants graces that have the "effect" of "sanctifying" Christians and at the same time of including them in the mission of salvation through worship and service. The words of *Lumen gentium* 44, addressed to religious but alluding to their baptismal consecration, are the following: "Through such a bond a person is totally dedicated to God by an act of supreme love, and is committed to the honor and service of God under a new and special title" (*LG* 44).[52] The latter is in no way extrinsic to baptismal consecration, but reveals its inherent capacity more clearly.

After pointing out what these consecrations have in common, let us examine what is peculiar to "religious" consecration. Its "effect" is to facilitate a "renouncing the world" (*PC* 5). Vatican II uses this specific phrase so as to distinguish the religious from the laity; the Council thus declares that the religious state is not a middle course between "clerical" and "lay" (*LG* 43); furthermore, with the aid of the comparative "ampler" (plenius), a description favorable to consecration through the evangelical counsels (*PC* 5), the Council points out what is peculiar to the grace received by religious.

Each of these three points would require a full treatment so as to bring to light all the theological and spiritual richness they contain. Here we shall explain, in a manner as condensed as possible, the result of our reflection.

In this context "world" has its original monastic meaning.[53] It does not refer to what is evil in itself—sin, Satan, his works, and pomps[54]—but to goods, such as marriage, riches and autonomy, which one renounces by following the evangelical counsels of Jesus Christ. By declaring that religious consecration "provides an ampler manifestation" of gospel values than does baptism, the Council indicates that the "effect" of this renunciation of the "world" is an enhancement of the same traits that were imprinted on the souls of religious by baptismal consecration.

Since the Constitution *Lumen gentium* 43, 2, states that the religious state "is not an intermediate one between the clerical and lay states," and since it is affirmed in *Lumen gentium* 44, 4, that "the religious state does not belong to the hierarchical structure of the Church,"[55] we can conclude from these texts that "the effect" and "the term" of religious consecration corroborate the grace already received by Christians through their baptismal consecration. In this case, we must ask ourselves whether or not there is identity of consecration between the baptized and the professed. Can we imagine that the religious subsequent consecration could create a certain distinction between the two? We must answer in the affirmative.

The reason for this distinction is that the religious renounce the "world" and by this very fact lose the "secular" condition that characterizes "laymen."[56] This fact allowed the Council to declare that the religious state "belongs inseparably to the life and holiness of the Church" (*LG* 44). By having affirmed that the religious dedicate "their entire lives to God's service through an act of special consecration" (*PC* 5), the Council teaches us that, through a nonsacramental means, namely religious profession, God bestows graces that have the effect of producing a true and particular consecration.

Once we have reached this conclusion, it remains to show more clearly how it is possible that a true consecration exists that intensifies that of baptism and confirmation, and whose "term" permits Christians to participate more deeply in the salvific priesthood of Christ, according to one of its aspects.

What Characterizes the Consecration by Vows?

In order to answer this question, we first intend to make a "nonadequate" distinction between what is "typical" of nonsacramental consecration and what is "peculiar" to it. Its peculiarity, that is, renunciation of the world, is the cause of what is "typical" of it; the peculiarity cannot be found in other consecrations, especially in those of baptism and confirmation with which we are making a comparison. On the other hand, the grace of baptism confers the "typical," though to a different degree. Our subsequent remarks attempt to shed more light on this initial distinction.

Whoever understands the mentality of Vatican II will easily

concede the following three statements, which have already been developed in our expositions:

1. every grace of consecration allows the person who receives it to share in the consecration and mission that the Father confers on Christ who in turn conveys it further through the action of the Holy Spirit;
2. to designate this participation, the Council uses various phrases that have as their common denominator the notion of sharing in the priesthood of Christ, the unique and supreme Priest of the New Testament;
3. this priesthood involves two elements that are inseparably joined together: being at the same time "offering" and "victim."

This last statement opens up the path we intend to follow so as to point out what is "typical" of nonsacramental religious consecration.

Let us anticipate the insight that we shall have to demonstrate with aid of the texts of the Council: the grace of consecration, by means of one or three evangelical counsels, calls for an intensification of "being a victim." And from this requirement, we can and must draw other conclusions: dependence, humility, and increased service. Vatican II treats this "typical" aspect of nonsacramental religious consecration by considering it as being a "sign."

In the third paragraph of *Lumen gentium* 44, we find the basic text that concerns us. Before presenting this paragraph sentence by sentence, we must point out that it is a synthetic conclusion of what is stated in the two preceding paragraphs. Here is the first sentence:

> The profession of the evangelical counsels, then, appears *as a sign* which can and ought to attract *all the members* of the Church to an effective and prompt fulfillment of the *duties of their Christian vocation* (LG 44).[57]

The "sign" that this consecration has as its effect, as indicated by the italicized words, exists so as to be an incentive for all Christians to fulfill without faltering ("impegre") the duties of their Christian vocation. Obviously, by using the word "officia," the Council does not refer to pleasant obligations, but to painful ones, ensuing from the common Christian vocation. It seems, therefore, that the effect of this sign is understood as "apologetical": what is considered here is the aspect of sacrifice that consecrated religious freely embrace for the love of Christ.[58] We believe that, in the Council's thought, the "sign" cannot be viewed merely as something exterior, but indeed as an expansion of the interior grace received, to which a consistent acquiescence is to be given.[59]

Therefore, we can maintain that what is "typical" of this consecration consists in a more intense participation in the priesthood of Christ who chose to be "victim" so as to save the world.

The second sentence of the paragraph under analysis comes to the same conclusion. However, since the second further reinforces and explains the first, we must present it:

The People of God has no lasting city here below, but looks forward to one which is to come. This being so, the religious state by giving its members *greater* freedom from earthly cares *more adequately manifests* to all believers the presence of heavenly goods already possessed here below. Furthermore, it not only *witnesses* to the fact of a new and eternal life acquired by the redemption of Christ. It *foretells* the resurrected state and the glory of the heavenly kingdom (*LG* 44).[60]

The comparative adverb "more" (*magis*) is repeated twice: the writer of the text was clever enough to put them together as much as he could. The first *magis* indicates the *particular* of the religious state (freedom from earthly cares); the second *magis*, which nuances the three verbs we have italicized, represents what is "typical" of the grace of consecration. Taken together, these three verbs (manifest, witness, and foretell)—without specifying if each of them corresponds to an evangelical counsel—illustrate what we might call, after St. Paul, the wisdom and power of the cross (1 Cor. 1:25).

This "more" of the cross present in the religious state makes radiant in it what it has in common with other states. Since we intend to emphasize the content of the real grace operative in this "sign," we cannot pass over in silence the fact that the text characterizes the religious state as manifesting more perfectly "the heavenly goods already possessed here below."

This view is reinforced in the third sentence that, however, presents it from a different angle, that is, in relation to "the life of Christ."

> Christ also proposed to His disciples the *form of life* which He, as Son of God, accepted in entering this world *to do the will of the Father*. In the Church this same state of life is *imitated with particular accuracy* and perpetually exemplified (*LG* 44).[61]

We want to point out the expression "be exemplified . . . in the Church," which could be translated "be made present," since the Latin verb used by the Council undoubtedly alludes to religious life as being "the sign," and at the same time the actualization of what is represented.

Having noted this, let us focus on the italicized words. We might summarize the doctrinal content of this very important paragraph in this way: Vatican II presupposes and teaches that the choice "of imitating" and "following" the *form of life* of the Son of God is salvific and represents an essential condition for salvation.[62] Thus, Vatican II teaches that God gives special graces that constitute the consecration of a state of life. Whoever receives them can more faithfully follow the form of life that Christ chose for himself and proposed to his disciples.

Lumen gentium 42 refers to religious as those who "embrace poverty with the free choice of God's sons" (*exinanitio*), in explicit reference to Ephesians 2:7–8: "who more closely follow and more clearly demonstrate the Savior's self-giving" (*LG* 42).[63] In this same passage, it is stated that those who "subject their own will to another person on God's behalf, in pursuit of an excellence surpassing what is commanded (*ultra mensuram praecepti*) . . . liken themselves more thoroughly to Christ in His obedience" (*LG* 42).[64] In spite of the emendments to which Chapters V and VII of *Lumen gentium* were subjected,[65] we are fully entitled to compare number 42 with number 44. The content and even the expressions of both are equivalent.

We consider to be normative the remark made before in relation to what is "typical" of nonsacramental consecration, namely, that it bestows the grace required to participate, in a specific way, in the salvific priesthood of Christ. Therefore, the comparative adverbs by which the Council characterizes this consecration, and especially those we have examined and which in themselves are more generic and unspecified ("provides an *ampler* manifestation of the baptismal consecration" [PC 5]; and "he is *more intimately* consecrated to divine service" [LG 44]) must be understood to refer directly to the "victimal" aspect proper to all consecration. Thus, religious "more fully" and "more intimately" attain to the full meaning of baptism without undermining the value of the indispensable sacrament.

We have attributed this normative significance to the paragraphs of *Lumen gentium* 44 because of the remarkable density of the doctrine they contain. This theological richness sheds light on the following phrases: "it is a state consecrated to God" (LG 45) through which the Church manifests its maternal concern; the "magis," which we find in *Lumen gentium* 46, alluding to the value of the evangelical counsels so as to "pattern the Christian after that manner of virginal and humble life which Christ the Lord elected for himself, and which his Virgin Mother also chose"[66]; and, finally, the fact that this consecration "adorns the Bride of Christ with the unswerving and humble loyalty of religions" (LG 46).

We have purposely omitted a few words from the third paragraph of *Lumen gentium* 44, in order to enhance their meaning all the more. They will serve as a conclusion to all we have said about what is "typical" of nonsacramental consecration. In connection with the "religious state," it is said that "to all men it shows wonderfully at work within the Church the surpassing greatness of the force of Christ the King and the boundless power of the Holy Spirit" (LG 44).[67]

It is evident that the virtue of Christ glorious and the power of the Holy Spirit are fully manifest whenever religious in the Church want to be and become voluntary, loving, and grateful victims, a desire which, as we have said, constitutes what is "typical" of the religious state. This state requires all the virtue and power mentioned in this text, if the baptized are to accept it and to persevere in it, since only with the help of divine grace can they live out this consecration for the good of the Church and the World.

Once the religious "state" is comprehended in terms of the blood of Christ's sacrifice and his condition as salvific victim, the conclusion drawn by the Council can be seen to correspond to all that has been exposed in this essay: "the religious state constituted by the profession of the evangelical counsels . . . belongs inseparably to the life and holiness of the Church" (*LG* 44).[68]

Conclusion

At the end of this essay, we can assert that the Council presents "religious" consecration as constituting a state that enjoys a special role in the People of God. If we choose to designate this state as a "casta sacra,"[69] and qualify it with terms taken from sociology, we should not try to place it among the "high" social classes, but among the lowest, those of the outcast. Indeed, the gift of God induces a Christian to become a servant and a "victim" in an unambiguous and intense way; although a Christian chooses a religious vocation, its efficacy as a consecration is due to God himself, who is its first and main agent. Therefore, the "profession" and the self-giving it implies "confer a consecration." When God consecrates, as when he calls, he prepares and helps a Christian to accept the "consecration." He confers real graces, which have an existential import even in the case of a "nonsacramental consecration."

The consecration conferred by baptism and confirmation bestows a grace prior in importance to any other subsequent "consecration." Therefore, baptism provides the fertile furrow in which "religious" consecration may take root.

The double meaning of the concept "consecration" (to make and to dedicate) and its double purpose (to worship and to serve) first appertain to baptism and confirmation, but reach their culmination in "religious" consecration because of the latter's increased evangelical intensity. This is what the Council expresses in various ways. Yet the Council, especially when it focuses on the "victimal aspect" of religious consecration, best indicates the inseparability between sacramental and nonsacremental forms of consecration and their distinctiveness for the good of the Church as it carries out its evangelical mandate for the world along with Christ and in the power of the Holy Spirit. Living out the vows must correspond to this divine "consecration," if it is to bear fruit and nurture the world with the sanctifying energy that is the wisdom of Christ and the love of the Spirit that come from and lead ahead to the Father.

Translated from the Spanish by Louis-Bertrand Raymond
and Philip Rosato.

Notes

1. Let us quote only the opinion of N. Hausman, "La vie religieuse apostolique selon Vatican II," *NRT*, 107 (1985), 658–674. On page 658, the author says: "La consécration ecclésiale et al destinée missionnaire constituent ainsi, nous paraît-il, l'essentiel de l'enseignement conciliaire sur la vie religieuse." His remarks, which should not be restricted to the missionary aspect, have a particular authority because this article synthesizes a thesis presented at the Faculty of Theology and Canon Law of the Catholic University of Louvain, in June 1985.

2. We refer to the documented study of A. Restrepo, *De la "vida religiosa" a la "Vida consagrada,"* presented as thesis at the P.U.G., 1974, 3 vol., a thesis supervised by Father Jean Beyer and partly published, with the subtitle, "Una evolución teológica" (Rome, 1981). See, in the same sense, the well-written article of F. Morlot, "Consacrazione sacerdotale e consacrazione nei consigli evangelici," *Vita Consacrata*, 7 (1971), 638–657. The author does not present the subject in its full extent, limiting himself to the society founded by Father de Clorivière, but he develops it along the same lines as A. Restrepo. The title of Father J. Galot's book is also suggestive: *Porteurs du souffle de l'Esprit. Nouvelle optique de la vie consacrée* (Paris, 1967).

3. For example, M.-D. Chenu, *Les laïcs et la "Consecratio mundi,"* Unam Sanctam 51, c (Paris, 1966), 1035–1043, with a bibliography on pages 1052–1053. It should be noted that the author repeats in substance the content of his article, "Consecratio mundi," *NRT*, 86 (1964), 608–618; L. Mendizabal, "La Consacración religiosa y el sentido de los votos," *Manresa*, 37 (1965), 225–248; J. Galot, *Porteurs du souffle de l'Esprit. Nouvelle optique de la vie consacrée*, 60–62.

4. Here are, in chronological order, some articles and books that we consider to be important for our subject: J. Beyer, *La consécration à Dieu dans les Instituts séculiers*, AnGregoriana 141 (Rome, 1964); L. Mendizabal, "La Consagración religiosa y el sentido de los votos," *Manresa*, 37 (1965), 225–248; U. Rocco, "Battesimo e professione religiosa," *Perfice Munus*, 40 (1965), 157–162; J. Leclerq, "Professione religiosa, secundo battesimo," *Vita Religiosa*, 3 (1967), 3–8; B. Secondin, "Battesimo e professione religiosa nel misterio della Chiesa," *Vita Religiosa*, 3 (1967), 203–214, 299–311; G.G. Ranquet, *Consacrazione battesimale e consacrazione religiosa* (Alba, 1967); J. Beyer, *Die vita per consilia evangelica consecrata* (Rome, 1969). The author puts together the articles published in *Periodica*, during the years 1966–1968; M. Olphe-Galliard, *Chrétiens consacrés. Thèmes et documents* (Paris, 1971); J. Beyer, "La consacrazione nella Chiesa," *Vita Consacrata*, 7 (1971), 138–150; A. Bandera, "La consacrazione a Dio per mezzo dei consigli evangelici," *Vita Consacrata*, 7 (1971), 345–358, 431–441, 521–531, 609–616; F. Morlot, "Consacrazione sacerdotale e consacra-

zione nei consigli evangelici," *Vita Consacrata*, 7 (1971), 638–657; J. Garcia Paredes, "Confirmación y vida religiosa. A la luz de la consagración de las virgenes en la Iglesia Romana," *Vida Religiosa*, 34, (1973) 275–286; X. Ochoa, "Excursus historico-doctrinalis circa sensum institutionalem consecrationis religiosae," *Commentarium pro religiosis*, 55 (1974), 193–221, 289–312; E.C. Meyer, "Is Religious Life a Sacrament?" *Review for Religious*, 33 (1974), 1100–1120; D. Bertetto, "La Consacrazione religiosa," *Vita Consacrata*, 10 (1974), 321–326; G. Martelet, "La consacrazione secolare," *Vita Consacrata*, 11 (1975), 577–590; R. Regamey, "Consacrazione religiosa," *Dizionario degli Istituti di Perfezione*, 2: 1607–1613; A Pigna, "La consacrazione religiosa," in E. Ancelli (ed.), *Vita Religiosa. Bilancio e Prospettive* (Rome, 1976), 117–149; G. Ghirlanda, "Ecclesialità della vita consacrata," *Vita Consacrata*, 13 (1977), 26–32, 231–237; G. Scalvini, "La mistica del voto religioso," *Nuova Rivista di Ascetica e Mistica*, 2 (1977), 193–215; G. Rambaldi, "Consacrati a Dio in Cristo per evangelizzare," *Vita Consacrata*, 14 (1978), 540–548; G. Lesage, "Evoluzione e portata del vincolo sacro nella professione religiosa," *Vita Consacrata*, 15 (1979), 74–95; A. de Bonhomme, "La consacrazione per mezzo dei consigli è una consacrazione nuova?" *Vita Consacrata*, 15 (1979), 35–47; M. Fitzpatrick, "A Contemporary Understanding of the Vows," *Review of Religious*, 39 (1980), 378–388; R. Tyron-Montalembert, "Le renouveau conciliare de la consécration des vierges," *Vie Consacrée*, 53 (1981), 357–369; M.J. Shoenmackers, *Genèse du chapitre VI "De religiosis" de la Constitution sur l'Eglise "Lumen Gentium"* (Rome, 1983); G. Jelich, *Kirchliches Ordensverständnis im Wandel. Untersuchungen zum Ordensverständnis des Zweiten Vatikanischen Konzils*, Erfurter ThS 49 (Leipzig, 1983), 151–173; A. Boni, "La vita consacrata nell'età patristica," *Vita Consacrata*, 20 (1984), 777–789; P. Molinari and P. Gumpel, "Il capitolo VI della Costituzione dogmatica sulla vita religiosa nell'immediato pre-concilio. I Lavori di preparazione del Concilio. I Lavori conciliari," *Vita Consacrata*, 20 (1984), 815–896; P. Molinari and P. Gumpel, "La dottrina della Costitutione dogmatica "Lumen Gentium" sulla vita consacrata," *Vita Consacrata*, 21 (1985), 3–137; O.G. Girardi, "Vocazione e consacrazione nella esortazione Apostolica 'Redemptionis donm,' " *Vita Consacrata*, 21 (1985), 399–415. Also, we must not forget the articles in note 5.

5. To prove our assertion, it will be sufficient to recall the controversy between A. Boni and P. Molinari, which was published in the review *Vita Consacrada* (VC). This controversy was triggered off by A. Boni's article, "La vita religiosa nel suo contenuto teologale," VC, 7 (1971), 265–276, to which P. Molinari replied in his own, "Divino obsequio intimius consecratur," VC, 7 (1971), 417–430; P. Boni retorted with "Domino se specialiter devovent," VC, 7 (1971), 764–781;

P. Molinari answered back with "Domino se peculiariter devovet et divino obsequio intimius consecratur," VC, 8 (1972), 401–432. See also the intervention of A. de Bonhomme at the International Congress of Canon Law (14–19 February 1977, P.U.G.), published in *Periodica*, 67 (1978), 373–390, and translated into Italian in VC, 15 (1979), 35–47. The author, besides recalling the divergence of opinion between A. Boni and P. Molinari, which we just pointed out, says that R. Regamey, J. Galot, and J. Beyer defend the opinion that religious consecration is special, and that, on the contrary, J.M.R. Tillard denies it. A. de Bonhomme agrees with the position of the three aforementioned theologians (pp. 389–390).

6. To justify our contribution, it might be sufficient to quote this sentence of P. Molinari: "In vista della grande importanza che la dottrina conciliare cerca la consacrazione dei religiosi riveste per la loro vita ed anche per la teologia *che certamente può e deve ancora essere sviluppata* su questo punto, ho ritenuto opportuno . . . ," VC, 8 (1972), 432. To the necessity indicated in the words we have italicized corresponds, without any doubt, the subsequent contribution of the articles of P. Molinari and P. Gumpel mentioned in note 4. However even these authors, like the others, as far as we can notice, do not have in mind all the texts of the Council referring to the "consecrate-consecration."

7. On this subject matter, see what P. Molinari says in his article, "Domino se peculiariter devovet . . . " (cf. note 5, pp. 429–430). From now on, when we place in parentheses (note. . . .) with a corresponding number, the reader should know that we are referring to the notes of this chapter.

8. It appears that L. Cabielles de Cos has a position different from ours in his long article, "Vocación universal a la santidad y superioridad de la vida religiosa en los capítulos V y VI de la Const. 'Lumen Gentium,' " *Claretianum*, 19 (1979), 5–96. As we can see on pp. 42–50, and as is summarized on p. 91: "En síntesis, y por lo que a este tema se refiere, las perspectivas que se perciben en el Concilio para la futura teología de la Vida Religiosa son: superación del perfeccionismo en los consejos; profundización exégetica en cada uno de ellos; separación definitiva, con sus consecuencias, de la virginidad frente a los otros dos; superación de la terminología misma, eliminando quizás hasta la palabra 'consejo.' Todo esto supone superar el texto conciliar; pero es seguir las pistas que el mismo Concilio ha abierto," We shall indicate further another conclusion of what the author considers to be a "surpassing" (superación). We are content with observing that there are various ways to approach the texts of the Council.

9. Here we refer to the data provided by the work published by the Catholic University of Louvain, in Philippe Delhaye, M. Gueret, and P. Tombeur (eds.), *Concilium Vaticanum II. Concordance, Index, Listes*

de fréquence, Tables comparatives (Louvain, 1974). The term "consecratio" appears twenty-four times and "consecrare," twenty-one times, in all their forms. See pp. 136–137. The term that interests us appears in AG (three times), AA (one), CD (four), GS (one), LG (fourteen), OT (two), PC (five), PO (nine), SC (four), and NP (preliminary explanatory note 2).

10. See *Oxford Latin Dictionary* (Oxford, 1969) for "consecro-areaviatum," and for "con-sacro" (p. 411), and the verb "sacro" (p. 1675, Oxford, 1980).

11. In the *Lexicon totius latinitatis* of Aegidio Forcellini, published by F. Corradini (Patavii, 1940,), Vol. I, it is said of "consecro": "est idem quod sacro, seu ex profano sacrum religiosumque facio, diis dico" (p. 798).

12. Among the various meanings of "consecro," as given by A. Forcellini (note 11), it seems to me appropriate to point out the literal meaning: (1) which is used "absolute" (consecrabantur agri); or "cum dativo personae," which is equivalent to "addicere" (dedicate to); (2) "consecrare aliquem est inter deos referre et deum facere. Hinc ponitur et de Romanis imperatoribus qui post mortem inter deos referebantur." These two meanings appear fundamental to me: one, "dedicate," and the other, "make." Concerning "dedicate," see the distinction made between "consecrare" and "dedicare" toward the end of the chapter, which can be summarized: "quaecumque dedicantur consecrata sunt, non contra." Although, sometimes, the two verbs are used as equivalents.

13. In the *Lexicon* of A. Forcellini, we read: "7. Item apud scriptores Ecclesiasticos consecrari dicebantur qui baptismate aluebantur, quippe qui hoc sacramento famulatui divino addicebantur. 8. qui sacris ordinibus insignuntur imprimis episcopi" (note 11).

14. Notice that the Council uses various terms to designate the same content. In some cases, it explains it further (e.g., in LG 28, referring to priests); in other cases, it gives a shorter and more condensed locution (PO 3). Regarding the "religious," the Council avoids giving a definition though a few Fathers had asked for it, and gives as equivalent "the vows," "the profession," and "the consecration through the evangelical counsels." The essence alone of this consecrating effort is considered. Father Galot used in this broad sense the word "religious" (note 2), p. 5. Sometimes, I also use the expression "nonsacramental consecration" to designate the same content.

15. As can be noted in our exposition, we have touched lightly on many aspects of the "consecrate-consecration." We have kept in mind some aspects that seem to confirm our interpretation: e.g., what is said of the consecration conferred by holy orders, which is the hierarchical communion ["*unum idemque sacerdotium* et ministerium Christi ita participant (bishops and priests)] ut *ipsa unitas consecrationis* missionisque requirat" (italics added) (*PO* 7).

16. Chapter II of the Decree *PO* deals with the ministry of priests and, following the order of *LG* 28, it places first the ministry of the word of God, in spite of the opposition of a few Fathers (No. 4). Number 5, which speaks of the office of sanctifier, corresponds to No. 3 of the first text. The text "emendatus" will undergo alterations. As for what concerns us, we must point out that the Commission rejects the proposition of modus No. 20: "Deleantur verba 'ministrante Episcopo.' " See *AS*, IV/ VII, 145. And see also the commentary of J. Frisque, "Le Décret presbyterorum Ordinis," in P. Colin (ed.), *Les Prêtres. Formation et ministère,* Unam Sanctam 68 (Paris, 1968), 144–145, 148. The answer of the Commission is significant because the text clearly indicates that the main "agent" is God, and the bishop is the minister, although, according to *OT* 2, the bishops must consecrate (consecrent) the suitable candidates. We can point out more than one "agent" of the same "consecrate," not exluding but ranking them properly.

17. In the "textus emendatus," No. 12 corresponds to No. 11 of the preceding (cf. *AS*, IV/VI, 369). Its content is definitive, even though it had to go through many alterations. This No. 12 is the first of Chapter III of *PO* dealing with the perfection of priests. The first sentence of this number, according to J. Frisque (cf. note 16) is a kind of preface to the whole chapter: "elle—et nous pouvons ajouter tout le numéro—fonde, au point de vue doctrinal, le lien entre le ministère et la vie des prêtres" (p. 164). The alterations brought about to the definitive text are numerous, but they do not modify the sentence that we have transcribed.

18. With regard to the text of *LG* 28, let us remember that it belongs to Chapter III, which underwent many alterations. The "transmission of powers" is considered from a dogmatic rather than a historical point of view. Yet, it remains soundly and clearly established that Christ communicates his own consecration, and this, from our point of view, is conclusive. This consecration includes the ordination to God (worship) and the ministry (service), just as the mission is linked to the grace bestowed to carry it on. See the good commentary of A. Grillmeier on this number 28 in *LThK*, I, 247–252. As for *PO* 2, consult the commentary of J. Frisque (note 16), 137–140. Notice that the first paragraph of this No. 2 recalls the doctrine of the common priesthood that is oriented toward worship and service. In our second paragraph, the same two parameters appear, but they refer to the sacerdotal consecration received through the participation in the consecration of Christ.

19. The No. 2 of *OT* 2, written and rewritten so as to take into account the suggestions of Cardinals Bueno Monreal and Döpfner, and the Polish bishops, includes three paragraphs. We are interested in the second one: it deals with the vocation itself to priesthood, which is the result of the harmonious unity between the divine call and the call of the Church (cf. *Catechismus Romanus*, P. II, Chap. VII, Nos. 3–5). It should be noted that the main "agent" is the Holy Spirit, though, grammatically speaking, the "means" is "Spiritus Sancti sigillo." For the "consecratio mundi," see the article of M.-D. Chenu (cf. note 3). For a comprehensive view of the meaning, categories, and value of the concept "consecration," the article of Father J. de Finance, "consécration," *Dictionnaire de Spiritualité*, II, 1576–1583 is excellent. We keep our distance from the solution of M.-D. Chenu. The position of *PO* 3 looks far more convincing to us by giving to "consecratur" a strong sense of "dedication" coming from the same sanctifying grace.

20. It should be emphasized that the action of the Holy Spirit as "agent" does not suppress that of Christ, neither, therefore, that of the "minister" who administers the sacrament.

21. At the conclusion of the sentence, of which we have transcribed the beginning (note 17), the Council says: "simili modo Presbyteri, unctione Spiritus Sancti consecrati et a Christo missi, in seipsis opera carnis mortificant et hominum servitio totaliter se devovent, et . . ." (*PO* 12). With regard to the many alterations proposed about this second paragraph, the answer given to the modus 10 should be noted. This modus is expressed in four paragraphs: from a. to d. In paragraph b., it is proposed to change the sentence. The Commission refused to change it because the proposed sentence is very long and does not mention "Spiritus Sancti [et Sanctificantis]," (*AS*, IV/VII, 194). Hence, the weight of the sentence that interests us.

22. We refer to the article of P. Molinari, "Divino obsequio . . . ," 423–426, and "Domino se peculiariter devovet . . . ," 406–431, already mentioned (note 5). Also, P. Molinari and P. Gumpel, 107–109 (note 4).

23. P. Molinari asserts: "Per chiunque conosca il latino è infatti ovvio che il sense grammaticale della parola *consecratur* è passivo e non riflessivo" ("Domino se peculiariter devovet . . . ," 407, note 5). About this subject, A. de Bonhomme had already noted: "Sane non excluditur verbo *consecretur* significationem retransitivam (si consacra) tribui posse (cf. O. Reimann, *Syntaxe latine* . . . , 7th ed. [Paris, 1942], 221). Sed declaratio Commissionis Theologicae Concilii omne dubium excludit," p. 389, note 63 (note 5). We can quote J. Oleza, *Gramática de la lengua latina* (Barcelona, 1945), 240, n. 405, which fully agrees with this.

24. The subject "agente" of "liberari intendit," which may well be translated "he wants to free himself," is without doubt the person who takes the vows. Now the meaning of the conjunction "et," which may

be equivalent to "et re vera," "reapse" (A. Forcellini, Vol. II, 307 [note 11]), seems to be required, especially since the verb "consecratur" changes subject "agente." The phrase "et divino obsequio intimius consecratur" would thus repeat what precedes, according to the theological perspective proper to Vatican II.

25. For commentaries on this No. 44 and in general on Chapter VI of *LG*, which we have consulted, see that of P. Molinari and P. Gumpel, whose articles "Il capitolo VI . . . " and "La dottrina della Costituzione Dogmatica . . . ," which we have quoted in note 4. The first article, which is long and well-documented, deals with the question of the separation–union of Chapters V and VI (pp. 842–893), and the second one with Nos. 43 and 44 (pp. 97–114). The commentary of F. Wulf (*LThK* I, 284–313), focusing on the history of these two chapters (284–287) and appropriately pointing out the themes of No. 44 (306–307) and also its problematics, seems to be reserved regarding the endorsement of the teachings ensuing from this number. In our opinion, he is right, when in note 5 of p. 307, he states that, in regard to *Magno gaudio* of Paul VI (*AAS*, 56 [1964], 565–571), the Council avoids repeating the "strong" expressions (*AAS*, 567) of this speech of the pontiff while referring to it.

26. We have already transcribed, in note 20, the words of *LG* 10 to which we refer. Two points should be noted: the preposition "per" with the accusative indicates "the agent"; the word "regenerationem" is equivalent to "baptism," if one does not understand as an endyadis the phrase that then would be equivalent to "by the regenerating unction of the Holy Spirit." There would then be a question only of baptism, and not of confirmation, in our opinion. The reason for including the two sacraments in this text comes from the text of *AA* 3, which we can consider as parallel, and which makes a clear distinction between the two sacraments. It reads thus: "Laici officium et jus ad apostolatum obtinent ex ipsa sua cum Christo capite unione. Per Baptismum enim corpori Christo mystico inserti, per Confirmationem virtute Spiritus Sancti roborati, ad apostolatum ab ipso Domino depuntanur. *In regale sacerdotium et gentem sanctam* (cf. 1 P2, 4–10) *consecrantur ut. . . ."* The words italicized are equivalent to those of *LG* 10. Regarding confirmation and its relation to baptism, one should consult P. Fransen, "Firmung," *LThK*, 4, 145–151; G. Kretschmar, "Firmung," TRE 11, 192–204 (with a choice bibliography); and F. Cuttas, "Confirmation," DS 2:1412–1422. It seems to me that the relationship between confirmation and baptism can lead to a deeper understanding of the relationship between baptism and nonsacramental consecration through the evangelical counsels.

27. The Latin text says: "Qua propter conjuges christiani ad sui status officia et dignitatem peculiari sacramento roborantur et veluti consecrantur" (GS 48). Obviously, the ablative of "peculiari sacramento," in other words, marriage, indicates "the agent" of this "consecrantur." The particle "veluti," which tones down the affirmation, could already be found in Casti connubii of Pius XI, as it appears in the good commentary of B. Haring, in *LThK Suppl.* III, 423–434, without however appraising the meaning of this "veluti." In relation to our exact goal of pointing out "the agent" of "consecrantur," we also can prescind.

28. The texts are *LG* 28, *PO* 3, and *PO* 12. (1) *LG* 28: "Presbyteri, quamvis pontificatus apicem non habeant et in exercenda sua potestate ab Episcopis pendeant, cum eis tamen sacerdotali honore tonjuncti sunt et vi sacramenti Ordinis, ad imaginem Christi, summi atque aeterni Sacerdotis (Acts 5:1–10; 7:24; 9:11–28), ad Evangelium praedicandum fidelesque pascendos et ad divinum cultum celebrandum consecrantur, ut veri sacerdotes Novi Testamenti." These words belong to the same paragraph we already have transcribed (note 18). The ablative "vi sacramenti Ordinis" clearly indicates "the agent" of this "consecrantur," which obviously does not exclude other "consecrators" of a different rank. (2) *PO* 3: "Presbyteri Novi Testamenti, vocatione quidem et ordinatione sua, quodam modo in sinu Populi Dei segregantur, non tamen ut separentur, sive ab eo, sive a quovis homine, sed ut totaliter consecrentur operi quod Dominus eos assumit." This No. 3, which is the last of the first chapter of *PO*, speaks about the condition of the priest in the world: it complements what we have pointed out in note 18. It should be added that here, and with good reason, the "vocation" is presented also as being an "agent." While admitting "quodam modo" that vocation and ordination are set apart, we acknowledge that they convey special graces that are not bestowed on all. The use of "consecrentur" to correct all possible misunderstandings and reinforce the "non ut separentur" shows that the Council makes the meaning of "dedicate oneself" prevail in the concept of "consecrate." Therefore, to dedicate oneself to the work for which the Lord has assumed them, is to insert oneself into the Church and mankind, by answering to the dynamism of the grace received. See P. Colin, "Le prêtre un homme 'mis à part' mais non 'séparé,' " 261–274. (3) *PO* 12: "Ad illam vero perfectionem adquirendem peculiari ratione tenentur sacerdotes, quippe qui, Deo in Ordinis receptione novo modo consecrati, Christi Aeterni Sacerdotis viva instrumenta efficiantur ut. . . ." We have already dealt with this No. 12 and its second paragraph (note 17). We must add that the two "modi" affect the words we have transcribed in this paragraph and that can be found in Nos. 5 and 6 (*AS*, IV/VII, 1921–1931). The first one proposed that it be read "majori ratione" and "tenentur." The Commission rejected the first *modus* and maintained the "peculiari," and accepted the "tenentur." The second *modus* proposed that it be read: "in Ordinis receptione Deo specialiter consecrati," putting forward that the baptismal consecration had already been mentioned.

29. To know the alterations of this text and the significance of the changes made, and also the critique of the preceding text made by Bishop Abed of Tripoli, see the commentary of J.A. Jungmann, *LThK*, I, 74–77.

30. For the commentary of this No. 11, see especially P.J. Beyer, "Les Istituts séculiers," Unam Sanctam 62 (Paris, 1967), 375–384. The author, very competent in the subject, emphasizes the importance of the phrase added, "quamvis non sint instituta religiosa" (375–376); he notes that the term "religiosa" is equivocal (379), and that the consecration in the Church is an act of charity (380). See also the contributions of the same J. Beyer already mentioned in note 4. F. Wult (*LThK*, II 286–289) also sheds light on the content of No. 11, thanks to *Provida Mater* and *Primo feliciter* of Pius XII, two documents fundamental for secular institutes, and thanks to the alterations brought to the schemas. We attract the reader's attention to the ambivalence of the terms. Sometimes they are employed in a sense we can qualify as technical (as in the case of the word "religiosa"); elsewhere, in a broader sense (as here, "professio"). The same can be said of "in saeculo," which terms these institutes "saecularia"; they too renounce the "world," in the sense indicated before. The imprecision of the vocabulary can easily give the impression of being incoherent (cf. J. Beyer, *Les Instituts séculiers*, 383). However, we believe that well-founded and adequate solutions can be found.

31. We take the liberty of insisting on this issue: from our viewpoint, we consider that, according to the doctrine of the Council, it is beyond doubt an established fact that "consecration" has various agents, of which one does not exclude the other, but requires it. In keeping with the remarks of P. Molinari in his article, "Domino se peculiariter devovet . . . " (note 5), where he says "parlando della consacrazione religiosa [del Concilio] non dice mai che il religioso *se consecrato*, ma adopera sempre e ovunque la forma passiva 'consecratur' " (p. 402), an idea that he repeats in pages 403, 407, and 409, we can conclude with equivocation that the Council would have excluded from the role of "agent" the person who makes the profession. But there is nothing of the sort. We said and repeat that we accept as our own the interpretation of P. Molinari of *LG* 44. But, once more, Vatican II does not exclude the professed from the role of "agent." The text of *PC* 11, by itself, proves the opposite, Moreover, if we look for texts of the Council in which, referring to the "religious" consecration, it uses the verb "consecrare," we notice, to our astonishment, in view of the author's insistence, that besides the one of *LG* 44, there are only two: *PC* 1 and *LG* 45. The first text indicates as "agent" the profession; the second one has the phrase "statum Deo consecratum" coincide with "professionem religiosam." In both cases, we must not exclude as "agent" the human person who "consecrates himself," nor God who consecrates.

32. For the commentary, see that of F. Wult (*LThK*, II, 250–305), as introduction to the history (250–265), for what more directly deals with No. 5 (276–278). The commentary and study of G. Jelich (note 4) are still more elaborate; for the successive alterations of the text, see p. 89–126; and for the theological content, which includes also *LG*, pp. 127–284. In direct relation to our subject, see what he says in "Die Weihe als totales Engagement des Menschen" (pp. 161–162). We emphasize these words of his explanation: "Nach 'Perfectae caritatis' bringen die Ordensleute sich Gott dar. Sie weihen sich im Beforgen un Versprechen der Räte" (p. 161). G. Jelich proves it by referring to the three evangelical counsels, but without directly referring to *PC* 5. We believe this to be a negligence, since, on this point, he summarizes and condenses all the remaining texts regarding the consecration of the religious. This author emphasizes well the elements of vocation and grace, and also the fact that his divine element is consecrating, but not to the detriment of the human element, which both receives and consecrates (p. 162).

33. According to J. Oleza, *Gramática* (note 23), p. 194, the "quamdam" can have a "balancing" meaning or, on the contrary, a "toning down" meaning. I think it should be understood in the first meaning to conform to the text of *PO* 16, which, regarding virginity or celibacy, says: "nova et eximia ratione Christo consecrantur." Therefore, we have translated "quamdam" into "really."

34. See note 32.

35. Regarding the changes made in this text, the motives of "sacerdotal celibacy" and the aspect or foundation of its holiness, see J. Frisque (note 16), pp. 172–176, in direct relation to this second paragraph, pp. 174–175, where with just reason he notes that there is question of celibacy as "gift," and that the language used herein could be called "generic," as in *LG* 42 dealing with the same subject. Also the article of F. Wulf (*LThK*, III, 214–221). In *AS*, IV/VII, 212, we can see how the Commission answers the "modi" 17 and 21 jointly, and chooses the phrase "nova et eximia ratione Christo consecrantur," which passed into the definitive text and with which the Council partly meets the alterations proposed by 332 Fathers, and besides justifies the value of "sign."

36. For the history of this decree, see the commentary of S. Brechter (*LThK*, III, 10–21). Besides the explanation of the various alterations, we find in it the detailed results of votings on the "modi." This same author (pp. 112–117) comments on No. 38 and brings out the "reassuming" value of its first paragraph and the impact of the intervention of cardinal A. Bea on this same paragraph.

37. See the commentary of S. Brechter (note 36), which pertinently emphasizes that, given the nature of presbyteral priesthood—recalled here together with its first obligation, mentioned in No. 1 of this decree—we may take by way of conclusion the words we have emphasized in the translation, and which correspond to our purpose: all his life is also dedicated to the service of missions.

38. See note 28.

39. See R. Schulte, "La vie religieuse comme signe," in Unam Sanctam 51, c. III (Paris, 1966), 1153–1156.

40. I think that without doubt the word "consecration" replaces that of "sacrament of Orders." We should not fail to notice, since this confirms the interpretation we have given in note 32, that the verb "constituere" is also used in PC 5, on the subject of the "religious" profession.

41. See what we say further (note 42) to determine the value of this consecration.

42. See the commentary of Cardinal J. Ratzinger (LThK, I 238–359), pp. 352–354, which clarifies the meaning of NP regarding one of the most difficult problems for the Church, from the legal and historical point of view. Our interest is confined to bringing out the equivalence between the "fit" and the "constituitur" of LG 22 (note 21); and that this "fit" is afterwards expressed through "datur." We must not forget that these locutions coincide as regards their substance.

43. See the commentary of P.-J. Cordes (LThK, III, 170–178), which deals with all of this third chapter and in particular with this No. 7. He emphasizes that the relationship between priest and bishop is precisely based on "the unity of consecration and mission." He observes, as the difference between the two, that "la participación al servicio episcopal se concede al prebétero por el sacramento, su actuación por la misión canónica" (p. 171). J. Frisque (note 35) comments on this number on pages 152–154.

44. We have already mentioned this No. 12 and this paragraph (note 28), and also its second paragraph (note 17). We must add, regarding the words transcribed, that there were four modi (Nos. 1–4). The first one asked that the words "tamquam Ordinis Episcopalis cooperatores" be removed. The answer was: "non acceptatur." The second one saw a difficulty in the "configurantur," to which it was answered: "Ratio imaginis hic bene congruit." The third one, wishing that mention be made of human weakness, was accepted. The fourth one was rejected: it proposed to change the adjective "tantae" and was answered: "Stet textus. Ratio cogens non videtur" (AS, IV/VII, 192).

45. Regarding our own point of view, let two things be noted. The

problematics of "vows," of their "matter" and "perpetuity" remain marginal to our study. Concerning the vows, see, for example, C. Pujol,
"Los votos religiosos," *Espiritu*, 23 (1974), 19–52; and his intervention,
which was appreciated at the International Congress of Canon Law
(note 5) and mentioned in *Periodica*, 67 (1978), 507–510. Secondly, by
interpreting the word "consecratio" the way we do in the text, the term
of the comparatives used here by the Council appears clearly, namely,
"other sacred ties," if they are less firm and stable. We refer to the
assertion of L. Cabielles (note 8): "La consagración más intima y perfecta (el texto, con grand prudencia, no pone el termino de estos
comparativos) significada en los víncolos más presente a Cristo unido a
su Iglesia, es una sobreanadidura o una simple explicitación de la
consagración y vinculos del bautismo?" (p. 71). The "perfectior," therefore, does not refer to baptism, but also to the vows. The "intimius"
(more intimately) of the sentence that immediately precedes is quite
another matter. Later, we discuss this.

46. See *PC* 17.

47. Suffice it for our purpose to mention some texts qualifying objects destined for worship: for example, "sacra supellex" (*SC* 122) or
"sacrae supellectilis" (*SC* 128), "sacras imagines" (*SC* 125), "sacri al-
taris" (*PC* 6). The "Liturgia" is called "sacra" many times (*SC* 9, 22; *UR*
15), and also the "musica" to which the Council alludes (*SC* 44).

48. We refer to the opinion of F. Wulf, commenting on No. 2 of
PO (*LThK*, III, 146). The author brings out very well the first words of
this No. 2: the consecration and mission of Christ. And he states:
"ciertamente aquí la 'consegración' y 'misión' del sacerdocio de la Iglesia
tienen su origen y su modelo." And then he wonders what is their
content, and what is the relationship between them. He answers: "Der
Grundbegriff ist zweifelsohne der Sendung," although he notices afterwards that we must not conceive the mission in a merely external sense.
I wanted to clarify this relationship in the text. Y. Congar, for his part,
gives the preference to the "consecration." Cf. "Le Sacerdoce du nouveau Testament. Mission et culte," in Unam Sanctam 68, p. 243.

49. J. Neuner, commenting on this number (*LThK*, II, 331–333),
places these significant words at the beginning: "Der Artikel über der
Zälibat hat eine komplizierte Geschichte," which he justifies afterwards. But, in his final writing, everything flows as if the article had
been written with one stroke of the pen. The interventions of Cardinals
A. Bea and J. Döpfner, Bishops Mendes and Reuss, and many Fathers
who, in all, propose sixty "modi." One can read the answer to these
modi and their content in *AS*, IV/VII, 83–87. The sixth "modus"
asking to substitute "consequuntur" for "impetrantur" and to emphasize
the dependence of the Church received this answer: "In texto emen-
dato dicitur 'consequuntur.' Hoc modo perfectior caritas apparet ut

fructus *ipsius consecrationis Christo factae* et sic jam elucescit ejus aspectus ecclesialis" (p. 85). The italicized words indicate that the Commission suggests that the person who makes the profession "consecrates herself" to Christ, and that the "more perfect charity" is its fruit.

50. The texts of the Council to which we refer leave aside the "moment" or "time" when the candidate accepts his commitment to celibacy; as required by their theological content, they consider only the gifts that baptism, confirmation, priesthood, and even the diaconate confer.

51. What we refer to by the words "worship term" can be replaced by "service," and vice versa; these two elements of participating in the consecration and mission of Christ are closely linked together. "Worship," therefore, is already a "service," and the latter is a way of glorifying God. We insist on emphasizing another aspect of this point. If we compare the comparatives used here with those used by Vatican II in *LG* 42, and *PC* 12, 13, and 14, speaking in a different context about the same evangelical counsels, we notice that they coincide. The Council, therefore, brings to our notice as a teaching the "consecration" of the counsel as such.

52. Regarding the "modi" that have modified this sentence, see *AS*, III/VII, 130–131.

53. The meaning of the word "mundo" has been clearly expressed by A. Guillamont when he writes: "Mais, ce mot [kosmos], comme on le sait, est ambigu; ici [referring to the monastic conception] il désigne non pas ce qui est essentiellement mauvais, mais ce qui est relativement mauvais, dans la mesure où ce peut être un obstacle pour qui veut devenir parfait" (*Aux origines du monachisme chrétien. Pour une phénoménologie du monachisme*, Spiritualité Orientale 30 [Bégrilles en Manges, 1979], 222). On the same page, a little earlier, he writes: "La première de ces démarches [du moine] est le renoncement, en grec 'apotagé' ou 'apotaxis.' Il ne s'agit pas seulement du renoncement au mal et à Satan, comme l'était, pour tout fidèle, le renoncement baptismal; mais il s'agit de renoncer même à des choses qui, en elles-mêmes, ne sont pas mauvaises: la famille, non seulement celle que le moine fonderait s'il se mariait, mais aussi (nous le verrons) celle où il est né, sa parenté charnelle; puis les biens et al richesse de ce monde."

54. In the new Roman Ritual, concerning the baptism of children, we can choose between two formulas. In the first, the priest asks if one renounces Satan, all his works and pomps. Obviously, the answer is: "I renounce." In the second formula, it is first asked: "Abreneutiatis peccato, ut in libertate filiorum Dei vivatis?" and to complement, it is added "the seductions of iniquity" and Satan, "the author and prince of sin" (*Ordo baptismi parvulorum* [Vatican City, 1969], p. 30, No. 57).

55. Regarding the "modi" and answers, we insist on mentioning

those pointed out in Nos. 31 and 33. In No. 31, the Fathers ask for the suppression of the words "Status religiosus . . . inconcusse pertinet," because they are not clear enough. And, in the same sense, No. 33 proposes to suppress "inconcusse" "quia assertio est theologice et historice falsa." The Commission answered: "affermatio de professione consiliorum quae statum in Ecclesia agnitum constituit, certe stare potest" (*AS*, III/VII, 132). As for "ab Ecclesia structuram hierarchicam non spectet," as far as we can see, nobody raised difficulty.

56. Our reflections lead us to consider "Christian sanctity" as a "univocal" concept that can apply to all Christians. Fathers Molinari and Gumpel do not seem to share this opinion: after meticulously studying "the substantial unity of Christian sanctity and its differentiation, they conclude: 'siamo nel campo dell'analogia e non in quello della univocità" (*La dottrina della Costituzione dogmatica* . . . , note 4, p. 38). Perhaps we differ only in words. One can use the concept, e.g., "of man" in a strictly univocal sense, and yet there is room for the "diversity" of races and, with greater reason, of individuals. Second, the "secularity" considered by the Council, proper to "laymen" or "nonconsecrated" is different from the "secularity" that characterizes secular institutes. The latter has, as point of reference, the "nonsecularity" of religious, but not inasmuch as they renounce the "world," in the sense explained in note 53. More precision in the terminology can be desired; but, if it remains possible to save the proposition of the neighbor (namely, the Council, in the present case), P.A. Bonnet considers that "secularity" is characteristic of the "laypeople," but not exclusively; he gives an equal rank to the secular institutes, "De laicorum notione adumbratio," *Periodica*, 75 (1985), 227–271 esp. pp. 245–246.

57. See *LG* 44.

58. The *Relatio* with regard to the paragraph discussed here can be found in *AS*, III/I, 318. As a sample of the various reviews of this paragraph, we can mention three commentaries: (1) that of F. Wulf (*LThK*, I, 308–310), who considers the argumentation of this paragraph to be "colorless" when compared with the one that should have been presented (p. 309); (2) that of L. Cabielles (note 8), who deems that the writers "keep on thinking like perfectionists" (p. 72), which disqualifies the whole paragraph; (3) that of Fathers Molinari and Gumpel, *La dottrina della Costituzione dogmatica* . . . (note 4), which, in our opinion, presents the data objectively.

59. On this point, we agree with L. Cabielles (note 8), pp. 74 and 82. We do not consider to be appropriate the explanation of K. Rahner in his "Uber die evangelische Räte" (*Schriften zur Theologie*, VII, pp. 404–434), although he examines, in a masterly manner, the "objectivizing" value of the evangelical counsels in the fallen world, because, in my opinion, he empties it of its content of real grace (p. 427).

60. It should be noted only, since we have mentioned the commentaries in note 58, that the term of comparison of the comparatives is the other states of life.

61. Let us notice first that the Council speaks about the "form of life" that the Son of God accepted in entering this world, and that it refers, therefore, to the historical Jesus. It is presupposed that this "form of life" is salvific and, by this very fact, for all Christians an indispensable model. Second, the verbs "follow" and "imitate" have an equivalent meaning, as in the time of the first Christian generation. It must be pointed out that A. Schulz admits the equivalence of the two concepts in the New Testament, but "to a lesser degree" in his book *Nachforgen und Nachahmen* (Munich, 1962), p. 335.

62. We were amazed to observe an author like L. Cabielles, in the article we quoted many times, "Vocación universal . . ." (note 8), finding it hard to accept this doctrine of the Council. He seems to find a stumbling block in the way the Council argues in this passage and in others dealing with the consecration through the counsels; indeed, he questions whether "una mayor configuración . . . con el Cristo histórico lleve consigo una mayor configuración salvifica" (p. 74). The same difficulty reappears in pp. 76 and 81. It is true that the "configuratión," just like the "imitation" or "following" of Jesus, must be well understood as Vatican II, we think, presupposes it. Having said this, I consider that to get rid of the Council's argumentation, however embarassing it may be, it is not reasonable to assert, referring to Jesus, that the "historical Jesus is definitively outdated" (p. 91).

63. The term of the comparison is evident, and so is the salvific value of this "imitate."

64. This text is linked directly to the preceding one.

65. Besides what we have pointed out on this subject (note 25), see the commentary of G. Philips (*LThK*, I, 139–155), esp. 152.

66. See *LG* 46.

67. See *LG* 44.

68. To clear up misunderstandings, we want only to emphasize here that by bringing out the "typical," as we understand it, we do not deny all the links it has with the other aspects, and in particular with those of "offering" and "service." Our assertion must not be understood in an exclusive sense. All things form an organic unity, bound to and through Christ, within the Church, by the action of the Holy Spirit, to the glory of God the Father.

69. We are alluding to the phrase "casta consacrata" used by A. Boni in his article, "La vita religiosa" (note 5), p. 270, and only because it is of perfect use in enhancing our own point of view.

CHAPTER 44

Life Consecrated
by the Evangelical Counsels
Conciliar Teaching and Later Developments

Jean Beyer, S.J.

Summary

The Council found it difficult to define the position of the consecrated life, and to distinguish between "religious" and "secular"
consecrated life. It started a debate that enabled true doctrinal
progress to be made, and this was then extended by the papal
documents of Paul VI and John Paul II, and fostered deeper
doctrinal reflection. The 1983 Code benefited from this necessary reflection, and it is of help in further research. The essential
points of such research are as follows: the consecration of life
through the evangelical counsels, counsels and charisms, religious and secular consecrated life, typology and renewal, consecration to God and men, consecration as an act of love and a
Trinitarian act.

Vatican II was the first Council to deal with the consecrated
life within the broader framework of a renewed ecclesiology. It
had been difficult to define its true place, and to see the whole
importance of consecration through the counsels, and to distinguish religious and consecrated life. The last point was the subject of in-depth doctrinal study, which was virtually ignored by
the commissions responsible for drafting the texts.

What the Council did not itself accomplish would be the task of the renewal it set in motion. Bit by bit, stress would be laid on the essential place of consecration in the life, and the role of the counsels through which it is made. A clearer idea would be reached as to the nature of consecration, and also of the counsels as lived out according to different charisms, without exaggerating the importance of witness to the detriment of the primordial value of consecration as an act of love in a life wholly oriented toward union with God, the imitation of Christ, and the redemption of the world.

The Council saw a real doctrinal progress, which was continued in the papal documents and the reflection they fostered. These developments are sketched out in the present study.

Lumen gentium and Consecrated Life

In *Lumen gentium,* consecrated life is seen first of all within the context of the universal vocation to holiness, and is then expanded on in a special chapter under an erroneous title that, despite some vigorous protests, would not be changed[1]—although it would eventually be contradicted by a last-minute correction to the Decree *Perfectae caritatis,* stating that secular institutes are not religious institutes.[2] The source of this late addition, and also that of Chapter VI of the Constitution, is of help in discerning the value of the texts and how they should be interpreted.[3]

The Constitution *Lumen gentium* could not provide an overall picture of the life of the Church, and any deeper doctrinal analysis would have entailed major structural alterations.[4] The change made to the chapter on the people of God is significant,[5] since the stress laid on the episcopate left the presbyterial priesthood—and also the diaconate—in shadow.[6]

In reaction against a position that tended to claim that perfection was reserved to observance of the counsels,[7] what is known as the "religious" life was placed in a chapter in which all the different states of life were passed under review. On the request of the Fathers, religious were dealt with in a special chapter, which in their opinion corresponded better to the place and role of religious in the Church and the world.[8] In order to enable their voice to be heard and to coordinate their efforts, the Secretariat of Bishops (a name not without its ambiguities) was set up, but it was unable to bring about the introduction of important elements from the discourse *Magno gaudio* of Paul VI, in which the Pope stressed certain values that he hoped to see taken up in the Constitution.[9]

Religious Life or Consecrated Life

Had the title of Chapter VI wanted to express the breadth of the life to which it referred, it should have been entitled (as certain Fathers suggested) "The Profession of the Evangelical Counsels," or even "Life According to the Evangelical Counsels."[10] During the revisions of the text, "the consecration of the counsels"[11] was spoken of, and then "consecration by the counsels."[12] *Perfectae caritatis* would speak of "the excellence of the life consecrated by the evangelical counsels."[13] And the Code would draw its inspiration from this phrase, drafting the title of Part III of Book II as "Institutes of Life Consecrated by the Profession of the Evangelical Counsels,"[14] a title that in the definitive text would become "Institutes of Consecrated Life and Societies of Apostolic Life."[15]

Thus the term "institutes of consecrated life" is accepted in the Church today. However, there is still the question of the societies of common life, some of which state that they do not live a consecrated life, while others vigorously claim the opposite.[16] Any title that was both concise and exact would have to take into account problems that have not yet been fully resolved. For instance, hermits, even numbers of hermits, do not make up an institute,[17] as is also the case for consecrated virgins[18]; the order of widows was ignored, although it is at present undergoing a fresh renewal.[19] All in all, the best title would be: "Consecrated Life in the Church." Those who do not live this life can find their true canonical position elsewhere.[20]

Essential Elements

The slow awakening to the essential elements of consecrated life was important, starting with the Council, and despite the predominance of a monastic-cenobitic type of religious mentality.[21]

Emphasis was happily placed on the counsels as a gift of the Lord to his Church,[22] and also on the variety of the charisms and their specific identity.[23] Such collective charisms give rise to a brotherly life that is shared by those whom God calls.[24]

Consecration to God

Despite its doctrinal importance, the statement that God consecrates was overly restrictive.[25] Like the initiative of consecration, that of vocation is divine,[26] and this divine initiative calls forth a response that *Lumen gentium* did not pursue. Some people incorrectly choose not to see any special consecration here.[27] This position makes some doctrinal assumptions that are to say the least debatable. If God's choice is love, the response to this choice is a response of love[28] in a gift of self that allows the person to belong to God forever.[29] Such a response is possible only in Jesus Christ—in him, through him, with him, and like him; it reaches its culmination in his sacrifice,[30] and normally takes place in the Eucharist.[31]

Lumen gentium hardly provides a satisfactory solution as regards the nature of consecration. In this area, the perspective was still much more that of the vows of religion[32] than that of the act of love entailed in total self-giving. The perfection of consecration was seen as dependent on the sacred bonds taken on therein, and it was more perfect if these bonds were perpetual.[33]

In order to recognize the value of the bonds, the vow had to be seen as having a higher value than an oath or a promise.[34] The problem has now been slowly clarified: the strength of the consecration lies in the gift of love received from God, which is answered with the love that is expressed in the acceptance of the divine choice by the person who consecrates himself to God irrevocably.[35]

In order to be firm and stable, consecration presupposes the wish to give oneself totally and definitively, even if the bonds are in fact temporary[36] and have some form other than a vow.[37] One point was not clarified in *Lumen gentium,* and would not be by the rest of the Council: that of consecration *by* the evangelical counsels.[38] In what way do these counsels make up consecration, and why do we speak of a consecration by the counsels?

The Three Evangelical Counsels

The role of the counsels was highlighted in Chapter V on the universal vocation to holiness, and from this point of view, the separation of Chapters V and VI represents a division that need not have been made.

Having stated that holiness is fostered in a special way by the manifold counsels of the Lord to his disciples, *Lumen gentium* highlights the importance of the three major counsels, which are traditionally known as poverty, chastity, and obedience. The normal order is altered here for exegetical reasons—although these reasons are somewhat questionable.[39]

According to *Lumen gentium*, the first counsel is that of virginity.[40] This is then followed by those of obedience and poverty, according to Paul's exhortation to the Philippians (2:7–8) and the Corinthians (2 Cor. 8:9). This order is reversed in Chapter VI, which speaks first of chastity dedicated to God, and then of poverty and obedience,[41] viewing these counsels as a type of virginal and poor life that Christ chose for himself and his mother.[42]

Virginity is not only chastity dedicated to God. It is a precious gift given by the Father to certain people (cf. Mt. 19:11; 1 Cor. 7:7), and means consecrating oneself more easily and without any division of heart (*facilius indiviso corde*) to God alone.[43] It presumes celibacy, perfect continence, and the chastity proper to this state.[44] It is a special source of spiritual fruitfulness, and gives rise to the order of virgins,[45] although in order to be a total gift, it requires poverty and obedience as complementary elements: without these other two counsels, the gift would not be the total one of an undivided heart.[46]

The three counsels must also be seen as a unified attitude like that of the incarnate word, which was the expression of a single love of the Father, lived out in full dependence, in poverty of heart and in full obedience to the will of him who had sent him.[47] This filial aspect was suggested by *Lumen gentium*,[48] although the document did not expand on it. It is better understood today, so that the conciliar formula of "consecration *by* the evangelical counsels"[49] is clarified.

Consecration by the Counsels

Consecration by the counsels can be understood as integration into the divine filiation of the incarnate word, so that by imitating his filial attitudes in responding to the gift of the Father, we are united through love to Christ and his sacrifice. Through his voluntary death, Jesus is given, sanctified, and consecrated so that those who are one with him may also be sanctified and consecrated in giving themselves to the Father (Jn. 17:19). This consecration is based on baptism, and accomplished in the Eucharist. This latter point was not mentioned by *Lumen gentium*, although it forms the true center and heart of consecration by the counsels.[50]

The Constitution stressed the importance of the ministry of the Church, which receives the vows, and which, through its public prayer, calls down God's blessing on the consecrated person. It does this by linking the person to the eucharistic sacrifice, although the Church does not stand in for the person who consecrates himself to God; his or her consecration is personal, and is a response of love. It should have been stated how this union with Christ's sacrifice is brought about.[51]

Further, it is in the Eucharist that we understand that this consecration is not only love of God, but, through love of God, love of mankind. Pius XII had noted this when he spoke of a "consecration to God and to souls,"[52] a formula that expressed the attitude of Christ and of those who, in him and like him, consecrate themselves to the Father for the establishment of his kingdom and the building up of the Church. Hence, the ecclesial nature of any consecrated life.

The Ecclesial Character of Consecrated Life

Although it does not explicitly discuss the supremely ecclesial character of consecrated life, *Lumen gentium* does not completely ignore it. It has its place in the Constitution on the Church, and is, moreover, based on the gift of the counsels—a gift made to the Church—on the grace of the Lord who preserves it, and on the action of the Spirit who gives rise to it in the diversity of charisms—gifts that the Church interprets and approves.[53]

This ecclesial character of consecrated life is founded on baptism and is lived out in the Eucharist, where the Church is constituted and reunited, and lives and grows.[54] This gift, which is given to God who is loved above all things, becomes service and praise of God in a new sense,[55] and enables people to represent better the union of Christ with the Church, his bride.[56] This union with Christ means that consecrated life is a dedication to the whole Church,[57] which in turn means that each consecrated person works according to his or her vocation to establish and strengthen the kingdom of Christ within souls, and to spread it throughout the world.[58]

Typology and Autonomy of the Institutes of Consecrated Life

In accordance with different charisms, a typology of the consecrated life becomes constantly clearer. It also presupposes an autonomy, which enables people to live out the gift received, an autonomy that finds its strongest expression in a complete exemption.

If each institute has its own identity, life, and mission through its specific charism, it must express this as spirit and structure, which are constitutive elements of any ecclesial community.[59] The charism is not to be limited to the spirit of an institute, but is spirit *and* structures, inasmuch as the structures express its spirit. This means that each institute needs its own law—a need the Code would take into account.[60]

In order to gain a better understanding of its charism, each institute takes its place within the mystery of Christ that it must live out in order to manifest it to both believers and unbelievers.[61] This general norm would then be expanded on: the institute will imitate Christ in prayer on the mountain, Christ who proclaims the kingdom of God to the crowds, heals the sick and crippled, brings sinners to conversion, blesses children, and pours out his benefits on all—always in accordance with the will of the Father who sent him.[62] The secular institutes were forgotten in this listing. *Perfectae caritatis* would complete the list of different types,[63] and the Code would then give it a definitive form by improving on the text of *Lumen gentium*.[64]

If the gift made to the founder must be received, approved and protected,[65] this cannot be the responsibility of the institute alone: it is an ecclesial responsibility, involving all the faithful, and especially the hierarchy.[66]

The autonomy in question is not some sort of independence, and does not place the religious life "beyond the hierarchy."[67] On the contrary, it permits a better integration into the life of the Church, and thus entails a special dependence on the hierarchy, which recognizes and protects it.[68]

From this point of view, exemption is instructive: to start with, it protected the autonomy of the monasteries, while later it supported the pastoral activity of the mendicants and became an apostolic mission entrusted to the institute by the Supreme Pontiff. *Lumen gentium* recalled this ecclesial aspect of the autonomy of the institutes, an autonomy that must be understood in the light of the charism. An institute cannot be itself without an external autonomy that ensures its development and flourishing.[69] Exemption is a reinforcement of autonomy, both internal and external. It had not been suppressed, and is necessary to the identity of the institutes for which it has been recognized.[70]

The Place of Religious in the Structures of the Church

The position given to religious in the schema provoked a reaction of rejection. It was seen as a lack of respect, and the opposition it would encounter from certain bishops was clear.[71]

The Council of Trent had not been able to overcome the problem of exemption, which was, moreover, linked to the primacy of Peter. It was brought up again at Vatican II when episcopal prerogatives were being discussed.

How should religious be described? It is first necessary to discuss them. Confining them to a single chapter on the vocation to holiness meant that their identify and the importance of their state of life were lost, and their role in the Church was downplayed. In this connection, the order of the schema was important. Although it underwent revision, it did not follow the traditional order, which has not lost its influence and would have dealt with clergy, religious, and lay people.[72] There was a rejection of the thought of Pius XII, who saw religious as an intermediate state between clergy and laity.[73] The removal of religious from the "hierarchical" structure of the Church was more deeply felt, bearing in mind the divine constitution of the latter.[74]

Are religious outside the hierarchical structure of the Church? The point is to discover the meaning of "hierarchical." The term refers either to position or dependence on the hierarchy,[75] but which hierarchy? That of sacred orders: bishops, priests, deacons?[76] Or that of Church government: Pope, college of bishops, diocesan bishops?[77] Those who are not ordained are called "lay people." But who is ordained? At the time of the Council, minor orders still existed, and a person who had received tonsure was a cleric.[78] Today, there are three degrees of sacred orders: episcopate, presbyterate, and diaconate.[79] Is the diaconate a sacrament? This question has been asked, but has not been solved.[80]

"Hierarchical" can also have another sense—that of a harmonized and unified organic whole—and in this view every state of life according to divine law belongs to this structure, forming the unity of the Church. In this perspective, the distinction between clerics and lay people no longer holds. There are "laity and laities."[81] Religious live a state of life according to divine law, the counsels are a gift of the Lord, the charisms are a gift of the Spirit, and each type of consecrated life belongs to the fullness of the Church, manifests the mission of Christ and the Church, and reveals the depth of the Christian life. In this perspective, every form of consecrated life belongs to the hierarchical structure of the Church. When *Lumen gentium* used the term "hierarchical" in a partial sense, it practically denied it; however, stating that the religious life belongs to the holiness of the Church does not distinguish it. Every state of life belongs to the holiness of the Church, and each person must live and foster such holiness. All Christians are called to holiness.

The question was, therefore, not solved. Its solution will be found when their correct place is again given to the "orders" of persons that liturgical tradition has recognized within the eucharistic assembly, and thus also within the concrete life of the Church.[82]

Secular consecrated life raises another problem. Its inclusion in the diocesan clergy and also in the laity indicates that it does not alter the present condition of the people involved, but simply confirms and reinforces it. It was therefore important to recognize a twofold "state" of life for the same person, whatever the actual terminology used might be. As we shall see, the Code would face this problem.[83] However, we first examine the contribution of the other conciliar documents to the doctrinal reflection and analysis started by *Lumen gentium*.

The Contribution of the Conciliar Decrees

Four Decrees contributed further nuances or greater depth to the teaching of *Lumen gentium: Perfectae caritatis, Ad gentes, Christus Dominus,* and *Presbyterorum ordinis.*

There are two dominant elements in *Perfectae caritatis*: respect for the charisms, and the typology corresponding to the latter.[84] Its charism gives each institute the right to be and to remain itself, and a return to their sources eliminates anything not in keeping with the views of the founder. The Decree also warns against any updating that is not first and foremost a spiritual renewal.[85]

The essence of such renewal is consecration by the counsels. Article 1 takes up and expresses the position of *Lumen gentium* still better by placing the accent on perfect charity from the very outset,[86] and article 5 explains what makes up this consecration: it is a response to the divine call[87]; rooted in baptism,[88] it expresses a personal gift of self to God[89]; received by the Church, it commits the person to its service.[90] The example of Christ, and imitation of him, allow a sharing in his pouring out of himself and in his life in the Spirit.[91]

The counsels are a response to God's love. They presuppose a life hidden in God, in which love of neighbor has its source with a view to the salvation of the world and the building up of the Church.[92]

Perfectae caritatis represents a search for identity within this renewal, and expresses a more detailed typology. The more important articles concern the monastic life as lived without apostolic activities,[93] and in order to avoid too radical an attitude, article 9 would be drafted, placing the monastic institution after institutes dedicated to works of the apostolate.[94] Article 8 gives the essential elements of a life that is both communitarian and apostolic, and is applicable to every institute of apostolic life.[95] The principles linking action and comtemplation would be taken up again in the Code.[96] Lastly, in article 11, the secular institutes saw their ideal recognized: a fully consecrated life,[97] consecration to God and men,[98] integration into the midst of the world,[99] action on the world by using the means of the world,[100] consecrated secularity that acts as a leaven,[101] both among secular priests and among lay people.[102] There was a fortunate last-minute correction, so that it was stated that secular institutes are not religious institutes[103]—which was in contradiction of the very title of the Decree, and also of the ambiguity of *Lumen gentium.*

Ad gentes is also concerned in this typological research. It stresses the value of monastic life without any participation in apostolic activity,[104] although it does confirm the value of the latter for other religious institutes.[105] The document expresses the wish to see different forms of consecrated life take root in the young churches, so that the different aspects of Christ's mission and the life of the Church can be seen.[106] And, lastly, it hopes that the contemplative life can be established everywhere, since it belongs to the fullness of the presence of the Church.[107] Here again, we can see the emphasis on the ecclesial character of the different forms of consecrated life.

Christus Dominus provides further details on the position of institutes, and particularly religious ones, in the perspective of diocesan life.[108] Religious priests are part of the diocesan clergy without being diocesan clerics.[109] *Ad gentes* had placed them more clearly among the local *presbyterium*, or college of presbyters.[110] With the exception of wholly monastic institutes,[111] their collaboration is expected; their work is carried out under the authority of the bishop, and exemption is not in contradiction of this, since such exemption concerns above all the internal life of the institute.[112] This position gives clearer definition to that of *Lumen gentium*, and would be still further clarified later, when the autonomy of the institutes—both internal and external autonomy—would be better understood. This is because any collaboration presupposes full respect for the charism of each institute.[113]

The doctrinal contribution of *Presbyterorum ordinis* highlights the value of the evangelical counsels.[114] This document was produced late in the Council and replaced the "propositions" to which the schema on priests had been reduced. Its expansion gave it the appearance of a true conciliar constitution.

Those responsible for drafting the document avoided reference to the counsels, which tended at that time to be seen as confined to religious, although their hand was forced by circumstances: celibacy had to be given its proper place, the obedience due to the bishop was discussed, and a sober style of life was an invitation to suggest voluntary poverty. And this resulted in further analysis and explanation of the counsels and their relationship with the Eucharist and the priesthood.[115]

Although the priesthood of married men is mentioned,[116] the priestly ministry is seen as a call to a personal gift of self, an invitation found in the texts for ordination, which call for imitation of Christ in his gift to the Father for the salvation of the world, and this gift is to be made, if possible, with an undivided heart, through a response of love that seeks to be total. Each priest responds to this according to the vocation and grace given to him by God.[117] Obedience has its place in the context of the mission given in the name of the Lord. This obedience will be responsible and voluntary, and forms the priest to the image of Christ, who was obedient unto death.[118] The use of worldly goods will respect their purpose as goods to be shared for the common good,[119] although Christ invites each priest, according to the grace he has received, to imitate him who was rich but became poor in order to enrich us from his poverty.[120] This call to voluntary poverty crowns the progressive call represented by the priesthood as it is lived out.

Although the priest lives in the world, he is not *of* the world. He frees himself from any disordered concern in order to be able to listen to God, who speaks to him through daily life. Freedom and acceptance make a spiritual discernment possible with regard to the world and earthly things.[121] This latter aspect of the counsels is stated very clearly both for religious and for secular institutes, as also for every Christian who is moving toward the perfection of charity.

The Teaching of the Popes Since the Council

Paul VI followed the workings of the Council, and his discourse *Magno gaudio* and his decided intervention in favor of the secular institutes are proof of his respect for consecrated life. His Exhortation *Evangelica testificatio*[122] is of particularly outstanding importance in this connection. The document is addressed to religious, but this does not prevent the Pope from describing values that are common to every type of consecrated life.

Paul VI's position is clear. With regard to consecration, he recalls that the Council highlights the greatness of this freely given response to the call of the Spirit,[123] following the example of Christ, as represented by the total and irrevocable gift of self.[124] This gift consists of consecration by the counsels, a consecration made by religious,[125] and carried out within the Church and through its ministry.[126] This ministry is twofold (and this idea is new): that of superiors, even lay people, and that of the whole ecclesial community. Paul VI writes as follows:

Such is your consecration, made within the Church and through her ministry—both that of her representatives who receive your profession and that of the Christian community itself, whose love recognizes, welcomes, sustains and embraces

those who within it make an offering of themselves as a living
sign "which can and ought to attract all the members of the
Church to an effective and prompt fulfillment of the duties of
their Christian vocation, . . . more adequately manifesting to
all believers the presence of heavenly goods already possessed
in this world."[127]

This text gives a good summary of the value of consecration
made to God, its ecclesial character, and its witness value.

In the same document, Paul VI quietly takes up the question
of the types of religious life: a wholly contemplative life,[128] and
an apostolic life uniting action and contemplation.[129] The Pope
stresses the essential feature of the latter type of religious life,
stating that its members "are consecrated to the apostolate in its
essential mission, which is the proclaiming of the Word of God
to those whom he places along their path, so as to lead them
toward faith."[130]

This apostolic work is to be integrated into the diocesan pastoral ministry. At least at first glance, Paul VI seems to take up the
restrictive attitude of *Christus Dominus* with regard to exemption,[131] although he does state that this encompasses respect for
the specific character of each institute in virtue of its special
charism.[132] It is also in this text that the term "charism" appears
for the first time.[133] Paul VI uses three expressions in speaking of
charisms: "the charisms of the religious life,"[134] "the charisms of
founders,"[135] and the "the charisms of the various institutes."[136]
The term was already in use in doctrinal discussions, although
Vatican II did not use it.[137] Starting with Paul VI, it would
become normal in Church documents,[138] and John Paul II uses it
very frequently.[139]

In *Redemptionis donum*, John Paul II provided what we might
call a first summary of his teaching to religious. This document
illustrates the nature of consecration, the gift of God in the
call,[140] the call to a gift of reciprocal love, a gift of "spousal
covenant,"[141] a gift to Christ that is a gift of self to the Father,[142]
an act of love lived out in the Holy Spirit.[143] Consecration is
thus an act of love,[144] a Trinitarian act,[145] a consecration in
which apostolate and witness are rooted.[146]

The evangelical counsels are seen within the paschal mystery,
between the mystery of sin and that of justification and salvific
grace.[147] They are not only renunciations, but also have a posi-

tive value of love and communion.[148] The Pope states that each consecrated person must find his or her own role in Christ's redemption and his or her personal path of sanctification.[149] Stress is thus laid on an individual aspect, so that even within a group, the personal aspect of each vocation is brought out—an aspect rarely expressed in the constitutions or statutes of any institute of consecrated life.

The ecclesial role of consecrated life receives an ever broader space in the teaching of John Paul II: love of Christ expressed in consecration benefits the whole people of God; further, the Church is aware "that in the love that Christ receives from consecrated persons, the love of the entire Body is directed in a special and exceptional way to the Spouse who at the same time is the Head of this Body."[150]

Lastly, in *Redemptionis donum,* John Paul II takes up the idea of a "state of life" that is a special gift of God to the Church, a state of life defined by the counsels and thus moving beyond the counsels themselves,[151] a state of life chosen by those who make their "consecration to God and the profession of the evangelical counsels." Consecration and profession are thus distinguished from one another, and this distinction means that we must be more precise in identifying the differences, value, and connection of the elements of the single act of consecration.[152]

Consecrated Life in the New Code

The Code reflects the Council. Indeed, it does more: it links the Council to tradition, benefits from doctrinal progress that has taken place since the Council, and also takes into account present problems. Violations and distortions in consecrated religious life made it impossible to give greater freedom to various institutes,[153] while some, for other reasons, did not want it.[154]

With the Code, the term "institute of consecrated life" entered into current usage in the Church. With regard to the general title of this section, things would have been simplified if it had allotted a separate place to hermits, and to the orders of virgins and widows.[155] Societies of common life, which were suffering an identity crisis, did not allow a simpler title or a more systematic layout.[156] When these societies can find a solution that fulfills their aspirations, this part of the Code will then more correctly be entitled "Consecrated Life in the Church."

Within the Code, consecrated life receives a description rich in conciliar concepts,[157] while avoiding the outright statement that a person who commits himself to it consecrates himself to God.[158] And even if the formula of Pius XII is not repeated word for word,[159] it is present through the values it encompasses, even for the eremitical life.[160]

The 1983 Code has the merit of listing the essential features of religious life,[161] which needed distinguishing from secular institutes—although the latter did not receive any similar treatment.[162]

The secular institutes open the path further to reflection on states of life in the Church.[163] They were previously strictly separated,[164] and are distinguished from one another today on different levels. Thus, a lay person who is consecrated but not religious remains part of the laity, and a diocesan priest who is a member of a secular institute remains a member of the secular clergy. We are, therefore, faced with the problem of a twofold state of life. This problem also exists for the permanent, but married deacon: as a deacon, he is a cleric, but as a married person is he a layman? It is not surprising that the commission did not want to repeat the text of *Lumen gentium*,[165] which the Code did retain in another connection.[166]

These states of life are recognized particularly as having liturgical positions in the eucharistic assembly, professional ones in the life of the Church, and apostolic ones according to the various missions of the Christian laity.

The typology of consecrated life was not taken up in the Code. A project had been drawn up, but it was rejected, always for the same reasons as before.[167] Such a typology will one day be of major importance for an ecclesial life that is concerned over truth and renewal.[168] Moreover, a specific typology is coming to light among the secular institutes.[169]

An effort at clarification has been announced in order to see the counsels outside or beyond their practical applications in religious or secular life, or according to the different charisms.[170]

Stress must be laid on the position given to autonomy—even external autonomy—and exemption, and to collaboration with other institutes, the diocesan clergy, and the episcopate.[171] In these areas, firmly based general norms gather together the inordinately detailed indications found in *Christus Dominus* and in the Motu proprio *Ecclesiae sanctae*, which was concerned with the application of *Christus Dominus*. [172]

A more detailed study of the Code shows that it echoed the Council, improving on it on a number of points, thanks also to a more precise and more appropriate terminology.

Conclusion

The Council opened a debate on consecrated life that has not yet ended, setting in motion a doctrinal renewal, the full impact of which we still do not realize. The return to the charisms of founders encourages a true renewal, and an in-depth study and analysis of the nature and value of consecration highlights the divine vocation and the significance of consecration to God by the counsels. Lastly, Christ is given a central place. The charisms lead to a more faithful imitation of his mysteries, and his consecration provides the basis for that of those who consecrate themselves to him in order to consecrate themselves to the Father. His life as Son provides the evangelical counsels with their meaning and places them in the context of Trinitarian life.

These values restore an evangelical tone to consecrated life—a tone that a speculative doctrinal approach and a practice tending to uniformity had caused it to lose.

Further, the deeper and broader study and understanding of the ecclesial character of consecrated life allows full communion with the whole people of God.

In the face of this overall picture, we can see that the Council represented a call to a task of renewal that is being carried out in fidelity as a response to the action of the Spirit.

Translated from the French by Leslie Wearne.

Notes

1. The choice of this title was a compromise, but unfortunately it led to the belief that the secular institutes were religious; see AS, III/VIII, 127 *ad primum modum*. The secular institutes were not forgotten by certain Fathers; see their hopes on this subject as summarized in M. Schoenmackers, *Genèse du chapitre VI "De Religiosis" de la Constitution dogmatique sur l'Eglise "Lumen Gentium"* (Rome, 1983), 41–44.

2. In this regard, see J. Beyer, *De vita per consilia evangelica consecrata* (Rome, 1969), 51–53, which gives the document drafted by those in charge of secular institutes, and also the correction made on 27 October 1965, thanks to the intervention of Paul VI, in order to safeguard their identify.

3. We would refer to Schoenmackers, *Genèse du chapitre VI 'De Religiosis,'* and to the studies of P. Molinari and P. Gumpel, "La dottrina della Costituzione dogmatica *Lumen Gentium* sulla vita consacrata," *Vita Consacrata,* 21 (1985), 1–137, esp. Chapter VI, "sui Religiosi," 97–137.

4. This alteration in structure would have made it possible to pinpoint more precisely the different forms of life proper to the laity. In this connection, see J. Beyer, "Laïcat ou peuple de Dieu," *La Chiesa dopo il Concilio, Atti del Congresso Internazionale di Diritto Canonico, Roma, 14–19 gennaio 1970,* 2 vols. (Milan, 1972), I/1, 233–247. We also studied this question in *Du Concile au Code de Driot Canonique. La mise en application de Vatican II* (Paris, 1985), 60–65 ("Les ordres de Personnes").

5. This chapter was entitled "The People of God or the Laity." It was transferred and placed before the chapter dealing with the hierarchy. It would have been better to add here the subject matter dealt with in Chapter V, "The Vocation of all the Faithful to the Holiness of the Church," which was in fact proposed even at the time of the first general discussion, on 30 September 1963; AS, II/I, 351, 3c.

6. The priesthood contains two degrees: episcopate and presbyterate. The diaconate was considered at the Council from the pastoral point of view as permanent diaconate and diaconate of married men; see H.E. Lauenroth, *Der ständige Diakonat. Seine ekklesiologische Idee und kanonistische Verwirklung* (Regensburg, 1983). While the diaconate is part of a hierarchy of ordination, it is not necessarily part of the hierarchy or the functions of government, and the Council did not express itself on the subject of the sacramentality of the diaconate; see J. Beyer, "De Diaconatu animadversiones," *Periodica,* 69 (1980), 441–460.

7. In this connection, see an answer of the Secretariat of State of 13 July 1952, in J. Beyer, *Les Instituts séculiers* (Paris, 1954), 355–357; see also *NRTh,* 78 (1956), 930, note 24.

8. See Schoenmackers, *Genèse du chapitre VI "De Religiosis,"* 107–204.

9. *AAS,* 56 (1964), 565–571. The discourse of Paul VI is cited in a note. See *AAS,* 57 (1965), 5–75, esp. 49–53, notes 138, 140, 144. Schoenmackers, *Genèse du chapitre VI "De Religiosis,"* 292–293, gives the four *modi* to be introduced to Chapter VI. Cf. AS, II/VIII, 128–134, Modi 2, 16, 25, 40.

10. AS, III/VIII, 127.

11. Thus, the *textus prior* of No. 35: "Aestimanda est consecratio consiliorum evangelicarum"; see *AS*, III/I, 313.

12. Thus, the textus emendatus of 1964; see *AS*, III/I, 313.

13. The Decree *Perfectae caritatis* uses the expression in number 1d.

14. *Communicationes*, 7 (1975), 89–90, No. 30 of the *Relatio*.

15. *CIC*, lib. III, P. III, "De Institutis vitae consecratae et de Societatibus vitae apostolicae." This title was already in the text of the Code presented to the Pope in 1982 with a view to its promulgation.

16. With regard to these societies, see E. Cappellini (ed.), *La legge per l'uomo. Una chiesa al servizio* (Rome, 1980), 190–203 ("Le Società di vita comune"); and J. Bonfils, "Instituts religieux et sociétés de vie apostolique. Aperçus théologiques, canoniques et pastoraux," *Documents Épiscopat*, 11 (June 1983).

17. The solitary life was quietly recalled in *LG* 43a and *PC* 1b.

18. Virgins obtained their own ritual in 1978, and the Code noted this renewal in Canon 604.

19. On 24 February 1984, the Sacred Congregation for the Sacraments and Divine Worship confirmed the ritual for the "Blessing of Widows" approved by Cardinal J.M. Lustiger, Archbishop of Paris, for the "Fraternité N.D. de la Résurrection."

20. Such societies can today be recognized as personal prelatures (cann. 294–297), which enables candidates to be incardinated into the societies and also the establishment of their own seminaries. This would not have been the case had they been set up as public associations, except as authorized through special indult. This possibility of incardination was envisaged in Canon 691 of the 1980 draft.

21. Certain documents published by Schoenmackers, *Genèse du chapitre VI "De Religiosis,"* 303–320 (Doc. XIII–XV), are the best illustration of this mentality.

22. *LG* 43a: "Donum divinum quod Ecclesia a Domino suo accepit et gratia eius semper conservat." This divine gift is concretized in the charisms of foundation.

23. *LG* 43a: "Quasi in arbore ex germine divinitus dato mirabiliter et multipliciter in agro domini ramificata variae formae . . . variaeque familiae creverint."

24. *LG* 43a: "Illae familiae sodalibus suis adminicula conferunt . . . communionis in militia Christi fraternae."

25. "Deo summe dilecto mancipatur . . . Deo sacratus." It is not possible to construct a whole doctrine on the basis of the passive verb, although one fact is certain: it is God who has the initiative, and it is he who calls people to consecrated life. These discussions between various authors have been studied by A. de Bonhome, "Estne consecratio per consilia nova consecratio? Sententiae et argumenta," *Periodica*, 67 (1978), 373–390.

26. In actual fact, consecration by God is carried out in the call, if it is perceived and received as it should be.

27. Thus, A. Boni and J.M.R. Tillard, whose views are described by de Bonhome, "Estne consecratio per consilia nova consecratio?" 382–388.

28. This character of reciprocity would eventually be stressed by John Paul II; see note 141.

29. The "soli Deo vivit" would be highlighted by *PC* 5a, but was already expressed in Chapter V with regard to virginity, *LG* 42c: ". . . ut in virginitate vel coelibatu facilius indiviso corde *Deo soli* se devoveant."

30. In this regard, see Bonhome, "Estne consecratio per consilia nova consecratio?" 380–382.

31. The moment at which the consecration by the counsels is made (for example, within the celebration of the Eucharist) is one thing, but the role of the Eucharist in making any consecration on the part of man possible is another matter.

32. *LG* 44a.

33. *LG* 44a: ". . . tanto autem perfectior erit consecratio quo per firmiora et stabiliora vincula magis repraesentatur Christus cum sponsa Ecclesia indissolubili vinculo coniunctus." This text is problematic from various points of view, as we shall see. If the value of the *consecratio* depends on the extent of the bonds, we cannot deny that the consecration is also the act of the person who consecrates himself to God.

34. An oath swears before God to the truth of the commitment undertaken. A promise is not made to God—if it were, it would be a vow—but is made *propter Deum* and cannot be viewed as a simple promise. In this regard, see the Declaration of the Sacred Congregation for Religious of 19 May 1948, in Beyer, *Les Instituts séculiers*, 332–333.

35. This would be the position of Paul VI and John Paul II; see notes 125 and 145.

36. The 1917 Code had supported this aspect in Canon 488, 1°: ". . . temporaria, elapso tamen tempore renovanda"; these words stressed the importance of the personal decision, which goes beyond the commitment made through a temporary vow. Indeed, if a definitive commitment is made through a temporary vow that is to be renewed, it can be seen as conditional on the part of the Church and the institute, although it may be definitive in the will of the person making it.

37. As regards commitments other than vows, see M.P. Azaredo, *Sacred Bonds. A study of the application of "Renovationis causam"* (Rome, 1983).

38. We shall give the explanation of this consecration by the counsels in what follows.

39. See *LG* 39a, where the *concilia evangelica* seem to be the three counsels. They are distinguished from others in 42c: "Sanctitas Ecclesiae item speciali modo fovetur multiplicibus consiliis quae Dominus in Evangelio discipulis suis observanda proponit. Inter quae eminent." Virginity or celibacy, obedience, and poverty are named. Some exegetes hold that consecrated celibacy was explicitly counseled by the Lord, whereas the other counsels were not. The counsel of poverty given to the rich young man would be addressed to all Christians. However, we cannot forget the value of the example of Christ, as is emphasized in *LG* 43a, *PC* 1a, and Canon 575 of the 1983 Code.

40. *LG* 42c.

41. *LG* 43a; cf. *PC* 1c, 25.

42. *LG* 46b.

43. *LG* 42c; cf. *PO* 16b.

44. *PO* 16b, where "virginitas vel coelibatus propter regnum coelorum servatum" is spoken of. *PC* 12a speaks of "castitas propter regnum coelorum," and *PC* 12b and 12c of "continentia perfecta."

45. The citations of the Fathers are important here; see *AAS*, 57 (1965), 48, notes 133 and 134.

46. *LG* 44a stresses the totality of the gift as expressed in the three counsels: "totaliter mancipatur." This *totaliter* was questioned, but the text was maintained; see *AS*, III/I, 328.

47. In this connection, see J. Beyer, "Premier bilan des chapitres de renouveau," *NRT*, 95 (1973), 75–76; and "Valori essenziali da esprimere nelle Costituzioni di un Istituto Religioso," *Vita consacrata*, 22 (1986), 44–48.

48. *LG* 44c: "formam . . . vitae quam Filius Dei accepit." And 45b: "ad genus vitae . . . quod sibi elegit Christus."

49. *PC* 1d.

50. This union to the sacrifice of Christ is referred to without any emphasis in *LG* 45c: "oblationem eorum sacrificio eucharistico associans." See also *PC* 6b, where the relationship to the Eucharist is even weaker. Canon 607, §1, of the 1983 Code is more explicit: "donationem veluti sacrificium Deo oblatum quo tota existentia fit continuus Dei cultus in caritate." Cf. our study, "Natura della consacrazione di vita mediante i consigli evangelici," in "Una vuova disciplina della vita consacrata," in E. Cappellini (ed.), *Problemi e Prospettive di Diritto canonico* (Brescia, 1977), 154–161.

51. *LG* 45c.

52. Motu proprio *Primo feliciter* V, in *AAS*, 40 (1948), 283–286, esp. 285.

53. *LG* 43a; *PC* 1b; Canons 575–576.

54. *LG* 26a: "Eucharistia qua continuo vivit et criscit Ecclesia." *Ibid.*: "praesens est Christus cuius virtute consociatur una, sancta, catholica et apostolica Ecclesia." See also *LG* 28a: "[Presbyteri] suum . . . munus sacrum maxime exercent in eucharistico cultu . . . qua . . . vota fidelium sacrificio capitis ipsorum coniungunt."

55. *LG* 44a. See Canon 603, §1: "Suam in laudem Dei et mundi salutem vitam devovent."

56. *LG* 44a; *PC* 12a; Canon 671, §1: "vita religiosa *uptote totius personae consecratio* mirabile in Ecclesia manifestat conubium a Deo conditum."

57. *PC* 1c, 6a.

58. *LG* 44c; *PC* 5e.

59. *LG* 8a.

60. Canons 586, §1; 587, §1.

61. *LG* 45a.

62. *LG* 45a.

63. *PC* 11.

64. Canon 577.

65. *LG* 45a; this paragraph provided the inspiration for the Code in Canons 576; 577; 586, §2.

66. *LG* 44b: "Unde et Ecclesia propriam indolem variorum institutorum . . . teutur et fovet." Cf. Canon 586, §2.

67. The title of an article opposed to the religious life and its autonomy. See the response of Father J. Creusen in *NRT*, 55 (1928), 492–503. This mentality was also behind *LG* 44d. In any case, it is difficult to see the usefulness of this questionable statement.

68. *LG* 45b: "intuitu utilitatis communis."

69. *LG* 45b. We would note this important indication: "Ipsi sodales in officio erga Ecclesiam *ex peculiari suae vitae forma* adimplendo," which applies to all institutes of consecrated life. See, in what follows, the position taken in the Decree *Christus Dominus*.

70. If, from the pastoral point of view, a greater dependence on diocesan bishops is normal today, it cannot be said that exemption has been eliminated; it remains a greater autonomy, for which the religious congregations have no equivalent. Cf. V. De Paolis, "Gli Istituti di vita consacrata nella Chiesa," in A. Longhitano (ed.), *La vita consacrata* (Bologna, 1983), 53–141; on the subject of exemption, 137–140. The same position is found in J. Garcia Martin, "Exemptio Religiosorum iuxta Concilium Vaticanum II," *CpR*, 62 (1981), 193–205, 239–302; 63 (1982), 23–33, 135–154, 193–217.

71. See previous note 67.

72. A number of Fathers asked that the call to holiness be dealt with in the chapter on the people of God, to be followed by treatment of the hierarchy, religious, and lay people. This concern is understandable. The Code reverses the order in another way: first, it deals with the faithful, lay people, clerics, and their associations, then with the hierar-

chical constitution of the Church, and lastly with the consecrated life. As regards these changes, see J. Beyer, "Le nouveau Code de droit canonique. Esprit et structures," *NRT*, 106 (1984), 375–382.

73. See Apostolic Constitution *Provida Mater Ecclesia* 4, in *AAS*, 39 (1947), 116; and Allocution *Annus sacer*, in *AAS*, 43 (1951), 27.

74. Pius XII referred to the canons of the 1917 Code in order to say that clerics and lay people form orders of persons by divine law. Cf. Apostolic Constitution *Provida Mater Ecclesia* 4, in *AAS*, 39 (1947), 116. This position has been challenged, and not without reason. See the remarks made by various theologians and canonists, in Beyer, *Du Concile au Code de droit canonique*, 63, note 7.

75. The degrees of Orders are not as such hierarchical degrees. On this point, Canon 108 of the old Code seems more technical and precise. In the canon, the term *hierarchica* is used only for the hierarchy of sacred Orders and that of government. The term "hierarchical structure" of *Lumen gentium* is ambiguous.

76. Sacred Orders had been defined by Pius XII in the Apostolic Constitution *Sacramentum ordinis*, in *AAS*, 40 (1948), 5–7. The subject of the Constitution was the validity of the rites of ordination.

77. Cf. Canon 108, §3 of the 1917 Code.

78. Cf. Canon 108, §1 of the 1917 Code.

79. Minor orders were suppressed by the Motu proprio of Paul VI, *Ministeria quaedam* (12 August 1976), in *AAS*, 64 (1972), 529–534.

80. In this connection, see Beyer, "De diaconatu animadversiones," 441–460.

81. See the book of V. Portier, *Laïcus et laïcats dans le peuple de Dieu* (Paris, 1967).

82. Cf. our study, "Les ordres de personnes," in *Du Concile au Code de droit canonique*, 60–65.

83. Canon 711 of the 1983 Code.

84. PC 7–11.

85. PC 2e.

86. PC 1: "Perfectae caritatis per consilia evangelica prosecutionem."

87. PC 5a: "vocationi divinae responsum."

88. PC 5a: "in baptismatis consecratione intime radicatur."

89 PC 5a: "constituit peculiarem . . . consecrationem. . . . Soli Deo vivant." And 5b: "sui ipsius donatio."

90. PC 5b: "ab Ecclesia suscepta, eius servitio . . . addictos." And 5e: "Deum prae omnibus et unice quaerentes, contemplationem qua Ei mente et corde adhaereant, cum amore apostolico . . . coniungant."

91. PC 5c.

92. PC 6a.

93. PC 7.

94. PC 9a.

95. PC 8. This article was completely reworked, and took up the position of the superiors general expressed by M. van Kerckhoven, M.S.C. See the text and commentary in Beyer, *De vita per consilia evangelica consecrata*, 93–104.

96. Canon 675, §§1–3.

97. PC 11a: "veram . . . et completam." This contradicts the position of *Provida Mater Ecclesia*, which had built up a certain hierarchy of value between orders, religious congregations, societies of common life, and secular institutes. See *Provida Mater Ecclesia* 6–7, 9, in *AAS*, 39 (1947), 117–118.

98. PC 11a. The thinking of Pius XII is retained here, although it is less vigorously expressed.

99. PC 11a: "in saeculo" and "in saeculo degentibus."

100. PC 22a: "apostolatum in saeculo ac veluti ex saeculo . . . exercendum," which takes up the position of *Primo feliciter* II, in *AAS*, 40 (1948), 285, which A. Gemelli had expressed in his famous "Memorandum" of 1939 published in *Secolarità e vita consacrata* (Milan, 1966), 359–442, esp. 424, note 32.

101. PC 11b: "ut revera fermentum sit in mundo."

102. PC 11a.

103. PC 11a: "Instituta saecularia, *quamvis non sint instituta religiosa* veram *tamen*." We italicize the words introduced into the text on the request of Paul VI; see note 2.

104. AG 40b.

105. AG 40c. The terminology is to be regretted: "institutes of active life" was formally refused by the commission of religious in the drafting of *Perfectae caritate*.

106. AG 18c.

107. AG 18d.

108. CD 34–35.

109. CD 34: "ad clerum dioecesis pertinere dicendi sunt."

110. AG 20c.

111. CD 35a.

112. CD 35c.

113. CD 35a. It must be observed that there is a certain contradiction in insisting on the one hand on the identity of the institutes, and the call on the other hand to change their constitutions in order to allow a more direct and more intense apostolate.

114. PO 15–17.

115. PO 13c: "invitantur ut quod tractant, imitentur."

116. PO 16a.

117. PO 16b.

118. PO 15c.

119. PO 17d.

120. *PO* 17d.

121. *PO* 17a.

122. *AAS*, 63 (1971), 497–526; English translation in Flannery (ed.), *Vatican Council II: The Conciliar and Post Conciliar Documents*, 680–706.

123. *Evangelica testificatio* (*ET*) 7a: "invitamento Spiritus Sancti libere respondentes."

124. *ET* 7b: "Haec doctrina Concilii in claro lumine huius doni magnitudinem quod ipsi dare libere decrevistis, quodque . . . simile doni a Christo Ecclesiae suae impertiti perinde ac hoc absolutissimum est et irrevocabile."

125. *ET* 1: "Spiritualis magnanimitas illorum quo . . . Domino vitam suam consecrarunt." This position of Paul VI is important, and contradicts the unilateral position that wanted to see consecration as a purely divine prerogative. In this regard, see R. Regamey, *Paul VI donne aux religieux leur chartre* (Paris, 1971), 39–45.

126. *ET* 7b.

127. *ET* 7b. On the last point, Paul VI refers to *LG* 44c. With regard to heavenly goods, see *LG* 8a.

128. *ET* 8.

129. *ET* 9–10.

130. *ET* 9.

131. *ET* 50.

132. *ET* 11.

133. *ET* 11. Cf. F. Viens, *Charismes et vie consacrée* (Rome, 1983), 83; see also 55–100, where the author sets forth the teaching of Paul VI on the charisms of consecrated life.

134. *ET* 11.

135. *ET* 11.

136. *ET* 32.

137. *LG* speaks of "donum divinum" (43a), "spiritus fundatorum" (45a), and "vocatio in quam a Deo vocatus est" (47).

138. From this point of view, the document *Mutuae relationes*, in *AAS*, 70 (1978), 473–506, is important; in it not only is the teaching on charisms more developed (Nos. 11–12), but the elements are given for a spiritual discernment of new charisms (No. 51).

139. See Viens, *Charismes et vie consacrée*, 100–111, which is a study on the use of the term by John Paul II. Fuller information can be found in the volumes entitled *Jean-Paul II aux religieuses et religieux*, 1 (1978–1980), 2 (1981–1982), 3 (1983–1984). An index in each volume gives references to the teaching of the Pope on "Le Charisme propre de chaque institut" and "Charismes et vie ecclésiale."

140. *Redemptionis donum* (*RD*) 6a, in *AAS*, 76 (1984), 521; English translation by St. Paul Publications (Homebush, N.S.W., 1984).

141. *RD* 8c, 11b–c.

142. *RD* 14a; cf. 9a.

143. *RD* 10a.

144. *RD* 8b.

145. *RD* 8f; see also 15a–c.

146. *RD* 15a.

147. *RD* 13d.

148. *RD* 10a.

149. *RD* 13d.

150. *RD* 14a.

151. *RD* 14a; see also 13j.

152. *RD* 14a. For fuller information on *Redemptionis donum*, see our study "Redemptionis donum," *Vita Consacrata*, 21 (1985), 158–176.

153. The reference to the "ius proprium" was considerably reduced from the second draft (published in 1980) onwards, because of the obligation to define various points in the constitutions to be submitted for the approval of the competent authority.

154. Certain superiors general preferred that the law itself fix those things that would otherwise have been within the competence of the Roman congregations and therefore arbitrary.

155. Hence the difficulty in interpreting the terms "accedit" or "accedunt" of Canons 604 and 731. The term had already been used ambiguously in *LG* 41d: "Quibus accedunt."

156. Contrary to what *PC* 1d had done.

157. It suffices to refer to Canons 573; 574, §2; 575–578. For the religious life, to Canons 607–608; 618–619; 631, §1; 652, §2; 654; 662; 673–676. For the secular institutes, to Canons 710, 711, 713.

158. The term "consecrare" or "consecratus" was understood as a passive "consecrated by God," despite the contrary position of Paul VI (see note 125), and John Paul II (see note 140). The liturgical books also have the active sense; for example, the *Ordo professionis religiosae*, Editio typica (Vatican City, 1970), 111, in the example of the formula of profession: "Ego ad Dei honorem, firma voluntate impulses *intimius Ei me consecrandi*," and 121, giving the text to be inserted into Eucharistic Prayer IV: "quae . . . hodie *tibi perpetuo se consecrarunt.*"

159. See Canons 573, §1; 577; 591; 675, §§1–2.

160. See Canon 603: "in laudem Dei et mundi salutem."

161. Canons 607, §§1–3; 608.

162. The information found in Canons 710 and 713 needed synthesizing.

163. We have noted this problem from the viewpoint of the secular institutes; see Canon 711.

164. It is necessary to move beyond the position of Canon 107 of the 1917 Code, which influenced those of Pius XII and the Council, especially as found in *LG* 43b and 44d.

165. See the successive drafts of the present Canon 574. Canon 2, §1, of the 1977 draft read: "Status eorum qui in huiusmodi Institutis vitam fraternam agunt, *licet ad Ecclesiae structuram hierarchicam de se non spectet*, ad eius tamen vitam et sanctitatem pertinent et ideo ab omnibus in honore habendus est." The Eastern Code also avoids taking up this position; see *Nuntia,* 16 (1983), 10.

166. See Canon 207, §2, in which the "inconcusse" of *LG* 44d has disappeared.

167. See *Communicationes,* 13 (1981), 401–404.

168. It is certain that the present Code is defective in this regard, especially as concerns the canonic life and the monastic life.

169. In this connection, see the various studies on just pluralism among these institutes; cf. J. Beyer, "De iusto institutorum saecularium pluralismo," *Periodica,* 60 (1971), 500–506.

170. See Canons 598–601. We could also see a counsel expressed in Canon 602.

171. See Canons 586, §1; 591; 611; 678; 680; 682.

172. Cf. *CD* 35, and *Ecclesiae sanctae II* 22–40.

CHAPTER 45

The Task of Revising the Constitutions of the Institutes of Consecrated Life as Called for by Vatican II

Michel Dortel-Claudot, S.J.

Summary

Vatican II called on the institutes of consecrated life to revise their constitutions. This task has now been carried out, and is one of the most outstanding fruits of the Council, although little has been said or written about it. This article fills this gap by tracing the history of such revision from 1966 to 1986. It assesses the work achieved, and concludes that the objective set by the Council will finally be reached at the price of unflagging perseverance. The task now remaining is that of living out these renewed constitutions.

Vatican II called for the "up-to-date renewal" of religious life, and more broadly that of the institutes of consecrated life. *Perfectae caritatis* first lays down general guidelines for this vast task, and calls for the life, prayer, activity, and government of the institutes to be adapted to the needs of the apostolate, and to different cultures and circumstances, as well as to the actual physical and psychological circumstances of their members. It then draws the following practical conclusion: "For this reason,

constitutions, directories, books of customs, of prayers, of cere-
monies and such like should be properly revised, obsolete prescriptions being suppressed, and should be brought into line with
conciliar documents" (PC 3). In the next number, the conciliar
Decree gives the following wise warning: "All should remember,
however, that the hope for renewal lies more in greater diligence
in the observance of the rule and constitutions than in the multi-
plication of laws" (PC 4).[1]

The revision of the constitutions of the institutes of consecrated life has by now been achieved at least in its essential
aspects, and is one of the outstanding fruits of the Council,
although there has been little discussion on the subject outside
the institutes themselves.[2] This modest study is an attempt to
rectify this lacuna.[3]

The conciliar decision to revise the constitutions is the outcome of a line of reflection that began well before Vatican II, in
the time of Pius XII. As early as 1950, authorized voices were
stressing how necessary it was to adapt the specific law of religious families to the needs of today's world.[4]

Perfectae caritatis 4 gives some orientations for such revision:
making laws and deciding on norms is the special responsibility
of general chapters, with the approval of the competent authority of the Church as laid down by law. Such decisions will be
preceded by consultations carried out throughout the whole of
the institute in question. It was left to the Motu proprio *Ecclesiae
sanctae* (Part II) of Paul VI, of 6 August 1966, to provide more
detailed instructions:

1. It is the institutes themselves which have the main responsibility for renewal and adaptation. They shall accomplish
this especially by means of general chapters or, in the Eastern
rite, by *synaxes*. The task of general chapters is not limited to
making laws; they should also foster spiritual and apostolic
vitality.

3. In each institute, in order to put renewal and adaptation
into effect, a special general chapter is to be summoned within
two or, at most, three years. . . .

6. This general chapter has the right to alter, temporarily,
certain prescriptions of the constitutions—or, in Eastern rites,
of the "typica"—by way of experiment, provided that the purpose, nature and character of the institute are safeguarded.

Experiments which run counter to common law—and they should be embarked upon with prudence—will be readily authorized by the Holy See as the need arises.

Such experiments may be continued until the next ordinary general chapter, which will be empowered to grant a further prolongation but not beyond the date of the subsequent chapter.

8. The final approval of constitutions is reserved to the competent authority.

12. The general laws of every institute (constitutions, typica, rules or whatever other name is given to these) must, generally speaking, contain the following elements:

(a) the evangelical and theological principles concerning religious life and its incorporation in the Church, and an apt and accurate formulation in which "the spirit and aims of the founder should be clearly recognized and faithfully preserved, as indeed should each institute's sound traditions, for all of these constitute the patrimony of an institute" (PC 2b).

(b) the juridical norms necessary to define the character, aims and means employed by the institute. Such rules must not be multiplied unduly, but should always be clearly formulated.

13. A combination of both elements, the spiritual and the juridical, is necessary, so as to ensure that the principal codes of each institute will have a solid foundation and be permeated by a spirit which is authentic and a law which is alive. Care must be taken not to produce a text either purely juridical or merely hortatory.

14. From the basic text of the rules one shall exclude anything which is now out of date, or anything which may change with the conditions of time, or which is of purely local application. These norms which are linked with present-day life or with the physical and psychical conditions or situations of the subjects, should be entered in separate books, such as directories, books of customs or similar documents, whatever be their name.

17. Those elements are to be considered obsolete which do not pertain to the nature and purpose of the institute and which, having lost their meaning and impact are of no further assistance to religious life. But the idea of witness, which

religious life has for its function to show forth, must be kept in mind.[5]

Ecclesiae sanctae II 1–19 clearly indicated the path to be followed, although some doubts still persisted on certain important points.

The special chapter "has the right to alter, temporarily, certain prescriptions of the constitutions" (*ES II* 6). What does "*certain* prescriptions" mean? Should the institutes in question be satisfied with reworking or eliminating certain articles of the constitutions and adding others, but without any radical recasting of the text taken as a whole? Can the constitutions be drafted in such a way as to produce a truly new text that is still in conformity with *Ecclesiae sanctae II* 6 in respecting the purpose, nature, and character of the institute? When *Ecclesiae sanctae II* 13 warns that "care must be taken not to produce a text either purely juridical or merely hortatory," does it simply envisage the replacement of the odd page of the constitutions, while the bulk remains unchanged? Different authors felt called on to give their opinion on these various point between 1966 and 1968.[6]

After some hesitation, it was realized that in the case of many institutes, the simple modification of one or another article of the constitutions would not allow for the up-to-date renewal called for by the Council, and would in any case turn the text of the constitutions into a sort of patchwork. The idea of having new texts replace those in force, but on an experimental basis, was therefore put forward, and eventually came to be seen as a possible solution. Even so, it was stressed that *Perfectae caritatis* 3 certainly did not oblige institutes to draw up constitutions that were totally new from beginning to end. Those who wished could simply alter a certain number of articles in their specific laws—a choice that was generally taken by recently founded institutes, with constitutions that had been produced after 1950, and thus at a time when the trend toward renewal was already penetrating consecrated life.

Ecclesiae sanctae II 8 reserves definitive approval of constitutions to the competent authority. In institutes of pontifical right, this is the Apostolic See—which means the Congregation for Religious and Secular Institutes, the Congregation for the Evangelization of Peoples, or the Congregation for the Oriental Churches, according to the particular institute in question.[7] Before being approved, the text is examined according to an established procedure.[8]

In institutes of diocesan right, the competent authority changed after 28 November 1983, when the new Code of Canon Law came into force. Before this date, it was the task of each and every bishop of a diocese in which the institute had a community to approve its constitutions,[9] whereas after this date, the competent authority became the bishop of the principal seat of the institute, after consulting the bishops of the other diocese in which the institute is found; the purpose here is to safeguard the unity of an institute that is spread over a number of dioceses.[10]

Immediately after the Council, some people thought the institutes should assemble in general chapter in order to revise the constitutions at present in force and then *immediately* submit these revised versions for the definitive approval of the competent authority. Paul VI certainly wanted the task of renewal called for by Vatican II to begin without delay in all the institutes, and this is why the special chapter was to be convened "within two or, at most, three years"; this chapter could be divided into two separated sessions, separated by a gap that should not usually exceed a year (*ES II* 3). However, he also hoped that the institutes would prudently carry out some experiments, and then assess the advantages and disadvantages of these before making any definitive decision. This led to the idea of a period of time that should be neither too long nor too short, and at the end of which the renewed constitutions should be submitted for the approval of the Church: eight to twelve years was considered a reasonable time. After this, it became usual, even in documents of the Holy See, to refer to this period as the "period of experimentation."[11] The renewal constitutions were thus to be approved not after the special chapter, but after the second ordinary chapter celebrated after this special chapter, in other words, immediately following the third chapter to be held in the institute after 11 October 1966, the date on which *Ecclesiae sanctae II* officially came into force. The timetable eventually laid down was as follows: special chapter, convened after 11 October 1966; first ordinary chapter; second ordinary chapter; and, lastly, immediately following this second ordinary chapter, the definitive approval of the renewed constitutions.[12] For the sake of clarity in the present study, we refer to this second ordinary chapter as the "constituent chapter."

The Period of the Special Chapters (1967–1971)

The important general chapter called for by *Ecclesiae sanctae II* 3 was thus referred to as the "special chapter," because of the special task with which it was faced, whether it was in fact an ordinary or "elective" chapter or an extraordinary one. It was sometimes referred to as the "renewal chapter" or "aggiornamento chapter," although in the present study we keep the official title of "special chapter."

Between 1967 and 1971, the majority of institutes set about planning, and then celebrating, their special chapters—a courageous undertaking, and one for which it must be admitted that most of them were relatively unprepared. It may be wondered whether the maximum delay of three years imposed by *Ecclesiae sanctae II* 3 for the convocation of the special chapter was too short. With the hindsight provided by the twenty years that have passed since the promulgation of this Motu proprio, this is now a legitimate question. [13]

The institutes needed guidance, orientations, and instructions. They received the latter primarily from the lips of the Supreme Pontiff himself: between 1965 and 1974, Paul VI spoke to general chapters on about forty occasions, at special audiences or at audiences for the members of the chapters of a number of different institutes[14]; and apart from this, there were his many addresses on consecrated life, and his Apostolic Exhortation *Evangelica testificatio* of 21 June 1971.

The various authors also offered institutes their advice and suggestions, both on the manner in which special chapters should be planned and held, and on what should be said in the future constitutions. [15] For its part, the International Union of Superiors General provided precious assistance for female religious institutes. [16] *Ecclesiae sanctae II* 4 had made the following recommendation:

> In preparation for this chapter, the general council must arrange, by some suitable means, for an ample and free consultation of all the subjects. The results of this consultation should be made available in good time so as to guide and assist the work of the chapter. The consultation may be done at the level of conventual or provincial chapters, by setting up commissions, by sending out questionnaires, etc. [17]

It was the first time in the history of consecrated life that a free consultation was organized on such a vast scale and embracing such a wide range of subjects. Inevitably there were a fair number of misjudgments in the procedure followed, but above all in the evaluation of the results of such consultations. The fault lay less with the institutes themselves than with certain sociologists or psychologists who were acting as their technical advisers in this delicate process.

At the end of the period of the special chapters, and still in the heat of the moment, it was difficult to carry out any valid assessment of what they had accomplished, although a number of authors did make the attempt.[18]

Now that a certain amount of time has elapsed, it is easier today to reach judgment on the work produced by the chapters celebrated between 1967 and 1971.[19] In the first place, we consider the outward form of this production by taking a sample group of ninety-one institutes, which are chosen from a much larger number, and are fairly representative of the male and female religious congregations of simple vows from every country.

At this time, eighty-six of these institutes approved capitular texts that were to replace, on an experimental basis, the chapters of the constitutions then in force regarding the following subjects: the aim and spirit of the institute; the evangelical counsels; prayer life; community life; the apostolate. The other five institutes did not adopt new texts for these subjects to replace the texts then in force, but chose to retain the latter with the modification of a few articles.[20]

As regards the subject of government, seventy-five institutes out of the ninety-one adopted a new experimental text, while sixteen retained the one they had, or modified only one or two minor points—generally the procedure for electing delegates to general or provincial chapters.

As regards formation, the production of the special chapters depended on the Instruction *Renovationis causam*, promulgated by the Congregation for Religious and Secular Institutes in January 1969.[21] Chapters celebrated in 1967 and 1968 said nothing—or very little—about formation, whereas almost all those that met in 1969, 1970, and 1971 spoke about the matter, most frequently reproducing large extracts from this document.

In an overall perspective, what general impression do we draw from the texts approved by the special chapters? Let us answer this question, while leaving aside for the moment the sections of these texts concerned with the government of the institutes.[22] Simplifying things a little, we can distinguish two types of capitular texts. On the one hand, there were new rules of life that were satisfactory from the points of view both of the language used and of the requirements of consecrated life.[23] These texts represented a very valid draft for the future renewed constitutions called for by the Council. On the other hand, there were new rules of life that could in no way be seen as containing the seeds of constitutions: they neither provided a clear statement of the basic requirements of consecrated life nor laid down any practical norms.[24] Their language was abstract, full of jargon, and hard to understand, and fashionable concepts were mixed in with citations from Vatican II that were often incomplete and out of context. The whole impression was that of texts that would soon be dated and were certainly not built to last.[25]

During the period of the special chapters, the Congregation for Religious and Secular Institutes adopted a prudent and reserved approach, as can be seen in the letter of 10 July 1972 from its then Secretary, Archbishop A. Mayer, to the President of the International Union of Superiors General:

In a letter dated December 4, 1967 the Sacred Congregation for Religious and Secular Institutes requested institutes to send the acts of their special general chapter which were to be held according to the motu proprio, Ecclesiae sanctae, Part II, No. 3.

In making this request the Sacred Congregation wished to be aware of the experiments in progress and also to know if the chapters remained within the limits set by the motu proprio. This permitted modifications of the constitutions "ad experimentum" as long as the nature, end, and purpose of the institute would be preserved.

Following this letter, many institutes sent their capitular acts and this sacred Congregation has responded to many, making the necessary observations and also permitting experiments contrary to common law. . . .

In this period of experimentation the Sacred Congregation does not approve new constitutions. This does not prevent the acts of the general chapters from becoming immediately effective provided, as mentioned above, the purpose, nature and character of the institute are preserved (*Ecclesiae sanctae*, Part II, No. 6).

However, every derogation from common law must have a dispensation explicitly granted. In some cases, it might easily have happened that the Sacred Congregation omitted to call attention to some change contrary to the law in force. This would have been due to an oversight and may not be interpreted as an explicit concession. [26]

In this same letter, the Secretary of the Congregation drew attention to a certain number of omissions and distortions that were quite frequently to be seen in the texts produced by the special chapters: each vow must be clearly defined; the personal authority of superiors should not be watered down to some vague collective responsibility of communities and councils; the formula of religious profession must be the same for all those who make their vows; a passive voice is erroneously granted to those in temporary vows; decision-making powers are illicitly granted to the broadened councils that have been set up in many institutes; the religious habit is not dealt with properly; small communities are to have a local superior and must retain a religious life style.

The Period of the Intermediate Chapters (1972–1976)

As will be recalled, the timetable laid down by *Ecclesiae sanctae II* 6 was as follows: special chapter; then, first ordinary chapter; and lastly, second ordinary chapter (which we refer to as the "constituent chapter"), at the end of which the renewed constitutions are to be submitted for the definitive approval of the Church. This timetable was observed by the majority of institutes, although in some institutes not one, but two and sometimes three ordinary chapters were held between the special chapter and the constituent chapter, with the permission of the Holy See. In the present section, we therefore use the term "intermediate chapters" to indicate both the single first ordinary chapter, as envisaged in *Ecclesiae sanctae II* 6, and also the two or three ordinary chapters held between the special chapter and the constituent chapter (so that for some institutes, the latter became the third, or even the fourth, ordinary chapter after the special chapter).

It goes without saying that not all these intermediate chapters were celebrated between 1972 and 1976: some took place prior to 1972, and others well after 1976. We have simply taken these two dates as general reference points because the special chapters had almost all been held by 1972, and the series of constituent chapters really began in 1977.[27]

In these intermediate chapters, what happened to the capitular texts that had been approved by the special chapters? In order to answer this question, we must distinguish between the different groups of institutes:

1. The few institutes that had retained the articles of their preconciliar constitutions concerning the aim and spirit of the institute, the evangelical counsels, prayer life, community life, and the apostolate did not change their approach at their intermediate chapters.[28]

2. At the opposite end of the scale, a very small number of institutes completely recomposed and rewrote the new rule of life that had been approved *ad experimentum* at the special chapter, although this was certainly not done with a few to seeking definitive approval soon afterwards. This approach generally resulted in a text that was far inferior to the previous one, and that was vaguer, less spiritual, and tended even more to sidestep the issue of the real requirements of consecrated life.

3. The vast majority of institutes only partially modified the texts approved at their special chapters. In order to provide an objective overview of the content of these modifications, we must examine the different aspects of consecrated life:

(a) *The Aim and Spirit of the Institute*. Various institutes tried to increase their awareness of their own specific charism more deeply than had been the case at the special chapters, when this element had tended to be universally neglected.

(b) *Apostolic Activities*. At their special chapters, many institutes had adopted a new but wise approach to their activities, while always remaining faithful to their traditional mission as defined in their previous constitutions. However, many others had adopted imprudent approaches, systematically abandoning the tasks proper to the character of the institute, so that the range of apostolic tasks of the members was unduly broadened. In this second group of institutes, it was not possible to correct these mistaken orientations at the intermediate chapters, and, in some cases, they were in fact confirmed and reinforced.

(c) *Evangelical Counsels, Prayer Life, and Community Life.* In these areas, the problem varied according to the country concerned, and these differences had repercussions for the texts approved at the intermediate chapters. Simplifying matters considerably, we can summarize as follows: (i) In those institutes that were mainly French-speaking, or in which the French-speaking influence was predominant, the years 1967 to 1971 had often seen a sort of "crisis," with challenges to the authority of superiors, a falloff in sacramental life and prayer life, encroachments on poverty and the common life, an increase in the number of members living alone, and so on. The intermediate chapters that took place between 1972 and 1976, therefore, had to deal with this situation, so that in many cases—and particularly with regard to community life, poverty, and obedience—they approved texts highlighting the requirements of religious life that had tended not to be stressed by the special chapters. (ii) In those institutes that were mainly English-speaking, or in which the English-speaking influence was predominant, this "crisis" arose later, at the time of the intermediate chapters, so that under pressure from certain of their members, these chapters approved texts on community life, poverty, and obedience that were less in keeping with the obligations of the religious life than those of the special chapters had been. The situation was very similar in institutes with a Spanish-speaking majority, or in which the Spanish influence was predominant. (iii) In those institutes that were mainly Italian-speaking, or in which the Italian influence was predominant, matters were less obvious and tended to be spread out over a longer period of time, so that the approaches of the special chapters and intermediate chapters were more similar. The same can on the whole be said of institutes in which the German influence was predominant.

(d) *Formation.* Those institutes that had not been able to take the Instruction *Renovationis causam* into account at their special chapters made up for this at their intermediate chapters.

(e) *Government of the Institute.* Let us base ourselves on the sample of ninety-one congregations studied. As we said, at their special chapter, seventy-five of the ninety-one approved a new experimental text on government. We also said that at their special chapters, sixteen institutes had retained their preconciliar text or had changed it only very slightly. What did these sixteen institutes do at their intermediate chapters? Five still retained their preconciliar text. Eleven approved an entirely new text: in four institutes, this was made necessary by the division into provinces and regions, and in the seven others, it was the search for new but imprudent forms of government that led to this. Lastly, after their intermediate chapter, eighty-six out of the sample of ninety-one congregations (that is, 94.5 percent) possessed a text on government that was very different from that in force prior to Vatican II—and this percentage corresponds well with what we know of all institutes as a whole.

In our considerations, we did not make any judgment on the texts of the special chapters concerning government,[29] since it is more interesting and informative to examine all the texts on this subject approved between 1967 and 1976, in other words, during the periods of both the special chapters and the intermediate chapters. However, we need to go a little further back in order to do this.

Between 1967 and 1976 religious everywhere—even the least well qualified—started airing views on the government of their institutes. Authority became a subject of discussion even at the local community level, and the very organization of the institute was hotly debated. Each person would come up with his or her own diagram or chart, with arrows pointing in every direction, and ascending and descending lines—the former decidedly outweighing the latter in both number and intensity. "Life should move upwards," was a frequently heard cry, and this goes to explain the heavy strokes used for the ascending lines in all the diagrams produced at that time.

Certain words were outlawed from the texts, so that the verbs "to command," "to order," and "to direct" disappeared totally, or almost so. The verb "to govern" tended to be retained for major superiors, but was no longer used for the local superiors, who were now expected to "animate." The verbs "to decree" and "to decide" were no longer used for superiors, although they were retained for general and provincial chapters. The word "authority" lost its genetive, since the authority "of superiors" was no longer mentioned, and it was henceforth employed alone, so that people started talking of the "service of authority" in the province or the institute, as if it were some abstract reality without any personal support. It also became customary to use "authority-and-obedience" in tandem, which helped to make authority a depersonalized principle.

Between 1967 and 1976, the same key ideas became established everywhere: participation was extolled, the merits of collegiality were snug, and decentralization was encouraged. And despite the difficulties in pronouncing the word—let alone those involved in explaining it—the term "subsidiarity" was found on every tongue. The majority of institutes moved in this direction, and although this took place later in some than in others, such slight differences are irrelevant in the face of the breadth of the phenomenon. This orientation was undoubtedly a necessary stage, and its omission could well have entailed greater ills than the blunders and confusion that are so clear for us to see today. However, its universal dimension and its one-way character did mean that this ground swell of opinion entailed one major drawback, in that it made the institutes reflect on their type of authority and their governmental structures on the basis of outside ideas that were strongly in the air all around them, and not primarily in the perspective of their own specific identity and vocation. The changes made between 1967 and 1976 took as their model and reference points values that were brought into the institutes from outside, and that were sometimes very foreign to their particular traditions.

After this aside on the texts approved between 1967 and 1976 on the subject of government, let us confine ourselves again to the period of the intermediate chapters, which did in any case allow many institutes to assess the progress made so far and also the work still remaining to be done, and to gain a better understanding of what should be written in the renewed constitutions.[30] During this same period, the Congregation for Religious and Secular Institutes broke its reserve thanks to its new information bulletin *Informationes* (published in English under the title of *Consecrated Life*), and unobtrusively gave some orientations on the revision of constitutions and the role of general chapters in this connection.[31] Moreover, the congregation also made an unofficial first evaluation of the work accomplished by the chapters that had taken place since the Council, that is, between 1966 and 1976.[32] This evaluation ended with the following observation and invitation:

The time seems to have come for striking the balance with regard to the experiments made over these past ten years. Moreover, the prescriptions of the *motu proprio* "Ecclesiae Sanctae" invite religious who see that the time has come for drawing up definitive texts of renewed Constitutions to submit them to the Holy See for approval. These prescriptions embody the desire—rather generally expressed—to return to more stable norms, once the period of experiments is over.[33]

Toward the end of the period studied in the present section, the International Union of Superiors General set about a very wide survey of female institutes on the subject of their recent general chapters. The last question asked was as follows: "What in general is the predominant attitude in your congregation with regard to the provisional Constitutions?" And, among other things, the summary of the replies said the following, which deserves to be quoted: "Some congregations hope to continue to live in a spirit of searching and of adaptation to life in full evolution, so that they do not want any definitive Constitutions. Others are of the opinion that what is provisional does not yield good results."[34]

In the 1975–1976 period, therefore, the moment was almost upon the majority of institutes of consecrated life when they had to produce the now definitive text of their renewed constitutions, so that these could be presented for the approval of the Church. A good number of institutes was very apprehensive about this day of reckoning and would only too willingly have put it off indefinitely. These fears are seen in the survey of the International Union of Superiors General.[35]

The Period of the Constituent Chapter (1977–1986)

We have just referred to the fears existing at the end of the previous period. Two years later, how did the institutes feel about the prospect of having to provide themselves with constitutions that were stable and were no longer to be subject to the opinions of each successive chapter? There was a fairly rapid reversal of trends in this area between 1977 and 1978, marking a sort of watershed and a decisive step in the long process of renewal of the constitutions that had been set in motion by the

Council. If we consider the phenomenon in a worldwide perspective, the situation was as follows at the end of 1978: the vast
majority of institutes were aware that the moment seemed to
have arrived, ten or twelve years after the great turmoil of the
special chapters, to make some more definitive statements about
themselves, and they were seized by a wish to give birth to their
constitutions, as the written expression of their charisms.[36] The
Secretary of the Sacred congregation for Religious and Secular
Institutes noted this in the following terms in an official letter of
21 December 1978 addressed to his opposite number in the Sacred Congregation for the Evangelization of Peoples:

> . . . many religious feel the time has come to have clear,
> complete and stable constitutions to present to prospective
> candidates the specific characteristics of their congregation.
> Desirous, too, of expressing in writing all that is best in them,
> the institutes feel it is vital for them to "say what they are
> about" and to have it recognized and approved by the Church.
>   This attitude, which has been evident for some time, in-
> duces this Sacred Congregation to support and encourage the
> efforts being made on all sides toward the preparation of defini-
> tive constitutions, in addition to the fact that the institutes
> which have already obtained this approbation have experi-
> enced great satisfaction and an increased vitality.[37]

"The time has come!" was the watchword of the time, and
John Paul II gave it the form of a universal instruction in his
address of 14 November 1979 to the members of the Fifth General Assembly of the International Union of Superiors General:

> After the years of experience aimed at updating religious life
> according to the spirit of the Institute, the time has come to
> evaluate objectively and humbly the attempts made, to recog-
> nize their positive elements, and any deviations, and finally to
> prepare a *Rule of stable life,* approved by the Church, which
> should constitute for all the sisters a stimulus to deeper knowl-
> edge of their commitments and to joyful faithfulness in living
> them.[38]

The institutes were therefore ready to make the last move from
their experimental renewed constitutions to the definitive ones.

Even so, some did ask for a further delay of two or three years, in order not to be influenced by the time factor, and therefore to be able to plan their constituent chapters more effectively. The Secretary of the Sacred Congregation for Religious and Secular Institutes refers to this factor in his previously cited letter of 21 December 1978:

> . . . when really special conditions, studies on the charism of the founder, structures of the congregation, or the concept of its mission demand a longer period of reflection, it would seem that in general a delay of 2 or 3 years is sufficient without prolonging the experimental period to 1986–1987.
> As a general rule, this Sacred Congregation grants necessary extensions up to 1983 or 1984. If the ordinary chapter is not scheduled by that date, the institutes can easily arrange to convoke an extraordinary chapter, an act fully justified by the importance of the matter.[39]

In point of fact, the Holy See caused no difficulties over postponing the date by which constitutions were to be presented for approval until 1981, 1982, or 1983, but a delay until 1984, 1985, or 1986 was granted only for serious and exceptional reasons.[40] Most constituent chapters were held between 1977 and 1983,[41] with very few taking place earlier, and very few later, and the majority undoubtedly taking place between 1980 and 1982.

What was the attitude of the Holy See, and, more specifically, that of the Sacred Congregation for Religious and Secular Institutes, between 1979 and 1983, which was the most important period in the broader one at present under consideration? Did it play any active role—and if so, which one—with the institutes as a group with regard to the actual content of the constitutions? Did it promulgate any true norms on this subject that were applicable to consecrated life as a whole? We must state that the Congregation adopted a more nondirective attitude, and its officials only gave their opinion on the actual content of the future constitutions discretely and on rare occasions:

1. The first such occasion during this period was on 23 February 1979, at the monthly meeting between the Council of the "16" and the Sacred Congregation for Religious and Secular Institutes.[42] The subject under study was that of the constitutions,

their drafting, and their approval, and with regard to this very topical problem, the Council of the "16" asked some questions of the members of the Congregation who were present. Some of the answers were as follows:

> SCRSI has already given thought to the possibility of issuing norms or criteria, or at least an official explanation of the norms in *Ecclesiae Sanctae*. On the other hand, it wishes to leave Institutes quite free: they need this freedom while drafting their Constitutions. . . .
>
> The criteria for the approval of Constitutions . . . can be reduced to two main ones, viz., Are the Constitutions in conformity with the official documents of the Church? and Do they express the Institute's charism clearly? . . .
>
> SCRSI has a duty to check on each Institute's fidelity to its charism. . . . If any doubts or difficulties arise, both sides should attempt to remove them, in great mutual trust. . . .[43]

2. The Congregation again gave its views on constitutions at the end of 1979, in an article that appeared in its news bulletin.[44] This article was written in a relatively free manner, and having recalled the instructions of the Council and of *Ecclesiae sanctae II*, it draws attention to some specific points:

> Some institutes wondered if it would not be better to await the promulgation of the new Code of Canon Law. As a matter of fact, the new Code is not expected to make substantial alterations in the present one; and if some article in the revised constitutions will need to be changed, it will always be easy to find a suitable opportunity of inserting the required refinements. . . .
>
> . . . the constitutions must give an orientation suited to inspire the apostolic activity to be carried out according to the distinctive charism. . . . All forms of apostolic or charitable activity cannot be undertaken. . . .
>
> It is particularly important to know what material should be included in the constitutions and what should be put in the other books.

This article also gives some general indications on the content of the constitutions and the type of language to be used.

3. The Congregation also made its opinion known to some

extent in the spring of 1980, in the form of an "interview" granted by Sister Mary Linscott to the editors of the bulletin of the International Union of Superiors General.[45]

Thus, as we said, the Congregation adopted a more or less nondirective attitude between 1977 and 1980, which corresponds to the period when the institutes were preparing to produce their definitive constitutions. However, this did not prevent it from fulfilling its duty of answering bishops who had the task of approving the constitutions of institutes of diocesan right that fell under their authority[46]; nor from giving its opinion on the draft texts that certain institutes, particularly large ones, spontaneously submitted to it even prior to their constituent chapters; and nor again from making the necessary remarks on the constitutions definitively approved by general chapters and submitted to its examination for official approval.

4. On 26 February 1982, the meeting between the Council of the "16" and the Congregation took the evaluation of the renewal of constitutions as its subject. In the name of the Congregation, Father L. Ravasi first described the process of approval and recalled in very general terms some important points that must be found in constitutions, and then noted what seemed to be the most positive aspects of the new constitutions:

The seriousness of the work undertaken and the amount of time, energy and other resources invested in it.

Charism is often expressed in felicitous terms: the ecclesial aspect of religious life is emphasized without constraint.

Their biblical, theological and spiritual richness.

The variety of style, formulation and redaction.

Constitutions often remind one of a garden full of flowers, in which asceticism, spiritual orientations, etc., are happily blended. They are not merely "normative": they also bring a light spiritual breeze.

In the course of the discussion that immediately followed this, Cardinal Pironio, Archbishop Mayer, Sister Mary Linscott, and Father Ravasi also noted aspects of the new constitutions that might be seen as negative:

Some texts are too short; others are too prolix.

The essential points of the legislation should be in the

Constitutions, which in that sense ought to be sufficiently complete.

Sometimes too much is left in the *Directory*, to the detriment of the Constitutions which are thus impoverished.

Some texts, but this is very rare, contain orientations that are not in agreement with the Church's doctrine.

Quotations are taken out of their context; hence there is the danger of changing the meaning of official documents such as *Perfectae caritatis* and *Ecclesiae sanctae.*

An option for the poor is excellent, but sometimes the way it is expressed is less good.

Some Constitutions are excessively marked by the context where they originated.[47]

5. Lastly, in 1983, the Sacred Congregation for Religious and Secular Institutes devoted a large issue of its news bulletin to the renewed constitutions, with contributions from the Cardinal Prefect and twelve other people—members or consultants of the Congregation and other experts.[48] The aim was not that of promulgating official norms, but of helping those institutes that still had to produce their definitive constitutions by giving them the benefit or orientations based on a number of years of experience. (We were already in 1983!)

The new Code of Canon Law was promulgated by John Paul II on 25 January 1983, by which time probably two-thirds of the institutes had already celebrated their constituent chapters. Did this cause any problem in drafting their definitive constitutions? We must honestly admit that it did not, except on a few decidedly minor juridical points. There are various reasons for this fact. In the first place, the final draft of the new Code had been completed and sent out to those who had a right to receive it in the course of the summer of 1980. Thus, although the institutes of consecrated life did not see it, the experts who acted as their advisers did have the document, and judged that as far as the canons on consecrated life were concerned, the final text would not be very different from this draft—a guess that proved correct. The constitutions drafted in 1981 and 1982—and this includes a large percentage of those voted on prior to 25 January 1983— therefore, had an eye on the Code that was soon to appear. Moreover, from fall 1980 onwards, the competent Roman Congregations (for the institutes of pontifical right) and the Bishops (for those of diocesan right) examined and corrected the constitutions submitted for their approval in the light of this final draft of the Code.[49] Now, bearing in mind the amount of time normally taken in examining constitutions, this represented almost all the texts approved by the institutes in 1979 and 1980 as well. We must, therefore, draw the following conclusion: only those constitutions approved by general chapters between 1975 and 1978 were not able to take into account the 1980 draft of the new Code either when they were being drafted or at the time of their examination; and, when all is said and done, this represents only a small number of institutes.[50]

The Definitive Renewed Constitutions

After the first stumbling steps of the special chapters, the successes or blunders of the intermediate chapters, and the necessary evaluations, a "common doctrinal approach" concerning the content of the definitive renewed constitutions gradually took shape. This was made possible by the general goodwill of the institutes, the cooperation of the majority of their members, and the orientations that the Sacred Congregation for Religious and Secular Institutes gave when the time was ripe, neither too early nor too late.[51] The experts who helped the institutes in their reflections from 1979 to 1986 also made their contribution to the formulation of this common doctrinal approach.[52]

According to this approach, the definitive renewed constitutions—those approved by the constituent chapters—must be a rule of life in the deepest sense of the term for the institute and its members, a rule of life composed and drafted in such a way that the consecrated members can fix their hearts on it and return to it again and again in reading and in personal and community prayer. Its language must be clear, and easy to memorize. In order for constitutions to be able to withstand the test of time, they must be phrased in simple and timeless words: jargon and language too closely linked to our age should be avoided in constitutions, because what is fashionable today may mean little tomorrow.

Constitutions are not only a work to be used for meditation or spiritual reading, although it is a good thing if they can be used for these purposes too. They must tell the consecrated person what he or she should be living and what his or her style of life should be, and, therefore, they cannot be limited simply to statements of principles of spiritual theology, and descriptions of purely interior attitudes, movements of the soul, and sentiments of the heart. Side by side and as thoroughly mixed as possible, they must contain both the spiritual principles that inspire the life and activity of the consecrated person, and also the fundamental requirements flowing from these principles in the sphere of action and behavior. Constitutions must contain a true program for consecrated life, with living and well-defined lines. They will only be a rule of life to the extent that they indicate a path that is clear enough for people to follow without becoming caught up in the words.

By bearing all this in mind, the constitutions will in the first place define the spirit of the institute, its nature, its mission in the Church, and the type of apostolic service proper to it—in other words, the various elements that go to make up its specific charism. The description of the latter certainly cannot be limited to two or three short phrases so general that they could be applied to any form of Christian life.

The constitutions will then define the requirements with regard to the evangelical counsels, community life, and prayer life—elements that must be seen as absolutely fundamental to the institute according to its own specific charism and to what is called for by any consecrated life. They must also define the object of the vows, drawing their inspiration from Canons 599, 600, and 601. And, lastly, they will provide the necessary norms as to formation, government, administration of worldly goods, and separation from the institute.[53]

Traditionally, the specific law of an institute encompasses not only its constitutions, and maybe one of the great Rules to which it refers back, but also other normative documents that are not subject to the approval of the Church and are thus easier to revise. In 1966, *Ecclesiae sanctae II* 14 said: "These norms which are linked with present-day life or with the physical and psychical conditions or situations of the subjects, should be entered in *complementary codes,* such as directories, books of customs or similar documents, whatever be their name."[54] These complementary codes are usually issued by the general chapter of an institute, although they can be issued by other authorities such as

the superior general and his council. It is up to the constitutions
to provide the necessary instructions in this regard. [55]

According to the common doctrinal approach, the following
have their place in such separate codes and not in the constitutions: anything that is likely to vary from one period to another;
anything that it must be possible to adapt to new circumstances
and needs as these occur; anything that is clearly secondary; and
purely technical rules that any social organization must observe
for its smooth running. [56]

Apart from its complementary code, which will be valid for all
territories, can an institute have certain specific rules for each
province? The answer is that this is possible, but on condition
that the constitutions explicitly allow for this, stating clearly the
spheres in which the provinces can have their own rules and also
saying who has the power to lay down such rules. In order to
safeguard the unity of the institute, these special rules must not
be too numerous and must concern practical points or minor
juridical details. [57]

How should the relationship be seen between the principle
code—in other words, the constitutions—and the complementary
code? There are various possible solutions, and each institute will
choose the one most suited to its nature and requirements. [58]

Do the texts approved by the constituent chapters and then
amended during the process of official approval correspond to the
ideal we have sketched out here?

We can without any hesitation reply affirmatively, at least for
the vast majority of institutes. They are as a whole now in possession of renewed constitutions that are objectively of great value,
and we can say that the hopes expressed in *Perfectae caritatis* 3
have been fulfilled in essence. The objective the Council set
itself will finally have been reached at the cost of a considerable
effort—an effort maintained, with various high and low points,
for between eleven and seventeen years, according to the institute in question. [59] It is too early to undertake a scientific study of
the content of the renewed and approved constitutions. [60] Even
so, what we can see so far makes it possible to reach a very
positive preliminary overall judgment on this content, both for
institutes of diocesan right and for those of pontifical right. [61]

Earlier in this study, we were led to express some reservations
as concerns the texts on government approved by general chap-

ters between 1967 and 1976. How would we now evaluate those approved by the constituent chapters?

The change in language seen between 1967 and 1976 remains. The banned words did not reappear, and institutes continued to be allergic to the terminology of a previous period ("command," "order," "forbid," and so on). On the other hand, however, the key words that were used in the 1967–1976 period to convey certain convictions and views then current came to be employed with more discernment between 1977 and 1986. The terms "collegiality," "subsidiarity," "coresponsibility," and "animation" are found less frequently in the definitive constitutions than in the texts produced in previous years. This is partly because of normal erosion, so that these terms came to lose their initial impact, but also because people reflected more deeply on the true meaning of these different concepts when the time came to set about drafting their definitive constitutions.

These concepts are still used, but in a more judicious and wiser manner now. For example, the word "collegiality" is now used only for general and provincial chapters, and is no longer applied in the context of the various councils and communities. The word "subsidiarity" has been cut down to size, and is no longer taken as a synonym for "autonomy." The word "animation" is no longer used completely on its own to define the role of superiors, and other words are now added to fill this concept out and provide greater nuance. Use of the word "coresponsibility" has shown that it is full of ambiguities, which is why it was handled with greater prudence at the constituent chapters: if it is simply taken as emphasizing that all the members of the same institute, the same province or the same community must feel morally responsible for the common good, it should be retained, whereas if it means that everybody shares to an equal extent in decision-making, it should be rejected. The various institutes came to a relative unanimous understanding in this connection between 1977 and 1986.

Was the proper and inalienable role of the superior—a role that cannot be watered down into some vague collective responsibility of the council or community—rediscovered at the constituent chapters? The answer would appear to be affirmative as far as the major superior is concerned, although the answer is less certain for local superiors.[62] Almost all the definitive constitutions provided a satisfactory description of the authority proper

to the major superior, in contrast to the wooliness and imprecision of the texts produced between 1967 and 1976.[63] His relationship to the council was clarified,[64] and, on a deeper level, it
was more clearly stressed that although animation is necessary,
the role of the major superior must go well beyond simple animation, even though the actual form of this role may differ widely
from one institute to another.

The necessary rectifications were thus made at the constituent
chapters, primarily because reflection on the government of the
institute had been preceded by reflection on the specific identity
of the institute itself—something that the lack of time, the impossibility of a proper perspective, and the general context had not
previously allowed. However small it may be, every institute has
its own heritage of reference points on the basis of which it can
define its government. However, these points need to be examined and clarified. And the period of the special chapters, and in
part that of the intermediate chapters, were not favorable to this
type of study, which requires peace and quiet, and discernment;
the merits of these periods are undoubtedly to be sought in another sphere. However, the period of the constituent chapters,
which saw a great emphasis on the individual riches of each
institute, made it possible to rediscover such reference points, so
that the government of each institute could then be better defined in function of its charism.

What we have just said about the section of the definitive
constitutions concerned with government goes to confirm our
very positive overall judgment of these constitutions.

On the worldwide scale, we do not have very much information on the way in which the definitive constitutions of institutes
of diocesan right have been examined by the bishops concerned
before being approved. We know more about how those of institutes of pontifical right were dealt with by the Holy See, and
particularly by the Sacred Congregation for Religious and Secular Institutes, and what type of corrections were usually called for
before approval was granted. There were very few cases in which
the Congregation asked that the new constitutions be totally
rewritten,[65] and this goes to show the quality of the work of the
constituent chapters.

The following are the points that the Congregation most often
requested: a more precise definition, couched in more specific

terms, of the apostolic aim of the institute; a better formulation of the object of the vows, particularly the vow of poverty; the correction of ambiguous terms with regard to the authority of superiors and the functioning of councils; the insertion of specific obligations envisaged by the new Code, particularly as concerns community life and life style.[66] Their examination by the competent authority, therefore, made it possible to improve the content of the constitutions approved by the constituent chapters still further—as the institutes themselves were often fair enough to recognize.

It must be observed that the new Code of Canon Law, whether in the form of the first draft of 1977, that of 1980, or the text definitively promulgated on 25 January 1983, contributed considerably to the quality of the renewed constitutions.[67] In the first place, it takes into very serious account the great variation between different institutes of consecrated life and presents this diversity as a source of wealth for the Church. It then calls on the institutes to remain faithful to themselves and states that each must safeguard its own spiritual heritage. And this is why it recognizes and guarantees the freedom they need in order to express their authentic charism in their constitutions. It does so by constantly referring the institutes to their own specific law. In a considerable number of cases, it does not lay down any universal norm, and confines itself to saying that on a given point, it is up to the constitutions, or more broadly the specific law of the institute, to make suitable provisions, taking into account the nature of the institute in question. On several occasions, it also formulates universal norms, but leaves to specific law the possibility of laying down different, or even contrary, norms on the same subject. Lastly, in a few instances it lays down universal norms, but states that specific law can add others if it judges this to be helpful.[68]

As Father Gambari has clearly stressed,[69] the amount of freedom thus left to institutes so that they can define their charism better and express it through suitable juridical norms means that their constitutions are now of greater importance than before, and this in turn means that the responsibility of the institutes that have drafted their definitive renewed constitutions, or still have to do so, is all the heavier.

Eighty-six percent of the religious institutes of pontifical right that come under the Sacred Congregation for Religious and Secular Institutes, as we said at the outset of this article, are now in possession of their definitive renewed constitutions.[70] And the percentage is very probably the same if we consider all the institutes of consecrated life throughout the world, whether of pontifical or diocesan right. It is higher in certain countries where almost all institutes have finished their new constitutions, and lower in others because a hard core of institutes is still opposed to the idea of *definitive* constitutions or refuses to submit them for the approval of the Church.[71]

Whatever the figures may be, consecrated life is now as a whole faced with the true problem: that of accepting and living out these new constitutions. In the end, this is where the real question lies.[72] The revision of the constitutions as called for by Vatican II was never an end in itself, but was a means in the service of a much greater objective: that of the up-to-date renewal of consecrated life. In the perspective of the universal Church, the revision of constitutions can now be said to have taken place, at the price of considerable effort and unflagging perseverance. This represents a great step forward, but it will not produce the fruits expected by the Council unless all consecrated men and women truly live from these new texts that have been so patiently produced. History has shown that the holiness of institutes is not automatically in proportion to the objective beauty of their constitutions. A good religious is not the one who meditates on the rule and is able to savor its full depth; rather, it is the one whose whole existence is a living rule. True conversion to the gospel, in accordance with the charism of each institute as this is expressed in its newly approved constitutions, is only just beginning.

Translated from the French by Leslie Wearne.

Notes

1. In this article, we use the following abbreviations: *BulUISG,* Bulletin of the International Union of Superiors General (English translator's note: cited in French except in the case of direct quotations in the main text, which are taken from the English-language edition); COM, *Comunidades, boletín bibliográfico de vida religiosa y espiritualidad; CpR,* Commentarium pro Religiosis; SCRSI, Sacred Congregation for Religious and Secular Institutes; *ES II,* Motu proprio *Ecclesiae sanctae* of Paul VI, Part II (6 August 1966), in *AAS,* 58 (1966), 757–787;

InfSCRSI, Informationes SCRSI, news bulletin of the Sacred Congregation for Religious and Secular Institutes, Italian edition (English translator's note: cited in its original version, except in the case of direct quotes in the main text, in which case the English-language edition, published under the title *Consecrated Life,* is used); IUSG, International Union of Superiors General; REPSA, Religieuses dans les professions de santé, 106 rue du Bac, Paris; *RfR, Review for Religious;* SC, *Studia Canonica; VieC, Vie Consacrée; VitaC, Vita Consacrata;* VRel, *Vida Religiosa; WAYSup, The Way,* Supplement. (English translator's note: in keeping with the style used in other articles in the present collection, abbreviations are not used in the main text, but only within parenthesis or in the notes.)

2. What is the present situation with regard to the revision of constitutions? The following are the figures for the 1,400 religious institutes of pontifical right dependent on the SCRSI (the universal Church at present has about 2,500 approved religious institutes either of diocesan or pontifical right, so that this represents 56 percent of the total number of religious institutes): 900 new constitutions have already been approved, and 200 others have already been submitted to the SCRSI and are at present being examined; this means that a total of 1,100 new constitutions have certainly been approved by general chapters, in other words, 78.5 percent of all institutes of pontifical right dependent on the SCRSI; see Sister Mary Linscott, "I criteri pratici di rinnovamento," *InfSCRSI,* 11/2 (1985), 165. There are 300 institutes that have yet to present their new constitutions to the SCRSI. We can make a reasonable guess that about 100 of these have already approved their new constitutions in a general chapter but have not yet submitted them for approval because of extra time needed for refinements to the text, and printing—and sometimes translating—it. This brings the number of institutes of pontifical right dependent on the SCRSI that are now in possession of their new constitutions to 1,200, or 86 percent. Thus, on 1 October 1986, this left only 200 institutes, or 14 percent, that had not yet finished revising their constitutions.

3. The only studies to have dealt with this subject in any depth would appear to be the following: M. Dortel-Claudot, *Les Congrégations religieuses se donnent une Règle de vie stable. Le travail accompli de 1977 à 1981 dans les Instituts pour élaborer leurs nouvelles Constitutions* (Paris, 1981); Linscott, "I criteri pratici di rinnovamento"; E. Sastre Santos, "De normis ad Codices Congregationum religiosarum congruenter recognoscendos," *CpR,* 59 (1978), 138–175; *idem,* "Los Códigos de las Congregaciones Religiosas ante el tercer Capítulo general de renovación," *Claretianum,* 21–22 (1981–1982), 157–228. The revision of the constitutions called for by *Perfectae caritate* 3 refers to both religious and secular institutes of consecrated life, and also to societies of apostolic life. In the present article, although we speak more specifically of reli-

gious institutes, our analysis and reflection apply equally, *mutatis mutandis*, to secular institutes and societies of apostolic life.

4. Sastre Santos, "De normis ad Codices Congregationum religiosarum congruenter recognoscendos," 155–158. Among the authors to have pointed out the need to modify the specific law of institutes well before Vatican II, we would note: B. Frison, "The Constitutions of Religious Institutes and modern trends," *The Jurist*, 18 (1958), 149–176; E. Gambari, "Accommodata renovatio Constitutionum jurisque particularis statuum perfectionis," in *Congressus generalis de Statibus perfectionis, Romae 1950—Acta et documenta*, 1 (Rome, 1952), 525–531.

5. English translation in Flannery (ed.), *Vatican Council II*, 624–628. The instructions given in *ES II* are in part taken up by Canon 587 of the new Code of Canon Law: "§1. In order to protect more faithfully the particular vocation and identity of each institute, its fundamental code or constitutions must contain, besides what must be observed according to can. 578, fundamental norms about the governance of the institute and the discipline of members, the incorporation and formation of members, and the proper object of sacred bonds. §2. A code of this kind is approved by the competent authority of the Church and can be changed only with its consent [*ES II* 8]. §3. In this code spiritual and juridical elements are to be suitably joined together; however, norms are not to be multiplied unless it is necessary [*ES II* 12–13]. §4. Other norms established by the competent authority of the institute are to be suitably collected in other codes, which can moreover be fittingly reviewed and adapted according to the needs of places and times [*ES II* 14]."

6. P.M. Boyle, "Experimentation," *RfR*, 27 (1968), 518–538; B. Frison, *Rinnovamento nello Spirito e delle strutture* (Rome, 1968), 67; J.B. Fuertes, "De competentia Capituli Specialis," *CpR*, 48 (1967), 259–270; J.F. Gallen, "Experimentation concerning articles of the Constitutions," *RfR*, 27 (1968), 335–342; A. Gutierrez, "Regula et Institutum relate ad accommodatam renovationem," *CpR*, 48 (1967), 67–70; *idem*, "Constitutiones congruenter recognoscantur," *CpR*, 48 (1967), 271–292; *idem*, "La revisione delle Costituzioni," in *Il Capitolo speciale* (Milan, 1967), 73–125; *idem*, "Consultationes. An Capitulum speciale," *CpR*, 49 (1968), 224–226; L. Gutierrez, "De natura juridica Capituli specialis religiosorum," *CpR*, 48 (1967), 241–258; L. Ravasi, "Il Capitolo delle Costituzioni," *Vita Religiosa*, 2 (1966), 464–467.

7. 1,400 religious institutes are dependent on the SCRSI, 54 on the Sacred Congregation for the Evangelization of Peoples, and 33 on the Sacred Congregation for the Oriental Churches.

8. The procedure followed by the SCRSI is described by Sister Agnès Souvage, "Processus de l'approbation des nouvelles Constitutions," *InfSCRSI*, 9/1 (1983), 153–161.

9. In actual practice, this procedure can be very complicated. This

is why, in an exceptional case in 1979, the SCRSI granted a French bishop, on his request, the faculty of approving the constitutions of an institute of diocesan right in the name of the three other bishops concerned; see Prot. no. 29067/79. Later, between 1980 and 1982, it was no longer willing to grant the bishops of principal houses this type of faculty, and encouraged them to reach a direct agreement with the other bishops for the approval of the constitutions of institutes of diocesan right.

10. Canons 587, §2, and 595, §1.

11. The term was probably ill-chosen, since it could lead to ambiguity, and some institutes did indeed believe, whether in good or bad faith, that with the blessing of the Church, they had been granted a type of *mardi gras* of several years in which anything went.

12. It was foreseen that the date of this approval would vary from one institute to another, since the interval between two chapters normally corresponds to the length of term in office of the superior general, and this is not always the same. In institutes where this term is six years, and where the special chapter also coincides with an elective chapter, the experimental period is therefore twelve years. In institutes obliged to convene the special chapter during the term in office, and in those in which the term is less than six years, the experimental period is from eight to eleven years; however, this still seemed sufficient. On the other hand, where the term in office of the superior general is ten years, the period between the special chapter and the second ordinary chapter could be as much as twenty years, which would have been the case for the De La Salle Brothers.

Following the special chapters, doubts arose as to the way of calculating the last year of the experimental period. Some institutes inserted a chapter of affairs between two elective chapters separated by six years: Should this administrative chapter be seen as one of the two ordinary chapters spoken of in *ES II* 6? In other institutes, the chapter following the special chapter was purely elective, and no evaluation of the texts approved by the previous chapter was carried out: Should this chapter then be counted for the purposes of *ES II* 6? There was some confusion over these various problems. The experts who were consulted were uncertain in their replies, and the institutes generally chose the interpretation that allowed them to extend the experimental period as much as possible; see particularly Frison, *Rinnovamento nello Spirito e delle strutture*, 67. We now know that *ES II* 6 should have been interpreted as follows, even if it meant requesting a dispensation in case of difficulty: any chapter, whether elective or not, and whether assembled at the end of a normal or shortened term, must be counted for the purposes of *ES II* 6.

13. As is correctly noted by Sister Mary Linscott, ex-President of the

IUSG and, for a number of years, a member of the SCRSI, where she works as coordinator of the office entrusted with examining and approving the renewed constitutions, in "I criteri pratici di rinnovamento," 163: "Non c'erano precedenti per questo tipo di assemblee capitolari . . . e la scadenza improrogabile del tempo era molto breve (ES II 3). Non era affatto sorprendente che i capitoli generali speciali fossero risultati ardui; una esperienza pasquale di gioia e sofferenza. Mai era accaduto che tutti i religiosi del mondo avessero tenuto tanti capitoli generali insieme, in un periodo di due o tre anni; mai che i capitoli generali, tenuti nello stesso tempo, avessero avuto come ordine del giorno la revisione e il rinnovamento di tutta la vita e la missione degli istituti; che ai capitoli fosse stata data l'autorizzazione di sperimentare, seppur temporaneamente, su prescrizioni di costituzioni. Il compito era enorme e gli istituti religiosi l'affrontarono con coraggio e buona volontà. Che ci fosse una certa tensione e confusione era inevitabile."

14. A list of the addresses of Paul VI to general chapters, with the necessary references, can be found in COM, 3/9 (1975), 2–4 ("Fichero de Materias").

15. A. Diez, "De commissionibus capitularibus," CpR, 48 (1967), 312–322; G. Escudero, Capítulo especial. Guía para un Directorio (Madrid, 1968); "Expériences communautaires: préparation du Chapitre général spécial," VieC, 40 (1968), 48–53; B. Frison, "Renewal of Religious," SC, 1 (1967), 45–78; J.B. Fuertes, "De parando Capitulo," CpR, 48 (1967), 351–365; J.F. Gallen, "Constitutions of Lay Congregations," RfR, 25 (1966), 361–437; idem, "Constitutions without canons," RfR, 27 (1968), 452–508; idem, "Proper Juridical Articles of Constitutions," RfR, 27 (1968), 623–632; E. Gambari, Il Rinnovamento nella Vita Religiosa (Milan, 1967), 227–244; A. Guy, "La contribution des canonistes à la révision des Constitutions des communautés religieuses," SC, 1 (1967), 205–221; J. Jimenez Delgado, "Medios más eficaces prescritos por el Concilio para la renovación de la vida religiosa," Confer, 10 (1967), 337–369; M.B. Pennington, "The new Constitutions, a life charter," SC, 2 (1968), 77–98.

16. "Revision of the Constitutions," BulUISG (English edition), 5 (August 1967), 4–19; "Procedure of the Chapter," BulUISG (English edition), 6 (November 1967), 2–14; "Renewal of Constitutions," BulUISG (English edition), 10 (November–December 1968), 1–27.

17. Sister Agnés Sauvage, "Agenti del rinnovamento," InfSCRSI, 11/2 (1985), 170.

18. For example: J. Beyer, "Renewal Chapters: First Reflections," WAYSup, 11/14 (1971), 88–114; idem, "Primo bilancio dei Capitoli di rinnovamento," VitaC, 8 (1972), 161–190; idem, "Premier bilan des Chapitres de renouveau," NRT, 95 (1973), 60–86.

19. The way in which the special chapters were planned and the

different phases of the work carried out by them are well analyzed in G. Scarvaglieri, "Coinvolgimento dell'Istituto nella revisione delle Costituzioni," *InfSCRSI*, 9/1 (1983), 61–87. Moreover, the author continues his interesting analysis well beyond 1971. What he calls the "Fase terza: Sperimentazione e verifica" (pp. 71–72) corresponds to what we call the "period of the intermediate chapters, 1972–1976." What he calls the "Fase quarta: Rifinitura del testo e conclusione del lavoro" (pp. 72–73) corresponds to what we call the "period of the constituent chapters." Various institutes have published information on the way in which they planned their special chapter, and we have an example of this in *BulUISG*, 7 (1968), 1–20.

20. What we have observed on the basis of this sample of ninety-one texts corresponds fairly well to the judgment of Linscott, "I criteri pratici di rinnovamento," 164: "Alcuni istituti hanno seguito strettamente le norme date, revisionando i testi approvati e sopprimendo prescrizioni cadute in disuso, riportando i documenti in linea con il Concilio (*PC* 3). Moltissimi, tuttavia, non hanno revisionato i loro testi. Li hanno, invece, semplicemente riscritti."

21. Instruction on the Renewal of Religious Life, *Renovationis causam* (6 January 1969), in *AAS*, 61 (1969), 103–120; English translation in Flannery (gen. ed.), *Vatican Council II*, 634–655.

22. We examine this point in due course, at which time we consider both the texts on government produced by the special chapters and those produced by the intermediate chapters.

23. At the special chapters, the institutes that had drafted new experimental texts to replace the constitutions then in force were happy to refer to them as a "rule of life." In this connection, see the modest survey we carried out in 1977, on the basis of a sample group of seventy-seven institutes: M. Dortel-Claudot, *Que mettre dans les nouvelles Constitutions, Règles de vie ou Normes des Congrégations religieuses?* (Paris, 1977), 24–26.

24. Sauvage, "Agenti del rinnovamento," 171: "Reagendo alle prescrizioni anteriori, fortemente minuziose, alle quali per lungo tempo, erano stati sottomessi, i Capitolanti vollero preparare delle Costituzioni puramente spirituali, talvolta anche poetiche, eliminando con cura tutte le norme concrete, fossero pure quelle inerenti alla vita spirituale, comunitaria, apostolica, alla formazione e persino al governo."

25. Viewed in the worldwide perspective, and considering the new rules of life of institutes of both diocesan right and pontifical right, the satisfactory rules of life happily outnumbered the unsatisfactory ones.

26. *RfR*, 31 (1972), 805. Text of the letter of the SCRSI of 4 December 1967, to which Archbishop Mayer refers, is found in *BulUISG*, 7 (1968), 21.

27. Some institutes celebrated their constituent chapters as early as 1975 or 1976, but these were exceptions.

28. Earlier, we gave the figure as five out of a sample of ninety-one congregations with simple vows (see p. 96 above).

29. See p. 97 and note 23.

30. In this connection, we would emphasize the clarification provided by two well-known and influential experts: J. Beyer, "Le Costituzioni rinnovate," *VitaC*, 11 (1975), 65–85; E. Gambari, "Orientamenti per la revisione e l'elaborazione delle Costituzioni," *VitaC*, 10 (1974), 201–210. We should also note the contribution of other authors from various countries: J. Alvarez Gomez, "Balance de una renovación emprendida," *VRel*, 36 (1974), 85–98; A. Bocos Merino, "El Capítulo obra de todos," *VRel*, 36 (1974), 99–120; C. Domeño Lerga, "Objetivos y metodología de un Capítulo," *VRel*, 36 (1974), 129–138; M. Dortel-Claudot, "L'obéissance dans les nouvelles Constitutions des Instituts religieux de vie active," *VieC*, 48 (1976), 285–295; T. Dubay, "Composing new Constitutions, style and content," *RfR*, 34 (1975), 757–780; J.A. Echevarria, "Los Capítulos de renovación," *COM*, 9/3 (1975), 49–47; J. Gallen, "Revision of the Constitutions," *RfR*, 33 (1974), 376–385; idem, "Writing Constitutions," *RfR*, 33 (1974), 1323, 1338; idem, "Typical Constitutions," *RfR*, 34 (1975), 191–223; idem, "Canon Law for Religious after Vatican II. Writing Constitutions," *RfR*, 35 (1976), 102–111; B. Garcia Fernandez, "¿Qué se puede esperar y qué no se debe esperar de un Capítulo?" *VRel*, 36 (1974), 139–146; A.-M. Labarre, "Plus qu'une expérience, un départ," *Vie des communautés* religieuses, 30 (1972), 286–288, J. Lopez Garcia, "Modo práctico de preparar un Capítulo," *VRel*, 36 (1974), 121–127; J. Lozano, "Revision of the Constitutions: Meaning, Criteria and Problems," *RfR*, 34 (1975), 525–534; S.T. McCarthy, "In Search of New Wine Skins," *RfR*, 32 (1973), 818–828; M.L. Orsy, "How to Write good Constitutions," *RfR*, 32 (1973), 482–489; W.A.M. Peters, "How to Write good Constitutions," *RfR*, 32 (1973), 1294–1301; J. Rousseau, "Le Code fondamental des Constitutions des Instituts religieux," *SC*, 10 (1976), 195–233; B. Rueda, "Un Capítulo, para el mundo de hoy," *La vida religiosa hoy* (Madrid, 1974), 325–370; G. van den Broeck, "Le nuove Costituzioni degli Istituti Religiosi," *VitaC*, 8 (1972), 1–12. The articles by Alvarez Gomez, Bocos Merino, and Domeño Lerga cited at the beginning have been collected in a book entitled *Los Capítulos de renovación* (Madrid, 1974).

31. "Orientations pour la révision des Constitutions," *InfSCRSI*, 1/1 (1975), 60–65; "Natura e Finalità dei Capitoli generali," *InfSCRSI*, 2/2 (1976), 215–227; "Les voeux du Chapitre général," *InfSCRSI*, 1/1 (1975), 168–169.

32. "Les Chapitres généraux depuis le Concile. Premier bilan," *InfSCRSI,* 3/1 (1977), 83–100.

33. *Consecrated Life,* 3/1 (1977), 76.

34. "Tendance dans les Chapitres généraux," *BulUISG,* 41 (1976), 31.

35. Sister Mary Thaddea Kelly, "Nouvelles Constitutions, une interpellation," *BulUISG,* 37 (1975), 13, referred to this in 1975: "Dans certaines Congrégations, on voudrait ne pas avoir à affronter la question des Constitutions. Devrait-on en avoir? Sont-elles nécessaires? Un oui tout simple mais puissant est la réponse."

36. This movement, which had its source in the institutes themselves, was probably encouraged by those experts who spoke between 1977 and 1978 about constituent chapters and the need to start planning them. We would cite the following: Anon., "Index articulorum pro redigendis Constitutionibus," *CpR,* 59 (1978), 191–200; "Ultimos Capítulos de renovación," *VRel,* 44 (1978), 403–476; J. Beyer, "Il Diritto capitolare," *VitaC,* 14 (1978), 462–471; *idem,* "Le Droit capitulaire," *L'Année canonique,* 22 (1978), 61–70; Dortel-Claudot, *Que mettre dans les nouvelles Constitutions?; idem,* "Pourquoi des nouvelles Constitutions?" *VieC,* 50 (1978), 295–302; *idem, What should be included in the New Constitutions, Rules of Life or Norms of Religious Congregations?* (Rome, 1978); D. Gottemoeller, "Readiness for New Constitutions," *RfR,* 36 (1977), 560–564; F.G. Morrissey, *La rédaction des Constitutions à la lumière du nouveau droit des Religieux* (Ottawa, 1978); D.F. O'Connor, "Guidelines and Practical Issues in the Drafting of New Constitutions," *RfR,* 37 (1978), 753–776; J. Alvarez Gomez, "Líneas-fuerza de las Constituciones renovadas," *VRel,* 44 (1978), 34–49; M. Said, "Le rôle du droit particulier des Instituts dans le renouveau de la vie consacrée," *BulUISG,* 44 (1977), 13–27; 45 (1977), 4–18; Sastre Santos, "De normis ad Codices congregationum religiosarum congruenter recognoscendos," 138–186; V.J. Sastre, "Qué está pasando con las nuevas Constituciones?" *VRel,* 4 (1978), 34–49; J. Torres, "Las Constituciones renovadas," *VRel,* 44 (1978), 1–83, esp. 7–11 ("Renovar las Constituciones").

37. *Consecrated Life,* 5/2 (1979), 201–202.

38. *BulUISG* (English edition), 52 (1980), 7.

39. *Consecrated Life,* 5/2 (1979), 201. In 1980, Sister Mary Linscott, "Constitutions: une interview avec Sr. Mary Linscott, snd, de la Sacrée Congrégation pour les Religieux et Instituts Séculier," *BulUISG,* 53 (1980), 17, had to explain the procedure to be followed in order to obtain an extension of the experimental period: "La Sacrée Congrégation retient le principe d'*Ecclesiae Sanctae* et pense qu'il est bon, dans la mesure du possible, que le texte soit présenté après le deuxième Chapitre ordinaire suivant le Chapitre de renouveau; mais, en certains cas

particuliers, elle accepte de considérer une prolongation du temps as-
signé. Pour cela, elle examine chaque cas en particulier, et demande que
l'Institut concerné exprime les raisons de sa requête, donne un aperçu du
travail déjà réalisé sur les Constitutions, et indique le programme qu'il
s'est proposé pour la prolongation du temps, afin d'assurer l'achèvement
de l'entreprise à une date raisonnable."

40. The following figures illustrate this point. Since a certain discretion is necessary in this area, there are no official statistics. We therefore rely on our personal memory. At the end of March 1981, 177
religious institutes had alrady consulted us with regard to their definitive constitutions, telling us of the work they had accomplished or
intended carrying out. Out of the 177, about 30 had requested and
obtained permission to postpone their constituent chapter to 1981 or
1982; 18 had obtained permission to postpone it until 1983; 3 until
1984; 4 until 1985; and 2 until 1986. Thus, 9 institutes out of the 177
(or 5 percent) had obtained permission to postpone their constituent
chapter until 1984, 1985, or 1986, the year of their ordinary chapter.
The previous ordinary chapter, which, according to the timetable set by
ES II 6, should have approved the definitive constitutions, was held in
either 1978, 1979, or 1980. For these very far-flung international institutes, convening an extraordinary chapter between two ordinary chapters would have required a great deal of extra travel and expense, and
permission for postponement was granted for this reason. To the best of
our knowledge, no institute has obtained permission from the Holy See
to extend the experimental period to 1987. Moreover, we do know of
the case of one institute that in 1980 asked permission to wait until
1987 before submitting its constitutions for approval, but that had its
request refused.

41. For further information on the planning of the constituent chapters and their work, see: Dortel-Claudot, *Les Congrégations religieuses se
donnent une Règle de vie stable*, 39–66; *idem*, "Les Chapitres généraux
aujourd'hui. Étude," *BulUISG*, 59 (1982), 32–55, and *REPSA*, 297
(1983), 387–402; M.K. Hollow, "Development of a Constitution,"
RfR, 40 (1980), 801–809; Scarvaglieri, "Coinvolgimento dell'Istituto
nella revisione delle Costituzioni," 72–84. In the same article, Scarvaglieri writes, p. 68: "Da dati emersi si rileva che circa ¾ degli Istituti
hanno impiegato come tempo per la revisione delle Costituzioni da 11 a
16 anni." If we consider that the planning of the special chapters
generally began in 1967, his conclusions jibe well with our own: from
1967 to 1977 is eleven years; and from 1967 to 1982 is sixteen years.

42. The Council of the "16," which is made up of eight female
superiors general and eight male superiors general, elected, respectively, by the Assembly of the International Union of Superiors General and by that of the Union of Superiors General, is the group dele-

gated to act as permanent representatives of both female and male religious institutes to the Holy See. This group, which was set up in the wake of Vatican II in a spirit of dialogue and mutual collaboration has a monthly work session with the Cardinal Prefect, the Secretary, the Under-Secretary, and some other members of the SCRSI.

43. Council of the "16," Minutes of the meeting of 23 February 1979, pp. 2–3; Consejo de los Dieciseis, "Constituciones. Su redacción, su aprobación," *VRel,* 45 (1979), 272–275.

44. "Decisions and Guidelines. The Revision of the Constitutions," *Consecrated Life,* 5/2 (1979), 195–200.

45. "Constitutions: An Interview with Sister Mary Linscott, S.N.D., of the Sacred Congregation for Religious and Secular Institutes," *BulUISG* (English edition), 53 (1980), 8–19.

46. Sometimes a bishop who has the task of approving the constitutions of a religious institute of diocesan right begins by sending the text to the SCRSI in order to receive its opinion. With regard to the constitutions of secular institutes of diocesan right, we would note in passing the following element that has been introduced in recent years by rulings of the SCRSI: the bishop of the principal house can, in accordance with Canon 595, §1, approve the renewed constitutions of a secular institute of diocesan right, but before doing so, he must submit the text to the SCRSI and obtain its *nihil obstat.* This measure, which does not apply to religious institutes or to societies of apostolic life, was dictated by wisdom, since in many dioceses people are not at all familiar with secular institutes, which are a recent form of consecrated life; moreover, a number of secular intitutes have been founded only recently and their renewed constitutions are in fact their first ones, so that the intervention of the Holy See is justified on the basis of Canon 579.

47. Council of the "16," Minutes of the meeting of 26 February 1982, pp. 3–4.

48. *InfSCRSI,* 9/1 (1983), 1–182: Cardinal E. Pironio, "Constituciones renovadas," 3–12; F. Iglesias, "Orientamenti Conciliari e del Magistero," 46–60; G. Scarvaglieri, "Coinvolgimento dell'Istituto nella revisione delle Costituzioni," 61–87; V. Macca, "Le Regole nel rinnovamento della vita religiosa," 88–97; A. Gutierrez, "El nuevo Código de derecho canonico y el derecho interno de los institutos de vida consagrada," 98–115; V. Macca, "Le Costituzioni tra teologia e diritto," 116–125; M. Dortel-Claudot, "Le Code complémentaire," 126–139; J. Torres, "Approbación ecclesiastica de las Constituciones; significato y alcance," 140–152; A. Sauvage, "Processus de l'approbation," 153–161; Y. Damiani, "Les Instituts Séculiers et le renouvellement des Constitutions," 162–166; B. Baroffio, "Presentazione ed assimilazione delle Costituzioni: Considerazioni generali," 167–177; A. Galliani, "Presentazione ed assimilazione delle Costituzioni: Un'esperienza concreta," 178–182. An excellent summary of this important issue of the SCRSI newsletter is found in: "Le nuove Costituzioni occasione per un rinnovamento," *Testimoni*, 17 (15 October 1983), 7–10.

49. At the 26 February 1982 meeting of the Council of the "16" with the SCRSI, Father L. Ravasi had this to say: "Although the new law has not been published, it is taken into account in the process of approving the new orientations" (Council of the "16," Minutes of meeting of 26 February 1982, p. 4).

50. Those institutes that approved their constitutions between 1975 and 1978 were able to correct various articles in the light of the new Code, at the time of the first or second ordinary chapter following their constituent chapter. This revision was all the easier since their constitutions had been approved at the outset for a limited period of from five to ten years, in accordance with the practice that ended to be followed by the SCRSI between 1975 and 1979; see Dortel-Claudot, *Les Congrégations religieuses se donnent une Règle de vie stable*, 33–34; Linscott, "I criteri pratici di rinnovamento," 165.

51. In the 1979–1983 period, it was possible to make clear statements on certain subjects that would have been impossible between 1972 and 1976 without giving rise to violent reactions, and that could only have been said in 1977 and 1978 with a great deal of circumspection and circumlocution. Our opinion on this point must be shared by any fair-minded person who is familiar with the various currents of opinion that have passed through the institutes of consecrated life from the time of the special chapters until today. Let us illustrate this evolution by considering one specific element: the new constitutions must contain an article that states clearly that the members of the institutes of consecrated life must obey the Pope precisely in virtue of the vow of obedience. This is nothing new, and specialists in constitutions have always been aware of it. Even so, any reference to the need for such an article at a meeting of male and female religious of all institutes, held in France in 1973, would undoubtedly have provoked protests, or at least grumbling and a deaf indignation, in a good proportion of those present. In January 1977, when we presented our course *Que mettre dans les Constitutions?* (see note 36) in Paris, we were successful in having a great number of items accepted by many institutes with relatively up-to-the-minute views. However, we also clearly felt from the atmosphere in the hall that any reference to what was to be written in the constitutions regarding obedience to the Pope would have led to a complete loss of credibility—and indeed of listeners—and we therefore made an on-the-spot decision against mentioning this point. However, four years later, in March 1981, in the same conference hall and before a similar audience, we were able to discuss this point quite openly and without any risk of a similar reaction;

see Dortel-Claudot, *Les Congrégations religieuses se donnent une Règle de vie stable*, 84–86. This would be in agreement with the remark of Linscott, "I criteri pratici di rinnovamento," 168: "La maggior parte dei testi di Costituzioni rivedute dimostravano un notevole miglioramento di qualità agli inizi degli anni '80."

52. *WAYSup*, 36 (1979), the whole issue entitled "Revising the Constitutions"; S. Alonso, "Significación y contenido de las Constituciones renovadas," in *La vida espiritual de los Religiosos* (Madrid, 1981), 153–183; D.J. Andres, *El Derecho de los Religiosos. Comentario al Código* (Madrid, 1984), 25–30; D. Bertrand, "Des constitutions religieuses un enjeu pour l'Eglise," *VieC*, 55 (1983), 25–30; J. Beyer, "Costituzioni religiose e diritti fondamentali," in *Diritti umani, dottrina e prassi* (Rome, 1982), 555–573; idem, "Valori essenziali da esprimere nelle Costituzioni di un Istituto Religioso," *VitaC*, 22 (1986), 43–58, 287–299, 367–379; M. Cerletty, "Some Practical Helps for the Development of Constitutions," *SC*, 14 (1980), 155–170; M. Dortel-Claudot, "Les nouvelles Constitutions. Premier et second Livres," *VieC*, 52 (1980), 41–49; idem, "Que mettre dans les nouvelles Constitutions?" 20–36; idem, *Les Congrégations religieuses se donnent une Règle de vie stable*, 67–87; idem, "Quelques points essentiels des Constitutions. Comment les formuler?" *VieC*, 53 (1981), 232–245; idem, "El Código complementario," *Cuadernos Monasticos*, 19 (1984), 457–467; G. Earle, "Discovering the Constitutions," *WAYSup*, 36 (1979), 124–130; N.M. Ford, "Why Religious Revised their Constitutions," *RfR*, 42 (1983), 218–225; J.F. Gallen, "Constitutions and Directory," *RfR*, 40 (1981), 759–772; S.L. Holland, "Can. 587," in Canon Law Society of America, *The Code of Canon Law. A Text and Commentary* (New York, 1985), 459–460; L. Hughes, "Revision, the Law and the Chapter," *WAYSup*, 36 (1979), 58–70; S.M. Joss, "Constitutions and Cultural Problems," *WAYSup*, 36 (1979), 113–123; M. Linscott, "The Service of Religious Authority: Reflections on Government in the Revision of Constitutions," *RfR*, 42 (1983), 197–217; M. Milligan, "Charism and Constitutions," *WAYSup*, 36 (1979), 45–57; D.F. O'Connor, "Some Observations on Revised Constitutions," *RfR*, 38 (1979), 771–779; idem, "Constitutions and the Revised Code of Canon Law," *RfR*, 42 (1983), 506–513; C. Osiek and K. Hughes, "Constitutional Hermeneutics: on the Interpretation of Constitutions," *RfR*, 45 (1986), 57–68; E. Sastre Santos, "Los Códigos de las Congregaciones religiosas ante el tercer Capítulo General de renovación," *Claretianum*, 21–22 (1981–1982), 157–228; E.M. Strub, "Constitutions, for Whom?" *WAYSup*, 36 (1979), 103–112; J. Walsh, "The Difficulties of Revision," *WAYSup*, 36 (1979), 5–17.

53. Canon 587, §§1 and 3.

54. See Canon 587, §4.

55. Should there be one or more complementary codes? Canon

587, §4, uses the plural in order not to exclude any possibility. In the case of most small institutions, a single complementary code may be enough, while other institutes, because of either their size or the complexity of their organization, need several complementary codes, each one devoted to a specific sphere. There is the same freedom and the same possibility of diversity as regards the name to be given to the complementary code (or codes). Here we use the term "complementary code," because this is in line with *ES II* 14, but institutes are obviously free to use other terms.

56. Does this mean that the complementary code is to be simply juridical and practical and not involve any spiritual considerations? Definitely not: institutes are free to produce a complementary code that is either purely juridical and practical, or both spiritual and practical.

57. Andres, *El Derecho de los Religiosos,* 27–30; M. Dortel-Claudot, "Le code complëmentaire," *InfSCRSI,* 9 (1983), 126–139; *idem,* "El Código complementario," 457–467.

58. The solutions adopted by the various institutes eventually fell into one of the four following categories: (1) constitutions and complementary code, making up two separate booklets; (2) constitutions and complementary code placed in the same book, with the constitutions as the first part, and the complementary code as the second; (3) in the same book, each chapter of the complementary code is placed immediately after the corresponding chapter of the constitutions; (4) the norms of the complementary code are not placed separately, but are distributed at the most suitable points throughout the actual body of each chapter of the constitutions, and, in order to make a distinction, they are printed in italics or in smaller type, and are slightly indented.

59. Sauvage, "Agenti del rinnovamento," 172: "Attualmente, le Costituzioni rinnovate, di circa due terzi degli Istituti di diritto pontificio, hanno avuto l'approvazione della Santa Sede, ed è doveroso riconoscere che i testi proposti racchiudono in sé un autentico valore spirituale ed apostolico. . . . Il risultato dunque è positivo, anche se il cammino percorso è stato, talvolta, lungo, scabroso, difficile." Linscott, "I criteri pratici di rinnovamento," 168: "La maggior parte dei testi di Costituzioni rivedute dimostravano un notevole miglioramento di qualità agli inizi degli anni '80. . . . La terminologia potrebbe suscitare ancora difficoltà, la sistemazione del materiale potrebbe far sorgere problemi e non sono esclusi possibili deviazioni dovute ad interpretazioni sbagliate o soggetive dei testi conciliari come dall'assolutezza dell'esperienza in vigore, alle spese della tradizione viva. Ma nell'insieme il lavoro che ora si sta svolgendo sulle costituzioni è di alta qualità."

60. Some institutions have presented the general lines of their renewed constitutions in various publications, for example: G. Crocetti, "La novità dello Spirito nelle Costituzioni rinnovate: l'adorazione eucaristica nella Regola di Vita dei Sacramentini," *VitaC*, 22 (1986), 323–331; A. Pedrini, "Novità di accenti nelle Costituzioni rinnovate: Francesco di Sales e le Costituzioni salesiane rinnovate," *VitaC*, 22 (1986), 480–493. Even so, very few studies have so far been carried out with a view to presenting the content of the renewed constitutions taken as a whole, although we would note the following. (1) As regards the *apostolate:* M. Dortel-Claudot, "Le service de l'homme aujourd'hui. Regard sur les nouvelles Constitutions des Instituts religieux féminins de vie apostolique," *VieC*, 58 (1986), 20–30; *idem*, "Le service de l'homme selon les nouvelles Constitutions des Instituts religieux féminins de vie apostolique," *REPSA*, 309 (1985), 375–380. (2) As regards *community life:* "Che cosa dicono le Costituzioni rinnovate," *InfSCRSI*, 11/1 (1985), 137–138. (3) As regards *obedience:* M. Dortel-Claudot, *Obéir aujourd'hui dans la vie religieuse; Pourquoi? A qui? Comment? Etude à partir de 145 nouvelles Constitutions votées au Chapitre général de 1978 à 1984*, Travaux et conférences due Centre-Sèvres 6 (Paris, 1985). (4) As regards *government:* G. Scarvaglieri, *Modelli di Governo generale* (Rome, 1983); *idem*, "Modèles de gouvernement général: description," *BulUISG*, 67 (1985), 46–56; E. de Montebello, *Expansion et décentralisation. Structures nouvelles établies dans les Constitutions des Instituts religieux féminins*, Dissertation for the Faculty of Canon Law of the Gregorian University (Rome, 1986); M. Dortel-Claudot, *Les structures de gouvernement et de participation des Congrégations religieuses*, Travaux et conférences due Centre-Sèvres 3 (Paris, 1984), 35–80; *idem*, "Le strutture di governo e di partecipazione delle Congregazioni religiose. Il Consiglio generale," *VitaC*, 21 (1985), 779–792; *idem*, "Il Consiglio generale allargato," *VitaC*, 21 (1985), 860–870; *idem*, *Le strutture di governo e di partecipazione delle Congregazioni religiose*, Quaderni di Vita Consacrata 9 (Milan, 1986). (5) As regards certain more exterior aspects of the renewed constitutions, such as the layout, the overall structure, the order of chapters, and titles: Dortel-Claudot, *Les Congrégations religieuses se donnent une Règle de vie stable*, 39–66.

61. Having taken part in the drafting of the texts of a great number of institutes of diocesan right both in French-speaking countries and elsewhere, we can give our personal testimony in this sphere: the renewed constitutions of institutes of diocesan right are definitely as good as those of institutes of pontifical right, and there are even some that are small masterpieces and that are of a much higher quality than those of some great international institutes.

62. Dortel-Claudot, "Le strutture di governo e di partecipazione delle Congregazioni religiose," 775.

63. Among other things, the following have been clearly accepted as proper to the provincial, or to the superior general of institutes without provinces: (1) assigning each religious his or her community and personal apostolic mission; (2) making a regular canonical visitation to the houses; and (3) approving the "community statutes" and the "apostolic projects" of the communities.

64. In both the texts and practice, the following are now better distinguished: (1) the decisions that the major superior can take alone, without even listening beforehand to the opinion of his counsellors; (2) those that he can take only after consulting the members of his council as gathered in session; (3) those that he can take only with the consent of his council; and (4) those that must be the object of a "collegial vote" of the council.

65. It is difficult to suggest a figure, but we would guess that this represents not more than 2 percent of all the constitutions examined between 1975 and 1986.

66. Certain canons of the new Code are often referred to in the written remarks of the SCRSI in order to allow institutes to fill in various lacunae in the text submitted or to make the necessary corrections: Canon 666 (on observing discretion in the use of the means of social communication); Canon 667, §1 (some part of the religious house must be reserved for the community); and Canon 669, §1 (on the religious habit). It must be admitted that negotiations between the Holy See and a number of superiors general on this last point have been long and laborious, although in the end the institutes have—humbly and to their credit—agreed to make the requested additions to their texts.

67. The 1977 schema was of course familiar to all the institutes to which it was officially sent out with a view to soliciting their remarks and suggestions. We have already described the circumstances that meant that the constitutions voted on in 1979 were able to profit from the 1980 schema, either while they were being drafted, or during their examination for approval (see pp. 107–108 above).

68. The present article is not the right context in which to give a list of the canons of the new Code that grant institutes the freedom of which we are speaking. Such a list is found, together with extensive explanations and comments in various works, in particularly the following: J.F. Gallen, "Guidelines for Conforming Constitutions to the New Code," *RfR*, 42 (1983), 748–758; E. Gambari, *Il nuovo Codice e la vita religiosa* (Milan, 1984), 121–235; *idem*, "Relaciones entre el nuevo Código de derecho canonico y el de 1917, en referencia a las Constituciones. El nuevo Código y el derecho proprio," *Confer*, 22 (1983), 563–581; A. Gutierrez, "El nuevo Código de derecho canonico y el derecho interno de los institutos de vida consagrada," *InfSCRSI*, 9 (1983), 98–115; M.B. Pennington, "The New Code of Canon Law and the New Legislation of the Religious Institute," *The Jurist*, 42 (1982), 192–196; L. Ravasi, "Nuovo Codice, nuove Costituzioni, nuovo

Direttorio," in *Il Nuovo Diritto dei Religiosi* (Rome, 1984); B.L. Thomas, "Constitutions and Canon Law," *WAYSup*, 50 (1984), 47–60.

69. "Incidenza del Codice di Diritto Canonico sulle Costituzioni e le altre fonti del Diritto proprio," in Union of Superiors General, *Animazione e Governo: XXIX riunione 23–26 maggio 1984* (Rome, 1984), 65–83.

70. See note 2.

71. R.A. Hill, "The Community and the Option of Non-Canonical Status," *RfR*, 41 (1982), 542–543, referred to this phenomenon: "A large number of religious institutes during the past several years either have already sent revised texts to Rome or have requested guidance from the Congregation about the matters which should be found in their constitutions. The responses to a number of them have been made public and these have greatly clarified the mind and intent of the Congregation with respect to the matters which it considered essential to authentic religious life and which, therefore, have to be spelled out in all fundamental codes. In many congregations in North America the details of required constitutional elements have occasioned considerable consternation and, in some instances, resentment and further exacerbation of divisions among the members. In some cases, and in a few public statements, the suggestion is being put forward that *the community refuse to submit or resubmit its constitutions for approval by the Holy See.* This is being referred to as the option of non-canonical status."

72. It is significant that little has yet been written on this subject. Even so, we would indicate the following: J. Aubry, "Orar con las Constituciones," *VRel*, 44 (1978), 76–82; B. Baroffio and A. Galliani, "Presentazione ed assimilazione delle Costituzioni," *InfSCRSI*, 9 (1983), 167–182; A. Bocos Merino, "Convertir las Constituticiones en instrumento de renovación," *VRel*, 44 (1978), 64–75; E. de Montebello, "Comment accueillir des Constitutions)" *REPSA*, 300 (1984), 152–157; J.M. Palacios, "Responsabilidad de los religiosos ante las nuevas Constituciones," *VRel*, 44 (1978), 50–63. We would note that the meeting of the Council of the "16" with the SCRSI on 26 March 1982 discussed the subject of "The Role of the Superior General as 'the animator of communities' in view of helping them to live according to the new Constitutions"; see Council of the "16," Minutes of the meeting of 26 March 1982, pp. 6–8.

CHAPTER 46

Priestly Celibacy
from the Canonical and
Psychological Points of View

Rev. Giuseppe Versaldi

Summary

Starting with an analysis of the question of priestly celibacy as it was discussed and presented by the Second Vatican Council, the article examines the documents of the magisterium that followed the Council until the promulgation of the new Code of Canon Law in 1983, with a view to assessing the acceptance and further study of the conciliar proposals. After a necessary word on the significance and legitimacy of the canonical norm, the difficulties in the life of priests are examined with reference to the postconciliar crisis. A critical examination of the replies provided by the psychological and sociological sciences shows an encouraging agreement between the disciplinary norms and the real help need by those in difficulty, with particular emphasis on the need for a greater effort to provide a formation that combines traditional methods with those offered by the human sciences if the latter are correctly used in the service of vocational values.

Introduction

Among the expectations raised by John XXIII's announcement of the Second Vatican Council on 25 January 1959, those concerning a reform of the discipline of the Latin Church on priestly celibacy not only received a good deal of attention, but often became a sort of rallying point for the call for other radical changes in the Church. However, there was nothing in the expressed intentions or in the official declarations of the magisterium to support any such hypothesis: it was the fruit more of energetic clammering outside the Church and was fanned by the media, which appointed themselves spokespersons in this area. However, it never took shape in the Council Hall in the form of a proposal for the abolition of celibacy.

Thus, if we examine the drafting process of the Decree on the Ministry and Life of Priests (*Presbyterorum ordinis*), which is the conciliar charter on the priesthood, we can realize the lack of proportion between the previously mentioned expectations of a change in the rules on celibacy and the opinion of the Council Fathers. After their rejection of the schema containing the twelve principles, *De vita et ministerio sacerdotali*, which on 13 October 1964 opened discussions of the priestly ministry on the Council floor, the Fathers examined a fuller schema proposed by the relative commission. In the course of its work, this commission had already discussed celibacy at length: on the one hand, 121 Fathers had requested a presentation of the foundations of the doctrine of the Church on the fittingness of priestly celibacy, and on the other, 118 Fathers sought confirmation of the principle that preisthood and matrimony are not essentially incompatible. In neither case were the current norms in force in the Latin Church ever challenged, as was shown by the discussion of the same Fathers on the new text presented by the commission, which highlighted differences in the stress to be given to the subject of the retention of priestly celibacy. Discussion of the schema began on 14 October 1965 and was preceded by the well-known intervention of Paul VI, which was read in the Council Hall on 11 October 1965 by Cardinal Tisserant, and in which the Pope stated that public discussion of the law on priestly celibacy was inopportune and called on the Fathers who so desired to express their opinion on this subject to do so in writing. Bishop Larrain, President of the Conference of Bishops of Latin America sent a cable to the Pope denying unofficial rumors that the bishops of Latin America were in disagreement on the present law on priestly celibacy, thus demonstrating the outside pressure to which the Council assembly was being subject. The commission set to work on the schema accepted by the Fathers (1,507 for and 12 against), and once more the problem of priestly celibacy required lengthy discussion—although not on its retention or abolition, but rather on the way the law should be formulated so as to safeguard all the values involved, as well as the diversity of the Eastern Church, and also with an eye to ecumenical dialogue.

On 12 and 13 November 1965, the new schema was approved without any prior discussion: the vast majority approved the schema, although there were 5,671 *placet iuxta modum* that the commission had to examine. Once again the ruling on celibacy was not easy to formulate: 110 Fathers asked for reference to the practice of the early Church as seen in 1 Timothy 3:2–5 and Titus 1:6; 71 Fathers did not want any mention of the practice of married priests in the Eastern Church; 2 Fathers wanted explicit treatment of the married and unmarried clergy, while 68 Fathers did not want any mention of married priests; 5 Fathers wanted the Council to recognize the legislation of the Eastern Church in the same way that it confirmed the present legislation of the Latin Church; 289 Fathers rejected the distinction between theological reasons and pastoral reasons for priestly celibacy and stated that the foundation was in the special consecration to Christ with which the priest places himself completely at the service of the kingdom of God; 123 Fathers wanted the Council to confine itself to citing the legislation at present in force without expressing any opinion.

The text amended according to the *modi* that had been considered valid by the commission was put to the vote on 2 December, obtaining 2,243 approvals, 22 rejections, and 3 invalid votes. The vote on final form was on 7 December 1965 and was confirmed with 2,390 for and only 4 against. Thus, Paul VI was able to promulgate the Decree on the same day with the formal formula.

It therefore seems clear that *within* the Council and among the Fathers themselves, there was never any real or significant movement toward an alteration in the existing legislation of the Latin Church with regard to priestly celibacy. On the other hand, there was a great deal of discussion both in the commission and on the Council floor with regard to the formulation and presentation of the doctrine on priestly celibacy, in which there was undeniable difficulty in reconciling and integrating different values, such as priesthood, matrimony, celibacy, the legitimate diversity between churches, charisms, persons, freedom, institution and authority, the common good, charity and justice, ecumenism, and so on.

The final text of the Decree *Presbyterorum ordinis* as approved represents the most balanced formulation the Fathers could reach in integrating all the values involved in priestly celibacy. The text of number 16 starts with praise of "perfect and perpetual continence for the sake of the kingdom of heaven [as] recommended by Christ the Lord (cf. Mt. 19:12)," which is immediately referred to the priesthood within an historical framework: it "has always been highly esteemed in a special way by the Church as a feature of priestly life" inasmuch as it is "at once a sign of pastoral charity and an incentive to it as well as being in a special way a source of spiritual fruitfulness in the world," thus repeating what the Council itself had stated in the Constitution *Lumen gentium* 42. This is followed by a word about the quality of the link between celibacy and priesthood: "It is true that it is not demanded of the priesthood by its nature," with explicit reference to the practice of the early Church (1 Tim. 3:2–5; Tit. 1:6), as well as the tradition of the Eastern Church. The Fathers explain the "many ways in which celibacy is in harmony with the priesthood": since the priestly mission is wholly "dedicated to the service of the new humanity," so celibacy leads priests "more readily to cling to him [Christ] with undivided heart," to "dedicate themselves more freely in him and through him to the service of God and of men," and to be "less encumbered in their service of his kingdom," so as to "become better fitted for a broader acceptance of fatherhood in Christ." According to the Council, celibacy thus becomes a *proclamation* to humanity of exclusive dedication to the mission of "espousing the faithful to one husband" and also an *evocation* of the marriage between Church and Christ that will be fully manifested in the world to come and of which celibate priests become a "living sign." Another historical reference on the movement from a context of recommendation (*commendabatur*) to one of legislation (*lege impositus est*) precedes the Council's statement on the relationship between priesthood and celibacy: the Fathers confirm the obligation of celibacy for the Latin Church, although they restrict it to "those destined for the priesthood." This statement is followed by exhortations to fidelity and perseverance, despite the worldly mentality according to which "perfect continence is considered by many people to be impossible." Lastly, reference is made to the means for obtaining and preserving the gift of celibacy: prayer of imploration to God, and the observation of ascetical rules.

It should be observed that other conciliar documents also mention priestly celibacy in a way in complete accordance with this text of *Presbyterorum ordinis*. Thus, although the Constitution *Lumen gentium* 29 opens the way to the possibility of the permanent married diaconate, in all other cases, it confirms the ruling on celibacy. And the Decree on Priestly Formation, *Optatam totius* 10, calls on candidates to the priesthood to embrace priestly celibacy "not only as a precept of ecclesiastical law, but as a precious gift of God," and with a view to formation to priestly celibacy, it indicates the need for a proper knowledge of the dignity of Christian marriage, although candidates are invited to "recognize the greater excellence of virginity consecrated to Christ."

These conciliar declarations were certainly not able to put an end to discussion, nor to resolve the problems that nourished it. Since then, and in view of the persistence of objections and also the crises of many priests who request dispensation from celibacy, with the consequent problems, both pastoral and for canonical administration, a great number of articles and books have appeared, aimed at explaining the current legislation and its foundations. I feel that it is helpful to take a look at the path followed by the Church through the postconciliar upheavals in order to show the contribution of the magisterium, and thus to evaluate the problem of priestly celibacy from the canonical and psychological points of view—two perspectives that offer interesting prospects. On the one hand, in the Latin Church, priestly celibacy is laid down by canonical norms in which the "convenience" or "fittingness" of its bond is given, whereas, on the other, the choice and living out of such a state entails psychological processes of the human person that are studied by the science of psychology. A combination of these two perspectives makes it possible to throw new light on the value of priestly celibacy, and also helps solve the problems that often bring people to a crisis— or at least contributes toward such a solution.

The Path Followed by the Magisterium from the Second Vatican Council to the New Code of Canon Law

When the Council closed, it had offered the Church the following contributions:

- confirmation of the existing legislation for the Latin Church with regard to priestly celibacy;
- greater reflection on the reasons for the fittingness of the bond between priesthood and celibacy;
- orientations on the means to be used in formation and perseverance in the state of priestly celibacy.

After the Council, there were many pronouncements and statements by the magisterium, and examination of these can help us to understand the concern and interest over this question.

1. The Encyclical *Sacerdotalis coelibatus* of 24 June 1967 marked the fulfillment of the promise made by Paul VI during the Council. The Encyclical deals with all the most important aspects of priestly celibacy: apart from confirmation of the present system, further in-depth attention is given to the reasons for the fittingness of the bond, and objections are answered (Nos. 1–33); there is an analysis of the history of the Church, with the well-known difference between Latin and Eastern Churches (Nos. 34–49); consideration is then given to the effect of celibacy on human nature (Nos. 50–59); lengthy consideration is given to formation for priestly celibacy and to how it is lived out in priestly life (Nos. 60–82); cases of desertion are then examined, together with the problem of dispensations (Nos. 83–90); and, lastly, reference is made to the fatherly role of the bishop and to the contribution that all the faithful can offer their pastors (Nos. 96–98).

2. The contribution of the Sacred Congregation for Catholic Education concentrated on a more specific point: on the express request of the 1967 Synod of Bishops, the Congregation prepared a document that was published on 6 January 1970 under the title *Ratio fundamentalis institutionis sacerdotalis* (known in English as *The Basic Plan for Priestly Formation*). The document speaks of the need to create "the necessary conditions" for the full and joyful observance of priestly celibacy (No. 48). Freedom of choice on the part of the candidate requires: understanding of

the gift of celibacy and respect for the married state; interior and exterior psychological freedom; emotional stability, including "suitable education in matters of sex" and a "chaste love of persons" that is to be experienced and shown "gradually . . . with sound and spiritual discretion"; the practice of mortification, custody of the senses, and the "natural means favorable to mental and physical health" (No. 48).

3. The Synod of Bishops itself offered a document on *The Ministerial Priesthood*, entitled *Ultimis temporibus*, on 30 November 1971. In this document, celibacy is spoken of in authoritative terms, confirming the decisions of the Council. It discusses the basis and motivations for the bond between priesthood and celibacy, and the "need to preserve celibacy in the Latin church" through the present law (168 *placet*; 10 *non placet*; 21 *placet iuxta modum*), rejecting the ordination of married men even in special cases unless authorized by the Supreme Pontiff. It then describes the conditions that can foster celibacy: growth in interior life, human balance through well-ordered social integration, fraternal relations with other priests and with the bishop, and adequate preparation through understanding of the positive reasons for celibacy in the faithful and total service of God.

4. Following the call of the Encyclical *Sacerdotalis coelibatus* to issue instructions for those who must form future priests, in 1974, the Sacred Congregation for Catholic Education published *A Guide to Formation in Priestly Celibacy*, which examines the specific question of formation. It is the fullest and most systematic document specifically on this subject. Even in the foreword, the correct approach to the task of formation can be seen: "Holy celibacy is a 'precious gift' which God freely gives to those whom he calls. Those so called, however, have the duty to foster the most favorable conditions so that this gift might bear its fruit" (No. 1). After confirming the value of celibacy and the reasons for it, as well as its link of fittingness with the ministerial priesthood even in the midst of contemporary difficulties, it confirms the need, but also the insufficiency, of exterior canonical laws, in order to affirm the need for education to celibacy, so that "a person entering this state of life must not see himself so much taking on a burden as rather receiving a liberating grace" (No. 16), and the purpose of formation is therefore "to form a responsible and mature man into a perfect and faithful priest" (No. 16).

Part II gives the aim of seminary training as that of forming personalities that are "integrally human, Christian and priestly" (No. 17). Formation in human maturity ("a man who has brought to reality his vocation as a man," No. 18) calls for a free, conscious and responsible ability to will "the good," emotional, and sexual integration, and self-control. Formation in Christian maturity has the same requirements and "comes about by a gradual growth in the faith, by the adoration of God, . . . by growing more perfect in Christ, and by contributing to the building up of His Mystical Body" (No. 24). Formation to priestly maturity entails the same requirements of human, emotional, and sexual maturity within the specific framework of the priestly personality, which is that of the "shepherd of souls, on the model of Jesus Christ, Teacher, Priest, and Pastor" (No. 29).

Part III provides guidelines for seminary training and speaks of the role of the educator and his task of discernment, of sex education, education in celibacy, education in priestly asceticism, problems of emotional integrity, and the difficulties inherent in the whole process of formation.

Part IV speaks of the educational purpose of the seminary as an institution that must provide an educational atmosphere, in which spiritual life and ecclesial charity are expressed, and that allows contact with the world along certain specific lines and for specific purposes.

The conclusion highlights the primacy of divine grace, but proper space is also given to the conditioning of the "psychic mechanisms of man" on which the educational action works in order to bring about those conditions that "make the human person a valid instrument for the work of divine grace" (No. 90).

5. The new Code of Canon Law (1983) is the fruit of the Second Vatican Council and marks the completion of the task of renewal as set by the Council. Following the orientations given by the Council Fathers, it in substance confirms the previous legislation, but with certain variations, some of them important:

• with reference to the abolition of tonsure and minor orders, the clerical status now includes only diaconate, presbyterate and episcopate;
• the introduction of the permanent diaconate, with the possibility of accepting "married men, provided they be of more mature age" (LG 29), has led to the existence of two categories of deacons: celibate ones and married ones;

- with regard to married deacons, contrary to the previous ruling on celibacy, they are not called on to live in continence, and are allowed the use of marriage (Canon 1037);
- the old rule is, however, confirmed according to which marriage is no longer possible or valid after ordination (Canon 1087), without any exception being made for the permanent diaconate, although there is a possibility of dispensing from the impediment arising from the order of the diaconate for marriage in cases of danger of death, and this is reserved not to the Holy See but to the local Ordinary (Canon 1079);
- Canon 1037 lays down that all those who are admitted to the presbyterate and unmarried candidates who are admitted to the permanent diaconate must publicly undertake before God and the Church, in the prescribed rite, the obligation of celibacy.

This legislation is supported by abundant canonical material referring to the formation of candidates:

- Canon 241 states that admission to the major seminary is conditional on the presence of the capacities to exercise the sacred ministry, taking into account the candidates' "human, moral, spiritual and intellectual characteristics, their physical and psychological health and their proper motivation";
- Canon 247 confirms the need for "suitable education" for observance of the state of celibacy with full awareness of the duties and responsibilities—as well as the difficulties—of the priestly life;
- the need for careful formation is stressed in Canon 1027, whereas Canon 1028 calls on the bishop or competent superior to instruct candidates prior to ordination on the obligations they are to undertake, and then the following Canon 1029 states that he is to admit only those who enjoy "a good reputation, good morals, and proven virtues, and other physical and psychological qualities which are appropriate to the order to be received";
- together with the minimum ages (25 years for the presbyterate, 23 years for the transient diaconate, 25 years for the unmarried permanent diaconate, and 35 years for the permanent married diaconate), Canon 1031 also calls for "sufficient maturity";
- "insanity" and other forms of psychological infirmity that, in

the opinion of experts, make candidates incapable of exercising the ministry, are irregularities according to Canon 1041, 1°;
- Canon 1044 lays down the impediment to the exercise of orders already received by those who are affected by such infirmities;
- Canon 1051 gives the criteria that the Ordinary is to bear in mind in the investigation of the qualities required of the ordinand: a testimonial is required from the rector of the seminary concerning the necessary qualities, that is, sound doctrine, genuine piety, good morals, and suitability for exercising the ministry, and, after a careful investigation, his physical and psychological health; the bishop can also use other means that seem helpful for an accurate evaluation;
- the suitability of the candidate, according to Canon 1052, must be "proved through positive arguments," and if there is any doubt, the ordination is not to take place.

The Code also lays down penalties for those who do not fulfill the obligation they have assumed:

- Canon 1394 lays down an automatic (*latae sententiae*) suspension—apart from the loss of office laid down in Canon 194, §1, 3°—for a cleric who attempts even a civil marriage; persistence in his line of behavior entails progressive deprivations, and even definitive loss of the clerical state;
- concubinage or scandalous permanence in external sin against the sixth commandment are to be punished with suspension, and other more serious penalties if the cleric persists in such scandal (Canon 1395).

In comparison with the 1917 Code, the new Code gives more attention and provides fuller details as to the criteria for the discernment of vocations and the formation of candidates. It no longer speaks solely from the moral and spiritual point of view, but also gives information on the physical and psychological qualities needed for the priestly state, and the use of the human sciences. There is almost no alteration as regards the steps to be taken in cases of nonfulfillment of obligations, and the same can be said of the criteria and procedures for dispensation from celibacy, which are still reserved to the Holy See, in accordance with the specific norms on this subject issued by the Sacred Congregation for the Doctrine of the Faith in 1980.

Two observations can be made on the basis of this schematic overview of the interventions of the magisterium with regard to the question of priestly celibacy between the time of the Council and the promulgation of the new Code:

1. the substantial confirmation of the traditional appreciation of the value of the celibacy of priests in the Latin Church;
2. a constantly increasing concentration on the question of formation in celibacy, as can be seen from both the quantity and the quality of the individual documents and of the norms of the new Code.

The Question of the Person's Response to the Call to the Celibate Priesthood

Not only does canonical legislation have theology as its foundation, and the salvific mission of the Church as its aim,[1] but it is specifically given in order to provide practical assistance in the common life of the members of the Church, and must therefore have a pastoral function: the law is for persons, in order to help in the fulfillment of their Christian ideal according to the particular vocation of each person within the Church.

As far as canonical legislation on priestly celibacy is concerned, there has been a great deal of criticism and not a little confusion precisely as to the function of canon law. An example of more recent criticism can be seen in what was said at a so-called "Synod of Married Priests" held at Ariccia in Italy in August 1985. One of the so-called five "Catholic truths" approved by the participants rejects canon law on celibacy as illegitimate, since it is said to be in violation of "a fundamental human right" conferred on the apostles and on all proclaimers of the gospel by Christ himself—that is, the right "to be accompanied by a Christian sister as wife (1 Cor. 9:5)."[2]

This approach is questionable even in exegetical and historical terms, but is completely mystifying in logical and juridical terms in the light of a correct ecclesiology. As Cardinal Höffner had previously observed,

. . . a good number of discussions on the law of celibacy seem to presume that candidates to the priesthood possess some juridical right—what might be called a "subjective" right—to be ordained, and that this right subsists even when the candidate wants to combine priesthood and matrimony. No such right exists. It is, rather, the acceptance of the candidate on the part of the bishop that is the deciding factor in this matter.[3]

Another of the "five truths" of the same synod would appear to prove the accuracy of Cardinal Höffner's accusation, inasmuch as it states that

. . . any community has the right to have the ministers necessary to it and to this end can present suitable candidates, and the apostolic authority established by Christ has the duty to ordain those candidates who are recognized as suitable with the imposition of hands.[4]

Canon law clearly places no restriction on the freedom of persons who have the *right* to a juridical state—in this case, that of the ministerial priesthood. However, it does lay down the conditions for actually entering such a state. In other words, canon law imposes celibacy on nobody, but it does restrict the priesthood to those who are also called to celibacy. And this decision is in line with the duty of the hierarchical Church to discern the authenticity of the priestly vocation at specific times and places: the condition of the call to celibacy as a requisite for the priestly vocation is still held to be valid and fitting by the highest representative of the unity and authenticity of the Church—in other words, an Ecumenical Council. And since "the call to the priesthood cannot in any way be separated from the way in which the Church calls, authentically interpreting the voice of the Spirit, it is nonsense to speak of the obligation of celibacy being 'imposed' on those called to the priesthood."[5]

There is thus no violation of the rights and freedom of the individual in canon law, which simply lays down rules for the practical fulfillment within the Church of what has been discerned.under the inspiration of the Holy Spirit and is proposed for the good of the faithful. The discernment of the bond of fittingness between priesthood and celibacy seems to be ever more clearly rooted within the history of the Church well before any legislative formulation. Cardinal A.M. Stickler rightly warns against

. . . anachronistic concepts and evaluations, as, for example, when it is stated *sic et simpliciter* that for many years there were married men in the Church even up to the highest level of the dignity of government, in other words, up to the papacy, and that only in the twelfth century was ecclesiastical celibacy introduced into the Western Church.[6]

Even if it is true that "from the beginning married men were admitted to all orders, and thus to the clerical state, . . . they were bound to perfect continence from the moment they received sacred orders."[7] And the first written law as regards celibacy already reflects this approach, as can be seen in Canon 33 of the Council of Elvira at the beginning of the fourth century. This canon ruled out the possibility of marriage after ordination, which then formally became a diriment impediment to matrimony at the Second Lateran Council (1139). Stickler concludes that "the twelfth century therefore did not see the introduction of celibacy, but the confirmation of the invalidity of matrimony for clerics *in sacris* who attempted marriage, which had as such always been prohibited."

We can, therefore, say that from the point of view of the history of the Church, the direction taken by development is that of an ever greater confirmation of the fittingness of the bond between priesthood and celibacy.[8]

From the point of view of pastoral theology, the reasons for this fittingness are clearly given in the previously cited documents of the magisterium, especially the Encyclical *Sacerdotalis coelibatus*. I think it is interesting to note the contribution of H. Urs von Balthasar[9] on the subject of the difference between the priestly state and the religious state (or that of the counsels), since this can lead to further insights into the balance of the position of the Church, which does not claim the necessity but confirms the fittingness of the bond between priesthood and celibacy. According to von Balthasar, "The priesthood is primarily an ecclesial function, an objective ministry, and, on the basis of this ministry, subsequently a way of life," while "The way of the counsels is primarily a personal way of life that subsequently became an ecclesial way of life—similar, therefore, to the official ministry."[10] The objective element of the salvific function is, therefore, the predominant factor in the ministerial priesthood, while the subjective element of representing Christ in his total gift to the Father in poverty, obedience, and virginity is the predominant factor in the state of the counsels. Because of the objective sufficiency of the ministry of Christ, the person of the priest is not seen as the primary element; rather, "The official and, therefore, impersonal mark of the minister must always be present in the priesthood so that the personality of Christ may shine through with greater clarity." It would therefore be wrong on the part of the priest to make any attempt to "identify himself as subject with his office, to bring office and person into congruence by dint of strenuous effort in order thereby 'to be equal to' his office." In the state of the counsels, on the other hand, the person of the consecrated person is in the foreground, inasmuch as he

> . . . has the privilege of representing the way of the Redeemer in the Church and for the Church; of renouncing everything that Christ renounced in order thereby to bear witness, by the gift of his own existence, to the vitality and permanence of the answer by which the Church accepts the challenge of Christ's word and essence. [11]

It seems to me that this difference in emphasis (which is not opposition) of the elements entailed in the calls to the priesthood and to consecrated life can provide a basis for the nonessential need for the bond between priesthood and celibacy; that is, it shows the objective and gratuitous character of the salvific mission of Christ, which can work in the priestly ministry even through a recalcitrant instrument. And this same view that leads to rejection of the necessity of the link between priesthood and celibacy also leads to the conclusion that it is fitting, inasmuch as "the two forms of election are, as it were, complementary." Thus, "The priest, who by reason of his office is the bearer of Christ's grace, can find no other and no better answer to this grace than to be subjectively the kind of priest Christ wants him to be." And von Balthasar goes on to state that

> It is in no way correct to say that, of itself, the priestly function demands of the individual a less great and less perfect gift of self than does the grace of election to the state of the counsels. The opposite would be more true: The greatness of

the priestly vocation demands of the one called to it the fullest gift of which he is capable.[12]

In this perspective, obedience, poverty, and perfect chastity, which are essential for consecrated life in the form of vows, are supremely fitting for the priestly state even without the form of a vow. Von Balthasar examines the two types of vocation in the New Testament, and sees Peter, who is married, as "the representative of the official priesthood," and John and Paul, who are virgins, as "the representatives of that personal and interior priesthood that is the explicit following of the High Priest 'who offered himself unblemished unto God' (Heb. 9:14)." However, the complementary relationship between the two states is eventually seen when Peter is asked for a greater love than the others (Jn. 21:15):

When it is a question of learning something from or about the Lord, Peter can no longer rely, as he has hitherto done, on John's greater love. . . . He must also become the embodiment of love. . . . Consequently, an effort is required of both of them: of John, who, in a spirit of renunciation and out of love for the Lord and for the Church, transfers to Peter his primacy of love; and of Peter, who may assume his primacy of office only if he assimilates to himself personally this greater love that is John's. The "tension" between love and office was thus overcome.

This shows the delicate balance between the difference and fittingness of the two states, which complement one another, and reach their highest point in unity: "The Lord's sole purpose in bringing about this decisive transfer of power was to achieve unity. Earlier, Peter had been given a function that was to engage and absorb his whole being."[13]

Having confirmed the legitimacy and fittingness of the bond between ministerial priesthood and celibacy, both from the formal and practical viewpoints, we are now faced with another equally clear question: the difficulty many of those called to the ministerial priesthood have in fulfilling the demands of the choice of celibacy. Although, as we have seen, the history of the Church teaches that the direction discerned and formally established by law has been that of a celibate priesthood, it is also true that for a long time "celibacy was in large part violated" and "for some regions we can say it practially fell into disuse."[14] And in the present period, we again find similar crisis conditions, as is seen in defections from the priestly state and also in the requests for dispensation from the celibacy taken on with priestly ordination.[15] The crisis in priestly celibacy has fostered various studies and surveys, especially in Europe and the United States, and the following are just two examples:

1. an official study on celibacy in the Netherlands called for by the bishops of that country in 1967, and carried out by the University of Nijmegen; the answers to a questionnaire sent out to diocesan priests as well as to subdeacons throughout the country showed that only 27 percent wanted the present legislation to be retained, whereas 46 percent wanted its abolition, and 27 percent did not give a definite answer because they wanted pluriformity[16];
2. in the United States, a survey of the diocesan clergy published in 1968 revealed that 62 percent of the clergy thought that diocesan priests should be free to choose between marriage and celibacy, with a predominance of this opinion among the younger clergy (72 percent of those under thirty-five years of age).[17]

Even if these trends and opinions refer only to certain areas of the worldwide Church and seem to become weaker as time passes, they could be used in support of the objections that have always been raised against the bond between priesthood and celibacy. In his Encyclical *Sacerdotalis coelibatus*, Paul VI recalled that "There are also some who strongly maintain that priests by reason of their celibacy find themselves in a situation that is physically and psychologically detrimental to the development of a mature and well-balanced human personality" (No. 10). Formation for the priesthood would then be contrary to human freedom and dignity, inasmuch as "the degree of knowledge and power of decision of a young person and his psychological and physical maturity fall far below—or at any rate are disproportionate to— the seriousness of the obligation he is assuming, its real difficulties and its permanence" (No. 11). We may here recall the older and more radical objection according to which the priest, as a man, is not capable of controlling his own passions and therefore of fulfilling the commitments of celibacy—an argument already used at the Council of Seleucia (or Persian Council) in 486 A.D.!

These and other possible objections, and the possibility of providing an answer to them, directly involve the human sciences—those sciences that study human nature in its existence and actions, and that can be of help in interpreting facts in the light of meanings and values drawn from the theological and biblical sciences.

And there have in fact been a good number of studies aimed at providing an answer and explanation for the phenomenon of the crisis in the priesthood, although there is an important premise for any evaluation of these studies. Research and interpretation on the social and psychological levels must observe at least two conditions in order to be acceptable:

1. There must be agreement or at least compatibility between the object of research and the anthropological premise implicit in the work instrument. In our case, this means that there must be harmony between the significance of priestly celibacy as it is seen in the ecclesial perspective and the anthropological premises implicit in psychological and sociological science that is used, with its own autonomous method, in research in this field. It is clear on the one hand that neutrality is not possible for the sciences that study man in his significance and aims precisely as regards the content he is called on to fulfill, and on the other hand that if the anthropological view implicit in these sciences does not accept—or distorts—the value and significance of priestly celibacy, any attempt at an interpretation of the latter as its exists is misleading and inadequate. The observation of L.M. Rulla concerning the Christian vocation in general can be applied to the specific case of priestly celibacy:

> . . . an athropology of Christian vocation cannot borrow from other anthropologies without making an appropriately critical analysis of their basic presuppositions and of the dialectical differences of horizon that may exist between their views of the human person. [18]

2. The second condition for an accurate investigation is that it must be open to *all* the possible explanations, with an in-depth study that makes it possible to gain the greatest possible understanding and not only a description of the phenomenon.

These two conditions are connected, since it is obvious that reduction in meaning and value in the anthropological sphere easily opens the way to restrictions on hypotheses and on the deterministic explanation of the phenomena.

I confine myself to citing some studies that have been carried out with the aim of understanding and explaining the phenomenon of the present-day crisis in priestly celibacy from a sociological and psychological point of view, in order to assess not only the results, but also the respect shown for the necessary conditions for a serious investigation in this field.

1. The study carried out by the National Opinion Research Center (NORC) in 1972[19] sought to discover why priests leave their ministry. The choice of variables (age, family tensions, inner-directed personality, religious experience, contemporary values, work satisfaction, loneliness, the desire to marry, future plans) tends for the most part to indicate that the research is based on a model in which the view of the priesthood is oriented more to the role than to self-transcending values. This means that the priesthood is seen more as a means to reach self-realization than as a gift of self. The result of this research is therefore weighted in advance toward the discovery of the correlation between the level of satisfaction or frustration, and perseverance or abandonment of the priesthood, without considering the other possible explanations of such satisfaction or frustration, either with regard to self-transcending values or with regard to possible conflicts or problems within the person. It is therefore no surprise to discover that those who have left the priesthood were found to be further advanced toward self-realization than those who remained, more open to change and more critical of traditions, and that they viewed the ministerial priesthood as a transitory and modifiable institutional role without any substantial difference from the priesthood of all the faithful. Those who have left the priesthood tend to find justification for their own decision to leave, which reduced the tension they felt. In any case, the fact that all the possible explanations of such tension were not checked, as well as the lack of any longitudinal control, divests the research of its value as proof. In the light of the facts, the entry into the priesthood of those who have then left it is inexplicable if it is not admitted that something has also changed in the subjects in question, because had they held their present ideas, they would not have become priests. Further, one result of

the study seems to indicate that one possible explanation can be sought in another direction: in the long run, twice as much tension is found in the marriages of expriests than in other marriages, which would indicate the possibility that the tension, which is reduced when the man leaves the priesthood, tends to recur within the new role after a period of relief. And this throws doubt on the model on which the study was based.

2. Another study that can be examined is that presented by W. Mönikes,[20] which was carried out on a sample of forty-six expriests and ninety-eight priests who had persevered. In this case, too, the range of concepts underlying the hypotheses considered and the variables taken into account is insufficient, so that the results are predetermined. Priestly commitment is seen in terms of conformity to the role, and the difficulties are explained in terms of conflict between the characteristics of the person and conformity to this role. No consideration is given to the possibility of conflicts within the personality of the subjects, so that it appears that these conflicts can only spring from the confrontation with the institution and the institutionalized role. There is no allowance for any other view than that of conformity to the role, and the possibility is therefore ignored that the motivation of conformity to the role can be interior acceptance of self-transcending values and the free gift of self. It is therefore not surprising that in this study, too, we find that in comparison with those who have remained in the priesthood, expriests are less dogmatic, less authoritarian, less rigid, and more extrovert. They conform less to orthodoxy, prefer social and group life, and their attitudes toward the concept of the priesthood are more innovative and progressive. In general, expriests describe themselves in favorable terms and the institution of the Church in unfavorable terms. However, in this study, too, there is no answer to the question of the entry of these persons who then left the priesthood, unless it is admitted that they changed in the meantime. This should lead to analysis of the subjects and not only of the relationship of conformity with the role in order to explain difficulties and abandonment.

3. On the other hand, a study that takes account of the requirements for a correct explanation of possible crisis in priests is that found in *Entering and Leaving Vocation: Intrapsychic Dynamics* by L.M. Rulla, F. Imoda, and J. Ridick.[21] This study starts from anthropological premises that are in harmony with the object of

the investigation, and consideration is given to all the possible variables that can influence the priestly vocation, beginning with the intrapersonal sphere, and then going on to analyze interpersonal relationships in the light of the self-transcendent values proper to the vocation examined. The study formulated hypotheses, which were then checked against a longitudinal study of 247 young men (religious and seminarians) and 433 women religious in the United States, and a control group of 107 laymen and 136 laywomen. The following conclusions are drawn from the complex analysis of the material collected, for which we refer to the text cited:

(a) When entering their vocation, the majority of the subjects (60 to 80 percent) demonstrated a psychological fragility, as seen from central and subconscious vocational inconsistencies; in other words, they were disturbed by promptings and tendencies that were centrally opposed to the vocational ideals consciously and freely accepted, although the subject was not aware of this opposition.

(b) These central and subconscious inconsistencies tend to persist, even after the formation period.

(c) These same inconsistencies hinder the capacity to internalize vocational values—that is, the capacity to act as motivated by vocational ideals and not by defensive or utilitarian reasons.

(d) There is a significant difference between those who persevere and those who leave their vocation with regard to this capacity for internalization, since even when they entered those who leave were considerably more inconsistent than those who then persevere; indeed, according to the authors, such inconsistencies lead subjects to unrealistic expectations with regard to the role they are to fill, and they will then be disappointed by the objective reality, with a parallel weakening in their capacity to internalize values; this leads either to alienation or to a smaller apostolic success, thus opening the way either to abandonment of the vocation, or to a priestly life that is lived out without further reference to ideals (in other words, the tendency to use the vocation as a sort of "nest").

(e) The authors also use other similar studies to explain the link existing between frustration and alienation in the lives of priests, and the temptation to feel celibacy is the obstacle to overcoming the difficulties: because of the defensive function that sexuality possesses as a result of its plasticity and ubiquitousness, any disturbance or difficulty of the personality can use sexual behavior as an outlet or defense. Thus, it is not surprising that when frustrations begin to be felt in vocation "these frustrations may seek some outlets in sexual phenomena,"[22] so that such subjects come to see matrimony as the possible solution to their problems.

(f) The increase in the numbers of those leaving the priesthood since the Second Vatican Council does not mean that the fragility of the subjects has increased, but depends rather on factors that encouraged it to come to the surface. The authors bring out three possible social and cultural factors that have had an influence not in creating the causes of the problem but in its manifestation: (i) institutions and authority have reduced coercive pressure in order to leave more room for personal freedom, and this has caused the surfacing of those fragilities of certain subjects that could have been hidden by a more rigid structure; (ii) the conciliar renewal in fact meant that many traditional ideas and attitudes were challenged, so that fragile subjects saw the already weak attraction of objective values decrease; (iii) a tendency to pay more attention to the exercise of the priestly role and possibly less attention to the need to internalize vocational values, almost in compensation for a previous lack of attention to free experimentation with these same roles—and in fragile subjects, due to the above-mentioned inconsistencies, such experimentation has led to an increase in frustration and opened the way to further departures.

As can be seen from this brief and incomplete summary, the authors take into consideration both internal and external elements, and come to an explanation of the entire vocational process from entry to departure, supporting their conclusions with a serious and meaningful survey and investigation.

It can therefore be said that the present difficulties concerning celibacy appear to be a manifestation of a more complex vocational crisis, and thus more a consequence than a determining factor, as L.M. Rulla wrote in a recent publication.[23] This means that it is not celibacy (and the law with which it is linked to the priesthood) that is the source of the difficulties in the vocational life, but rather the fragilities of the subjects—fragilities not adequately resolved during formation—that make the choice precarious, and with time give them the feeling that celibacy is an undue restriction and make them see matrimony as the solution to their difficulties. We certainly cannot conclude from this that all those who have left the priesthood were psychologically fragile: it is simply one explanation of the prevalence of such processes, although it does not rule out the possibility of errors springing solely from circumstances or of choices that are impossible to carry through because of real and serious pathological factors that were not immediately recognized. However, as the authors themselves stress in a later publication,[24] not only is fragility significantly present in priestly crises, but it constitutes a restriction on effective freedom because of the influence of unconscious elements that are present in the person and are contrary to what he consciously wants to become. (This is the second dimension introduced by Rulla as a guide for theoretic reference.[25])

Faced with these results of research by the human sciences into the crisis and abandonment of the choice of the celibate priesthood, it must be concluded that the solution of the crisis should be sought in an adequate formation, which must aim at eliminating those central unconscious inconsistencies that are the source of the process that can lead to departure. It is therefore neither a matter of reconsidering the bond of fittingness between priesthood and celibacy, nor of lifting the law that restricts the priesthood in the Latin Church to those who are also called to celibacy. Indeed, apart from divesting the significance of celibacy and also the priesthood of their splendor, the abolition of this law would not be of any advantage to those in difficulties, while it would deprive those who now live it with fidelity and effectiveness of a certain support. Rulla also states that "the law of celibacy enhances the vocational consistency and effectiveness of people whose degree of consistency allows the law to work," while "people with unconscious conflicts de facto do not benefit from such positive influence of the law," although its abolition would offer them "another easy way to evade facing their real personal problem,"[26] which, after some temporary relief, tends to reappear in the new matrimonial state (as is shown by the previously mentioned higher level in marital conflictuality in the marriages of expriests as compared with ordinary marriages). The true solution for these people is not a change in their state, but a change in themselves in the form of an intensive effort to remedy their inconsistencies and to orient them toward the self-transcendent values of the priestly vocation and not only toward the role.

Some Concluding Suggestions

We have seen that there are underlying theological and pastoral reasons for the fittingness of the bond between priesthood and celibacy. The human sciences show that the difficulties spring chiefly from the fragility of persons who are not adequately formed and trained to live out the values of their vocations (and not only celibacy), but that, in time, the need to free themselves of celibacy comes to be seen as the hoped-for solution to their insatisfaction, although this then tends to recur within the new matrimonial state. It therefore becomes important to uphold the significance and value of the bond between priesthood and celibacy through the law of the Church, but at the same time to improve traditional formation, which does not seem capable of reducing the fragility of these people.

The history of the Church in the area of priestly celibacy can be of help in this task. The Church has used laws and disciplinary measures to help people to understand and live out the value of priestly celibacy, although for centuries it was unable to eliminate contrary trends and inconsistencies, until it stopped relying solely on disciplinary norms and began to give serious and radical encouragement to the work of formation, thus leading to the institution of seminaries.

Similar orientations are also found in the present-day magisterium. We have merely to recall what Paul VI wrote in his Encyclical *Sacerdotalis coelibatus* 65: ". . . care should be taken for the progressive development of his [the candidate's] personality through the means of physical, intellectual and moral education directed toward the control and personal dominion of his instincts, sentiments and passions." Similarly, in *A Guide to Formation in Priestly Celibacy* 38, we read that candidates should be selected "in accordance with modern, psychological diagnosis, without losing sight of supernatural factors and of the complexities of human influences on the individual." In the light of the results of psychological and social studies, it seems necessary to integrate the traditional formation methods with those placed at our disposition by modern psychology, if we want to resolve those central and unconscious inconsistencies that leave people so fragile that in the new social and cultural environment they can be led to an explicit abandonment of the vocation they had previously accepted. However, in my opinion, in order to be valid, this approach must begin with those who have the task of forming candidates for the priesthood, as the Council recalls in the wise words of *Optatam totius* 5:

> The training of students depends not only on wise regulations but also, and especially, on competent educators. Seminary superiors and professors should therefore be chosen from among the best and should receive a careful preparation in sound doctrine, suitable pastoral experience and special training in spirituality and teaching methods.

These educators "must be capable of understanding the deep underlying dynamics in subjects who enter into vocation . . . and of avoiding any projection of their own personal problems onto the young men they are called on to help."[27] The essential priority of the formation of educators was taken up in the document *A Guide to Formation in Priestly Celibacy* 39, which states: "Without careful preparation anyone who undertakes this task, one of the most difficult in the educational field, cannot possibly produce any positive results." However, it does not seem to me that norms proportionate to these priority requirements have been offered in the new Code of Canon Law. Although Canon 253 does lay down the conditions for teaching in seminaries, I can find no parallel canon indicating the essential elements involved in acquiring the capacity and skill needed by superiors for the overall formation of students. Despite this, Canon 1051 assigns the superior in charge of formation or the rector the task of providing a testimonial on whether the candidate has the necessary qualities! Having seen how deep and hidden the fragility of candidates can be, we can obviously understand how difficult it is today to carry out such discernment if those in charge of formation do not combine and integrate the traditional tools with those offered by a healthy and serious psychology. The possibility of errors in the discernment of vocations (with regard both to the existence of the supernatural call, and to the level of formation attained by the person who has been called) is also proportionate to the training that superiors have received. And the risk is clearly not negligible if the new norms issued by the Sacred Congregation for the Doctrine of the Faith in 1980 regarding the canonical procedure for dispensation from priestly celibacy state that the Congregation will consider not only the cases of priests who have long since left the priesthood and now wish to regularize irreversible situations, but also

. . . the cases of those who should not have received priestly ordination because the necessary aspect of freedom of responsibility was lacking or because the competent superiors were not able within an appropriate time to judge in a prudent and sufficiently fitting way whether the candidate really was suited for continuously leading a life of celibacy dedicated to God (No. 5).

It is not easy to interpret this provision, since it is difficult to see why it is easier to distinguish the causes of departure retrospectively than it was during and at the end of formation, unless we now possess different tools, or unless we confine ourselves to considering only the most extreme and obvious cases. Even so, it is beyond doubt that the inconsistencies discussed, which are the predominant cause of departures, do *not* make a person *incapable* of freely taking on and stably living in priestly celibacy, although they are still the source of such difficulties and frustrations as to make the choice of departure easy for the reasons given. The majority of cases would therefore be ineligible for dispensation, but this is acceptance only if, during formation, candidates are offered *all* the forms of possible assistance by people who have been properly trained, as well as the use of all the educational tools available, both the traditional ones and those offered by modern science that are in keeping with vocational values. It would be unjust if, on the one hand, candidates to the priesthood were not provided with all the assistance possible, thus allowing a fragility that has an insidious effect over time, and if, on the other hand, they were then denied dispensation when the solution of the fragility that has led to their departure is considerably more difficult to deal with than it was at a younger age and within a formative structure aimed at resolving it. It is certainly wise and just to remind bishops that they should provide priests in difficulty with assistance "so that they may more easily and joyfully safeguard the duties undertaken on the day of ordination," together with the help of their "priestly brothers, friends, relatives, physicians and psychologists" (*Norms for the Laicization of Priests* 6). Even so, it is undeniable that at that point, the task is considerably more difficult, and it must be undertaken with the use of any instruments that were previously ignored.

It therefore seems helpful to begin the task of formation by taking into account any possible psychological fragility springing from unconscious inconsistencies. This would not only lead to a fall in the number of departures, but would also make it easier to carry out a discernment in the cases of requests for dispensation. Indeed, if a priest does arrive at departure, despite the help provided by Church discipline, despite an adequate formation, and despite timely assistance in subsequent difficulties, it would be easier to distinguish cases of a lack of good will from those of error in discernment as to the individual's capacity. The restriction of the concession of dispensation to the latter would then be in keeping with charity and justice, since anybody who leaves through a lack of good will has failed to fulfill a commitment freely undertaken and thus does not have the right to expect the Church to support his choice, because this would compromise the common good and also the good of the priest himself, who would be deprived of a constant call to return to fidelity to God.

The various elements of our study show convergence between conclusions drawn from different perspectives: the value of the bond between priesthood and celibacy is supported by theological and pastoral reasons, and canonical science places its normative and disciplinary system at the service of this bond, while a correct analysis of information drawn from the human sciences shows the need to integrate retention of the present legislation with an increase and improvement in the work of primary formation for those who decide to take on the celibate priesthood. This convergence of conclusions is encouraging, but it is also demanding inasmuch as it must not be left on the theoretical level but must be translated into concrete attitudes and corresponding commitment on the part of the various people concerned, so that the witness of celibate priests may make this treasure of the Latin Church shine forth ever more bright.

Translated from the Italian by Leslie Wearne.

Notes

1. Apostolic Contitution *Sacrae disciplinae leges* (25 January 1983).
2. In *Avvenire* (1 September 1985), 4.
3. J. Coppens (ed.), *Sacerdozio e Celibato* (Milan, 1975), 784.
4. In *Avvenire* (1 September 1985), 4.
5. G. Versaldi, "Il Celibato sacerdotale," *La Revista del Clero italiano*, 57/9 (September 1976), 778–787.
6. A.M. Stickler, *Il Celibato ecclesiastico nel Codex Iuris Canonici rinnovato* (Vatican City, 1984), 71.
7. *Ibid.*, 72.
8. Cf. H. Crouzel, "Celibato e continenza ecclesiastica nella Chiesa primitiva: i motivi," in Coppens (ed.), *Sacerdozio e Celibato*, 451–504.
9. H. Urs von Balthasar, *The Christian State of Life* (San Francisco, 1983).
10. *Ibid.*, 267.
11. *Ibid.*, 268–269.
12. *Ibid.*, 275.
13. *Ibid.*, 281–285.
14. A.M. Stickler, "Evoluzione della disciplina del celibato nella Chiesa d'Occidente dalla fine dell'età patristica al Concilio di Trento," in Coppens (ed.), *Sacerdozio e Celibato*, 505–560.
15. From the *Annuario statistico della Chiesa* for 1983: in 1973, among the secular clergy, there were 1,868 departures, and this figure had decreased to 603 in 1983; the requests for dispensation from celibacy had risen from 371 in 1964 to 1,026 in 1968.
16. *Inchiesta ufficiale sul celibato in Olanda* (Brescia, 1969).
17. J.H. Fichter, *America's Forgotten Priests* (New York, 1968).
18. L.M. Rulla, *Anthropology of the Christian Vocation. Vol. 1: Interdisciplinary Bases* (Rome, 1986), 20.
19. National Opinion Research Center, *The Catholic Priest in the United States* (Washington, DC, 1972).
20. W. Mönikes, *Zur Analyse von Rollenkonflikten ehemaliger Priester der romisch-katholischen Kirche*, doctoral thesis (Bonn, 1973).
21. L.M. Rulla, F. Imoda, and J. Ridick, *Entering and Leaving Vocation: Intrapsychic Dynamics* (Rome, 1976).
22. *Ibid.*, 249.
23. L.M. Rulla, *Depth Psychology and Vocation* (Rome, 1971), 248.
24. L.M. Rulla, F. Imoda, and J. Ridick, *Antropologia della Vocazione Cristiana. Vol. 2: Conferme esistenziali* (Casale Monferrato, 1986).
25. Rulla, *Anthropology of the Christian Vocation*, Vol. 1.
26. Rulla, *Depth Psychology and Vocation*, 233–234, 249–250.
27. Rulla, Imoda, and Ridick, *Entering and Leaving Vocation*, 265.

PART VIII

RELIGION
AND
RELIGIONS

CHAPTER 47

Christianity and the Non-Christian Religions in their Relationship to Religious Experience

Johannes B. Lotz, S.J.

Summary

Religious experience and Christian revelation interpenetrate one another. Hence, in a hidden manner, revelation is at work in the non-Christian religions that derive from religious experience. Conversely, revelation is rooted in man through religious experience. This unity is threatened by two extremes. The disintegration of revelation into relativistically misinterpreted religious experience was brought about by modernism. The Christianity of that period responded by separating revelation from religious experience. In contrast to these positions, the Second Vatican Council sought to restore the unity of the Christian and human dimensions. This effort gave many the opportunity of dispersing the Christian element into the human element after the Council. In contrast, others strove to attain a new separation of the Christian element from the human element. In the face of this situation, it is the urgent task of the present moment to fight with all our forces for a balanced synthesis between the Christian and human elements, and especially for the rooting of revelation in religious experience, for which there are numerous opportunities.

Experience and/or Revelation?

According to a widespread conception, Christianity is one religion among others, and it is seen as a compliment to describe it as one of the great world religions. The title of this study, however, contrasts Christianity with the non-Christian religions. Consequently, it cannot be called a religion in the same sense as the others, or maybe it cannot be considered a religion at all. We may ask what the reasons are for this contrast, and whether they are so persuasive as to render this contrast comprehensible, and, indeed, decisive.

The Second Vatican Council throws light on these questions in its Declaration on the Relation of the Church to Non-Christian Religions. This declaration begins with the words *Nostra aetate* and points out that today more than ever before all peoples "form but one community," since they all have a meeting point in God as their common origin and their common destiny (*NA* 11). Furthermore, "his providence, evident goodness, and saving designs extend to all men" (*NA* 1). They "look to their different religions for an answer to the unsolved riddles of human existence" (*NA* 1). This lifts them up to a "certain awareness" and "recognition" of the hidden Godhead, which "results in a way of life that is imbued with a deep religious sense" (*NA* 2). This is specified in detail for Hinduism, Buddhism, and above all for Islam, and is even further emphasized for the rich "common spiritual heritage" that links Christians with Jews or the religion of the Old Testament (*NA* 2–4). Christianity "rejects nothing of what is true and holy in these religions" (*NA* 2).

These statements study the agreement of non-Christian religions with Christianity. What, however, must be stated concerning the difference between these two fields? We must certainly see a difference of degree, inasmuch as Christianity contains in a complete and perfect form what remains fragmentary and imperfect in non-Christian religions. This is to be understood as concerns the material content, not as concerns the degree to which it is carried out, for non-Christians are very often superior to Christians in their fidelity and zeal. The extraordinary claim that is already contained in the difference of degree also points to the essential difference, without which the former would appear to be nothing other than an offensive attack. But the essential distinction leads back to the sources from which the two forms of religious consciousness are derived; for if Christianity did not dispose of a source over and above the source of non-Christian religions, its claim would be incomprehensible and presumptuous.

The history of religions shows that the source of these religions is religious experience, which the Council calls "experience of God" (GS 7). This is accessible to all individuals and peoples, and develops within history, in the course of which it takes on a multitude of forms. In contrast, Christianity lives from "divine revelation," to which the Council reserves its own Dogmatic Constitution *Dei verbum*. Revelation reaches its climax in Christ, and it is entrusted to the Church, which transmits it to us and interprets it for us, which in turn produces an historical development with manifold expressions.

The duality of the sources produces numerous questions that have flared up afresh, especially in response to the Council. What must be shown is whether religious experience truly gives what is denied by atheism. Furthermore, the contemporary demand for rationality is not very favorable for this study, as it either requires a rational basis for religion, or else claims that religion cannot be reconciled with rationality or that when it is examined rationally, it dissolves into nothing. If we admit religious experience, we are faced with the further question of whether revelation (which goes beyond it and completes it) exists, and of the relationship between them. Does experience take place entirely independently of revelation, or is revelation always already at work in experience in a hidden way? And does religious experience always need to refer back to revelation lest it go off the rails and be unable to express itself perfectly? Conversely, what is the relationship of Christinaity to religious experience? Does the former include or exclude the latter? The latter thesis is the premise adopted by those who consider that although the non-Christian religions are nourished from religious experience, this is in no way the case for Christianity, which they consider has its roots in faith that corresponds to revelation, and thus it cannot be said to derive from experience. What is more, they say, faith cannot be reconciled with experience; if a person decides in favor of faith, he must renounce experience, and the very attempt to link the two is almost bound to end up with experience driving out faith, and hence with the decline of Christianity and a return to the non-Christian religions.

Religious Experience and the Grace of Christ

In order to respond to all these questions, we start by examining religious experience, or experience of God.[1] Through experience, people encounter preexistent reality in their corporal presence. This always occurs with reference to the visible world with its human beings and objects. More precisely, experience includes not only the external dimension or the things surrounding the person who is experiencing, but also the interior dimension, or what he himself is or what is happening within him. There is a difference between this and the experience of God, who transcends the world and is not directly accessible to us because of his hidden nature. For this reason, he can be reached only by indirect experience, or experience mediated by the world. Many consider this to be impossible, and thus they either deny the existence of God (atheism) or draw him into the world (pantheism), or else they consider that he cannot be experienced but is accessible only by logical reasoning.

In contrast to this, we shall list three experiences in which the natural dimension can gain a glimpse of the supernatural dimension or the human dimension can, and often does, gain a glimpse of the divine dimension. The experience of overwhelming *fear* tears away every worldly support and throws us into nothingness. Instead of losing everything here, the individual will gain everything if he or she manages to attain the unshakable bearing force hidden yet present in this abyss. The experience of this final loneliness detaches a person from his or her human "you," while at the same time giving a hint of the divine "you," which alone reaches into his or her innermost core and thus finally fulfills him or her. The experience of meaninglessness makes life appear to have so little to offer that it seems not to be worthwhile, or else to produce only disgust and weariness. A night such as this shows how every earthly meaning is only preliminary and hence insufficient. This leads humanity already to strive after the definitive meaning that justifies everything and through which it is touched by the divine fullness of meaning.

The three experiences prompted by a lack of something lead on to the positive fulfillment that corresponds to them. Sometimes this fulfillment overcomes a person even without first experiencing the lack; here the person is gripped by the unshakable foundation, by the fully beatified "you," or by the meaning that illuminates all. This may occur in many ways, whether through nature, art, or human encounters. In each case, what is experienced in these or other ways requires further clarification until God's countenance is thrown into more or less clear relief, and awestruckness is transformed into religious veneration or adoration. The process we are speaking of here embraces humanity with all its forces, and demands the devotion of a person's entire personality down to the very innermost depths.

The awakening of religious awareness is developed in countless stages and an immense variety of forms. This leads to the growth of religions as paths to salvation that are built by people themselves to lead them to God. Although he has not yet expressly encountered these people, Christ is active in them in a hidden manner, as is also witnessed by the Council, according to which they "often reflect a ray of that truth which enlightens all men" (NA 2). This is an echo of the gospel, which states that Christ is "the true light that enlightens every man . . . coming into the world" (Jn. 1:9). The following text is also apposite here: "I, when I am lifted up from the earth, will draw all men to myself" (Jn. 12:32).[2]

Thus, although the non-Christian religions also live from the truth and grace of Christ, these attain their full development only when they become effective *expressly*. Insofar as this is not achieved, religions remain incomplete and imperfect, wandering off on all kinds of false trails concerning both insight and behavior. This shows their need for redemption, which they can obtain from Christ alone. Interiorly, they are referred to this because God's will to save includes all people (NA 1), as is also witnessed by holy scripture: "God so loved the world that he gave his only Son" (Jn. 3:16). It follows that religious experience, on which religions draw, is ordered toward divine revelation, with which it is always imbued.[3] This finds its confirmation in the growing contemporary unity of peoples, thanks to the numerous elements of Christian truth that expressly make their way into the various religions, as can be seen in the case for the eight beatitudes as concerns Hinduism.

Clarification of Religious Experience

Religious experience is prepared for its encounter with Christian revelation through the further clarification already mentioned. This completes what is incomplete, perfects what is imperfect, and eliminates error. Experimentation itself leads to the form, thus purified, of this experience, and this brings to ever clearer expression the twofold etymological meaning of religion, namely, the careful observation of what is incomparably significant, and reconnection with the absolute foundation of all. In this unceasing human experimentation—which is not only intellectual but also existential or universal—its religious profundity is gradually thrown unequivocally and overwhelmingly into relief. In this way, the various religions approach Christianity, even though they remain marked by sin, as Paul, who was driven by holy zeal, pointed out in his letter to the Romans with regard to the Jews and the Greeks (Rom. 1:4).[4]

Reflection on experimentation and what is experienced, which is the specific task of philosophy, is connected with progressive experimentation in this process of clarification of religious experience. It must be admitted that many of its orientations produce misinterpretations, or even the destruction of the experience, thus leading to pantheism or atheism. This shows that it is also in need of redemption; yet as redemption begins to exercise its power over it, philosophy is purified in its original specific character and becomes capable of making a decisive contribution toward justifying, purifying, and determining, and thus toward consolidating religious experience.

Here, transposition of consciousness from the foreground to the background has a role to play. Although in the former this is already ever necessarily at work, it usually escapes attention and is thus often forgotten or even denied, and is thus only rarely given its full importance. Foreground consciousness is concerned with the things and people we find in the world, whereas background consciousness proceeds by mediating these to the world containing all things and people, indeed, to all-embracing universal reality. To put it another way, in the part we always already experience the whole; in the penultimate, the ultimate; in the relative, the absolute; and, finally, in the worldly and human, the divine.

Our era is mostly acquainted only with the experimentation of objects within the world, and it is closed regarding all that lies beyond it. It must, therefore, first be opened afresh for experimentation of the profound dimension of the metaphysical and thus metaworldly foundation of all objects. Only in this framework, which Heidegger calls that of being, does religious experience originate and develop, and thus humanity gains it proportionally to the actualization of interiorization from the foreground to the background, and this is achieved not only with the intellect, but with the whole of the human person.[5]

Clarifying reflection on religious experience can take as its starting point three actions performed by human beings, namely, knowing, willing, and forming. Inasmuch as knowledge attains truth, it already always orders the individual or particular into the universal or whole, for only in this way is the absolute viewpoint opened up through all the relative perspectives: it is from here that the object is seen as it is in itself, and not just as it appears in a limited perspective. Inasmuch as the will attains freedom, it strives after limited goods in the perspective of the limitless One who is good and who unites in himself all that is good; since only this is able to satisfy our will, it is irresistibly attracted by the limited goods or is capable of choosing them in freedom. Insofar as the activity of "forming" attains beauty, it renders the absolute of the background visible in the relative of the foreground, or else it works out a transparency for the former in the latter. The individual who is receptive to this thus experiences the divine basis of the work of art, or at least according to one or another of the rays it emits.

Taking these as its starting point, clarifying reflection understands that the all-embracing whole, the limitless good, and the absolute basis coincide and can be completed through other viewpoints. Its task is particularly to render clear the metaworldly and personal nature of the last of these, as today these attributes often fall into the twilight of a pantheizing flirtation with an impersonal absolute: here a noncritical syncretistic assimilation with religious attitudes of the Far East can be observed at work.

As concerns the metaworldly or supernatural attribute, the whole, the limitless, and the absolute are perceived only when transcendence is ascribed to them in the sense of total independence of all that is partial, limited, and relative. By contrast, insofar as (as in Hegel) the whole, the limitless, and the absolute find their fulfillment solely in the partial, the limited, and the relative, respectively, the whole, the limitless, and the absolute remain under the constraint of the partial, the limited, and the relative, respectively, and thus they are not truly themselves, or else self-identity is always transpierced with nonidentity.

As concerns the personal attribute, this is given in a person solely inasmuch as he or she enters into the whole, the limitless, and the absolute, whereby he or she gains the perfect return to himself or herself, or his or her self-identity. In contrast to this, an animal cannot go beyond the partial, the limited, or the relative, and thus it attains only an incipient return and wanders off in self-alienation. Thus, the whole, the limitless, or the absolute in its purity as guaranteed by transcendence is essentially personal or a person, and so not the divinity per se, but God, the absolute, the limitless One.

Considered more precisely, God's metaworldly and personal attributes are intimately linked to one another; indeed, they include one another. The personal attribute is prefigured in the metaworldly attribute inasmuch as the personal attribute gives the whole, the limitless, or the absolute its unsullied purity or its full self-identity, which is equivalent to personal self-possession. Conversely, it is only in the personal attribute that the meta-worldly attribute attains its full expression, since only the freedom that is given with the person can guarantee the entire independence of the whole from the part, of the limitless from the limited, or of the absolute from the relative.

We must add that God's perfect or infinite transcendence is the basis and reason for his equally perfect and infinite *immanence* in the world or in people and things, and thus responds to the concern of pantheism in a purified form. For God's absolute independence includes the absolute dependence of the world or of people and things. This, however, means that all that is relative obtains its position only in the absolute God, by whom it is brought into being and sustained. Since dependence on the absolute reaches into the innermost depths of what is relative, everything exists only through the fact that God intimately indwells it.[6]

Revelation in Deed and Word

As our account has shown, redeemed philosophizing, through the reflection that is its specific task, makes an essential contribution to clarifying and establishing religious experience, which thereby shares yet more profoundly in redemption than was the case in the development of experimentation through experimentation itself. However, redemption is worked out in completion of religious experience through divine revelation, as we have just mentioned. Here, humanity's own efforts are taken up and thus fulfilled in the willing encounter of God's grace. Hence, a person is not solely directed toward the light that is innate, but is illumined by the light of God himself, which shines out in Christ. Christ is "the true light that enlightens every man . . . coming into the world" (Jn. 1:9).[7] Vatican II confirms that everyone shares in this light when it states that "God can lead those who, through no fault of their own, are ignorant of the Gospel to that faith without which it is impossible to please him" (AG 7). Since revelation is the basis for faith, it reaches all in a hidden fashion, and this includes those whom it does not reach explicitly. Nonetheless, it remains the mandatory task of the Church to lead all people in a manner that is also explicit to the revelation that finds its perfection in Christ. This is given decisive prominence by the Council:

> She [the Church] proclaims and is in duty bound to proclaim without fail, Christ who is the way, the truth and the life (Jn. 14:6). In him, in whom God reconciled all things to himself (2 Cor. 5:18–19), men find the fullness of their religious life (NA 2).

In order to define revelation more precisely, we must distinguish revelation by deed from revelation by word. The former is effected by God's calling his creatures into being; in these works of his, he communicates himself to us and becomes accessible to us: "Ever since the creation of the world his invisible nature . . . has been clearly perceived in the things that have been made" (Rom. 1:20). This is brought about by God's both being perceptible behind his works and directing his Word to us. Thus "in many ways," he has "spoken" to us; thus, formerly the patriarchs and prophets, but in latter times, "his Son" were the bearers of his message (Heb. 1:1f.). He is the witness who surpasses all the others, because he is "in the bosom of the Father," and "has made known" to us what he himself has seen from all eternity (Jn. 1:18). Thus, "truth came through Jesus Christ" (Jn. 1:19), and we must follow the admonition: "Listen to him" (Mt. 17:5).

Humanity's response to revelation by deed is religious experience with its interpretation partially through experimentation itself and partially through philosophical reflection. Humanity responds to revelation through faith, whereby it entrusts itself to God who speaks to it, and assumes his message into its convictions and life. Religious experience and faith interpenetrate one another, for the former is perfected by the latter, but the latter is also prepared for and set in motion by the former. This perfecting is achieved in two stages, corresponding to faith as healing and as elevating grace. As healing grace, faith offers the help needed by religious experience in order to attain maturity despite its human limitations and its infirmity as derived from original sin. As elevating grace, faith opens up the mysteries of God that are inaccessible to religious experience, although religious experience does also produce indispensable premises for faith.

Healing and Elevating Grace

Thomas Aquinas contributes to a further clarification of the healing grace of faith at the beginning of his *Summa Theologiae*. Although he teaches that humanity is capable of reaching God by the force of its own reason, he nonetheless observes that the full truth is reached only by few people after a long time, whereas for most people it remains mixed with many errors.[8] This is the basis for the statements of the First Vatican Council which, although it declares that a person can rise by intellectual powers to the fully developed image of God, nevertheless immediately adds that it is to be ascribed to divine revelation that even in the present condition of humanity, everyone can reach this without excessive difficulties, with full certainty, and without any error.[9]

"Present condition" means the state in which humanity now finds itself on account of original sin and personal sin through the ages. This does not remove the fundamental capacity for experiencing God, but considerable difficulties stand in the way of actual experience, and divine revelation offers help in overcoming these. This help is not absolutely but only morally necessary, since the essential perceptibility remains, and it is only the existential capacity for actualization that is impaired.[10]

Faith as healing grace is intimately connected with faith as elevating grace, in that the former is ordered to the latter. Religious experience develops first of all as humanity's ascent to God, since it reaches from the level of creation. Correspondingly, the non-Christian religions also move in the same direction; they are represented as the work of humanity or as paths of salvation on which it has embarked. However, on closer consideration, humanity's ascent is based on God's descent, inasmuch as this is the only way in which a person can be capable of reaching God; in other words, God has opened up access for humanity by means of his creatures. It follows that the ways of salvation built by humanity are in the last analysis granted by God. If humanity wished to exclude this foundation, its religions would be so presumptuous as to deprive its religious efforts of their very roots. Inasmuch as faith as healing grace indicates such links, it prepares religious experience for the structure of Christianity that is given with elevating grace.

Furthermore, religious experience is freed from error by faith as healing grace, its incompleteness is completed, and its authentic context is perfected. In this way, it takes on a form that is in agreement with the expression of Christianity as prefigured in elevating grace. In this perspective, too, religious experience is thus prepared for Christianity through healing grace.

Revelation and faith as elevating grace go beyond religious experience inasmuch as they open up a wholly new area of truth and life. We are admitted to sharing in the Trinitarian life of the one God, as the eternal Father gives us divine sonship through his Son's becoming man and working our redemption. As true children of God, we are "born of God" (Jn. 1:13), and we are not only called God's children, but are this in all truth (1 Jn. 3:1). Just as we received human nature through birth from our mothers' wombs, by our birth from the eternal Father, we are "partakers of the divine nature" (2 Pet. 1:4). The new life given in this way brings new truth that unveils for us the mysteries it contains and that we proceed to accept in faith.

In this way, religious experience is perfected by faith, and Christianity is introduced. However, since faith has its starting point in revelation from God, Christianity is not the work of people, but is rather the path of salvation built for humanity by God himself, and thus this path is essentially different from the non-Christian religions. Furthermore, Christianity cannot be seen as their equivalent, as a way of salvation like them, alongside or among others. On the contrary, it presents itself as the peerless path to salvation that is superior to all others. It includes the religion of Old-Testament Judaism as a preliminary stage, which also has its origins in divine revelation. Certain elements both of the Christian and the Jewish revelation have been taken up into Islam, and these, as we have already indicated, can also be found in other religions.

On account of its specific nature as described here, Karl Barth preferred no longer to call Christianity a "religion." This shows a dual meaning attributed to the word. In its broader meaning, it indicates every path of salvation of humanity to God, and in its more restricted sense, by contrast, it covers only a path of salvation developed by humanity itself to reach God. As is easy to see, Barth has the more restricted meaning in mind: in this sense, it is true to say that Christianity is not a religion, especially as, according to Barth, it remains tied to sin and hence to error. However, predominant linguistic usage follows the broader meaning, according to which Christianity is also a religion. Nevertheless, this does produce the danger that it may be too closely associated to the other religions and may end up being taken as one of them. Hence, better justice is done to the unique character of Christianity if we contrast it to the religions as something specific and thus refrain from calling it a religion. Even so, we can follow current linguistic practice, provided we respect the specific character of Christianity.[11]

Religious Experience and the Christian Faith

Inasmuch as Christianity lives in the first place from revelation and faith, it does not detach itself from religious experience; indeed, it can in no way exist without it. On the contrary, it opens up humanity to God and makes it receptive to God's action. Indeed, it develops a person into a "hearer of the word," as Karl Rahner puts it: a person who looks out for what may be a word from God and who is ready and capable of receiving it.[12] At the same time, Christianity is augmented by the fact that it is plunged in religious experience, with humanity's profound dimension, whereas without being rooted in this way, it is in the majority of cases only externally acquired. Taken on by others, it is appropriated only rationally, without assuming flesh and blood. By contrast, inasmuch as it becomes one with religious experience, it shares in the character of the latter, which involves the whole human person, and thus itself becomes experienced Christianity. Moreover, this penetration is already achieved by the fact that the revelation and faith of Christianity contain in themselves the basic features of religious experience that had its origins in humanity; they need only their full development and thus lead to experienced faith from within. This is further deepened and perfected by "spiritual experience" (DV 8), that is to say, through the experience that the Holy Spirit effects in us, completing and animating the grace of faith by his gifts. Only a faith that is experienced in this way can face the contestations, especially of our times, and more particularly so when it rises to the level of mystical clairvoyance.

As appears clearly from the foregoing, the revelation and faith of Christianity in no way essentially exclude religious experience. On the contrary, already in their basic structure and all the more in their fully developed form, they circumscribe experience that thus belongs to their constitution. Hence, thanks to its specific nature, faith is open to religious experience, and thus it is no longer true to its nature if it opposes it and drives it out as though it were something hostile to it. In such circumstances, there is often a relativizing conception of faith at work, according to which faith with its provisional truth simply disappears as soon as experience with its definitive truth comes to the fore.[13] However, the fact of the matter is that faith is not a preliminary stage of experience, but rather that experience is the preliminary stage of faith that leads into it without suppressing or destroying it.[14]

In order to clarify the interpenetration of religious experience and Christian faith further, the structural and existential viewpoints must be distinguished from one another. From the structural point of view, the Christian faith as fulfilled by religious experience is evidently superior to religious experience alone, which lacks the explicit encounter with Christian faith. From an existential point of view, however, or according to the actualization that is actually lived out, religious experience and the religions that issue from it can be superior to Christian faith, as can be seen time and again from history. If we are to gain a proper appreciation of this contrast, we must never forget that it must in no way be observed as a general principle; on the contrary, there is also Christianity as lived out fully as well as non-Christian religions that fall short of the full actualization of their demands.

Nonetheless, this contrast surprises us, and we must discover the reason for it. This is no doubt because Christianity comes down from above, whereas the religions ascend from below. Now with the specific nature of what is Christian, the grace of God is given, which in the final analysis is the origin of all that humanity possesses, although this does not exclude its collaboration but, rather, includes it. However, it is possible and it frequently occurs that humanity expects to receive everything from the grace of God alone, and neglects his collaboration. Consequently, we find a divergence between the call of Christianity and the actual life of the Christian individual. Conversely, the adepts of non-Christian religions do not take the grace of God expressly into account, but, on the contrary, feel they are reliant on their own efforts, which therefore often rise to amazing feats and exceedingly harsh practices as well as ingenious methodical systems geared at a remarkable actualization in life of the demands specific to each of the respective religions.

The Disintegration: Modernism and Psychology

In our considerations so far, we have set forth certain of the basic features both of the distinction, as given by revelation, between the Christian faith and human religious experience, and also of the inner unity of this faith and this same experience. Now it is our task to examine important deviations from these contexts, and particularly those whose influence has been felt in the postconciliar period. Here, on the one hand, we have the disintegration of Christian revelation into religious experience, and, on the other hand, the separation of the Christian religion from religious experience. These two tendencies are connected inasmuch as the struggle against disintegration leads to an exaggerated separation, which rebounds into a new disintegration. It is possible to overcome each of these extremes only when the matured twofold unity of revelation and experience is achieved, and this is the goal striven after by the postconciliar development.

The tendencies collectively designated as modernism arrived at the disintegration. This movement came into being at the turn of the twentieth century, and it still exerts an influence on the present-day situation as the questions it raised are not entirely resolved, despite the condemnations of the Church. This battle centered around the relationship of Christianity with religious experience and thus with history, since experience is developed within history. The reply of modernism constituted a short circuit, since it more or less set Christianity on the same level as the non-Christian religions and consequently fell short of its indispensable specific nature. Its attempt at reconciling Christianity with the modern consciousness, characterized by experience and history, failed inasmuch as it led to the disintegration of Christianity. This was all the more radical as the movement slid into a relativistic and irrationalistic interpretation of experience under the influence of history.[15]

Depth psychology is not free of this disintegration, as it is developed by C.G. Jung. His book *Psychology and Religion* already indicates by its title that psychology is innately superior to religion and thus is normative for it.[16] Christianity is viewed in the same way and consequently dissipated into a psychologically interpreted religious experience. It is characteristic of Jung "that it is not a matter of the question of faith, but one of experience" (*PR*, 180), which, however, is "to be taken as what its value is for the individual who has this experience"; here there is "no objective criterion" (*PR*, 91), and thus it is interpreted subjectively. Although religion is an indispensable component of the life of the psyche, today religion is mostly annihilated to the point of the "death of God" (*PR*, 162). Nevertheless, religious experience cannot constitute the basis for "a kind of proof of the existence of God"; on the contrary, we are limited to the "archetypal image of the divinity" (*PR*, 108). Jung knows only "the interior God" (*PR*, 107); he does not wish to equate him with the God of the "profession of faith" (*GesW*, XI, 690). Lastly, God is referred to as being "always the overwhelming psychic factor" (*PR*, 146), who can "signify a power that blesses or destroys" (*PR*, 156). All religions derive from this kind of experience: "Confessions are codified and dogmatized forms of original religious experiences" (*PR*, 16); accordingly, Christianity is only "the formulation of a situation that was prevalent at the beginning of our era and during a series of centuries that followed" (*PR*, 175).[17]

Separation of Experience and History

We have clarified the question of the disintegration of divine revelation into human experience by two examples. It is necessary to protect the autonomy of Christianity against this dissolution, which steals from Christianity the specific element proper to it and thus destroys it. However, this all too easily drove the defendants of Christianity into the other extreme, namely, its separation: the dissolution of Christianity into the purely human led them to separate it from the human dimension. Here an evident role was played by a misunderstanding both of Christianity and of the human dimension.

Christianity was seen all too one-sidedly as revelation by word, whereas revelation by deed, which belongs intimately to it, and above all religious experience were accorded too little attention; indeed, they were largely forgotten. Even those authors who still referred back to revelation by deed went no further than its rational discursive development, and they can hardly be said to have gone on to religious experience, which is at its basis. This failed to assure the inalienable specific character of revelation by word but, rather, endangered it by losing sight of its roots in religious experience. Christianity separated from religious experience is estranged from humanity because it disappears into an abstract distance and is deprived of its living power of attraction.

As concerns the human dimension, the separation was accentuated by the fact that the followers of modernism and psychologism held a view of religious experience in which it ceased to be God's revelation in deed, for they interpreted it as an irrational event springing forth from the subconscious, so that humanity is trapped within its own experiences and does nothing but circle within itself and around itself without ever reaching God, who is infinitely greater.[18] Anyone attempting to implant divine revelation in word into religious experience so greatly misinterpreted in this way is bound to destroy it at the very outset. However, since the defendants of the autonomous character of Christianity frequently no longer saw religious experience except in its misinterpreted form, they were obliged to reject the thesis of revelation in word being rooted in religious experience. For the same reason, they were capable of recognizing revelation in deed as being authentic only in its rational form, and thus they incorporated only this aspect into revelation in word, which they therefore definitively separated from religious experience. Thus, the effect of this misinterpretation of religious experience on those defending the autonomous character of Christianity consolidated the process of separation of relevation in word from religious experience on the basis of a justification that was only apparently valid.

Since religious experience develops within history, history is inseparably linked to experience, and thus it must be recognized and taken seriously, along with experience. The same is true of revelation, which is developed within history as revelation both in word and in deed.[19] However, history poses the basic question of whether historical existence opens up for us only perspectives that are limited within time, and that are hence relative, or whether it also gives us access to truth beyond time, which is hence absolute.[20]

Unfortunately, modernism and psychologism view historicity as relativization, and hence exclude us from absolute truth, granting us access only to relative perspectives. However, since for Christianity, the attaining of absolute truth is of essential importance, the plunging of Christianity into history as misinterpreted in this way becomes equivalent to its dissolution into the likewise misinterpreted human dimension. Those who fought in defense of the autonomous character of Christianity against this disintegration were often influenced by this false interpretation of history, so that they remained oblivious of its true sense. This is why it seemed to them that it was possible to save Christianity from disintegration only by separating it from history. In this way, revelation in word was separated from history for the sake of its metahistorical content, which rendered it prey to a rigidly static, lifeless conceptuality. The same can be observed for revelation in deed, the innate historicity of which was suppressed lest its truth be lost. However, parallel to this, the historical existence of humanity went on, while Christianity became progressively estranged from it, banished as it was into an unreal metahistoricity. As it lost its internal unity with humanity to a far too great an extent, it pined away to a superstructure that became devoid of life, since it had only a perpetually diminishing share in the living character proper to humanity, and consequently no longer had much or anything more to do with experience, which is one of humanity's distinguishing features.

Return to Experience: Difficulties

The crisis inherent in this situation was clearly perceived by the Second Vatican Council, which explains why it took pains in many ways to bring Christianity back close to humanity and to root it in its experience. This was above all the direction taken by the Pastoral Constitution on the Church in the Modern World (*Gaudium et spes*). The same direction was taken by the reform of the liturgy with the introduction of the language of the people (*Sacrosanctum concilium*). In this context, we can also situate the Decree on Ecumenism (*Unitatis redintegratio*) and the Declaration on Religious Freedom (*Dignitatis humanae*), as well as the Declaration we have already cited on the Relation of the Church to Non-Christian Religions (*Nostra aetate*). In all the documents, we find evidence of the effort to break through the shackles of separationist isolation and to open up new paths to the unity of Christianity with humanity. Without any doubt, this brought a breath of fresh air into Christian life, which aroused many hopes and found its expression in many different efforts at renewal. Here we should mention the widespread practice of meditation and the charismatic movement with its link back to the early Church.[21] The message of freedom engendered particular enthusiasm. The Council proclaims that Christ "by his obedience unto death, opened the blessed way of the liberty of the sons of God to all men" (*LG* 37). Here the Council refers to Saint Paul's statement: "You were called to freedom" (Gal. 5:13).

However, the abuse of freedom was not lacking. Warnings against this are already to be found in the New Testament (Gal. 5:13 and 1 Pet. 2:16), and it often degenerated into unbridled capriciousness. Driven on by the burning desire to overcome the separation between the Christian and human dimensions, many plunged into a dangerous watering down of Christianity. Thus, mysteries of the faith were frequently brushed aside or reduced to aspects of human existence, and here the divinity of Christ in particular began to be eclipsed. The same occurred as concerns moral behavior, the norms of which often evaporated, to be adapted to the inclinations of people, conditioned by time. In order to eliminate the separation without the disintegration, not only must Christianity be attuned to the specific character of the contemporary human dimension, but the latter must also be purified in the perspective of the Christian dimension.

Despite all the efforts made, the attempts we have mentioned have not been successful in effectively eliminating the separation. It is still true that Christianity often does not arrest people's attention and fails to reach their hearts. For many it has nothing to say and leaves them indifferent, which is why they turn away from it and often quietly abandon it. They consider it has nothing to offer them, and so they take no interest in it. A reason for this can be found in the fact that a contemporary person demands experience, without which his or her attention can hardly be arrested any more.[22] Our Church services following the liturgical reform are often so impoverished, especially when almost mechanically performed by an overworked and somewhat superficial priest, that they can hardly be said to communicate any experience any more. The same holds good for Christian communities, which often can hardly be said to offer the welcoming embrace of true community to all, and thus no longer have any hold on the majority. Consequently, many people, especially the young, turn to ideological associations that promise them religious and community experience for which in certain sects they are often prepared to make incredible sacrifices for fascinating gurus. The yearning for narcotics is part of the same picture, and this has already troubled and destroyed large numbers of people.

Return to Experience: New Points of Departure

In order to overcome the separation and avoid the disintegration, Christians are today following paths that aid human and spiritual experience to break through. In this way, they are preparing the interpenetration of experience and Christianity, whereby not only is experience developed and purified, but Christianity is brought to bear as a living experience. However, since this procedure finds few points of departure in the Christian tradition, lost in the process of separation and hence rigidified, these people enrich themselves from the wisdom of the Far East, which has come closer to us through the contemporary growing unity of the world. This produces very rich ideas of a methodical nature that must, of course, be carefully distinguished from the ideological background of Buddhism or Hinduism. However, since this distinction is not always sufficiently clearly drawn, it brings about a new disintegration of Christianity, whereby instead of an encounter with the personal God, we find a pantheizing assimilation into an impersonal absolute and an attitude that is closer to self-redemption than to redemption as granted by God's grace in Christ. This state

of affairs represents a totally new chapter in the relations of Christians with the non-Christian religions. Although we are at the
very beginning of this new chapter, we receive significant help
from the open attitude of the Council.

This new contrast demands first of all an awakening of the
Christian tradition that is in no way to be seen as the poor
relation of the East and that transmits to us the Christianity, rich
in experience, of former centuries. This awakening is rendered
easier by the fact that this tradition never actually died out, but
has continued to be active to the present day in many of its
directions and in certain circles. It is above all in the contemplative orders that the traditional spirituality is handed on not only
through theoretical instruction, but also through practical training. The interior life radiates from such islands as these by means
of lectures and courses, quiet retreat days, and especially by stays
in monasteries, and reach the ever more numerous people who
realize how much they are in need of this deeper dimension. In
this way, rationalistic reductionism is gradually being overcome.
It had neutralized the effect of spiritual exercises, but in its place
people are now once again learning to use and to profit from the
methodical instruction of the masters of the West, amongst
whom we would mention Ignatius of Loyola. Integrated into this
context, the wisdom of the Far East has had—and continues to
have—important help to offer for the renewal of a living, profound religious experience. The whole fullness of this cannot, of
course, be attained without the operation of the Spirit of God,
who "helps us in our weakness" by his gifts that grant us experience (Rom. 8:26ff.).

The basic attitude here matures slowly, and renders fruitful the
hearing of the word of God, which we encounter in the Holy
Scriptures and in preaching. If we study "the goodness of the
Word of God" (Heb. 6:5) not only scientifically, but apply it to
ourselves personally and let ourselves be gripped and changed by
it, we shall grow ever more powerfully into religious experience.
Here precious help is given by preaching, even when it is addressed to one who is already himself gripped and changed.[23]
Liturgical celebration has the same effect when it is performed as
an event that raises people above the level of everyday life and
leads them into profundity. Through its words and actions, the
celebration of the Mass is particularly able to convey religious
experience. At the same time, holy actions performed in com-

mon create a community that is animated from within, and this supports the individual and fills him with joy. It continues beyond its bounds into the profane world through works of charity, and it provides secutity. [24]

Hearing the word of God and liturgical celebration become effective for religious experience to the extent that meditative interiority is alive in them. This has embarked on a new and very promising beginning in our days through the unification of the Christian tradition with ideas from the Far East. It is increasingly practiced by clergy and laity, both young and old, and they achieve considerable depths of profundity. Here they proceed from conceptual thought to metaconceptual experience. Instead of concerning themselves with ideas they themselves have produced, they let themselves be reached, overwhelmed, and changed by the most intimate mysteries, by the divine foundation and the reality of grace. They enter into the hidden dialogue in which humanity truly encounters God and is united with him, with the incarnate and risen Christ as mediator. The whole person, including his or her bodily nature, shares in the success of this process, and therefore bodily posture and breathing are of considerable importance. The untiring practice of this meditation produces to a great extent the purification and development as well as the full power of religious experience. Its maturity is greatly assisted by the aid of a life-giving spiritual father. This leads to the meditative character of the individual's whole existence, which affects his everyday life, even for the least of the brethren (Mt. 25:31–46). [25]

By following the path we have indicated here, we are responding to the fundamental concern of the Council, which was to renew and deepen the unity of the Christian and human dimensions. The Christian dimension becomes human as it fulfills with a surfeit of riches the expectations of the human heart that reach their climax in religious experience. [26] The human dimension becomes Christian as a person is soaked in the Spirit of God and receives the grace of the divine life, becoming "the spiritual man" (1 Cor. 2:15). In this way, the separation is overcome without the disintegration, and thus at the same time the true relationship of Christianity with the non-Christian religions is manifested. Christianity surpasses them insofar as revelation in word and grace are not dissolved into what is purely human. It indwells them insofar as the Christian dimension is ever at work within them in a hidden manner. Thus, it is not separated from them, and they move toward it as to their fulfillment.

Translated from the German by Ronald Sway.

Notes

1. J. Lotz, *Transzendentale Erfahrung* (Freiburg im Breisgau, 1978).
2. P. Rossano, "Teologia e Religioni: un problema contemporaneo," in R. Latourelle and G. O'Collins (eds.), *Problemi e Prospettive di teologia fondamentale* (Brescia, 1980), 359–378.
3. R. Latourelle, *Révélation dans le christianisme et les autres Religions* (Rome, 1971), 41–74 ("La Spécificité de la Révélation chrétienne").
4. K. Rahner, "Das Christentum und die nichtsch nichtchristlichen Religionen," in *idem, Schriften zur Theologie,* 5 (Einsiedeln, 1962), 136–158; J. Heislbetz, *Theologische Gründe der nichtchristlichen Religionen,* Quaestiones disputatae 3 (Freiburg im Breisgau, 1966); H. Fries, "Religionloses Christentum," in C. Hörgle *et al.* (eds.), *Wesen und Weisen der Religion* (Munich, 1969), 267–281; P. Schwarzenau, *Der grössere Gott. Christentum und Weltreligionen* (Stuttgart, 1977); A. Schweitzer, *Das Christentum und die Weltreligionen* (Munich, new edition, 1978); W. Strolz and H. Waldenfels (eds.), *Christliche Grundlagen das Dialogs mit den Weltreligionen* (Freiburg im Breisgau, 1983); W. Strolz and S. Üda (eds.), *Offenbarung als Heilserfahrung im Christentum, Hinduismus und Buddhismus* (Freiburg im Breisgau, 1983).
5. The foundation of experience in the absolute is a link between West and East: H. Waldenfels, *Faszination des Buddhismus. Zum christlich-buddhistischen Dialog* (Mainz, 1982).
6. Since today it is often the case that all that is left of religious experience is the experience of nothingness, B. Welte, *Das Licht des Nichts. Von der Möglichkeit neuer religiöser Erfahrung* (Dusseldorf, 1980), takes his lead from this and shows how the initially ambiguous idea of nothingness can give rise to a new religious experience. See also: H. Waldenfels, *Absolutes Nichts* (Freiburg in Breisgau, 1976); H.S. Hisamatsu, *Die Fülle des Nichts. Vom Wesen des Zens* (Pfullingen, 1975).
7. According to K. Rahner, God's will to save implies that in each individual a hidden, nonverbalized revelation event takes place.
8. Thomas Aquinas, *Summa Theologiae,* q. 1, a. 1.
9. DS, 3004–3005.
10. J. Lotz, *In jedem Menschen steckt ein Atheist* (Frankfurt, 1981), 118–129.
11. H. Kahlefeld *et al.* (eds.), *Christentum und Religion* (Regensburg, 1966).

12. K. Rahner, *Hörer des Wortes. Zur Grundlegung einer Religionsphilosophie* (Munich, 1963²).

13. Thus, the human dimension deviates, for example, if someone comes to the experience of Zen and then considers that he or she no longer needs Christianity because he or she has now attained something greater.

14. In recent years, there has been a movement away from Christianity to the religions of the Far East. One of the principal reasons for this is the demand for experience that these religions appear to fulfill, whereas in Christianity, it is thought that this longed-for fulfillment is no longer to be found because of the lack of experience. Here we have a powerful stimulus for Christianity to develop the experience that is proper to it.

15. L. Scheffczyk, "Wirkungen des Modernismus auf Theologie und Kirche," in A. Langner (ed.), *Katholizismus und philosophische Strömungen in Deutschland* (Paderborn, 1982), 43–58; N. Trippen, "Gesellschaftliche und politische Auswirkungen der Modernismuskrise in Deutschland," in *ibid.*, 59–103.

16. Zurich, 1940.

17. Recently, religious experience has been likewise relativized in K. Walf (ed.), *Stille Fluchten. Zur Veränderung des religiösen Bewusstseins* (Munich, 1983). This work contains the following titles: "Derivations of God from the impersonal absolute, or the interior self under the influence of Jung"; "Feminist theology"; and "Neomodernist disintegration."

18. DS, 3475–3481.

19. K. Rahner, "Weltgeschichte und Heilsgeschichte," in *idem, Schriften zur Theologie*, 5, 115–135.

20. W. Kasper, *Das Absolute in der Geschichte* (Mainz, 1965); *idem, Glaube und Geschichte* (Mainz, 1970); *idem, Absolutheit des Christentums*, Quaestiones disputatae 79 (Freiburg im Breisgau, 1977).

21. This finds convincing expression in the writings of H. Mühlen.

22. E. Biser, "Glaube in dürftiger Zeit," *Stimme der Zeit*, 108 (1983), 169–181, esp. 179: "Alles Interesse konzentrierte sich auf das Erfahrungsmoment." Also: ". . . richtete sich die religiöse Sinnerwartung so entschieden auf die Erfahrungsdaten, dass diese geradezu zur Bedingung der Glaubensbereitschaft wurden." "Gib mir Erfahrung, und ich glaube, lautete der unausgesprochene Grundsatz."

23. J. Goldbrunner, *Bibelkurs. Besinnungen auf die Heilsgeschichte*, 3 vols. (Freiburg im Breisgau, 1983–1984).

24. J. Pieper, *Zustimmung zur Welt. Eine Theorie des Festes* (Munich, 1963).

25. J. Lotz, *Kurze Anleitung zum Meditieren* (Frankfurt, 1973).

26. J. Lotz, *Was gibt das Christentum dem Menschen? Grunderwartungen und Erfüllung* (Frankfurt, 1979).

CHAPTER 48

From Monologue to Dialogue
in Conversations with Nonbelievers
or The Difficult Search
for Dialogue Partners

Bernd Groth, S.J.

Summary

The Second Vatican Council also wished to enter into dialogue with nonbelievers. For this purpose, and also for the study of the phenomenon of atheism, a special Vatican secretariat *pro non credentibus* was set up. On the basis of the experiences of this secretariat, this article concentrates on three problem areas concerning dialogue with nonbelievers: (1) the meaning of dialogue with nonbelievers must be understood from the changed attitude of the Church with respect to the world; (2) despite the importance attributed to this dialogue by the Church, it appears to be difficult to find dialogue partners; and (3) this experience gives rise to certain theological considerations.

———
———

Since 1965 there has been a special "Secretariat for Nonbelievers"—a novelty in the history of the Church.[1] The secretariat has a twofold task: (1) "the study of atheism, in order to examine its various causes more thoroughly," and (2) "as far as is possible, to start a dialogue with nonbelievers themselves, who sincerely accept collaboration."[2] The setting up of this secretariat with its special goals was intended to be a response to the desire of the Second Vatican Council, which stated that the Church was concerned with a deeper understanding of modern atheism and its manifold causes (cf. GS 21b). Here the Council is of the opinion that all people should also work together "to establish right order in this world where all live together. This certainly cannot be done without a dialogue that is sincere and prudent" (GS 21f).

The Secretariat for Nonbelievers has now been in existence for twenty years, and this is sufficient grounds for according a rather more thorough consideration to certain questions concerning the Church's attitude to the nonbelieving world. What is the true significance of the dialogue with nonbelievers for the Church itself? What has been achieved since the Council in order to gain a deeper understanding of atheism? Lastly, what is the situation concerning dialogue and collaboration with nonbelievers? The considerations that follow are concerned with these and similar questions, and are principally concentrated on three areas: (1) the meaning of the dialogue with nonbelievers can be seen from the changed attitude of the Church with respect to the world; (2) despite the importance attributed to this dialogue by the Church, it appears from statements made by representatives of the Secretariat for Nonbelievers to be difficult to find dialogue partners; (3) this experience on the part of the secretariat has produced certain information for the desired dialogue itself as well as for a deeper understanding of contemporary atheism.

The Changed Attitude of the Church

The Second Vatican Council marked a fundamental turning point in the Church's attitude to the world. This transformation is above all reflected in the Pastoral Constitution on the Church in the Modern World, *Gaudium et spes*, but also in other documents—for example, the Decree on Ecumenism, *Unitatis redintegratio*, or the important Declaration on Religious Freedom, *Dignitatis humanae*. This new attitude on the part of the Church has been described as being a change "from opposition to dialogue,"[3] for since the beginning of the "modern age" (seventeenth to eighteenth centuries), there had been a sometimes harsh contrast between the Catholic Church and "the world."

Although this contrast was at its most extreme during the pontifi-
cates of Gregory XVI and Pius IX in the nineteenth century, it
continued by and large right up to the Second Vatican Council.
It was only with the Council that "dialogue with all men" was
sanctioned (cf. GS 92) as the proper attitude of the Church to
the modern world. The basic nature of this decision is revealed in
a text from Pope Paul VI's "dialogue encyclical" *Ecclesiam suam*
(1964), found in the center of the document:

> As is clear, the relationships between the Church and the
> world can assume many mutually different aspects. Theoreti-
> cally speaking, the Church could set its mind on reducing such
> relationships to a minimum, endeavoring to isolate itself from
> dealings with secular society; just as it could set itself the task
> of pointing out the evils that can be found in secular society,
> condemning them and declaring crusades against them, so also
> it could approach so close to secular society as to strive to exert
> a proponderant influence on it or even to exercise a theocratic
> power over it, and so on. But it seems to Us that the relation-
> ship of the Church to the world, without precluding other
> legitimate forms of expression, can be represented better in a
> dialogue, not, of course, a dialogue in a univocal sense, but
> rather a dialogue adapted to the nature of the interlocutor and
> to factual circumstances (the dialogue with a child differs from
> that with an adult; that with a believer from that with an
> unbeliever). This has been suggested by the custom, which
> has by now become widespread, of conceiving the relation-
> ships between the sacred and the secular in terms of the trans-
> forming dynamism of modern society, in terms of the pluralism
> of its manifestations, likewise in terms of the maturity of man,
> be he religious or not, enabled through secular education to
> think, to speak, and to act through the dignity of dialogue.[4]

The Pope thus gives two possible attitudes of the Church
toward the world with regard to such dialogue, although he then
rejects both. The first attitude strives for a separation of Church
and world (a minimum of relationship), whereas the second proposes to mix the two spheres (influence and domination). Both
these wrong attitudes can be explained by the "divine and human
constitution" of the Church.[5] This creates a dual tension: "utopian" and "apocalyptic." Both of these tensions reproduce, as it
were, the dual reality of the Church on the historical and social

levels. The apocalyptic tension tends toward the separation of Church and world, despising "earthly" values and hence overemphasizing what are understood as "heavenly" values. This tension can escalate to the point of opposition between Church and world. In contrast to this, the utopian tension aims at acceptance of the reality of the world in order to Christianize this reality, so as to build up a Christian world. Whereas the apocalyptic temptation consists of despising the world (*contemptus mundi*) and fleeing the world (*fuga mundi*), the utopian temptation is to let the state degenerate into an instrument of religion (*instrumentum religionis*), with the help of which the Christian society (*societas christiana*) is to be built up.

Roughly speaking, in the first centuries of Christianity, separation of the Church and the world was predominant. In the Middle Ages, there was largely a reciprocal interpenetration of the two spheres. The opposition we have just mentioned between Church and world in modern times was also behind a radical refusal of modern values (for example, freedom of religion and conscience, tolerance) on the part of the Popes. In contrast to this, at least in theory and principle, encounter and dialogue are nowadays the determining features of the relationship between Church and world.[6] Suspicion and mistrust have been replaced by the "sympathy" with which the Church attempts to view the world.[7] Consequently, the Council also emphasizes the close solidarity of the Church with the whole human family in the Preface to its Pastoral Constitution:

> The joy and hope, the grief and anguish of the men of our time, especially of those who are poor or afflicted in any way, are the joy and hope, the grief and anguish of the followers of Christ as well. Nothing that is genuinely human fails to find an echo in their hearts. For theirs is a community composed of men, of men who, united in Christ and guided by the Holy Spirit, press onwards towards the kingdom of the Father and are bearers of a message of salvation intended for all men. That is why Christians cherish a feeling of deep solidarity with the human race and its history (GS 1).

The same spirit prompted the Council to try to present the Church as a "service" rather than a "power." Thus, we read in the Decree on the Missionary Activity of the Church, *Ad gentes:*

The presence of Christians among . . . human groups should be one that is animated by that love with which we are loved by God, who desires that we should love each other with that self-same love. Christian charity is extended to all without distinction of race, social condition, or religion, and seeks neither gain nor gratitude. Just as God loves us with a gratuitous love, so too the faithful, in their charity, should be concerned for mankind, loving it with that same love with which God sought man. . . . Christians ought to interest themselves, and collaborate with others, in the right ordering of social and economic affairs. . . . The Church, nevertheless, has no desire to become involved in the government of the temporal order. It claims no other competence besides that of faithfully serving men in charity with the help of God (AG 12a–c).

Thus, the Council clearly and unambiguously refuses the utopistic temptation. It justifies its refusal with the quite different task entrusted to Christ's disciples:

They are not working for the merely material progress or prosperity of men; but in teaching the religious and moral truths, which Christ illumined with his light, they seek to enhance the dignity of men and promote fraternal unity, and, in this way, are gradually opening a wider approach to God (AG 12d).

The "soul," as it were, of the Church's new attitude to the world is universal dialogue, which integrates the Church into the whole human family. In the framework of this universal dialogue, the dialogue with nonbelievers maybe has a decisive role to play. It will show how seriously the Church takes its new attitude to the world.

For our part, our eagerness for such dialogue, conducted with appropriate discretion and leading to truth by way of love alone, excludes nobody; we would like to include those who respect outstanding human values without realizing who the author of those values is, as well as those who oppose the Church and persecute it in various ways. Since God the Father is the beginning and the end of all things, we are all called to be brothers; we ought to work together without violence and without deceit to build up the world in a spirit of genuine peace (GS 92e).

This text refers to the task of the Secretariat for Nonbelievers,[8] which is precisely that of ensuring that the nonbelievers, the opponents of the Church and its persecutors, as spoken of in *Gaudium et spes* 92, are not excluded from the universal dialogue.

The Difficulty in Finding Dialogue Partners

What results have been obtained so far in the dialogue with nonbelievers? The task with which the secretariat was entrusted seems extraordinarily difficult, not to say completely impossible. Paul VI had already expressed doubts as to whether it was possible to have a dialogue with those who deny the very existence of God:

The first of these circles is immense. Its limits stretch beyond our sight and merge with the horizon. It is that of mankind as such, the world. We gauge the distance that lies between us and the world; yet we do not consider the world a stranger. All things human are our concern. We share with the whole of mankind a common nature; human life with all its gifts and problems. . . . We realize, however, that in this limitless circle there are many, very many unfortunately, who profess no religion; and we are aware also that there are many who profess themselves, in various ways, to be atheists. We know that some of these proclaim their godlessness openly and uphold it as a program of human education and political conduct, in the ingenuous but fatal belief that they are setting men free from false and outworn notions about life and the world and are, they claim, putting in their place a scientific conception that is in conformity with the needs of modern progress. This is the most serious problem of our time. We are firmly convinced that the theory on which the denial of God is based is utterly erroneous. . . . Dialogue in such conditions is very difficult, not to say impossible, although, even today, we have no preconceived intention of excluding the persons who profess these systems and belong to these regimes. For the lover of truth discussion is always possible. The difficulties are enormously increased by obstacles of the moral order: by the absence of sufficient freedom of thought and action and by the perversion of discussion so that the latter is not made use of to seek and express objective truth but to serve predetermined utilitarian ends. This is what puts an end to dialogue. The Church of Silence, for example, speaks only by her sufferings. . . .[9]

From the general context, it is clear that here the expression "denial of God" (*negatio Dei*) implies principally atheism as propagated in socialist states where the Church is deprived of the right to religious propaganda. In view of the difficult situation of the Church in these countries, the Pope did not wish to give up the hope that "they may one day be able to enter into a more positive dialogue with the Church than the present one which we now of necessity deplore and lament."[10] We must, moreover, not overlook the fact not only that the militant atheism of the socialist states exists, but that atheism is a very widespread phenomenon of our times,[11] which also includes what is known as indifferentism.

The experiences of the Secretariat for Nonbelievers concerns the practical dialogue between believers and nonbelievers would, however, seem at first to point in a different direction. The "springtime of dialogue"[12] that flourished in the years immediately following Vatican II is linked with the conversations of the Society of St. Paul, which took place in Salzburg (1965), Herrenchiemsee (1966), and Marienbad, Czechoslovakia (1967). Christians and Marxists, especially intellectuals on both sides, spoke together, and this guaranteed a certain openness from the very outset. The invasion by the Warsaw Pact states closed the period of the "Prague Spring," which had also rendered possible the springtime of dialogue between Christians and Marxists. The Secretariat for Nonbelievers was behind the foundation of the German-language periodical *Internationale Dialog-Zeitschrift*, which was unfortunately short-lived (1968–1974).[13] Apart from various research projects and consultations, "the public dialogue between believers and unbelievers was a rare occurrence, and when it did take place, it produced only meager results."[14]

A particular difficulty seems to be that of awakening interest in such dialogue on the part of nonbelievers who are not Marxists. Most nonbelievers appear to show no interest in dialogue.[15] Yet this lack of interest is surely sometimes based totally on the conviction that they can learn little or nothing from believers and that they cannot even begin to hold a discussion with them because of their dogmatism?

In 1980, Monsignor (later, Cardinal) Paul Poupard, the former Rector of the Institut Catholique in Paris, succeeded Cardinal König as head of the Secretariat for Nonbelievers. Poupard spoke of the difficulty in finding suitable dialogue partners in two interviews he granted in 1985 to the German publications *Der Spiegel* and *Herderkorrespondenz*. In the interview in *Der Spiegel*, [16] a number of critical questions were put to the president of the secretariat. It was stated that the Church obstinately refused pertinent answers to problems of modern life. Hence, the interviewer continued, nonbelief was a necessary consequence for many. Poupard countered this by stating that people had not yet properly discovered the modern answers of the Council. The editors of *Der Spiegel* also felt the Church was lacking in the capacity to learn that is seen in science, which learns from its mistakes. It is like trying to fit a square peg into a round hole to try to reconcile the search for truth with the claim that one already possesses it. The criticism was concentrated on the basic question of "whether the Church is capable of thinking so openly that nonbelievers will listen to it once more." The cardinal replied to this that however much the Church might reform itself, the basic problem was that man wants to be God. In the last analysis, the question at stake is which nonbelievers one is talking to. Poupard admitted the difficulties his secretariat had to overcome in this respect.

> In contrast to the other two pontifical secretariats concerned with dialogue—the Secretariat for the Promotion of the Unity of Christians and the Secretariat for Non-Christians—I have no dialogue partners on the international level. There is no forum for international atheism, since many atheists are inclined towards individualism.

The editors wanted to know why, for example, he did not have talks with the Italian Marxists who were seeking a dialogue wth the Catholics. The cardinal replied that this was a task for Italian Catholics. Then, *Der Spiegel* suggested, the dialogue is really a monologue. The cardinal replied: "I will admit that we have great difficulties in being taken seriously by people as valid dialogue partners."

Shortly after this, a brief reflection on the problems of this interview in *Der Spiegel* appeared in the Catholic periodical *Christ in der Gegenwart*.[17] The author of this article observed that the interview was impressive evidence of the rift that continued to exist between the religious and secular worlds of language and thought. As an example of this, he cited the problem of reconciling the search for truth and the possession of truth, and Poupard's distinction between a hierarchical ordering of the Church, which derives from the gospel, and the contemporary division of the Church into Congregations, the Holy See, and the Vatican, which is the work of people. The editors found this distinction simply incomprehensible. The author of the article was doubtless not so far off the mark when he concluded:

> Armed with a language which is at best comprehensible only within the Church, we cannot fight the battle with atheism. It is of no use either simply to have a better public relations machine, or to replace old forms of publicity, apologetics and "propaganda" with a more lively Church management. The dialogue with atheism should and must enter a new phase. For this, Christians need the courage to develop a new language which will break up the old models and penetrate the doubts of our existence.

In the *Herderkorrespondenz* interview with Cardinal Poupard,[18] the same question is raised concerning specific dialogue partners:

> But what is the situation as concerns dialogue partners, especially in the case of the secretariat? . . . Agnostics and atheists, apart from state atheism of a communist type, are not generally very organized people, or if they are, they are more likely to organize themselves against the Church than for a dialogue with it.

Here the cardinal's reply is the same as in the *Der Spiegel* interview:

> You are right. In comparison with the other dialogue secretariats, the search for dialogue partners is more difficult in our

case. . . . As the heritage of the Enlightenment, the Encyclopedists and European free-thinking, we have a long tradition of
"free spirits." Those who follow this tendency, whether they be
a-religious, agnostics or atheists, are mostly people who do not
take kindly to others speaking in their name. The only association with which the secretariat has maintained very stable relations is the International Association of Humanists in Utrecht.
They are free-thinkers in the sense of the Enlightenment.

Unfortunately, this conversation did not dwell any further on
this problem, but then turned its attention to other subjects.

Practical and Theological Consequences

Although the following considerations concentrate on the difficulty of the Secretariat for Nonbelievers in finding dialogue partners, we would not contest the fact that here and there discussions
between Christians and nonbelievers were and still are possible.
Here we would exclude the problem of dialogue between Christians and Marxists from socialist states. The secretariat's experience is primarily concerned with the geographical area of the so-
called "Western World" (Western Europe and North America).
Granted the complexity of the overall problem, here we can naturally not deal with all the questions that can be posed in this
connection. We therefore venture into only three problem areas
which, however, seem to be particularly important.

1. Despite the position of Cardinal Poupard, who refused in
his conversation with *Herderkorrespondenz* to speak of a "contemporary post-Christian situation,"[19] we have little difficulty in
recognizing the contemporary situation as being not only "post-
Christian" but also "postatheist." Whether we describe the new
situation as "secular" or not is really not of such great importance. During the latter years of his life, the late Karl Rahner
untiringly drew attention to this quite new situation:

The atheism we are faced with nowadays is not—despite all the
contexts that should not be denied—the atheism of the Enlightenment, nor is it the atheism presumed as evident or propagated
by criticism of religion in the nineteenth century, especially in
Feuerbach and Marx. Whilst contemporary atheism may once

again appear in the most varied forms with very different social premises, all contemporary atheisms do present common premises and features which permit us to speak of contemporary atheism in the singular. It is always an atheism conditioned by contemporary rationalistic and technical society.[20]

Rahner is of the opinion that despite all its readiness for dialogue, the Church has not yet recognized the reality of the situation to a sufficient degree. Thus, true contemporary atheism is as follows:

The majority of contemporary atheists in the East and in the West consists of people for whom the question of God is not a problem that really troubles and torments them. To a great extent, the experience of the existentially unavoidable nature of the question of God still needs to be wakened.[21]

Rahner's observations can easily be filled out and confirmed by sociological research. According to the sociologist Gerhard Schmidtchen, contemporary social systems

. . . have long since left the phase of actual secularization, and they produce their own independent truths, lifestyles and personal identities, or else deformations of these, which no longer bear any relation to the Christian message or to anything that could, even by the broadest of interpretations, be understood as such.[22]

In this context, Schmidtchen refers to Max Weber, who at the turn of the twentieth century saw the "religious features" effaced in modern industrial societies. Schmidtchen understands "dechristianization" as the modern society's no longer needing Christianity, but organizing everything itself. The process of dechristianization generates a social situation in which

. . . the Church's message of how one should live, believe and feel slides into the area of the incomprehensible. What the Church has to say can then no longer be put into practice in everyday life. For many, participation in Church life means being penalized by conflicts of orientation.[23]

In the second part of his article, Schmidtchen analyzes dechristianization as the "enfeeblement of ecclesiastically institutional
Christian identity." Formerly, he says, there was a Christian
presence in our society, extending well beyond the framework of
the active parish. However, he considers that in the long run,
"outside the institution of the Church, there can be no Christianity that can be meaningfully called by this name."

2. If all this is true, we may ask the theological question of
whether we can still meaningfully speak of atheism as "nonbelief" or as a conscious negation of God. What does it really
mean for theological reflection and the Church's preaching if we
are now confronted with a situation that, to adopt the words of
Karl Marx, no longer needs even "the atheistic mediation"?[24] In
the act of nonbelief, there is still something of a conscious refusal
of something with which one has come to grips, a negative
response. But as regards modern atheism, this can no longer be
said to be the case. Rather, the word "God" no longer plays any
role in the modern understanding of reality.

Here we must contradict Karl Rahner, who considered that
the word "God" could not disappear, but would remain.[25] Of
course, he was right inasmuch as the word "God" will survive in
dictionaries. However, it will no longer possess any existential
meaning for people, since they no longer have any idea of what is
to be understood by it. Hence, contemporary nonbelief is based
on a deeper problem. If we are to take the sociological description of the situation into account, the contemporary spiritual
situation must be described in theological terms as a situation of
"God-less-ness." Above all, in the contemporary dialogue with
nonbelievers, we have the task of

. . . bringing the discussion on language concerning God out
of the area of simple misunderstandings and, rather, of polariz-
ing it to the actual antithesis which becomes visible only once
the problem of atheism is developed in the context of the
problem of Godlessness.[26]

In biblical language, "Godlessness" means that man is incapable
on his own of building up a relationship with God. It is God who
takes the initiative in this relationship. He leads man, as it were,
out of his Godlessness (cf. Rom. 4:5; Eph. 2:12).

3. The biblical experience of God includes observations that

are sometimes all too easily swept under the rug. The initiative always comes from God: he shares himself, turns to man and speaks to him. Left to himself, man is capable only of "idols," which are therefore criticized by the prophets as the work of human hands and have nothing to do with the living God of the Bible. It is not man who seeks and encounters God, but the opposite that is true: God seeks man out. The Old Testament expresses this experience in the explanation of the name of Yahweh as "I am that I am" (Ex. 3:14). In the New Testament, God seeks out man in Jesus Christ (cf. Eph. 2:12).

If we now confront the contemporary spiritual situation with the biblical experience of God, we reach a negative conclusion: the question of God is no longer one that worries secular humanity. Its situation does not even permit the posing of this question. Humanity and its experience of the world no longer give it any occasion for this. On the other hand—from a positive point of view—this means that the question of God is only posed in its real significance when the individual is confronted with the Christian message, which claims to be the "Word of God" (cf. DV 1–6). It is only when someone is struck by the Christian message that he begins to wonder what the word "God" means in this context. If it is true that in the Christian message, it is God who communicates himself, "belief" in the Christian sense means living in communion with God. From this point we may, so to speak, ask retrospectively what the individual was before his encounter with the Christian message, and in what theological situation he or she was living. The answer to this retrospective question can be given with Saint Paul: "You were at that time separated from Christ, alienated from the commonwealth of Israel, and strangers to the covenants of promise, having no hope and without God in the world" (Eph. 2:12).

There is one last problem. How can we speak of God today, in the situation we have described, in a way that makes it clear that we are really speaking of God? How can access be conveyed to secular man to the reality that the Christian message refers to as God? Since the Bible itself introduces God as the Creator (cf. Gen. 1–2), God must be presented as he "without whom nothing is." Thus, language about God must acquire a meaning that speaks to our reality. This means we can speak about God only if we are basically speaking of human reality. This leads to the following demand as a rule for dialogue: when Christians speak of reality, it must be made comprehensible why they then also speak of God.[27] This "rule of context," which here can only be roughly indicated, is intended to avoid statements concerning God being considered meaningless, and thus to unblock dialogue.[28]

However, the rule of context and all that has been said concerning it are still not enough. Alongside the so-called "golden rule" (cf., for example, Matthew 7:12: "Whatever you wish that men would do for you, do so to them"), a second basic rule of dialogue can be formulated.[29] Readiness for discussion and the effort at comprehensibility are not enough to ensure real dialogue. The will for dialogue must be practically expressed by my enabling my dialogue partner to enter into dialogue with me. Understanding the other means giving space for expression. This is also fundamentally true for the Church's dialogue with nonbelievers. And it could then permit the previous monologue actually to become a dialogue.

Translated from the German by Ronald Sway.

Notes

1. In its edition of 9 April 1965, *L'Osservatore Romano* announced the setting up of a Secretariat for Nonbelievers. Cardinal Franz König, Archbishop of Vienna, was nominated by Pope Paul VI as the first President, and Father Vincenzo Miano, S.D.B., the first Secretary.

2. On the basis of the statements of Vatican II on atheism (cf. GS 19–21), the aims of the secretariat were specified by the Apostolic Constitution *Regimini Ecclesiae universae* of 15 August 1967, from which the quotations are taken; AAS, 59 (1967), 920.

3. Cf. the editorial "Dall'opposizione al dialogo. La 'svolta' del Vaticano II nel rapporto tra Chiesa e mondo moderno," *La Civiltà Cattolica*, 3256 (15 February 1986), 313–324.

4. AAS, 56 (1964), 609–659, here 643–644; English translation by the Vatican Press (Boston, 1964), 37.

5. Cf. SC 2; LG 8a; Salvatore Nicolosi, *Utopia e apocalisse. Cristianesimo e temporalità* (Rome, 1982), 15ff.

6. Concerning this rough outline, cf. Nicolosi, *Utopia e apocalisse*, 16–64; Giuseppe De Rosa, *Il dialogo con gli atei* (Rome, 1965), 1–12.

7. Cf. De Rosa, *Il dialogo con gli atei*, 8; also the editorial "Dall'opposizione al dialogo," 322f.

8. Cf. the commentary on this passage by C. Moeller, *LThK*, 3, 590.

9. AAS, 56 (1964), 650–652; English translation 43–45.

10. *Ibid.*, 654; English translation 47.

11. The expression employed in the text, describing atheism as "the most serious problem of our time" (*res gravissima, quae nostris contingunt temporibus*) refers, strictly speaking, only to militant atheism as mentioned here. The text does not permit us to employ this expression for atheism in general, as many authors do, referring to this passage.

12. Cf. Francesco Skoda, "El diálogo entre creyentes y no creyentes en la experiencia del Secretariado para los no creyentes," *Atheism and Dialogue*, 20/1 (1985), 71–76, esp. 76; cf. also Paul Poupard, "A vingt ans," *Atheism and Dialogue*, 20/1 (1985), 58.

13. Skoda, "El diálogo entre creyentes y no creyentes," 75.

14. *Ibid.*, 74.

15. *Ibid.*

16. "Die Befreiung ist eine herrliche Sache. Kurienkardinal Paul Poupard über Gläubige und Ungläubige in der Welt," *Der Spiegel*, 28 (1985), 137–149.

17. "Einst Dialog, heute Monolog? Wie ein neues Gesprach mit dem Atheismus möglich ist," *Christ in der Gegenwart*, 37 (1985), 244.

18. "Atheismus ist ein nachchristliches Phänomen. Ein Gespräch mit Kardinal Paul Poppard," *Herderkorrespondenz*, 39 (1985), 264–269.

19. *Ibid.*, 268f.

20. K. Rahner, "Kirche und Atheismus," *StdZ*, 199 (1981), 3–13.

21. *Ibid.*, 6.

22. G. Schmidtchen, "Die gesellschaftlichen Folgen der Entchristlichung," *StdZ*, 196 (1978), 543–553, here 544.

23. *Ibid.*, 546.

24. K. Marx, "Ökonomisch-philosophische Manuskripte von 1844," *MEW* 1, 546.

25. Cf. K. Rahner, *Grundkurs des Glaubens. Einführung in den Begriff des Christentums* (Freiburg/Basel/Vienna, 1977[8]), 54–61.

26. G. Ebeling, *Dogmatik des christlichen Glaubens*, 1 (Tubingen, 1979), 179. Ebeling discussed this problem in detail; cf. "Die Botschaft von Gott an das Zeitalter des Atheismus," *Wort und Glaube*, 2 (Tubingen, 1969), 373–395.

27. Cf. K. Rahner, "Schöpfungslehre," *Herders Theologisches Taschenlexikon*, 6, 352: "Wir sagen gerade, wer u. was Gott ist, indem wir sagen, dass wir Geschöpfe sind." This is also the meaning of Bultmann's famous statement, in "Welchen Sinn hat es, von Gott zu reden," in *Glauben und Verstehen* 1, 28: "Es zeigt sich also: will man von Gott reden, so muss man offenbar von sich selbst reden."

28. Cf. R. Schaffler, *Fähigkeit zur Erfahrung. Zur transzendentalen Hermeneutik des Sprechens von Gott* (Freiburg/Basel/Vienna, 1982), 16ff.

29. Cf. G. Calogero, *Logo e dialogo. Saggio sullo spirito critico e sulla libertà di coscienza* (Milan, 1950), 51ff.

CHAPTER 49

Human Rights and Freedom within Official Atheism

Ivan Fuček, S.J.

Summary

The teaching of the Council on human rights was sparse and fragmentary, but was taken up and developed by the International Theological Commission in a work published in 1984. The present study takes as its starting point one of the sections entitled "The Second World." An analysis of the historical and ideological changes that have taken place in countries with "real socialist" regimes clearly shows the lines of thinking that lie behind their specific constitutional laws. It is equally easy to see the difference between their foundation and their view of humanity and those of the international charters and the teaching of Vatican II. Finally, we can see how a shared terminology is belied by different contents, implementation and approaches in the sphere of social, economic, political and personal rights.

This subject is closely linked to the teaching of the Council on atheism (GS 19–21) and falls within the study of human *rights*, which have over the past ten years been the subject of scientific investigation with the use of various disciplines: philosophy, law, sociology, politics, economics, ethics, and Protestant and Catholic theology, to which we should add studies by other religions and the adherents of various other lines of thinking.

The present work takes as its starting point theoretical and

199

practical *official atheism,* which still prides itself on encompassing
the essence of classical marxist anthropology, the ethics of which
is reflected in the specific structure of society. Although atheism
may have taken on slightly different features than those current
at the time of the Coucil twenty-five years ago (GS 19), "systematic atheism" (GS 20) is still following the same path, since a
closed system does not as such tend to recognize the present
symptoms of exhaustion. The reflection of experts on *scientific
atheism* has changed perspective. For example, the debate between science and religion has lost its clearcut quality. The same
can be said of the *atheistic humanism* of Hegel and Feuerbach
("God for man is man himself") and that of Nietzsche ("God as
man's competitor"). And the *social atheism* of Marx is aging. The
problems involved in atheism today tend, rather, to take the
form of indifferentism, secularism, and practical materialism.[1] In
the face of the various expressions of the development of atheism
as phenomenon (GS 19), we must once more stress that "systematic atheism" (GS 20), that is, marxist atheism, is the same as
ever.

The reader should not be surprised if the present study uses as
its documentary basis a study issued by the International Theological Commission in 1984 under the title *The Dignity and Rights
of the Human Person.*[2] The fact is that the need arose to gather
together the various texts on human rights that were scattered
through the Constitutions, Decrees, and Declarations of Vatican
II—few in number, it is true—in order to study them further and
evaluate them in a Christian theological perspective, and then
offer the fruit of this investigation in the form of suggestions or
possible practical solutions for international organizations.

The work of the International Theological Commission, therefore, represents the natural sequel to conciliar thought. Indeed,
we can fearlessly state that the key to the subject of human rights
as expressed in the documents of Vatican II can be found precisely in the work of the commission. As far as the subject in the
present chapter is concerned, our attention will be basically concentrated on the section entitled "The Second World."[3] This
expression is used to indicate "the world which has for its common characteristic what is called 'real marxism' " (para. a), and
the text deals exclusively with theoretic and practical official
marxist atheism in countries in which it is still in vogue, de-

fended, propagandized, and used as an instrument at the service of marxist education.

The International Theological Commission has carried out a theological study—the first of this type in the history of the Catholic Church—in order to reach a rational judgment in the light of faith, not only on the rights of the "second world" in particular, but also those of the whole world, leaving aside the fact that in the case of the rights of the "second world," and especially those of the USSR, there is an ethical background that has the aim of building the "ethical state." This is certainly not the place to launch into the endless discussion between marxist ethics in general and the possibility of its foundation in particular. Confining ourselves to the facts, I am personally convinced that official Soviet ethics draws on the fundamental and most important principles of its praxis from its own constitutional and legislative law, while its starting point is classical marxist anthropology, and this is taken as a presupposition for the present study, which will make use of it as necessary.

We are then faced with the basic question of whether this atheism imposed on citizens can become an imitation of organized religion, a new state religion, or maybe an official antireligion. In order to answer this question,, we shall use as our point of reference the new charter of rights and freedoms of the USSR, in other words, the Brezhnevian Constitution of 1977 (= C77). We have chosen this document because it is the only one that claims to be a model document not only for the constitutional law of "real socialism" (art. 1), but also for constitutional law throughout the world.[4] It is based on classical marxist doctrine, and thus does not recognize human rights (which it does not even mention), and particularly the right to freedom of political and religious thought, and of conscience, in the sense found in the international charters.[5] The Council has this to say about such socialism:

> Among the various kinds of present-day atheism, that one should not go unnoticed which looks for man's autonomy through his economic and social emancipation. It holds that religion, of its very nature, thwarts such emancipation by raising man's hopes in a future life, thus both deceiving him and discouraging him from working for a better form of life on

earth. That is why those who hold such views, wherever they gain control of the state, violently attack religion, and in order to spread atheism, especially in the education of young people, make use of all the means by which the civil authority can bring pressure to bear on its subject (GS 20).

Around this official line there is a whole range of revisionists and neomarxists whose interpretation of marxism is not in accordance with the doctrine of the classical fathers (Marx, Engels, Lenin), nor with that of the party, the Communist Part of the USSR (the CPSU), nor with that of the marxism at present in power—particularly that of the constitutional charters and the juridicial codes: the constitutions of Lenin (1918 and 1924), Stalin (1936), and Brezhnev (1977).[6] Although this pluralism is illegal, it is a recurrent phenomenon and is increasingly found among marxist thinkers, to the extent that we can now consider that there are a number of different "marxisms."[7] We are faced with the "evolution of marxism itself" and the "differing complexions of postmarxist theorizing" (para. a). A number of neomarxists accuse official marxism of having betrayed and distorted the teaching and intention of the great marxists. They see today's "real socialism" (para. a) as presenting forms and dispositions of social life that were condemned by Marx himself, whose thought did not envisage a politics of force, the suppression of personal freedom, or any extreme severity toward those who do not observe official doctrine ("dissidents" or "those who think differently"), the consequences of which extend to a loss of every freedom. According to these thinkers, we are faced with a regression into a "premarxist" state, so that the so-called "capitalistic" western democracies guarantee and protect the rights and freedoms of the workers better through union supervision in the workplace, détente between the classes, and many other social safeguards.[8]

When it moves on to study rights in the "second world," the following terse statement of the document of the International Theological Commission becomes clear: ". . . we meet various difficulties, the principal ones possibly being the evolution of marxism itself and the differing complexions of postmarxist theorizing" (para. a).

The document does not linger any further over the evolution of marxism, nor over the differences in postmarxist theories.

Instead, it emphasizes its intention of considering only the forms of marxism that are practiced today in specific political regimes (para. a). As a result, the aim of the present work can only be a fairly faithful commentary on the text of the basic document of the commission, through the use of the same work instruments. It is not a question of sketching a philosophy or a history of rights, but rather of drawing a comparison between three views of humanity: that of marxist constitutional law, that of the international law of the charters, and the Catholic one as represented by this document of the International Theological Commission.[9] Our method follows that of the document.

Historical and Ideological Outline

The basic document of the International Theological Commission calls the reader's attention to the essential difference between real socialism and Christianity—and also the international charters—on the subject of rights and freedoms when it refers to

. . . the forms of marxism that are practiced today in those political regimes in which constitutions and laws indicate ways of looking at man and of acting so different that while human rights are recognized in words, these words are then interpreted quite differently (para. a).

In order to gain a better idea of this "way of looking at man" in the 1977 Soviet Constitution, we must move a step backwards and consider two of the premises of leninism, in order, on the one hand, to pinpoint its difference from marxism, and, on the other, to discover how the concept of rights is not in line with the genuine thought of Marx. These changes have also influenced the constitutional basis of the rights of the citizens of the USSR in the "way of looking at man" and the actual "way of acting," in other words in the dignity of the human person and his or her ethical activity.

Lenin differs from Marx and Engels on three particular points.

The first point is the theory of revolution. For Marx and Engels, the socialist revolution called for a very high level of development of the productive forces, with victory being ensured in almost all developed countries, but under specific conditions of an objective economic and social nature. Lenin modified all three theories: revolution starts from a less developed capitalist country, does not break out simultaneously in all countries, and conditions of a solely subjective political nature are sufficient. Furthermore, Lenin supported permanent revolution. [10]

The second doctrinal and practical divergence concerns the communist party. Marx and Engels wanted a workers' party that would include the whole working class, and not a party that would constitute a force "directing the class." [11] On the other hand, at the Seventh Congress in 1918, Lenin created the "Communist–Bolshevik–Russian Party," placing it before the class. This leninist character of the party would later extend to all communist parties throughout the world, continue in the new name of the "Communist Part of the USSR" (CPSU) received at the Nineteenth Congress (in 1952) under Stalin, and be reinforced in the 1977 Constitution, article 6a: "The leading and guiding force of Soviet society . . . is the Communist Party of the Soviet Union."

The third point of divergence concerns religion. In theory, Lenin is in agreement with Marx when he declares that religion is the opium of the people:

> Man makes religion, religion does not make man. In other words, religion is the self-consciousness and self-feeling of man who has either not yet found himself or has already lost himself again. [12]

However, they differ on the practical aspect. While Marx and Engels ideologically refer back to the "mythological school" (Bauer, Robertson, Drews), the "historical school" (Strauss, Renan, Harnack), and the doctrine of the "Tubingen school" (Strauss, Feuerbach, Chr. Bauer), Lenin follows a path of his own that is more propagandistic and demagogic, not to say aggressive, and is very close to that of the eighteenth-century French encyclopedists—a path that had in fact already been "opened up" by Engels. The fact that the struggle of the encyclopedists has nothing to do with marxism is irrelevant as regards ideology and praxis: what counts is their atheistic approach and the fight against the Christian religion. [13] This commitment to such a fight is indeed found in the statutes of the Soviet Communist Party

(1961): "The member of the party must . . . carry on a decided battle against . . . religious prejudices" (art. 2).[14] The 1977 Soviet Constitution, for its part, states that "Citizens of the USSR are guaranteed freedom . . . to conduct . . . atheistic propaganda" (art. 52).[15]

A second premise is the historical development of a concept of law that is different from the original thought of Marx. This is another element that influences the view of man as well as the "constitutions and laws" (para. a) of real socialism, and the 1977 Constitution in particular. We can and must immediately state that this law is not and cannot be "natural" but positive. For this reason, marxist law is situated by its nature exclusively in the positive field. As regards its existence, two periods are envisaged: the first would be "transitory" (and is still in existence today), and the second will be "permanent" (in the final classless society) and will come into being after the decline of every law, and indeed after the disappearance of the state. This doctrine goes back to Marx and Engels, whose precise thinking is not easy to reduce to one univocal interpretation. At first, Marx did not even use the term "law" because it was tainted by bourgeois conceptions. Later on, after he has understood that it is rooted in economy and history, apart from a simple juridical discipline, he takes up its analysis, breaking with modern law, criticizing ontological opinions of idealist philosophy and the theses of scholastic philosophy, and proposing a new ontology of his own that accepts only the one reality of the material. Under the influence of Hegel, Feuerbach, Spinoza, eighteenth-century French and English materialists, and certain ancient philosophers, such as Heraclitus and Democritus, Marx formulates two fundamental theories: (1) the law is a constituent component of the history of economy as dictated by economic evolution; and (2) the law is neither immutable nor universal and outside the categories of time, space and history, since man's being neither is nor can be an immutable reality. There is thus no natural law—which, furthermore, was a bourgeois system in the hands of the ruling classes, a slave and feudal system that was instrumentalized by capitalists, who wrongly attributed a universal value to law. So, for Marx, in comparison with historical materialism, all doctrines prior to him were conservative philosophies allied to the ruling class.[16]

We do not need to investigate Marx's concept of law further.

We would merely note his utopistic doctrine on the decline of the law and the state, inasmuch as they have a merely informative significance for our subject on the gnoseological level. This disappearance will take place when the conditions for the existence of law and state have definitively disappeared. A "transitional" time, "X," is still needed—that of the "dictatorship of the proletariat"—in which the victorious proletariat must itself take on the task of acting as the instrument of law and state.[17]

Following the stages in the development of marxist law, and leaving aside many names (Kautsky, Plekhanov, Bukharin, and others) and their opinions, not all of which are fully in accordance with official marxism, it must be said that a twofold element again plays an important role: different practical and pragmatic requirements are always brought about by new historical trends. Thus, the development foreseen by Marx and Engels generally does not take place. Lenin, and indeed Stalin, would follow the path imposed on them by specific conditions that tend more to strengthen the law and the state than to bring about their decline. This is why the doctrine of E.B. Pašukanis was condemned: his fidelity to Marx's thought on such decline was considered dangerous.[18] Since then, juridical operations have tended to be instruments of the CPSU. Stalin, Vishinsky, and Judin laid down the norms according to which theoreticians of the law should think and act.[19] Law in real socialism today has characteristics similar to those of capitalist law, for example, etatism, normativism, positivistic concept of law, and superstructure (the CPSU) that constitutes and establishes laws. Even so, the specific character of a new form of socialist law is more clearly seen in the 1977 Constitution. It is democratic inasmuch as it manifests "a socialist state of the whole people, expressing the will and interests of the workers, peasants, and intelligentsia, the working people of all the nations and nationalities of the country" (art. 1). Its aim is not an exploration but the building up of communism: "The supreme goal of the Soviet state is the building of a classless communist society in which there will be public, communist self-government" (Pr. 1). The law is a means of progress and not of reaction, because "major matters of state shall be submitted to nationwide discussion and put to a popular vote (referendum)" (art. 5).

The external forms of the law are no longer "rigid" either, since the first principle of law is that of "democratic centralism":

"Democratic centralism combines central leadership with local initiative and creative activity and with the responsibility of each state body and official for the task entrusted to them" (art. 3); "The Soviet state and all its bodies function on the basis of socialist law" (art. 4a).

Thus, while "striving for the further development of socialist democracy" (Pr. m, iii), in the meantime, the 1977 constitution defines "the rights, freedoms and obligations of citizens" (Pr. m, vi) in accordance with marxist-leninist ethics. It is clear from the 1977 Constitution that the law as thus established will increasingly become an instrument of socialist education (arts. 9, 25, 45). Despite everything, it is believed that once the norms have become unnecessary, "socialist social relations" (Pr. l) will be perfected, to the point of their transformation into "communist relations" (Pr. l), and the process of law will move toward its definitive decline.[20]

Different Bases of Rights

While still respecting the methodology of the basic document of the International Theological Commission and using the same moral-theological language proper to semiotics, we shall now consider the essential aspects of this difference between the "way of looking at humanity" and the "way of acting" (para. a) under "the forms of marxism that are practiced today in certain political regimes" (para. a), and the view of man found in the international charters (which are endorsed by those regimes) and our Christian one.

This methodology is more inductive than deductive or dialectical inasmuch as it leads us from the immediate to the distant and final, and from specific premises to universal conclusions. Meanwhile, the object of the present section is the foundation or basis of rights found in those "constitutions and laws," and, specifically, the present Soviet Constitution, as compared with the United Nations charters and the International Theological Commission document.

This comparison will provide a clearer picture of the "basis of the basis," in other words, the view of humanity and its dignity as seen in three different perspectives. "The problem is stated not merely as a piece of information, but because of the Christians

who live, co-exist, in such places and who are required to cooperate. They are more or less tolerated as citizens, although they are
viewed with suspicion" (para. a).

There is no doubt that today's Christian must, on the one
hand, be "aware of his own specific Christian identity which
involves obedience, even on earth, to the 'paradoxical' laws of
God's kingdom,"[21] and, on the other hand, of "the intimate ties
that link him to all men of good will."[22] Within this framework,
we can see the three clearly distinct bases of human rights and
freedoms.

The foundation of human rights within the framework of a
state of the new type such as the Soviet Union is in function of
the origin and of the goal, while it is identified with the authority
of the state itself. The origin is identified with the "Great October Socialist Revolution . . . under the leadership of the Communist Party headed by Lenin" (C77, Pr. a). This state is of "a new
type, . . . the basic instrument for defending the gains of the
revolution and for building socialism and communism" (*ibid.*).
The expression "the leadership of the Communist Party" indicates the state as apparatus, or the supreme effective authority;
"the Soviet state" indicates the state as community, or the stable
order of the community (or collectivity) of the peoples resident
in the territory of the USSR; and "of a new type," like "the
instrument for defending the gains of the revolution and for
building socialism," indicates the first and second stages of the
same revolution. In this context, the word "communism" fore-
shadows the third stage, or, in other words, the final stage of
evolution. These expressions show fairly clearly that the communist society is seen as the final aim of the present Soviet political
community.[23] The aim of the new type of state will therefore not
be of a liberal nature in the sense of defending the property of
individuals—and still less in that of the most ordinary and recent
teaching of the magisterium of the Catholic Church, according
to which the common good can only be defined in relation to the
dignity of the human person and therefore cannot be reduced
simply to economic values (GS 71).[24] The ultimate aim will be
more that of a totalitarian state, with, after Stalin, some nuances
and innovations introduced by Khrushchev and Brezhnev and
upheld by Gorbachev.[25]

In the first (historical) part of the Prologue, the 1977 Soviet
Constitution speaks of "socialism," "a socialist society" and "the

Soviet people," and of "new opportunities for growth of the forces of socialism" (paras. b–c), in other words, the first stage of evolution. Stress is laid on the fulfillment of "the aims of the dictatorship of the proletariat" and the statement that "the Soviet state has become a state of the whole people" (para. d). This latter statement, which is ambiguous even as it stands, becomes problematic if we compare it with the next sentence: "The leading role of the Communist Party, the vanguard of all the people, has grown" (para. d). The Soviet state has now become the state "of the whole of the people," while the role of the party grows as "vanguard of all the people."

The second part of the Prologue describes the present situation in the USSR (in other words, the second stage of communist evolution), in which "the creative forces of the new system and the advantages of the socialist way of life are becoming increasingly evident" (para. e) and "powerful productive forces and progressive science and culture have been created" and "more and more favorable conditions are being provided for the all-round development of the individual" (para. f). In the present situation, "a new historical community of people has been formed—the Soviet people" (para. g), with "mature socialist relations," "equality of all," and "fraternal cooperation" (paras. g–h). The law of life (or praxis) of Soviet society is "concern of all for the good of each and concern of each for the good of all" (para. i). It is, therefore, "a society of true democracy" (para. j), the political system of which ensures "the combination of citizens' real rights and freedoms with their obligations and responsibilities to society" (para. j). Sočetanie (= combination, union) means harmony between rights and obligations. Even so, in this important second part of the Prologue—and the same applies to the whole of the 1977 Constitution—we do not find expressions such as "human rights" or "human rights and freedoms." There is never even the slightest reference to the person as an individual. Here again, as in anciet Greek absolutism, the individual is totally absorbed by the state, the society (the collectivity), "the people," democracy—in other words, by the internal collectivity, with which he is almost identified.[26] What we have then is an excessive exaltation of society at the expense of the individual and the dignity of the human person. According to marxist doctrine, man has no "natural," innate, intangible right that has not been successively established, drawn up or otherwise derived, and this is in total contrast to the doctrine of Vatican II, which, despite the fact that it stresses the importance of the life of society, states that the human person "is and ought to be the beginning, the subject, and the object of every social organization" (GS 25).

> . . . there is a growing awareness of the sublime dignity of the human person, who stands above all things and whose rights and duties are universal and inviolable. . . . The social order and its development must constantly yield to the good of the person, since the order of things must be subordinate to the order of persons and not the other way around (GS 26).

The situation of man within the framework of the Soviet state becomes even clearer in the third (or "eschatological") part of the Prologue (the third stage of communist evolution), which describes the final struggle of the CPSU and the whole people (paras. l–m). There is a description of the aim of the Soviet state, or the path toward final victory: "The supreme goal of the Soviet state is the building of a classless society" (para. l). In order to attain this goal, it is necessary to "lay the material and technical foundation of communism, to perfect socialist social relations and transform them into communist relations, to mold the citizen of communist society," and so on (para. l). It is therefore clear that apart from the state, which is identified with the political community, the Soviet citizen is left with no value springing simply from his birth and proper to him as a human being. In this case, the person of the individual does not have a personal goal that transcends that of the state, so that the yardstick for moral behavior is that of the state and the party—in other words, the struggle for the final victory of communism (art. 6b). The whole person of the individual and all of his or her relationships must be ordered and subordinated to the socialist political society and consequently to its sovereign authority.

Without stopping to consider the degree to which this Soviet model draws its inspiration from the teaching of Hobbes and Hegel, or that of Marx, Engels, and Lenin, we can decidedly state that the 1977 Constitution reveals an exaggerated exaltation of the state, both theoretical and practical, in which the human person is only a minor component. The aim of the Soviet state is, therefore, supremely ideological—"the final victory of communism"—and is established independently of the good of the individual citizen, whose other possible interests are sacrificed to it. "The interests" of society or of "present and future generations" (arts. 17, 18) are often highlighted in the 1977 Constitution, so that when it is stated that in such a society the conditions exist for "the all-round development of the individual" (Pr. f; cf. art. 20), this never refers to the individual person as separate from the state, but solely as part of the collectivity. The value of the individual is solely a function of the state.

As far as authority in Soviet society is concerned, this is not the authority of patriarchal, inherited, or charismatic power, but that of legal and bureaucratic power organized into the various levels of governors, functionairies, and citizens. When it is stated that *The Soviet people, guided by the ideas of scientific communism . . . hereby affirm the principles of the social structure and policy of the USSR, and define the rights, freedoms and obligations of citizens, and the principles of the organization of the socialist state of the whole people"* (Pr. m; emphasis mine), there is no explanation as to who this "Soviet people" is, which is so powerful and is distinct from the state—indeed, distinct from "the whole people." Before trying to find an explanation, let us summarize the main elements of Brezhnevian theory: the Soviet state is a reality superior to man, so that the latter is subject to the former as a simple component. Even so, "the Soviet people" defines "the aims of the socialist state," the Soviet people defines "the rights, freedoms and obligations of citizens," and the Soviet people similarly establishes "the principles of the organization of the socialist state of the whole people" (Pr. m, vi). There are in fact two peoples, inasmuch as "the Soviet people" governs "the whole people." Obviously, the first "people" (that is, "the Soviet people") is above the socialist state, and is thus the supreme authority, identified with the common good in a very special way. And who is this suprapeople, suprastate, and supraauthority? According to the 1977 Constitution, the answer can only be the communist party, which is the supreme source of rights and freedoms for the Soviet citizen. The text in question states:

The leading and guiding force of Soviet society and the nucleus of its political system, of all state organizations and public organizations, is the Communist Party of the Soviet Union. The CPSU exists for the people and serves the people.

The Communist Party, armed with Marxism-Leninism, de-
termines the general perspectives of the development of society
and the course of the domestic and foreign policy of the USSR,
directs the great constructive work of the Soviet people, and
imparts a planned, systematic and theoretically substantiated
character to their struggle for the vicotry of communism.

All party organizations shall function within the framework
of the Constitution of the USSR (art. 6).[27]

When the word "force" (taken from the Statute of the CPSU,
Prologue, para. b) is linked with "armed" and "struggle," the tone
becomes somewhat military, even though, at first sight, we tend
to think more of ideological, political, and ethical force. The
"force" that "leads" is an expression not found in Stalin's 1936
Constitution (art. 126).[28] It was Brezhnev who restored the
CPSU, giving it the supreme position in Soviet society, so that it
is the main—if not the sole—force that leads the whole people,
including even the Supreme Soviet and the legislature. According to the explanation of Brezhnev himself, "in directing the
activity of the Soviets it [the CPSU] does not take their place,
but defines the functions of the organs of the part and the
state . . . , with concern for the further development of socialist
democracy."[29] The idea of "guiding" or "directing" toward goals
planned by the party belongs to Lenin, Khrushchev and Brezhnev, and was not included in Stalin's Constitution.[30] The concept of leading and guiding "the nucleus of the political system"
says much more than was said in Stalin's Constitution, which
still viewed the party as the "guiding nucleus" (art. 126). If the
CPSU leads and guides the "nucleus" (*jadrom*) of the whole political system and the state and public organizations, this means that
there is in fact nothing that is not led and guided by the party.
Step by step, we therefore come to see that the "Soviet people"
that defines the rights, freedoms, and obligations of the citizens,
and even the aims of the socialist state (Pr. m, vi) is an unparal-
leled authority.[31]

Leaving aside certain expressions such as "exists for the people," "serves the people," "armed with Marxism-Leninism," and
"directs the great constructive work of the Soviet people," let us
instead look more closely at the phrase "imparts a planned, systematic and theoretically substantiated character"—a phrase that
reveals a specific "scientific" character in line with the premises

of the materialist world view. "Scientific" thus means that the marxist-leninist doctrine or ideology is "understood as the supreme revelation of scientific knowledge," in the words of G. Codevilla.[32] There is no doubt, then, at the top of the pyramid of power in Soviet society, we find the CPSU, whose political, doctrinal, and ideological supremacy cannot be overruled within the structure of the state. The CPSU is the prime maker of the state and is, therefore, above the state, which serves it as its "basic instrument" (Pr. a), while the legislative order is an instrument subject to the state, and operates as such. The CPSU is, therefore, the primary and supreme source of the rights and freedoms of the Soviet citizen, in view of the fact that the 1977 Constitution sees man as "Soviet man" and not simply as "man"; in other words, it includes him within the Soviet system and its marxist-positivistic law, and cannot view him outside this framework inasmuch as man is an empty monad without any innate quality in this connection.

The Authentic, Innate, Universal, and Inalienable Source

The international documents show a diametrically different opinion. In the Charter of the United Nations (1945) and the Universal Declaration of Human Rights (1948), a man or woman is not a being stripped of the existential values belonging to the person, but a being whose dignity is rooted in his or her personal and ontological reality or existence. This dignity of the human person is the basis or source from which all human rights flow, because, as the Preamble to the latter declaration states, it is "inherent in all members of the human family" (para. a). Their "rights" are therefore "equal and inalienable" (para. a) and the "recognition of the inherent dignity . . . is the foundation of freedom, justice and peace in the world" (para. a). All human beings are "born free," are "equal in dignity and rights," are "endowed with reason and conscience," and "should act towards one another in a spirit of brotherhood" (art. 1).[33] Although the declaration extols an ideal that should inspire all human beings, it is in fact bereft of any juridical effectiveness, whereas two other pacts or treaties *are* juridically binding on the signatory states. These are the International Covenant on Economic, Social, and

Cultural Rights (= ESC), and the International Covenant on Civil and Political Rights (= CP), both of which came into force in 1976, and both of which were signed by, among others, all the members of the Warsaw Pact, led by the USSR. Both agreements have the same Preamble, which repeats the previously cited text of the Universal Declaration of Human Rights on the "recognition of the inherent dignity and of the equal and inalienable rights of all members of the human family" (para. a), but clarifies this with the observation that "these rights derive from the inherent dignity of the human person" (para. b).[34] The same statement is found in the Final Act of the Conference on European Security and Cooperation signed in Helsinki on 1 August 1975 by thirty-five states, including the Soviet Union. Out of the ten principles set forth, the seventh is the most relevant to us here: "Respect for human rights and fundamental freedoms, including the freedom of thought, conscience, religion or belief." It is explicitly stated that the source of all human rights is the "inherent dignity of the human person" (para. b) and that the most important task for the states involved is that of promoting and encouraging the "effective exercise of civil, politic, economic, social, cultural and other rights and freedoms all of which derive from the inherent dignity of the human person and are essential to his free and full development" (para. b).[35]

Thus, all human rights, and specifically fundamental human rights, "find their immediate source" in this dignity, and even when the human person "errs," he or she "always maintains inherent dignity and never forfeits his or her personal dignity" (para. n).[36] This is the authentic, innate, inalienable, universal, inviolable source, inasmuch as people are born equal in dignity and freedom. According to these international documents, we cannot start with the state or collectivity, and then move on to the individual who is subject to it. The only legitimate process is the one that begins with recognition of the personal right of every person (through measures to safeguard it), and then moves on to the community, in other words, the state, never forgetting that any provision laid down by the state comes in the final analysis from the individual (who is also citizen) and hinges on the tangible right of every individual as person, inviolable in his or her own inherent dignity (GS 26 and 29). The document of the International Theological Commission speaks in similar terms with reference to the same teaching:

The idea of the dignity of the human person and of the rights of man, which in a very special way were worked out under the influence of the Christian doctrine on man, have also been buttressed by all the statements of this century. Today, how-ever, whether through misinterpretation or direct violation, on the ground they too often are impeded or even disfigured.[37]

It is obvious that the international charters do not give any further explanation of the exact nature of this "human dignity." However, the document of the International Theological Com-mission does give further explanation, and we can discern two aspects of this teaching: a preliminary one on how the document sees the "hierarchy" of rights in reference to the dignity of the human person, and an underlying one on how it sees the "basis of the basis," in other words, the philosophical and theological question of where the dignity of the person itself has its basis. We would, of course, remain within the perspective of the document of the International Theological Commission, although there are other possible explanations. On the one hand, it is clear that not all rights are "natural" and hence "universal," and the document does not in fact deny this point (ITC 1.2). On the other hand, the dignity of the person, which is the basis of these equal rights for everybody, has very deep anthropological roots, and these are seen in the light not only of reason but also of faith.

The document of the International Theological Commission establishes a hierarchy of rights, which follows and improves on that of the international treaties of the United Nations—the International Covenants on Civil and Political Rights, and on Economic, Social and Cultural Rights[38]—subdividing the rights into three categories. The first category is made up of the essen-tial or major rights: some of these are fundamental or primary, for example, the rights to life (CP, art. 6), personal dignity (art. 10), equality (art. 26), freedom of thought, conscience, and religion (art. 18), not being harassed for one's personal opinions (art. 19), and so on; although the others are still essential or major, they are in fact nonfundamental rights, for example, cer-tain civil rights (CP, arts. 21, 22), political rights (arts. 9, 13, 17, 25), social rights (arts. 14, 15, 23; ESC, arts. 11–14), eco-nomic rights (ESC, arts. 6–9), and cultural rights (art. 15). The second category covers the very numerous nonessential or minor rights that exist in any society: they appear either as "consequences with a bearing on fundamental rights" (ITC 1.2) or as "conditions involved in practical application, and also as closely bound to the actual circumstances of times and places" (ITC 1.2); such rights are of themselves "less intangible" precisely as regards their formulation and any necessary reformulation in accordance with the historical progress of society, which any civil or ecclesiastical legislation must take into account in order to make sure it always avoids "denial of the fundamental rights themselves," especially in unusual and very difficult circumstances (ITC 1.2).

> When it comes to a judgment about the practical implementation of these lesser rights, the demands of the common good must be borne in mind or, in other words, the totality "of social conditions which make possible, for groups and for individuals, the full and timely attainment of fulfillment" (GS 26) (ITC 1.2).

The third category covers those human rights

> . . . which belong not to the strict requisites of the rights of nations as strictly obligatory norms, but are postulates for the human ideal of progress towards a universal "humanization." What is at stake here is the achievement of the highest human ideal and this is the obligation—since this is the desire of all citizens—of all those charged with the care of the common good and political life. International assistance may be necessary here in particular cases (Dec. 1948, end of Prologue) (ITC 1.2).

In view of the deepest metaphysical and theological (and not only psychological or sociological) roots of the expression "the dignity of the human person," we must be careful to avoid any ambiguity (ITC 1.2). It does not indicate an absolute autonomy, whether this is seen as some form of radical independence from God or as a type of atheism (GS 19, 20). We have already rejected similar forms, together with a relative autonomy that makes exaggerated claims regarding respect for "personal freedoms," although it does accept that this autonomy is "ultimately grounded in the supreme transcendency of God" (1.2). The point is to try to understand this relationship between creature and Creator. There are many interpretations (cf. GS 12, 14–16, 36), some of them apparently doubtful, and others confused—although this does not necessarily mean that they are exaggerated or mistaken. The path chosen by the International Theological Commission is that of "the theology of the history of salvation" (2.1.2), which may be one, but can be seen from different perspectives: thus we can have an ascending—or even "transcendental"—theological anthropology (for instance, that of Karl Rahner), or a descending, more traditional one (for instance, that of Hans Urs von Balthasar). The International Theological Commission chooses the descending path, and, therefore, starts with the creation, moves on to sin, and centers its approach on the mystery of Christ, in line with the thinking of Vatican II (GS 22, 32, 38, 45).[39] Although this choice is in itself questionable, it is perhaps more acceptable from the point of view of constitutional and legislative law, because of its continuity with traditional concepts of law, especially "natural law" or *ius gentium* (ITC 1.2), and is also maybe more suited to a systematization of a scholastic type of teaching. However, both paths are christocentric and theocentric, because if they were not, where would the basis of the dignity of the human person and of his or her rights and freedoms rest? In line with this, Cardinal Daneels had the following to say in the *Relatio post disceptationem* to *Mysterium hominis* at the 1985 Extraordinary Synod of Bishops:

Knowledge of God is the foundation of the dignity of each person; reverence towards God is the foundation of reverence towards neighbor and towards every creature. Without this theocentric dimension the defense and promotion of human rights—of such great importance for the Church today—will not only pass into mere "horizontalism" but will lack any foundation, and will ultimately be reduced to nothingness.[40]

In any case, the personalistic-immediate basis of the dignity, rights, and freedoms of man is man himself in his most intimately ontological structure (body-psyche-spirit) and everything needed for the intrapersonal dimension. This is followed by the interpersonal or social dimension, beginning with the distinction between the sexes (Gen. 1:27; 2:24), and with the human being's original vocation (the call to love), and then continuing with the vocation to marriage or celibacy, including family life as the first communion and community, which has its place in the lesser or greater community of society, the state and the Church.

The christological-remote basis is the person of the incarnate Son of God, the perfect image of the Father, who has redeemed us and made us the new creation in Christian dignity, "existing for the good of all" (ITC 2.2.3).

And the Trinitarian-final basis is God the Creator in his justice (2.2.1).

This exemplary progression through anthropological (philosophical and theological) basis, dignity of the human person and his rights, subsists even in the sinner: even in "the most wicked individuals," man is always an image of God the Creator, redeemed by Christ and grafted into him, so that he always bears "the likeness of the heavenly Adam" (cf. 1 Cor. 15:49).[41]

This doctrine differs totally from the Marxist-Leninist approach or any other atheistic positivism. "By means of this doctrine Christians have an original contribution to make in the universal effort to push on the quest for these rights" (ITC 2.2.2).[42]

Differences in Legislative Norms

The difference as to the basis of human rights is a result of differing anthropological conceptions—different views of the image of humanity, society, and the world. Real socialism gives priority to the collectivity in a perspective of we-you-I,[43] as against the priority of the international charters, Vatican II and the document of the International Theological Commission, which have I-you-we as their perspective. According to Marx, the collectivity eliminates the possibilities of an "abstract" and "immutable" right of the person. A.J. Vishinsky, former Soviet delegate to the United Nations, openly criticized this position in December 1948:

The draft declaration on human rights seems to accept that reactionary opinion directed against national sovereignty and is thus totally inconsistent with the principles of the United Nations. . . . Human rights cannot be envisaged apart from the state: the very concept of subjective right is bound up with that of the state.[44]

For its part, the Council answers with the concept of natural, immutable, and universal law. It "wishes to remind men that the natural law of peoples and its universal principles still retain their binding force. The conscience of mankind firmly and ever more emphatically proclaims these principles" (GS 79).

The material concerning the social rights that are part of Soviet social constitutional law is complex and rich, but special attention should be given to the approach to schooling, the freedom of choice of profession, and promotion in public and political employment. In each case, everything is oriented toward "the interests of society" (C77, arts. 13c, 17, 30b, 61, 62), which means that "each and every citizen must collectivize himself to the utmost" (ITC 3.1.3b).

There are undeniably positive aspects. The educational sector in the Soviet Union is being constantly improved and offers a vast range of possibilities and assistance: education is tax-free (C77, art. 45b), the majority of students receive a salary, and, although it may be minimal, it does still help with living expenses.[45] The task of establishing and perfecting a "uniform system of public education" throughout the whole Soviet Union is made more difficult by the number of nations and languages. The fifteen federated republics with their 270 million inhabitants are made up of one hundred different nations, each with its own language, a factor that not only jeopardizes uniform public education and "the opportunity to attend a school where teaching is in the native language" (art. 45b), but has also led to a number of provisions, which mean that on certain points in this sector, Soviet law is in fact ahead of that of the United Nations charters (ESC, art. 13a–d). However, unlike the conciliar view, it does not rule out any "monopoly of schools" (GE 6) or any "social and political slavery" (GS 29).

On the contrary, this system of education "serves the communist education . . . of the youth" (C77, art. 25); indeed, it "ensures," "serves," and "trains" a mature and convinced communist from infancy onwards. Such education is obviously bound to be antireligious or strictly secular, and is a clear atheistic ideological choice within the universal framework of schooling. This is stated in the 1961 Statute of the CPSU, which calls for a fight against "religious prejudices and other survivals of the past" (art. 2d), and is confirmed in the new 1986 Statute (Ustav), which repeats the same thing in article 2g entitled "Religious Prejudices" (reli-

gioznimi predrassudami), whereas in the 1986 Program of the
CPSU, the new project for atheistic education (*ateističeskoe
vospitanie*) envisages new efforts and greater commitment on the
part of all the people in order to make sure the new atheistic
attitudes and behavior are more firmly rooted.[46]

This is a far cry from the Council's claim of the "right to a
Christian education" (*GE* 2) and the statement that parents
have "a primary and inalienable duty and right in regard to the
education of their children" (*GE* 6) "in accordance with their
own religious beliefs" (*DH* 5). And it is also very different from
article 13c–d of the International Covenant on Economic, Social and Cultural Rights. Soviet parents do not enjoy any type of
alternative in the shape of schools different from those established by the public authorities. Nor do they have "the liberty . . . to ensure the religious and moral education of their
children in conformity with their own convictions" (CP, art.
18d). This is not simply a legislative omission, but a position
diametrically opposed to the international agreement that has
been duly ratified by the Soviet Union itself. Here we are dealing
with a true state monopoly on every educational level, except for
religious communities—in other words, schools dedicated exclusively to clergy formation and training, and, therefore, confined
to a strictly limited number of adult students, schools for the
religious formation of younger students being banned by law.[47]
However, from the point of view of international law, it is unacceptable that education in the Soviet Union should be exclusively aimed at creating a type of "socialist person" who is the
protagonist of communism, thus precluding any other type of
viewpoint.

The 1977 Soviet Constitution goes on to guarantee the right
to work in terms that are undoubtedly better than those found in
international law, and also the choice of profession, taking "due
account of the needs of society."[48] Among the basic freedoms,
the International Covenant on Economic, Social and Cultural
Rights includes "the opportunity to gain one's living by work
which one freely chooses and accepts" (art. 6a), and Vatican II
emphasizes the individual's right to "all that is necessary for
living a genuinely human life: for example, . . . the right freely
to choose one's state of life" (GS 26) and the "right to work" (GS
67). According to the International Theological Commission,
these rights "depend on justice" (3.2.1):

Man has a right in justice to all the means he needs to develop himself and attain fulfillment, subject to the common good. . . . A man cannot develop himself without the enjoyment of material goods and their use. On the other hand, as master of himself, he should have the rights to appropriate freedom and to co-responsibility (3.2.1).

It is in the choice of profession that candidates in the Soviet Union come up against many problems. Since professional or vocational training is reserved exclusively to the state, the possibility of benefitting from it is restricted according to the needs of the moment. For example, in entrance examinations, the predetermined number to be admitted means that a considerable percentage of applicants are rejected. What are the criteria for admission? Study certificates, reports issued by school or workplace, the inevitable membership of the youth branch of the CPSU (Konsomol), a certificate of good "ethico-political" behavior, and so on. There are also social types of advantages that influence such choices: preference is given to children of state employees, those who are active in the Konsomol, and the children of the political and bureaucratic intelligentsia, who have the advantage of very high-level backing with the CPSU. About forty percent of those accepted come from the higher levels of political society.[49]

As often happens with Marxist-Leninist doctrine, there is always a legal basis for religious and political discrimination. Thus, if one of the primary obligations laid down in the Statute of the CPSU is that of "carrying on a dedicated struggle against any manifestation of bourgeois ideology, . . . religious prejudices and other survivals of the past, observing the principle of communist ethics and placing the interests of society above personal interests,"[50] a professional or vocational selection process obviously becomes necessary. Candidates who belong to any other ideology or religion, in other words, those who do not observe "communist ethics," are excluded from the possibility of higher studies or professional training, and from jobs in the country's industrial and economic network. During the course of his studies, if an individual is suspected of not following the official state line to the letter, he or she will be expelled from the enterprise or combine that is underwriting his or her specialized training, thus definitively compromising his or her integration into the productive life of the country, and he or she will be classified as a "dissident" and placed in a category with those who do not share the official party line. Such expulsions are, of course, in accordance with the ethical uniformity of the state, in which each member is called on to become its best reflection.[51]

It is also interesting to observe how this attitude is contrary not only to international law but also to Soviet law itself. It is contrary to article 5 of the UNESCO convention against discrimination in the field of education and training[52]; it is contrary to article 18d of the International Covenant on Civil and Political Rights, where the individual's convictions are respected as something essential; it is contrary to article 13a of the International Covenant on Economic, Social and Cultural rights; and, lastly, it is contrary to Soviet law itself, which protects the rights of the citizen, and does not envisage the loss of employment because of religious convictions, as is in fact stated in article 42 of the penal code of the Russian Soviet Federated Socialist Republic in its amended form of 18 March 1966.[53] Choice of job or profession is, therefore, not an act of full personal freedom, but is made by the state and lies in the hands of the CPSU, which runs the whole organization of the country on the basis of the economic and political system of the collective, thus entailing inevitable discrimination on social, ideological, political, cultural, and religious grounds, Such a policy is quite obviously contrary to the "triad of fundamental principles," which provide the basis for a common interpretation of the human rights proclaimed and stressed by the International Theological Commission:

> Such a basis is to be found in that triad of fundamental principles, namely liberty, equality and participation. This triad underlies the rights attached to personal liberty, juridical equality and the exercise of the activites belonging to social, economic, cultural and political life. The links which exist between the elements of this triad exclude a one-sided interpretation, e.g., liberalistic, functionalistic or collectivistic (3.2.2).

Education and choice of profession open the way to important public positions that are open to all those who have the right qualifications: "Citizens of the USSR have the right to take part in the management and administration of state and public affairs. . . . This right is ensured by the opportunity to vote and to be elected to Soviets of People's Deputies and other elective state bodies" (C77, art. 48a–b). No mention is made of the possibility of election for citizens whose political opinions differ or who belong to any religious confession, even though the 1977 Constitution declares: "Citizens of the USSR are equal before the law, without distinction of origin, social or property status, race or nationality, sex, education, language, attitude to religion, type and nature of occupation, domicile, or other status" (art. 34a). However, it then adds that "the equal rights of citizens of the USSR are guaranteed in all fields of economic, political, social, and cultural life" (art. 34b), thus excluding the religious field. Now, on the basis of international law, the Soviet Union is obliged, without any restrictions or discrimination, to allow its citizens the possibility of "access, on general terms of equality, to public service in their country" (CP, art. 25c),[54] and we must understand this as including positions of power.

The Council, which does not on the whole have much to say about human rights, lingers significantly over the opportunity of admission and advancement in public and political employment, and over the right to vote:

> It is fully consonant with human nature that there should be politico-juridical structures providing all citizens without any distinction with ever improving and effective opportunities to play an active part in the establishment of the juridical foundations of the political community, in the administration of public affairs, in determining the aims and the terms of reference of public bodies, and in the election of political leaders (GS 75).

The Council had, therefore, already stressed those three fundamental principles subsequently taken up by the document of the International Theological Commission, that is, liberty, equality, and participation (3.2.2). In practice, not all young people of equal ability enjoy the same career opportunities in the public, political, cultural, economic, and social life of the Soviet Union. Moreover, an official or manager is promoted by nomination, which comes after a particularly searching political investigation, with a severe examination of the individual's political convictions and fidelity to the party. Although the laws may not make any specific reference to religious tendencies, citizens who show religious convictions are automatically rejected. Indeed, within the perspective of the struggle against religion, these citizens are subject to threats.[55]

Although it extols equality, at no point does the 1977 Soviet Constitution guarantee the possibility of "access, on general terms of equality, to public service in their country" (CP, art. 25c). And the articles on the electoral system (C77, arts. 95–102) state: "The following shall have the right to nominate candidates: branches and organizations of the Communist Party of the Soviet Union" and other bodies connected with the party (art. 100a), which means that all representatives are chosen exclusively by members of the party. Here, again, it is clear that Soviet constitutional social law recognizes only one type of individual or citizen.

Concluding Reflections

The Second Vatican Council spoke of human rights in relatively fragmentary fashion in four documents.[56] The most important text for rights under official atheism is that of *Gaudium et spes* 19–21, which does not give a specific treatment of rights and freedoms in atheistic regimes, but provides a sort of summary of the forms and causes of atheism throughout the world (GS 19), systematic atheism, particularly when in power (GS 20), and the attitude of the Church to atheism (GS 21). Further light is then shone on these remarks on atheism by other conciliar texts on human rights and freedoms that have a bearing on our study. The teaching of the Council on rights is sparse, implicit rather than explicit or developed, and was obviously suggested more by the period of the Council than by the specific requirements of the world and the Church today. The credit for having developed, systematized, and updated it must go to the International Theological Commission. Their work, which was suggested and supported by John Paul II, has made use of new information and new perspectives on the teaching on rights, drawn from the international charters of the United Nations and the Conference on European Security and Cooperation. While the charters end with the statement that the basis of human rights is the dignity of the human person, the document of the International Theological Commission continues with an anthropological and theological type of investigation, aimed at showing that the underlying basis of this dignity—humanity "in the image of God"—is found in God the Creator, Christ the Redeemer, and the Spirit the Sanctifier.

In this perspective, the primary question as the the basis of human rights becomes vital. The basis of Christian human rights is totally different from that found in the 1977 Soviet Constitution, and is closer to that of the charters, although the latter place their foundations on the anthropological and philosophical level, whereas the Christian basis proceeds from sacred scripture, is developed in philosophy, and ends in a theological reflection that is contemporary but is always carried out in the light of revelation. The distance between the basis of Soviet legislation on man and the conclusions of the International Theological Commission, which also encompasses the charters, therefore becomes unbridgeable—also because the two views of man are diametrically opposed. According to the doctrine of the 1977 Soviet constitution, which follows that of the classic fathers of Marxism, man possesses nothing by nature, has nothing in him that is immutable and eternal, has nothing from birth, and does not have any right that is prior to positive legislation. Everything he has in the field of rights is given to him by the specific collectivity to which he belongs. In its short text on the "second world," the document of the International Theological Commission uses the term "collective" or "collectivity" five times (3.1.3). The primary and ultimate reality to be served is not the human person, but the concrete collectivity; the goal of a person in the socialist concept is his or her economic, political, cultural good, and so on, whereas the ultimate goal is the classless communist society, which is progressively brought about until its final fulfillment at a certain moment "X" in time. Moreover, the criterion of good and evil (3.1.3.e) is based on those of the good and wellbeing of the collectivity and of its "interests," as the 1977 Soviet Constitution repeats a number of times. What possible meeting points can there be between this view and the Christian concept of a person as made in the image of God, created by the Father, redeemed by Christ the Son of God, and sanctified in the Spirit, and who has a destiny not solely of this world (a world of which a person is master in the name of God), but also an eschatological destiny that will be fulfilled in the vision of God?

It is equally difficult to reconcile the international law of the charters with Soviet constitutional law. Taking an example of

social rights, we saw that although the 1977 Soviet Constitution
speaks of equality, it in fact does not guarantee it at all, since it
recognizes only one type of person: in other words, the biddable,
uncritical citizen, who is ready to serve the state and the communist party and to pursue their aims. The same can be said of rights
of an economic character, and even more so of those of a political character. When defining the political system, the 1977 Soviet Constitution (arts. 1–9) does not even mention the quality
of rights as to "political opinion or any other type of opinion"
that is claimed in the International Covenant on Civil and Political Rights (art. 2a); nor does it mention it in articles 33–38,
which deal with the juridical equality of citizens. It is especially
significant that article 34, which is the most important in this
area, does not indicate even a trace of equality in the case of
opinions different from the official line. The 1977 Soviet Constitution claims for Soviet citizens the need that their rights and
freedoms always be "in accordance with the interests of the people" and have the aim of "strengthening and developing the
socialist system" (art. 50a). This ethical and "metaethical" yardstick is ever-present and is constantly stressed. Lastly, as far as
personal rights and freedoms are concerned, according to the
analysis of the document of the International Theological Commission, "the individual conscience does not exist but only the
collective conscience as mirrored in the individual" (3.1.3.f), so
that in the close relationship with the collectivity, the individual
is simply a part. The conscience is the mirror of the specific
social environment, and it is in the conscience that the collectivity speaks as norm and "objective" imperative. The conscience
develops side by side with the progress of the society, so that a
more developed society means a greater possibility of development for the conscience of the individual, which is the concrete
expression of the "interests," needs, progress, and responsibilities
of the specific collectivity in which the Soviet citizen lives.
Within the same field of personal rights, we must still consider
the concept of religion, which is also viewed in the perspective of
the economic order—or, more precisely, that of production levels. The person who lives in poverty and misery is incapable of
dragging himself out of this state on his own, and is shut in on
himself in his inferiority. He makes the mistake of looking for
help not from technical and scientific quarters, but from a transcendent being, who would be capable of making him happy,

except that he does not in fact exist. God then becomes one of the most dangerous "alienations," destroying man and reducing his productivity. Moreover, a still imperfect productivity leads to religious alienation. The conclusion is that after man has perfectly dominated nature, he will become the absolute master of the world, and since religion has no right to exist, it will be wiped out. However, since this eradication will not come about naturally, religion must be fought with every possible weapon, not the least of which is that of universal atheistic education, as we have seen in the program of the Communist Party of the Soviet Union recently signed by Gorbachev (1986).

The many forms of contradiction with the international law of the charters, and all the more so with the Christian view as expressed in the document of the International Theological Commission, are therefore very clear: the image of man is different, inasmuch as the human person is viewed as secondary to the ethical and ideological state; the basis of rights and freedoms is different, inasmuch as dignity is not seen as innate to the human person but as vested in the authority of the collectivity, or more exactly in the authority of the Communist Party of the Soviet Union; rights and freedoms are subordinated to the Marxist-Leninist collectivity and its aims, and universal freedoms are not envisaged as they are in the international charters the fundamental right to equality is oriented in the Marxist-Leninist perspective. The 1977 Soviet Constitution never uses the expression "human rights," and this reflects the typical way of thinking behind Soviet constitutional law.

Even when they use the same language, it is clear that the content of the documents of real socialism and that of the international documents take on different meanings. The words "social," "individual," "conscience," "religion," "right," "freedom," "matter," "world," "man," and "society" take on values of their own. For example, freedom "of conscience" (C77, art. 52a) is not conceived of as freedom of political opinion, since an opinion not in line with the common opinion of the society gives rise to contradictions in the sphere of conscience. Freedom of conscience is solely freedom "of speech," "of the press," and so on, but always within the precise limits of being "in accordance with the interests of the people" (art. 50a) and "in accordance with the aims of building communism" (art. 47a). Freedom "of religion" is never seen as referring to a world view that underlies the social, private, and public life of believers, encompassing family, school, and even political behavior. Religion is confined to the private sphere, with those who practice it always being viewed as involved in "prejudices of the past" in the words of Lenin. It therefore has nothing to do with public life, and freedom of religion is to be restricted to acts of ritual worship. It is thus normal for the Church to be separated from the state, but not in the same way as in western countries, where it enjoys full freedom in carrying out its own activities in every field. In real socialism, it is destined to disappear as soon as possible: this has always been the aim of communist society, and its recent 1986 program renews this commitment (section V, B). There is no basis in communist countries for a policy of tolerance toward Church and believers, and still less for religious freedom as this is meant in the international charters—even though these may have been ratified by the Soviet Union. On the other hand, this ambiguity as to terminology cannot continue, inasmuch as the philosophical anthropology and ethical axiology of official marxism have nothing in common with the anthropology and ethics created by a *ratio recte iudicans,* even leaving aside the light of faith. And this is why the International Theological Commission speaks as follows in the conclusion of its document:

> It is clear that the Marxist vocabulary on human dignity, rights, liberty, the person, conscience, religion, etc., differs altogether not only from the Christian teaching, but also from the concepts of international law as expressed in many charters. . . . In spite of these difficulties a wise and efficacious dialogue should be entered into and kept going (3.1.3.g–h).

Translated from the Italian by Leslie Wearne.

Abbreviations

ATS   *Ateisticeskij slovar* (Moscow, 1984)
CP   International Covenant on Civil and Political Rights
CPSU Communist Party of the Soviet Union
C77   Konstitucija Sojuza Sovjetskih Socialisticeskih

Respublik (=1977 Constitution of the Union of
Soviet Socialist Republics)
DCM   Dictionnaire critique du marxisme (Paris, 1982)
ESC   International Covenant on Economic, Social and
Cultural Rights
ITC   International Theological Commission
LCS   Biscaretti di Ruffia and Crespi Reghizzi, La
Costituzione Sovietica del 1977. Un sessentennio di
evoluzione costituzionale dell'URSS (Milan, 1979)
MEW   Marx-Engels Werke
Pr.   Prologue
RSFSR   Russian Soviet Federated Socialist Republic
SDG   Sowjetsystem und demokratische Gesellschaft. Eine
vergleichende Enzykopadie
UN   United Nations
USSR   Union of Soviet Socialist Republics

Notes

1. K. Marx, Zur Kritik der Hegelschen Rechtsphilosophie. Einleitung,
MEW 1 (Berlin, 1957), 378; G.M.-M. Cottier and G.A. Wetter,
"Atheismus," SDG, 1 (1966), 410–426; cf. H.-W. Schüte, "Athe-
ismus," in Historisches Wörterbuch der Philosophie, vol. 1, 595–599;
"Atheismus," in TRE, vol. 4, 349–436; A. Tosel, "Athésime," in
DCM, 61–63; "Religion," in SDG, vol. 5, 584–633.

2. W. Ernst et al., "Human Dignity and Human Rights. International Theological Commission Working Papers," Gregorianum, 65/2–3
(1984); ITC, "Theses de dignitate necnon de iuribus personae humanae," Gregorianum, 66/1 (1985); ITC, Les chrétiens d'aujourd'hui
devant la dignité et les droits de la personne humaine (Vatican City, 1985).
I have personally contributed to the work of the ITC, and have discussed this subject in the following works: "Il fondamento dei diritti
dell'uomo nella Costituzione sovietica," Civiltà Cattolica (1983/I), 222–
234 (in Portuguese, Cultura e fé, 21 [1983], 64–80); "I diritti eco-
nomici, politici e personali nella Costituzione de Breznev," Civiltà
Cattolica (1983/II), 232–242 (in Portuguese, Cultura e fé, 23 [1983],
31–43); "I diritti sociali nella nuova Costituzione sovietica," Civiltà
Cattolica (1983/II), 15–24 (in Portuguese, Cultura e fé, 22 [1983], 35–
47); "Marxismus huius temporis in potestate constitutus de iuribus et
libertatibus hominum," Periodica, 72 (1983), 273–308; "Libertà religiosa nel diritto costituzionale d'ispirazione marxista-leninista: con-

fronto col diritto internazionale ratificato dal marxismo-leninismo ufficiale," in F. Biffi (ed.), *I diritti fondamentali della persona umana e la libertà religiosa. Atti del V Colloquio giuridico (8–10 Marzo 1984)* (Rome, 1985), 637–641.

3. The original Latin text is found in *Gregorianum*, 66/1 (1985), 5–23; cf. "3.1.3. Mundus secundus," p. 19; this subsection is cited here according to paragraphs (e.g., para. a). English translation, *The Dignity and Rights of the Human Person*, published by the Furrow Trust (Maynooth, Ireland, 1985) (English translator's note: this English translation has been slightly amended at certain points).

4. The original Russian text is found in *Konstitucija (Oznovnoj Zakon) Sojuza Sovjetskih Socialističeskih Respublik*, ed. "Juridičeskaja literature" (Moscow, 1978), 15–46; English translation, *Constitution (Fundamental Law) of the Union of Soviet Socialist Republics*, published by the Novosti Press Agency (USSR, 1977); cited here as C77, and then, for example, art. 33a (= article 33, paragraph a).

5. C77, art. 36 c. Art. 50a, for example, guarantees information "in accordance with the interests of the people and in order to strengthen and develop the socialist system." Cf. arts. 34a–b, and 52a–b. Article 62a again stresses: "Citizens of the USSR are obliged to safeguard the interests of the Soviet state, and to enhance its power and prestige [*jego moguščestva i avtoriteta*]."

6. G. Wetter, "Marxismo," *Dizionario Teologico Interdisciplinare*, 2 (1977), 469–503; cf. my article "Il fondamento dei diritti dell'uomo nella Costituzione sovietica," 230–231.

7. S. Sirovec, *Ethik und Metaethik im jugoslawischen Marxismus. Analyse und Vergleich mit katholischen Positionen* (Paderborn/Munich/Vienna/Zurich, 1982).

8. Cf. W. Post, "Marginalien zu Karl Marx und Kommunismus," *Orientierung*, 31 (1967), 272–274.

9. Cf. my contribution to the work of the ITC, *Les chrétiens d'aujourd'hui devant la dignité et les droits de la personne humaine*, 116–126.

10. T. Schieder, "Revolution," in *SDG*, vol. 5, 692–721, esp. 710–717 ("Die Revolution in Theorie und Praxis des Marxismus . . . Lenins Revolution Strategie"); A.K. Wildman, "Lenin," in *SDG*, vol. 4, 1–29; C.D. Kernik and P. Scheibert, "Leninismus," in *SDG*, vol. 4, 29–50; J.P. Lefebvre, "Révolution," in *DCM*, 796–798; G. Labica, "Léninisme," in *DCM*, 508 –510. Post, "Marginalien zu Karl Marx und Kommunismus," 272, says, among other things: "Unklar bleibt jedoch, wie weit Lenin und seine Handvoll geschulter Revoluzionäre sich legitim auf Marx berufen können. Das Problem liegt vor allem darin, ob die von Marx prognostizierte Revolte nicht von ganz anderen Vorstellungen ausging. Nicht nur, dass Russland ein feudalischer Agrarstaat und kein industriellkapitalistisches Land war, nicht nur, dass Marx vom

Aufstand des Proletariats sprach und nicht von gut organisierten Revolutionskadern; auch die gesamte fundamental wichtige Dialektik von Theorie und gesellschaftlicher Praxis wurde insbesondere von Lenin, aber auch schon von Engels, uminterpretiert."

11. K. Marx and F. Engels, *Manifest der Kommunistischen Partei,* MEW 4 (1947/1948), 457–493, which includes the following (474): "Die Kommunisten sind keine besondere Partei gegenüber den anderen Arbeiterparteien. Sie haben keine von den Interessen des ganzen Proletariats gentrennten Interessen. Sie stellen keine besondern [in the Anglica edition of 1888 = sektiererischen] Prinzipien auf, wonach sie die proletarische Bewegung modeln wollen." Thus, in France, the communists join with the social democrat party; in Switzerland, they support the radicals; in Germany, the communist party joins forces with the bourgeoisie. Cf. *ibid.*, 492–493: "Die Kommunisten arbeiten endlich uberall an der Verbindung und Verstandigung der demokratischen Parteien aller Lander."

12. Marx, *Zur Kritik der Hegelschen Rechtsphilosophie, 378; English translation, "Contribution to the Critique of Hegel's Philosophy of Right,"* in R. Niebuhr, *Marx and Engels on Religion* (New York, 1971), 41. Marx also states (*ibid.*): ". . . criticism of religion is the premise of all criticism." A.G. Wetter, "Lenin e il Marxismo sovietico," in Facoltà Filosofica della Pontificia Università Salesiana (eds.), *L'ateismo contemporaneo*, 2 (Turin, 1968), 143–203.

13. V.I. Lenin, *Sulla religione* (Rome, 1957); C. Teklak, "Le fonti della concezione marxista di Gesù," *Antonianum*, 58 (1983), 244–262; G. Labica, "Réligion," in *DCM*, 774–780; J. Rajčak, *Gesù nella ricerca sovietica contemporanea* (Rome, 1985) ("un libro prezioso"—S. Virgulin).

14. *LCS*, 553.

15. Cf. *ATS*. Under the various entries for "Atheism" in this atheistic dictionary, there is a clear emphasis on marxist-leninist atheism, including the atheistic education of the collectivity in schools and in the formation of an atheistic mentality (pp. 32–45). It is very important to neutralize the influence of believing parents (pp. 43–44). Atheistic propaganda must be of a mass nature (*massovie formi*), to be filled out (*dolžni dopolnjatsja*) with individual work (p. 41).

16. Marx and Engels write about law in a fragmentary fashion, and such texts are scattered throughout their works: Marx, *Zur Kritik der Hegelschen Rechsphilosophie, 378–391; idem, Aus der Kritik der Hegelschen Rechtsphilosophie/Kritik des Hegelschen Staatsrechts,* §§ 261–313, MEW 1, 201–233; *idem, Zur Judenfrage,* MEW 1, 347–377; *idem, Das philosophische Manifest der historischen Rechtsschule,* MEW 1, 78–85; K. Marx and F. Engels, *Die deutsche Ideologie. Kritik der neuesten deutschen Philosophie in ihren Repräsentanten Feuerbach, B. Bauer und Stirner, und des deutschen Sozialismus in seiner verschiedenen Propheten,* MEW 3, 9–

530 (many texts from this book are to be considered); K. Marx, *Das Elend der Philosophie. Antwort auf Prudhons "Philosophie des Elends"* (German by E. Bernstein and K. Kautsky, with Foreword and Notes by F. Engels), MEW 4, 63–182 (few texts on law); *idem, Einleitung in Grundrisse der politischen Ökonomie (Rohentwurf) 1857–1858* (Berlin, 1953), 3–31; *idem, Zur Kritik der Politischen Ökonomie*, MEW 13, 3–160; *idem, Kritik der Gothaer Programms*, MEW 19, 11–32; F. Engels, *Herrn Eugen Dührings Umwälzung der Wissenschaft ("Anti-Dühring")*, MEW 20, 5–767 (in this large volume, the relevant texts must be searched for); *idem, Der Ursprung der Familie, des Privateigentums und des Staats. Im Anschluss an Lewis H. Morgans Forschungen*, MEW 21, 25–152.

17. MEW 21, 169; MEW 20, 262.

18. E.B. Pašukanis, *La teoria generale del diritto e il marxismo* (Bari, 1975); J. Michel, "Droit," in *DCM*, 289, explaining the thought of Pašukanis, says that in the field of law, he "est la figure majeure pour cette période," and stresses his view: "Si le droit n'a pas de réalité *sui generis*, il a bien une efficacité particulière. . . . Dans les années 1930, Pashukanis devra renier ses thèse sur le dépérissement de l'Etat et du droit, et c'est Vychinski, le juriste-procureur des grands procès de Moscou, qui aura alors pour charge de fixer officiellement la theorie du droit de l'époque stalienne."

19. M. Villey, *Rechtsphilosophie*, SDG 5, 532–553 (here 546).

20. *Ibid.*, 547–548.

21. ITC, *Theses de dignitate necnon de iuribus personae humanae.* Cited as ITC with the relative section and subsection numbers, except for subsection 3.1.3, "Mundus secondus," which is cited according to paragraphs (see note 3). Here ITC 3.1.1.

22. *Ibid.*

23. Cf. my article "Il fondamento dei diritti dell'uomo nella Costituzione sovietica," 222–234.

24. The magisterium has spoken on a number of occasions on the "legitimacy of private property" and its "social function": GS 71; John XXIII, *Mater et Magistra*, in *AAS*, 53, (1961), 430; John Paul II, *Laborem exercens*, in *AAS*, 73 (1981), 613; English translation, St. Paul Publications (Homebush, N.S.W., 1981), 58, where it is stated that the principle of private property in the teaching of the Church "diverges radically from the program of collectivism as proclaimed by Marxism and put into practice in various countries in the decades following the time of Leo XIII's Encyclical [*Rerum novarum*]. At the same time it differs from the program of capitalism practiced by liberalism and by the political systems inspired by it."

25. Let us take the example of "property." It is "exclusively of the state" (art. 11b). Then a distinction is made between "personal property," which was protected "by the law" according to the 1936 constitution (art. 10) and is now protected "by the state" (art. 13a), and "private property," which does not exist at all, since such a term is contrary to the goal of communism. Cf. R. Khalfina, *Propriété personnelle en URSS* (Moscow, 1976), esp. 87–95 ("Revenus et épagnes du travail"), and 93–107 ("Maison d'habitation et économie domestique auxiliaire"); C77, art. 23a.

26. L.I. Brezhnev, "O projekte Konstituciji (Osnovnoga zakona) Sojuza Sovjetskich Socialističeskich Respublik i itogach jego vsenarodnoga Obsuždenia" (4 October 1977), in *idem, Leninskim kursom,* 6 (Moscow, 1978). Brezhnev emphasizes the identification of man with the state: "L'uomo nuovo, che non separa se stesso dalla Stato, che considera gli interessi dello Stato e di tutto il popolo come la cosa propria vitale" (*LCS,* 482). Brezhnev writes as follows on the subject of "human rights": "E' proprio il tema della 'preoccupazione' per *i diritti dell'uomo* che noti esponenti del mondo capitalistico *hanno scelto in questi ultimi tempi come principale direttiva di marcia nella loro crociata ideologica contro i Paesi del socialismo*" (*LCS,* 494; italics mine). Even so, Brezhnev signed the Helsinki Final Act on 1 August 1975, Principle VII of which speaks of "human rights." Cf. *Prava celovjeka i sovrenennij mir* (Kiev, 1980); Academy of Sciences, *Prava ličnosti v socijalističeskom obščestve* (Moscow, 1981); Academy of Sciences, *Relizacija prav graždan v uslovljach razvitogo socijalizma* (Moscow, 1983).

27. Statute of the Communist Party of the Soviet Union, 1961, Prologue, para. c, states: "The party exists for the people and serves the people. It is *the highest form* of Soviet organization, *the force that directs and guides Soviet society.* The party directs the great creative activity of the Soviet people, and imparts an organized, planned and *scientifically based* character to *the struggle to attain the final aim, which is the victory of communism*" (italics mine).

28. *LCS,* 477.

29. Brezhnev, "O projekte Konstituciji," 533 (*LCS, 496*); *Istorija Komunističeskoj Partii Sovjetskogo Sojuza* (Moscow, 1980), a large universal manual of 800 pages; T.H. Rigby, *Communist Party Membership in the USSR 1917–1967* (Princeton, 1968); R.G. Wesson, *Lenin's Legacy: The Story of the CPSU* (California, 1978).

30. *Istorija Komunističeskoy Partii Sovjetskogo Sojuza,* 742–747. For the party of the Democratic Republic of Germany, cf. *Die neue Verfassung der DDR* (Cologne, 1974), 32–38.

31. There is no similar reference in the 1918, 1924, and 1936 Constitutions; at those dates, there was still no discussion of the conditions of a "developed socialism" (*Partija v uslovljach razvitogo socijalizma*).

32. This ideology, which describes itself as a "science," claims to be

the "supreme revelation," "nonostante il categorico e aprioristico rifiuto di una verifica dei principi su cui è costruita e sul metodo stesso del suo procedere," as is pointed out by G. Codevilla, "I diritti umani nelle costituzioni dell'Europa orientale," in G. Concetti (ed.), *I diritti umani. Dottrina e prassi* (Rome, 1982), 461. Cf. F. Gentile, "I diritti dell'uomo nella critica marxista," in *ibid.*, 631–644.

33. UN, *Statute of the International Court of Justice* (New York: 1983); UN, "Universal Declaration of Human Rights," in *The International Bill of Human Rights* (New York, 1985), 4–9. Cf. my article "Il fondamento dei diritti umani nei documenti internazionali," *Civiltà Cattolica* (1982/IV), 548–557.

34. UN, "International Covenant on Economic, Social and Cultural Rights," in *The International Bill of Human Rights*, 10–20; *idem*, "International Covenant on Civil and Political Rights," in *ibid.*, 21–40. It should be recalled that these pacts were approved by the General Assembly of the UN as early as 16 December 1966, but did not come into force until 1976; UN, *Human Rights International Instruments. Signatures, Ratifications, Accessions, etc.*, 1 July 1981, ST/HR/4/Rev3 (Geneva, 1981); UN, *The International Bill of Human Rights, XXX 1948–1978* (New York, 1978).

35. Italics mine; Conference on Security and Cooperation in Europe, "Final Act," in *International Legal Materials, Current Documents* (American Society of International Law), 14/5 (September 1975), 1292–1325; cf. *Sicherheit und Zusammenarbeit in Europa (KSZE), Analyse und Dokumentation 1973–1978*, H.A. Jacobsen, W. Mallman, and C. Meier (eds.), *Dokumentation zur Aussenpolitik*, II/2, *Wissenschaft und Politik* (Cologne, 1978), 917.

36. John Paul II, Letter *The signal occasion* to the Secretary General of the UN on the Thirtieth Anniversary of the Universal Declaration of Human Rights (2 December 1978), para. n, in Pontifical Commission "Iustitia et Pax," *Human Rights, The Social Teaching of John Paul II*, 7 (Vatican City, 1981), 11.

37. ITC 3.1.1.

38. Cf. note 34.

39. The second section of the ITC document deals with "The Theology of the Dignity and Rights of Man," and this section is in turn divided into two subsections, the first of which is entitled "In Some Theological Sources" (in turn subdivided into "The Biblical Perspective" and "The Roman Magisterium Today"), and the second of which aims at a systematic consideration of "The Dignity and Rights of Human Persons in the Light of the Theology of the History of Salvation" (in turn subdivided into "Man as Created," "Man the Sinner," and "Man as Redeemed by Christ").

40. *Relatio post disceptationem*, 2, to *Mysterium hominis*, 3; italics mine.

41. ITC 2.2.1–2.2.3. It can and should be said that the ITC document does not enter into any discussion of the basis of rights. On the whole, it assumes that this is known from the international charters. It then says that "in some respects" (citing John Paul II, Address to the Fifth Colloquium Juridicum, in *L'Osservatore Romano* [11 March 1984], 8), but without saying in which "respects," religious freedom "may be regarded as the basis of all other rights. Some, however, would claim this primacy for equality" (1.2). This can be deduced from the fact that, on the one hand, in order for man to be whole, his relationship with God must be safeguarded ("religious freedom"), but religious freedom presumes the truth of the human being with all his relationships (with God, himself, others, the world), the most fundamental of which is the vertical one; and if the latter is blocked, the human person is unable to reach his full development. Cf. G. Lo Castro, *Il Soggetto e i suoi diritti nell'ordinamento canonico* (Milan, 1985), 191: ". . . la ragione ultima del diritto canonico non sta nella specifica dimensione religiosa ma nella condizione umana." On the other hand, the "equality of all men" is certainly at the basis of every positive right, although it also assumes the ontological structure of the human being, which is then equal, universal, inviolable, and so on. Therefore, not even equality has its roots in the religious dimension, but merely finds an outstanding expression there.

42. Cf. various works by the members of the ITC, especially those of H. Hamel, C. Schönborn, and H. Schürmann, published under the general title "Human Dignity and Human Rights," *Gregorianum*, 65/2–3 (1984); E. Fuchs and P.A. Stucki, *Au nom de l'autre. Essai sur le fondement des droits de l'homme* (Geneva, 1985); "La dignità della persona umana: fonte dei diritti dell'uomo," in *Portare Cristo all'uomo*, vol. 3 (*Solidarietà*), Studie Urbaniana 24 (Rome, 1985), 897–983; S. Marcus-Helmons, "L'homme et ses droits fondamenteaux en Europe Occidentale," in R. Goldie (ed.), *Image of Man in Human Rights Legislation: Pilot Study on Human Rights*, FIUC (Rome, 1985), 21–36; P. Daubercies and C. Lefevre, *Le respect et la liberté. Droits de l'Homme, Raison et Foi*, FIUC, (Rome, 1985); S. Cotta, "Il fondamento dei diritti umani," in G. Concetti (ed.), *Diritti Umani. Dottrina e prassi* (Rome, 1982), 645–655.

43. This anthropology is described in a few words in the ITC document, 3.1.3.b: "According to 'historical materialism' man is not created by God (a myth distorting reality) but simply a result of the evolution of matter. Genuine human progress will be attained when the conditions of production and the human labor entailed are changed for the collective good by changing the economic structures, on which furthermore the whole so-called 'superstructure' is built and sustained. To attain this end each and every citizen must collectivize himself to the utmost."

44. H. Kelsen, *La teoria comunista del diritto* (Milan, 1956), 278.

45. O. Luchterhandt, *UN-Menschenrechtskonventionen, Sowjetrecht-Sowjetwirklichkeit. Ein kritischer Vergleich* (Baden-Baden, 1981), 104–105.

46. *LCS,* 553; "Ustav Komunističeskoj partii Sovjetskogo Sojuza," *Pravda* (7 March 1986), 8; "Programma Komunističeskoj partii Sovjetskogo Sojuza," *Pravda* (7 March 1986), 6 (V, B).

47. Luchterhandt, *UN-Menschenrechtskonventionen, Sowjetrecht-Sowjetwirklichkeit,* 102. It is well known that the 1977 Constitution allows "atheistic propaganda" (art. 52), which is in practice carried out through the use of every possible means, whereas religious propaganda is forbidden. On the other hand, in the first constitution (1918), Lenin allowed the following text: "The church is separate from the state and the school from the church, and the right of all citizens to freedom of religious and antireligious propaganda is recognized" (art. 13). However, in due course, Stalin decided to eliminate "religious propaganda" and to encourage only "antireligious propaganda," as we can see in the 1936 Constitution, art. 124. The final aim of this increased atheization is the building of the atheistic classless communist society (or collectivity). Cf. my contribution, "Libertà religiosa nel diritto costituzionale d'ispirazione marxista-leninista," 637–641.

48. C77, arts. 40a, 14a–c, 15b, 17, 13a, 23a, 60.

49. Luchterhandt, *UN-Menschenrechtskonventionen, Sowjetrecht-Sowjetwirklichkeit,* 33–35.

50. *LCS,* 553 (art. 2d).

51. Statute of the CPSU (1961), in *LCS,* 551–572.

52. Luchterhandt, *UN-Menschenrechtskonventionen, Sowjetrecht-Sowjetwirklichkeit,* 35.

53. *Vedomosti Verchovnogo Sovjeta RSFSR,* 12, 221, "O primenii statji 142 Ugolovnoga kodeksa RSFSR," 18 March 1966, 220.

54. V. Remnev, "The Societ Citizen and Administration," in Academy of Sciences, *Socialism and Human Rights* (Moscow, 1981), 118–130.

55. Luchterhandt, *UN-Menschenrechtskonventionen, Sowjetrecht-Sowjetwirklichkeit,* 42.

56. IM 5; DH 1, 2, 3, 5, 6, 7, 9, 14; GE 1, 2, 3, 6; and GS 21, 25, 26, 29, 42, 52, 65, 67, 68, 73, 74, 75, 76, 79, 82.

CHAPTER 50

Interreligious Dialogue in the Church's Evangelizing Mission

Twenty Years of Evolution of a Theological Concept

Jacques Dupuis, S.J.

Summary

Is interreligious dialogue an intrinsic dimension of the Church's mission? Is it a matter of preevangelization or of evangelization proper? Is it an end in itself, or does it represent a means ordained to the proclamation of the gospel? Vatican II did not answer these questions, nor is a unanimous answer given to them after the Council. The postconciliar period is, however, characterized by a clear evolution of the terminology bearing on the subject as well as of its theological aspect. This article studies some major landmarks in this evolution, leading to the recent document of the Secretariat for Non-Christians entitled "The Attitude of the Church Toward the Followers of Other Religions" (Pentecost 1984). Following this document, the article proposes a broad and comprehensive notion of the Church's evangelizing mission. Interreligious dialogue appropriately represents one of its integral dimensions: aroused as it is by the Spirit, true dialogue consists moreover in mutual evangelization between Christians and other believers. It remains, however, open to the proclamation of the gospel in which the mission of the Church culminates.

Words, like men, have a history and their evolution, far from being fortuitous, witnesses to our developing awareness of the realities that they are intended to convey. This observation, which can be verified in many theological areas, applies in a singular manner to the terms by which the Church has in the past defined her mission and tends to define it today; to the evolution of the terms corresponds a deepening of mission theology. Thus, "mission" (in the singular) or the Church's "missionary activity" is used today as a broad concept within which "missions" (in the plural) need to be understood; the priority of mission over missions shows that the Church's vocation is fundamentally the same in all places, even though degrees of development may differ.[1] A related, and even more profound evolution in missionary semantics consists in the progressive emergence in recent years of a broad concept of "evangelization" as comprehending the overall mission of the Church. Having followed this semantic evolution during and after Vatican II, D. Grasso rightly concludes: "The post-Conciliar Church keeps broadening more and more the term 'evangelization,' to make it express the totality of her mission. It could be said that in the Church everything is 'evangelization,' for she actualizes her mission in all that she does."[2] It is clear that a shift in mission theology underscores this new terminology. The mainstream of pre-Vatican II missiology, as is well known, had defined the goal of missions as "planting the Church." Characteristically, Vatican II, without repudiating this traditional view, combined it with another that at the time had begun to carry greater favor. Thus, we read, for instance in *Ad gentes* 6, that "the specific purpose of this missionary activity (in the 'missions') is evangelization and the planting of the Church among those peoples and groups where she has not yet taken root."[3] The combination of the two terms, legitimate as it is, shows that at Vatican II, "evangelization" had not yet uniformly taken up the broad comprehensive meaning by virtue of which it could become identified with the overall mission of the Church. This was to be a postconciliar development.

The present chapter is directly concerned with interreligious dialogue; specifically, with the role and significance that can, or must be assigned to it in the Church's mission. To solve this problem, however, attention must be paid to the semantic evolution of mission terminology in recent years. Is interreligious dialogue part and parcel of the Church's mission, or does it remain somewhat extrinsic to it, useful merely as a first approach to the others? Does it belong to evangelization proper, or must it be viewed as "preevangelization"? Can it be considered as an end in itself, or is it to be seen as a means ordained to the proclamation of the gospel? Is it, as the followers of the other religious traditions are often inclined to believe, the latest device put to use by the missionary Church to win new members over to herself? Can it eschew all proselytizing attitudes while claiming to give expression to the Church's evangelizing mission?

The answers to these questions have neither been uniform in Vatican II nor in post-Vatican II theology; nor are they uniform today. Nevertheless, a certain evolution can be followed through the last twenty years, tending to a growing appreciation of interreligious dialogue as in its own right an authentic expression of the Church's overall evangelizing mission. Our intention here is to follow this evolution through some important documents of the period under review, some of which belong in different ways to the Church's teaching authority, while others do not. The survey makes no pretense at being exhaustive; the documents covered may, however, be considered as representative landmarks. Opinions of individual theologians have been left out of consideration, though undoubtedly they often gave shape to, and are reflected in, the documents.

One more observation needs to be made by way of introduction. The place assigned to interreligious dialogue in the Church's mission depends in the first place on the theological evaluation that is made of the world's religious traditions and of their significance in God's overall saving plan for humankind as it is realized in history. The two are necessarily interdependent. A minimizing evaluation of the religions themselves will naturally lead to a negative view of the relation of interreligious dialogue to mission; conversely, a positive stand regarding the first will normally command an open attitude toward the other. Our analysis of the documents has, therefore, constantly to keep in mind their theological assessment of the religious traditions, in order to account for the role and place they assign to interreligious dialogue in the mission of the Church.

Analysis of Documents

The Encyclical Letter *Ecclesiam suam* and Vatican II

Pope Paul VI published his programmatic Encyclical Letter *Ecclesiam suam* on 6 August 1964, that is, between the second and third sessions of Vatican II. This is not without significance for our subject, as the Vatican II documents that were to deal with interreligious dialogue (NA, AG, GS) were still in the making. The Secretariat for Non-Christians had been created by the Pope less than three months before the date of the Encyclical (17 May 1964). It can be safely said that *Ecclesiam suam* marked the entry of dialogue into the new perspective that the Church's program for self-renewal implied; it was an important dimension of the openness to the world contemplated by the Council. The term "dialogue" itself made with the Encyclical its appearance into official Church documents.[4]

The Encyclical's main concern was, in the Pope's own words, "the problem of the dialogue (*colloquium*) between the Church and the modern world" (*AAS*, 56 [1964], 613). "The Church should enter into dialogue with the world in which it exists and labors. She has something to say, a message to deliver, a communication to offer" (*ibid.*, 639). Dialogue is conceived by the Pope as "a method of accomplishing the apostolic mission, a means of spiritual communication" (644). Distinguishing the various forms that the "dialogue of salvation" can take, he stresses "the supreme importance which the preaching of the word of God maintains . . . for the Catholic apostolate. . . . Preaching is the primary form of apostolate" (648). The Church, the Pope observes, must be ready to "enter into dialogue with all men of good will, within and without its own sphere" (649). The Encyclical goes on to draw a series of concentric circles "around the central point in which God has placed us (the Church)" (650); thus, it hopes to show how the dialogue of salvation implied in the Church's mission attains distinctly different categories of people. The Pope distinguishes four such concentric circles, starting from the most remote (the whole of mankind and the world), passing through a second (the followers of other religions), and a third (other Christians), and ending with the most intimate circle (dialogue within the Church herself).

The second circle is "made up primarily of those who adore the one, supreme God whom we too adore," not only the Jews and

Muslims, but "also the followers of the great African and Asiatic religions" (654–655). "Honesty," the Pope insists, "compels us to declare openly our conviction that there is but one true religion, the religion of Christianity and our hope that all who seek God and adore Him may come to acknowledge its truth" (655). Nevertheless, "we recognize and respect the moral and spiritual values of the various non-Christian religions," and are prepared to enter into, and to take the initiative for, a dialogue on such common ideals as promoting and defending religious liberty, human brotherhood, culture, social welfare, and civil order (655).

The section of the Encyclical ends on this note of a true, but cautious opening. Its theological evaluation of other religions as well as the scope it opens for interreligious dialogue remain limited. The role and place of this dialogue in the Church's mission is not further specified or explained.

A breakthrough had, nevertheless, been made which the Second Vatican Council could follow up. Coming to the Council documents, this is not the place for an elaborate analysis of their theology of world religions. Let us, however, caution that an objective evaluation must neither exaggerate nor underestimate what the Council actually affirms.[5] Some general observations will suffice. There exists in the Council documents, on the one hand, a tendency to recognize "elements of truth and grace" (AG 9), not merely in the individual religious life of followers of other religions, but also in some objective elements of the religious traditions themselves, whether these be "religious rites and culture" (LG 17), "religious endeavors (incepta)" (AG 3), or other "treasures which the bountiful God has distributed among the nations of the earth" (AG 11), and are found in their "religious traditions" (ibid.) These elements are seen as "a ray of that Truth (illius Veritatis) which enlightens all men" (NA 2). On the other hand, a close look at the texts reveals on the part of the Council a growing awareness of the universal influence of the Holy Spirit, well beyond the boundaries of the Christian fold, indeed throughout the world. The Spirit of God—who is also the Spirit of Christ—fills the universe (GS 11). Ad gentes and Gaudium et spes—both belonging to the last session of the Council—make explicit reference to this universal presence of the Spirit, in time and space: "Doubtless, the Holy Spirit was already at work before Christ was glorified" (AG 4); so is he in the world of today, in the aspirations of men and women everywhere for a better quality of life (GS 38, 1), for a social order more worthy of man (GS 26, 4), and universal brotherhood (GS 39, 3). His constant influence keeps alive in man the question of his religious destiny (GS 41, 1), offering him the light and the strength to measure up to it (GS 10, 2). Man has been redeemed by Christ and made a new creature in the Holy Spirit (GS 37, 4). In fact, the Spirit is now calling all to Christ, not only through the preaching of the gospel but already through the seeds of the Word (AG 15); he offers to all "in a manner known to God . . . the possibility of being associated to the Paschal Mystery" (GS 22, 5). Thus, enlivened and united in the Spirit of the risen Christ, humankind journeys toward the consummation of human history (GS 45, 2)—with a lively hope, which is the gift of the Spirit (GS 93, 1).

Such is the deep foundation upon which in the documents of the Council interreligious dialogue is based. It is not surprising to see the same documents appeal to the members of the Church to enter into the practice of interreligious dialogue. Such an exhortation is already found in *Nostra aetate:* "prudently and lovingly through dialogue and collaboration (*per colloquia et collaborationem*) with the followers of other religions, and in witness of Christian faith and life, acknowledge, preserve and promote the spiritual, moral and socio-cultural values found among them" (*NA* 2). Similar appeals are repeated both in *Ad gentes* and *Gaudium et spes.* Following Christ's own example, his disciples, "profoundly penetrated by the Spirit of Christ, should know the people among whom they live, and should establish contact with them. Through sincere and patient dialogue (*dialogo*) they themselves should learn what treasures a bountiful God has distributed among the nations of the earth. At the same time, let them try to illumine these treasures with the light of the Gospel, to set them free, and to bring them under the dominion of god their Savior" (AG 11). The *magna charta* of dialogue in Vatican II is *Gaudium et spes* 92—where the Council resumes in reverse order the four concentric circles previously drawn by the Encyclical *Ecclesiam Suam.* Where believers of other religious traditions are concerned, the text hopes that "an open dialogue may lead us all faithfully to receive the inspirations of the Spirit and to follow them ardently" (GS 92, 4). These are generous words, never spoken before by an ecumenical Council.

They do not, however, tell us the place that the Council assigns to interreligious dialogue in the Church's mission. This is where we need to remember, as noted earlier, that the terms "mission" and "evangelization" underwent an evolution during the Council that, moreover, did not end with the Council itself; they remained somewhat ambiguous throughout the Council, sometimes referring only to the missionary proclamation of the gospel, at other times extending more broadly to the entire missionary activity of the Church.[6] But even where mission and evangelization are given this broader meaning in the Council documents, no explicit mention is made of interreligious dialogue as constituting by itself one of its intrinsic elements. This silence can be verified in the key texts on dialogue referred to previously: in *Ad gentes* 11, dialogue is directly linked to the witness of life; as for *Gaudium et spes* 92, 1, after stating that "by virtue of her mission to shed on the whole world the radiance of the Gospel message . . . the Church stands forth as a sign of that brotherliness which allows honest dialogue and invigorates it," it becomes silent and proceeds no further. By virtue of her mission, we are told, the Church stands in a privileged posture for dialogue; the significance of interreligious dialogue itself in her evangelizing mission remains, however, unexpressed.

Theological Conferences and Congresses

It is not surprising that the question that Vatican II had left unanswered surfaced often in postconciliar discussions, in particular, in theological conferences and congresses. It was not without importance for the renewal of pastoral methods in those countries chiefly where Christians represented a tiny minority in the midst of a religiously plural society. Was entering into interreligious dialogue with others doing evangelizing work, yes or no? And, if not, what role did such dialogue have in the Church's mission? It is not possible to review all the theological meetings where these questions were asked in postconciliar years. Two have been selected that seem sufficiently representative.

In 1969, Sedos (Rome) organized a *Symposium on Mission Theology for Our Times*. We need only examine its Theological Conclusions of three precise points: the theology of religions, the concept of mission and evangelization, and the place assigned in it to interreligious dialogue.[7]

On the theology of religions: the Conclusions recognize the universal active presence of the Spirit. Yet, "the one and only pathway of salvation" is Christ, while, "as creations of man's religious genius in search of his destiny," other religions "cannot be paths of salvation" (I, 1, 1). However, the authentic religious values they contain, "purified and elevated by grace, . . . can be a means of arriving at the act of faith and charity that is necessary for salvation." In their rites and beliefs, "supernatural elements— wherever they may come from—" can also be found (I, 1, 2). In those religions then "there exists an ordination to Christ which can only be fulfilled by the proclamation of the Gospel," whereby the supernatural elements eventually contained in them are brought back to their source (I, 1, 3).

On mission and evangelization: it is mission work that allows those already oriented toward Christ "to reach full knowledge of His mystery" (I, 2, 1), revealing to them their true nature and the ultimate meaning and destiny of their life (I, 2, 2). The proclamation of the gospel under Christ's mandate is ordained to this end that "everything might gradually be subjected to His Lordship" (I, 2, 3).

On dialogue: "Missionaries never start from zero. Through dialogue, they must discover the authentic values present in non-Christian religions, in order to purify and elevate them by inserting Christ's Gospel in them. In this way, Christ will be manifested to non-Christians, not as a stranger but as the one they have been looking for" (I, 3, 1). Successful dialogue presupposes as necessary conditions identification with the others and an authentic meeting with them (I, 3, 2).

Summarily: the attitude toward the religious traditions of the world, though positive, does not appear fully consistent. But mission and evangelization remain primarily identified with the proclamation of the gospel; interreligious dialogue seems reduced to a means conducive to proclamation, to a method that provides it with a useful point of entry. This evaluation of dialogue strikes one as all the more unsatisfactory when compared with the more positive assessment that the same Conclusions make of the relationship between evangelization and development work: development work, provided it is done as Christian witness, "should be recognized as evangelization in the strict sense. . . . It is one of the ways of evangelization" (II, 2), even if it calls for proclamation (II, 2), the "second pathway of evangelization" with which it is necessarily tied up (II, 3). The contrast is striking: while development work is *a way of* evangelization, tied up as it may be with proclamation, interreligious dialogue is but *a means for* the proclamation of the gospel.

Soon after the Sedos Symposium, there took place at Nagpur (India) in 1971 an important *International Theological Conference on Evangelization and Dialogue in India.* Our task must again consist in examining the Final Declaration of the Congress, specifically its theology of religions and its understanding of the mission of the Church, in order that we may assess the role and significance it assigns to interreligious dialogue in relation to that mission.[8]

The "theological understanding of the religious traditions of mankind" is significantly positive. The Declaration sees Christ and his grace at work in them (12). An ineffable mystery, "which is called by different names but which no name can adequately represent" is active among all peoples of the world—the same which is "definitively disclosed and communicated in Jesus of Nazareth" (13). God's self-communication "extends to the whole of mankind in different ways and degrees within the one divine economy" (14). The fulfillment of man's destiny "can only be reached through man's positive response to the mystery which he discovers in his personal experience"; this destiny the Christian knows to be union with Christ, Liberator and Savior (15). "Since man is a social being, concrete religious traditions provide the usual context in which he strives for his ultimate goal. Therefore, the religious traditions of the world can be regarded as helping him towards the attainment of his salvation. . . . The different Sacred Scriptures and Rites of the religious traditions of the world can be in various degrees expressions of a divine manifestation and can be conducive to salvation . . . " (16).

Lest there should be any ambiguity, the Declaration affirms clearly that such a positive assessment of the religious traditions of the world does not in any way undermine the "uniqueness of the Christian economy" (16) or "lessen the urgency of the Christian mission." This mission is dealt with under the heading "evangelization." Evangelization is, however, conceived narrowly in terms of witnessing to and preaching Christ (18). "The mission of the Church," says the Declaration, "has to be realized through evangelization. By evangelization we mean the imparting of the good news of salvation in Jesus Christ . . . , not only through proclamation . . . but also through a life of Christian witness"

(19). In the context of religious pluralism, such evangelization is meaningful and necessary "because it communicates the explicit knowledge of Christ" (22).

Given this identification of evangelization with the proclamation of the good news, it is clear that, whatever value might be attributed to interreligious dialogue, it could not be considered as belonging to evangelization proper. The next section of the document gives, however, a very positive evaluation of dialogue: it results in a mutual enrichment of the Christian partners and the others (25); it aims at "mutual understanding, communion and collaboration." "By its very nature (it) . . . tends towards the ultimate vision of a perfect unification of all men which can be discerned in the convergent aspirations of the various religious traditions" (26). It is "good in itself, because it fosters mutual communication and edification" (27). From the fraternal exchange of spiritual experiences, there results, in particular, a "mutual spiritual enrichment." "This enrichment comes from the fact that in dialogue each partner listens to God speaking in the self-communication and questioning of his fellow-believers. It leads to a spiritual growth and therefore to a kind of deeper *metanoia* or conversion to God" (27).

Had not the term "evangelization" been in anticipation narrowed down to gospel proclamation, the positive assessment and rich description of interreligious dialogue contained in the Nagpur Declaration could have been expressed in terms of mutual evangelization beween Christians and others. This, however, is not said here.[9]

The 1974 Synod on Evangelization

As is well known, in view of each of the Synods of Bishops in Rome, the various episcopal conferences of the world are requested to send a Communication to Rome. In preparation for the 1974 Synod on Evangelization, as would be expected, the Asian episcopal conferences made the great religious traditions of Asia and interreligious dialogue their primary concern. It would be tedious to show the positive approach various Communications from Asia took toward this pastoral reality, sensitivity to which had been growing in recent years.[10] Nor is this required, for we possess a more broad-based document, which in general may be said to represent the approach of the Asian episcopal conferences to the subject. The First Plenary Assembly of the Federation of Asian Bishops' Conferences (FABC), which met in Taipei, Taiwan, 22–27 April 1974, in preparation for the Synod, published a Final Statement and some Recommendations. What do these documents have to say on our subject?[11]

Summarily: the preaching of Jesus Christ and his gospel assumes in Asia today "an urgency, a necessity and magnitude unmatched in the history of our faith in this part of the world" (8). The primary focus of this task of "evangelization" is the building up of a truly local Church (9); "in Asia especially this involves a dialogue with the great religious traditions of our peoples" (13). There follows a very positive appraisal of these religious traditions: they are "significant and positive elements in the economy of God's design of salvation" (14). "How . . . can we not acknowledge that God has drawn our peoples to Himself through them?" (15). Dialogue with them "will reveal to us also many riches of our own faith which we perhaps would not have perceived" (16), and teach us to receive from them (17), while "on our part we can offer what we believe the Church alone has the duty and the joy to offer to . . . all men" (18). Among the recommendations made by the Plenary Assembly figures Recommendation 3, which is to "evolve a working concept of evangelization that embraces, as integral to that concept, genuine dialogue with the great living religions of Asia and other deep-rooted forms of belief, such as animism" (p. 35; FAPA, p. 39). Speaking of the promotion of justice, the statement had remarked that "evangelization and the promotion of true human development and liberation, are not only not opposed, but make up today the integral preaching of the Gospel, especially in Asia" (23). In spite of a still hesitating terminology, what is desired is a broad concept of evangelization, of which both the promotion of justice and interreligious dialogue will be viewed as integral parts.

Passing on to the celebration of the 1974 Synod on Evangelization of the Modern World, it may first be observed that the Asian representatives, while sharing with the South Americans the concern for justice and liberation and with the Africans that for inculturation, made themselves, in the spirit of the Taipei Assembly, the advocates of an open theology of the great religious traditions of the world and of a positive approach to interreligious dialogue as intrinsically belonging to the Church's mission. Lack of space forbids examining individual interven-

tions closely;[12] we must limit ourselves to the reports of the
special secretaries and to the final documents of the Synod.
These various documents witness to the fluctuations suffered by
our theme during the Synod proceedings. In his report on the
first part,[13] D.S. Amalorpavadass, secretary, wrote: "Dialogue is
good in itself and is an end in itself because it fosters mutual help
and communion; it cannot, however, be severed from evangelization, nor does it dispense us from the duty to evangelize. Even
though theologically evangelization and dialogue are distinct,
nevertheless both combine together into one life in the case of
many Christians . . . " (16). Earlier, the same secretary had defined evangelization in terms of proclamation: "By evangelization
may be understood the proclamation, through words, works and
life of the good news of salvation of all men in Jesus Christ" (15).
The report of the secretary of the second part,[14] which followed
later, spoke differently. D. Grasso recalled the recent evolution
of the term "evangelization," which he said was being verified at
the Synod itself, toward a comprehensive notion embracing "the
entire mission of the Church" (16); he did not, however, allude
to the possible relation between interreligious dialogue and the
evangelizing mission.

The history of the Synod does not need to be recalled here.[15] It
is well known that the hope of publishing an elaborate final document was frustrated at the end. But it is worthwhile to examine
what the schema of the final document that was proposed to the
assembly had to say on our subject.[16] It read: "Interreligious dialogue must not be considered extrinsic to the Church's mission of
evangelization. . . . In itself it is already a concrete expression of
the mission of the Church. [In dialogue] the members of the
Church, impelled by love and a great reverence for the action of
the Spirit in other men, share with them their Christian experience. Interreligious dialogue, therefore, is good and needs to be
promoted as belonging to the Church's mission" (34). As it failed
to receive a positive preliminary vote, the entire schema of the
final document had to be abandoned; with it, the proposition
mentioned previously went by the wayside. The hope of an elaborate document having been shattered, the Synod decided to publish a short Declaration.[17] This text, however, though intending
to summarize the Synod's main orientations does this in a subdued
fashion, where the thrust of the Synodal work fails to come
through effectively. Of interreligious dialogue, it says the follow-

ing: "Confident in the action of the Holy Spirit which overflows the bounds of the Christian community, we wish to foster dialogue with non-Christian religions, so that we may reach a better understanding of the gospel's newness and of the fullness of revelation, and thus may be in a better position to show to others how the salvific truth of God's love is fulfilled in Christ" (11). Interreligious dialogue seems here reduced to a means conducive to the proclamation of the gospel; it is not in itself an expression of the Church's evangelizing mission.

The Apostolic Exhortation *Evangelii nuntiandi*

One year after the Synod, Pope Paul VI published the Apostolic Exhortation *Evangelii nuntiandi,* dated 8 December 1975, in which he meant to prolong the reflection of the Synod and to present its findings to the whole Church. Our analysis of this important document must limit itself to what touches directly on our subject.

The notion of "evangelization" set forth by the Exhortation is in more than one sense a broad one. Evangelization, which is the mission of the Church and her very *raison d'être* (14), involves the entire person of the evangelizer: his words, his deeds, and the witness of his life (21–22); as for its object, evangelization extends to all that is human, aiming as it does at the renewal of humanity and the transformation by the power of the gospel of human culture and cultures (18–20). Yet, this broad and inspiring view notwithstanding, the Pope, when defining evangelization, continues to have primarily in view the explicit proclamation of the gospel and all those Church activities that directly flow from it: "She [the Church] exists in order to evangelize, that is, to say in order to preach and teach, to be the channel of the gifts of grace, to reconcile sinners with God, and to perpetuate Christ's sacrifice in the Mass, which is the memorial of His death and glorious resurrection" (14). The proclamation of the gospel is so central to evangelization that often it is simply identified with it: evangelization is proclamation—that is, kerygma, preaching and catechesis (22). In any event, "there is no true evangelization if the name, the teaching, the life, the promises, the Kingdom and the mystery of Jesus of Nazareth, the Son of God, are not proclaimed" (22). On the other hand, evangelization only reaches its full development if the hearers' inner adherence is concretely expressed by their entering through the sacraments into the community of believers that is the Church (23).

The Pope meant to bring out "the reality of evangelization in all its richness, complexity and dynamism" (17), and his preoccupation to "evangelize man's culture and cultures" goes a long way in that direction. Yet the question must be asked about the place the Apostolic Exhortation assigns in the evangelizing mission to the promotion of justice and human liberation on the one hand, and to interreligious dialogue on the other.

Regarding the first, the Pope notes that evangelization involves "an explicit message, adapted to the different situation constantly being realized" (29). In today's world, this means that "the Church has the duty to proclaim the liberation of millions of human beings, many of whom are her own children, the duty of assisting the birth of that liberation, of giving witness to it, of ensuring that it be complete. This is not foreign to evangelization" (30). There follow important and necessary cautions against possible deviationns of human liberation work (31–37) and a restatement of the "specific religious finality of evangelization" (32). Nevertheless, the somewhat restrictive view on liberation work as "not foreign to evangelization" stands in contrast with the much more positive assertion of the 1971 Synod of Bishops, which in its document *De Iustitia in Mundo* had declared it to be "a constitutive dimension of the preaching of the Gospel" (6).[18]

What of the other question? What place does the Apostolic Exhortation give to interreligious dialogue in the Church's evangelizing mission? The role of the Holy Spirit as the principal agent of evangelization is stressed in so far as he animates the Church (75); but the Spirit is nowhere said to be at work in the world beyond the boundaries of the Church. This had been a basic affirmation of Vatican II and had not failed to surface in the Synod proceedings. *Evangelii nuntiandi*'s assessment of the other religions seems unduly negative. Positive values are recognized in them in the line of the Council, but, these notwithstanding, they are understood to carry but the echo of a sincere human quest and search for God. Even "the highest forms of natural religion" fail to establish "an authentic and living relationship with God," "even though they have, as it were, their arms stretched out towards heaven" (53). There is no room here to further discuss this evaluation of the other religions, a subject which the Pope himself says raises many questions to be further studied by theologians. [19] It must suffice to mention that it leaves little scope for interreligious dialogue and no room for it in the Church's evangelizing mission. In *Evangelii nuntiandi*, the followers of other religions are only considered "beneficiaries of evangelization"; it is to them in the first place that the proclamation of the gospel by the Church needs to be addressed. Thus considered, evangelization is one-way traffic; there is no room for mutual evangelization of Christians and others through interreligious dialogue.

John Paul II and the Secretariat for Non-Christians on "Dialogue and Mission"

We cannot review the entire teaching of the present Pope on the subject of other religions, evangelization, and interreligious dialogue. Some landmarks and representative texts must suffice here also. [20]

As would have been expected, John Paul II touched on the theme of the other religions in his first Encyclical Letter, *Redemptor hominis* (1979). He did so with a very open attitude. Does it not sometimes happen, the Pope asked, "that the firm belief of the followers of the non-Christians religions—a belief that is also an effect of the Spirit of truth operating outside the visible confines of the Mystical Body—can make Christians ashamed. . . .?" He recommended all activity designed to "coming closer together with" them "through dialogue, contacts, prayer in common, investigation of the treasures of human spirituality in which . . . the members of these religions are indeed not lacking" (6). "The Fathers of the Church," he added, "rightly saw in the various religions as it were so many reflections of the one truth, 'Seeds of the Word,' attesting that, though the routes taken may be different, there is but one single goal to which is directed the deepest aspiration of the human spirit as expressed in its quest for God and . . . for the full dimension of its humanity . . ." (11). "The missionary attitude always begins with a feeling of deep esteem for 'what is in man' (Jn. 2:25). . . . It is a question of respecting everything that has been brought about in him by the Spirit which 'blows where it wills' (Jn. 3:8)" (12). The Pope, as may be seen, insists on acknowledging the operative presence of the Spirit of God in the followers of the

other religions and bases on this theological foundation the significance of interreligious dialogue in the Church's mission.

Addressing the peoples of Asia from the Auditorium of Radio
Veritas, Manila, in 1981, the Pope returned to the same theme
with even more pressing accents.[21] The Church, today, he said,
"experiences a profound need to enter into contact and dialogue
with all these religions." What seems to bring together and
unite, in a particular way, Christians and believers of other religions is an acknowledgment of the need for prayer. "We trust
that whenever the human spirit opens itself in prayer to (the)
Unknown God, an echo will be found of the same Spirit who,
knowing the limits and weakness of the human person, Himself
prays in us and on our behalf . . . (Rom. 8:26). The intercession
of the Spirit of God who prays in us and for us is the fruit of the
mystery of the Redemption of Christ . . ." (4). "All Christians,"
the Pope concluded, "must . . . be committed to dialogue with
the believers of all religions, so that mutual understanding and
collaboration may grow; so that moral values may be strengthened; so that God may be praised in all creation. Ways must be
developed to make this dialogue become a reality everywhere,
but especially in Asia, the continent that is the cradle of ancient
cultures and religions . . ." (5). Even while the appeal has become more pressing, the doctrine remains that of the Encyclical:
the recognition of the operative presence of the Spirit in the
others turns interreligious dialogue, for the Church, into an important task and a felt need. It remains to state this doctrine
explicitly in terms of mission and evangelization.

Leaving incomplete our review of the pronouncements of the
present Pope,[22] we may pass on to the recent document of the
Secretariat for Non-Christians, which brings to fruition the reflection of many years and, as will soon be seen, expressly places
interreligous dialogue within the purview of the Church's evangelizing mission.[23] Published on Pentecost 1984, in celebration of
the creation, twenty years earlier on the same day, of the Secretariat for Non-Christians, the document is entitled "The Attitude of the Church Toward the Followers of Other Religions:
Reflections and Orientations on Dialogue and Mission." It has
been approved by the Pope, who in his address to the plenary
assembly of the Secretariat in which the document was finalized,
confirmed with his authority some important points contained in
the document itself.[24] The Pope remarked that "dialogue is funda-

mental for the Church" (2), based as it is "on the very life of God, one and Triune. God is the Father of the entire human family; Christ has joined every person to Himself (RH 13); the Spirit works in each individual. Therefore, dialogue is also based on love for the human person as such . . . and on the bond existing between culture and the religions which people profess" (2). Experience, the Pope went on to say, shows that dialogue "is carried out in many forms," which he evoked (4). He concluded that "dialogue finds its place within the Church's salvific mission; for this reason it is a dialogue of salvation" (5); nor is any local Church "exempt from this duty which is made urgent by continuous changes" (3). To understand the place of dialogue in the Church's overall mission, it is necessary, the Pope said, "to avoid exclusivism and dichotomies" (5)—dichotomies, it must be understood, that would sever interreligious dialogue from evangelization; exclusivism that would reduce evangelization to proclamation. The Pope explained: "Authentic dialogue becomes witness and true evangelization is accomplished by respecting and listening to one another (RH 12)" (5).

The document of the Secretariat makes the same points more explicitly. It gives interreligious dialogue a broad definition: "It means not only discusssion, but also includes all positive and constructive interreligious relations with individuals and communities of other faiths which are directed at mutual understanding and enrichment" (3). Its main concern is "the relationship which exists between dialogue and mission" (5). It must be noted—and regretted—that in the introductory section of the document, this relationship still seems to be conceived in terms of a dichotomy between evangelization and dialogue: mention is made of the "duties of evangelization and dialogue which are found together in the mission of the Church," and of the difficulties that can arise between them (7). This impression of a dichotomy is, however, soon dissipated. For, in its first part on mission, the document explains that the mission of the Church "is one but comes to be exercized in different ways according to the conditions on which mission unfolds" (11). It recalls that RH 15, echoing the 1971 Synod of Bishops, considered "the commitment to mankind, to social justice, to liberty and the rights of man, and the reform of social justice" "an essential element of the mission of the Church and indissolubly connected with it" (12). Promotion of justice, however, is but one aspect, while the intention of the document is to put together the "different aspects and manners of mission" (12). It does so in a text which, without pretending to be exhaustive, enumerates five principal elements of the "single but complex and articulated reality" of the Church's evangelizing mission. This important text has to be quoted at length:

> Mission is already constituted by the simple presence and living witness of the Christian life (cf. *EN* 21), although it must be recognized that "we bear this treasure in earthen vessels" (2 Cor. 4:7). Thus the difference between the way the Christian appears existentially and that which he declares himself to be is never fully overcome.
>
> There is also the concrete commitment to the service of mankind and all forms of activity for social development and for the struggle against poverty and the structures which produce it.
>
> Also, there is liturgical life and that of prayer and contemplation, eloquent testimonies to a living and liberating relationship with the active and true God who calls us to His Kingdom and to His glory (cf. Acts 2:42).
>
> There is, as well, the dialogue in which Christians meet the followers of other religious traditions in order to walk together towards truth and to work together in projects of common concern.
>
> Finally, there is announcement and catechesis in which the good news of the Gospel is proclaimed and its consequences for life and culture are analyzed.
>
> The totality of Christian mission embraces all these elements (13).

"The totality of Christian mission embraces all these elements"; nor is the list complete. Some observations may be made. The proclamation of the gospel through announcement and catechesis comes at the end ("finally"). And rightly; for mission or evangelization must be thought of as a dynamic reality or a process. This process culminates in fact in the proclamation of Jesus Christ through announcement (kèrygma) and catechesis (didachè). By the same token, however, the "liturgical life and that of prayer and contemplation" should have come even later and followed after the proclamation of Jesus Christ with which it is directly connected—as in Acts 2:42 to which reference is made—and of which it is the natural outcome. The order would then have been as follows: presence, service, dialogue, proclamation, sacramentalization—the last two corresponding to those Church activities that in the more narrow but not untraditional view made up evangelization. In the broad perspective adopted by the document, the "single reality" of evangelization is said to be at once "complex and articulated"; it is a process. This means that, while all the elements making up the process are forms of evangelization, not all have either the same place or the same value in the mission of the Church. Thus, for instance, interreligious dialogue precedes proclamation. It may or may not be followed by it; but only if it is, will the process of evangelization come to completion. For proclamation and sacramentalization are the climax of the Church's evangelizing mission.

The first part of the document ends by stressing once more "the important place (*l'importance*) of dialogue within the mission (19). Though our analysis of the document could end here, let us take note rapidly of some observations made in the second part, where dialogue is studied more closely. According to our document, dialogue is not only in itself a distinct aspect of evangelization; it is also an "attitude and a spirit," and as such, "the norm and necessary manner (*le style indispensable*) of every form of Christian mission, as well as of every aspect of it, whether one speaks of simple presence and witness, service, or direct proclamation." All the forms of mission enumerated earlier must be "permeated by . . . a dialogical spirit" (29). As for interreligious dialogue as a specific task of evangelization, which—it is said once more—"finds its place in the great dynamism of the Church's mission" (30), it itself can take on different forms: there is the dialogue of life, open and available to all (29–30); there is dialogue through a common commitment to deeds of justice and human liberation(31–32); there is intellectual dialogue in which specialists exchange on the level of their respective religious heritages to promote communion and fellowship (33–34); there is, finally, at the deepest level, the sharing of religious experiences, of prayer and contemplation, in a common search for the Absolute (35). All these forms of dialogue,[25] it may be said, are on the part of the Christian partner, ways of working toward the "evangelical transformation of cultures" (34) and opportunities of sharing with the others in an existential way the values of the gospel (35). The third part of the document, where the theology of "Dialogue and Mission" is further developed, need not be considered here.

Some Theological Consequences

From our review of the eventful evolution over the last twenty years of the theological concept of interreligious dialogue, and of the place and significance assigned to it in the Church's overall mission, it would seem that some theological conclusions can already be drawn.

A Broad Comprehensive Concept of Evangelization Is Needed

By a broad, comprehensive concept is meant here not only that the whole person of the evangelizer is involved: his words and deeds, the testimony of his life; not only either that evangelization extends to all that is human, seeking as it does the transformation by the gospel values of culture and cultures. The notion must also comprehend the various forms of Church activity that come under the purview of evangelization. It must embrace activities that do not belong to the proclamation of Jesus Christ and subsequent sacramentalization, in particular, the promotion of justice and interreligious dialogue. Both of these should be considered as in their own right authentic forms of evangelization. This supposes overcoming a long-standing habit of reducing evangelization to explicit proclamation and sacramentalization in the Church community, a task to which the promotion of justice and work for human liberation remains somehow peripheral and interreligious dialogue apparently foreign.[26]

Interreligious Dialogue as an Intrinsic Dimension of Evangelization

The 1971 Synod of Bishops emphatically declared the promotion of justice and participation in the transformation of the world a "constitutive dimension" of the evangelizing mission of the Church. The same can and should be said about interreligious dialogue.[27] In fact, rather than distinct parts, there is question of different elements or dimensions, better still of distinct forms, modalities, or expressions of a mission that is "a single but complex and articulated reality." The concrete forms that the evangelizing mission takes on in practice will depend to no small extent on the concrete circumstances of time and places, on the human context—social, economic, political, and religious—in which it is exercised. In the context of a rich variety of religious traditions, all of which continue to be even today for millions of their adherents the source of inspiration and values, interreligious dialogue will naturally be a privileged form of evangelization. There may even be circumstances in which, at least for some time, it is the only way open to mission.

Evangelization and the Overall Mission of the Church

"Evangelizing," Paul VI said in *Evangelii nuntiandi,* "is the grace and vocation proper to the Church, her deepest identity" (14). Once evangelization is understood as identical with mission, expressed though it is in a variety of forms, some distinctions long traditional seem to become obsolete. Such are the distinctions between preevangelization and evangelization, between indirect and direct evangelization, the basis for which was the identification of evangelization with the explicit proclamation of Jesus Christ.[28] The drawback of such distinctions was that all that went under the concept of pre- or indirect evangelization seemed to belong to the order of means, more or less conducive, and leading more or less directly, to the explicit proclamation of Jesus Christ in evangelization proper. Interreligious dialogue must, however, be conceived as good in itself, not as a means toward an end distinct from it; it is a form of evangelization in its own right.

Evangelization Culminates in the Proclamation of Jesus Christ

What has just been said about interreligious dialogue as evangelization in its own right does not take away from the fact that the proclamation of Jesus Christ represents the climax or summit of the evangelizing mission of the Church. The process of mission culminates in proclamation and sacramentalization. When, however, the transition will be made in reality from interreligious dialogue to proclamation must be left in each case to God's own time and Providence. Whenever and wherever this transition takes place, the Christian partner of dialogue beings to exercise a prophetic function. To him it now belongs to interpret the mystery of salvation that has been shared and lived together by the partners of dialogue, to identify Jesus who is the Christ as the source of this mystery, and to declare and proclaim him to others as the common Savior of all. Let us, moreover, remark, lest there should be any ambiguity, that circumstances may obtain in which proclamation is possible from the beginning of the evangelizing process. Such is the case with those groups of people that are sometimes called, unelegantly, "responsive areas."

Interreligious Dialogue: Mutual Evangelization under the Influence of the Spirit

But, independently of whether or not it will turn into proclamation, interreligious dialogue is in itself evangelization. It is in fact mutual evangelization, for in it the Christian and the other partner or partners evangelize each other under the influence of the Spirit of God.[29] The reason is that they live together—knowingly on one side, unknowingly on the other—by the same mystery of Jesus Christ, which becomes operative in them through the action of the Spirit. "Since Christ died for all, and since the ultimate vocation of man is in fact one and divine, we ought to believe," Vatican II declared in *Gaudium et spes* 22, 5, "that the Holy Spirit in a manner known to God offers to every man the possibility of being associated with the Paschal Mystery." The practice of interreligious dialogue verifies the concrete reality of what the Council affirmed on theological principle. The influence of the Spirit of Jesus Christ calls the partners of interreligious dialogue, together and through each other, to a deeper conversion toward God. This is mutual evangelization.

Conclusion

On set purpose, this chapter limited itself to answering the question: Is interreligious dialogue evangelization? The theology of dialogue lay beyond its immediate scope and has only been touched upon in so far as was required to answer the question.

How, and under which conditions is interreligious dialogue a genuine expression of the evangelizing mission of the Church; what demands, if it is to be true, does it make on the partners; what different forms can it take; where does it begin and where does it lead; what challenges does it raise and what fruits does it bear? All these questions must remain unanswered here. It belongs to a theology of liberation to show how and under which conditions action on behalf of justice is true evangelization; similarly, it is the task of a theology of interreligious dialogue to show how and under which conditions the same is true of dialogue.

Notes

1. A. Wolanin, "Il concetto della missione nei decreti 'Ad gentes' e 'Apostolicam actuositatem' e nella 'Evangelii nuntiandi,' " in M. Dhavamony (ed.), *Prospettive di Missiologia, Oggi* (Rome, 1982), 89–105.

2. D. Grasso, "Evangelizzazione. Senso di un termine," in M. Dhavamony (ed.), *Evangelization* (Rome, 1975), 21–47, esp. 43.

3. Y. M.-J. Congar, "Commentaire sur le Décret: Principes doctrinaux," in *Vatican II: L'action missionaire de l'Eglise* (Paris, 1967), 198–208.

4. The Latin text of the Encyclical does not, however, have *dialogus*, but consistently speaks of *colloquium*.

5. I may be permitted to refer to various essays in which I have examined the Council documents on this subject under various aspects. These have been reproduced in J. Dupuis, *Jesus Christ and His Spirit* (Bangalore, India, 1977), chapter IX, esp. 153–155; chapter XI, esp. 196–202. See also P. Rossano, "Sulla presenza e attività dello Spirito Santo nelle religioni e nelle culture non cristiane," in M. Dhavamony (ed.), *Prospettive di Missiologia, Oggi*, 59–71; also K. Kunnumpuram, *Ways of Salvation: The Salvific Meaning of Non-Christian Religions according to the Teaching of Vatican II* (Poona, India, 1971).

6. For "evangelization," cf. D. Grasso, "Evangelizzazione. Senso di un termine," 23–30, esp. 29–30.

7. The proceedings of the Symposium were originally published in French in "Salut et développement," *Spiritus* 10/39 (1969), 321–521, Conclusions: 518–521. English translation: *Foundations of Mission Theology* (Maryknoll, 1972), Conclusions: 165–168. Figures refer to those of the Conclusions.

8. The proceedings of the Nagpur Conference are published in M. Dhavamony (ed.), *Evangelization, Dialogue and Development* (Rome,

1972). The Final Declaration is found on pp. 1–15. Figures refer to numbers of the Declaration.

9. Much less is said in the "Report of the Special Committee on Evangelization, Dialogue and Development," which attempts to define the three terms. In this text, in which, however, only the responsibility of the committee members is involved, evangelization and dialogue are distinguished even more sharply. Evangelization "is the proclamation of the good news of salvation in Jesus Christ to men who do not know Him to bring them to the faith, and to fellowship in Him." Given this definition, whatever positive value interreligious dialogue may have, it remains outside the reach of evangelization. Text of the Report, *ibid.*, 17–20.

10. As a sample can be mentioned the Communication of the Catholic Bishops Conference of India (CBCI), the text of which is found in *Report of the General Meeting of the CBCI: Calcutta, 6–14 January, 1974* (New Delhi, 1974), 124–143.

11. *Evangelization in Modern Day Asia.* The First Plenary Assembly of the Federation of Asian Bishops' Conferences (FABC) (Hong Kong, 1974). Figures are those of the Statement. The same document is found in *For All the Peoples of Asia. The Church in Asia: Asian Bishops' Statements on Mission, Community and Ministry, 1970–1983. Volume One: Texts and Documents* (Manila, 1984), 25–47.

12. Characteristic of the trend were the interventions of Archbishop L.T. Picachy, President of the Indian Episcopal Conference and of Archbishop A. Fernandes, both speaking in the name of the CBCI. The full text of their interventions is found in D. S. Amalorpavadass (ed.), *Evangelization of the Modern World* (Bangalore, India, 1975), 124–134. "The Chuch in India," Archbishop L.T. Picachy said, "sees inter-faith dialogue as a normal expression of evangelization" (125); and Archbishop A. Fernandes : "Evangelization . . . embraces the entire mission of the Church. . . . Inter-faith dialogue and development work . . . must be considered authentic dimensions of the Church's work of evangelization" (129–130). An Italian summary of the interventions is found in G. Caprile, *Il Sinodo dei Vescovi: Terza Assemblea Generale* (Rome, 1975), 214–216, 423–435.

13. *De Evangelizatione Mundi Huius Temporis (Pars Prior). Mutua Communicatio Experientiarum, Synthesis Relationum et Interventionum Patrum* (Vatican City, 1974). References are to page numbers.

14. *De Evangelizatione Mundi Huius Temporis (Pars Altera). Themata Quaedam Theologica cum Experientiis Connexa Clarificantur. Synthesis Relationum et Interventionun Patrum* (Vatican City, 1974). References are to page numbers.

15. For a short account of the Synod, cf. J. Dupuis, "Synod of Bishops 1974," *Doctrine and Life*, 25 (1975), 323–348.

16. *Suffragatio circa Argumentum de Evangelizatione Mundi Huius Temporis* (Vatican City, 1974).

17. Latin text in G. Caprile, *Il Sinodo dei Vescovi: Terza Assemblea Generale* (Rome, 1975), 1011–1016; English translation in D.S. Amalorpavadass (ed.), *Evangelization of the Modern World*, 96–101.

18. The often quoted text reads as follows: "Action on behalf of justice and participation in the transformation of the world fully appear to us as a constitutive dimension (*ratio constitutive*) of the preaching of the Gospel, or, in other words, of the Church's mission for the redemption of the human race and its liberation from every oppressive situation" (*AAS*, 63 [1971], 924).

19. I refer the reader to some comments I made in *Vidyajyoti*, 40 (1976), 218–230.

20. We refer to P.G. Falciola, *L'Evangelizzazione nel Pensiero di Paolo VI* (Rome, 1980) and *Sulle Vie della Evangelizzazione con Giovanni Paolo II* (Rome, 1981).

21. *AAS*, 73 (1981), 391–398.

22. I refer to an article by T. Michel, "Islamo-Christian Dialogue: Reflections on the Recent Teachings of the Church," *Bulletin*, 59 (1985), 172–193, for a review of the teaching of Paul VI and John Paul II on the Church's relation with Islam in particular. The author also points to a growing openness to Islam and to a consequent deeper appeal for dialogue. Among more recent documents on the same subject, see especially the Speech of the Holy Father John Paul II to young Muslims during his meeting with them at Casablanca (Morocco), 19 August 1985 in *Islamochristiana*, 11 (1985), 201–208.

23. The Secretariat for Non-Christians had previously to its credit several publications on dialogue with specific religions: Hinduism, Buddhism, Islam, and the African Religions. The new document, however, besides having in mind other religions in general, sums up the Secretariat's experience of the last twenty years and is more theological. It is the outcome of a lengthy project initiated in 1979; its text has gone through four drafts previous to the formulation presented and voted for in the February–March 1984 plenary assembly.

24. The text of both the document and the Pope's address is published in several languages in *Bulletin. Secretariatus pro non-Christianis*, n. 56; 19, 2 (1984), 117–242. Figures refer to those of the Pope's address and of the document.

25. On the different forms of dialogue according to the document, see J. Dupuis, "Forms of Inter-Religious Dialogue," *Bulletin*, 59 (1985), 164–171; also in *Portare Cristo all'Uomo. Congresso del Ventennio dal Concilio Vaticano II, 18–21 Febbraio 1985. Volume I: Dialogo* (Rome, 1985), 175–183.

26. Some authors still speak of evangelization and interreligious dialogue as of two tasks of the Church's mission, adequately distinct from each other. Mission is then understood broadly as comprehending both those tasks, but evangelization remains narrowly identified with the proclamation of the gospel. Some examples will suffice. M. Dhavamony, "Evangelization and Interreligious Dialogue," in M. Dhavamony (ed.), *Evangelization* (Rome, 1975), 245–272, adopts this point of view. D. Grasso, "The Primacy of Evangelism in Mission Activity", in Sedos (ed.), *Foundations of Mission Theology* (Maryknoll, 1972), 104–110, identifies evangelization with proclamation, and distinguishes it from preevangelization. In an article entitled "Meeting of Religions: Indian Perspectives," in T.A. Aykara (ed.), *Meeting of Religions: New Orientations and Perspectives* (Bangladore, India, 1978), 7–24, Archbishop D.S. Lourdusamy, Secretary of the S. Congregation for the Evangelization of Peoples, considers evangelization (identified with proclamation) and dialogue as "two functions of the Christian existence," to which there correspond in Vatican II two distinct documents, *Ad gentes* and *Nostra aetate*, respectively, and in the Vatican two distinct dicasteries, the S. Congregation for Evangelization of Peoples and the Secretariat for non-Christians. Monsignor P. Rossano, "Theology of Religions: A Contemporary Problem," in R. Latourelle and G. O'Collins (eds.), *Problems and Perspectives of Fundamental Theology* (New York/Ramsey, NJ, 1982), 292–308, gives, however, a different interpretation: "The presence of both documents in the conciliar corpus is enough to show how specious the claim is that mission and dialogue in the Church are mutually exclusive. It should also be noted that whenever *AG* speaks of mission it always associates with it the word dialogue, while *NA*, regarded as the *magna charta* of dialogue, does not hesitate to speak of the Church's duty to 'ever proclaim Christ,' 'the way, the truth and the life' (2)" (303); dialogue is "an element and necessary aspect" of the Church's missionary commitment (*ibid.*)— without, however, mission and evangelization being here explicitly identified. In "Sulla presenza e attività dello Spirito Santo nelle religioni e nelle culture non cristiane," 59–72, Monsignor Rossano writes in the same vein: "I due atteggiamenti, del dialogo e della proclamazione, dell'ascolto e dell'annuncio, non si elidono a vicenda, ma si incontrano proprio nell'area dello Spirito che è alla radice di entrambi" (70). In "Dialogue in the Mission of the Church," *Bulletin. Secretariatus pro non-Christianis* 57; 19, 3 (1984), 265–269, M. Zago, the present Secretary of the Secretariat for non-Christians, writes while presenting the recent document of the Secretariat: "Dialogue was established to be intrinsic to mission, included within mission in the broad sense, as is the whole of the Church's activity which springs from the command of Christ. . . . " He adds less felicitously: "In this sense, dialogue is clearly distinguished from evangelization . . . , thus once more identified with proclamation (268). On the contrary, in addressing the recent meeting of the Episcopal Commissions for Inter-Religious Affairs of FABC, in Sampran, Thailand, 23–30 October 1984, Monsignor F.A. Arinze, Pro-Prefect of the Secretariat for Non-Christians, expressed himself very clearly, saying: "We share the mystery of Christ by the work of mission and mission includes dialogue with those who do not believe in Christ. Interreligious dialogue between Christians and non-Christians is one of the ways in which we Christians bear witness to Christ, *in which we evangelize*, in which we live our faith, in which we work for the coming of God's Kingdom" (unpublished; emphasis added). Here interreligious dialogue is unmistakably considered as one way of mission, which, in turn, is identified with evangelization.

27. We prescind here from the discussion whether the 1971 Synod of Bishops should have spoken of "integral part," rather than of "constitutive dimension."

28. The distinction between preevangelization and evangelization must not be attributed too easily to Pope Paul VI himself in his Mission Message, 1970, in which he explained the relationship between evangelization and development. The Pope affirmed that, while evangelization always retains its "essential and intentional priority," development may, in particular circumstances, be given "pastoral priority." The original Italian text went on: "Si parla di pre-evangelizzazione, cioè l'accostamento dei futuri cristiani per via di carità . . . " (AAS, 62 [1970], 538). The English text has: "There is first *what some refer to as* preevangelization (emphasis added); the French text: "on parle de préévangélisation" (Documentation catholique, 67 [1970], 811).

29. On the Holy Spirit and the Church's evangelizing mission, see J. Dupuis, *Jesus Christ and His Spirit*, 245–258; also Archbishop D.S. Lourdusamy, "The Holy Spirit and the Missionary Activity of the Church," in M. Dhavamony (ed.), *Prospettive di Missiologia, Oggi*, 45–58; Monsignor P. Rossano, "Sulla presenza e attività dello Spirito Santo nelle religioni e nelle culture non cristiane," *ibid.*, 59–72; "Esprit et évangélisation," *Spiritus*, 20/75 (1979), 115–183.

CHAPTER 51

Evangelization and Dialogue
in Vatican II
and in the 1974 Synod

Mariasusai Dhavamony, S.J.

Summary

Paul VI summarized all the vitality of the Church toward the world in dialogue (*Ecclesiam suam*). Thus the term and the spirit of dialogue entered into all the Conciliar documents. First, evangelization and dialogue are explained. The relation between the general and particular mission of the Church is made precise; the role of the local churches in evangelization is stressed. Evangelization indicates both the first proclamation of the gospel and the whole ministry of the Word and the whole mission of the Church. Dialogue implies both search for truth and sharing it and the establishment of right order among people in collaboration through mutual respect and love. Religions contain both positive and negative elements, worthy of respect in their true and good elements, and prepare people to receive Christ and his message in which they find their fulfillment. Thus, evangelization and dialogue are inseparably related. In the 1974 Synod, dialogue is admitted as an integral part of the mission of the Church.

Introduction[1]

Around 1960, there happened what we might call the greatest single religious event since the Reformation, the person of Pope

John XXIII and the event of the *aggiornamento* that he set in motion. The changes for which Pope John and the Council he inaugurated were responsible are well known. *Aggiornamento,* Unity of all Christians, and Dialogue with Non-Christians and Non-believers characterize this period. But dialogue as a form of thought and action of the Catholic Church in the world today is basic to *aggiornamento* and Christian unity. For Pope Paul VI summarized all the vitality of the Church toward the world in dialogue: "To this internal drive of charity which seeks expression in the external gift of charity, we will apply the word 'dialogue.' The Church must enter into dialogue with the world in which it lives. It has something to say, a message to give, a communication to make."[2] Dialogue entered almost unawares, together with the Johannine spirit, into the spiritual design of the Council itself right from its first session. In fact, Pope Paul spelled out the motives that impel the Church to dialogue, the methods to be followed, and the ends to be attained in his Encyclical *Ecclesiam suam.* From this moment, the term and the spirit of dialogue entered into all the conciliar documents and determined their tone and content. Two of the terms in the title of this chapter have to be explained before we deal with the problem of the relation between evangelization and dialogue. Hence, we shall divide the exposition as follows: (1) evangelization; (2) interreligious dialogue; (3) the relation between evangelization and interreligious dialogue first in Vatican II and then in the Bishops' Synod on Evangelization (1974).

Evangelization and Dialogue in Vatican II

Evangelization

The term "evangelization" as used by the Council has a precise meaning: "The special end of this missionary activity is the evangelization and the implantation of the Church among peoples or groups in which it has not yet taken root" (*AG* 6). It is still more clearly expressed thus: "Therefore she [the Church] makes the words of the Apostle her own, 'Woe to me if I do not preach the Gospel' (1 Cor. 9:16), and accordingly never ceases to send heralds of the Gospel until such time as the infant churches are fully established, and can themselves continue the work of evangelization" (*LG* 17). Evangelization means the preaching of the gospel of Jesus Christ. In the apostolic formula: *the gospel of Jesus Christ* (AG 6), Jesus Christ is the subject of the gospel in as far as he has been the first to have brought and promulgated it on earth; he is also the object of the gospel in as far as the gospel speaks of him and is himself; finally, the genitive can be taken as one of authority in as far as the evangelical message is preached by the disciples of the risen Christ by express command of him and with his influence either on the preachers or on the listeners.[3] "By her proclamation of the gospel, she [the Church] draws her hearers to receive and profess the faith, she prepares them for baptism, snatches them from the slavery of error, and she incorporates them into Christ so that in love for him they grow to full maturity" (LG 17).

This way of understanding evangelization raises some problems in the interpretation of the teaching of the Council on this point. First of all comes the problem of relating the general mission of the Church, which is one and coextensive to the existence of the Church herself, to her special missionary activity. The general mission of the Church "is carried out by means of that activity through which, in obedience to Christ's command and moved by the grace and love of the Holy Spirit, the Church makes itself fully present to all men and peoples in order to lead them to the faith, freedom and peace of Christ by the example of its life and teaching, by the sacraments and other means of grace. Its aim is to open up for all men a free and sure path to full participation in the mystery of Christ" (AG 5). This general mission of the Church is exercised in different conditions. Where there has not yet been Christianity, the Church has to proclaim the good news and cannot still have a sacramental ministry nor can it exercise an indigenous theological activity. Thus, the differentiation in the exercise of the unique mission of the Church comes both from the spiritual situation of the human groups to the benefit of which this mission is exercised and from the activities that the Church uses and the method it follows in relation to each situation. Therefore, the missionary activity is distinguished from the pastoral activity and from the ecumenical activity. It is better not to consider this distinction between the missionary activity and the pastoral activity as between two specifically different activities of the same genus. For to hold that when the Church is founded, the missionary activity ceases and that one passes to pastoral activity is to exaggerate the distinction that has its truth at the formal plane.[4]

The Council sees the fulfillment of evangelization in the "planting of the Church" (AG 6). The concept behind this expression is the Church in the singular, unique and universal, extending beyond its present human limits, to new people, new cultures, and new societies. What is stressed is the centripetal movement of assimilation. This outlook reflects the ecclesiology of Vatican I; the accent is put on the primacy of the Pope; it reflects the devotion to the Common Father of the faithful; finally, it shows the desire of the newly established weak communities to find support from the rock that is Peter. On the contrary, Vatican II gives a different formulation: "until such time as the new Churches are established" (LG 17). Here, the expression in its plural form is to be noted. Obviously, missionary dynamism has been influenced here and usefully clarified by the present historical movement in which the desire for autonomy and the achievement of independence by the young nations show themselves again again after the collapse of western world imperialism. The rediscovery by Vatican II of the "autonomy," with and under St. Peter's successor, of the bishops in their own sphere is found here. The Decree on the missionary activity explicitly recognized the extreme importance of the establishment of the local Churches as the aim of missionary activity. This new emphasis marks the method of evangelization in the future. Rather than moving toward an excessive centralization in which the unity of Latin style and the direct intervention of central authorities would contribute to creating uniformity, missionary activity will tend more than in the past to give an increasingly important place in the formation of communities to local elements and to "authenticity." It could be a matter of the languages of the forms of the eucharistic and sacramental liturgy, even of the way of exercising authority; in brief, it will be a matter of allowing all possible freedom to spontaneity, both particular (of the episcopal community) and local (of a definite cultural or political society). A good many powers have been undoubtedly put into the hands of Episcopal Conferences and of individual bishops.

Evangelization synthesizes all the activities that conduce a non-Christian to meet existentially, to understand experimentally, to accept in all liberty and conscience, the only true God and him whom he had sent, Jesus Christ. This responds to the central preoccupation expressed by St. Paul: "provided Christ be announced." This proclamation assumes diverse grades and forms that are all missionary by reason of their intention, also when one cannot explicitly proclaim Christ because it is impossible or premature in certain situations. This is consoling for those missionaries who are not directly employed in the proclamation of Christ, but form only part of it through participation, i.e., through witnessing. The Council describes this witnessing, dividing it into witnessing by life and witnessing by word (AG 11–14). Witnessing by life is less explicit, more austere, but also more constant and more convincing. Its effect and force can be expressed thus: "Your religion must be very good for having made you so good."

In sum, the term "evangelization," which has become current in the last twenty years in the various conciliar documents, indicates not only the first proclamation of the gospel to non-Christians, but also the whole ministry of the Word and the whole mission of the Church.[5]

Interreligious Dialogue

The Council speaks very often about dialogue, but it will be difficult to find a definition of it in its documents. However, we come across two significations. The first is described thus: "The search for truth, however, must be carried out in a manner that is appropriate to the dignity of the human person and his social nature, namely by free enquiry with the help of teaching or instruction, communication and dialogue. It is by these means that men share with each other the truth they have discovered, or think they have discovered, in such a way that they help one another in the search for truth" (DH 3). Dialogue is the means of seeking after truth and of sharing with each other the truth they have found or think that they have found, thus helping one another in the search for truth. The second sense of dialogue is derived from texts such as the following. "Although the Church altogether rejects atheism, she nevertheless sincerely proclaims that all men, those who believe as well as those who do not, should help to establish right order in this world where all live together. This certainly cannot be done without a dialogue that is sincere and prudent" (GS 21). Here dialogue is a means of collaboration in establishing right order in the human society and thus contributing to the common good of people, both be-lievers and nonbelievers.

The dialogical approach in all activities of the Church has been explained time and again in the documents of the Council and more fully elaborated by Pope Paul VI in his Encyclical *Ecclesiam suam*. The Council speaks of the ecumenical dialogue (UR 4), of the interreligious dialogue (NA), and of dialogue with nonbeliev-ers (GS 21), of dialogue in the missions (AG 11, 15). It is obvious that the principles on which each type of dialogue rests and the themes that it deals with are partly different from those that charac-terize other types of dialogue. However, the various forms of dia-logue cannot be disassociated one from the other. As the Council says: "For our part, our eagerness for such dialogue, conducted with appropriate discretion and leading to truth by way of love alone, excludes nobody" (GS 92). The Council has realized that modern man seeks dialogue as a privileged means of establishing and developing mutual understanding, esteem, respect, and love, whether between groups or individuals. The dialogical approach consists in the will to understand the interlocutor more and more than to condemn him and in the respect shown to his dignity and liberty in face of pluralism; and in the attempt to discover the elements of truth contained in the views of the other, and in the exposition of one's own conviction in the face of the other's opposi-tion and slow assimilation. The dangers in dialogue are false irenism and syncretism; there cannot be weakness with respect to one's duty to one's own faith. The postconciliar Church has re-flected much on the issue of dialogue. See the publications of the three Secretariates for Christian Unity, for dialogue with non-Christians, for dialogue with nonbelievers. We can distinguish three forms of dialogue with the world, though they are not always and necessarily separable: dialogue as human encounter, doctrinal dialogue, and dialogue as collaboration at the level of action.[6]

Religions in so far as they contain true and good elements are worthy of respect. They help prepare the human society to re-ceive Christ and his message in which they find their fulfillment. Still more, in their authentic good values, they are already some-thing in which Christ acts and prepares in them and across them his complete coming. Thus, religions in their true and good elements are pre-Christian and pro-Christian. They are preparations for Christ. In all that is true and good, they tend to Christ, and, by his grace, they invisibly but really are already in contact with him (LG 16). But the ambiguity found in individual persons is also found in human non-Christian societies and religions. "This universal plan of God for salvation of mankind is not carried out solely in a secret manner, as it were, in the minds of men, nor by the efforts, even religious, through which they in many ways seek God in an attempt to touch him and find him, although God is not far from any of us. (cf. Acts 17:27); their efforts need to be enlightened and corrected, although in the loving providence of God they may lead one to the true God and be a preparation for the Gospel" (AG 3).

The Council did not have any illusions with respect to religions. There are positive and negative elements, as seen in the history of religions. In religions, there are deficiencies that are not limited only to individual feelings and shortcomings. There are determinate positions such as dogmatic relativism, fatalism, pantheism, magic, and moral deviations that are accepted as principles and hence vitiate some of the religious manifestations. There are deficiencies in the very essence and depth of some of their credo and precepts. Hence, religions need to be purified, assumed, and resurrected.

More specially, as we come to the analysis of the *Nostra aetate*, we face a problem. Since religions have both positive and negative aspects, one has to choose the way that is more opportune and adapted in the approach to religions. Though theoretically both aspects, positive and negative, should be comprised, practically, this equilibrium did not appear convenient to the Council Fathers for various reasons. The first reason is historical. The traditional attitude of the missionaries has been negative with regard to religions, insisting on their defects and shortcomings, sometimes with the lack of fairness toward them. Hence, a more positive attitude was taken by the Council. Second, the conciliar and pastoral preoccupation was not prone to condemnation and anathema. The spirit of reconciliation was adopted by trying to find what is positive and favorable, what is common to all partners, and present the Catholic position in the light of this reconciliation. The third reason is more profoundly theological. God's will of saving all people and his justice is positive. God does not want the death of the sinner, but that he or she be converted and live. A *fortiori*, God wishes that persons and ideas that appear just be put more in evidence than inasmuch as false and bad. So also the Church, sent by God, should recognize what is good and true in other religions. "Ever aware of her duty to foster unity and charity among individuals, and even among nations, she reflects at the outset on what men have in common and what tends to promote fellowship among them" (NA 1). In this context, the Council does not speak of the differences between Christianity and non-Christian religions. But, in other places, it speaks of the divergences and of the errors that are to be found in religions. "She [the Church] has a high regard for the manner of life and conduct, the precepts and doctrines which, although differing in many ways from her own teaching, nevertheless often reflect a ray of that truth which enlightens all men" (NA 2). "It [the missionary activity] purges of evil associations those elements of truth and grace which are found among peoples, and which are, as it were, a secret presence of God; and it restores them to Christ their source who overthrows the rule of the devil and limits the manifold malice of evil" (AG 9). Thus, the Council does not hesitate to speak in some way the whole truth; namely, both the positive and negative values, both the common and the specific elements in religions, as found in concrete situations.

The Council recommends dialogue in the following words: "The Church therefore urges her sons to enter with prudence and charity into dialogue and collaboration with members of other religions. Let Christians, while witnessing to their own faith and way of life, acknowledge, preserve and encourage the spiritual and moral truths found among non-Christians, also their social life and culture" (NA 2). Many qualities are needed in the dialogue partner. A theoretical and experiential knowledge of Christian life and an accurate knowledge of non-Christian religions are certainly required. Besides, he who does not know catechism, theology, experience of prayer, of grace, and of suffering cannot engage in dialogue fruitfully and profoundly. He ought to affront the great questions of humanity such as the nature of humanity, the sense and destiny of human life, etc. (NA 1). A superficial person will remain empty before such problems of life. The interreligious dialogue, if it has to pass beyond courtesy, is a very engaging function with diverse espects, styles, and progressive rhythm. The forms of dialogue, according to Nostra aetate, are the following. Christians have to witness to their own faith and way of life, for beautiful words without living according to them are lies. They are urged to acknowledge the spiritual and moral truths found among non-Christians, also in their social life and culture; that is to say, they have to know well the religion and culture of the interlocutor. Thirdly, they are asked to preserve and encourage these truths and to foster a genuine respect in promoting the truth found in others (NA 2). The redemptive plan of God is realized precisely by fulfilling in a divine, supernatural way what has real value already in the religious search of humanity. This is not competition but convergence, being already penetrated mysteriously by the Spirit of God.

The evaluation of non-Christian religions, according to the Council, can be explained thus. Religions attempt to overcome the unrest of the human heart in various ways. "So . . . religions which are found throughout the world attempt in their own ways to calm the hearts of men by outlining a program of life, covering doctrine, moral precepts and sacred rites" (NA 2). Secondly, this initiative should be illumined and healed. "This universal plan of God for salvation of mankind is not carried out solely in a secret manner, as it were, in the minds of men, nor by the efforts, even religious, through which they in many ways seek God in an attempt to touch him and find him, although God is not far from any of us (cf. Acts 17:27); their efforts need to be enlightened and corrected, although in the loving providence of God they may lead one to the true God and be a preparation for the Gospel" (AG 3). Thirdly, religions command respect as they seek after God and salvation. This does not mean that everything in them can be accepted and is to be esteemed as unconditionally good. More pointedly, there ought to be respect for the positive values in religions. At the same time, one ought to be aware of the unacceptable elements in them. Also, we have to note that these values are undergoing changes in radical and profound ways at present.

The problem of the salvific value of non-Christian religions was not explicitly treated by the Council. All men are universally called to salvation by the grace of God. The idea of divine appeal is addressed to all men and designates an inclusion of all the fragments of history. All that is true and good in religions constitute a preparation for the gospel. The possibility of salvation outside the visible Church is not put in direct relation with other religions as such in such a ways that these religions are described as ways of salvation. The possibility of salvation is linked to two components: salvific grace of God and obedience to conscience. Nothing prevents that this obedience could be practiced within the forms found in and offered by religions. This does not prevent that it is not religions but obedience and grace that are named ways of salvation.[7]

Evangelization and Dialogue

The initiative given by Vatican II for interreligious dialogue has raised some problems with respect to the relationship between dialogue and evangelization. Some Christians thought that the Church had renounced evangelization as a positive work of preaching the gospel to non-Christians and of converting them to the Catholic faith, and has substituted it by dialogue. The non-Christians have thought that dialogue was a new and more subtle form of evangelization. Hence arises the problem, both theological and pastoral, of reconciling dialogue and evangelization.

Sincere appreciation of what is true and holy in religions does not mean univocal and totally positive judgment of everything that is found in religions. The attitude toward religions should be one of comprehension and discernment, of sincere and patient dialogue. The purpose of dialogue is to discover in them providential elements and the ways of God toward humanity. The Council has wished to avoid that. From a unilateral evaluation of religions, we can conclude that they were willed as such by God, and thus are included in the history of salvation as ordinary ways of salvation, given by God as such. This will certainly destroy the missionary endeavor of the Church. "The sacred Council begins by professing that God himself has made known to the human race how men by serving him can be saved and reach happiness in Christ. We believe that this one true religion continues to exist in the Catholic and Apostolic Church, to which the Lord Jesus entrusted the task of spreading it among all people when he said to the Apostles, 'Go therefore and make disciples of all nations baptizing them in the name of the Father and of the Son and of the Holy Spirit, teaching them to observe all that I have commanded you' (Mt. 18:19–20)" (DH 1). From this, it is clear that the Catholic Church is the only ordinary way of salvation given by God. The Council did not wish to enter into discussion on the mode and the grade of belonging of religions to the history of salvation. It did not wish to pronounce on the content and nature of revelation contained in them, nor on the eventuality of their permanence until the end of the world. Besides, the Council says nothing on the historical origin of religion or religions, on the character of respective founders of religions, nor on the presence in them of the elements of the primitive revelation. Primitive revelation, given to the first parents of humanity, is affirmed (*DV* 3), but nothing is said about its nature, content, and conservation in history. The Council gives premises on all these problems in order to open new theological research on the profound and dynamic relation between Christianity and religions.

The signification of the mission of the Church in its relation to non-Christian religions, and of their values and limits present in them, is thus outlined by the Council. In explicit reference to whatever good is found sown in the minds and hearts of people or in the rites and customs of peoples, words such as *conservare, liberare, sanare,* and *elevare et consumare* are used (*LG* 17; *AG* 9). Referring to the spiritual and moral values of religions, the Council uses the words *agnoscere, servare,* and *promovere,* without prejudicing in any way the preaching and witnessing of Christ (*NA* 2). In order to accomplish this complex duty of purification, assumption, and elevation, evangelization ought to be integrated with dialogue. Dialogue and evangelization thus summarize the attitude of the Church in front of religions in the perspective of the plan of God.

There is also the reciprocal connection between dialogue and evangelization in the documents of the Council itself. The Decree on the Missionary Activity of the Church contains a whole paragraph that deals with dialogue:

> In order to bear witness to Christ fruitfully, they should establish relationships of respect and love with those men, they should acknowledge themselves as members of the group in which they live, and through the various undertakings and affairs of human life they should share in their social and cultural life. They should be familiar with their national and religious traditions and uncover with gladness and respect those seeds of the Word which lie hidden among them (*AG* 11).

On the other hand, the Declaration on the Relation of the Church and Nonchristian religions, which is dedicated to dialogue, states resolutely the necessity and urgency of evangelization and mission: "Yet she proclaims and is in duty bound to proclaim without fail Christ who is the way, the truth, and the life (Jn. 1:6). In him in whom God reconciled all things to himself (2 Cor. 5:18–19) men find the fullness of their religious life" (NA 2). This means that the Church wants to join evangelization and mission inseparably to dialogue. In carrying out the mandate of evangelization and mission, the Church wishes to adapt the method and spirit of dialogue. That is to say that evangelization will have to take into account the capacity for understanding and the existential situation of the interlocutors. Dialogue tends to reciprocal knowledge and understanding. It tends to increase the respect and esteem for religions, scrutinizing the action of God in them, gifts of God in them, and inducing a greater union and fraternity among people. Hence, dialogue enters into the basic duties of the Church. The Church cooperates in the realization of the universal plan of God in history in which all Christians are invited to rethink the patrimony of revelation, facts, and words revealed by God in function of great socio-cultural contexts of humanity, to stimulate a greater and more adequate intelligence of faith and favor the assimilation of the gospel on the part of these cultures. Thus are excluded syncretism, false particularism, false irenism, and is effected adaptation of Christian life to the genius and disposition of each culture. The Catholic unity is enriched by the variety of gifts and treasures of peoples.

Dialogue itself is a form of Christian witnessing; it is the genuine expression of fraternal relation to others. It is an encounter in which the authority of the Church is not put from the first as the previous condition, but in which the divine truth is attested in the human meeting. The model for this meeting is Jesus Christ and the Samaritans. In the communion of knowledge of problems, uncertainties, etc., dialogue is possible. It is not simply teaching but searching in common. The Christian has also to learn; even if he or she in the faith participates in the depth of divine wisdom, he or she can grow and advance, thanks to non-Christians. His or her own Catholic faith is deepened through dialogue with non-Christians. "Just as Christ penetrated to the hearts of men and by a truly human dialogue led them to the divine light, so too his disciples, profoundly pervaded by the Spirit of Christ, should know and converse with those among whom they live, that through sincere and patient dialogue these men might learn of the riches which a generous God has distributed among the nations" (AG 11).

The final question is whether interreligious dialogue itself is a specific activity, distinct from evangelization and mission proper.[8] We distinguish between dialogue as a specific activity and dialogue as interior spirit and methodology of approach which must shape all ecclesial action, such as evangelization, mission, pastoral activity, ecumenical activity, and the exercise of ministry itself and government. In other words, there is no evangelization without dialogue; but can there be dialogue without evangelization? Can a function of dialogue exist in the Church, together with evangelization and mission, which does not have the immediate object of evangelization and mission, but intends simply to obtain the objective aim of dialogue; namely, mutual understanding, a greater drawing together and a mutual spiritual advantage?

Dialogue and evangelization remain distinct activities and have their own well-determined scope. Dialogue has its own scope, namely, a common searching and sharing, so that the partners come closer together to the religious truth. The scope of evangelization is to the non-Christian to the faith in Christ and his message of salvation. Dialogue itself by its inner dynamism on the part of the Christian calls for evangelization, for no Christian can be insensible to the call of Christ that he witnesses through dialogue in the non-Christian partner. Although it is true that dialogue does not serve as a bait or means for the evangelical activity, it creates certain new truths and new light in the understanding of the religious truth in the partners, and this may well necessitate the Christian to preach the gospel. Thus, dialogue has its place in evangelization because the Christian partner takes consciousness of the other and comprehends the other and leads him to Christ and his message. There are in non-Christian religious people lights and graces of salvation that come to them from Christ without visible intervention of the Church. Christ is the Light of the world. Hence, there are lights that do not dispense people to receive the Light, nor the Church of the duty of carrying it to them. So also the graces that do not dispense people from receiving the Grace, nor the Church of proclaiming it. We are thus led at the heart of the mission: to recognize the dialogical structure. Mission cannot be defined only by the act of bringing light where there is only darkness, but that it is communion and partaking. This surpasses dialogue envisaged only as a means of contact or as testimony of the spirit of openness. It is question of an internal law of this vast operation that is called mission. If truths ought to encounter the Truth, and graces, the Grace, Truth and Grace ought from their side seek and receive graces and truths. This is recognized not only by the great missionary Encyclicals, for instance, *Evangelii precones*, but also by the Council (*LG* 17). They ought to lead to Christ. Thus, the Church has a revealing and recapitulating function toward the world.[9]

The 1974 Synod of Bishops on Evangelization

Both in the working paper prepared for the Synod and in the Synod itself, many different meanings of "evangelization" were given.[10] (1) The term can mean "every activity whereby the world is in any way transformed in accordance with the will of God the Creator and Redeemer." Certainly, it gives recognition to any work of the laity, religious, and priests in secular areas. It includes any activity done in accordance with God's will. But it is not sufficiently specific and not in harmony with the biblical meaning. Besides, the vagueness in the meaning lessens the urgency of the tasks more closely connected with the Word of God such as preaching, catechetics, sacramental ministry, etc. (2) The term also means "the priestly, prophetic and royal activity whereby the Church is built up according to Christ's intentions." This certainly indicates the specific nature of the mission of the Church; but it appears not sufficiently cosmic in its outreach and might give the impression of indifference to the legitimate aspirations of mankind in the relatively autonomous social, political, and cultural sphere. (3) The term has been taken to mean not only the first preaching of the gospel to those who have never adequately heard it before, but also the task of evoking one's Christian faith, fostering it, and bringing it to full maturity through the ministry of the Word and Sacrament. This understanding of evangelization might undermine the missionary activity of the Church toward the two-thirds of the world population who are non-Christian. Pope Paul VI observed that though certain elements must be present in any valid description of evangelization, but evangelization must not be reduced to any single one of them. "So evangelization has been defined by some as consisting in the proclamation of Christ our Lord to those who do not know him, in preaching, catechetics, baptism and the administration of the other sacraments. But no such defective and incomplete definition can be accepted for that complex, rich and dynamic reality which is called evangelization without the risk of weakening or even distorting its real meaning" (*EN* 17).

In this connection, it is interesting to note that in his opening address to the Synod, Pope Paul VI summed up the Christian view of other religions and the policy of the Secretariat for Non-Christians: "Likewise we cannot omit a reference to the non-Christian religions. These in fact must no longer be regarded as rivals or obstacles to evangelization, but as a field of lively, respectful interest and as the recipients of a deepening friendship." The discovery of the riches of the world religions is not a deterrent but an incentive to evangelization; it is a realization that God goes before us and has already prepared the way. The non-Christian religions represent an invitation to evangelization for they are essentially preparations for it.

The Fathers of the Synod in their message to the Church at the end of the Synod affirmed: "Being sure of the action of the Holy Spirit which goes beyond the limits of the Christian Communities, we desire to extend the dialogue to non-Christian religions in order to be more fully able to understand the newness of the Gospel and the fullness of revelation, and also to show to them that the salvific truth of divine love which finds its fulfillment in Christ."[11] In spite of this declaration, the term dialogue has never been used in any part of the *Evangelii nuntiandi*. This is a surprise especially in a document by Pope Paul VI, who dedicated his first Encyclical to dialogue, and who instituted the Secretariat for Dialogue with Non-Christians.

In continuity with the teaching of Vatican II and also in the many discourses, Pope Paul VI told the Christian of his duty to esteem and respect the non-Christian religions. The reasons for this positive appreciation are the following: (1) They represent the living expression of the spiritual lives of millions of peoples. (2) They embody the human search for God for thousands of years and that, although imperfect, is often made with the deepest sincerity and righteousness. (3) They have taught generations of people to pray. (4) They contain innumerable "seeds of the Word." (e) They constitute a true "preparation for the Gospel" (*EN* 53).

The problem of the theological understanding of religions is not treated in the *Evangelii nuntiandi*, especially, whether non-Christians are saved *in* and *through* their religions, so that these may be called "ways of salvation." But the Pope said enough of what can be at this stage affirmed about the non-Christian relgions and left the questions open for theologians to study. Above all, the Pope clearly affirmed that the non-Christians have the *right* to hear the gospel preached to them in its entirety and missionaries have the *duty* to proclaim it to them. No future theology of non-Christian religions will be able to diminish this obligation to preach the gospel to non-Christians. Pope Paul VI insisted on the uniqueness of Christ and the gospel, its universality, and the fact that Christ established the only ultimately true religion: "In other words, our religion effectively establishes with God an authentic and living relationship which the other religions do *not* succeed in doing, even though they have, as it were, their arms stretched out to heaven" (*EN* 53).

Religions are said to be incomplete searches for God. They cannot establish an authentic and living relationship with God. But are religions merely natural expressions without a supernatural element in them, as the following statement might suggest: "Accordingly, even in the face of the most admirable forms of natural religion, the Church judges that it is her special function, by virtue of the religion of Jesus Christ which she proclaims in her evangelization, to bring men into contact with God's plan, with his living presence, with his solicitude" (*EN* 53). Besides, *Evangelii nuntiandi* speaks of the action of the Holy Spirit outside of the Catholic Church (cf. 75); we can also extend this presence of the Holy Spirit in some way also in religions. Reference is made to the innumerable seeds of the Word (*EN* 53). The context of this affirmation is that religions possess a splendid patrimony of religious writings and have taught generations of men how to pray. There is no mention of the problem of inspiration and revelation of the non-Christian sacred writings. This is left to the study and reflection of the theologians.

With regard to the identity of the Christian message before non-Christain religions and ideologies, the Pope recognizes that it is necessary to integrate what is valuable in them in evangelization and appeals at the same time to maintain by all means the purity and unity of the Catholic faith and of the doctrine of the Church. Christianity seems to lose its identity in recent times. If

God becomes a cosmic force and is not a person or if he is
identified with the human person in what is the most noble in
him, we lose sight of the identity of the Christian God. Also
when one insists in such a way that the seeds of the Word are
expanded in all religions, one forgets that it is necessary to pass
from "the unknown God" to Christ, the God who reveals himself. To assert that to "the anonymous God" corresponds "the
anonymous Christian," i.e., the man who is assured of salvation
by the mere fact that he is an honest man, is to forget that if the
ways of the salvific grace of God are not known to us, Christ has
established a normal economy of salvation that passes necessarily
through Jesus Christ (*EN* 26).

The Christian salvation is as much identifiable as the identity
of the Christian God in the *Evangelii nuntiandi*. The Church is
the continued presence of Christ to all men. The action of God's
grace and the good will of men are admitted by the council to be
the means of salvation for those who do not know Christ or the
Church (*LG* 16). This is often interpreted as to imply that it is
sufficient for non-Christians to obey their conscience. This is to
simplify things, and with *Lumen gentium*, it is also necessary to
see the texts where salvation is much more attached to the action
of the grace of Christ inciting men to the search of truth and
love. If good will is sufficient, it is so in the measure in that it
cooperates with the graces offered by Christ. Insistence on the
supernatural action of grace is necessary (*EN* 14).

Some think that the age of explicit proclamation is over, since
we are living in a period when orthopraxy, liberty, and permis-
siveness are stressed. One has to be satisfied with bearing witness
to the gospel by an authentic life. Moreover to preach Christ will
be to make an attempt on the liberty of consciences. *Evangelii
nuntiandi* clearly teaches the necessity not only of bearing witness, but also to explicit preaching of the gospel (*EN* 42), while
also stressing authenticity (*EN* 76). There has been also a false
interpretation of the conciliar teaching on the liberty of conscience. Some identify the liberty of conscience and free examination or free thought and believe that it entails abandonment of
objectivity and search for truth. Some contest all authority,
doctrinal, moral, pastoral, of the hierarchy. The Council's teaching on religious liberty can be summarized thus. It is a question of
proclaiming the Good News and the mercy of God and not to
enslave men. The response to the preaching of the gospel is only

valid if it comes from sincere and full liberty without any coercion. The truth and the good have their own value and claim, recognized as inestimable even for those who do not accept it.[12]

With respect to the relation between evangelization and dialogue, there is only an implicit reference in the *Evangelii nuntiandi*.[13] The work of evangelization is the essential message of the Church. Dialogue with non-Christian religions is an integral part of the mission of the Church. On the one hand, "the action of the Holy Spirit is extended beyond the frontiers of Christian communities." On the other, interreligious dialogue is made so that it may contribute to the better understanding of the newness of the gospel, of the plenitude of the Christian revelation, and to be able to show them better the salvific truth of love of God that is accomplished in Christ (*EN* 11).

Notes

1. The English translations of the conciliar documents are taken from Austin Flannery, O.P. (gen. ed.), *Vatican Council II*, New Revised Edition (Northport, 1984). The translation of *Evangelii nuntiandi* is taken from Austin Flannery, O. P. (gen. ed.), *Vatican Council II* (more postconciliar documents) (Northport, 1982).

2. *Ecclesiam suam* 64–65.

3. See M. Zerwick, *Graecitas biblica* (Rome, 1966), 13.

4. Y. M.-J. Congar, "Theologische Grundlegung (Nos. 2–9)," in J. Schütte (ed.), *Mission nach dem Konzil* (Mainz, 1967), 143ff.

5. D. Grasso, "Evangelizzazione. Senso di un termine," in M. Dhavamony (ed.), *Evangelization* (Rome, 1975), 21–47.

6. V. Miano, "Dialogo," in *Dizionario del Concilio Ecumenico Vaticano Secondo* (Rome 1969), 999–1000.

7. J. Ratzinger, "Konzilsaussagen über die Mission ausserhalb des Missionsdekrets," in J. Schütte (ed.), *Mission nach dem Konzil*, 28ff.

8. See P. Rossano, "Dialogue," *Bulletin*, 2 (1967), 143ff.

9. Y. M.-J. Congar, "Eglise et Monde," *Esprit* (1965), 356–357.

10. See *L'evangelizzazione nel mondo contemporaneo*, *Documento Preparatorio al Sinodo 1974* (Vatican City, 1973). *L'Eglise des cinq continents. Principaux textes du Synode des évêques. Rome, 1974* (Paris, 1975).

11. See *Osservatore Romano*, 27 Nov. 1974.

12. Ph. Delhaye, "L'Evangelisation chrètienne aujourd'hui," *Esprit et Vie* (1976), 66ff.

13. See M. Fitzgerald, "La Evangelii nuntiandi e le religioni del mondo," in *L'annuncio del Vangelo oggi* (Rome, 1977), 609–627.

Chapter 52

The Catholic Church
and the Jewish People

Reinhard Neudecker, S.J.

Summary

This essay is essentially a critical commentary on the Conciliar Declaration *Nostra aetate* 4 and the two documents by the Commission of the Holy See for Religious Relations with the Jews, published in 1974 and 1985, and, as such, it should enable the reader to become well acquainted with the complex and difficult problems of Jewish–Christian relations. A serious attempt has been made to give an accurate account of the concerns, viewpoints, and questions of the Jews. One section gives an evaluation of Pope John Paul II's visit to the Synagogue of Rome on 13 April 1986.

The Conciliar Declaration *Nostra aetate* 4 had long and, for the most part, painful antecedents, extending from the time of the New Testament down to the horrors of Auschwitz. These will be mentioned in the commentary on the Vatican "Notes," which were published on 24 June 1985.

After the shock caused by the slaying of six million Jews, Christians and Jews alike raised their voices and urged the Christian Churches to combat anti-Semitism and to work toward establishing a positive attitude toward the Jewish people. The Ten Points of Seelisberg, drawn up by an international conference of Christians and Jews on 5 August 1947 and addressed to all churches,

had great significance and influence, even on the conciliar Declaration and other Catholic documents on Christian–Jewish relations. The most important declarations that followed Seelisberg
were the Statement of the World Council of Churches on the
Christian Approach to the Jews (Amsterdam, 1948); the Proposals of Bad Schwalbach (1950), drawn up by Protestant and Catholic theologians; the Resolution on anti-Semitism of the World
Council of Churches (New Delhi, 1961); and the Statement of
the Department of World Mission of the Lutheran World Federation of the Church and anti-Semitism (Løgumkloster, Denmark,
1964).[1] When we consider the immediate antecedents to the
conciliar Declaration, the following three petitions to the Council
should be mentioned in particular: the petition of the Pontifical
Biblical Institute of 24 April 1960; the request of the Institute of
Judaeo–Christian Studies of Seton Hall University of 24 June
1960; and the important memorandum, which still merits consideration, of the Apeldoorn working group, which met on 28–31
August 1960.[2]

The decisive impulse toward a conciliar Declaration on the
Church and the Jewish people came from Pope John XXIII,
whom even Jews called "John the Good." As Apostolic Nuncio
in Bulgaria and Turkey during the period of Nazi terrorism, he
had saved thousands of Jews from deportation. As Pope, he had
the words *perfidus* and *perfidia iudaica* removed from the liturgical
prayers of Good Friday, and he also had a negative-sounding
passage in the Consecration to the Sacred Heart of Jesus suppressed. In June 1960, he received the Jewish historian Jules
Isaac, who had played a determining role in drawing up the Ten
Points of Seelisberg. In October 1960, he greeted a group of
American Jews with the Biblical words: "I am Joseph, your
brother." On 18 September 1960, he asked Cardinal Bea to
prepare a draft for a declaration on the inner relations between
the Church and the Jewish people.

The Declaration *Nostra aetate* had a very difficult and troubled
development in the council,[3] which recalls in many ways the
tragic bimilennial history of relations between Christians and
Jews and makes it seem almost miraculous that the declaration
ever appeared. Indiscretions, intrigues, near-eastern misunderstandings and fears, especially of a political nature, all became
entangled. In addition to this, there was what could be called
"Christian obstinacy," a certain inability to understand, found

among some Christians at the Council. They were mentally unprepared for the topic, and all too much children of a time when
the relations between Church and Synagogue had been "the
stepchild of theology" (J. Oesterreicher). The result of all this
was that the Declaration was constantly being changed and
never being fit into its projected plan. During these turbulent
times, Cardinal Bea proved himself to be "the true father of the
Declaration" (J. Oesterreicher). The first draft, the "Decretum
de Iudaeis," presented to the central commission in June 1962,
appeared in November 1963 as Chapter IV of the schema on
Ecumenism; in the spring of 1964, the Declaration appeared in
the appendix to this schema. But then, because of the insistence
of those who opposed it, the Declaration was to be greatly shortened and inserted into the schema on the Church. It was a
broader vision, that of Pope Paul VI in particular, of the human
family as brothers and sisters, and as children of God, which
brought it about that this declaration finally became, in November 1964, the core of a new conciliar Declaration on the Relation
of the Church to Nonchristian Religions. On 28 October 1965, a
vote was taken on this Declaration, with 2,221 ballots in favor,
88 opposed, and three invalid. The extraordinary significance
that Paul VI attributed to this Declaration is revealed in the
words that he used that same day in promulgating it: "The
Church is alive! Well, then, here is the proof, here the breath,
the voice, the song. . . ." The Pope then spoke of those adher-
ing to other religions, mentioning "especially the Jews, of whom
we ought never to disapprove and whom we ought never to
mistrust, but to whom we must show reverence and love, and in
whom we must place our hope."[4]

The Conciliar Declaration *Nostra aetate*

Besides being one of the first important commentaries on it,
the agitated history of the Declaration just mentioned has left its
traces in the document. For example, in comparison with the
first draft,[5] it will be immediately noted that some expressions
that have a pleasant ring have been eliminated: "The Church,
the Bride of Christ, acknowledges with a heart full of gratitude. . . ." "She rejoices. . . ." "The Church loves this people."
"Whoever despises or persecutes this people does injury to the

Catholic Church." The final wording is that of a rather sober, at times diplomatic-sounding document, which is still, because of the changes that were made in it during the process of its maturation, to be preferred on the whole to the first draft. Moreover, it is now found within the larger context of the Declaration on the Relationship of the Church to Nonchristian Religions, a fact which must obviously be taken into account in its interpretation.

The foreword to this document (*Nostra aetate* 1) gives the reason for, and the purpose of encounters with non-Christian peoples and religions: "In her task of fostering unity and love among men, and even among nations, she [the Church] gives primary consideration in this document to what human beings have in common and to what promotes fellowship among them."

The text of *Nostra aetate* and of the two later documents of the Commission for Religious Relations with the Jews must be explained here in some detail, since surveys have shown that many of the readers to whom these writings are addressed have little, if any, knowledge of them.

The statements of *Nostra aetate* 4 may be arranged as follows:

1. *The Special Bond That Links the Church with the Jewish People.* The Church acknowledges that the beginnings of her faith and of her election are found already in the Patriarchs, in Moses and the Prophets. She has received the Old Testament from the Jewish people. She draws sustenance from the root of the good olive tree (cf. Rom. 11:17–24). By his cross, Christ has reconciled Jews and Gentiles, making them both one in himself.

2. *The Special Position of the Jewish People Even after Christ.* According to Romans 9:4–5, "they have the adoption as sons, the glory, the covenant, the giving of the 'law,' the worship and the promises; they have the patriarchs and from them is Christ according to the flesh." Also from the Jewish people sprang Mary, the Apostles, and most of the early disciples. And despite the rejection of the gospel by many Jews, they still remain beloved of God because of their fathers, since he does not repent of the gifts or calls he makes (Rom. 11:28–29). The Church awaits the day at the end of time on which all people will be united (Zeph. 3:9; cf. Is. 66:23; Ps. 65:4 Rom. 11:11–32).

3. *The Fostering of Mutual Understanding and Respect.* This is to be achieved especially by biblical and theological studies and fraternal dialogue.

4. *The Question Concerning the Death of Christ.* "True, authori-

ties of the Jews and those who followed their lead pressed for the
death of Christ (cf. Jn. 19:6); still, what happened in his passion
cannot be blamed upon all the Jews then living, without distinction, nor upon the Jews of today." The Jews have not been
repudiated or cursed by God. In religious instruction and sermons, all should take pains not to teach anything out of harmony
with the truth of the gospels and the spirit of Christ.

5. *Anti-Semitism*. The Church, which repudiates all persecutions, "deplores the hatred, persecutions, and displays of anti-
Semitism directed against the Jews at any time and from any
source." Christ freely suffered his passion and death because of
the sins of all humanity.

The declaration has been greeted as a kind of milestone in the
history of Jewish–Christian relations. For the first time, a council has spoken expressly and appreciatively about the Jewish people and the special ties that connect the Church with them. Of
course, there have been some criticisms of the document. But a
better knowledge of the history of the text would have tempered
these criticisms to some extent. Cardinal Bea himself had written: "In fact we do not think at all that this is a document which
is perfect in all respects—something which, in any case, is hu-
manly impossible—and that therefore it must be defended at all
costs and in each and every detail."[6]

Observations and Questions on *Nostra aetate*

Regarding 1. The Church has received from the Jewish people
the so-called "Old Testament" or more precisely, it should be
said, the Old Testament and the New Testament.[7] But did she
not also, together with the Scriptures, receive in some way the
manner of interpreting them? In any case, it is certainly true that
the Church, at its origins, received the Old Testament in the
form that it was lived and understood by the Jews at the time.
And in his comparison of an "exegete" (that is, one who knows
how to deal correctly with the Bible) with the head of a house-
hold who brings forth both new and old from his rich storehouse
(Mt. 13:52), Jesus adopts basically the Pharasaic-Rabbinic mode
of text interpretation that, in dialogue with the biblical text,
aims at uncovering revelations that were both old and ever new.
A higher regard for the Jewish understanding of Scripture could
be evidence of the fact that the Church, according to Romans

11:17–24 is still today nourished (present tense!) from the root of the good olive tree.

Regarding 2. (a) The expression "because of their fathers" is sometimes considered, by the Jews, to be somewhat offensive. Actually, a unilateral emphasis on this expression, which is also frequently found in Jewish literature, could induce one to limit the reason for the divine love to only the distant past, without considering the steadfastness, even to the acceptance of martyrdom, of so many Jews throughout history up to our own days. Even in the hell of Auschwitz, Jews have professed and invoked the name of God.

(b) The hope that some day all peoples will be united under the sovereignty of God is based on the thought expressed in Romans 11:11–32. The Pauline view, which had been expressed even more clearly in the first draft, should not be understood in the sense that the Church "awaits the return of this people" without recognizing the fact that there must also be a return on her part.

In addition to the view expressed in Romans 11, which even a Catholic exegete once described as being "somewhat naive," the New Testament makes use of other figures to describe the same reality. The Parable of the Two Sons (Lk. 15:11–32), which already some Fathers of the Church, especially Augustine, applied to Jews and Christians, should explain more clearly, for example, the incomplete state in which the younger brother (the Christian), as well as the older, is found. There is no individual salvation. The banquet can only reach its joyful climax when the elder brother (the Jew) takes his place at the table. Only then can the father, who until that time goes from one to the other to win them over and to reconcile them to each other, be fully present.[8] It is obvious that the vision of Luke 15 must be enlarged today in order to include all the other non-Christian brothers and sisters as well.

Regarding 3. According to *Nostra aetate* 2, dialogue and collaboration should be conducted with prudence and love and in a way that bears witness to Christian faith and life. The accent on Christian witness frequently raises a suspicion among Jews that in the Judaeo-Christian dialogue, the Church is aiming at the conversion of the Jews. Such an interpretation is to be excluded, as is evident from many postconciliar documents.[9] This finds its foundation to a great extent in the Pauline view mentioned before, according to which, at the end of time, the Jewish people will of themselves join the Church (Rom. 11:11–32).

Regarding 4. When we consider the difficult relations between religion and politics, the frequently obscure problems connected with jurisdiction in lands occupied by the Romans, and the problem of the so-called anti-Judaism in the New Testament, which still needs much more investigation, the statement about "Jewish authorities and those who followed their lead" in reference to the death of Jesus is a matter of some dispute. "Viewed historically, those responsible for the death of Jesus were: 'a small group of Jews, a Roman, and a handful of Syrians who belonged to the Tenth Cohort stationed in Palestine' (Cardinal F. König). And all these were forgiven by the Lord on the cross."[10]

Regarding 5. The theme of anti-Semitism is again taken up in *Nostra aetate* 5. Any discrimination or harassment is rejected, and a definite reason for this is given: an anti-Semite or anyone who refuses to act in a loving way toward certain persons, cannot call upon God who is the father of all. He has understood nothing of God, for "he who does not love does not know God" (1 Jn. 4:8).

During the conciliar debate of 28–29 September 1964, a number of the Fathers favored the Church's admission of guilt to the Jewish people. Bishop Elchinger of Strasbourg asked: "Why can we not draw from the Gospel the magnanimity to beg for forgiveness, in the name of so many Christians, for so many and so great injustices?"[11] Before this, Cardinal Bea, in a conference in Rome, had already recalled the solemn words with which Pope Paul VI had asked pardon of non-Catholic Christians for all the guilt that could be imputed to the Catholic Church for the painful divisions among Christians. Regarding the attitude of the Church toward the Jews, the cardinal stated: "Here perhaps we should confess many faults, faults of the Church herself as well."[12] On 13 August 1985, Pope John Paul II spoke in Yaoundé (Cameroon) about the failure during the course of history on the part of "people belonging to Christian nations"; and he continued: ". . . we ask fogiveness of our African friends who, for example, suffered so much under the slave trade."[13] Strange to say in light of this, a request for the forgiveness of the Jewish people has been expressed only on a regional basis.[14]

The Declaration *Nostra aetate* is not an ultimate that cannot be surpassed. At the press conference on the day of its promulgation, Cardinal Bea observed: "The Declaration on the Non-christian Religions is indeed an important and promising begin-ning, yet no more than the beginning of a long and demanding way towards the arduous goal of a humanity whose members feel themselves truly to be sons and daughters of the same Father and act on this conviction."[15]

Since then, the Church has continued along this route for twenty years, and it has already made notable advances. Dialogue groups, secretariats, and commissions have been established on national and regional levels. Numerous documents, some of which have already been mentioned, have been composed, often as the result of dialogues between Christians and Jews. Among these, the Document of the Pastoral Council of the Catholic Church in the Netherlands (5–8 April 1970), the Statement of the French Bishops' Committee for Relations with Jews (16 April 1973), and the Working Paper of the Study Group "Jews and Christians" of the Central Committee of Roman Catholics in Germany (8 May 1979) have been especially important. The sig-nificance of the statements of the American Bishops' Conference (March 1967 and November 1975) lies particularly in its indica-tion of concrete means of action and its emphasis on the special tie existing between the Jewish people and the land of Israel.[16]

On 22 October 1974, Paul VI established the Commission for Religious Relations with the Jews, which has issued two docu-ments for the universal Church that are based on national or regional studies: the "Guidelines" of 1 December 1974 and the "Notes" of 24 June 1985, which will now be examined.

Guidelines and Suggestions for
Implementing *Nostra aetate*

The document begins with some basic observations: "Deeply affected by the memory of the persecution and massacre of Jews which occurred in Europe just before and during the Second World War," the Council effected a decisive change in the his-tory of relations between Jews and Catholics. And after two thousand years "too often marked by mutual ignorance and fre-quent confrontation," as a result of this conciliar Declaration, many steps have been taken to promote a new relationship be-tween Jews and Christians. The spiritual bonds and historical ties

that link the Church to Judaism condemn all forces of anti-
Semitism and discrimination as being opposed to the very spirit
of Christianity.[17] Christians must strive "to acquire a better
knowledge of the basic components of the religious tradition of
Judaism," and "to learn by what essential traits the Jews define
themselves in the light of their own religious experience."

1. *Dialogue.* Where there have actually been relations between
Jews and Christians, these have seldom risen above the level of a
monologue. Dialogue presumes that each side wishes to attain a
better knowledge of the other, which in turn leads to a deeper
understanding of one's own traditions. It demands respect for the
other as he/she is, and above all for his faith and religious convictions. "In virtue of her divine mission, and her very nature, the
Church must proclaim Jesus Christ to the world (*Ad gentes* 2),"
but in order to not give offense to the Jews, Catholics must take
care to maintain the strictest respect for the religious freedom of
others while bearing witness to their own faith. Because of "an
unfortunate past," for which "Christians[18] will certainly recognize their share of responsibility," there is still "a widespread air
of suspicion."[19] In order to not offend, even involuntarily, others
with whom one is engaged in a friendly talk or scholarly discussion, "it will be vital to guarantee, not only tact, but a great
openness of spirit and diffidence with respect to one's own prejudices." Under certain circumstances, "a common meeting before
God in prayer and silent meditation" might be recommended,
since this is a source of that humility, openness of heart and mind
that are necessary for a deep knowledge of one's own self and
others.

2. *Liturgy.* With respect to the question of the liturgy, which,
because of its common elements, is important for the Judaeo-
Christian dialogue, the first concern should be with the reading
of the Old Testament. "An effort will be made to acquire a better
understanding of whatever in the Old Testament retains its own
perpetual value (cf. *Dei Verbum* 14–15), since that has not been
cancelled by the later interpretation of the New Testament.
Rather, the New Testament brings out the full meaning of the
Old, while both Old and New illumine and explain each other
(cf. *ibid.*, 16)." In commenting on Scriptural texts, emphasis
should be placed on "the continuity of our faith with that of the
earlier Covenant, in the perspective of the promises." Particular

efforts should be made to give a correct interpretation to those passages that may seem to place the Jewish people in such a bad light. And special attention should be given to "those phrases and passages which Christians, if not well informed, might misunderstand because of prejudice" (for example, "the Jews" in the Gospel of St. John, "Pharisees, "Pharisaism").

3. *Teaching and Education.* In recent years, a better understanding has already been achieved in several areas: It is the same God who speaks both in the Old and New Testaments; Judaism in the time of the New Testament was a complex reality; the Old Testament and the tradition based on it is not simply a religion of justice, fear, and legalism; Jesus and the Apostles had their origins in the Jewish people, "and although his teaching had a profoundly different character, Christ, nevertheless in many instances, took his stand on teaching of the Old Testament." Judaism did not end with the destruction of Jerusalem, but continued to develop a tradition rich in religious values, "although we believe that the importance and meaning of that tradition were deeply affected by the coming of Christ."[20] Concerning the question of the trial and death of Jesus and of the eschatological expectation, the statements of Vatican II are repeated. Information concerning these questions should be given in catechisms and religious textbooks, history books and the mass media as well as in schools, seminaries, and universities. Exegesis, theology, history, and sociology should promote scientific research on problems that touch Judaism and Jewish–Christian relations. "Wherever possible, chairs of Jewish studies should be created, and collaboration with Jewish scholars encouraged."

4. *Joint Social Action.* This is based on the common understanding of the human person as image of God; it grows out of love of the same God and through collaboration for the good of humanity, it can do much to foster mutual understanding and esteem.

The "conclusion," besides giving some practical suggestions to bishops for implementing the conciliar Declaration, stresses the significance of Jewish–Christian relations even in those regions where there are no Jewish communities. The Church as such, when she meditates upon her own mystery, meets the mystery of Israel. There is, furthermore, an ecumenical aspect; "The very return of Christians to the sources and origins of their faith . . . helps the search for unity in Christ, the cornerstone."[21]

In the opinion of both Christians and Jews, the "Guidelines" have been greeted as a genuine advance because of their depth and balance. From the Jewish viewpoint, they have, however, been criticized mainly on two counts. The mention of a divine mission to proclaim Jesus Christ to the world has been a source of renewed distrust, and it has again raised the question as to whether or not the Church in its dialogue is not ultimately concerned with the conversion of the Jews. Furthermore, there is no reference made to the bond of the Jewish people for the land and the state of Israel, which had been previously stated by, among others, both the Pastoral Council of the Catholic Church in the Netherlands and the French Bishops' Committee for Relations with Jews.[22] As a matter of fact, if the document had maintained the principle that it had itself proposed, that the Jewish reality should be accepted the way it is understood by the Jews themselves, it could not have overlooked this point. The reason for the omission, which is probably responsible also for the late appearance of the "Guidelines," is apparently to be found in the premature and unauthorized publication (*The New York Times*, 11 December 1969) of a working paper that was thought to be a draft for an official pronouncement. In this text, which had been elaborated at the request of the Vatican's Secretariat for Promoting Christian Unity, were these important words:

> Fidelity to the covenant was linked to the gift of a land, which in the Jewish soul has endured as the object of an aspiration that Christians should strive to understand. In the wake of long generations of painful exile, all too often aggravated by persecutions and moral pressures, for which Christians ask pardon of their Jewish brothers, Jews have indicated in a thousand ways their attachment to the land promised to their ancestors from the days of Abraham's calling.
>
> It could seem that Christians, whatever the difficulties they may experience, must attempt to understand and respect the religious significance of this link between the people and the land. The existence of the State of Israel should not be separated from this perspective; which does not in itself imply any judgment on historical occurrences, or on decisions of a purely political order.[23]

Notes on the Correct Way to Present the Jews and Judaism in Preaching and Catechesis

This new document is "the result of a long and patient drafting."[24] Although it has made notable progress, especially in the treatment of the Jewish roots of Christianity, the relation of Jesus to the Pharisees, the presentation of the Jews in the New Testament, and the State of Israel, certain aspects of this instruction have been a source of disappointment and, at times, of severe criticism on the part of both Christians and Jews. It has also been said that there were not sufficient preliminary consultations and that it was published under the pressure of time. These criticisms are corroborated by the fact that already, from the time of its release to the press, some improvements were being made.

The text begins with some "preliminary considerations," which are followed by six sections and a conclusion.

1. *Religious Teaching and Judaism.* The importance of a correct presentation of the Jews and Judaism is emphasized in an observation made by Pope John Paul II: "Work that is of poor quality and lacking in precision would be extremely detrimental" to Judaeo-Christian dialogue (No. 6). Some important conditions for such a presentation are also mentioned: it should be done "in an honest and objective manner, free from prejudices and without any offenses" (Pope John Paul II in the "Preliminary Considerations"). Care must be given to respect essential traits through which Jews define themselves in the light of their own religious experience (No. 4). It is not surprising that after only twenty years of dialogue, these lofty principles have not yet been fully developed.

These are the main passages, at times difficult to understand, which deal with the relations between the Church and Judaism:

5. The singularity and the difficulty of Christian teaching about Jews and Judaism lies in this, that it needs to balance several pairs of ideas which express the relation between the economies of the Old and New Testaments: Promise and Fulfillment, Continuity and Newness, Singularity and Universality, Uniqueness and Exemplariness. . . .

7. "In virtue of her divine mission, the Church" which is to be "the all-embracing means of salvation" in which alone "can be obtained the fullness of the means of salvation" (*UR* 3),

"must of her nature proclaim Jesus Christ to the world" (cf. *Guidelines and Suggestions* I). Indeed, we believe that it is through him that we go to the Father (cf. Jn. 14:6): "and this is eternal life, that they know thee the only true God and Jesus Christ whom thou hast sent" (Jn. 17:3). Jesus affirms that "there shall be one flock and one shepherd" (Jn. 10:16). Church and Judaism cannot then be seen as two parallel ways of salvation; and the Church must witness to Christ as the Redeemer for all, "while maintaining the strictest respect for religious liberty in line with the teaching of the Second Vatican Council (Declaration *Dignitatis Humanae*)" (*Guidelines and Suggestions* I).

Further: The Jews "have been chosen by God to prepare the coming of Christ" (No. 8); "the definitive meaning of the election of Israel does not become clear except in light of the complete fulfillment (Rom. 9–11)" (II, No. 1).

In texts such as these, Jews see themselves defined in Christian categories and not presented as they perceive themselves to be, in the light of their specific religious experience. They feel that in these statements, they are deprived of their own identity. "Judaism is not seen as a legitimate path to salvation."[25] The election of the Jews, then, would consist solely in a preparation for the coming of Christ. "If this is the sole basis for their chosenness, and they are excluded from salvation as long as they do not accept Jesus, they remain in an inferior status."[26] This is deemed by the Jews to be a return to the ecclesiastical triumphalism that characterized the past. They sense a return to the saying "Extra ecclesiam nulla salus (There is no salvation outside the Church)," which is, according to W. Kasper, "a highly ambiguous phrase" that can be misunderstood "in the sense of a narrow-minded restriction of salvation."[27]

This situation reveals the need for dialogue between Jews and Christians also on a precisely theological level. The insights of such dialogue could possibly lead to, among other things, a new theological language, to "new wine in new skins." Such a language can occasionally be heard already today. Pope John Paul II has coined some significant expressions in this regard. In his address of 6 March 1982 to delegates of episcopal conferences for relations with Judaism, he said: "We shall be able to go by diverse—but in the end convergent—paths and with the help of the Lord, who has never ceased loving His people (cf. Rom. 11:1), to reach true fraternity in reconciliation, respect, and full accomplishment of God's plan in history."[28] In his address to the participants in a Colloquium on *Nostra aetate* held 19 April 1985, the Pope spoke of "our respective vocations as Christians and as Jews."[29] Theological language of this kind is approved by Jews.

2. *Relations between the Old and the New Testament.* The reason for the detailed exposition of this theme is "to show the unity of biblical Revelation (O.T. and N.T.) and of the divine plan," for it is from here that the problem of the relation between the two Testaments derives. This is a problem that must be resolved primarily with the help of typology. "Typology however makes many people uneasy and this is perhaps the sign of a problem unresolved" (No. 3).[30]

The most important statements are contained in paragraphs 5–7:

5. It should be emphasized that typological interpretation consists in reading the Old Testament as preparation for and, in a certain sense, outline and foreshadowing of the New (cf., e.g., Heb. 5:5–10, etc.). Christ is henceforth the reference-point of and the key to the Scriptures: "the rock *was* Christ" (1 Cor. 10:4).

6. It is true then, and it needs to be stressed, that the Church and Christians read the Old Testament in the light of the event of the death and resurrection of Christ, and that on these grounds there is a Christian reading of the Old Testament which does not necessarily coincide with the Jewish. Thus Christian identity and Jewish identity should be carefully distinguished in their respective reading of the Bible. . . .[31]

7. Typological reading manifests all the more the unfathomable riches of the Old Testament, its inexhaustible content and the mystery of which it is full. . . .

Despite the strong emphasis on typology, this is not the only way suggested for interpreting the Old Testament. Mention is also made of its own proper value as Revelation (No. 7); and with reference to the different ways in that the Scriptures are understood by Jews, it is said that Christians are not "hindered from profiting, but with discrimination, from the traditions of Jewish reading" (No. 6).

On this point, the diocese of Rome had earlier, in January 1983, given a much more positive opinion:

> Reading the Old Testament together is particularly recommended, so that the light shed by Jewish tradition in its different modes (normative, narrative and mystical) may help to develop an approach to the sacred text which can be especially helpful in plumbing the depth of the Word of God."[32]

The Jewish understanding of Scripture, which, as noted before, Jesus had in common with the Pharisees and with "normative" Judaism, despite some differences with them (cf. Mt. 5:21–48) and a certain aversion to legalistic "exegesis," seeks to show, in a dialogue with the biblical text, the unfathomable riches of the Old Testament, its inexhaustible content, and the mystery with which it is filled. "Turn it (the Torah) over, and turn it over yet again, since everything is in it!"[33] In this way, the Scriptures never become "old"; rather their revelation is ever new.[34] Thus taken, the sixth section of the "Notes," with its mention of the "continuous spiritual fecundity" of postbiblical Judaism, certainly includes high praise for the Jewish interpretation of Scripture.

3. *Jewish Roots of Christianity.* This section is one of the most positive parts of the document. The use of the expression "Jewish," and not "Old Testament" roots, as found in the title cannot be sufficiently stressed, given some virtually ineradicable misunderstandings. The background of the New Testament is not so much the Old Testament as it is known today through the historical-critical method, but the Old Testament as it was lived and understood in the time of the New Testament.[35] Without a knowledge of their Jewish milieu, neither the historical Jesus nor the New Testament can be understood. Unfortunately, this document discusses only the major elements of the Palestinian milieu, which, however, certainly do represent the decisive background for early Christianity. But other movements such as apocalyptic and the world of Hellenistic Judaism must also be considered, for they also left clear traces in the New Testament.

The most important statements of the section may be briefly quoted:

> Jesus was and always remained a Jew.[36] . . . Jesus is fully a man of his time and of his environment—first century Jewish Pales-

tinian society. . . . Jesus' relations with biblical law and its interpretations, be they more or less traditional, are undoubtedly complex. . . . But there is no doubt that he wished to submit himself to the law (cf. Gal. 4:4). . . . His relations with the Pharisees were not totally nor at all times polemical. Of these there are many proofs. . . . Jesus shares, with the majority of his contemporary Palestinian Jews, some pharisaic doctrines: the resurrection of the body; certain forms of piety such as alms-giving, prayer, fasting (cf. Mt. 6:1–18) and the liturgical practice of addressing God as Father; the priority of the commandment to love God and neighbor (cf. Mk. 12:28–34). . . . Like Jesus himself, Paul also used methods of reading and interpreting Scripture and of teaching his disciples which were common to the Pharisees of that time. This includes the use of parables as seen in Jesus' ministry, as well as the manner in which both Jesus and Paul supported conclusions with quotations from Scripture. . . . If in the Gospels and elsewhere in the New Testament there are all sorts of unfavorable references to the Pharisees, these should be seen against the background of a movement which was both complex and diversified. Moreover criticisms of various types of Pharisees were not lacking even in rabbinical sources (cf. the *Babylonian Talmud,* tractate *Sotah* 22b, etc.).[37]

The document does not deal specifically with the differences that actually existed between Jesus and the Pharisees.

4. *The Jews in the New Testament.* This section is concerned particularly with the negative statements about the Jews found in the New Testament, that is, with what has been called its anti-Judaism and even anti-Semitism. With reference to the long and complicated process of the redaction of the New Testament, it states:

> It cannot be ruled out that some references which are hostile or less than favorable toward the Jews have their historical context in conflicts between the nascent Church and the Jewish community. Certain controversies reflect circumstances of Christian–Jewish relations as they existed long after the time of Jesus.

The development of these conflicts, which lead finally to the parting of the ways, is mentioned only briefly. There already

were conflicts between Jesus and certain categories of Jews. The
majority of the Jewish people did not believe in Jesus. This latter
fact, accentuated by the Christian mission, especially that
among the pagans, "led inevitably to a rupture between Judaism
and the young Church."

The history of this first decisive conflict has not yet been
sufficiently investigated.[38] One must start from the fact that, in
response to the life, death, and resurrection of Jesus, there arose
a movement within Judaism that became more and more separated from the main currents of its own religion. Among the
factors that played an important role in this process were, on the
one hand, a particular attitude toward the Scriptures, which is to
be explained at least partially by an expectation of an imminent
Parousia, and, on the other hand, the problem created by an
ever-increasing number of Christians who had been converted
from paganism. The Scriptures were interpreted in reference to
Jesus, whose position was still further exalted by a series of messianic titles. According to Paul's interpretation of the law, the
pagans who became Christians had no need of prior conversion
to Judaism. They consequently remained as foreigners to the
Jewish people. And by the fact that they claimed to be the
people of God based on a New Covenant, they even entered into
a kind of rivalry with the Jewish people. In face of all these
developments, the Judaeo-Christians found themselves to be in a
difficult situation.

On the other side, during the period that followed the Jewish
War and the destruction of the Temple (70 A.D.), the Pharisees
began a reorganization and unification of the Jewish people that
was effected largely by establishing a binding juridical order and
fixing a certain number of religious obligations. This included
admonitions and measures directed against marginal groups such
as the Judaeo-Christians and other "heretics." According to Rabbi Eleazar of Modiin (end of the first and the beginning of the
second century), "he who profanes the Sabbaths, or despises the
festivals, or openly shames his fellowman, or nullifies the covenant (circumcision) of our father Abraham, or gives the Torah a
meaning contrary to its right one, even though he is learned in
the Torah and has good deeds to his credit, has no share in the
world to come."[39] Of some obvious significance was the inclusion
of the Judaeo-Christians in the "benediction" concerning heretics (*Birkat ha-Minim*)[40] in the Eighteen Benedictions (*Shemoneh*

Esreh) of the daily liturgy. The malediction that was invoked upon the Roman authorities and different groups of heretics, including the Judaeo-Christians ("Nazarenes"), was at the time probably expressed somewhat as follows: "May there be no hope left to the apostates, and do Thou speedily uproot in our days the kingdom of arrogance, and may the Nazarenes and heretics perish in a moment. 'Let them be blotted out of the book of the living, and not be written with the righteous' (Ps. 69:29). Blessed be Thou, O Lord, who humblest the arrogant!" Our sources do not tell us if the intent of the Pharisees was to exclude the Judaeo-Christians from the synagogue with this imprecation. However, its consequence, and very likely that of other measures as well, was that the Judaeo-Christian Christians no longer took part in the Jewish liturgy. John 9:22, 12:42, and 16:2 speak of exclusion from the synagogue.[41]

The last paragraph of this section takes up "the delicate question of responsibility for the death of Christ," and, despite the advances that have been made in the last twenty years through Jewish–Christian dialogue, it uses the same expression as the past: "authorities of the Jews and their followers." The document would have been better received if the words spoken during the press release had been inserted into the text itself: in view of our own participation as sinners in the death of Christ, "the historical intervention in Jesus' passion of those few Jews and some Romans becomes a very secondary matter. The *Credo* of the Catholic Church has always mentioned Pontius Pilate, and not the Jews, in relation to the death of Christ."[42]

5. *The Liturgy.* In this section, brief mention is made of what Jews and Christians have in common and of the Jewish roots of Christian liturgy, a matter which has not yet been sufficiently studied.

6. *Judaism and Christianity in History.* This section deals essentially with three themes: (1) the land and the state of Israel, (2) the history of the Jews since 70 A.D., and (3) the Holocaust.

(1) The text on the land and the state of Israel has been drawn up with particular care. In their far-flung diaspora, Jews have preserved the memory of the land of their forefathers at the very center of their hope (Passover *Seder*).

Christians are invited to understand this religious attachment which finds its roots in Biblical tradition, without, however, making their own any particular religious interpretation of this relationship (cf. *Declaration* of the U.S. Conference of Catholic Bishops, 20 November 1975).

The existence of the State of Israel and its political options should be envisaged not in a perspective which is in itself religious, but in their reference to the common principles of international law.

The text is acceptable, but a decisive word in favor of Israel's right to exist and its security as a state would have been welcomed, a statement similar to that of the French Bishops' Committee for Relations with the Jews, for example; "Beyond the legitimate divergence of political options, the conscience of the world community cannot refuse to the Jewish people, who had to submit to so many vicissitudes in the course of their history, the right and means for a political existence among the nations."[43] Pope John Paul II had earlier spoken in a similar fashion. In his apostolic letter *Redemptionis Anno* of 20 April 1984, he states: "For the Jewish people who live in the State of Israel and who preserve in that land such precious testimonies to their history and their faith, we must ask for the desired security and the due tranquility that is the prerogative of every nation and condition of life and of progress for every society."[44]

It is to be hoped that these words concerning the land and the State of Israel will soon be followed by concrete deeds, for "it is the duty also of the Christians to confirm the sovereignty, freedom, even the mere existence of the country that has given its Jewish citizens a home and has strengthened a healthy self-esteem of Jews everywhere."[45]

The text concerning the state of Israel has been considerably criticized by Jews, who are particularly disturbed by the fact that in their opinion the document gives no real religious significance to the state of Israel. The International Jewish Committee on Interreligious Consultations (IJCIC) has declared in the name of its member organizations, the American Jewish Committee, the Anti-Defamation League of B'nai B'rith,[46] the Jewish Council of Israel on Interreligious Consultations, the Synagogue Council of America, and the World Jewish Congress: "Modern Israel is emptied of any possible religious significance for Christians. Even Israel's profound religious significance for Jews . . . is mentioned in such recondite fashion as to be unrecognizable."[47] A press release of the Jewish Council in Israel on Interreligious Consultations, given on 24 June 1985, contains a similar statement and adds the following observation: "The Council regrets the failure to recognize that the document's affirmation of the continuing status of the Jews as the Chosen People implies the continuing validity—for Christians as well as for Jews—of the divine promise of the land to the Jews."[48]

On the other hand, H. Siegman, Executive Director of the American Jewish Congress, has defended the position taken in the "Notes" mainly on the grounds that Jews themselves are not in agreement regarding the religious significance of the state of Israel (on whether it is a religious phenomenon, and in particular whether its rebirth is to be considered as the beginning of an eschatological process): "The Vatican document's suggestion that Catholics view the State of Israel in the perspective of 'common principles of international law' is precisely correct."[49]

(2) The history of the Jews since the destruction of the temple (70 A.D.) is touched only briefly. Nevertheless, the fact is recognized that the Jewish people, especially in their far-flung diaspora have given to the world "a witness—often heroic—of its fidelity to the one true God" and exalted him "in the presence of all the living" (Tb. 13:4). This clearly implies that Christians too should heed this witness. The permanence of the Jewish people has been accompanied by a continuous spiritual creativity in the rabbinical period, in the Middle Ages, and in modern times. The faith and the religious life of the Jewish people are professed and practiced still today. The "negative balance" in Jewish–Christian relations during the course of two thousand years is not carefully considered but only mentioned in passing. Nevertheless, just before the publication of the "Notes," there appeared in La Civiltà Cattolica, a periodical authorized by the Vatican, two feature articles (for which the periodical accepts responsibility), one on "Jews" and the other on "Jewish-Christian Relations."[50] Perhaps what is said there about the history of the Jews since 70 A.D.[51] could be seen as completing what is expressed in the "Notes."

A survey of the painful history of the relations between Jews and Christians, a history not yet sufficiently investigated and assimilated, must begin with the New Testament and the controversies mentioned therein. These have their source in antagonisms, part of which were inner-Jewish and part of which were due to relations with pagan-Christians. At the time of their

conversion, pagan-Christians were not always completely free of
their well-known pagan anti-Semitic heritage. A times, their
negative attitude toward the Jews was simply reinforced by
pseudotheological "Christian" arguments.[52] As the young movement became the church of primarily pagan–Christian orientation, gradually the original inner-Jewish conflicts were no longer
understood as such, and the texts in question were frequently
interpreted as a reflection of an almost irreconcilable opposition
between Jews and Christians, and even of a rejection of Judaism
that went back to Jesus himself.[53] New Testament texts were
thus at times distorted, misused, removed from their context,
and made coresponsible for an ever more intensive anti-Judaism
(an antagonism on religious ground, not always clearly distin-
guishable from anti-Semitism based on racism). For the now
normative Pharisaic–Rabbinic Judaism, such texts, if not the
whole New Testament, frequently appeared to be anti-Judaic or
anti-Semitic slander coming from a foreign religion, one opposed
to Judaism. Naturally, the Jews reacted to all of this, a reaction
reflected already in some New Testament texts and later in some
Patristic ones.[54] In comparison with Christian anti-Judaism, especially that in effect after Christianity became the state religion,
Jewish "anti-Christianism" was of relatively little significance.

Care must be taken, however, not to judge the anti-Judaism of
the past by modern standards. "Love of truth certainly requires
that we acknowledge possible errors. But the same love and justice
also demand that we should refrain from judging statements made
in other times, using standards that were established only centuries later, standards based on progress in explaining the doctrine,
achieved by the Church only in our days."[55] Anti-Judaism can
never be simply equated with a hatred for Jews.[56] It is largely a
consequence of a Christian apologetic that sought to clarify and
justify its own faith in the face of Judaism. The continuation of
Judaism after Christ and after the destruction of the Temple, the
persistent expectation among the Jews of the Messiah's arrival, the
continuous failure of the Christian mission among the Jews, and
occasionally the attraction that the Jewish religion has had for
some Christians, presented at that time an enduring challenge to
the Church, and raised questions concerning her claims. Within
the narrow framework of an "either-or" mentality, it was argued: if
Judaism is right, Christianity must be wrong; "if Jewish worship is
honorable and significant, ours can only be a lie and a trick."[57] As

a consequence, the Christian religion was frequently defended and promoted in a triumphalistic way by using allegorical and typological interpretations of the Old Testament, by a gross exaggeration of some New Testament positions and the projection of an image of Judaism that fitted that concept. All this was, above all, at the expense of the Jewish people, since they were frequently accused of deicide, of having broken the covenant with God. They were also spoken of as rejected by God as his chosen people and replaced in this role by the Church. But, as a consequence of their own separation from their "root" (Rom. 11:17–24), the Christians also suffered negative consequences, since "spiritually we are Semites" (Pius XI).[58]

In addition to written attacks, there were verbal attacks against Jews. Even when John Chrysostom, a zealous preacher and Father of the Church, spoke with the "good" intention of strengthening and informing Christians in their faith, and dissuading Christian women from visiting the synagogue on Sabbaths and feast days, statements such as the following can in no way be justified: "It (the Synagogue) may be called a brothel, a place of unlawfulness, a quarter for evil spirits, a fortress of the devil, the ruin of souls, the steep slope and mortal abyss for every kind of perdition; still, no matter how it may be described, it can never be given (with terms such as these) the name it deserves."[59] Particularly fearsome were the Good Friday sermons that were taken at times as an invitation to the burning of synagogues and bloody riots. We can only mention in passing the different forms of discrimination, of slander (Jews were accused, for example, of desecrating the host, ritual murders, poisoning of wells, and the spreading of the plague), of forced baptisms, enclosure in ghettos, persecutions, banishments, and massacres (especially in connection with the Crusades and the eastern European pogroms); and, on the other hand, the positive measures employed by Popes, bishops, and secular authorities, as well as the attitude of countless Christians who took seriously the commandment of loving one's neighbor and so protected the Jews.[60]

Religious motives are obviously not sufficient to explain the complex phenomenon of hostility toward Jews. These motives are perhaps themselves an expression of a more extensive aberration to be found on a sociopsychological level and manifested in the form of distrust, intolerance, rejection, or aggression when there is need to deal with something or someone that is "different." For example, one who is successful on a commercial or scientific level encounters envy; "the stranger" is often made the scapegoat for business or social problems.

Hostility to the Jews reached a climax with the arrival of racial ideology in the second half of the nineteenth century. In the face of an all-pervading anti-Semitism, a Jew could not save himself by assimilating to his Christian surroundings or even through conversion, a fact that was frightfully proven in the attempted genocide by German National Socialism.

(3) Concerning the "Holocaust," the "Notes" state that catechesis should help in understanding "the meaning for the Jews of their extermination during the years 1939–1945, and its consequences" (No. 25). Although Christian culpability in the Holocaust has been admitted on a regional level,[61] and although Pope John Paul II in his allocution to the representatives of the Jews in Mainz on 17 November 1980 spoke of "a false religious view of the Jewish people, which in the course of history was one of the causes that contributed to misunderstanding and persecution,"[62] it is both surprising and deplorable that the "Notes" have passed over the meaning of the Holocaust for Christians. However, this omission was rectified during the press conference: there is a question regarding its meaning "also for us, whom it also obviously concerns" (English text); it is a question "of a tragedy which is obviously also ours" (Italian text). Can this statement be understood as a sense of Christian coresponsibility for the Holocaust? At times, it appears that Christians wish to deny any complicity in the Holocaust on the grounds that it was a completely godless terrorism and that the perpetrators of it had nothing to do with Christianity. But this overlooks the fact that the anti-Semitism of National Socialism appealed at times to the New Testament and to Church history for its justification.[63] In 1946, Julius Streicher, a Nazi criminal and editor of the infamous weekly *Der Stürmer,* declared before the Nuremberg court that in accusing him, the reformer Martin Luther was himself being accused, for he had only carried out what Luther had ordered every righteous and believing person to do.[64]

7. *Conclusion.* Here special mention is made of "a painful ignorance of the history and traditions of Judaism, of which only negative aspects and often caricatures belong to the commonly held ideas of many Christians. That is what these notes aim to remedy."

The Pope's Visit to the Synagogue of Rome
(13 April 1986)

What was obvious to Jesus, Peter, and the first Christians is now, after almost two thousand years of separation of Jews and Christians, no longer without its problems. Some Christians who had no knowledge of the current Jewish–Christian relations were at first rather perplexed by the announced visit of the Pope to the synagogue of Rome. In the neighborhood of St. Peter's, a few followers of the suspended Archbishop Lefèbvre distributed handbills with the headline: "Stop, Pope, do not go along with Caiphas!" These handbills also accused the Pope of changing the Christian religion. Many other Christians had, on the other hand, come to recognize anew, especially after the Second Vatican Council, the historical and spiritual roots of the Church in the Jewish people, and for them the visit to the synagogue was no surprise. They saw the Pope's desire to visit the Roman synagogue as just an advance along the path taken by John XXIII and Paul VI.

In the eyes of some Jews, especially those of strict orthodoxy, the Pope's visit to the synagogue was not so simple. One could ask, for example, whether the presence of Christians in the synagogue did not somehow compromise the strictness of Jewish monotheism. The Pope was, at any rate, fully aware that being inside the synagogue was due to "generous hospitality," for which he has repeatedly expressed his gratitude.

Possible reservations and hesitations on the part of Jews over the delicate situation created by the presence of Christians at a Jewish religious ceremony were met in different ways. One of the Scriptural texts chosen to be read was Micah 4:1–5, a text that leaves no doubt that the Jews will follow their way "for ever and ever" in the name of the Lord their God. The Pope and Chief Rabbi Elio Toaff were to read no Psalm together. No prayers (except for the Psalms) were spoken aloud, although there was a brief pause for silent prayer. The choir solemnly proclaimed faith in the Messiah yet to come. No convert to Christianity had been invited.

It is only natural that some central concerns of the Jews were mentioned in the synagogue, since Jews from America, Europe, and Israel had hoped, especially after his visit to the synagogue had been announced, that the Pope would take a stand on some current issues. The President of the Jewish Community of Rome as well as the Rabbi drew particular attention to anti-Semitism and to the Holocaust. Psalm 124, recited by Rabbi Toaff, also touched this theme. In their addresses, both Jewish leaders expressed a particular concern—not taken up by the Pope—for the recognition of the state of Israel by the Holy See. The reading of Genesis 15:1–7 fits into this context. In contrast with the opinion widely held in liberal Judaism, which no longer identifies the Messianic era with the arrival of a personal Messiah and the return to Sion, Rabbi Toaff declared:

> The return of the Jewish people to its land must be recognized as a good and an inalienable gain for the world, because it constitutes the prelude—according to the teachings of the prophets—to that epoch of universal brotherhood to which we all aspire, and to that redemptive peace that finds it sure promise in the Bible. The recognition of Israel's irreplaceable role in the final plan of redemption that God has promised us cannot be denied. [65]

This view is hardly approved by Christians; many Jews do not share it either.

In his discourse, the Pope did not intend to present any new themes regarding Christian–Jewish relations. He nevertheless made some significant affirmations that may also be indicative for the future. He spoke of a "general acceptance of a legitimate plurality on the social, civil, and religious levels." With the words of the Council, he deplored all expressions of anti-Semitism directed against the Jews at any time and by anyone: "I repeat: 'By anyone.' " In this way, by including the Church and certain Popes, he replied to discreet allusions in the two Jewish speeches. He expressed his "abhorrence" for the genocide decreed against the Jewish people during the Second World War. He recalled that in 1979, when he visited Auschwitz, he paused in particular before the memorial stone with its Hebrew inscription and prayed "for so many victims from various nations." The central theme of the papal discourse was, however, concerned with the three most important points from the conciliar Declaration *Nostra aetate:*

1. *The Special Bond that Links the Church with the Jewish People.*

The Jewish religion is in a certain way "intrinsic" to the Christian religion. "We therefore have a relationship with Judaism which we do not have with any other religion. You are our dearly beloved brothers and, in a certain way, it could be said that you are our elder brothers."

2. *The Jews as a People Have No Ancestral or Collective Guilt for What Happened to Christ during His Passion.* "The Lord will judge each one 'according to his own works,' Jews and Christians alike" (cf. Rom. 2:6).

3. *The Jews Are Not "Repudiated or Cursed."* On the contrary, they are "beloved of God, who has called them with an irrevocable calling" (cf. Rom. 11:28–29).

The reaffirmation and proclamation of these convictions should be, as the Pope emphasized, the decisive contribution of his visit to the synagogue. It is to be hoped that the words and gestures will attain the desired effect. Millions of men and women who had never heard of *Nostra aetate* learned from the Pope, whom they saw on the television screen, the deepest convictions of the Council on which rest the present relations of Catholics with the Jewish people. They also heard that each of these two religions, Judaism and Christianity, has the right "to be recognized and respected in its own identity." They learned that the Jewish–Christian dialogue must be deepened "in loyalty and friendship, in our respect for one another's intimate convictions." They heard that during the dark years of racial persecution, there were not only failings on the part of Christians, but positive actions as well. In Rome, for example, the doors of religious houses, churches, and buildings of the Holy See had been opened in order to afford safety and refuge to many Jews. Those who witnessed this historic encounter between the Pope and the Rabbi were invited by both to cooperate on a worldwide level "in favor of the human person . . . of his dignity, his freedom, his rights. . . ." Above all, the viewers were able to see that the head of the Catholic Church, without any triumphalism or any intention of drawing Jews away from their own religion, but with simplicity and a readiness to listen, appeared as a brother among brothers. They experienced a "rediscovered brotherhood" that was also expressed in a final embrace of the Pope and the Rabbi, a gesture that was immediately copied by Jews and Christians, with joy and gratitude frequently mingled with tears. All this reflected the spirit that the Pope had invoked when he said with the Psalmist: "See how good and beautiful it is when brothers live in harmony . . ." (Ps. 133).

The effect this historical event will have on the relations between the Church and the Jewish people, as well as on the relations of the Church with other religions, cannot yet today be fully evaluated in all its significance.

Jewish Points of View

The questions and concerns of the Jewish people and their contributions to the development of Jewish–Christian relations can only be treated here in a brief and summary fashion. The preceding exposition has already shown that individual Jews and Jewish organizations have contributed to the genesis of the conciliar Declaration and postconciliar documents, and that their concerns have, to a great extent, been taken up.

If two brothers have not conversed with each other for an all too long time, but have fought, insulted, and injured each other, and have lived entirely apart, it is not surprising that the elder brother is not immediately overjoyed by the friendly overtures of the younger, especially if he is chiefly to blame for their falling out. Rather, one has to imagine that the elder brother asks himself with some suspicion if the other is sincere in his intent, or if he is not, rather, moved by some less noble motives. The comparison limps, of course. The younger brother, who wishes to converse with the older cannot, for example, be immediately compared with the Christian. And there is no question of a single Christian and a single Jewish brother. There are many kinds of Christians, and some of these, despite the Council and national bishops' conferences, have paid no attention whatever to an invitation to talk with their Jewish brothers and sisters. Others have shown the greatest reserve in speaking with them, and still others are little interested in any kind of reconciliation, in changing themelves, in recognizing the other as their brother, in taking him seriously, much less in learning from him. But neither is the Jewish brother a single person. There are many kinds of Jews (and there is no teaching authority in Judaism that can be compared with that of the national bishops' conferences, much less with that of a Pope or of an ecumenical council). There are some Jews who, as soon as they perceive in the younger brother a sign of change, go forth to meet him with trust and kindness.[66] Others are hesitant to encounter him. And, before they are willing to speak about the mysteries of their own calling and their own way, they would rather speak about points of conflict and the guilt of the past. Others are still reluctant, since they are suspicious of the sudden change of their brother or, because of the past, find it very difficult to recognize the other as their brother.

Mutual but also divergent interests and concerns have brought Jews and Christians together in common dialogue.[67] The Jews' preoccupation with the safety of their people has been met with the desire of Christians to end the horrors of anti-Semitism and to radically change a basically negative attitude toward the Jews that has endured for nearly two thousand years. The fact, however, that Christians, reflecting their own mystery, encounter Judaism as a fundamental and positive value, has no such counterpart for the Jews. But for them, Christianity is deeply written into their painful history. Up until the present, Jewish-Christian dialogue has been mainly concentrated on the issue that are perhaps of greater interest to Jews than to Christians. In these areas, significant progress has already been made, particularly concerning questions of anti-Semitism, the state of Israel, the evaluation of the Pharisees, the so-called anti-Judaism in the New Testament, and the recognition of the spiritual creativity in Judaism after the time of Christ. Among the problems still to be treated are mentioned, on the Jewish side, the question of the role of the Christian theology in anti-Semitism, the role of the Church in some dark phases of history (for example, the Crusades, Inquisition, expulsion of Jews, Holocaust), support for the state of Israel and its recognition by the Holy See.

Now that some of the original goals of the dialogue have been reached, and a renewed vision of Judaism poses "questions to many aspects of Catholic theology, from Christianity to ecclesiology, from the liturgy to the sacraments, from eschatology to the relation with the world and the witness we are called to offer in it and to it,"[68] today Christian interest is moving more toward theological dialogue. But at the present time, such an interest is shared by only a few Jews. Among the reasons for this is a still prevalent suspicion that the ultimate, though concealed, motive for Jewish–Christian dialogue is still Christian proselytism. There is also the not uncommon fear that theological dia-

logue favors a still further assimilation of the non-Jewish environment, and that the number of mixed marriages between Jews and
Christians could continue to increase. On a more theological
level, there are three main reasons that militate against a Jewish
participation in theological discussions:

1. Theology has a subordinate place in Judaism. Some Jews are
even of the opinion that theology is a non-Jewish affair. Although there are some theologians in Judaism, and there have
been attempts since the Middle Ages to develop a systematic
theology, and even though some Jews of liberal tendency regard
theology as desirable, it is, on the whole, considered to be of very
little advantage. Less religious Jews consider such attempts to be
regressive. Orthodox Jews as a rule judge this to be an obstacle
and threat to faith.[69] On the other hand, what appeals to Jews—
and to Christians!—is an imagistic-narrative "theology," such as
arose from the biblical heritage in the pharisaic–rabbinic epoch,
and as it is found also in Jesus.

2. Theology is extensively concerned with concepts (for example, sin, penance, grace) that are stamped with Christian notions
and are therefore "necessarily sectarian."[70]

3. Many Jews are hesitant or reluctant to share the mystery of
their own religious experience with outsiders. "This is fully understandable and should be not only respected but also admired."[71]
What is proper to the Jewish religious experience is identified in
the rabbinical texts with the oral Torah (oral tradition), which
God has destined for the Jews alone.

> Rabbi Judah Ben Shalom said: Moses wanted the Mishnah
> (oral Torah) to be written as well. But the Holy One, blessed
> be He, foresaw that the nations of the world would translate
> the Torah, read it in Greek, and say: "We too are Israel!" So
> the Holy One, blessed be He, said to him: "If I were to write
> for them (the Jews) the whole of my Torah, they (the Jews)
> would be accounted as strangers" (Hos. 8:12), because the
> Mishnah is the secret of the Holy One, blessed be He, and the
> Holy One, blessed be he, reveals His secret only to the righ-
> teous, as it is said: "The secret of the Lord is for those who fear
> him" (Ps. 24:14).[72]

Beneath such texts lies the conviction that God's relation to
Israel is of a special profundity and uniqueness, and that it can-

not be readily extended to other peoples or religions. God reveals himself to each people in His own way. Christians must, therefore, leave it up to the Jews to offer whatever they want to share of their experiences. Christians have no rights in this regard.

However, despite all such reservations, we cannot avoid theological dialogue. This is already proven by the fact that many subjects taken up in Jewish–Christian dialogue have important theological aspects. Here and there, Jewish and Christian theologians have in fact already taken the first cautious steps. Also of great significance is the fact that chairs for Jewish–Christian studies have been erected in Jewish universities and that the New Testament and early Christian literature are being taught in some Rabbinical seminaries.

It is hardly for Christians to judge the stimulus and enrichment that Jews can obtain from their encounter and dialogue with Christians. In any case, the widespread conviction that Jews have nothing to learn from Christianity is changing.[73] Some early judgments that were formed largely as the result of Christian anti-Judaism and anti-Semitism are disappearing with quite extraordinary rapidity. A reexamination of Jewish understanding of Jesus and of Christianity has been taken up in some circles. Here and there, a revision of Jewish textbooks has also begun. Particular significance has been attributed to the collaboration among Jews and Christians in the promotion of peace and social justice.

Reflections and Prospects

1. Since the new relations between the Church and the Jewish people have existed for only a relatively brief period of time, we must still start with the fact that our knowledge of each other is as a rule extremely limited or even nonexistent. One encounters limitations even with regard to "experts" who are engaged in Jewish–Christian dialogues. Those who take part are frequently appointed by certain organizations and are chosen at times for basically "diplomatic" reasons, yet they are expected to be able to handle all kinds of different problems. But it is obviously impossible for anyone to be truly competent in all the questions that pertain to his own spiritual and religious world[74] much less in those of his partners in dialogue.[75] The consequences of this is that experts in

Jewish–Christian relations are not always sufficiently esteemed in individual, specialized groups. Jewish–Christian relations are, however, such an important matter that the very best Jewish and Christian historians, exegetes, patrologists, theologians, and legal experts should be involved.

2. Before such specialized groups engage in dialogue, it is recommended that the "solutions" to important questions on Jewish–Christian relations should be slowly and cautiously proposed. It is better to see problems and leave them alone than to answer them poorly. Pope John Paul II has consequently noted that, in this area, "work of poor quality and lacking in precision would be extremely detrimental."[76]

3. The limits of dialogue, especially of theological dialogue, should also be noted here. One cannot arrive at what is proper to religious truth simply through a process of reasoning. What is meant by Torah to a Jew, or by Jesus to a Christian, is hardly to be grasped through rational debate or understanding of concepts.[77] The ultimate approach is only to be found in a religious experience, which is at the core of every religion. With its emphasis on "a common meeting before God in prayer and in silent meditation," the "Guidelines" have provided the right direction. Although modest beginnings have already been made,[78] it is precisely here that the greatest difficulties are encountered; they are at least partially due to the unfortunate history of Jewish–Christian relations in the past.[79]

4. In the larger context into which Jewish–Christian relations have been placed by the Council, it could prove to be easier to pass over the differences and to discover what is common. In the experience of transcendence, there is neither Jew nor Christian (cf. Gal. 3:28). Both "lose" and both gain. The scarcely begun dialogue with non-Judaeo-Christian religions can be both a challenge and an enrichment if Christians and Jews are willing to engage in it seriously. In eastern meditation halls, one can already today encounter Buddhists or Hindus together with Jews and Christians.

5. The motives for a Christian interest in Judaism and in the Jewish people are still frequently all too self-centered. Christians are often only in search of a better understanding of the New Testament, the roots of Christianity, the Christian liturgy, or the resolution of Christian problems. When will Christians consider the Jews as important in themselves?

6. This raises the serious question of whether or not we, as Christians, have hitherto sufficiently observed the basic rules of dialogue, that is, of listening. From the very fact that, according to Romans 11:17–18, "the wild olive" should not exalt itself over the old branches, it is the Jews who should begin the dialogue. Only when we have listened to what they have to tell us, and only when we have gazed at the witness that Jewish martyrs have given over the centuries down to the horrors of Auschwitz, can we speak to them about ourselves in humility and perplexity, and also of how God has revealed himself to us Christians in their brother Jesus.

7. Today, there is hardly any Church document on the Jews that does not condemn anti-Semitism. But words are not enough, as was already suggested in the first draft of the *Decretum de Iudaeis* of June 1962. "A condemnation of anti-Semitism is today, after Auschwitz, no longer sufficient. What is needed is true solidarity with the Jews."[80]

8. Jewish–Christian collaboration in the search for peace and social justice on a worldwide level should be of the greatest importance.[81] If Jews, on the basis of the painful experiences of their own people, stand up before the Christians and the world to see to it that others do not experience a similar misfortune, then a loud, united voice will be raised in favor of those without rights, the oppressed, the homeless, the starving, and the victim of torture. According to Matthew 7:21 and 25:31–46, it is precisely by works such as these, and not by the articles of faith or even their belonging to their own religious community, that Christians will be judged, since these deeds are ultimately decisive.

Translated from the German by M. Joseph Costelloe, S.J.

Notes

1. The most important pre- and postconciliar documents are to be found primarily in the following collections: H. Croner (ed.), *Stepping Stones to Further Jewish-Christian Relations: An Unabridged Collection of Christian Documents* (London/New York, 1977), which contains *Nostra aetate* 4, pp. 1–2, and the "Guidelines," pp. 11–16; *More Stepping Stones to Jewish-Christian Relations. An Unabridged Collection of Christian Documents 1975–1983* (New York, 1985), which contains the "Notes," pp. 220–232; M.-T. Hoch and B. Dupuy (eds.), *Les Eglises devant le Judaïsme: Documents officiels 1948–1978* (Paris, 1980); K. Richter

(ed.), *Die katholische Kirche und das Judentum. Dokumente von 1945– 1982* (Freiburg/Basel/Vienna, 1982); G. Cereti and L. Sestieri (eds.), *Le Chiese cristiane e l'ebraismo, 1947–1982* (Casale Monferrato, 1983). In Rome, the documents can be found at the SIDIC Center (Service International de Documentation Judéo-Chrétienne), which edits a periodical in French and in English under the same name. We wish here to express our gratitude to the personnel of the Center for their kind assistance in helping find these documents. Occasionally, existing English translations have been slightly altered in light of the original texts.

2. See J.M. Oesterreicher, "Declaration on the Relationship of the Church to Non-Christian Religions. Introduction and Commentary," in H. Vorgrimler (ed.), *Commentary on the Documents of Vatican II*, vol. III, (New York/London, 1968), 8–17.

3. *Ibid.*, 17–136.

4. *Ibid.*, 129.

5. *Ibid.*, 40.

6. Augustin Cardinal Bea, *The Church and the Jewish People: A Commentary on the Second Vatican Council's Declaration on the Relation of the Church to Non-Christian Religions* (London, 1966), 12.

7. So according to the statement of the Lutheran World Federation of Løgumkloster (*Stepping Stones*, 86).

8. On the Seventy-Fifth German Katholikentag, which was held in Berlin in 1952, under the question: "Where is your brother?" the parable was continued as follows:

The elder son gave no reply to the father's urgent invitation to the banquet for his brother who had been lost and returned. Instead, he went away and walled up the door between the rooms that had been given him by his father and the rest of the farm. He put a fence around his part of the fields and henceforth stayed away from the rest of the land. Both brothers married and dwelt beside one another, but their mutual alienation became ever more hostile and hateful. Since the family of the once-lost brother increased much more than that of the elder, the latter, out of timidity, withdrew yet more. The family of the younger brother gradually forgot their relationship to the others and in the end had nothing but contempt for them whom they deemed to be completely at odds with their common ancestor.—It thus happened that one day the youngest son of the once-lost brother, in a fit of blind rage, beat to death one of his little cousins, of whom (plural!) he had heard so much evil, just as Cain had done to Abel.

The old father, when he heard of this, rose up, went to the door of the house and cried out with a loud voice: "*Where is your brother?*"—A shudder ran through the family of the once-lost brother. There was a change of heart, and through love they began to seek the love of their estranged brothers. And at the end of days the whole family was reconciled and joined together in the perfect banquet which has no end in all eternity. Amen.

This text is quoted by K. Thieme in his essay "Augustinus und der 'ältere Bruder.' Zur patristischen Auslegung von Lk. 15:25–32" in *Universitas, Festschrift für Bischof Dr. A. Stohr*, vol. I (Mainz, 1960), 84–85 = *Freiburger Rundbrief*, 13 (1960/61), 26.

9. In his frequently cited article, "Study Outline on the Mission and Witness of the Church," (*More Stepping Stones*, 37–55), T. Federici has spoken of an "unwarranted proselytism." The same has been said with greater clarity and authority in various ecclesiastical documents: in dialogues, "proselytizing is to be carefully avoided" (U.S. National Conference of Catholic Bishops, *Stepping Stones*, 18); "any intention or design for proselytism must be rejected as contrary to human dignity and Christian conviction" (Pastoral Council of the Catholic Church in the Netherlands, *Stepping Stones*, 51); any "disloyal attempt to detach the other from his community and draw him to one's own . . . must be excluded not only out of respect which must apply to dialogue with any person, but for a particular reason, . . . that the Jews as people have been the object of an 'eternal Covenant' " (French Bishops' Committee for Relations with Jews, *Stepping Stones*, 64); "it is fundamentally prohibited to Jews and to Christians to seek to move the other to become disloyal to the call of God which he has received" (Central Committee of Roman Catholics in Germany, *More Stepping Stones*, 116).— Concerning the question of mission to Jews within Protestantism, see the Ecumenical Considerations on Jewish–Christian Dialogue of the World Council of Churches in *More Stepping Stones*, 174.

10. K. Rahner and H. Vorgrimler (eds.), *Kleines Konzilskompendium* (Freiburg/Basel/Vienna, 1966), 352.

11. Oesterreicher, "Declaration on the Relationship of the Church to Non-Christian Religions," 77.

12. Cereti and Sestieri (eds.), *Le Chiese cristiane e l'ebraismo*, 54.

13. *L'Osservatore Romano* (English edition), 9 September 1985, 3.

14. "In Germany we have particular cause to ask forgiveness of God and of our Jewish brethren" (German Bishops' Conference of 28 April 1980, *More Stepping Stones*, 142). Cardinal J. Glemp has noted that in the process of reconciliation among Christians, words alone are not enough: "When, through the service of the Church God grants us pardon, the Church herself decides the conditions. She therefore speaks to us of an examination of conscience, of repentance, of a resolution of amendment, of the confession of sins, and, for serious sins, she requires an indication of their number and circumstances. God wishes to know what he forgives. A man also has the right to know what he forgives. According to the same criteria, he also has the right to know the full extent of the evil endured and committed. Only this

way, which is hard and difficult, can lead us to an honest way of acting" (sermon preached in Rome on 7 December, 1985, on the occasion of the twentieth anniversary of the exchange of letters of reconciliation between the Polish and German bishops).

15. Oesterreicher, "Declaration," 130.

16. In documents on a diocesan level can be found guidelines for mixed marriages between Catholics and Jews (*More Stepping Stones*, 70–108).—Some of the numerous ecclesiastical documents on national or regional levels give the impression that their authors have hardly engaged in dialogue with Jews. Occasionally, an ideal picture, with little concern for reality, is given of what the Jews should be according to Christians. Also, at times, the concept of the "Chosen People" is too exaggerated.

17. This thought is often expressed in documents of Christian churches. "To despise members of the Jewish people as Jews . . . means to betray Jesus himself" (Kirchentag of the Evangelical Church in Germany, in Cereti and Sestieri (eds.), 22). Anti-Semitism "represents a demonic form of rebellion against the God of Abraham, Isaac and Jacob; and a rejection of Jesus the Jew, directed against his people. 'Christian' anti-Semitism is spiritual suicide" (Lutheran World Federation, *Stepping Stones*, 86).

18. Of course, here the reference is above all to ecclesiastical authorities.

19. According to the important document published by the Faith and Order Commission of the World Council of Churches on the Church and the Jewish People (Bristol, 1967), Christian witness should be manifest "not so much in explicit words but rather by service" (*Stepping Stones*, 81).—"How could they (the Christians of Europe) preach 'Christ crucified' to the pitiful heap of surviving relatives of six million martyred Jews?! How could they bring the 'gospel of love' in the name of him who once said, 'by their fruits shall ye know them'?!" (J.J. Petuchowski, "The Christian-Jewish Dialogue," in J.J. Petuchowski, *Heirs of the Pharisees* [New York/London, 1970], 154; the article first appeared in *Lutheran World*, 10 [1963], 373–84).

20. The meaning of this clause is not entirely clear.

21. In a discussion with Cardinal Bea in Rome in 1966, Karl Barth observed: "But let us not forget, there is only one important ecumenical question: our relation to Israel" (*SIDIC* 1, No. 3 [1968], 17). The same idea has been expressed by the Faith and Order Commission of the World Council of Churches (*Stepping Stones*, 82–83).

22. *Stepping Stones*, 50 and 63–64.

23. The text of the working paper has been published by the Institute of Jewish Affairs in conjunction with the World Jewish Congress (*Christian Attitudes on Jews and Judaism. A Periodical Survey*, 10 [1970], 8).

24. Monsignor J. Mejía, former Secretary of the Commission for Religious Relations with the Jews, at the press release on the day of the document's publication ("Viva coscienza del patrimonio comune a tutti i livelli," *L'Osservatore Romano* [Italian edition], 24–25 June 1985, 7). An English text was also distributed at the press release. It is not in complete agreement with the printed translation of the Italian text in *SIDIC* 19, No. 2 (1986), 5–7.

25. Press release of the Jewish Council in Israel on Interreligious Consultations, 24 June 1985; see *Christian Life in Israel*, 17 (Fall 1985), 4.

26. G. Wigoder, "Retreat by the Vatican," *The Jerusalem Post*, 25 June 1985 [international ed., 6 July 1985, 13].

27. W. Kasper (ed.), *Absolutheit des Christentums*, Quaestiones Disputatae 79 (Freiburg/Basel/Vienna, 1977), 7.

28. Cereti and Sestieri (eds.), 340; *SIDIC* 15, No. 2 (1982), 28.

29. *L'Osservatore Romano* (English edition), 29 April 1985, 3 = Insegnamenti di Giovanni Paulo II, vol. VIII, 1 (1985), 1080 (in English). Also, in some ecclesiastical documents at a national level, a new theological language can be found that often takes up biblical affirmations. The "everlasting covenant," which God has made with the Jewish people (Gen. 17:7; see Rom. 11:29) is recalled; "for Christendom the Covenant was renewed in Jesus Christ" (French Bishops' Committee for Relations with Jews, *Stepping Stones*, 61); "in Christ the Church shares in Israel's election without superseding it" (the "Israel Study Group" of American Christian scholars, in Cereti and Sestieri (eds.), 188; *SIDIC* 6, No. 3 [1973], 33); Jews and Christians are in "companionship" traveling to "the same goal which is the reign of God" (study group "Jews and Christians" of the Central Committee of Roman Catholics in Germany, *More Stepping Stones*, 115).

30. The Catholic historian and cultural critic F. Heer has written about typology and not without exaggeration: "This, the greatest robbery in the history of the world from the Jewish viewpoint (and a true Christian, who takes himself seriously, must take account of it), reduces the Old Testament to the service of the Christian Church. What was created in the course of more than a thousand years by Jewish prophets . . . now becomes the booty of the 'New Israel,' the Church, as the inalienable inheritance of the Church" (*Gottes erste Liebe* [Munich, 1967], 54).

31. The late Jewish scholar S. Sandmel had expressed this idea in a pointed manner: "Possessing the Old Testament in common, the two traditions understand it in quite divergent ways, almost as if it were not the same book" (*Two Living Traditions: Essays on Religion and the Bible* [Detroit, 1972], 117). The typological explanation of Scripture has, as will be mentioned, also contributed to the fact that the Old Testament, such a central basis for both Jews and Christians, became one of the factors in the bitter separation between the two groups at the time of the early Christians.—Today one wants to arrive at least on a scientific level, at a common understanding of the Old Testament. The scientific exegesis of Scripture has a limited, and with respect to a literature such as that of the Bible, a too limited goal: this is to discover what the particular author really meant. The result can, therefore, be neither "Jewish" nor "Christian," and the question was asked as to whether a scientific commentary on the Bible written by a Jew can be regarded at all as "Jewish" (J.J. Petuchowski, *Wie unsere Meister die Schrift erklären* [Freiburg/Basel/Vienna, 1982], 28).

32. Number 142 of the directives edited by the Diocesan Ecumenical Commission (*Verso l'unità dei cristiani. Sussidio per una pastorale ecumenica nella diocesi di Roma* [Rome, 1983], 38 = *More Stepping Stones*, 148).

33. *Mishnah*, Avot 5, 22.

34. The designation of the Jews as "the people of God of the Old Testament" is therefore only partially correct.

35. The *Kommentar zum Neuen Testament aus Talmud und Midrasch* by H.L. Strack and P. Billerbeck shows how essential the Jewish background is for the interpretation of the New Testament. When it is critically used, it is still one of the most important resources for understanding the New Testament. Jewish authors who write about Jesus frequently give considerable weight to the explanation of the Jewish milieu of the time. According to Cardinal Daniélou, the books written on Jesus in our time by Jews are those that contribute most to making Jesus known (*Encounter Today*, 7 [1972], 108).

36. This statement must, of course, be prudently understood. The historical Jesus was a Jew. The risen Christ whom Paul encountered and whom the mystics have been experiencing until today cannot be contained in categories of this type (cf. Col. 3:10–11).

37. According to *The Jewish Encyclopedia*, 9, 665, the seven now famous classes of Pharisees are the following: "1. 'the shoulder Pharisee,' who wears, as it were, his good actions ostentatiously upon his shoulder; 2. 'the wait-a-little Pharisee,' who ever says 'Wait a little, until I have performed the good act awaiting me'; 3. 'the bruised Pharisee,' who in order to avoid looking at a woman runs against the wall so as to bruise himself and bleed; 4. 'the pestle Pharisee,' who walks with head down like the pestle in the mortar; 5. 'the ever-reckoning Pharisee,' who says, 'Let me know what good I may do to counteract my neglect'; 6. 'the God-fearing Pharisee,' after the manner of Job; 7. 'the God-loving Pharisee,' after the manner of Abraham."

38. See, however, the working paper "Christians and Jews" of the Evangelical Church in Germany (*Stepping Stones*, 137–142). Also,

L.H. Schiffman, *Who was a Jew? Rabbinic and Halachic Perspectives on the Jewish-Christian Schism* (New Jersey, 1985).

39. *Mishnah,* Avot 3,11; Avot de-Rabbi Nathan 26.

40. On the "benediction" concerning heretics, see P. Schäfer, *Studien zur Geschichte und Theologie des rabbinischen Judentums* (Leiden, Netherlands, 1978), 46–52.

41. That the exclusion (of the Judaeo-Christians) was not the only and absolutely necessary way of dealing with the situation seems to be expressed in a Talmud version cited by Abraham b. Azriel (thirteenth century). In his *Arugat ha-Bosem,* we read in reference to Ps. 118:3: "It is thus written in *Berakhot:* 'A man always pushes his companion away with the left hand, and he draws him near with the right. Not in the manner of Saul who pushed away the Edomite Doeg with both his hands, and not in the manner of Rabbi Akiva, who pushed away Jeshu (Jesus) with both his hands' " (E.E. Urbach (ed.), *Arugat ha-Bosem,* III [Jerusalem, 1962], 310–11).

42. J. Mejía, *L'Osservatore Romano* (Italian edition), 24–25 June 1985, 7.

43. *Stepping Stones,* 63.

44. *L'Osservatore Romano* (English edition), 30 April 1984, 6; *Insegnamenti di Giovanni Paolo II,* vol. VII, 1 (1984), 1072 (in Latin).

45. Oesterreicher, "Declaration," 131.

46. Since then, the Anti-Defamation League has left the IJCIC.

47. Press release of 24 June 1985.

48. See *Christian Life in Israel,* 17 (Fall, 1985), 4.

49. "Rome and Jerusalem: The Religious Meaning," *The Jerusalem Post,* 2 September 1985, 8.

50. "Chi sono gli Ebrei oggi?" *Civiltà Cattolica,* 136, 1 (March 1985), 521–533; "Problemi e prospettive del dialogo tra cristiani ed ebrei," *Civiltà Cattolica,* 136, 2 (April, 1985), 3–18. The second article has not found agreement on every point.

51. Pages 4–10 of the second article.

52. See the Statement by the French Bishops' Committee for Relations with Jews: *Stepping Stones,* 61.

53. In this vein, the well-known theologian A. Schlatter was of the opinion that "Judaism has never had a more powerful opponent than him (Jesus)" (*Wird der Jude über uns siegen?* [Velbert, 1935], 6).

54. See *Civiltà Cattolica,* 136, 2, 5–6.

55. Bea, *The Church and the Jewish People,* 16.

56. On the following, see H. Schreckenberg, *Die christlichen Adversus-Judaeos-Texte und ihr literarisches und historisches Umfeld* (1.–11. Jh.) (Frankfurt/Bern, 1982), esp. 15–40 (introduction) and 563–573 (concluding remarks).

57. PG 48, 852 (Schreckenberg, 325). This way of thinking, which in discussions of themes such as this (for example, the "New Covenant" in Jer. 31:31–34) is still to be encountered today among Christians and Jews, can finally be overcome only on the level of deep religious (mystical) experience.

58. *La Documentation Catholique*, 39 (1938), 1460, cited in A. Bea, *The Church and the Jewish People*, 13, note.

59. *PG*, 48, 915 (Schreckenberg, 326).

60. When the Jewish poet and writer E. Fleg was asked to write a history of the sufferings of the Jews, he replied: "If I were to do a work of this kind, it would rather be a history of friendship for Jews that I would write, for if we had not had at all times friends more powerful and more numerous than our enemies, we would no longer exist. All through our history, we have been continually helped and saved, and this, too, is one of its essential aspects" (*La Conscience Juive* [Paris, 1963], 9).— Pope Paul VI also recalled the positive, but still scarcely investigated, aspects of Jewish–Christian relations in the course of history, as, for example, in the fruitful spiritual exchange during the Middle Ages (*Osservatore Romano* [English edition], 23 January 1975, 3; *Insegnamenti di Paolo VI*, vol. XIII [1975], 29–30 [in French]).

61. The pastoral letter of the German bishops of 23 August 1945 states the following: "Many Germans, also from amongst us, . . . have remained indifferent . . . at the time of the crimes; many through their attitude supported the crimes, many themselves have become criminals. Serious responsibility falls upon those who because of their position were able to know what was happening among us and who, through their influence, could have prevented such crimes and did not do so, indeed have rendered possible these crimes and in this way showed themselves to be in solidarity with the criminals" (Richter (ed.), *Die katholische Kirche und das Judentum*, 63). In 1980, the Synod of the Evangelical Church in the Rhineland declared: "Stricken, we confess the coresponsibility and guilt of German Christendom for the Holocaust" (*More Stepping Stones*, 208). The declaration of the Swiss Bishops' Conference of 12 July 1979 speaks of the "coresponsibility of Christians" for the "millions of tortures and deaths of Jews in the near and remote past," and "that in the time of National Socialism, weak faith, cowardice, weakness and guilt were evident, not infrequently, also in Switzerland" (C. Thoma, *Die theologischen Beziehungen zwischen Christentum und Judentum* [Darmstadt, 1982], 23).

62. *Osservatore Romano* (English edition), 9 December 1980, 6 = *SIDIC* 15, No. 2 (1982), 26; *Insegnamenti di Giovanni Paolo II*, vol. III, 2 (1980), 1274 (in German).

63. Cardinal Bea, Conciliar address of 19 November 1963 in A. Bea, *The Church and the Jewish People*, 157.

64. H.-J. Gamm, *Judentumskunde*, Fourth Edition (Frankfurt, 1962), 140.

65. *Christian Jewish Relations*, 19, No. 2 (1986), 50. The speeches of the Pope, Rabbi Toaff, and the President of the Jewish Community of Rome were first published in English translation in *L'Osservatore Romano* (English edition), 21 April 1986, 6–8, and then in *Christian Jewish Relations* 19, No. 2 (1986), 49–56.

66. S. Sandmel has embodied this attitude in an exemplary way. As a reply to the Conciliar declaration, he composed the following: "A Proposed Declaration: 'The Synagogue and the Christian People' ":

The Synagogue views the Christian people as among its offspring. It acknowledges that Christian people have laudably spread the message of the Synagogue among people and in areas of the world beyond where the Synagogue had penetrated. The Christian people have adapted that message to their own character and their own ways of thinking and speaking, and they have both preserved much which is familiar to the Synagogue and also created much which is not. Man, in his weakness, has been incapable of maintaining unbroken unity. Neither the Synagogue nor the Church has been free from division, and a by-product of such division has been irreligious hatred, bitter recrimination, and persecution, both within and without. Since hatred, recrimination, and persecution are irreligious, the Synagogue laments all such manifestations within its past, and respecting the present and the future repudiates them as inauthentic manifestations of the spirit of Judaism. The Synagogue holds that its message must spread not by power or by might, but only by the Spirit of God and in the love of mankind.

The Synagogue is aware that Christian assemblies, lamenting and disavowing the Christian persecution of the Jews, have spoken in recent times in the same vein. The Synagogue welcomes these pioneer utterances.

All men are wont to remember grievances out of which attitudes of vindictiveness arise; therefore the Synagogue reminds its loyal sons of the biblical injunction (Leviticus 19:18): "Thou shalt not take vengeance nor bear any grudge against the children of thy people but thou shalt love thy neighbor as thyself." The Synagogue cannot, and does not, hold innocent Christians of our day responsible for the persecutions of the past, nor all Christians responsible, in the present or the future, for the misdeeds which may come from some.

The Synagogue continues to look forward to that day when all men, of all countries, colors, and beliefs, will become spiritually united. Since all universals are attained only through particulars, the

Synagogue is committed to the perpetuation of itself against all forms of dissolution. It understands "the election of Israel" as imposing on it a heavier obligation to God, not as an unseemly preferment. It welcomes into its midst all those who voluntarily wish to enter. It does not seek to dissolve the institutions of its offspring (= of the Christians), nor does it cherish, as a proximate or remote goal, the abandonment by Christians of their Christian loyalties. Rather, it desire that its offspring attain and maintain the spiritual heights which they often nobly expressed.

The Synagogue envisages the unity of mankind in a lofty spiritual bond, enabling men both to preserve the institutions which they hold sacred and to transcend them (*We Jews and You Christians* [Philadelphia/New York, 1967], 144–146).

67. The comment of H. Siegman, "What impels Christians to dialogue is theology, but what impels Jews is history," which has been widely quoted since the publication of his important article ("A Decade of Catholic–Jewish Relations—A Reassessment," *JES*, 15 [1978], 243–60) does not do full justice to the facts.

68. Cardinal J. Willebrands, President of the Commission for Religious Relations with the Jews, in a conference given in Rome on 17 April 1985, on the occasion of a colloquium on the twentieth anniversary of *Nostra aetate* (*Face to Face*, 12 [Fall, 1985], 12).

69. See L. Jacobs, "Theology," *EncJud*, 15: 1103.

70. See S. Sandmel, " 'Biblical Theology'—A Dissent," *Central Conference of American Rabbis Journal* (January, 1959), 15–20; "Reflections on the Problems of Theology for Jews," *JBR*, 33 (1965), 101–12 (= Two Living Traditions, 53–69).

71. Cardinal Willebrands, on 17 April 1985 (*Face to Face*, 12 [1985], 12).

72. *Tanhuma* B., Wa-yera 6.

73. Already in 1963, the Jewish scholar J.J. Petuchowski wrote:

Has not the time come for us to exchange views . . . , and to do so with a willingness to learn and to understand, rather than to score points in a debate? Is it not just possible that perchance one's own inherited concepts would profit by some widening of horizons? Need the Jew remain in ignorance of the Christian saint's *unio mystica* with his God, or the Christian oblivious of the *amor Dei intellectualis* of the devoted Talmud student? Such are the lines along which we can visualize the "dialogue" ("The Christian–Jewish Dialogue," in *Heirs of the Pharisees*, 153).

74. The well-known Jewish scholar D. Flusser has written: "This situation must be realized by Christian partners in the Christian–Jewish dialogue: among many Jewish participants in these talks, knowledge of Judaism is quite poor" ("Reflections of a Jew on a Christian Theology of

Judaism" in C. Thoma, *A Christian Theology of Judaism* [New York, 1980], 8). Must one say the same about their Christian partners to the Jews engaged in dialogue?

75. For example, some treatises on the Jews written by Christians in recent times reveal very little knowledge about postbiblical Judaism and its sources.—A Jewish scholar who had taken part over many years in Jewish–Christian dialogues was still of the opinion that every Catholic must say the Rosary daily and must confess his or her sins every time before receiving Communion (at every Mass!).

76. "Notes," I, 6.

77. This applies also to the concept of the Messiah, which is ever taken up in Jewish–Christian dialogues. This title often creates more confusion that clarity. Jesus himself seems to have avoided the designation of Messiah since, because of its different connotations (not least that of a "political" character), it could have contributed more to a misunderstanding of him than to deeper understanding.

78. In the United States, the National Council of Churches and the Union of American Hebrew Congregations have drawn up guidelines for joint religious services: "Jews and Christians in Joint Worship: Some Planning Principles and Guidelines," *Ecumenical Bulletin*, 44 (1980), 33–39.

79. In 1976, when an American Rabbi, who for years had taken part in Jewish–Christian dialogue, was to be given an honorary doctorate by a Catholic university, the suggestion made by Christians to say the Our Father was refused.

80. Declaration of the assembly of delegates of Pax Christi on the fortieth anniversary of the "Reichskristallnacht" (K. Richter [ed.], *Die katholische Kirche und das Judentum*, 91).

81. In this sense, John Paul II, in an address to American Jews, has expressed his admiration for the Jewish–Christian collaboration in the drive against hunger in Ethiopia and the Sahel zone (*L'Osservatore Romano* [English edition], 4 March 1985, 5).

CHAPTER 53

The Church Looks at Muslims

Ary A. Roest Crollius, S.J.

Summary

Vatican II opened a new era in dialogue between Muslims and Christians. This dialogue is still in its early stages, but progress has been made in mutual acquaintance and theological reflection. The explicit reference in the conciliar texts to the shared Judeo-Christian heritage indicates a possible orientation for a Christian theology of Islam in the shared search for the eschatological and messianic justice that has a normative effect for living together civically in the modern, pluralistic world.

The statements of Vatican II on Islam had a deep impact on relations between the Church and different groups in the Muslim world. The third chapter of the Declaration on the Relation of the Church to Nonchristian Religions is of special interest. This is not the place to go into the origins of this document, which are closely linked to the formulation of the attitude of the Jews. As regards Muslims, there is also a short passage in the Dogmatic Constitution on the Church that states that Muslims have a special relationship to the plan of salvation (LG 16). The difference between these views and those of the past has been pointed out repeatedly.[1] The setting up of the Secretariat for Non-Christians in 1964, and also the emphasis on "dialogue" in the Encyclical *Ecclesiam suam* of the same year,[2] contributed considerably to the establishment and implementation of this approach within relations themselves.

In the years following the Council, there would be a real avalanche of writings and declarations, on the Christian side,[3] on the value and methods of dialogue in general, and more particularly of that with Muslims. And there would also be an impressive succession of international meetings for dialogue between Muslims and Christians, and of visits between representatives of the different religions and their counterparts.[4] However, while the existence of the Secretariat for Non-Christians and the analogous section of the World Council of Churches meant that it was relatively easy to agree on representatives on the Christian side, the same was not true on the Muslim side. Sometimes the latter has been represented by political or academic bodies, and sometimes by private persons or heads of state.

It is not easy to assess the impact of these meetings on relations between Muslims and Christians. With regard to theoretical and doctrinal expression, for Catholic Christians, the past twenty years can be said to have been a period of discovery of the nature of dialogue, and of apprenticeship in how it actually works, as Paul VI wrote in his Encyclical *Ecclesiam suam*, and as the Council proposed.[5] The most recent documents of the Secretariat for Non-Christians, *The Attitude of the Church Towards the Followers of Other Religions: Reflections and Orientations on Dialogue and Mission*,[6] would appear to indicate that the period of enthusiasm—sometimes a little ingenuous and without clear objectives—for dialogue is drawing to an end. And this could also reassure those who claim the need for proclamation.

On a more practical level, Christians can be seen to have considerably developed their knowledge of the Islamic religion and cultures, especially in countries where there has been more recent Muslim immigration. In such situations, where Christians and Muslims live in the same country without feeling the weight of history,[7] it has been more especially possible to see the blossoming of "dialogue of life" and "dialogue of works."[8] In other parts of the world, it can be seen how attitudes that have grown up and taken root over centuries are not easily altered in a few decades, although even in such situations there are signs of a desire to draw nearer together and work together.

Muslim reaction to dialogue is relatively scarce. It is observed that among Christians, there is coexistence between "aggressive missionaries and humble dialoguers,"[9] and some Muslims say that

"the mission chapter of Christian history, as we have so far
known it, had better be closed,"[10] while others believe that "dialogue is but another form of mission" and see it more as an
opportunity to pursue the Islamic mission, or *da'wa*.[11] It would,
therefore, seem that there is justification for the statement that
"in the encounter with the Church Islam is divided within itself
between a sense of attraction and one of repulsion."[12] The main
reasons behind an attitude of repulsion or rejection are as follows:
the observation that the Church, especially in the West, has not
managed to create a just and ethically responsible society; the
missionary movement, which is seen as seeking to exploit the
position of economic, political and cultural inferiority of the
Islamic peoples; the studies of orientalists (even though such
scholars are not always Christians), which are also often referred
to as being further attempts to weaken Islam; finally, the
doctrinal positions of Christianity in which Muslims say they
cannot recognize the purity of monotheistic faith. On the other
hand, the need to work together for peace and justice continues
to act as a spur to dialogue with Christians.[13]

One of the great obstacles in the way of progress in dialogue is
the lack of knowledge the two parties have of the religion of
those who believe and live differently. It is especially difficult to
distinguish between the different groups and trends that are
found among the followers of another religion. Non-Muslims
tend to see the trends of fundamentalism and restoration as the
only representative aspects of Islam, and this impression is height-
ened by the fact that terrorist elements often make use of motivations and slogans referring to the Islamic religious heritage. On
the one hand, all this makes dialogue more difficult, but, on the
other, more necessary. Prejudices must be overcome in order to
reach an objective understanding of the social and religious circumstances and attitudes of the other party.

New Beginnings for a Theological Reflection

In the field of more or less institutional dialogue between
Muslims and Christians, both groups must still become accustomed to the new situation of religious and cultural pluralism
that is a constantly growing feature of every society and nation,

whereas in the field of theological reflection, we can say that new approaches and prospects are beginning to open up.

The statements of the Second Vatican Council on Islam are primarily to be seen within a pastoral context. The text of the Declaration on the Relation of the Church to Nonchristian Religions, *Nostra aetate*, is clearly exhortative. And the Dogmatic Constitution on the Church, *Lumen gentium*, then indicates a line of theological reflection: "But the plan of salvation also includes those who acknowledge the Creator, in the first place amongst whom are the Muslims: these profess to hold the faith of Abraham, and together with us they adore the one, merciful God, mankind's judge on the last day."[14]

It should be noted that the text speaks specifically of Muslims, and not of Islam. At the same time, however, elements of the faith and religious approach of Muslims are mentioned. These elements are not used here as arguments to prove that the plan of salvation also embraces Muslims, but seem to be seen more as signs of the presence of Muslims—as such, and thus with their religion—within the plan of salvation. Now, the elements mentioned belong to the core of the confession of faith common to the Judeo-Christian tradition, and the evocation of biblical monotheism is reinforced with the reference to Abraham. In this way, the conciliar text offers a precious orientation for further theological reflection. In order to be authentic, such reflection must take into consideration the historical fact of the spread of biblical monotheism in its Judeo-Christian form in a world in which men look for salvation and seek to attain it by different paths. In other words, a theology of non-Christian religions that does not take into account the facts of the religious and cultural history of humanity is bound to remain abstract.

Studies carried out in recent years on the theological and Christian interpretation of Islam enable us to formulate a "working hypothesis" for contacts between Christians and Muslims. The implementation of these contacts in the actual circumstances of life together in this world will show whether or not the hypothesis can be presented as a "thesis." The hypothesis is as follows: Islam lives from a religious experience that can be viewed in phenomenological terms and interpreted in theological terms as the expectation of the salvation proclaimed and brought about in Christ.

The Religious Experience that Gave Rise to Islam

The most important postconciliar work in the attempt to clarify the "theological location" of the Prophet of Islam is undoubtedly Claus Schedl's *Muhammad und Jesus*. [15] The author took the present Islamic scriptural tradition as authentic for Muslim believers themselves, and tried to interpret it within the perspective of the Islamic faith. Although some of the expressions used in the book might profit from further nuancing, the author makes the important observation that the religious experience of the Prophet of Islam was a conversion to the one God who had already revealed himself in the religions of the Book—in other words, in those of the Jews and the Christians. Schedl showed that the stress should be laid more on Christianity. [16] This could justify giving serious reconsideration to the now old observation of Schoeps that Judeo-Christianity, which has disappeared from Christian orthodoxy, has been preserved down to our days in Islam. [17] According to Schedl, too, the Koran demonstrates a good knowledge of Syriac and Semitic christology, and the koranic text should be read against the background of Semitic Christianity of the early centuries. [18]

It can be seen here that any "theology of anonymous Christians"[19] is completely inadequate in the theological consideration of Islam, which, from the very beginning of its preaching, took up a very clear position toward Christ and the Semitic Christian tradition. The intention of the koranic preaching was that of presenting the truth about Christ in the midst of a great variety of sects. This intention must also be recognized by Christians with a view to a doctrinal dialogue for a meeting in truth. At the same time, Christians must rethink their Judeo-Christian past. It is clear that general theological constructions are of little value here. However, there is a vast task awaiting historians of religion.

The Cultural Values of the Modern World

Every religion contributes to the structure of social life by means of values, norms, and rules that are proclaimed by the religion in question. In this perspective, every religion has a formative function with regard to culture, and since religion and culture are never perfectly identical, it becomes possible, by means of various acculturating processes, to form a cultural ecumene that embraces a variety of religions. It can be seen that humanity is today caught up in a process of expansion and deeper extension of a modern cultural ecumene that is influenced in Christian terms. This is especially true of the various types of "humanism" that have developed in western Europe and that have left an indelible stamp on the civic coexistence of nations.[20] In a particular way, it is difficult to think of the progressive assertion of the inalienable dignity of the human person without the influence of Christianity. The abolition of slavery, the assertion of the dignity of women within monogamous marriage, and the freedom of conscience and religion are other values that have attained fuller expression thanks to the light thrown on them by the ideals put forward by the gospel, even though they do as such belong to natural law. A number of the elements in the Universal Declaration on Human Rights itself can be seen in this perspective.

Although alternative "declarations" have been formulated on the Islamic side,[21] the very fact that Muslims feel challenged by the question of human rights shows the existence within Islam of a humanism that has its roots in faith in the one God, who is the creator and judge of humanity. A clear expression of this "converging humanistic and personalistic dynamism" between Christians and Muslims as based on faith in the same God can be found in the discourse of John Paul II at the meeting with young Muslims in Casablanca on 19 August 1985.[22] In this address, the witness of the one God and that of the dignity of the human person are viewed as sources of inspiration to work together in the present world in view of the world to come.

It must therefore be stated that for both Christians and Muslims, the humanistic and personalistic task has its roots in religious faith, and that at the present point in the history of peoples and civilizations, the formulation of these ideals does have a decidedly Christian stamp.

The Hope of Salvation

When considering a specific religion, the Christian theologian must become a phenomenologist and historian of religions, or at least take lessons from specialists in these areas. In R.C. Zaehner, we meet a student of religions who confesses that he has "an allergy to theology in general, and German theology in particular,"[23] while he willingly draws inspiration from authors such as Saint Francis de Sales. Zaehner sees the Second Vatican Council as an event of decisive importance in the religious history of humanity, in which the Catholic Church is called to become increasingly the religion for the whole human race, precisely by opening itself to the specific role that each of the great religions plays in this development. In certain earlier writings, Zaehner based himself on a typology of religions as phenomenologically observed and historically verified, and thus saw a convergence of the "great religious families" of humanity toward the Christian religion.[24] In his last great book, he sees convergence toward the doctrine of the incarnation as taking place, despite the texts of the different sacred books. "What similarity there is proves not that there is an inner unity underlying all the great world religions, but that there is in man a craving for an incarnate God strong enough to force its way into the most unpromising religious systems."[25] Such craving for salvation is not presented as a "theological" deduction, but as an observation made on the basis of an impartial and objective study of the scriptural and doctrinal documents of the various religions.

As far as Islam is concerned, a number of elements require further reflection in order to clarify their theological status. In the first place, it must be noted that for Muslim believers, the hope of salvation opens out to the salvific action of the transcendent and merciful God, from whom salvation is looked for as gift and grace.[26] In the second place, the same revelation of eschatological salvation and of the path leading to it through conformity of life, is seen in koranic preaching as gift and grace.[27] Moreover, the emphasis on the transhistorical character of salvation, and on the need to turn to God in prayer in order to be saved, shows that for the Muslim faith, salvation cannot be attained simply through man's natural powers.[28] Lastly, with regard to the figure of the savior who opens the eschatological era, Islam is closer to what we might call the "Semitic christology" of the Son of Man, the Servant and exalted One of God, than to speculations on the Logos.[29]

"The Ascending Way"[30]

At the beginning of the koranic preaching, the ideal proposed is that of service of one's neighbor, particularly the poor. The "ascending way" is described as follows: "It is the freeing of a bondsman; the feeding, in the day of famine, of an orphaned relation or of a needy man in distress."[31] On the other hand, placing one's trust in riches leads to damnation: "Woe to all back-biting slanderers who amass riches and sedulously hoard them, thinking their treasures will render them immortal! By no means! They shall be flung to the Destroying Flame."[32] There is no doubt for the Koran that love of wealth and any form of self-centeredness go together with a lack of openness to the salvation that comes from God. Love of this world makes a person insensitive to eschatological hope. The radical nature of this preaching, which exhorts its hearers to brotherly charity and humble trust in God, evokes the gospel preaching, which can be seen as a model for it. The Koran lists the following qualities as distinguishing the followers of Christ: compassion and mercy, freedom from pride, uninterrupted attention to prayer, generosity in almsgiving, and hope of the Last Day.[33] Thus, in the form of "ascent" through poverty, meekness, and humility, the image of Jesus has also been handed down and developed in Islam.[34]

It is not surprising that Islam has been unable to recognize the image of Jesus and the ideal of his followers in all the circumstances in which they have encountered the latter in the course of history. What was expected of Christianity was too different from the reality of Christians as they in fact found them. In order to reach an objective theological evaluation of Islam in the history of salvation, it is important that study should be carried out on the Judeo-Christian context of koranic christology, and on its originality in the midst of the heresies found at the time of the first koranic preaching. In the second place, it is important to recognize the positive effects of the coexistence of believers in the one God in today's world. All this will make it easier to clarify the present expectation of salvation within Islam, in a context of supernatural faith that seems to converge toward that fullness of justice foretold in the *Magnificat* and the Sermon on the Mount. Massignon pointed out that these gospel texts retain an apocalyptic value inasmuch as they foretell the triumph of the downtrodden and poor: "Those who lack everything, except their incorporeal thirst for Justice, invincibly cling to the latter with all their hope."[35]

The converging dynamics of this expectation is also recognized by Islam, and this has consequences for an organization of civic coexistence in conformity with the authentic values and ideals of the respective religious traditions. "Then will the righteous servant of God and the meek 'inherit the earth.' "[36]

These expressions seem to indicate how Christians and Muslims can accept the exhortation of the Council to highlight the best of their shared past within a perspective of faith: ". . . for the benefit of all men, let them together preserve and promote peace, liberty, social justice and moral values" (NA 3).

Translated from the Italian by Leslie Wearne.

Notes

1. R. Caspar, "Le Concile et l'Islam," *Etudes*, 324 (1966), 114–126; A. Roest Crollius, "Vaticano II e le religioni non cristiane," *RassTeol*, 8 (1967), 65–74.

2. *AAS*, 56 (1964), 609–659.

3. At the Canterbury meeting (3–9 August 1969), the Mission and Evangelization Commission of the World Council of Churches decided to set up a subcommission for dialogue, and this took shape in the section for dialogue between people of different beliefs and ideologies, which was approved by the Central Committee of the WCC in Addis Ababa in January 1971.

4. A short well-documented history of "organized dialogue" between Christians and Muslims is found in: M. Borrmans, "The Muslim-Christian Dialogue of the Last Ten Years," *Pro Mundi Vita Bulletin*, 74 (September–October 1978), 22–35 (Chapter II, "Recent History of Organized Dialogue"); and Ahmad von Denffer, *Dialogue between Christians and Muslims* (Leicester, 1980), 20–35 (Part 1, "A Survey").

5. Apart from the Declaration *Nostra aetate*, which deals directly with the attitude to non-Christian believers, we must highlight the importance of the Pastoral Constitution *Gaudium et spes*, which also deals with dialogue with followers of other religions (GS 92). Various parts of the text of this Constitution indicate the main themes that have in fact then been discussed in various dialogue meetings.

6. Published in six languages in *Bulletin*, 19 (1984), 117–242.

7. The Council specifically exhorts us to forget the "quarrels and dissensions" of the past (NA 3). Sad to say, such tensions do not belong only to the past.

8. The importance of such dialogue is also pointed out by the Council when it calls on Christians and Muslims "together [to] preserve and promote peace, liberty, social justice and moral values" (NA 3). The document mentioned in note 6 repeats the exhortation in Nos. 29–32.

9. Von Denffer, *Dialogue between Christians and Muslims*, part 1, 7.

10. Isma'il R. al-Faruqi, "Islam and Christianity: Diatribe or Dialogue," *JES*, 5 (1968), 45–77, here 51.

11. Ahmad von Denffer, *Some Reflections on Dialogue between Christians and Muslims* (Leicester, 1980), 14, 18. In the same spirit, Pope John Paul II has been publicly invited to embrace Islam in an open letter from the President of the Center for the Islamic Da'wa in Durban; see T. Farias, S.J., "Muslim Response to the Call for Dialogue," *Salaam*, 6 (1985), 55–58.

12. C.W. Troll, S.J., "Der Dialog zwischen Muslimen und Christen," *SdZ*, 110 (1985), 723–734.

13. T. Michel, S.J., "Muslim Approaches to Dialogue with Christians," *Islam and the Modern Age*, 15 (1984), 37–50. The last pages of this article offer a good bibliography on Muslim approaches.

14. LG 16.

15. Claus Schedl, *Muhammad und Jesus. Die christologisch relevanten Texte des Koran* (Vienna/Freiburg/Basel, 1978).

16. *Ibid.*, 165.

17. H.J. Schoeps, *Theologie und Geschichte des Judenchristentums* (Tubingen, 1949), 342. A fresh look at the enormous amount of material provided by P. Crone and M. Cook, *Hagarism, the Making of the Islamic World* (Cambridge, 1977), could enrich our knowledge of the Judeo-Christian environment in which Islam was born.

18. Schoeps, *Theologie und Geschichte des Judenchristentums*, 565–566.

19. K. Rahner, "Die anonymen Christen," *Schriften zur Theologie*, 4 (Freiburg, 1965), 545–554.

20. This fact is also recognized by the Islamic scholar Fazlur Rahman, "Revival and Reform in Islam," in *The Cambridge History of Islam*," 2 (Cambridge, 1970), 632–656, here 656. The author doubts whether the Islamic world has the ability to assume an attitude of critical and constructive discernment toward the various cultural elements of the contemporary world.

21. R. Caspar, "Les déclarations des droits de l'homme en Islam depuis dix ans," *Islamochristiana*, 9 (1983), 59–102.

22. The address was given in French: *Islamochristiana*, 11 (1985), 193–200. The same issue of this journal gives Arabic and English translations.

23. R.C. Zaehner, *Concordant Discord* (Oxford, 1970), 11.

24. R.C. Zaehner, *At Sundry Times* (London, 1958). In the introduction to the French translation of the work, *Inde, Israël, Islam* (Brussels/Paris, 1965), 46–47, J.-A. Cuttat provided a concise formulation of Zaehner's "thesis."

25. Zaehner, *Concordant Discord*, 443.

26. Among many texts in the Koran, Sūra 93 offers a clear descrip-

Ary A. Roest Crollius, S.J.

tion of the experience of God's mercy in the person of the Prophet of Islam, and the experience of grace within the community of believers is referred to in 3:103. In general terms, the expectation of salvation as grace and gift is expressed in the prayer that opens the Koran, Sūra 1.

27. Revelation in general is considered as a sign of God's mercy (44:5–6), more specifically koranic mercy (7:203; 21:107; 29:51), and also the mission of Jesus (19:21).

28. This is demonstrated in our studies "Death as a Theme in Qur'ānic Preaching," *Studia Missionalia*, 31 (1982), 161–165, and "The Prayer of the Qur'ān," *Studia Missionalia*, 24 (1975), 223–252.

29. L. Massignon, "L'Homme Parfait en Islam et son originalité eschatologique," *Eranos Jahrbuch*, 15 (1947), 287–314, stresses the Semitic–Arab character of the idea of the *Insān-al-kāmil* in Islam, unlike the Iranian or Hellenistic conceptions. In this perspective, the closeness between the theories of *ḥaqīqa muḥammadīya* and the Christian Logos, as pointed out by Zaehner, *Concordant Discord*, 440–441, deserves fresh consideration.

30. The Arabic word *al-'aqaba* used in Sūra 90:11–12 can be translated thus. The question asked by A. Bausani, in his commentary *Il Corano* (Florence, 1961), 714, would seem to be justified: "Vi sarebbe qui forse una somiglianza con la nota similitudine evangelica della 'via stretta' della virtù?" Traditional exegesis sees it as the path of the righteous, with all that this entails in the way of the struggle against selfishness and the attractions of evil.

31. Sūra 90:13–16; cf. 92:18–19; 93:9–11. English translation by J.J. Dawood (Harmondsworth, 1983).

32. Sūra 104:1–4; cf. 89:17–24; 92:8–11; 107:1–3.

33. Sūra 57:27; 5:82–85; 24:37.

34. The principal source for these traditions is M. Asin Palacios, *Logia et agrapha Domini Iesu apud Moslemicos scriptores, asceticos praesertim, usitata*, Patr. Or. 13 (1919), 331–431; 19 (1926), 530–624. Cf. also Y. Marquet, "Les Iḫwān al ṣafā' et le christianisme," *Islamochristiana*, 8 (1982), 129–158.

35. Massignon, "L'homme parfait en Islam," 292: "Ceux qui sont spoliés de tout, sauf de leur soif immatérielle de la Justice, y adhèrent de tout leur espoir, invincibles."

36. Mahmoud M. Ayoub, *Roots of Muslim–Christian Conflict* (mimeographed, Toronto, 1983), 48–49: "If domestic policies and foreign policy in the West could be truly christianized and the world of Islam in all its apsects could be islamized, then 'Dār al-Islām' could include the Church and the Church would see the entire world as the 'mystical body of Christ.' Then will the righteous servant of God and the meek 'inherit the earth' (Qur'ān 21:105 and Mt. 5:5)."

PART IX

QUESTIONS OF THEOLOGICAL FORMATION

CHAPTER 54

Biblical Theology
Its Revival and Influence on Theological Formation

Emilio Rasco, S.J.

Summary

The article consists of seven sections: "Biblical themes" and "biblical theology." The metaphors used by the Council concerning Scripture and theology. The preceding situation and unfinished projects. Scripture–theology discussion. The decisions of the Council. The fruits produced in theological fields. From the first fruits to the dynamism of hope.

"Biblical Themes" and "Biblical Theology"

If I am not mistaken, the expression "biblical theology" cannot be found either in the documents of the Council or in the important Encyclical of Pius XII, *Divino afflante Spiritu*.[1] But in the Council, there is no lack of expressions virtually equivalent to what can be called a "biblical theology," not in the concrete sense of a separate discipline as such, with a specific content of its own, but as a presentation of Holy Scripture in its entirety or of one of its integral parts (the Old Testament, the New Testament, Paul, John, etc.) rising above pure exegesis to give an overall view or to serve as foundation for dogmatic or systematic theology, as we shall see further on.

The documents of the Council, and in particular the Constitution *Dei Verbum* and the Decree *Optatam totius*, link Holy Scripture and theology in two main ways by using metaphors and by the expressions "themes of revelation" or "biblical themes."[2] It is difficult to see why there was no explicit mention of "biblical theology." I do not think it was because of the *de jure* difficulties that this discipline raises, namely, that being a concrete subject matter and genetico-historical at the same time, it is enlightened by faith according to Catholic thinking.[3] No trace of this problem can be found in the texts dealing with this theme at the time of the Council. On the contrary, there is no doubt that by "biblical themes," the Council Fathers meant biblical theology in a general sense. We read in the *Relatio de modis propositis et examinatis*: "In general, number 16 of *Optatam totius* pleased very much because it gives a firm opinion on some basic principles of the renewal of theological studies in the seminaries: the importance of biblical theology is emphasized . . . the preeminent biblical themes, at the same time, back up as much as possible the effort nowadays devoted to bring more closely together theological research, patristics, liturgical and spiritual life and the problems of pastoral."[4]

Further on, in an objection, the phrase "biblical theology" is mentioned as if it were immediately implicit in the text; and the answer clarifies the way in that biblical themes and biblical theology are brought together: "Hoc punctum est historia salutis in vita Ecclesiae semper in actu, ut praecipue in magnis thematibus biblicis apparet."[5]

Of course, the expression "biblical theology" had already been used in an important document on theological formation, even though, perhaps, this document did not stimulate the response hoped for. I am referring to the Instruction *De Sacra Scriptura in Clericorum Seminariis et Religiosorum Collegiis recte docenda*, of 13 May 1950.[6] In addition to other equivalent expressions, the instruction recommends that libraries contain the best works "on biblical theology,"[7] and that the best students be given free courses in *biblical theology*, among others.[8]

The basic text on this subject is found in the previously mentioned number 16 of the Decree *Optatam totius* on priestly formation:

Students should receive a most careful training in holy Scripture, which should be the soul, as it were, of all theology.[*9] After a suitable introductory course, they should receive an accurate initiation in exegetical method. They should study closely the principal themes of divine revelation and should find inspiration and nourishment in daily reading and meditation upon the Sacred books.[**10]

As can be seen, the themes are mentioned in two phases: as crowning biblical study, which begins with the "introduction," is followed by "exegesis," and culminates with the "themes"; and as the foundation of dogmatic theology, which starts from the "biblical themes" and goes on to the eastern and western Fathers and the exposition of systematic theology.

But why was the expression "biblical theme" used as the equivalent of "biblical theology"? I think it was in the air, as if it were thus perceived, especially in the French-speaking environment. A. Gelin had published a small book in 1946 that had wide circulation, *Les idées maîtresses de l'Ancien Testament*. In the introduction, after asserting that the history of the Old Testament is our history, he added: "Les grandes *thèmes*, les grandes constantes en doivent toujours être repris. . . . Citons en terminant quelques-uns de ces *thèmes*. . . ."[11] And the author enumerated a whole series of "themes": regarding vocation, the *inferma mundi*, faith, etc. Shortly afterwards, in 1950, J. Guillet[12] published a little book appropriately entitled *Thèmes bibliques*, which seemed in the first words of its preface to allude to Gelin: "Ces quelques thèmes ne couvrent pas toute la Bible. Ils n'en représentent pas même forcément les *lignes maîtresses*. . . ." Though it is not presented as a complete study, this work is not far from the idea of a biblical theology: "Essai pour étudier le vocabulaire religieux de la Bible, pour ressaisir, à travers l'histoire de quelques mots et de quelques images, les richesses de la religion d'Israël et le mouvement qui la conduit à Jésus-Christ." Lastly, let us mention a dictionary, the title of which changed significantly from *Vocabulaire biblique* to *Vocabulaire de théologie*

---

[*]Cf. Leo XIII, Encyclical *Providentissimus Deus*, 18 November 1893: AAS, 26 (1893–1894), 283.

[**]Cf. Pontifical Biblical Commission, *Instructio de Sacra Scriptura recte docenda*, 13 May 1950: AAS, 42 (1950), 502.

biblique.[13] This work, which has gone through many editions and numerous translations, was undoubtedly a high point in the growth of biblical theology presented in a form appropriate to biblical themes. And almost spontaneously, this expression is repeated four times in the preface: *les thèmes théologiques principaux, les thèmes majeurs de la révélation,*[14] and *thème majeur.* It involved "une initiation au langage de la Bible, en vue d'ouvrir les voies à une théologie biblique."

It was common then to talk about the biblical theme, especially in the environment we mentioned. But there is no doubt that there was a background to this, and I think that it is to be found in the articles that had been appearing in the *Theologisches Wörterbuch zum Neuen Testament,* which was published from 1933 on.[15] These studies, which were prevalently diachronic, constituted veritable monographs on biblical theology and possessed all the necessary historical and philological apparatus, which a later synthesis would utilize as a required scientific foundation.

It seems evident to me then that the Council used the expression "biblical themes" to refer to biblical theology. In this way, it already suggested the unity that must exist between biblical and systematic theology.

This aspect, together with other reflections on Holy Scripture, is treated in another basic text that uses various metaphors. We read, in fact, in *Dei Verbum:*

> Sacred theology relies on the written Word of God, taken together with sacred Tradition, as on a permanent foundation. By this Word it is most firmly strengthened and constantly rejuvenated, as it searches out, under the light of faith, the full truth stored up in the mystery of Christ. Therefore, the "study of the sacred page" should be the very soul of sacred theology.* The ministry of the Word, too—pastoral preaching, catechetics and all forms of Christian instruction, among which the liturgical homily should hold pride of place—is healthily nourished and thrives in holiness through the Word of Scripture.[16]

---

*Cf. Leo XIII, Encyclical *Providentissimus:* EB 115; Benedict XV, Encyclical *Spiritus Paraclitus:* EB 483.

The Metaphors Used by the Council Concerning
Holy Scripture and Theology

In relation to theology, J. Ratzinger[17] clearly distinguished the three metaphors used by the Council: the first one, Holy Scripture as "foundation"; without a unique and lasting foundation, like that of Scripture *una cum Traditione*, theology could not be built or developed. If this image seems somewhat static, the second metaphor of strength and youth (*roboratur semperque juvenescit*) immediately gives it a vital dynamism. Surprisingly enough, this image comes from a rather reductive text, namely, *Humani generis*, [18] and within this historical-theological context, the phrase lost some of its weight. That is why Ratzinger states clearly: in *Humani generis*, "the concern for a special kind of limitation on exegetical work to support the positions of the magisterium (*der lehramtlichen Vorlage*), turned out to be absolutely ineffective, and all its weight comes from the immediate relation to Scripture which our text demands of theology."

The third metaphor also appears in the Decree *Optatam totius*, and it is that of Scripture as "soul of theology." Various authors, such as Liloir, Grelot, and Hamel, [19] have emphasized the profound significance of this expression, which would, if it were taken seriously, give a totally new slant to theology. Grelot had pointed out the differences of context of the *Providentissimus Deus* of Leo XIII, the *Spiritus Paraclitus* of Benedict XV, and Vatican II, but it was chiefly Hamel who most accurately pointed out the value and limits of this metaphor in its prehistory. In the *Providentissimus*, the phrase expresses a desire rather than a necessity: "Illud maxime optabile est et necessarium, ut ejusdem Divinae Scripturae usus in universam theologiae influat disciplinam ejusque prope sit anima."[20] And a little further on it is declared: "Neque id cuiquam fuerit mirum, qui reputet, tam insignem locum inter revelationis fontes Divinis Libris deberi, ut, nisi eorum studio usuque assiduo, nequeat theologia rite et pro dignitate tractari." This does not prevent the pontifical document from making a distinction—dogmatic theology for the young, "ipsa demonstratio dogmatum ex Bibliorum auctoritatibus" for serious and erudite theologians.[21] E. Hamel correctly states of *Ex Bibliorum auctoritatibus* that this phrase about Scripture is, as it were, the announcement of the thesis[22] that the

experience of many centuries "proposed and established" the
truths of the faith *ex Divinis potissimum Litteris.*[23]

Benedict XV presented the formula in a still more apologetic
context of defense of dogmas when commemorating St. Jerome,
and it is unfortunate, because he could have used it more aptly
when treating of Scripture as food for spiritual life or as a special
source for the ministry of the Word. The Supreme Pontiff wrote
in 1920:

> Deinde, ut res postulaverit, argumenta ex Scriptura petenda
> sunt, quibus fidei dogmata illustremus, confirmemus, tueamus.
> Quod ille [Hieronymus] mirifice praestitit, adversus sui tem-
> poris hereticos dimicans: quos ad refellendos, quam acuta,
> quam solida e locis Scripturae arma desumpserit, omnia ejus
> opera luculenter ostendunt. In quo, si eum imitati erunt nostri
> Scripturarum interpretes, id profecto consecuturum est—quod
> decessor Noster in Encyclicis Litteris "Providentissimus Deus"
> "maxime optabile et necessarium" dixit—ut "ejusdem Scrip-
> turae usus in universam theologiae influat disciplinam ejusque
> prope sit anima."[24]

The phrase of Leo XIII, very open in itself but already en-
closed in the framework of the theological ideas of the time, had
even less relevance in 1920, and, in fact, the quotation is not
closely linked to the task of fighting against adversaries and heretics. But Hamel rightly pointed out that the idea of Scripture as
soul is, while not expressly mentioned as such, concerned with
preaching.[25] Indeed, concerning the ministry of the Word, the
Encyclical is worded as follows: "Neque enim eorum sermo habet
aliquid, cum momenti ac ponderis, tum ad effigendos animos
efficacitatis, nisi a sacra Scriptura informetur ab eaque vim suam
ac robur mutuetur."[26] According to a classic doctrine on the soul,
the *informatio* is the basic element, from which *vis* and *robur*
spring. Hamel is right: the phrase would be better placed if it
were tied to the quotation of Leo XIII on the soul of theology.
But this would have required going beyond the closed framework
that considered Scripture an eminently apologetic weapon.[27]

Number 24 of *Dei Verbum* ends with recognition of the close
link that exists between preaching and sacred Scripture. This
theme is not precisely that of the present study, although it is
closely connected to it, and it will, therefore, not be developed

here. Nor can we fail to mention that in Chapter II of the Decree on the Ministry and Life of Priests, *Presbyterorum ordinis*, which deals with priestly functions, the Ministry of the Word is considered before the sacramental, and, in particular, the eucharistic ministry. If it were possible, the whole of number 4 would have to be quoted, but let us confine ourselves to these few words: ". . . in every case their role is to reach not their own wisdom but the Word of God. . . ."[28]

The Preceding Situation and Unfinished Projects

To be in a position to appreciate fully the renewal and the influence that "biblical theology" has had on theological training thanks to the conciliar precepts, we must remember what the situation was not so long ago. Only thus will we be able to see clearly and grasp what has changed, if indeed there has been a change. In 1943, Pius XII published his magnificent biblical Charter *Divino afflante Spiritu*. This Encyclical entered directly into dialogue with biblical scholars, but also proposed a whole new program of biblical studies. Nevertheless, whether because the pontifical document did not have immediate application to study plans, or because of the difficulties the world was involved in in 1943, neither the system nor the programs changed much, despite the fact that for exegetes, this represented a breath of fresh air. Accordingly, in order to make the recommendations of the Encyclical more effective, the Pontifical Biblical Commission, with the approval of the Pope, in May 1950, *Silentibus jam armis*,[29] published an Instruction *De Sacra Scriptura recte docenda*.[30] It should be noted that the Instruction was not intended for theology faculties or for specialized institutes, because it was supposed that these centers were already doing a great deal even if it was for the benefit of very few, but rather for seminaries and the study facilities of religious orders. The study plan drawn up is truly admirable. It deals with knowing, on a solid scientific basis, Scripture *secundum omnes ejus partes*, together with the major problems of a historical or doctrinal order; and with providing a solid foundation for preaching. The Commission acknowledges that there will probably not be enough time available, and that this means that the professor must make choices, among which there should not fail to be what we could call a "compendium of biblical theology," even though the term was not used when the Commission said:

> Huic autem utilitati tum tantum recte satisfiet, cum magister clare monstraverit, quae sint praecipuae doctrinae tam in Vetere quam in Novo Testamento propositae, quae revelationis a primis initiis usque ad Christum Dominum et Apostolos cernatur progressio, quae inter Vetus et Novum Testamentum intercedat ratio atque conjunctio; neque omittat apte ostendere, quanti momenti spiritualis, nostris quoque temporibus, sit Vetus Testamentum.[31]

Other points were also suggested in this *ratio*. It must be confessed that it was almost impossible, if not utopian, to insert them into the already loaded program of the main and secondary subjects of theological study. To stir the waters, more than a document exclusively dedicated to Scripture was needed.

But along with liturgical renewal, which was strong at that time, interest in the Bible and biblical studies was making progress, as may be appreciated just by glancing at the periodicals of those years. And that is where the study of the "biblical themes" we mentioned came in and, as it were, interjected itself. But the fact remains that the general outline of theological studies remained impervious. Professors of Scripture certainly changed their outlook within their own fields, and many professors of fundamental and dogmatic theology felt the need for change. But that change did not come. A shock was needed, and that is exactly what the Council provided—Samson brought the edifice down.

The Scripture–Theology Discussion

It is true that for its part, theology had been much renewed. In particular, in certain countries and in many faculties in Europe and in some in North America, there were theologians teaching who would, at the appropriate time, give decisive assistance to the Council Fathers of Vatican II. In the most diverse fields— biblical, liturgical, ecclesiological, and ecumenical—it was they who furnished orientations until then unthinkable, and even looked upon with some suspicion. Theology was in fact abandoning a dead end, not without difficulties and fears, even though its traditional configuration, especially in some parts, had not been radically changed, and Sacred Scripture, and in particular biblical theology, had hardly touched it. The Word of God, doubtlessly with greater attention to its genuine meaning, continued to be a *locus*, a "proof of the thesis," as it had been for centuries. Change was not readily accepted. Thus, an article of L. Alonso Schökel, which presented a factual situation, gave rise in some Roman circles to an exaggerated reaction.[32] Before the opening of the Council, and even in its early stages, the Scripture–Theology relationship was warmly debated. We could mention just a few studies, of G. de Broglie,[33] J. Levie,[34] L. Scheffczyk,[35] M. Peinador,[36] and J. Michl.[37] In 1962, H. Vorgrimler published a book entitled *Exegese und Dogmatik* in which, among others, he gathered together studies on the subject by K.H. Schelkle (1958), K. Rahner (1961), H. Schlier (1957), E. Schillebeeckx (until then unpublished), and R. Schnackenburg (1961).[38]

Although their judgments, nuances, and practical approaches are not always alike, there are nevertheless points on which the majority of the studies are in agreement, namely, that the separation, indeed the mistrust or opposition between the two branches must come to an end. Scripture cannot be used as an *armamentarium*, a "proof of the thesis." Years later, in 1969, a theologian, J. Alfaro, would point out with great perspicacity the main defects of this "regressive" method.[39] But Vatican II gave the most conclusive reason when in number 24 of the *Dei Verbum* it stated that "Sacred Theology relies on the written Word of God, taken together with Sacred Tradition, as on a permanent foundation. By this Word it is most firmly strengthened and constantly rejuvenated, as it searches out, under the light of faith, the full truth stored up in the mystery of Christ. Therefore, the 'study of the sacred page' should be the very soul of sacred theology."[40] Long before, Leo XIII, after recalling that Scripture must influence the whole of theology because it is as if its soul,[41] quoted the decisive words of St. Thomas: "Non enim accipit [theologia] sua principia ab aliis scientiis, sed immediate a Deo per revelationem."[42] It is true, as Alfaro rightly pointed out, that St. Thomas took a different road in his *Summa Theologiae.*[43]

Outside the conciliar assembly, but often influencing the discussions inside the Vatican, the debate remained animated, and at times it intensified. It is impossible even to mention the various positions. When the documents finally reached their definitive form, it was apparent that the old study plan had to be discarded. The earlier efforts of *Divino afflante* in 1943 and the Instruction in 1950 had not had a significant impact and the reason, which the Instruction had foreseen, was evident—the lack of room in the curriculum. That is why specific proposals were soon forthcoming to make Scripture truly the soul that animates, rejuvenates, and invigorates theology. The Sacred Congregation of Seminaries and Universities published an issue of its periodical almost exclusively dedicated to this problem, which contained articles by prestigious authors such as Vagaggini, Benoit, Grelot, and Leloir.[44] The Encyclical governing ecclesiastical studies, the *Deus scientiarum Dominus* published by Pius XI in 1931, was obviously far out of date. However, a new charter could not be improvised without prior plans, pilot projects, etc. The issue of *Seminarium* that we mentioned contained various suggestions. Benoit, in a first plan that would not modify existing *ratio*, proposes a way of "integrating" biblical theology with exegesis and systematic theology, which would certainly require close collaboration among the professors. But a still more radical reform can be envisaged that would obviously involve changes in the present study plan, a new structure really, which would follow a progressive and historical course, from the primordial data of Revelation up to the inclusion of elements found in modern philosophy and culture.[45] Pierre Grelot proposes a different orientation, drawn from the Instruction of 1950, which, as we have mentioned, was never put into practice.[46]

In the last analysis, the whole problem can be reduced to two points. The first is that the professor of Scripture must have at his disposal a reasonable amount of time (it will never be enough) to devote to his subject matter, in accordance with the orientation of the Council, and this comes down to three points: the elements of "introduction," the role of "exegesis," and "biblical themes," or if it be preferred, based on what has been said here, "biblical theology." In all of this, the professor must also never lose sight of the progress of his students in the spiritual life and of their training for pastoral work.[47] The second point concerns professors of fundamental and dogmatic theology, and, in truth, it presupposes a preparation that is, if not highly specialized, at least very solid as regards Scripture.[48] Only thus will they be in a position to start from revealed matter with a truly reasoned and enriched presentation and then succeed in linking it to patristic and dogmatic theology and philosophical–theological ideas.

The Decisions of the Council

Having thus briefly illustrated the situation, let us turn to number 16 of the *Optatam totius*. We mentioned that "biblical theme" was used twice, and this point has not always been given the attention it deserves. The first time it appears as the culmination of exegetical study, and the second time as the first step in theological activity. Perhaps the wording of the official documents that began to implement the conciliar precepts fell short. Thus, in the *Normae quaedam* of 1968, which partly updated the *Deus scientiarum Dominus* and partly prepared the way for a new constitution, we read:

29. Institutio theologica ita recognoscatur ut, minime neglecto momento necessariae penetrationis speculativae, tradatur dimensionibus quae ad doctrinae sacrae indolem intrinsece pertinent, nempe: biblica, patristica, historica, liturgica, pastorali, spirituali, missionaria, oecumenica.[49]

The biblical dimension is but one of a long series; it seems to me that the document does not reflect the precepts of the Council. Meanwhile, the Apostolic Constitution was published, which abrogated that of 1931, together with the Norms of 1968 that prepared it. On 15 April 1979, John Paul II promulgated *Sapientia christiana*.[50] The text here comes closer, and even more important, it quotes the *Dei Verbum* explicitly. Before setting forth the biblical part in detail, it indicates in article 66 the goal of the faculty of theology:

Facultas Sacrae Theologiae eo tendit ut doctrina catholica, ex divina Revelatione maxime cura hausta, methodo scientifica sibi propria alte perspiciatur et systematice enucleetur; atque humanorum problematum solutiones sub ipsius Revelationis lumine sedulo investigentur.

Therefore, not only must Catholic doctrine spring from revelation, but current problems should be examined in its light. The following article is inspired by *Dei Verbum* 24, which it quotes: "Art. 67, §1. Sacrae Scripturae studium sit velut anima Sacrae Theologiae, quae in Verbo Dei scripto, una cum viva Traditione, tanquam in perenni Fundamento nititur."[51] The second paragraph surveys the other theological disciplines. I think that compared with the *Normae quaedam,* this represents a return to the letter and spirit of Vatican II.

One particular point regarding the arrangement of subjects is open to discussion, and that is the advisability of introducing the subject specifically called "biblical theology," of the Old or the New Testament or both, to the extent that the complexity and breadth of the subject matter permit. It is well known that "biblical theology" entails a whole series of problems about its true nature, its development (historical, genetic, and mixed), its unity as a science, etc. It is disputed whether, even within the New Testament, we should speak of biblical theology or biblical theologies.[52] In this instance, this subject is explicitly assigned to the biblical faculty at the Pontifical Biblical Institute,[53] but not in other instances. For example, Alfonso de la Fuente does not think that it ought to be presented as a specific discipline,[54] whereas J. Alfaro considers it "advisable for faculties of theology to offer courses specifically on biblical theology."[55] I know from experience that this course is, despite its difficulties, of great help to students. An overall view deepens and ties together whatever they have studied about the synoptic gospels, about Paul, about John, etc. The course is profitable not only for those who specialize in biblical studies, but also in a particular way to students in other degree courses (fundamental, moral, dogmatic, and ecumenical theology, etc.), so that they may personally grasp the historical character of revelation and go beyond what Alfaro perspicaciously calls "the mirage of a linear continuity between the themes of the Old and the New Testament."[56] It is still not unusual to run into simplistic assertions about *the* christology, *the* soteriology, or *the* eschatology of the New Testament. Future dogmatic theologians, having as accurate a panoramic view as possible, will be able to gain much in theological sensibility.

Fruits Produced in Theological Fields

At this point, the problem that presents itself is what renewal, what influence has Vatican II produced in theological training by declaring that the Word of God must be its soul? In answering this question, there is the risk of a subjective interpretation. We will have to limit ourselves to giving a few indications and to seeing what those personally concerned think or say. A further proof would be all the pastoral ministry, catechesis, and preaching of the Word, and finally, the Christian life itself of those who are being instructed. Further analysis of that kind would go beyond the limits of this essay and we are therefore excluding it from consideration.

A first indication comes from the students themselves who, without being single-minded about it, are much attracted to optional courses, seminars, etc., on openly biblical themes. The specifically scriptural courses are followed with considerable interest, and, in the dogmatic courses, they appreciate the biblical aspect being taught with abundant detail. One result that is beginning to be felt is not only the increasing number of students aspiring to the licentiate in theology with biblical specialization, where it exists, but also the great number of doctoral dissertations on biblical subjects. Some few are of a distinctly technical character, but those in which biblical theology offers possibilities of development tend to be more numerous. By just perusing the most recent dictionaries of theology, ethics, and spirituality, we can see that a considerable portion of them is being dedicated to the biblical aspect of their respective subjects.

In the second place, we can question those involved in and responsible for training, that is, the theologians, moralists, canonists, and others. After disputing for years about the relationship between Scripture and Tradition and having finally established that the Word of God has preeminence in theology, it now occupies a truly worthy place in teaching and in books. To be thorough, it would be necessary to take this treatise by treatise, but it will suffice to look, for example, at works that deal with the problems of concern to the various theological fields.

The collective work *Problemi e prospettive di Teologia Fondamentale* provides a general idea of the field of fundamental theology.[57] Just from a quick reading of this, the decisive role played by Sacred Scripture in this "new image of fundamental theology" is immediately evident, even in this preliminary stage, where the ground is being cleared to prepare the way for later construction. In all these studies, and in particular in those that in some way introduce the student to study of the Christian event, the scriptural basis is solid and full.

It is, of course, in the dogmatic area that the "themes of revelation" meet with a more radical influence. Systematic theology, as we pointed out before, maintained an animated, and at times difficult, dialogue with exegesis. Some authors, such as Schnackenburg[58] and Alfaro,[59] had already identified or developed these "themes" that theology needed to deepen. It would be interesting to compare these study projects with what has been realized. That a great deal has been accomplished is the impression given by reading, for example, the studies edited by K.H. Neufeld in *Problemi e prospettive di Teologia Dogmatica.*[60] The editor calls to mind, by reference to the *Sapientia christiana,* that the study of Scripture must be the soul of theology,[61] and an expert also deals with this relationship.[62] Others concern themselves with themes such as revelation, the gospel, dogma, and the unity of Scripture and dogma.[63] The studies contain numerous biblical quotations, but the most important fact about them is not that but rather that they are imbued with biblical theology.

While dogmatic theology had reduced Scripture to about a hundred proofs, the moral theology taught in theological courses in fairly recent times had more the flavor of Aristotelian or stoic ethic than of gospel or Pauline ethics. The Council itself in number 16 of its decree *Optatam totius* had called this particularly to the attention of ethicians when it declared:

Special care should be given to the perfecting of moral theology. Its scientific preparation should draw more fully on the teaching of holy Scripture and should throw light on the exalted vocation of the faithful in Christ and their obligation to bring forth fruit in charity for the life of the world.[64]

This being so, one moral theologian rightly asked whether Scripture were not the soul of moral theology.[65] The problems in the moral theology field were particularly difficult because, among other reasons, of the necessary connection between ethics and the surrounding world that is so different from the biblical world (itself so varied) not only as regards the Old Testament, but the New Testament as well. Furthermore, recent exegesis had adversely criticized some of the few "biblical" arguments of the moralists. Consequently, Hamel had good grounds to ask himself why and how we should turn to Scripture. In truth, the moralists had felt the need for renewal long before the Council, but the task was arduous—the biblical texts were difficult to apply and the danger of disintegration and of a facile "biblicism" was real. In various nations, in Italy,[66] Belgium,[67] and France,[68] biblists and moralists went to work together. Paul VI personally outlined the role of Scripture in an important speech to the International Theological Commission.[69] Was everything then taken care of? "Peu s'en faut!"[70] replied one moralist. However, this same author, after mentioning the extremely difficult relationships between the Bible and moral theology, points out that the influence of the Word tends to be deeper, more constant, and more varied. Obviously, the moral theologian must possess an excellent and continuous biblical training: "C'est à ce prix seulement qu'il saura mettre les immense richesses de la Bible au service de la théologie morale, sans réduire en rien l'autonomie de cette dernière."[71]

The concern for renewing ethics with the help of Scripture is seen in studies encompassing various aspects of ethics. In the collective work *Herausforderung und Kritik der Moraltheologie,*[72] we find a whole section entitled "The Biblical Foundations." Less explicit, but perhaps more diffuse, is the biblical presence in the studies *Problemi e prospettive di Teologia Morale.*[73] Moral theology is encountering problems that must be dealt with in an entirely new way, problems of war, of sexuality, of intercommunications, and of leisure time, or problems completely unknown to preceding generations, such as everything that involves the manipulation of human genetics. Much still remains to be achieved, but it is undeniable that from preconciliar moral theology to what is currently being taught, a great deal of progress has been made in the right direction. For if specific solutions to today's problems cannot, and at times ought not, be presented, general orientation and fundamental principles may be laid down that prepare the way for a truly Christian existence.

The Council did not connect canon law directly with Scripture (is this fact due only to the redaction the text or could it be that the connection was too difficult to make?), but rather with the "mystery of the Church,"[74] and through this medium, an indirect relationship with the Word of God can be reestablished. This is not the place to go deeper into this relationship. I shall confine myself to mentioning the earnest desire that at least some canonist circles have to establish an invigorating contact between ecclesiastical law and the gospel. In April 1976, for example, French canonists met in Paris to study "L'enracinement du droit canonique dans l'Ecriture."[75] At the beginning of the discussion, A. Passicus[76] put a series of theoretical and practical problems on the table that started from a conception of the Church formulated in new terms and not exclusively as *societas perfecta* regarding its relationship with the world, its missionary situation, ecumenical requirements, and the demands that consideration of the ecclesial community as "the people of God" entail. The problem immediately arose and was presented as to what could be looked for and hoped for from Scripture, not as an extrinsic recourse nor one to models already outdated, but rather a recourse to Revelation as a matter of institutional continuity. In fact, the discussion ended with an effort to refine the concept of "divine law" and to find its place within the deposit of revealed truth. These are fundamental problems and questions that a canonist has posed in all freedom and sincerity. On that occasion and for the purpose of opening a dialogue, excellent Christian (and one Jewish) biblists were listened to attentively, group discussions were held, and a series of conclusions were reached relative to excellent *desiderata* of the assembly to be reflected in the new Code of Canon Law then in preparation. As Dom W. Witters, O.S.B.[77] said:

> Enfin le Nouveau Testament présente le Christ lui-même comme la Norme ultime en tant qu'il est lui-même l'Amour, en tant que donateur de la Loi d'Amour, de l'Agapé divine, en tant aussi qu'instituant l'Eglise et lui assurant la permanence de sa présence par le don de l'Esprit. C'est de cetter manière que le droit canon trouve sa racine et sa source dans le Nouveau Testament. Evangile vécu dans et par une Eglise; le droit canon aura donc un perpétuel besoin de revenir à cette source, de confronter ses positions avec cette source, de demeurer en rapport vital avec cette source sans négliger pour autant la Tradition.[78]

An analysis, which would, of course, go far beyond our present purpose of the principles that inspire and the norms that are detailed in ecclesiastic law in the new Code of Canon Law, would show how and to what extent these and other proposals received satisfactory treatment. If the Council is to exert its influence in having the Word of God reflected in all the aspects of theological thought and the theological life of the Church, a new sensitivity may perhaps be needed so that Christians may find in the specific norms that guide them a reflection and almost a translation of the gospel.

From the First Fruits to the Dynamism of Hope

The present period of the Church cannot be divided, in a simplistic way, into "before" and "after" the Council, as Yves Congar commented with a sensibility that is traditional and, as one might say, eschatological.[79] Vatican II was not a goal, but rather a stage,[80] one which gave, however, without any doubt, as this theologian constantly repeats, a dynamism,[81] the energy of which will last a long time, as happened with previous Councils. And if there was no lack of abuses in practice, and if some even talked about crisis, it was not due to the Council, as Congar has shown through careful analysis, even though a certain responsibility[82] may be attributed to it, a responsibility that is at bottom, however, not completely negative:

> Par la franchise des débats, par l'ouverture à des apports longtemps ignorés, exclus, condamnés, par une saine critique interne poursuivie à la lumière des exigences tant de la mission que de l'Evangile, l'inconditionnalité du système hérité de la Contre-Réforme et de la Restauration antirévolutionnaire du XIX siècle, avait été dissoute. . . . Des courants d'idées, des attitudes trop longtemps tenues à distance ont pénétré par les portes et les fenêtres enfin ouvertes. La crise est venue *aussi* par là.[83]

Regarding the theme we have been treating, there was no lack of inspiring beginnings even before the Council such as the *Divino afflante Spiritu,* and even a detailed study plan such as the Instruction of 1950. What was lacking was an initial spark and suitable combustible material for making the fire catch. Furthermore, if Vatican II had perchance not done more than give the directions on which we have just commented, nothing would have been achieved. Nor was the *Dei Verbum* sufficient, which, despite its great importance, has yet to develop all its potential. There was need for a whole broad renewed outlook—ecclesiological, ecumenical, missionary, a new positioning of the Church relative to the world, an opening, and not just for the clergy, to the sacred sources of the liturgy and theological concerns, in order that the brief suggestions of the Council on the relations between Scripture and theology might give their fruits.

However, we have not reached this ideal. Concerning Scripture as the soul of theology, one writer put it this way: "Nous sommes à tous les niveaux, loin du compte."[84] There is still a long way to go to return to the inexhaustible fountain. Not even the official documents, it is said, are yet impregnated with the biblical Word, and it is not just a matter of filling them with scriptural quotations.[85]

That is the reason why Paul VI himself did not hesitate to point out or develop points that had not been treated or developed in Vatican II. In addressing Scripture scholars in 1970, he insisted on the indispensable aspect, studied so much today, of the textual interpretation process. This is a very important theme, said Paul VI, "basta considerare che la sua risonanza raggiunge anche la teologia, la catachesi, la mentalità dell'uomo di oggi."[86] (It suffices just to consider that its echo reaches theology, catachesis, and the mentality of the people of today.) This process of interpretation requires that the meaning of Scripture be made applicable to the present salvific moment, that it encompass and involve in the problem the very person of the interpreter, and that there be established between the text and the exegete a certain common character, because only thus can there be true fidelity to the Word and to the person of today.[87]

A few years later, Paul VI did not limit himself to mentioning the theme of hermeneutics and to insisting on the necessary integration of the diachronic method with the synchronic (themes that the Council had not had an opportunity to touch upon), so as to grasp the message of the text better, but he also added what follows, which is along the lines that we have been pursuing:

> C'est seulement de la sorte que les fruits de l'exégèse pourront servir à la fonction kérygmatique de l'Eglise, à son dialogue, s'offrir à la réflexion de la théologie systématique et à l'enseignement moral, et devenir utilisables pour la pastorale dans le monde moderne. On voit nécessairement se profiler ainsi, vous le comprenez, une réelle continuité entre la recherche exégétique et celle de la théologie dogmatique et morale. Da même, on voit se dessiner concrètement l'exigence de "l'inter-

disciplinarité" entre le bibliste, le spécialiste de la théologie dogmatique, celui de la théologie morale, le juriste et l'homme engagé dans la pastorale et dans la mission.[88]

And the Pope recalled regarding this a few of the most important phrases of the Council, which we have already quoted abundantly.

There has been, therefore, since the necessary shock given by the Council, a good deal of movement and a dynamism full of hope. The new generations understand how beneficial the change of atmosphere has been, now that there is a strong biblical component in their theological training. From these new generations, helped by exegetes and theologians working together, the Council will receive its true "reception," deep and impregnated with faith, which will be able to make the life of the Church fruitful on her dynamic pilgrimage toward the full realization of Christian hope. This will be the work and the gift of the great secret artificer of the Council, the Holy Spirit.

Translated from the Spanish by Louis-Bertrand Raymond and Edward Hughes.

Notes

1. But it is almost described in these terms in the Encyclical: "in illis quidem opportune allatis, quantum ad exegesim conferre possint, ostendant potissimum quae sit singulorum librorum vel textuum theologica doctrina de rebus fidei et morum, ita ut haec eorum explanatio non modo theologos doctores adjuvet ad fidei dogmata credenda confirmandaque, sed sacerdotibus etiam adjumento sit ad doctrinam christianam coram populo enucleandam, ac fidelibus denique omnibus ad vitam sanctam homineque christiano dignam agendam adserviat." (*Ench. Bibl.*, 551). Such a doctrine is subsequently, in No. 552, called *interpretatio theologica*. See further on the terms used by the *Instructio* of 1950.

2. See s.v. "Temi biblici" of T. Federici in G. Garofalo (director) in collaboration with T. Federici (chief ed.), *Dizionario del Concilio Vaticano II* (Rome, 1969), col. 1894–1896; C. Vagaggini, "La teologia dogmatica nell art. 16 del decreto sulla formazione sacerdotale," *Seminarium*, 16 (1966), 819–941, esp. 833ff.; P. Grelot, "L'enseignement de la Sainte Ecriture," *Seminarium*, 16 (1966), 853–874, esp. 873ff.: "Qu'est-ce qu'un thème biblique?" See esp. J. Alfaro, "El tema biblico

en la enseñanza de la teología sistemática," *Gregorianum,* 50 (1969), 509–542.

3. On this difficult problem, see G. Segalla, *Introduzione alla teologia biblica del Nuevo Testamento; Problemi* (Milan, 1981). The bibliography on this subject is enormous: see, e.g., R. Schnackenburg, *La théologie du Nouveau Testament. Etat de la question,* Studia Neotestamentica, Subsidia I (Bruges, 1961), 13, together with the important articles quoted of F.M. Braun, H. Schlier, C. Spicq, among others.

4. *AS* vol. IV, periodus IV, pars IV (Vatican City, 1977), 42.

5. *Ibid.,* 103.

6. *Ench. Bibl.,* 582–610.

7. No. 602. It would be interesting to do some research on the books that were then considered the best on biblical theology.

8. No. 605.

9. Notice the resemblance of this phrase "maxima divinae Revelationis themata" to the expression "thèmes majeurs de la Révélation," which we find in the prologue of the biblical dictionary that is quoted in note 13.

10. *Documentos del Vaticano II. Constituciones, decretos, declaraciones. Edición de bolsillo, con introducciones históricas, esquemas y copiosos índices* (Madrid, 1967); *OT* 16, 346–347.

11. A. Gelin, P.S.S., *Les idées maîtresses de l'Ancien Testament,* Lectio divina 2 (Paris, 1959), 8.

12. J. Guillet, *Thèmes bibliques. Etudes sur l'expression et le développement de la Révélation (Théologie,* 18) (Paris, 1954). The author thus describes the book (p. 7): "Essai pour étudier le vocabulaire religieux de la Bible, pour ressaisir, à travers l'histoire de quelques mots et de quelques images, les riches ses de la religion d'Israël, et le mouvement qui la conduit à Jésus-Christ."

13. *Vocabulaire de théologie biblique,* published under the direction of X. Leon-Dufour and J. Duplacy, A. George, P. Grelot, J. Guillet, M.-F. Lacan (Paris, 1970). This book was redacted between 1958 and 1961. About the change of name, see XV.

14. We have already pointed out the resemblance of the expression to the one found in *OT* 16: "maxima divinae Revelationis themata."

15. Initially edited by G. Kittel, and subsequently by G. Friedrich. The first volume is dated 1933, the last, 2 October 1979.

16. *Documentos del Vaticano II,* 130–131.

17. *LThK, Das zweite Vatikanische Konzil,* II (1967), 577.

18. *Humani generis* was published on 12 August 1950, shortly after the Instruction on biblical training. The text of the Encyclical says: "Quapropter sacrorum fontium sacrae disciplinae semper juvenescunt; dum contra speculatio, quae ulteriorem sacri depositi inquisitionem negligit, ut experiundo novimus, sterilis evadit" (*Ench. Bibl.,* 611).

19. L. Leloir, O.S.B., "La sainte Ecriture, âme de toute la théologie," *Seminarium*, 16 (1966), 880–891; Grelot, "L'enseignement de la Sainte Ecriture" *Seminarium*, 16 (1966), 853–874, esp. 873ff.; E. Hamel, "L'Ecriture, âme de la théologie," *Gregorianum*, 52 (1971), 511–535.

20. *Ench. Bibl.*, no. 114.

21. *Ibid.*, no. 114.

22. Hamel, "L'Ecriture," 514.

23. *Ench. Bibl.*, no. 114.

24. *Ibid.*, no. 483.

25. Hamel, "L'Ecriture," 519.

26. *Ench. Bibl.*, no. 484.

27. No. 21 of *DV* contains other metaphors and comparisons that, however, do not directly link Scripture with theology. Among these there is that of "the pure and perennial source of spiritual life," which comes from *Divino afflante Spiritu* (*Ench. Bibl.*, 567), but the document of the Council does not quote Pius XII.

28. *Documentos del Concilio Vaticano II*, 348.

29. *Ench. Bibl.*, 585.

30. *Ibid.*, 582–610.

31. *Ibid.*, 594.

32. L. Alonso Schokel, "Argument d'Ecriture et théologie biblique dans l'enseignement théologique," *NRT*, 91 (1959), 337–354. Monsignor A. Romeo, who has a position in the Congregation of Seminaries, took the occasion of this article to express a strong reaction: "La Enciclica *Divino afflante Spiritu* e le *opiniones novae*," *Divinitas*, 3 (1960), 385–456. The negative aspect of certain articles that appeared in *L'Osservatore Romano* at that time, including some authored by cardinals, cannot be ignored. For further details, see J.R. Scheifler in L.A. Schokel (ed.), *Concilio Vaticano II. Comentarios a la Constitución Dei Verbum sobre la divina revelación* (Madrid, 1969), 604–607.

33. G. de Broglie, "Sur la primauté de l'argument d'Ecriture en théologie," in L. Bouyer, *Du protestantisme à l'Eglise* (Paris, 1950), 247–250.

34. "Les limites de la preuve d'Ecriture Sainte en Théologie," *NRT*, 71 (1948), 1009–1029.

35. "Biblische und dogmatische Theologie," *TTZ*, 67 (1958), 193–202; the author later returns to the theme, "Die Auslegung der Heiligen Schrift als dogmatische Ausgabe," *MTZ*, 15 (1964), 190–204.

36. "La integración de la Exégesis en la Teologia," *Sacra Pagina* (Gembloux, 1959), I, 158–179.

37. "Dogmatische Schriftbeweis und Exegese," *Bz*, 2 (1958), 1–14.

38. Mainz, 1962 (Italian translation, 1967).

39. J. Alfaro, "El tema biblico en la enseñanza de la teologia sistematica," *Gregorianum*, 50 (1969), 516.

40. *Documentos del Concilio Vaticano II*, 130.

41. See *Ench. Bibl.*, 114, and what has been said before.

42. *Ibid.* The quotation is from St. Thomas, *ST*, I, q. 1, a. 5, ad 2.

43. Alfaro, "El tema biblico," 513ff.: "El ejemplo más elocuente de esta ausencia del dato biblico total, como punto de partida de la reflexión teológica lo ofrece precisamente la *Summa Theologiae* de S. Tomas; las *quaestiones* no surgen de la previa exposición de la doctrina bíblica, sino casi exclusivamente de la reflexión sistemática y de la discusión escolástica."

44. This concerns No. 4 of Year 17, new series Year 6, of the review *Seminarium*, from which we previously quoted the articles.

45. For further details, see the article of this author in *Seminarium*, especially 487ff.

46. P. Grelot, "L'enseignement de la Sainte Ecriture," *Seminarium*, 16 (1966), 853–874.

47. The Instruction of 1950 had already recommended that steps be taken to have the Sunday pericopes explained (*Ench. Bibl.*, 597). Bear in mind that with the liturgical reform, the number of readings increased. A whole course probably would not suffice for that, but neither would it be necessary: what is essential is that the professor provide a "method" for reading these passages.

48. In some places, there has been close collaboration by inviting the Scripture scholar to present the biblical aspect in a systematic way, which in theory is excellent; but the method is not easy and, in practice, has not always worked. See also Alfaro, "El tema biblico," 540.

49. See *Normae quaedam ad Constitutionem Apostolicam Deus scientiarum Dominus de Studiis academicis Ecclesiasticis recognoscendis* (Vatican City, 1968), No. 29, p. 21. The situation is hardly better in the *Adnexum B*, art. 27 (p. 57), where Sacred Scripture comes at point (d), after fundamental, dogmatic, and moral theology.

50. John Paul II, *Constitutio Apostolica "Sapientia christiana"* (Vatican City, 1979).

51. See *Documentos del Vaticano II*, 130–131.

52. See, among many others, the works already quoted of G. Segalla, *Introduzione alla teologia del Nuevo Testamento, Storia, Problemi*, or of R. Schnackenburg, *La théologie du Nouveau Testament*. Regarding the Old Testament, see G.L. Prato, "Dalla 'Rivelazione come Storia' all 'Storia teofanica,' " *Rassegna metodologica di teologia biblica*, in C. Casale Marcheselli (ed.), *Parola e Spirito; Studii in onore di Settimio Cipriani*, Vol. I (Brescia, 1982), 549–573.

53. Compare *Sapientia Christiana*, art. 71, and the *Ordinationes Sacrae Congregationis pro Institutione Catholica ad Const. Apost. "Sapientia Christiana" rite exsequendam* with *Pontificium Institutum Biblicum*;

Statuta (Rome, 1985), art. 46: "biblical theology" is the chief and obligatory discipline.

54. See *Concilio Vaticano II. Comentarios al Decreto "Optatam totius"* on priestly formation (Madrid, 1970); A. de la Fuente, "Formación intelectual," 495.

55. Alfaro, "El tema biblico," 541.

56. *Ibid.*, 536. See also p. 521 on the divergences, discontinuities, omissions, deficiencies, partial simplifications, and hasty syntheses.

57. R. Latourelle and G. O'Collins (eds.), *Problemi e prospettive di Teologia Fondamentale* (Brescia, 1980), a work of many collaborators.

58. Schnackenburg, *La théologie du Nouveau Testament*, 37–40, 103–112.

59. Alfaro, "El tema biblico," 532ff. presents a whole range of themes "which have not been sufficiently integrated into the study of systematic theology."

60. K.H. Neufeld (ed.), *Problemi e prospettive di Teologia Dogmatica* (Brescia, 1983).

61. *Ibid.*, 11.

62. X. Leon-Dufour, "Teologia e Sacra Scrittura," 43–70.

63. See also L.F. Ladaria, "Che cos'é un dogma? Il problema del dogma nella teologia attuale," 97–119.

64. *Documentos del Vaticano II*, 398ff. Excellent presentation of the invitation of the Council in J. Fuchs, "Theologia moralis perficienda. Votum Concilii Vaticani II," *Periodica de re morali canonica liturgica*, 55 (1966), 498–548.

65. E. Hamel, "L'Ecriture, âme de la théologie morale?" *Gregorianum*, 54 (1973), 417–445.

66. See T. Goffi (ed.), *Fondamenti biblici della teologia morale* (Brescia, 1973).

67. See M. Gilbert, "Recontre entre moralistes et exégètes," *RTL*, 5 (1974), 127–128.

68. See the work of many authors: *Ecriture et pratique chrétienne*; Congrès de l'ACFEB Angers, Présentation par Paul de Surgy, *Lectio divina*, 96 (Paris, 1978).

69. "Les sources de la connaissance morale chrétienne," *AAS*, 67 (1975), 39–44.

70. E. Hamel, "Ecriture et théologie morale, un bilan (1940–1980), *Studia Moralia*, 20 (1982), 178–193; quotation, p. 191.

71. *Ibid.*, 192.

72. Herausgegeben von G. Teichtweiter u. W. Dreier (eds.), *Herausforderung und Kritik der Moraltheologie* (Würzburg, 1971).

73. T. Goffi (ed.), *Problemi e prospettive di Teologia Morale* (Brescia, 1976).

74. Decree *OT* 16: "Similiter in iure canonico exponendo et in historia ecclesiastica tradenda respiciatur ad Mysterium Ecclesiae. . . ."

75. See "L'enracinement du droit canonique dans l'Ecriture," *L'Année canonique* (Paris, 1977), t. 31.

76. "Quel droit pour quelle Eglise: quelques questions fondamentales pour un nouveau type de réformes," *ibid.*, 19–37.

77. "Conclusions des travaux de groupes," *ibid.*, 221–232.

78. *Ibid.*, 226.

79. Y.M.-J. Congar, *Le Concile de Vatican II. Son Eglise peuple de Dieu et Corps du Christ*, Théologie historique, 71 (Paris, 1984), 7, 69.

80. *Ibid.*, 90.

81. *Ibid.*, passim; see, for example, 66, 67, 110.

82. *Ibid.*, 69–70.

83. *Ibid.*, 70.

84. *Ibid.*, 90.

85. *Ibid.*, 104.

86. See *AAS*, 62 (1970), 615–619; quotation, p. 616.

87. *Ibid.*, 616–618. See the article of D. Dupont, O.S.B., "Storicità dei Vangeli e metodo storico dei vangeli (*sic*: it should read: 'dell 'exegisi') nella Costituzione dogmatica *Dei verbum*, in A venti anni dal Concilio. Prospettive teologiche e giuridiche (Palermo, 1984), 50–73.

88. *AAS*, 66 (1974), 235–241; quotation, p. 239.

CHAPTER 55

The Study of the Fathers
of the Church
in Priestly Formation

Antonio Orbe, S.J.

Summary

Among the difficulties mentioned in number 16 of the Decree *Optatam totius* dealing with the role of patristics in the training of priests, there is a fundamental one. Is theology, as it is presently taught in seminaries and universities, in possession of the means required to give to the students a sound formation in the doctrine of the holy Fathers? The present essay points out the most serious obstacles, both theoretical and practical, which such a formation meets, and how to overcome them.

Subject Matter and Problems

In number 16 of *Optatam totius* we read: "Dogmatic theology should be so arranged that the biblical themes are presented first. Students should be shown what the Fathers of the eastern and western churches contributed to the fruitful transmission and illumination of the individual truths of revelation, and also the later history of dogma. . . ."

The study of the Fathers, or patristics, is said to belong the discipline of dogmatic theology and to follow the study of Scripture.

Patristics consists of the contribution, made by the Fathers of

361

the eastern and western churches, to the faithful transmission and explanation of the individual truths of revelation. The paragraph takes for granted the positive nature of the writings of the holy Fathers.

However, it does not state how the Fathers made this contribution: as exegetes of the Old and New Testaments? As witnesses to the apostolic tradition concerning the truths of revelation? Or as exponents of the truths revealed both within and beyond the Scriptures? This third description best explains both the meaning of *Optatam totius* and the traditional image of the Fathers themselves: they were witnesses to a tradition inherited from the apostles, and scholars qualified to transmit and interpret in an authentic way the truths revealed within and beyond the Scriptures.

It is indeed especially in connection with the Bible that the Fathers are well known. In their preaching and writings, they were, and considered themselves to be, first and foremost qualified exegetes of the Old and New Testaments. They were not exegetes by the simple fact that they interpreted the Scriptures. The great heretics also explained the Scriptures and relied on the literal meaning of the Bible. But the Fathers presented themselves as authentic exegetes of the eastern and western churches, capable of studying and expounding the truths revealed by Scripture. By this very fact, they unlocked the truths recorded in revelation by means of the key by which alone to understand them with full confidence: the tradition of their local churches. They knew that by wandering from this *paradosis*, one can neither read nor find in the sources of revelation the truths the Spirit of God has announced to us.

The Fathers, of course, pose difficult problems for us:

(a) *The Problem of the Boundaries between the Christian and the Non-Christian Tradition.* No one questions the authority of Origen and his influence as an exegete; this was the case in the East (e.g., Eusebius, the Cappadocians, Didymus) and in the West (St. Hilary, St. Ambrose, St. Jerome, Rufinus). Through Origen, the tradition of Philo made its influence felt in the Church. Many of the Fathers offer as ecclesiastical exegesis one that in great part stems from Philo. What credence can be attributed to such a tradition that pretends to be inspired by apostolic thought in its purest form? And what guarantee of credibility do the Fathers themselves provide us when, like St. Ambrose, they are well aware of their dependence on Philo and nevertheless christianize this non-Christian tradition, by including it into a symbiosis with the apostolic tradition?

(b) *The Problem of Compatability.* For one and the same biblical text, we find in the Fathers a thousand interpretations, many of which are contradictory. What is asserted by one of them is expressly condemned by another. Which of these thousand interpretations embodies the true tradition? And if we are certain about none, on what criteria can we rely in those uses when we are presented with conflicting interpretations: some appealing to the letter, others to the spirit, or to moral allegory, or to an historical exegesis or to a christological interpretation? The frequency of a certain approach does not constitute a proof of its rectitude, as is exemplified by the predominance of the Alexandrian or Origenian exegetical tendencies that won broad recognition merely for reasons of a literary nature.

These difficulties, although serious, do not detract from the authority the Fathers possess as exegetes. Their authority is all the more great because, in temporal terms, they are closer to the sources of revelation. The great authors of the second century treat the Scriptures in a way very much in agreement with them; the authors of the fourth century and the following ones were not able to attain the same degree of harmony.

The plurality of opinions found in the Fathers is reflected by dogmatic theologians at the present time. The Fathers are cited by them to confirm a certain exegesis. First, the sacred text is interpreted on the basis of a grammatical and literary analysis alone, as if Homer or Hesiod were in question; then, only if they serve the purpose of the theologian, recourse is had to the Fathers. If the latter do not agree with a particular contemporary exegesis, they will be passed over; but if they agree, they will be quoted. Far from providing the dogmatician a rule of interpretation so as to discover the truths of revelation, the Fathers are introduced for the additional erudition they supply. Since it is in conformity with rational principles, the only exegesis worthwhile at present is a purely literal one. Thus, the Fathers are either appealed *ad eruditionem* or *ad solatium,* provided they confirm the dominating interpretation, or they are neglected altogether, whether or not they agree with the prevailing interpretation.

Those who speak of biblical or exegetical theology, thereby generally mean dogmatic theology. According both to logic and to its own implicit axioms, dogmatic theology is based on biblical theology. But the latter is then said to be based on a very free and actual exegesis of the text. What meaning, therefore, can patrology have for dogmatic theology if, exegetically speaking, *per se* it contributes nothing, and is valid only *per accidens*, as a source of confirmation?

Here one arrives at the core of the problem. It is understandable why Protestant theology attaches little importance to the Fathers and why any dogmatic theology that is rationally guided only by the Scriptures leaves aside the Fathers. This is the main defect that nowadays marks theologians: logically speaking, the study of the Fathers has become superfluous. Therefore, one must decide in favor of one of the terms of the following dilemma: either to approach the sources of revelation, as the Fathers did, and follow the main lines of their biblical exegesis; or to relegate the Fathers to the domain of historical erudition, without feeling obliged to endorse an exegesis that, at one time, thought itself to be the guardian of the truth.

It takes much courage to admit this dilemma, and still more courage to choose its second term. Most theologians have little difficulty in acknowledging the teaching of *Optatam totius*; however, *in theory*, they acclaim the value of the Fathers without following the means they employed to transmit and proclaim the revealed truths, but *in practice*, they completely leave them aside.

This is not the only misinterpretation of which current dogmatic theology is culpable, but, eventually, it should be denounced.

The Challenge of Teaching Patristic Theology

In the following argument, two points are presumed: (a) the positive contribution of the Fathers in transmitting and proclaiming the revealed truths; and (b) the necessity of assimilating this contribution in a contemporary way in order to approach the sources of revelation, as the Fathers did, without rupturing the continuity of Christianity.

Two questions arise here:

1. Is it possible at the present time to provide theology students with a formation in patristics?
2. If so, how can we manage to do it? What pedagogy should be adopted in such a theological formation?

It is still possible to offer students a formation in patristics, although it is becoming more and more difficult. Obstacles are to be found, in the first place, within the students themselves.

At present, students know neither Greek nor Latin. If they are not even acquainted with Latin, it is utopian to provide them a formation in patristics. Translating the Fathers into modern languages impoverishes them, and renders many of their insights, and even their basic notions, quite unintelligible. Translation thus deprives the original terms of vigor and charm, since they are polyvalent in themselves and can be understood only in relationship to other analogous terms. Translations also impede making spontaneous comparisons between the text of the Scriptures, the personal style of a particular author, and its similarity with the style of other Fathers or of conciliar statements. Thus, translations have limits of all kinds—exegetical and dogmatic—that block any endeavor to comprehend the Fathers. If mastering Latin is very important, then mastering both Latin and Greek is still more important. The great Fathers, as well as the great Councils, made use of Greek or Latin.

In the second place, students today are overburdened with subjects. Since patristics is a difficult subject, it should be taught seriously or not at all. It has to be assimilated personally; presenting the Fathers only through lectures entails confusing science with erudition. In such a case, it would be better if patristics was omitted.

On the other hand, obstacles arise from the professors of theology.

First of all, it should be said that patristic theology—the matter in question here—is not to be confused with patrology. The latter may or may not be included in Church history, but it can never be a part of dogmatic theology. As a discipline dependent on Church history, patrology will have the scope and importance that the time dedicated to history concedes to it.

Here are some of the difficulties that the theology of the Fathers confront:

(a) The teacher of dogma, besides mastering biblical theology, must also teach patristics. At the present time, it is an apparently unrealizable luxury to distinguish the biblical from the patristic and the systematic theologian. Thus, the number of dogmatic disciplines keeps increasing at the expense of the time the students should dedicate to other disciplines: biblical, patristic, and systematic. The result is that professors are unable properly to teach the students all three of them.

Reduced to its viable dimensions, the difficulty lies in the teacher. Where, at present, can one find a professor who has mastered these three disciplines? The name of Juan de Maldonado comes to mind, or that of Francis of Toledo, professor of philosophy and scholastic theology, exegete of John, Paul, and Luke.

The present excessive specialization of professors does not allow students to receive a global formation; it results in erudition, that is, superficial knowledge that cannot form the students in a sound fashion.

Does this mean that at the present time the theologian with broad experience in exegesis, patristics, and systematics is obsolete? Obviously; this question is not pertinent today. No professor can master the three fields in an eminent and advanced degree. It would even be unusual if a professor could master both biblical and systematic theology. Because of the complexity of the biblical and systematic disciplines, patristics is very often sacrificed quite easily on grounds of realism. Interested only in making an elementary effort at bibliographical erudition, the *dii majores* are preoccupied with the questions in fashion. Why should the present need for biblical and speculative insights be sacrificed in favor of the study of the Fathers?

It does not seem that professors of dogma are opposed *in theory* to patristics; in fact, many of them would like to master all three of the previously mentioned disciplines. But, *in practice,* they cannot manage to do it. Forced to narrow their vision, they yield to the prevailing atmosphere and leave aside patristics. After presenting an exegesis of Scripture, professors move on to the academic modules determined by topics that can be grasped by the students. Consequently, one could ask whether an unrealizable paragraph like *Optatam totius* 16 does anything more than envision an ideal form of training; or, at the very best, does it officially approve those professors who, by sacrificing as unrealizable a formation based on all three disciplines, decide to train students solely by stressing the Bible and the Fathers, while neglecting speculative theology? In other words, since professors cannot emphasize all three disciplines, they choose two of them *ad libitum*. And if time does not allow for two of them, they content themselves with the one that suits them better.

It would evidently be dangerous to apply restrictions to other disciplines that are not inappropriate when patristics are involved. This fact itself indicates what esteem, even in theory, patristics enjoys is usually kept in the background, to nobody's astonishment.

(b) Can professors of theology, assigned to teach patristics to their students, honestly train themselves in this field as well as in exegesis and systematics? If, *in fact*, they do not usually receive such a training, this perhaps is due: (1) to not having been trained in all three fields, even though such preparation was available; and (2) to the impossibility of simultaneous training in all the fields.

Here one confronts another difficulty: How to train the trainers so that they are competent in the three fields and can afterwards teach them to their students? This question does not so much concern the seminaries as the universities. Supposing that an equal competence in the three fields is not provided to future professors at the present time, one can wonder if an ecclesiastic university will ever be able to give them such a formation. Will it be able to correct the deficiencies of the recent past, and so structure the disciplines that future professors might learn all three once the latter have been given absolute priority over more marginal subjects?

The proposals of *Optatam totius* are intended to help universities to determine the required educational structure that will be adequate to form academics who will have seminarians as students.

A university can form its students in many diverse ways. Yet the most common way is to multiply courses that, although they maintain a strict dogmatic unity, rest on a common denominator more generic now than ever, since the social sciences, psychology, and mass media are ranked among the classical disciplines and enjoy easy access to the sanctuary of theology.

This common practice explains the ambiguity of university formation even in the area of dogmatics. Theological disciplines multiply as a result of the confusion between basic theology and its various application. Such profusion of disciplines does not enhance theology itself. One who in the name of theology wishes to learn practical ways of translating it will eventually master many things, but not know theology.

A syllabus that values fields of application as much as basic classical disciplines does not foster the mission entrusted to the ecclesiastic universities; it deceives not only theological science, but also the Church itself by placing primary value on disciplines that do not even deserve to be considered secondary. There is the serious danger that ecclesiastical universities grant degrees to students who have not been trained in the three basic theological disciplines. It is, therefore, most urgent to give real priority once again to the great disciplines in such a way that this priority is conveyed in facts and not just in words and promises. Rather than leaving the three fields aside or postponing knowledge of them until a future date, academics will then attain skills in biblical, patristic, and speculative theology so that they will be able to give their students a sound formation.

Consequently, it is up to the university:

(a) First, the university is to recruit professors in the three basic disciplines. A few professors are needed in biblical theology and not only in exegesis. An exegete might train other exegetes, but not those competent in understanding the dogmatic relevance of Scripture. Some professors are needed in patristic theology and not merely in patrology. Only a patristic theologian can train others in the theology of the Fathers. The same can be said regarding speculative theology. A student devoted to a methodical study of these three disciplines can manage to synthesize them.

It is all the better if a university has at its disposal specialists in each of the various dogmatic disciplines. Provided they help the students learn the three basic disciplines, the method they employ will provide a sound dogmatic formation.

Do the universities have professors in the three disciplines who are capable of instilling in their students knowledge of their specialty? It is likely that the great majority of the students, even if this is the case, will give up pursuing a balanced formation. But then the fault will lie not with the university, but with the student or with circumstances extraneous to the theological disciplines themselves.

(b) Second, it is the responsibility of the university to apportion, according to their merit, the time to be dedicated to the basic subjects as well as to such concrete issues as examinations and written work.

To avoid excessive *specialization* that prejudices the study of the main subjects, universities should not put various disciplines on equal terms, and thus sacrifice the essential to the secondary.

They should not facilitate the study of superficial subjects by maintaining a clear distinction between what is academic and what is pastoral. They should also make sure that theology does not degenerate either into an easily assimilated history of dogma or into a repetition of the present stress on the literary value of ecclesiastical texts.

Obviously, only a few universities have a sufficient number of professors who have mastered and teach basic disciplines (exegesis, patristics, and systematics). Due to the lack of patristic theologians, there are few who intend to teach principally this discipline. If present circumstances continue, it will be difficult in the future to find professors competent in the Fathers.

But even in that case, emergency measures would not be lacking. There will be always a gulf between the ideal case of providing a solid foundation, and the realistic case of providing some formation.

Within the field of patristics:

1. it is possible to comprehend it only as regular students of a patristic theologian over a period of time,
2. it is possible to master patristics by assiduously reading a great work such as the *Dogmata Theologica* of D. Petau. M.T. Scheeben prepared himself to teach patristics by meticulously reading and studying Father Petavio. Another work worth studying is *Etudes sur la sainte Trinité* by Th. de Régnon. A keen mind is capable of opening itself in indirect ways to the universe of the Fathers. Thus, direct schooling can be replaced by personal reading that can arouse interest in a thorough study of patristics.

Fortunately, even without extant professors who measure up to Petau, dogmatic studies on the Fathers or on heretics are nowadays numerous; if one's reading is well chosen and organized, it can substitute for study of the classical patristic theologians. By following one's elementary interest in dogmatics, by consulting competent professors, by browsing through well-endowed libraries, and by choosing a solid subject for a thesis, one can advance to a profound and lasting appreciation of patristics.

But finding the way is not enough; one has to follow it by working assiduously. By selecting an important theme and by persevering in pursuing it, one can arrive at success: *nemo repente fit summus.*

Mastering the dogmatic teaching of the Fathers in an indirect way opens up broad horizons; however, one must experience the delight and *pathos* of patristics by means of direct exposure.

Even if students cannot find a living master to initiate them into patristics, other paths can be taken. (a) The students can write a dissertation on the theology of the Fathers; they should choose for their *subject* a Father whose doctrine is vigorous, and for their *theme* a major question. A sound method, combined with an excellent author's treatment of a worthwhile subject, leads to a thorough formation in patristics. The dissertation comes first; later, further studies on the same theme can be made, which are based either on the author originally chosen or on another. From the point determined by the dissertation, their knowledge of patristics increases in extent and depth. The more significant and suggestive the fixed point is, the easier the further writings will be and the greater their doctrinal value.

If producing a dissertation frightens students, they may be up to doing a translation, a different way of being initiated into patristics; they should choose a basic work, known for its quality and its breadth, and meticulously translate it into their own language. Innumerable problems of all kinds will emerge at every step; their total solution cannot be found by a reader, however shrewd he or she is, but by the patient translator who, contrary to all expectations, discovers by means of long lost words and allusions, the sole and decisive key to the text.

(b) Or, the students can make a personal synthesis of articles or works on patristics. Theological reviews and bibliographies might be useful. Each person has his certain preference and will often find certain themes appealing and want to study them thoroughly, at least by means of an indirect method. Although the latter is not ideal, it has a certain value. In most cases, only what is feasible produces results, and is all the more commendable because it directs one toward works of greater value. With a little experience and a sense of orientation, the students can avoid reading works (articles, studies, or monographs) of minor importance and concentrate on those associated with well-known names. This implies frequenting the library so as to choose publications, so that what is not absorbed from teachers is gained by habitual reading of the best recent literature.

(c) Another advisable solution lies halfway between writing a dissertation and synthesizing unknown works on the Fathers: selecting a theme from one of the Fathers, seeking advice from an expert, and developing it into an article to be published. The student can thus deepen and widen his or her field of study. Professorial fear feeds on illusions: nothing can be more efficient than to transcend in some way the ever-narrow limits of human knowledge. Whoever does one thing badly, will not find it difficult to do a hundred things worse. One should let oneself go and stop worrying.

If no one thoroughly masters *all* of theology (exegetical, patristic, and speculative), neither does anyone thoroughly master *all* of patristics. But one can still master the three disciplines to some modest extent; the formation of priests requires nothing more. Moreover, mastering the appropriate method of a discipline is sufficient. It will be enough if the method appropriate to each of the three disciplines is applied to teaching dogma. By teaching, one becomes a teacher. The formation of the students will profit from the subtlety that the professor has instilled in them by the very methods he has used to comprehend the Scriptures and the Fathers.

To be a perfect professor of dogmatics, one neither has to be acquainted with all branches of dogmatic theology, nor even to know one thoroughly. One need only approach the three basic disciplines with a sound method; a professorial formation *in fieri* will result in the similar ongoing formation of the students.

Given the reality of human limits, there is only one way by which to progress in patristics: the sacrifice of breadth for depth, so that one enters into a narrow field.

Reflections and Endeavors To Find a Solution

As is the case with any science, the more one progresses in theology, the more one grasps its unity and appreciates the simplicity of its first principles. Therefore, now at the end of this essay, one can understand what in the beginning could not be understood. Such an understanding would be aided by the following few remarks:

1. One should not undertake the reading and study of the Fathers in their entirety. If one has time to go deeper into

patristics, one should first choose those few Fathers who, from the dogmatic point of view, are highly esteemed. While all acknowledge the merit of studying St. Ambrose, the writings of St. Hilary, though more difficult, are always instructive regarding dogma. Whoever is well acquainted with the bishop of Poitiers will have made much progress in patristics, much more indeed than if he had broadened the scope of his study to all the other Fathers of the western Church (apart from St. Augustine). One who assiduously reads a single great author and eventually assimilates his *forma mentis,* draws the most fruit from the study of patristics. Such a person will have comprehended not only one Father, but also the dogmatic horizon stretching behind him. He will have clarified the main principles of his thought, and grasped many of the connections between the earlier study of patristics and the contemporary one. Thus, he will understand that patristics is still being created. It is a discipline that is *in fieri.*

2. As far as possible, do not enter too hastily into a Father's writings. One cannot accept his thoughts without prejudice or comprehend his vocabulary, his questions, and his exegesis, until one grasps his *forma mentis,* his way of reasoning. This depth is not possible if many Fathers are studied at once or if one advances too quickly. No matter how much time is dedicated to them, the Fathers always yield more benefit than expected; they have a living sense of dogma, and the greatest among them possess a modernity that surpasses in quality and depth many other readings. One must resonate with one Father, acquaint oneself with his theology, and assimilate his formulas; only in this way can one explain him to the students. This process will avoid the risk of teaching a dead theology, which was kept in the archives among the dead, and in the name of erudition is offered to modern students. In general, whoever studies the great Fathers of the Church and does not manage to discover perennial themes in his writings, can assume that he did not understand them. In this case, he will find it hard to highlight their true value and to present their message as one that applies to all times.

3. One should not presume that all the Fathers present the same theological message, or that studying them is equally easy. Their categories differ very much from ours. The introductions found in modern editions are of great help, since they spare us difficulties of all kinds. If the ordinary student of theology, for lack of time, cannot directly pursue a substantial patristic theme,

it would be advisable to teach him—by means of a seminar or a short thesis—how to read attentively some major text of the early Fathers. Usually, the more ancient they are, the more difficult and rich in every respect is their message. As the themes they debated become clearer and the number of authors involved increases, their writings become more impersonal and degenerate into literary tracts that they exchange among themselves. In the earlier centuries, however, this phenomenon is less frequent. Hence, there is a striking freshness in the works of the apostolic Fathers: St. Justin, Theophilus of Antioch, St. Irenaeus, Tertullian, Hippolytus, and Origen.

On these grounds alone, it would not be advisable to recommend to a student who is ready to initiate the study of patristics an author who from the point of view of dogma is second rate, has little personality, or simply collected the teachings of the other Fathers. Nor should he be advised to study an ancient Father like St. Clement of Alexandria, whose doctrine is original, but weak in dogmatic content.

Salvo meliori judicio, only a few Fathers of the eastern and western Churches deserve to be studied *today* because their dogmatic tracts can provide a sense of vigor to present-day theology. Although many of the Fathers testify to the great truths of revelation and proclaim them in an admirable *pastoral* manner, they are commendable *with regard to dogma,* and would therefore take up valuable time, to the detriment of the student's formation.

4. One should not become distracted by an extended study of patrology, a field that is praiseworthy in itself, but irrelevant to theological formation. Neither grammar nor philology, neither history of culture nor literature are dogmatic topics. Scholarly critics still take interest in the Fathers. But since there is a decadence of dogmatic studies and an increase in other merely literary approaches, it is time for a change of course. In this respect, St. Augustine is a noteworthy example. Previous scholars were interested in the bishop of Hippo as the doctor of grace, the Trinity, and the Church. Nowadays, critical studies are interested in his life, his literary formation, his religious psychology, or his labor as a pastor of the African Church. The great number of his works may indeed invite many monographical literary studies. But one should not hesitate to deal, once again, with the theme of grace, for example, by using new refined methods that are scrupulously genetic. One could compare this theme with the

parallel themes of Pelagius, in order at the same time to trace the trajectory of Augustine's thought, before and after Pelagius, and in relation to the Pelagius he was acquainted with. Who will dare to dedicate his life to such a project? Not even a specialist. Even less the professor of dogmatics who is already engaged in other questions.

Outlined above is a solution, a very relative solution: to work on monographs of augustinian dogmatics. Not to be satisfied with an indirect knowledge. To renounce superficial erudition for the sake of serious study of the great minds of yesterday.

5. One should not be astonished to note that with time the frontiers of patristics are changing. A contemporary reader of the *Dogmata Theologica* of D. Petau has the impression: (a) that former patristic scholars were interested in a host of themes, mainly because they were very sensitive to the fine points of dogma; (b) that many subjects, which were then of interest, are not interesting any longer, and that conversely, there is now interest in themes that were once ignored.

The themes studied and the themes ignored, although in various ways, have an influence on dogmatic theology. Some are major, others are minor; some are perennial, others passing. One should follow one's instinct, amid such a flood of works, so as to isolate themes that are simply in vogue, leave them aside, or give them only the importance they deserve.

One has to be quite optimistic to believe that the progress of human technology and the normal development of the sciences can assure perspectives on the truth, and lead beyond the ephemeral. Today, just as in the past, trends of thought connected to problems that are psychological in origin and geographically limited vanish just as quickly they appeared. Within a few years, ideologies and personalities are passed by.

To avoid following trends, theologians must first of all conjoin biblical theology and patristics without confusing them; they must stress the study of positive sources by making use of criteria that are also positive in nature. Because the Fathers are important especially as exegetes of the two Testaments, scholars will avoid passing trends all the better if they link patristics with knowledge of the revealed sources.

The *positive* value of the Fathers as intepreters of revelation consists of their testifying to a *positive*, apostolic, and verifiable tradition in the Churches, in opposition to the unwarranted traditions that heretics freely propagated. The *positive* criteria of this tradition were not based on the personal knowledge of the Fathers, whether they be Irenaeus, Hilary, or Augustine, but on the ecclesial tradition that they represented.

Naturally, just as the heretics put forward *their* positive traditions so as to interpret the sources, the Fathers could *think* they were guardians of a positive tradition, without at all possessing it. At this point, the *holiness* of the Fathers must be brought to mind as a decisive factor and a supplementary criteria. Their virtue as instruments docile to the Holy Spirit guarantees the truth of their testimony. This same Spirit, which inspired the sources of revelation, granted the Fathers, both officially as pastors of the Church, and individually as *holy* pastors, the dogmatic instinct that protected them from qualified errors and doctrinal deviations. Deviations are easier found in the thought of a man who is spiritually inattentive than in that of one who is united to God.

Even nowadays, *caeteris paribus*, a holy theologian in close union with God, as St. Bonaventure or St. Thomas were, better testifies to the truth. In contrast, the theologian who pays more attention to men than to God is more in danger of wandering from the great themes of theology, so as to follow ephemeral trends of thought. The Spirit of God cleanses the eyes of the mind so that it can see the treasures of God. As this was the case in the era of the Fathers and in the Middle Ages, so it is now. If theology has always been drawn to tangential themes at the expense of the substantial ones, patristic scholars at present must stand with the Fathers, and by human and divine means (with a clear body and mind [cf. Irenaeus, *Epideixis* 1–21]), not let themselves be distracted by other factors.

6. One should not to expect too much on the short term from studying patristic theology. The Fathers were at times wrongly quoted by scholars who *a priori* lent them no credibility, so as to provide an argument as naïve as this one: *Omnes Patres uno ore consentiunt.* This is the best way to discredit and neglect them with impunity.

For each of the dogmatic tracts, it would be beneficial to quote them, by making a synthesis similar to a proof from Scripture. Ideal, but unfeasible. There is a middle course between a facile and simple and a personal and complete presentation. There are many ways to acquire information from the Fathers concerning various dogmatic topics. When it is impossible to do otherwise, this information will be sufficient to construct a proof drawn from the Fathers. But, with good intentions, one can do more.

Just as there is no patristic theologian who can cover his whole field, each of the Fathers mastered only some basic doctrines. Most of the time, it is enough to know their particular opinion, without wasting energy in trying to cover a vaster field. Major theological questions are usually linked together by the Fathers. Once one has gone deeper into a serious issue, a point of reference is had so as to give a firm opinion on other questions by means of some supplementary study. What one did not manage to grasp clearly with the means at one's disposal will be achieved with time, after consulting additional bibliography. Assiduous reading of the great patristic theologians (monographs and classical works) can spare one much research. While not leaving aside the Fathers themselves, their works will offer resistance to a first reading, a second, and a third one, but a little less to a fourth; and they will yield elements adequate to prove ideas which until then kept running through one's head, but are now laid down in a simple text.

7. One should not confuse the patristic theologian with one who does research on the Fathers. Normally, it is up to the researcher to look for new treasures—either to publish unpublished texts, notes, or aspects until then unknown, or to find the clue to old riddles—and thus to widen the field of knowledge in various directions. In general, the researcher is looking for new discoveries.

The patristic theologian's task is to be acquainted with the doctrines of the Fathers, whether they are new or not, and to make them accessible to students. The field of his study is boundless. And to widen his view of dogmatics, he has no need of new doctrines to be added to those already known. It is more important to go deeper into them, to establish connections, and to throw light on them through insights until then ignored and through new relationships among concepts. A theologian masters patristics better if he has a talent for linking the dogmas of the Fathers: he does not content himself with multiplying insights or bringing up new problems: on the contrary, he discovers points of comparison in order to illumine in a clearer and simpler way problems already considered. He offers a synthesis of themes in which no single positive aspect is sacrificed; he unifies what is complex; he goes back to the point where the dispersion of themes took place, and explains them as they were before being dispersed.

The patristic theologian should reach this point, since all major dogmatic questions have common origins. And whoever locates them at their source will understand them *in fieri* as vital conjectures. Such a work does not require many tools, but a vast knowledge of literature. First and foremost, it requires much reflection on the key texts, and much insight so as to perceive the connection between one aspect and another, one testimony and another, one truth and another; between the anthropological and the strictly theological; and between the soteriological and the psychological. These subtle distinctions are understandable to neither the philologist nor the historian of dogmas, but to the theologian equally experienced in exegesis and speculation.

These remarks should encourage those professors who do not have at their disposal a large collection of books and who feel frustrated when confronted by the vast works of the Fathers. Many times, even those who are surrounded by specialists in the Fathers, and who consult all the monographs and articles on the subject, are able to publish books that in many respects are complete but still remain insensitive to dogmatic themes. This is one of the many modern paradoxes. Specialists in patrology, especially theologians, remain insensitive to the major themes of theology, to which any seminary teacher is more sensitive.

Thus, a field of great value opens up before the modest teacher of dogma. By reading a good edition of the Fathers, he will be able to discover a horizon of far greater beauty than that perceived by many specialists; he will be able to study it personally and expound it to his students. He must not let himself be led astray by the common temptation to be content with easy erudition. By allowing himself to go deeper into his subject matter, he will comprehend the real questions. A well-chosen Father of the Church will make his task far simpler.

Translated from the Spanish by Louis-Bertrand Raymond.

CHAPTER 56

Absence and Presence
of Fundamental Theology
at Vatican II

René Latourelle, S.J.

Summary

On the basis of the texts that have inspired the reform of ecclesiastical studies, the essay observes that the Council completely ignored fundamental theology as a distinct discipline—an omission that has had disastrous effects on the formation of pastors and faithful alike. It was not until 1976—in other words, eleven years after the Decree *Optatam totius*—that the Congregation for Catholic Education published a document that spoke of fundamental theology and its specific task. And its official status was eventually recognized by the Constitution *Sapientia Christiana*. Fortunately, fundamental theology found riches in the conciliar texts in the form of attitudes and content, and has been able to draw a great deal of benefit from these.

According to the *Normae quaedam*, it was in response to the conciliar Declaration on Christian Education of 28 October 1965 (GE 11) that the Congregation for Catholic Education proposed a certain number of guidelines[1] aimed at setting in motion the process of revision that had been called for. The Declaration had stated:

The Church anticipates great benefits from the activities of the faculties of the sacred sciences. . . . Therefore the ecclesiastical faculties, having made such revision of their own statutes as seems opportune, should do all in their power to promote the sacred sciences and related branches of learning, and by the employment of modern methods and aids they should train their students for higher research.[2]

On the same day, the Decree *Optatam totius* stated the great importance of the formation of priests, and gave some fundamental principles for such formation (*OT* Introduction).

And the impetus provided by the Council in fact gave rise to a spectacular renewal, which has affected both the quality and the length of ecclesiastical studies. In the thought of the Council and of the *Normae quaedam*, faculties of ecclesiastical studies must show a scientific stringency comparable to that of the best civil faculties.[3] The Decree *Optatam totius* lists, and thereby recognizes, the following among theological disciplines: Holy Scripture, dogmatic theology, patristics, liturgy, moral theology, canon law, Church history, study of the separated churches, and that of other religions (*OT* 16). In the wake of this Decree, certain disciplines experienced a fresh upsurge of vitality, and, in some cases, an unexpected popularity.

Paradoxically, however, a Decree that sets out to confirm laws tested by age-long experience, and to introduce new elements in response to the new conditions of our age (*OT* Introduction), makes no reference at all to classical apologetics, nor to fundamental theology, although the latter term was in very wide use at the time of the Council. Whereas the 1931 Apostolic Constitution *Deus scientiarum Dominus* (art. 27) presented fundamental theology as the first of the theological disciplines, the conciliar Decree simply ignores it altogether. This omission bears a heavy responsibility, coming as it did in the midst of an ecclesial crisis that was concerned with the very problems of fundamental theology. It is true that the conciliar documents do contain some extraordinarily rich texts from which fundamental theology has been able to benefit, but these fragments were not able to replace the structure that needed restoring and not demolishing.

If fundamental theology was not crushed by this blow, but on the contrary renewed itself with remarkable vitality, this is because of the unremitting labors of a handful who labored again on the task of classical apologetics, returning to the beginning and testing the firmness of each piece of the structure, so as to rebuild what is now known as "fundamental theology."

In the polarity between the absence and the presence of fundamental theology at Vatican II, it must be admitted that the pole of "absence" is decidedly predominant, both with regard to terminology and also with regard to the explicit concerns of the conciliar documents. The balance was happily reestablished, although only slowly, in the period between the Council and the promulgation of *Sapientia Christiana.*

The *Normae quaedam* (No. 26) state that the reform of ecclesiastical studies called for by the Church draws its inspiration from a certain number of conciliar texts, which are then listed. We shall use these texts as the framework for showing the absence of fundamental theology as a theological discipline in the conciliar documents. Our analysis will follow the chronological order of appearance of the documents in question, except that we shall use the Declaration *Gravissimum Educationis* as an introduction.

The Disappearance of Fundamental Theology

The Declaration on Christian Education

We have already cited a passage from this Declaration in which the Council Fathers call for a revision of the constitutions and methods of ecclesiastical faculties (GE 11), and we shall now reproduce the paragraph in which they give the reasons for this request, saying that it is to the faculties of the sacred sciences that the Church

> . . . confides the very grave responsibility of preparing her own students, not only for the priestly ministry, but especially either for teaching in the institutes of higher ecclesiastical study, or for the advancement of learning by their own investigations, or finally by undertaking the even more exacting duties of the intellectual apostolate. It is the function also of these faculties to promote research in the different fields of sacred learning. Their object will be to ensure that an ever-growing understanding of sacred revelation be achieved, that the inheritance of Christian wisdom handed down by former

generations be more fully appreciated, that dialogue with our separated brethren and with non-Christians be promoted, and that questions arising from the development of thought be duly solved (GE 11).

It appears clear that the text looks to the reform of studies for an increased understanding of already existing disciplines and not the abandonment of an important discipline such as fundamental theology. The Decree *Optatam totius* seems not to have seen it as making such a call. On the other hand, *Gravissimum Educationis* only pointed out one aspect of fundamental theology: that of a boundary discipline in dialogue with other Christian churches and other religions. It says nothing about its special task within Christianity itself as a service to believers—in other words, as reflection on the facts of God's intervention within human history, in Jesus Christ and through Jesus Christ, the Son of the Father.

The Constitution on the Sacred Liturgy (4 December 1963)

This Constitution recommends that teaching of the liturgy should be "ranked among the compulsory and major courses in seminaries and religious houses of studies. In theological faculties it is to rank among the principal courses" (SC 16), and this recommendation was repeated by the Decree on the Training of Priests (OT 16).

The Decree on the Means of Social Communication (4 December 1963)

On the same date as *Sacrosanctum concilium*, the Decree *Inter mirifica* shows the sensitivity of the Church to problems of communications. Although the document is short and relatively superficial, it does express the wonder of the universal Church in the face of new communication techniques and the possibility of applying these in the service of evangelization. In our opinion, the "wish to communicate with the men and women of our time is expressed much more decisively in the work of the Council as a whole than in the Decree *Inter mirifica*. It was then vigorously confirmed by Paul VI in *Ecclesiam suam* in 1964, considered in greater depth in *Communio et progressio* in 1971, and revealed its full development in *Evangelii nuntiandi* in 1976. Communication is now seen as a dimension of the Christian faith and as a specific feature of the mission of the Church.

Be that as it may, at the time of the Council, in 1963, the Decree on the Means of Social Communication, *Inter mirifica,* states that "priests, religious and laity should be trained at once to meet the needs described above. They should acquire the competence needed to use these media for the apostolate" (*IM* 15).

The Decree on Ecumenism (21 November 1964)

The Decree on Ecumenism, *Unitatis redintegratio,* observes that theology should not be explained in polemical terms, a rule that applies especially to questions concerning relations with our separated brethren. And it must be admitted that such attitudes have contributed to the discrediting of a certain type of apologetics of the past, which was both aggressive and belligerent, as if the Catholic Church bore no share of the responsibility for the tragedy of the Reformation (*UR* 7 and 8). All the other theological disciplines must be taught in an ecumenical spirit (*UR* 10).

The Decree on the Training of Priests (28 October 1965)

The conciliar document with the most direct bearing on theological studies is *Optatam totius Ecclesiae renovationem,*[4] a Decree apparently without any history, since volume 68 of the Unam Sanctam Series, edited by J. Frisque and Y.M.-J. Congar, devotes only three pages to the history of the document, and when it was voted on, it received 2,318 *Placet* as against 3 *Non placet*— a general judgment that it deserved, although the text does give rise to some important reservations.

Its positive aspects are numerous. The training of priests is centered on the mystery of salvation, and on Christ, who is the center of this mystery. If we want to understand the document, we must read it within the conciliar context of presence in the world. We must also bear in mind the specific theological approach adopted by the Council in its treatment of the questions that are the object of the Constitutions on revelation, the Church, the liturgy, and the Church within the world. This approach is based on Scripture, and its constant concern is to show the impact of each mystery on the spiritual and pastoral life of the Christian people, and an openness to dialogue with the world and the various religious families, both Christian and otherwise.

A theology that is thus centered on the history of salvation is called to renew itself at its source and in its extensions: at its source, through a theology that is biblical, patristic, and liturgical; and in its extensions through a theology that is pastoral and spiritual. We would emphasize, further, that in this history of salvation the object of the divine call is man, for it is man who is both challenged and saved.

In terms of philosophy, the Decree declined to present St. Thomas as the sole and universal master, preferring a more general expression, although it does indicate him later as guide to theological reflection, recommending philosophy students to acquire "a solid and consistent knowledge of man, the world and God. The students should rely on that philosophical patrimony which is forever valid" (OT 15). The reasons for this caution are, in the first place, the notion of philosophical research itself, which proceeds not through authority but through the study of actual facts, and, secondly, the diversity of the cultural circumstances in which students live. The ever-valid and enduring heritage referred to undoubtedly includes the philosophical principles of St. Thomas, even if he is not specifically named, for he remains a master and an example for all because of his creative activity, his intellectual vigor, his willingness to compare faith and reason, the fruitfulness of his intuition, the power of his systematization, and the blending in him of knowledge of God and life in God.

Theological studies are described in number 16. In a statement of principle, the Decree declares that theological disciplines should be taught in the light of faith and under the guidance of the magisterium, in such a way that students can draw pure Catholic teaching from divine revelation, entering deeply into its meaning, making it the nourishment of their spiritual life, and learning to "proclaim, explain, and *defend* it in their priestly ministry."[5]

The Latin word *tueri* (preserve, protect, defend) indicates a traditional function of classical apologetics, but neglects its main function, which is that of reflecting on the mystery of God's intervention in history and on the signs of this intervention.

The Decree then lists and briefly presents the main theological disciplines; Holy Scripture, dogmatic theology, moral theology, canon law, Church history, liturgy, study of the different Christian churches, and study of other religions. The only disciplines graced with any methodological details are Holy Scripture, dogmatic theology and moral theology, and dogmatic theology is treated especially favorably. We have read (in the *Acta Synodalia*) the written interventions of various bishops and conferences of bishops on the point dealt with here: frequent mention is made of Holy Scripture, the liturgy, pastoral theology, and spiritual theology, but fundamental theology is completely ignored. Despite its very decided effect on pastoral life, this discipline had apparently not yet appeared in the field of awareness of the Council of Fathers.

The Decree indicates five steps that should be followed in the teaching of dogmatic theology (*OT* 16): (a) in the first place, there is the presentation of biblical themes; (b) the contribution of the Fathers of the eastern and western churches to the faithful transmission and elucidation of each of the revealed truths will also be shown; (c) students will then make an effort to enter more deeply into the mysteries of salvation and perceive their interconnection; this work will be carried out under the guidance of St. Thomas; (d) students will be taught to recognize the mysteries that are always present and active in the liturgical actions and whole life of the Church; and (e) students must learn to seek the solution to human problems in the light of revelation, to apply its eternal truths to the changing conditions of human affairs, and to express them in language that our contemporaries will understand.

One of the positive aspects of this presentation is the important position attributed to the sources of theological reflection: scripture, tradition, liturgy. It is not a question of *proving* theses, but rather of grasping, savoring, and learning more about the depths of revealed mystery, for this mystery is not so much shadow as overabundance of light.

We can only applaud this renewal of perspectives that works to the benefit of scripture, dogmatic theology, moral theology, canon law, liturgy, and Church history. However, we must deplore the silence in which fundamental theology is shrouded. It is difficult to avoid the impression that to a large extent this Decree reflects the view of dogmatics specialists. Moreover, the composition of the first group[6] of the Theological Commission in 1969 speaks volumes on the influence of dogmatic theologians at the time of the Council: dogmatic theology is omnipresent, exegesis is decidedly secondary, and fundamental theology is almost completely ignored.

The Constitution on Divine Revelation (18 November 1965)

The richest contribution of the Council to fundamental theology comes from the Constitution *Dei Verbum* on the nature and object of revelation, on Christ, the mediator and fullness of revelation, on Scripture and Tradition, and on their relationship to the magisterium (*DV* 2–10). In number 19, the Constitution unequivocally states the historical nature of the gospels, although it follows the Instruction of the Biblical Commission (1964)[7] and distinguishes three levels or stages in their history: Jesus, the apostles, and the evangelists. And all these subjects are of major importance for fundamental theology.

As regards theology, the Constitution states that it

. . . relies on the written Word of God, taken together with sacred Tradition, as on a permanent foundation. . . . For the sacred Scriptures contain the word of God and, since they are inspired, really are the word of God; and so the study of the sacred page is, as it were, the soul of sacred theology.[8]

The contribution of *Dei Verbum* is so great that we shall return to it in connection with the presence, if only implicit, of fundamental theology at the Council.

The Decree on the Missionary Activity of the Church (7 December 1965)

The Decree *Ad gentes* contains some paragraphs that concern theology, and indirectly fundamental theology. Thus, it states that spiritual life and doctrinal and pastoral formation should be closely blended in the training of local clergy, and that the mystery of salvation should be studied as it is set forth in the Scriptures and as it is found in the liturgy (AG 16).

At a later point (AG 26), the Decree emphasizes that missionaries must above all receive a solid training in Scripture, in catechesis in order to learn to present the revealed mystery, and in the history of religions in order to have access to the spirits and hearts of the peoples to be evangelized. Moreover, it adds, a certain number of missionaries "should be more thoroughly prepared in missiological institutes, and other faculties and universities" (AG 26). Lastly, it states that professors in seminaries and universities must "instruct the young as to the true condition of the world and the Church, so that the need for a more intense evangelization of non-Christians will be clear to them and feed their zeal" (AG 39).

The Pastoral Constitution on the Church in the Modern World (7 December 1965)

Gaudium et spes is a document of considerable originality. For the first time, and in a text that is the longest in the whole history of Church Councils, the Constitution calls on the Church to awaken to the deep changes affecting human society, so that it can be present to contemporary men and women "in language intelligible to every generation . . . answer the ever-recurring questions which men ask about the meaning of this present life and of the life to come, and how one is related to the other" (GS 4). The Constitution presents Christ as the only true response to the mystery of man: "In reality it is only in the mystery of the Word made flesh that the mystery of man truly becomes clear" (GS 22). Christ is the key to the human enigma—the key that deciphers, interprets, and transfigures man. In the final analysis, it is Christ alone who reveals man to man. The Constitution thus refers to the most important sign of the credibility of Christianity, in other words, its ability to give a meaning to man and his problems, although it does so in a pastoral context, and without any thought of the mission of fundamental theology.

At a later point, the document refers to another no less essential sign of credibility: the witness of a life in conformity with the gospel. It says that priests should

> . . . build up by their daily behavior and concern an image of the Church capable of impressing men with the power and truth of the Christian message. By their words and example, . . . let them show that the Church with all its gifts is, by its presence alone, an inexhaustible font of all those resources of which the modern world stands in such dire need (GS 43).

Lastly, it devotes a whole chapter (GS 53–62) to the vital relationship between faith and culture. More precisely, it states that "theological research, while it deepens knowledge of revealed truth, should not lose contact with its own times, so that experts in various fields may be led to a deeper knowledge of the faith" (GS 62e). It also says that the theological sciences should constantly "seek out more efficient ways—provided the meaning and understanding of them is safeguarded—of presenting their teaching to modern man: for the deposit and the truths of faith are one thing, the manner of expressing them is quite another" (GS 62a). Pastoral work must contribute in a special way to ensuring this harmony between culture and Christianity.

For our part, we are of the opinion that fundamental theology is the unrivalled locus for this necessary encounter between faith and contemporary culture, for its specific object is the Christian revelation in all its fullness—in other words, as mystery, and also as reality incarnate in human history and language.

The Consequences of Abandonment

One by one, we have examined all the conciliar texts that were used as source or reference in drawing up the *Normae quaedam*. And nowhere have we found even the slightest explicit reference to classical apologetics, or to fundamental theology—a term that was in normal usage well before the Council. After declaring itself the promoter and reformer of ecclesiastical studies, the Council quite simply abolished an age-old discipline, or at least ignored it to all intents and purposes.

The *Normae quaedam*, which were issued on 20 May 1968, are

the faithful reflection of this conciliar operation. Note 12 to number 30 reproduces word for word the list of the theological disciplines found in *Optatam totius* (exegesis, patristics, liturgy, dogmatic theology, moral theology, spiritual theology, pastoral theology), thus in turn omitting fundamental theology. In number 35, which deals with the second cycle, the document speaks of specializations in the biblical, patristic, dogmatic, moral, pastoral, historical, ecumenical, missiological, liturgical, and spiritual fields. Again, there is absolute silence on the subject of fundamental theology, unless it is included in the *etc.* which brings the list to a close! The fact that the mystery of Christ is presented as the unifying center of all the theological disciplines does not change the facts of the problem in any way. We find it impossible to understand how the commission of experts who worked at drafting the *Normae quaedam* could have either unconsciously or deliberately omitted any mention of this discipline.

In the absence of any support from the Council, seminaries and faculties gave in to the temptation to sacrifice a discipline about which the magisterium itself did not seem to care. Some university centers with a long tradition did of course resist this trend, and did not throw fundamental theology overboard. A case in point is the faculty of theology of the Gregorian University, which not only retained fundamental theology in the first cycle, but also—despite the silence of the *Normae quaedam*—created a specialization in fundamental theology, which is flourishing with ever-growing success because it answers an absolute imperative of the Christian faith and offers more than 100 separate lecture courses and 20 seminars spread out over two years.

However, this was not the reaction of many seminaries and faculties. As dean for twelve years, we were able to examine the records of thousands of students from every part of the world. In the majority of cases where we had to remedy study programs, the shortcoming tended to lie in the area of fundamental theology. In some places, it was dismembered and reduced to a number of fragments that were then inserted with varying degrees of success in other disciplines: the historicity of the gospels into exegesis, revelation–tradition–inspiration into the introduction to theology, and so on. The subject of the signs of credibility was simply skipped, or partially treated when occasion arose within exegesis (for example, the subject of the miracles of Jesus). In other places, fundamental theology no longer exists at all, and it is considered that the introductory course to the mystery of Christ is a sufficient substitute. Lastly, there are places where, under the influence of *Dei Verbum*, fundamental theology has been reduced to the study of revelation and its transmission, so that it has lost half its territory, and particularly the whole area of credibility and of its necessary dialogue with other religions and other Christian churches. In short, by splitting up fundamental theology and linking its concerns to other disciplines like the debris of some bankrupt inheritance, fundamental theology has been robbed of its specific task. Furthermore, theology has failed in part of its mission (that of confirming its brethren in the faith) and led to the shipwreck of thousands of believers, who found themselves unarmed in the face of troubling questions that were too difficult to be dealt with without the help of specialists.

How on earth was such a lack of discernment possible, and how could such an aberration take root—and do so despite the warning signals that were flashing on all sides against the gathering tidal wave threatening the whole of the West?

Let us look at the facts. One year prior to the Decree *Optatam totius*, an Instruction of the Biblical Commission on the historical truth of the gospels[9] referred clearly to the school of form criticism and its chief proponent, Bultmann, accusing them of drawing their inspiration from rationalist principles and throwing doubt on the existence of a supernatural order of a revelation properly so-called, and of miracles and prophecies. All these questions concern fundamental theology, but even so *Optatam totius* did not even mention it one year later.

We are in fact convinced that a certain number of Christians—and, indeed, theologians—have absorbed varying doses of Bultmannian poison either directly or indirectly through translations. Lacking sufficient critical sense, they have taken on the empty glitter of an outmoded rationalism. Some of them may also have found in Bultmann the expression of their own skepticism disguised as science. One thing, though, is certain: Bultmann's rationalism and his inaccurate interpretation of the origins of Christianity have accounted for thousands of victims.

Bultmann proposed a simplification of Christianity, which is in fact nothing short of a caricature. His views are well enough known: Jesus is only a man, the last in a list of Old-Testament prophets; there is such a break between kerygma and history that we know practically nothing about the life and personality of

Jesus; if the early Church gave him the titles of Son of God,
Lord, and Savior, this was done for "marketing" reasons, in other
words, so that he could compete with the Greek divinities; when
the New Testament speaks of the miracles and resurrection of
Jesus, it is using the language of myth, under the influence of
hellenism and gnosticism, since the modern scientific mentality
cannot accept the idea of miracle—or that of the resurrection of
the dead; lastly, Jesus is certainly not the Savior of humanity in
the Catholic meaning of the term, but simply the historical locus
chosen by God to tell men of their salvation through faith. All
this is perfectly logical, its only fault being that it is no longer
Christianity. [10]

While Bultmann was carrying out his work of demolition, the
Council was silent over fundamental theology—the discipline
that could have countered it on several major fronts. The question of the identity of Jesus and the historical signs that substanti-
ate his claim as the Son of the Father is at the very heart of
Christianity. In this respect, we would very happily have seen a
Constitution as short and condensed as Dei Verbum, but on
Christ and the problems of christology, added to the three documents on the Church (Lumen gentium, Gaudium et spes, and Ad
gentes), since Christ was just as much in need of rehabilitation as
the Church was.

Theology cannot escape the need to reflect on the relationship
between faith and history, and on the unity of the glorified
Christ and Jesus of Nazareth. The Christian faith presumes a link
of continuity between the phenomenon of Jesus and the interpretation of this phenomenon by the early Church, for it is in the
earthly life of Jesus, and in his death and resurrection, that God
manifested himself, and this is what provides the foundation of
the Christian interpretation of this life as the only authentic one.
If the apostles were able to confess Jesus as Christ and Lord, he
must have performed actions, and assumed behavior, attitudes,
and language that allowed such an interpretation. If such a justification is not undertaken on the basis of the gospels, Christianity
crumbles in the first of its claims, and does not come from Christ,
Son of God, God-with-us.

Remaining within the context of fundamental theology, let us
linger a moment over this real conspiracy against the miracles of
Jesus and their historical truth. The ground seems to be shaky
and full of pitfalls even among exegetes and dogmaticians. It is

considered bad form to speak of miracles: it is best not to attribute Jesus with a type of activity that upsets contemporary man, since, as Paul VI observes, "we measure Christ with a human yardstick."[11] As we know, it is now man who tells God which actions he can or cannot perform. In this context, talking about the miracles of Jesus as events that really took place means placing his popularity at risk. And who would want to run such a risk? It is better to follow Bultmann. Similarly, people view the exorcisms carried out by Jesus as a reaction to universal evil, since it is obviously impossible that Jesus could have been attacking a personal and dark power whose kingdom he had come to destroy. His miracles of raising people from the dead are simply cases of reanimation, or amazing examples of the power of religious suggestion.

However, it is indeed miraculous that at the very moment when people are challenging the various actions of power carried out by Jesus that would accredit him as the Son of the Father, we have seen a universal rise and proliferation of religious sects with a great thirst and truly infantile credulity for the marvellous. Surely it would be helpful at this point to study the specific facts of Jesus' miracles as works of salvation, calling us to faith and conversion?

At the end of this sketch of the crisis brought on by the abandonment of fundamental theology as a specific discipline, we would recall a thought voiced by Monsignor Blomjous in February 1967, at a theological meeting held in Rome to plan the synod that was to take place in September. He observed that the Church was being shaken by a "crisis of credibility," and said that many people think that "the Church does not keep its promises, because the hopes raised by the Council and the principles of reform it announced have not yet been implemented."[12]

The problems of fundamental theology, and particularly of christology (for example, the divine identity of Jesus Christ, the relationship between the earthly Jesus and the Christ of faith, the salvific work of Jesus, and the knowledge and awareness of Jesus), have become so acute that they have been the subject of meetings of the International Theological Commission in 1980, 1983, and 1985.[13] Since the Council did not discuss these questions, it is obvious that the texts produced at these meetings could not seriously base themselves on its work.

We would repeat our question: How are we to explain the

silence of the Council and the *Normae quaedam* on apologetics and fundamental theology? We would examine some possible explanations:

1. Should we imagine that the Council was ashamed to refer to a discipline that had been discredited by its long-time aggressive, polemical attitude, and its constant readiness to cross swords with any imaginary or real adversary? This explanation does not hold water, because from 1960 onwards the term "fundamental theology" was universally used (*Deus scientiarum Dominus* itself spoke of fundamental theology as early as 1931) to indicate a discipline that had undergone such drastic plastic surgery that it needed a new passport as identification.[14] Each year since 1964, Jean-Pierre Torrell has produced an excellent survey of fundamental theology in the *Revue thomiste*, and for its part, the review *Concilium* regularly devotes an issue to the problems of fundamental theology. Since 1960, works on fundamental theology have been proliferating at an amazing pace.

Moreover, if we are to talk of an allergy to apologetics or fundamental theology, how should we describe the teaching in many theological centers of a dogmatic theology that has for a long time centered on the proving of "theses," and has been much more concerned over classifying these same theses (*theologice certa, de fide, de fide definita*) than giving them flesh and blood in order to bring them to life so that they can in turn give life to students? And what about the manuals of moral theology that are real arsenals of prescription, proscriptions, prohibitions, and infractions? Christianity would appear to be more a code than a life, more a breaking in and a discipline than an education and a vocation.

It must be admitted that the situation of apologetics was no more serious than that of the other theological disciplines. However, the error of the teachers of fundamental theology was maybe that they were more open in their self-criticism. The truth is that the crisis was as broad as the Church itself. It must of course be said that the attitudes of dialogue, service, conversion of heart, and searching for meaning that were introduced by the Council have cleansed the atmosphere for all the theological sciences. However, while certain disciplines actually benefited from special treatment, fundamental theology did not even get a look in.

2. Should we maybe say that the professors of fundamental

theology did not exist? No; such a statement would be equally unfounded, as can easily be seen from a list of names that represents only a small proportion of the great numbers of those at work: Bini, Boublik, Bouillard, Brinktrine, Bulst, Colombo, Darlap, De Bovis, De Broglie, de Lubac, Dejaifve, Dhanis, Dulles, Dumont, Dunas, Fries, Gaboardi, Geffré, Granat, Guitton, Hładowski, Holstein, Horvath, Javierre, Kern, Klinger, Kolping, Kopeć, Kubiś, Kwiathowski, Lang, Latourelle, Liégé, Locatelli, Marlé, Metz, Monden, Mouroux, Myszkow, O'Collins, Patfoort, Pinard de la Boullaye, Skalicky, Stirnimann, Söhngen, Thils, Torrell, Tromp, Waldenfels, Walgrave, Wicks, and Zedda. These men toiled under difficult conditions in order to renew a discipline that must periodically reexamine itself more than is the case for others (because it is a boundary discipline, with windows that open onto the human sciences), facing new risks and setting off along new paths.

Although the review *Seminarium* has published work on many interesting subjects, it has never thought it necessary to devote an issue to fundamental theology. On the other hand, a group of twenty professors undertook the task of producing and editing a 500-page work on contemporary fundamental theology for the Problemi e Prospettive Series produced by Editrice Queriniana in Brescia, Italy. And, by a happy coincidence, it is the only work in the whole series that now exists in five languages (the English edition is entitled *Problems and Perspectives of Fundamental Theology* and is published by Paulist Press), while the others exist only in the original Italian, or at most in one other language. And who says that there is no interest in fundamental theology?

3. Let us now move on to the real reasons for the silence of the Council and the *Normae quaedam* on the subject of fundamental theology. A first reason is to be sought in the lack of awareness of the problems of fundamental theology among certain dogmatic theologians of that period. By its very nature, fundamental theology is in constant dialogue with the other theological disciplines and with all the human sciences, but we should like to be sure that exegetes and dogmaticians develop in a similarly open world.

4. A second reason is found in the inability of the Church at the time of the Council to face the problems that had arisen in the field of fundamental theology. Then, as is so often the case, instead of admitting this temporary inability and immediately

setting in motion a vast research operation, a policy of silence and omission was preferred. And it was the professors of fundamental theology who had to undertake this vital research, but without any support.

The Rehabilitation of Fundamental Theology

Reality is stronger than any theory, and fundamental theology is concerned with problems that are too serious and too real to be ignored: the historical origins of Christianity; the reality and identity of Jesus; the historical reality of his message and his actions, especially his miracles and his resurrection; and the intention and nature of his plan for the Church as founded by Peter and the apostles. It is possible to hide our heads in the sand for a while like ostriches, but the problems do not go away and are always waiting there at the gates of the city—or the Church. We can refuse to look at them, but we cannot conjure them away. It is obvious that the tone must change, especially in the present climate of ecumenism, but the actual function of fundamental theology always remains the same. Apart from this, the questions it deals with constitute a unified whole, which means that fundamental theology is a separate sector of theology.

This brings us to a brief definition of the *specific character* of this discipline. The question that fundamental theology is alone in treating, that dogmatic theology does not deal with as such, and without which fundamental theology itself would lose its *raison d'être*, is one single block: the *credibility-of-the-revelation-of-God-in-Jesus-Christ*. The identifying feature of fundamental theology is revelation as "believable," although we must immediately state that here the believable, like the "believed," is Jesus Christ, who is both fullness of revelation (revealing and revealed) and sign of this revelation, which he himself is in person, inasmuch as he is the bearer of his own identity. The unifying center of fundamental theology which is thus its identifying element, is this confirmation of Christianity, according to which the overwhelming, unprecedented intervention of God in the person, history, flesh, and language of Jesus Christ is a justifiable assertion and is thus believable and the possible object of a decision of faith. Fundamental theology takes as the essence of its task the question of the credibility of the *whole* of the Christian revelation (with its individual mysteries). The considerations of fundamental theology are not only concerned with "what we believe," but first and foremost with "why we believe" (1 Pet. 3:15). If Jesus stands among us as the Son of the Father, and as the Totally-Other, it must be possible to identify him as such. He must allow us to glimpse something of the glory he possesses as Messiah and Lord. If this is not so, the epiphany of God in Jesus Christ is truly unbelievable, and if the Church is then incapable of saying what its basis is for stating that "Jesus is Lord," it fails in its first claim, and is left in a position where all it can offer is a new gnosis.

From the point of view of the believer, we would say that although faith may be the total trusting of man to God, it is not some uninformed abdication or the bankruptcy of reason driven to fideism and incapable of establishing the rightness of its choice. The person who commits himself to Christ must have valid reasons for doing so—reasons that can be explained in a logical line of thought. The believer can and must be able to "test" the solid nature of the reasons for his commitment. However, a simple believer would usually not be able to describe these reasons in detail, and it is the task of the theologian, as the servant of the Church community, to show that the option of faith has a basis and is reasonable.

When fundamental theology is seen in these terms it is obviously not a discipline that can be offered or omitted, but a necessary task that the Church cannot shirk without betraying its mission both to believers and also to unbelievers who come to it with questions. If theology stopped reflecting on the reality of God's intervention within history in Jesus Christ, and on the option of faith as a reasonable decision, it would be signing its own death sentence.

In all honesty, exegesis and dogmatic theology cannot claim to face this task in all its breadth. Not only are the questions of fundamental theology serious ones, they also require treatment from a special perspective, and with the mentality of someone who by profession stands at the crossroads of history, philosophy, exegesis, and dogmatic theology. If these questions are not dealt with in all their fullness and given satisfactory answers, they encourage doubts and misgivings in the depths of people's consciences, and these can be transformed into crises of faith and even be the cause of total shipwreck.

There are also other questions that concern fundamental theology, but more as a boundary discipline in dialogue with other religions, other Christian churches, other cultures, and the human sciences. Although this outward gaze is necessary, it should not distract fundamental theology from its primordial task, which is that of reflection on the revelation of God in Jesus Christ as a reality that is accessible, meaningful, identifiable, and thus believable. The very heavy emphasis of the Council on ecumenical dialogue and dialogue with other religions, together with its total silence about fundamental theology, blurred the perspectives.

After what we have just said about how essential fundamental theology is as a theological discipline, it is easy to understand that it could not simply disappear, even if *Optatam totius* and the *Normae quaedam* did not mention it.

Indeed, in the period extending from Vatican II in 1965 to *Sapientia Christiana* in 1979, fundamental theology made a slow reappearance, which was followed by its forthright presentation as a separate theological discipline, and then by its consecration as the *principal* discipline in *Sapientia Christiana*. But why should this period of catacomb life have been needed before it could rediscover what had in fact been stated in 1931 in *Deus scientiarum Dominus?*

This slow return to the light of day can be seen in the six documents that we shall now analyze.

The Basic Plan for Priestly Formation (or *Ratio fundamentalis*) (6 January 1970)

In its "Preliminary Remarks," this document[15] is presented as an attempt at a response to the Decree *Optatam totius* in the training of priests. And since the Decree did not mention fundamental theology, we should not expect any revolutionary creativity on the part of a text that was based on the Decree, addressed to episcopal conferences, and left the greatest freedom to the latter in drawing up their local "plans." Even so, as we shall see, fundamental theology does find its first crumb of comfort in the document.

Number 42 of the "General Rules" recommends that at the beginning of the philosophy and theology course, there should be an "introduction to the mystery of Christ and the history of salvation,"[16] and in number 62, the text adds that this introduction to the mystery of Christ should also help to provide a foundation for the personal faith of the students. Note 148d to number 70 emphasizes that philosophy formation must take into account the "daily more overwhelming growth of atheism and the trend towards divorcing faith from religion."

Theology studies, which must last for at least four years (No. 76), must view Holy Scripture as the soul of all theology, hence, the importance of exegesis and a knowledge of its methods, and of an integrated presentation of the whole of Scripture and the principal chapters of the history of salvation (No. 78).

Liturgy must from now on be considered a major discipline (No. 79). Dogmatic theology is described in the terms of *Optatam totius* (OT 16), although it is added that the attempt at plumbing the depths of the mysteries should be carried out with the support of St. Thomas as Master.[17] In short, the sources of theology (Scripture, Tradition, liturgy, history of dogmas) must be studied and reflection carried out under the direction of St. Thomas, in order to penetrate more deeply into the mystery of salvation.

The document then adds a rider that is clearly secondary:

> And although it now needs to be adapted to this ecumenical age and to the circumstances of the day, one should not neglect what was called *Apologetics*, which is concerned with the preparation necessary for the gift of faith and with the rational foundations of a living faith in relation to the sociological conditions which influence the Christian life in a particular way.[18]

Apologetics is referred to as a discipline of the past ("illa tradere quae sub nomine Apologeticae *veniebant*"), although its still relevant value is recognized in paving the way for faith and providing a foundation for the option of faith. The formulation betrays the clear influence of the Decree on Ecumenism, *Unitatis redintegratio*, and the Pastoral Constitution on the Church in the Modern World, *Gaudium et spes*.

The text of *The Basic Plan for Priestly Formation* was drafted in 1970, at a time when the term "fundamental theology" (a broad, all-encompassing, and positive concept) had replaced that of "apologetics" and was experiencing a remarkable renewal, so that the document lags very sadly behind the times. Speaking of the renewal of fundamental theology in the very period between 1960 and 1970, we recently wrote:

> After it had exorcised the ghost of the old apologetics and had dissociated itself from the very name with which it had been linked, the "new style" apologetics experienced the joy of a second spring. . . . All this found concrete expression in the definitive adoption of the name "fundamental theology" as indicative of its new image and new identity.[19]

The *Basic Plan* goes on to speak of moral theology, pastoral theology, Church history, canon law, and also of ecumenism and the history of religions (No. 80), but without realizing that in doing so, it is referring to the task of fundamental theology and its outward gaze.

Basically, in the much broader present context and from our point of view, this document seems disappointing, and more or less a repetition of *Optatam totius*. Even so, it does represent a slight advance for fundamental theology, inasmuch as it refers to a part of the mission of the latter in its mention of the terms "apologetics," "ecumenism," and "history of religions." But it is still far too little!

Letter on the Theological Formation of Future Priests (Rome, 1976)

Eleven years would pass after the promulgation of the Decree *Optatam totius*, and eight years after the *Normae quaedam*, before we would find the term "fundamental theology" used in an official Church document and before we would hear explicit discussion of the task of this discipline in a letter of the Sacred Congregation for Catholic Education. Although this discipline is mentioned in sixth place—that is, last of all, after Scripture, patristics, dogmatic theology, moral theology, and pastoral theology—it does receive two whole pages. This new departure is undoubtedly not unconnected with the presence of two professors of fundamental theology on the committee entrusted with drawing up the document.

The letter[20] rightly observes that today's priests, who are fewer in number, must take on broader tasks and face hitherto un-known problems requiring a more advanced and updated doc-trinal preparation (No. 4). On the other hand, the laity are more critical, better informed by the mass media, and live in a pluralis-tic environment; moreover, there are many lay people who have attended theological schools and faculties. If priests do not want to be left behind, but want to be able to provide answers to very acute problems, they need a vigorous, deep, and finely honed theological knowledge (Nos. 7–8). Now a good number of these problems involve fundamental theology. The questions of the faithful tend to concern the divinity of Christ, the unique fea-tures of Christianity, and the value of the gospels, more than the Trinity and the theological virtues. It has taken a long time for people to bow to the evidence in this matter.

We would add that new facts and situations present theol-ogy—and especially fundamental theology—with new tasks. Thus, we have the ecumenical question, the break between culture and faith, and direct dialogue with human sciences, without the traditional mediation of philosophy (Nos. 11–14). The need to answer such a wide variety of questions has led theology to a process of "atomization" (No. 69) and to a theo-logical pluralism (No. 65) that threatens to transform itself into a pluralism of faith (No. 123). There is, therefore, a strongly felt need for unity, synthesis, and systematization, especially on the level of basic or institutional courses. We are personally of the opinion that the atomization so deeply deplored is in large part due to the abandonment of fundamental theology, since it performed the precise function of ensuring the harmonization of the central truths and peripheral problems of theology by link-ing them all to the essential center of the mystery of Christ, and by showing the type of relationship they have with the mystery of Christ—and this is particularly true when dealing with the question of non-Christian religions and the separated churches.

The text considers fundamental theology in all its breadth, independent of the system according to which the material is spread out over different academic levels (basic degree, license, doctorate). It looks at fundamental theology in its primary and specific mission, as well as in its secondary tasks as a boundary discipline.

(a) Fundamental theology first and foremost studies the fact of the Christian revelation and its transmission in the Church. It studies the primary fact and the primary mystery of Christianity, which is the basic material of all the theological disciplines (No. 107). It is then presented as an introduction to dogmatic theology, and also as a coextensive dimension of all theology insofar as theology must answer the questions raised by students and by the milieu in which they will develop as future pastors (No. 108). Seen from within—that is, from within Christianity—fundamental theology, therefore, has the essential task of reflecting on the reality of Christianity as the work of God revealing himself to us in and through Christ, and on the reality of the Church as willed by Christ to carry on his work in the world (No. 109).

(b) As a boundary discipline, fundamental theology is in dialogue with the other historical religions in order to show the unique quality of Christianity, and also with the various forms of atheism and modern indifference, and with the human sciences that have shaped the mentality of contemporary men and women but also created problems that call on theology and catechesis to find fresh answers (No. 109).

(c) In this new historical context, in which Christianity is challenged by history, language, religions, philosophies, and cultures, fundamental theology can be seen by believer and nonbeliever alike as a logical and valid train of reasoning, illustrating how the mystery of Christ as present in the Church not only illuminates and interprets the human condition, but also raises it up and fulfills it in its relationship with the God of salvation (No. 110).

(d) It must be stressed that fundamental theology is not a simple anthropology, but an introduction to the fullness of the mystery of Christ and thus to theology as sacred science (No. 111). Such reflection is helpful in bringing pastors of souls to maturity, and freeing them from any inferiority complex in the face of the human sciences, so that they can use the latter without becoming slaves to them. It also provides believers with the assurance needed in order to confess their faith courageously (No. 112): "Always be prepared to make a defense to any one who calls you to account for the hope that is in you" (1 Pet. 3:15).

The document concludes that fundamental theology must be considered necessary for theological and pastoral formation, and

that it must, therefore, be given a place in curricula corresponding to its importance.

Despite the fact that it does give due recognition to the rise of
the problems of ecumenism, other religions, and the human
sciences, it is to be regretted that the major subject of credibility
or the historical signs of revelation are not explicitly mentioned
by the document. Even so, we should rejoice over this fresh air,
suddenly blowing in from the open sea and sweeping through
theology like a breath of spring. Fundamental theology, which
was thought to have been abolished, is alive and well. But it
certainly needed a long time to find evidence of this!

European Episcopal Conferences

In 1978 and 1979, the bishops' conferences of France, Germany, and Italy published documents on the theological curriculum for future priests.

(a) The French text has the aim of leading the student
through a spontaneous religious experience to reflected and structured theological knowledge. Without any reference to fundamental theology, the program is divided into three stages: (i) an
introduction to the mystery of Christ, (ii) a course on revelation
based on Dei Verbum, and (iii) a course on faith.[21]

(b) The program of the German Conference of Bishops also
begins with an introductory course, but unlike the French program, it specifically mentions fundamental theology and lays
stress on the objective content of the course rather than its
functional relationship to the student.[22] Fundamental theology is
seen as providing the foundation and legitimation of the option
of faith, on the basis of the facts given by revelation, and with a
view to the contemporary mind-set. As regards content, the
course deals with religion and religions, revelation and faith, the
Church as condition and mediation of faith. Fundamental theology is part of the systematic disciplines.

(c) Although it was published in 1980, in other words, a year
after Sapientia Christiana, the text of the Italian Conference of
Bishops[23] refers principally to the 1976 Letter of the Sacred Congregation for Catholic Education on the Theological Formation
of Future Priests, often literally reproducing it word for word, but
with amazing omissions on the relationships between faith and
reason, and Christianity and other religions.

The Constitution *Sapientia Christiana* (29 April 1979)

Finally, on 29 April 1979, the Apostolic Constitution *Sapientia Christiana*[24] was promulgated, succeeding *Deus scientiarum Dominus*, of 24 May 1931—after a lapse, that is, of about half a century.

As is normal in documents of this type, the Constitution confines itself to principles and orientations, and to the general form of the organization of studies. Its main aim is that of ensuring a deep fidelity from theology, by means of constant reference to the Word of God, great docility to the magisterium but without stifling the freedom of research, and a deep sense of ecclesial responsibility. According to the Constitution, theology can be reduced neither to simple exegesis, nor to simple theological reflection as divorced from its sources and the magisterium, nor again to the simple historical dimension. Theology cannot be some unilateral view, but entails an organic understanding of all the mysteries, as centered on Christ.[25] ". . . care must be exercised that all the disciplines are taught with order, fullness, and with correct method, so that the student receives harmoniously and effectively a solid, organic, and complete basic instruction in theology. . . ."[26]

As in *Deus scientiarum Dominus*, fundamental theology is given pride of place as an obligatory discipline, with stress on the fact that it must take into account the problems of ecumenism and the history of religions.[27] This amounts to a consecration of the existence and status of fundamental theology in its twofold—inward and outward—gaze. However, sixteen years had been needed in order to come full circle and restore fundamental theology to a position that had been forgotten by the Council, especially by the Decree *Optatam totius*, and by the *Normae quaedam*.

The Contribution of Vatican II
to Fundamental Theology

Although study of the conciliar texts may be disappointing from the point of view of terminology and the explicit status attributed to fundamental theology, it would be unfair not to recognize the positive contributions of the Council in the form of inspiration and renewal of perspectives, which have been assimilated by fundamental theology, giving it new life.[28]

The Theme of Revelation

The most important doctrinal contribution obviously came from the Constitution on Divine Revelation, *Dei Verbum*.[29] This dogmatic presentation of revelation in no way makes up for the need for an apologetics of revelation, although it does make good a serious shortcoming in traditional apologetics, which was constructed more or less on the narrow foundations of a quasi-nominal definition of revelation.

The Constitution does not neglect any of the essential aspects of the fact that it is at the heart of fundamental theology—in other words, the free intervention of God in Jesus Christ, this self-manifestation and self-giving of God that gives Christianity its unique character. The Constitution first of all considers the mystery of revelation: nature, object, purpose, economy, mediator. It then goes on to consider revelation in its historical unfolding: the promise and preparation of the Old Testament, then the epiphany of God in Jesus Christ, together with the signs of this epiphany, and lastly, its acceptance by man's faith under the action of the Spirit (*DV* 2–6). It deals with the transmission of revelation by Tradition and inspired Scripture, both of which give life to the people of God, and both of which are interpreted by the magisterium of the Church, which is hearer and also servant of the Word (*DV* 7–13). The Constitution recognizes the importance of literary genres in the interpretation of Scripture. On the other hand, it emphasizes the need for an ecclesial reading of the texts on the basis of solid literary and historical research. It energetically confirms the historical value of the gospels. Lastly, the role of the Evangelists is given its due importance within the overall process of the formation of the gospel tradition (*DV* 19). Of course, not every point is covered, but the Constitution does mark an important step in the history of the Council.

The various points in the Constitution do not all have an equal impact on fundamental theology. We shall note three in particular, because of the deep-reaching changes they have caused.

(a) *The Actual Structure of the Economy of Revelation.* Tra-

ditional apologetics had an invincible tendency to confuse
revelation-as-word with revelation through words. It thus gave
very careful attention to the formal teaching of Jesus, especially
his parables, but attributed only a secondary importance to his
example, his works, and his behavior—a subject intended above
all to nourish piety. If miracles were discussed, for example, this
was done in order to emphasize their witness value in confirming
the mission of Jesus as sent by God, and, therefore, the truth of
his message. Now *Dei Verbum* (Nos. 2 and 4) states that revelation is accomplished through the intimate union of actions and
words, both of which are constitutive elements of revelation.
This *sacramental* structure of revelation (real event and word of
interpretation) represents the most notable revolution introduced by *Dei Verbum*. Theology, and fundamental theology in
particular, has not yet completely assimilated the implications of
this basic principle.

(b) *The Incarnational Principle.* The incarnation of the Son of
God represents the time of fullness, the moment when the rhythm
of history speeds up and is concentrated in the person of the Word
made flesh. The newness is radical and absolute: not only does
God enter into history; he does so by taking on human flesh, with
all the risks and limitations of language, culture, and institution.
Christ does not only bring revelation: he is the Revelation itself,
the epiphany of God in human history. This incarnational principle is expressed in a condensed form in *Dei Verbum* 4:

> . . . he himself [Jesus Christ, the Word made flesh] . . . com-
> pleted and perfected Revelation and confirmed it with divine
> guarantees. He did this by the total fact of his presence and
> self-manifestation. . . . He revealed that God was with us, to
> deliver us from the darkness of sin and death, and to raise us
> up to eternal life.

It follows that revelation and incarnation belong to the same
mystery of the raising up of human nature and expression, and
also that all the dimensions of man are taken up and used to serve
as expression for the absolute Person of the Son.

(c) *The Absolute Centrality of Christ in Revelation and in Faith.*
Since Christ is both God the Revealer and God the Revealed,
the mediator and the fullness of revelation (*DV* 2 and 4), it
follows that he occupies a position within Christianity that distin-

guishes it from all other religions. Christianity is the only religion whose revelation is incarnated in a person who presents himself as the living and absolute truth. Other religions have had founders, but none of these (Buddha, Confucius, Zoroastra, Mohammed) proposed himself to his disciples as object of faith. Believing in Christ means believing in God. Christ is not simply the founder of a religion: he is both immanent within history, and the absolutely transcendent One, the One among millions, the Unique, Totally-Other.

When *Dei Verbum* recalls the unique Christian keynote, it is protecting fundamental theology against the various forms of relativism and syncretism that could contaminate its dialogue with other religions. If Christ is the fullness of revelation, inasmuch as he is God-among-us, it follows that he is himself the sole authentic interpretation of all the forms of salvation preceding, contemporary with, and succeeding his historical coming. The religions of salvation have a positive relationship to Christian revelation, although the quality of their content and the closeness of their relationship must be clarified. Only Christ is the "fullness of religious life" (*NA* 2). Even the Old Testament does not have an absolute and infallible interpretation of its own revelation, since it does not yet know the definitive word, who dissolves its ambiguities, sheds light on its images, and eliminates its shadows. Only Christ makes perfect understanding of the Old Testament—and indeed of all the religious experiences of humanity—possible. Only the gospel of Christ as proclaimed by the Church constitutes an event that interprets itself totally and infallibly, since the principle of interpretation here is God himself in Jesus Christ. The word does not bring light to the non-Christian in the same way as the Christian. The different religions can be seen as rays of this truth that lights every man who comes into this word (*NA* 2). In connection with them, we can speak of an "illumination" or "manifestation" that God makes of himself through the cosmos, through knowledge or in other ways (Rom. 1:19; Jn. 1:9) in order to show the action of the word on humanity. Nothing escapes this clarifying action, which is the source and criterion of all truth.

The Signs of Credibility

For fundamental theology, this absolute centrality of Christ as proclaimed by *Dei Verbum* in turn entails a renewed theology of the signs of credibility. This contribution to the theme of credibility is seen in the Council less in the form of a specific treatment of the signs than in that of a renewal of perspectives, especially in *Dei Verbum*, *Lumen gentium*, *Ad gentes*, and *Gaudium et spes*. As we know, the questions of approach and perspective have a determining value in theology, as in any discipline, arousing interest and attraction, or irrepressible repulsion. In this connection, it would be difficult to exaggerate the importance of the conciliar contribution to the theology of the signs of credibility.

(a) A first observation concerns the highlighting of the actual reality of the signs. The apologetics of previous centuries began by studying the specific signs of revelation, in other words, the miracles and prophecies. This procedure assumed too easily as if it went without saying (or in any case did not mention the fact) that the signs that enable us to identify Jesus are not exterior to him, but flow from Christ as personal center of irradiation. Before speaking of signs, we must, therefore, speak of the first Sign, which includes all the others—in other words, Christ himself.

Unlike Vatican I, which directly proclaimed the divine origin of the Christian message on the basis of the miracles and prophecies, Vatican II adopts the perspective of the person. Just as it personalized revelation, the Council personalizes the presentation of the signs, which are not seen as separate pieces accompanying Christ's message, like a passport or an ambassador's seal on a letter guaranteeing its authenticity. On the contrary, Christ is the Fullness of revelation, and the Sign of the authenticity of his own revelation (*DV* 4). And all the individual signs are simply the multiform rays of this epiphany of the Son among men.[30]

Jesus in Person, in his innermost being, is the Light and the Source of light, and this is why he performs actions, proclaims a message, and brings a hitherto unseen, unimagined, and unexperienced quality of life and love into the world, and also why he makes us consider the question of his real identity. The actions, message, and behavior of Jesus belong to another order, manifesting the presence of the Totally-Other within our world. He who is so close is in reality the transcendent One; he who is one among millions is the unique One; the homeless preacher is the all-powerful One; he who is condemend to death is the Thrice-Holy; he who is crucified is Life. Jesus is among us as the same as us and at the same time as the Totally-Other. This simultaneous twofold presence is a sign and challenge for us. There are signs of weakness in him, but also sufficient signs of glory to help us penetrate the mystery of his true identity. Jesus himself is the Sign that must be deciphered, and all the individual signs point toward him like a converging beam. Any study of the signs must, therefore, begin with a study of Christ as the primary and fundamental Sign, and then move on to the sign that is inseparable from him—in other words, the Church, his Body and his Bride.[31] Let us now move on to the individual signs.

(b) In the first place, we have the miracles. The rare texts of Vatican II that speak of the miracles of Jesus all share the fact that they link them closely to the person of Christ, giving them both a revelatory and a confirmatory function (*DV* 2 and 4). Through their revelatory function, they are the gospel in action, the kingdom in visibility (*LG* 5), rendering the announced salvation visible. "The miracles of Jesus also demonstate that the kingdom has already come on earth" (*LG* 5). Where Christ is found, the power of the salvation of the living God is at work. The Decree *Ad gentes* develops the same theme: ". . . Christ went about all the towns and villages healing every sickness and infirmity, as a sign that the kingdom of God had come" (*AG* 12).[32] And, lastly, the Declaration on Religious Freedom, *Dignitatis humanae*, contributes an important detail that is found nowhere else in the official documents of the magisterium:

> For Christ, who is our master and Lord and at the same time is meek and humble of heart, acted patiently in attracting and inviting his disciples. He supported and confirmed his preaching by miracles to arouse the faith of his hearers and give them assurance, but not to coerce them (*DH* 11).

(c) The sign of the Church, which was proposed by Vatican I "as a great and perpetual motive of credibility," seems to have been eliminated by Vatican II. However, this is certainly not the case. The truth is that the process of personalization that referred all the signs of historical revelation back to the personal center of Christ, worked equally in favor of the sign of the Church[33]: it is Christians themselves, through their lives of holiness, and communities of Christians, through their lives of unity and charity, who actually produce the sign of the Church. It is by perfectly living out their condition as children of the Father, redeemed by Christ and sanctified by the Spirit, that Christians show other people that the salvation proclaimed and bought by Christ is truly among us, for man's disobedient and rebellious heart is transformed into an obedient and filial heart. This concentration and personalization brought about by Vatican II are indicated in the appearance of the new term, "witness." The concept understood by Vatican I as the sign of the Church should now be sought in the category of witness, which is a major theme, reappearing as a sort of leitmotiv, especially in *Lumen gentium* (Nos. 12, 35, 38–42), *Ad gentes* (Nos. 6, 11, 15, 21, 24, 37), *Gaudium et spes* (No. 43), *Presbyterorum ordinis* (No. 3), and *Perfectae caritatis* (No. 25). The words "testimony" and "witness" (both as noun and verb) are found over 100 times in conciliar documents. Because the saints reflect the features of Christ, they are "witnesses to the truth of the Gospel" (*LG* 50).

Martyrs represent the most advanced point on the path of witness, because they are signs of the greatest love. Although it does not mention the new forms of contemporary martyrdom, which are linked to every type of torture, the Council returns time and again to the need and value of this highest witness of the Christian life. Priests (*PO* 3), missionaries (*AG* 24), and lay people (*LG* 42) "must be prepared to confess Christ before men and to follow him along the way of the cross amidst persecutions" (*LG* 42). The Council makes two statements on the value of martyrdom: it is the greatest manifestation of charity, and also an outstanding gift, a sign of love, and a remarkable grace: "Martyrdom makes the disciple like his master, who willingly accepted death for the salvation of the world, and through it he is conformed to him by the shedding of blood. Therefore the Church considers it the highest gift and supreme test of love" (*LG* 42).

The Council's emphasis at this point on the element of witness is made out of fidelity to revelation itself, which was both *docere* and *facere*, so that its transmission through the centuries encompases just as much the living of a certain style of life as the preaching of a message. Communicating the gospel means that the person who "communicates," who proclaims salvation, is also the living witness of a faith that has already illuminated and transformed his life. Otherwise, there is a risk that the gospel will remain an ideology, a system, a gnosis, or an ethics.

(d) The Council hardly mentions the subject of the fulfillment of the Scriptures in Jesus Christ. *Dei Verbum* states briefly that the "New Testament was hidden in the Old, and the Old was made manifest in the New," for although Christ established a new covenant in his blood, the books of the Old Testament, which are fully taken up in the gospel message, attain and show forth their full meaning in the New Testament, to which they in turn bring light and explanation (*DV* 16). It is obvious that despite some excellent studies,[34] this theme of traditional apologetics needs so great a renewal that fundamental theology is for the moment able to offer only suggestions indications and the bare bones of orientations.

(e) A serious criticism of classical apologetics concerned the question of meaning. Having established, on the basis of external arguments, that Jesus was sent by God and founded a Church, classical apologetics drew the conclusion that we must receive from this Church everything that we must believe, thus ignoring—at least in practice—that the Christian message is supremely intelligible, and that in itself this fullness of meaning already constitutes a powerful motive of credibility. Revelation is believable not only because of the exterior signs accompanying it, but also because it reveals man to himself; indeed, it is the only key to understanding the mystery of man. We should, therefore, not try to isolate factual reality from the meaning of revelation. Ancient apologetics did not dare face this question, no doubt in order to avoid encroaching on the sphere reserved to dogmatic theology. However, the obvious result of this was the creation of a break between the fact and the content of revelation.[35]

Jesus is not simply a breaking through of God into human history; his coming reveals man to himself, interpreting and transfiguring him. This is the perspective opened up by *Gaudium et spes*. The Constitution asks the fundamental question, "What is man?" and answers by presenting Christ as the only true response to this mystery. Christ is the key to the human cryptogram, the summing up of all anthropology, the one who gives him his true meaning, for he is the new Man, the new Adam of the new creation and of the new status of humanity (*GS* 22).

The key to the mystery of man is that, in Jesus Christ, God wants to beget each man anew as a son and inspire him, breathing into him his Spirit, who is a filial spirit. Far from being foreign to man, revelation is so deeply bound up with mystery that without it he could not know who he is.[36]

The Council, especially in *Gaudium et spes*, therefore, high-lights a motive of credibility that was too often neglected by classical apologetics: the capacity of Christianity to decipher human problems. Although the Council was definitely not thinking in terms of fundamental theology, the latter can in fact see this perspective, which should also be shared by dogmatic theology in the face of each of the mysteries, as a good belonging firstly to itself. Just as fundamental theology considers revelation in its overall aspect, whereas dogmatic theology studies each of the individual mysteries, fundamental theology considers revelation inasmuch as it throws light on the whole human condition and gives it its underlying meaning. And this is what Pascal, Blondel, Guardini, Teilhard de Chardin, Gabriel Marcel, K. Rahner, M. Zundel, and many others have done.

(f) We shall not repeat here the need for fundamental theology to enter into dialogue with other religions, the separated churches, other philosophies, and the human sciences, for the 1976 Letter of the Sacred Congregation for Catholic Education on the Theological Formation of Future Priests explicitly mentions this dialogue as a task of fundamental theology (No. 110).

However, it does seem important to emphasize the theme of the relationship between faith and culture as developed in *Gaudium et spes* (Nos. 53–62)—a relationship that has even received concrete expression in the creation of the Council for Culture.[37]

Although revelation was born without the thought forms and expressions of a specific time and environment, it must reach men and women of every era. *Gaudium et spes* lays stress on the fact that the Church has the mission of using the resources found in different cultures in order to make the gospel present and find the language suited to each culture. Now if theology is the normal mediation between faith and culture, it seems to us that fundamental theology is the privileged context for this encounter. The deepest changes in contemporary society are found on the level of the human sciences, especially history, philosophy, linguistic sciences, psychology, sociology, and ethnology. Since the object of fundamental theology is the study of the christic revelation as mystery and as reality incarnated within history, culture, and langauge, it seems to us that this particular discipline is the obvious context for this mutual questioning between faith and culture.

Evaluation of a Trial

Twenty-five years after the Council, how are we to evaluate the trial undergone by fundamental theology, with its official disappearance in *Optatam totius* and the *Normae quaedam,* and its subsequent rehabilitation, or at least its tardy reappearance, in the Letter of the Congregation on the Theological Formation of Future Priests and in *Sapientia Christiana?* There is no sense in denying that this long silence was a source of great suffering for professors of fundamental theology.

Even so, apologetics—or what is now fundamental theology—is used to being attacked. Professors of fundamental theology did not wait for the encouragement of the Council before starting on their self-examination and continuing their service of the Church by working for the renewal of their discipline. Apart from this, apologetics had a good deal to answer for: for centuries it had crossed swords with others without giving any quarter, and polemicized in unbending tones. It was in need of conversion. Its two or three decades in the catacombs will have done it good on the whole, for they will have given it the opportunity to reflect on its nature, method, identity, and status.

Fundamental theology has emerged from its trial purified and rejuvenated, more modest, more aware of the complexity of the problems to be dealt with and better equipped to deal with them, and more concerned with the search for meaning and intelligibility than with sledgehammer arguments. Instead of seeing itself in terms of a crusade and opposition, it presents itself in terms of proposition. It has moved from impassioned rhetoric to calm but critical explanation. It is aware that twentieth-century men and women are less interested in refutations than in attention to their problems, together with a serious presentation of the meaning of Christianity for the human condition. And this is the task it must take on, even if there were no adversary as such. As regards its organization in the teaching sphere, it is better structured, more centered on its essential tasks, and more christocentric.

Although it was never even mentioned by the Council, it does recognize that it owes the Council a great deal, in the form of the attitudes the latter developed throughout the Church (dialogue, service, conversion, a renewed search for meaning), and also in the form of perspectives, especially with regard to the subjects of revelation, the absolute centrality of Christ, the personalization of the signs of credibility, and the search for the meaning of man and his problems. It has benefited greatly from these riches, which have helped to make it more attractive, and indeed given it a "new image." Bearing in mind all these good things it has thus received, fundamental theology deliberately adopts an attitude of magnanimity.

Translated from the French by Leslie Wearne.

Notes

1. Sacred Congregation for Catholic Education, *Normae quaedam ad Constitutionem apostolicam "Deus Scientiarum Dominus" de studiis academicis ecclesiasticis recognoscendam* (Rome, 1968).

2. GE 11: "A scientiarum sacrarum Facultatum operositate plurimum exspectat Ecclesia. . . . Quare ecclesiasticae Facultates, propriis ipsarum legibus opportune recognitis, scientias sacras et cum sacris connexas impense promoveant et recentioribus quoque methodis et auxiliis adhibitis, ad altiores investigationes auditores instituant." For the remainder of our article, we shall give the original Latin text only in cases where the literal formulation of the Latin seems necessary for discussion of the texts. In other cases, we shall make use of the recognized official translations.

3. *Normae quaedam*, 44, note 18.

4. With regard to *Optatam totius*, the following may be consulted: AS, vol. III, III/VII, 793–971; III/VIII, 14–44, 171, 222, 228, 234–235, 239–359; IV/IV, 11–134, 171–172, 225–226, 392; III/V, 593–606; J. Frisque and Y.M.-J. Congar (eds.), *Les Prêtres, Décrets "Presbyterorum ordinis," et "Optatam totius,"* Unam Sanctam 68 (Paris, 1968), 187–189; J. Sauvage, "Orientations conciliaires pour la formation des prêtres," *Vocation* (January 1966), 193–223; "Optatam totius Ecclesiae renovationem," *Catholicisme*, 10/44 (1983), 105–106; J. Guyot, "Introduction au Décret sur la formation des prêtres," *Documents conciliaires*, 2 (Paris, 1965), 115–127; A. Wenger, *Vatican II, Chronique de la troisième session* (Paris, 1966), 381–390; R. Laurentin, *Bilan de la troisième session* (Paris, 1965), 235–238; *id.*, *Bilan du Concile* (Paris, 1966), 257–262; R. Latourelle, *Theology: Science of Salvation* (New York, 1969), 114–123, 141–145; L.-B. Gillon, "Le programme des études ecclésiastiques," *Seminarium*, 18 (1966), 327–338; C. Vagaggini, "La teologia dogmatica nell'art. 16 del Decreto sulla formazione sacerdotale," *Seminarium*, 18 (1966), 819–841; G. Colombo, "L'insegnamento della teologia dogmatica alla luce del Concilio Vaticano II," *La Scuola Cattolica*, 95 (1967), 3–33; G. Baldanza, P. Brocardo, *et al.*, *Il Decreto sulla formazione sacerdotale* (Turin, 1967), 441–471.

5. *OT* 16. The original text reads as follows: "Disciplinae theologicae, in lumine fidei, sub Ecclesiae Magisterii ductu, ita tradantur ut alumni doctrinam catholicam ex divina Revelatione accurate hauriant, profunde penetrent, propriae vitae spiritualis reddant alimentum eamque in ministerio sacerdotali annuntiare, exponere atque tueri valeant."

6. *La Documentation catholique,* 66 (1969), 495.

7. Instruction *Sancta Mater Ecclesia,* published by the Biblical Commission, in *AAS,* 56 (1964), 712–718.

8. *DV* 24: "Sacra Theologia in verbo Dei scripto, una cum Sacra Traditione, tamquam in perenni fundamento innititur. . . . Sacrae autem Scripturae verbum Dei continent et, quia inspiratae, vere verbum Dei sunt; ideoque Sacrae Paginae studium sint veluti anima Sacrae Theologiae."

9. In *AAS,* 56 (1964), 713: "Quidam enim hujus methodi fautores praejudicatis opinionibus rationalismi abducti, supernaturalis ordinis existentiam et Dei personalis in mundo interventum, ope revelationis proprie dictae factum, miraculorum et prophetiarum possibilitatem et existentiam agnoscere renuunt."

10. R. Latourelle, *Finding Jesus through the Gospels: History and Hermeneutics* (New York, 1978); *id.*, *The Miracles of Jesus and the Theology of Miracles* (Mahwah, NJ, in press).

11. Audience of 18 December 1968, in *L'Osservatore Romano* (English edition) (26 December 1968), 3.

12. G. Mollard, "Après le Concile," *Esprit,* 35 (1967), 359.

13. International Theological Commission, "Quelques questions touchant la christologie," Part I, *Esprit et vie,* 90 (1980), 609–620; "Théologie, christologie, anthropologie," Part II, *Esprit et vie,* 93 (1983), 2–10; an English translation is in preparation.

14. R. Latourelle, "A New Image of Fundamental Theology," in R. Latourelle and G. O'Collins (eds.), *Problems and Perspectives of Fundamental Theology* (Ramsey, NJ, 1982), 42–58.

15. Sacred Congregation for Catholic Education, "Ratio fundamentalis institutionis sacerdotalis," in *AAS,* 62 (1970), 321–384; English translation, "The Basic Plan for Priestly Formation," in National Conference of Catholic Bishops (ed.), *Norms for Priestly Formation* (Washington, DC, 1982), 17–60.

16. *Ibid.* 42a: "Haec initiatio . . . generatim apte coniugitur cum introductione in mysterium Christi et historiam salutis, quae ineunte curriculo philosophico-theologico iuxta Concilium habenda est."

17. *Ibid.* 79: "Ope speculationis, S. Thoma magistro, mysteria salutis plenius penetrare eorumque nexum perspicere alumni addiscant."

18. *Ibid.* 79: "Nec omittatur, spiritu oecumenico et forma hodiernis circumstantiis accommodata, illa tradere quae sub nomine *Apologeticae* veniabant, et quae praeparationem ad fidem fideique fundationem rationalem et vitalem respiciunt, ratione habita etiam elementorum ordinis sociologici, quae in christianam vitam peculiari modo vim exercent." The second edition of the *Basic Plan*, in 1985, makes no change in the 1970 text, although in note 188, it does mention the 1976 Letter on the Theological Formation of Future Priests, which explicitly mentions fundamental theology.

19. Latourelle, "A New Image of Fundamental Theology," 42.

20. Sacred Congregation for Catholic Education, *La formazione teologica dei futuri sacerdoti* (Rome, 1976): English translation, "The Theological Formation of Future Priests," in NCCB (ed.), *Norms for Priestly Formation*, 63–95.

21. French Episcopal Conference, "La charte des études des séminaires français," *La Documentation catholique*, 8 (1979), 373–389.

22. German Episcopal Conference, *Rahmenordnung für die Priesterbildung* (Bonn, 1978).

23. Italian Episcopal Conference, *La formazione dei presbiteri nella Chiesa italiana* (Rome, 1980).

24. John Paul II, Apostolic Constitution *Sapientiae Christiana* on Ecclesiastical Universities and Faculties, in *AAS*, 71 (1979), 469–499; the text is also found in *Seminarium*, 32 (April and September 1980), 259–297; English translation in NCCB (ed.), *Norms for Priestly Formation*, 227–245; Sacred Congregation for Catholic Education, "Norms of Application for the Correct Implementation of the Constitution," in *ibid.*, 247–261. Several articles on the Constitution appeared in *Seminarium* in 1980, for example: F. Marchisano, "La Legislazione academica ecclesiastica. Dalla Costituzione apostolica *Deus Scientiarum Dominus* alla costituzione apostolica *Sapientia Christiana*," *Seminarium* 32 (1980), 332–352; A. Javierre, "Criterios directivos de la nueva Constitución," *Seminarium*, 32 (1980), 353–371; R. Spiazzi, "L'Università e la Facoltà ecclésiastica nel contesto ecclesiale e culture odierno," *Seminarium*, 32 (1980), 372–411; F. Biffi, "La comunità universitaria, le sue componenti, le sue autorità," *Seminarium*, 32 (1980), 436–487; G. Pelland, "La Faculté de théologie," *Seminarium*, 32 (1980), 505–521.

25. *Sapientiae Christiana* 67b, and "Norms of Application" 50 and 52.

26. "Norms of Application" 52.

27. *Ibid.*, 51b.

28. In this connection, see our article: R. Latourelle, "Das II. Vaticanum. Eine Herausforderung an die Fundamentaltheologie," in E. Klinger and K. Wittstadt (eds.), *Glaube im Prozess. Christsein nach den II. Vatikanum. Für Karl Rahner* (Freiburg im Breisgau, 1984), 597–614.

29. However, it would be an exaggeration to see *Dei Verbum* as a totally new beginning. If we may be forgiven for pointing this out, well before its promulgation, we published a *Theology of Revelation,* which went through twenty-five editions in different languages. And when we published what was chronologically the first commentary on *Dei Verbum*—in *Gregorianum,* 48 (1966), 685–709—we simply inserted it into the second edition of *Theology of Revelation* without having to make any alterations to the body of the work because of some new element contributed by the Council.

30. Latourelle, "A New Image of Fundamental Theology," 49–50.

31. This is why we began our study of the theme of credibility with a work entitled *Christ and the Church, Signs of Salvation* (New York, 1972).

32. See also, Latourelle, *The Miracles of Jesus and the Theology of Miracles* (Mahwah, NJ, in press).

33. Latourelle, *Christ and the Church, Signs of Salvation,* 19–29.

34. In this connection, see especially: P. Grelot, *Sens chrétien de l'Ancient Testament* (Paris, 1962); *id.,* "Relations between the Old and New Testaments in Jesus Christ," in Latourelle and O'Collins (eds.), *Problems and Perspectives of Fundamental Theology,* 186–204,; P.-M. Beaude, *L'accomplissement des Écritures* (Paris, 1980).

35. Latourelle, "A New Image of Fundamental Theology," 39.

36. We attempted to present this in an abridged form in: R. Latourelle, *Man and His Problems in the Light of Jesus Christ* (New York, 1983).

37. *L'Ossservatore Romano* (21–22 May 1982). The 1984 Synod of Bishops also emphasized the importance of the inculturation of Christianity and the Christianization of cultures.

PART X

NEW PROSPECTS

CHAPTER 57

The Bible in Different Cultures
A Study Group Work Report*

FritzLeo Lentzen-Deis, S.J.

Summary

Exegesis is the first step in hermeneutics or in the application of the sacred text to the concrete life of a local church. However, it must take several aspects of culture into consideration. On the basis of *Dei Verbum* and *Gaudium et spes,* and with the assistance of *Inter mirifica,* a group of students from all over the world has examined the progress in methods, and the rules for an intercultural exegesis and for its practical application (starting points, problems, norms, dead ends, positive results, prospects, and reactions).

The Second Vatican Council responded to expectations of the time concerning the Church's concern for culture. The Church must not speak in an abstract, archaic, almost incomprehensible language, but rather, it should speak to all in their context. It must meet them in the principal task of the present time, that of reacting responsibly to their own period and its demands. John XXIII had already expressed this when announcing his decision to convoke the Council, employing memorable words that were so often referred back to during the Council, saying the Church must recognize and take into account "the signs of the times."[1] During

*This essay is also a mark of the author's gratitude to the benefactors and collaborators of the Church aid organizations *Adveniat* and *Missio.*

the Council, this concern was recalled again and again. Serious opposition to an expressed and formal conciliar declaration on culture and the world resulted from the strictly ecclesial and religious character of the Council. By its very nature, it could really only speak directly to Christians within the Church.[2] The difficulty inherent in the question itself was also pointed out. This consisted in the fact that neither the concept nor the implications and consequences of what is generally referred to as "culture" are understood by all in the same sense, nor are they entirely clear.[3] However, the original intention at the convocation of the Council and the eager expectation of many Christians meant that this concern could not be shelved. Specific and powerful stimulus was also to be found within the Church, e.g., the discord between the message of the gospel and its social consequences in a considerable number of countries and in the economic organization of many parts of the world. Thus, Dom Helder Camara, who was at that time the Auxiliary Bishop of Rio de Janeiro and Secretary of the Brazilian Bishops' Conference, worked untiringly toward drafting a conciliar document "on the Church in the world."[4] This drafting process took from the beginning of January 1963 to 7 December 1965. The text of the Pastoral Constitution *Gaudium et spes* had to be entirely rewritten six times. The reasons for this were the difficulties we have just mentioned, as well as the differing basic concerns, mentalities, and terminologies of the Council Fathers, who represented various countries and many levels and cultural groups within the Church. An extraordinarily vast amount of work was required in order to draft this text on the part of the bishops and experts on the commission entrusted with this task (which was often divided into ten subcommissions). Despite all the difficulties in comprehension and the resistance, a broad consensus had appeared concerning the necessity for a declaration of this type on culture. The Council Fathers had expressed this opinion on repeated occasions during sessions, and references to this effect can also be found in the writings and discourses of Popes John XIII and Paul VI. It is well known that under the leadership of Karol Wojtyla, who at that time was Archbishop of Krakow, a group of Polish bishops also produced a contribution to this Constitution.[5] And it was in connection with this conciliar text that the advice and influence of the Protestant observers at the Council and contact with the World Council of Churches played an important role.[6] However, we must also mention other conciliar texts. Although these are concerned directly with the Church and Christians, and do not have "culture" and "the world" as their principal object, they do give a very clear account of how Christians must behave in today's world in all its aspects.[7]

In this report, we shall consider primarily the significance of the various cultures, especially non-European ones, for an adequate interpretation of the message of the Bible. It is based on practical collaboration and dialogue with non-European students of biblical sciences in Rome and West Germany. Its point of departure is a new experience with the Bible that is starting especially outside Europe. Consequently, we shall start with a brief account of this phenomenon.

A New Departure

Since the Second Vatican Council, the Bible has become, in a new sense, the most important means for spreading and strengthening Christian faith. This is not to say that the Bible had not always previously played a fundamental role in the life of the Church. In the past, the Bible made a decisive contribution to all manifestations of Christian culture. However, one may say that the Bible was administered primarily by the "official" preachers of the Church.[8] A clear example of this is Christian art, which was decisive for cultural life in general, as in the Middle Ages. Very many of the subjects of this art were biblical figures or themes. However, this art was principally at the service of the Church's preaching and was supervised by Church authorities, or was even entirely dependent on the ecclesiastical powers. A lay artist could express his understanding of the Bible only within the permitted framework. Thus, the Bible was above all in the hands of the clergy, of students of theology, and of monks and nuns. The individual Christian, especially the layman, read it only under the supervision of the competent authorities, if he wished to give his interpretation a lasting form within the culture of society. The Bible had its most prominent place in the Liturgy, where it was officially read in public, explained and commented on. Naturally, it had its established place in teaching, in instruction, in fundamental theology, and in the defense of the faith. This form of contact with the Bible, as carried out according to such traditional customs, is thus still normal and predomi-

nant, especially in old Catholic countries, where the new event
we are discussing has not yet really been noticed.

However, new experiences with the Bible as the decisive
means of gaining a deeper knowledge of the faith and of its fresh
proclamation are moving large groups of people in the Churches
of Latin America, Asia, India, and Africa. What has happened
here? There is not only a small, albeit qualified, minority that
reads the Bible. There are not only the authorized preachers who
read the Bible in public and explain it. The Christian people
take an active part in incorporating the word of God into daily
life.[9] A beginning of this new movement often occurred in the
Liturgy of the Word at Holy Mass, at which the Bible has been
read in the language of the people since the Council. A second
point of crystallization was frequently the shared reading of the
Liturgy of the Hours by a small group—for example, a basic
community. However, it was also possible that a convinced cate-
chist or a religious community living in close contact with the
people of the world around them or a zealous priest began, at first
in a small circle and then with more numerous participation, to
read the Bible in common with members of the parish and in
general with people of good will. In these meetings, it was not
only the leader who was the animator of the assembly, but many
of the people addressed those present and expressed their own
understanding of the word of God for the present moment. Their
opinion was discussed, others expressed their agreement or made
new observations, restrictions, or modifications. In a common
process of consideration, meditation, and discussion, the word of
the Bible gained a new resonance for people. It was experienced
as speaking directly, offering consolation, help, and instruction,
and it was integrated into life. In many cases, especially in Latin
America and in Africa, groups and communities made practical
decisions for common action in Bible readings of this kind.

We might describe this new departure by saying that the Bible
has found a new place in common reading and discussion by the
people of the Church. This situation has a whole series of important implications.[10] We shall take it as the starting point for our
considerations, since it opens up new vistas for all churches and
thus for all Christian cultures.

Yet this new "life form" of the Bible in the countries we have
mentioned is identical with the old preconciliar use on one important point: this manner of reading the Bible and interpreting

it in common takes place (with very rare exceptions) in close connection with the bishops.[11] The people and their pastors are united in the opinion that this new breakthrough concerns them all. Thus, many believers, priests, and bishops greet this new spiritual departure with genuine joy. Naturally, there is also resistance, especially from those who think it will lead to changes in the internal structure of the Church, or those who fear serious social and political consequences of the biblical message.[12]

Considering the Question in a Specific Group

We shall now give an account of the specific efforts of a group of students at the Pontifical Biblical Institute and the Pontifical Gregorian University in Rome, and St. George's Philosophical and Theological College in Frankfurt to take a serious look at the previously mentioned new reading of the Bible by the people in each of their churches, in their countries, and their continents. While preparing their licentiates or doctoral dissertations, these students have tried to examine these processes by means of scientific exegesis and to apply them to biblical hermeneutics and the pastoral situation in their home cultures.

It is worth mentioning that all the participants in this study group are Catholic, although there is a good deal of contact with Protestant and Orthodox friends, and some of these non-Catholic Christians take part in seminars and in the summer course. All of the participants have practical pastoral experience. Many of them are priests, but the nuns and laypeople involved have already done pastoral work in their own countries. This is also true for the German participants from the Frankfurt college. Many of them have already studied or worked in Latin America or elsewhere abroad. Before joining, all of them must have completed at least a visiting semester together at a seminar with the other participants, either at the Biblical Institute in Rome or at the college in Frankfurt. In Rome, the participants usually live in colleges run by their home countries (there are one or more of these colleges for each continent, where priests or students to the priesthood can live during their studies), in the study houses of their orders, or else privately. However, they meet regularly during seminar sessions, at communal liturgical celebrations and at a series of social occasions. During their stay in Frankfurt, they live together. One condition is that all participants be able to speak the principal European languages. In order to study, the Bible they must learn the biblical languages and the classical exegetical methods. The studies carried out in common, the emphasis on communal living, and numerous social encounters foster discussion and exchange of opinions. The group lives together for at least a year, and, afterwards, many participants remain in it or keep in close contact.

The study group adopted the following method: the texts are always examined first according to the rules of conventional biblical exegesis, but from the outset, it is borne in mind that the preaching of the Bible must take place within the various cultures. Attention must be paid here to the churches' efforts at "inculturation" in their own countries. However, in their exegesis, all the members wish to take expressly into account the fact that "interculturation" must also figure alongside inculturation, if this deepening and proclamation of the faith is to be authentic.

The model of this inculturation is to be found in the Bible, but it is then methodically expanded on and further developed. In the New Testament, the Church is seen as a vast community of numerous local churches in communication with each other. The growth and flourishing of the life of faith in one place should be heard of and experienced by all other communities. Difficulties and adversities, whether from outside or within are of relevance not only for the individual local church but affect all. Thus, it is evident that advice and concrete help, admonition and correction, are not only tasks that must be fulfilled within an individual community, but also apply to the relationships between communities. In this case, they go beyond the bounds of the individual culture. This leads to a series of tasks that involve consideration of exegetical method. However, let us first outline the questions that particularly interested our group.

The Gospel as a Cultural Task

All the non-European (non-North Atlantic) Bible students of this group bring with them a firm conviction, much stronger than that of their European companions, that the Bible directly concerns life. This is connected to their incipient skepticism regarding scientific exegesis, which they find alien and abstract.

By contrast, many are amazed by the sincere interest of so many average and simple believers who offer a considerable part of their income to Church aid organizations such as the episcopal organization for Latin America, Adveniat, and who clearly feel personally involved in the destiny of Christians and the Church in far distant continents.

While they themselves begin their biblical studies under the impulse of an apostolate with biblical foundations, they find their own experience expressed in the renewal movements in ancient Israel and in the beginnings of the Church in the New Testament. The formation of *a Christian language of proclamation*, which is clearly recognizable in the New Testament, shows them an inculturation of the gospel into the Jewish and Hellenistic Jewish world, which can be compared to the new language of the Church in their own countries. The foundation and formation of the groups of disciples and apostles by Jesus about which the gospel tradition gives many details, the great project for the future, as well as the building of the *first communities* according to the Acts of the Apostles, the Letters of the New Testament, and the Revelation of John, all show them a form of community life involving men and women in their concrete social context. The first pages of the Bible show the building up of the world as man's life-task as willed by God. God created man and placed him in the "garden" created by Him, "to till it and keep it" (Gen. 2:15). From the time of the Patriarchs until the final destruction of the Temple, Israel is always shown in a concrete way as the People of God in the context of a world that must be formed and that is often hostile. In numerous bits of information, the New Testament offers, from the beginnings of the Church, an image of a Christianity that is forming a concrete internal culture for itself. Inasmuch as family structures, manual work, economic life, and also social conditions of the time (e.g., slavery) affected the internal life of the communities, it can be recognized externally that gospel and culture cannot be separated. In the Bible, this process of growth is already represented as an historical process that must continue far into the future—indeed, until the Lord's ultimate second coming, which will bring history to its fulfillment.

However, this poses some essential questions for the interpretation of the Bible today (and for theology in general). The second chapter of the conciliar Constitution *Gaudium et spes* was decisive in helping this group formulate these questions correctly, in

defining inculturation, and, above all, for the further consideration leading to the concept of interculturation. It is well known
that the introductory article number 53 avoids defining culture,
since this could hardly have been profitable given the differences
of opinions between "philosophers, sociologists, anthropologists
and ethnologists."[13] Nevertheless, this much considered "description of the phenomenon," which was arrived at after so many
corrections and conflicts, can certainly be said to represent one
of the best bases for discussion of the present problem—a fact
confirmed by the experience of the study group.

We shall now give the principal points of how a person's
activity corresponds to his or her essential capacities and affects
his or her surroundings and hence the world and nature. A
person develops through knowledge of the world and his or her
work. In this way, he or she forms social life in all its expressions.
This takes place in moral and institutional progress to the benefit
of many, even of all mankind. Hence, culture is positively as-
sessed in this conciliar document. In contrast to the Marxist
definition of culture as the by-product of an infrastructure of
wealth and leisure, all of a person's activities are included in it,
especially work. In the paragraph of article 53, we find the historical and social aspects of culture applied to sociological and ethnological questions. "Thus, too, is created a well-defined, historical
milieu which envelops the men of every nation and age, and
from which they drew the values needed to foster humanity and
civilization." This amounts to a recognition of the need for many
cultures and their diversity.[14] This is the basic position of the
present group in its considerations.

The Question of Unity in Diversity

As a place of study, Rome itself imposes upon students an
awareness of the plurality of the one universal Church. It also
makes clear the mutual interest of the various local churches, all
represented in Rome, which are already in dialogue with each
other because of existing institutional and traditional ties. For
this study group, the references found time after time in the Bible
to the solidarity of the tribes and parts of the People of God and
their common goal as pilgrims in the Old Testament, or the
original church "of the pillars" in Jerusalem, held in greatest

veneration by all communities founded by St. Paul—metaphors of this reality are abundant—are all part of the scriptural argument for the unity of all individual churches in the universal Church.

This unity and solidarity mean that no one must be indifferent to a flourishing spiritual and active life of faith anywhere in the world. If the churches in Latin America, for example, in their particular situation of political development and concern for helping to change rigid social and sociopolitical structures according to Christian principles, base themselves on the Bible in a new way and have success among the faithful, this must also be reflected in exegesis and theology. According to the Bible, powerful spiritual life anywhere necessarily radiates to other communities. This is to be found in the earliest experiences of apostolic preaching, and the letters of St. Paul refer to it. He writes concerning the Thessalonians: "So . . . you became an example to all the believers in Macedonia and in Achaia. . . . Your faith in God has gone forth everywhere . . ." (1 Thess. 1:7–8). In the Letter to the Colossians, we find another such indication: ". . . the word of truth, the gospel which has come to you, as indeed in the whole world it is bearing fruit and growing—so among yourselves" (Col. 1:5–6). Just as the Apostle in his letters wished to form the life of faith of his communities in harmony with the practice and teaching of all others, going as far as the very Judaeo-Christian mother church of Jerusalem, so today the local churches throughout the world have the same task.

Early Christianity, even at that time, had to face the problem seriously that we are again experiencing today as one of the most urgent problems of the Church. This is the question of "unity in diversity." The New Testament describes Christianity as a group of Christians of Jewish and pagan origins with a great many problems in adapting. The practical difficulties and conflicts between these two groups, with their origins in different cultures and religious attitudes, become visible in the background of the gospels, and then more clearly in the New Testament letters. The problem is stated expressly especially in Paul's writings. According to the intentions of Jesus and the admonitions contained in Paul's Letters, Christians should represent a single People of God. They are the Body of Christ. The New Testament itself energetically rejects splits and schisms in the Church. By contrast, it also clearly shows the differences between Christianity from Jewish and heathen origins. The gospel tradition bears witness to the passage of the new religion from the Jewish land of origin into the Hellenistic world. Paul's letters deal expressly and at considerable length with the behavior of Christians of pagan origin within the community.

Thus, questions are clearly raised that must be properly "translated" for people of today. Despite the apparent similarity of the problems, the difference in time of the biblical texts—at least two thousand years—must be taken into account, and this interval involves real cultural differences. So one of the first concerns of this research group is to find an adequate exegesis, especially of the Pauline theology of "Jews and Gentiles," in order to provide a bridge to the cultural differences of today's culture groups within the Church.[15] This will then facilitate a corresponding representation of the unity of the local community and of the whole Church in words and, above all, in images taken from their own countries and cultures.[16]

It is clear that this effort is not simply identical with inculturation, which is

> . . . the integration of the Christian experience of a local church into the culture of its people, in such a way that this experience not only expresses itself in elements of this culture, but becomes a force that animates, orients and innovates this culture so as to create a new unity and communion, not only within the culture in question but also as an enrichment of the Church universal.[17]

As concerns this latter element—that is, "enrichment of the Church universal," as an effect on the whole Church, or as benevolent recognition leading to implementation, experienced as enrichment, on the part of the universal Church—inculturation does not totally correspond to that which particularly concerns our group. Inculturation is jointly experienced and implemented by the participants of this study group in their various countries. However, this group wishes to emphasize a further aspect of the formation of culture, the influence of culture and the attaining of culture in the very act of "translating" the Bible, and they wish to accomplish this consciously and reflectively: the fruitful, guiding, animating, and enriching power that comes from the influence of other cultures. The interrelations of languages, works, behavioral models, institutions, and all kinds of texts are to be considered essential to this research project. We use the terms "texts" and "contexts" because they are familiar to us and because they have the advantage of being used in other sciences. The written work we wish to produce will not by any means be a series of abstract "language games." On the contrary, the rules we must develop here have a validity that extends far beyond the literary work. The language games that exist between the elements of the texts and between the texts and the readers or listeners are in point of fact behavioral games and have corresponding effects. They must be classified within culture as formation indicators or as stimuli for creative or destructive activity.[18] By expressing ourselves in this way, we show both the horizons and the methodical implications that this study group wished to take into account. These methods are not only literary and linguistic. They involve more recent sociological and behavioral theory. Thus "context theology" should not be made to adhere to a closed or limited system. We shall now indicate certain steps in this method.

Negative Aspects of Culture

We cannot integrate the Bible into our own time without first taking into account the way Christians have made use of the Bible in previous history. In any case, we cannot consider the culture of the Christian world as totally positive. The actions of people today—who have filled the world with a system of institutions, customs, and many different kinds of behavioral models— are also blemished because of omissions, mistakes, and sins on the part of Christians. During the process of secularization, principles and ideological stances worked to deprive religion of its influence in public life as much as possible. Important personal values, freedom, and human dignity were diminished in the interests of material gain or power. The conciliar Constitution *Gaudium et spes* was correct in listing alongside the positive elements of culture a series of "antinomies," with which contemporary humanity is faced in its eager acceptance of progress.[19] On the basis of the fundamental outline we have given here, our study group drafted a formulation of their concerns, and this must be taken into account before considering any individual situations or specific texts. At the present time, there are at least three serious objections to Christian preaching and its use of the Bible:

1. European Christians seriously neglected the basic principles of love of neighbor, respect for human dignity, and the most fundamental justice when they colonized other continents. The Christian faith was then *de facto* linked with subjugation to western culture. Westernization was, in most countries, linked with industrialization. This has often resulted in the blaming of Christianity for the negative consequences of colonization and modernization.

2. In many areas in which other religions still predominate, important religious and moral principles of the Bible and of Christianity are already known from the Bible itself or from history. The Christian missionary finds that many ideas and principles of Christianity have already been adopted by other forms of society or even other religions, so that many people do not see the need to go further and to accept the whole of the Christian religion. Many people from these sorts of countries have a predominant feeling of aversion to the institutionalized Church. They hold Jesus in esteem but reject the ecclesial organization. They find many Christian principles already present in their own cultures and traditions and feel many of their own ethical customs to be better adapted to their own countries, while others have already been adopted and adapted from the West. It needs to be made clear in a convincing fashion why the Christian faith still needs to be preached.

3. History, and especially the present, offers abundant proof to the effect that Christians themselves have not been overly concerned with unity. The Bible was and is used in different ways, both in theory, and, above all, in practice. There is a pluralistic multiplicity of Christian churches. The tendency to adopt only certain aspects of biblical or Christian ideas thus appears to be legitimized by the example of Christians themselves.

Therefore the previously mentioned principal problem of the unity of the Church in a multiplicity of cultures can be broken down into a series of questions: (a) To what extent is it possible today to imitate the intercultural origins of Christianity? (b) How far can adaptation to another culture go? (c) At what point does translation into other languages, cultures, and customs begin to involve and change what is essential to Christianity? (d) Is the image of the Church found throughout the New Testament normative—or, what does the New Testament teach concerning the development and growth of the Church, and so on?

Bases for a Working Hypothesis

We consider very careful study of the external and internal motives of the author or compiler to be indispensable in the investigation of a literary text or any witness to culture. All research on man, and, therefore, quite certainly all scientific investigation in the field of history and religion, requires as a precondition that the observer have the greatest respect for the opinion of the other. What Husserl calls "cognition by empathy" is demanded. The very principles used in describing the object of investigation—in texts, for example, the "literary genre"—must be established not from the researcher's preconceived ideas, but from the documents and witnesses themselves or from their context.

During this project, these and allied basic hermeneutical principles are continuously reexamined. In many cases, the group found that a serious impediment to intercultural interpretation was the frequent, almost innate tendency on the part of the participants tacitly to see and to presume their own cultures as "the best," and to take them as the basis for judging everything else. Only when one makes the effort to recognize and understand the reasons why people do things, can one recognize that other solutions, models of life, customs, gestures, and symbols can be useful—perhaps even more useful than one's own. In discussion, we found time and again that in many cultures, especially when using archaic or mythical ideas, the *concept of the person* has not been as clearly defined as it is in western philosophy. Nevertheless, in the cultures comprised within the experience of this study group, the following convictions are definitely present: (a) the conviction of a person's basic aspiration to knowledge of the truth (understanding, also on the part of the individual, who must and should know); (b) the conviction of the responsibility of the individual (conscience, capacity for good and bad decisions, and behavior) and that of the group or community as well (this is often clearer and more convincing in archaic cultures, which impose corresponding sanctions, than in the modern western consciousness); and (c) a conviction of an innate and inalienable vocation of a person to what western culture calls "freedom."

The group realizes the consequences of the fact that this inalienable, essential vocation of a person to personal freedom has been considerably underestimated in several cultures. In certain ancient Central and South American tribes, the man in the family unit exercised an almost absolute domination, and the tribal leader in many old cultures of Polynesia, Asia, Africa, and America predominated—and this was also not unknown in the early history of Europe. This can also be sensed in the psychological dependence on the part of members of a "clan" on the wishes and expectations of the other members, who often do not realize their situation. On the other hand, the valuable advantages of a close membership to extended communities is useful for interpreting the Bible, which can, both in the Old and New Testaments, teach modern people new—because it was much tested by experience—yet ancient wisdom.

Thus, the fact that *Gaudium et spes* avoids the concept of "person" in Articles 15–17 was noted by the group not so much with surprise as with a certain approval, although in Christian philosophical and theological debate, this concept has played such an important role. It is certain that in the fundamental definition of man as a person, we find one of the most valuable messages of Christianity to all cultures, and the form "person" may be extremely useful. However, there can be no doubt that other expressions such as "man," "tribal member," etc., which are normally used to express social relations, can be used just as well in its place.[20] Thus, *Gaudium et spes* speaks in detail of the essential structures of society and the fundamental relationship of the person to the community.[21]

The basis for the hermeneutical rule "*cognition only by empathy for reasons and motives*" is awareness of the respect for human dignity, which must be required and preserved. It can be summarized in three fundamental conditions: understanding, conscience, and freedom. This awareness is apparent in all the conciliar documents with the exception of the Decree on the Means of Social Communications, *Inter mirifica*—which, however, can be explained by the fact that it was proposed to the Council in a hurried fashion and that its approval at the voting was linked to the call for a pastoral document that was to be produced after the Council in a form suited to the present day. It is well known that the commission entrusted by the Council with drafting this document spent seven years at its task, and the document was finally published on 23 May 1971 in the form of a Pastoral Instruction with the significant title *Communio et progressio*. Our group studied this text carefully and believes that it can serve as a guide even to exegesis of the Bible for the present day.

Further Development of Theological Ideas

The group was particularly interested in *Inter mirifica*, [22] mentioned previously as being the only "preconciliar" text among the documents promulgated by the Council. In this text—particularly as concerns the hermeneutic directions mentioned or presumed—the development desired by the Council can be most clearly distinguished. The Decree deals with two main points: "teaching and guidance" for the correct use of the press, radio, television, and films, etc., and their use as a means for evangelization and the apostolate. We would draw attention to an important sentence in Article 5: "There exists . . . in human society a right to information on the subjects that are of concern to men either as individuals or as members of society, according to each man's circumstances." Here the human dignity previously mentioned is seen and emphasized as a premise for responsible behavior. [23] Forming public opinion is a necessary process in the life of a society, and this holds true for all communities. There is no reference in this document to man's essential vocation and that of the community from which it ensues. However, a fundamental means of forming opinion and of preparing man for responsible collaboration is demanded—namely, dialogue. It was also clear in the formulations of the Decree regarding the way in which means of communication are to be used, its particular emphasis on the concept of "Church," and the command to preach. Mass media are not really seen as the bearers of communication—something to be expected automatically in human society, aspiring to the communication of truth in dialogue and participating in the self-fulfillment of the individual and the community. They are seen, rather, as tools or vehicles of religious and moral preaching that is to be conducted under the ultimate responsibility of the hierarchy.

The Church is seen in a rather one-sided way as an institution that administers the truth and makes erudite statements and rules of conduct. "Preaching" appears to have been understood as "imparting knowledge." Furthermore, there is no consideration of the responsibility of lay people who create these media on their own initiative and who place them at the disposition of religious. This is precisely because the media are conceived of as being coopted into the service of the Church. In other words, the basic concept of "revelation" appears one-sidedly as "imparting knowledge of an established truth," and the Church appears one-sidedly to be a managerial apparatus for the imparting of this truth and the reliable administering of the media.

This corresponds to neoscholastic terminology that perpetuates a world view in which everyone recognizes an absolute religious truth as the supreme value, and the final responsibility for this is entrusted to the Church. In contrast, the modern world sees the Church as a cultural institution alongside others, which must justify itself before the critical judgment of reason in broad dialogue encompassing all the cultural, scientific and religious contributions of mankind. Its claim to evangelization is not recognized automatically, but must show itself to be appropriate in each individual case.

Revelation is mainly sought in the experience of a person, who confirms it as sustaining and giving meaning to his or her life. The Church then appears more as the community of a People of God than as the mystery of the presence of God. In this community, one is granted a share, since here one can experience final significance and definitive wisdom.

In the other conciliar texts, we always find, alongside these traditional formulations, contemporary expressions that take into account the progress made in the development of self-awareness and independent reasoning. In point of fact, these formulas employed by the conciliar texts, which are biblical and less scholastic—hence more narrative, since they describe contemporary experience—and which are sometimes considered pastoral, correspond better to the expectations of nonphilosophically educated, nonwestern cultures. At least this is the opinion of many members of this study group, who also find it easier to identify themselves with them than with customary theological terminology. We need no particular proof to demonstrate that in Latin America, Africa, India, and Asia, that is, in new forms of basic communities or in the context of liberation theologies, such expressions as "community" or "the People of God" are preferred, as emphasizing participation and experienced communion. A model of the proclamation of faith conceived of in terms of "communications theory" rather than "cognition theory" meets with spontaneous assent because of the process of convincing dialogue based on and confirmed in love and service of concrete experience. This is the way that the Church is represented in *Lumen gentium*,[24] and this view is also found in all the other documents. The Introduction to *Gaudium et spes* is explicit: *mysterio Ecclesiae penitius investigato* ("having deeply studied the mystery of the Church," GS 2).

Some General Results of the Research

Initially, the study group naturally had to consider the question of the hermeneutic perspective of the Christian message, which must be especially alien to other cultures. In the first place, this must cover everything that is called eschatological and claims to have an absolute, definitive meaning that is valid for all people. Difficulties of the same sort are raised by a dogma that appears only in later parts of the Bible, but which is firmly accepted within the corpus of Christian teaching, namely, that concerning the resurrection of the dead, and the whole Easter mystery in general and the events that occurred in the primitive community in Jerusalem connected with the appearances of the risen Christ. All of these questions are linked with those that recur periodically concerning the historical evaluation of the Jesus tradition in the gospels.

A summer course was held and a month was spent in impassioned debate on the texts of the gospels in this connection. It started with the question of exorcism, which the African members interpreted in a very realistic and fundamental way on the basis of their own experience with their indigenous customs and religions. A series of essays and articles was thus written, calling repeatedly for better knowledge and appreciation of literary genres.[25]

A further field of investigation, which has not yet been completed, is that of the "language" of Christian preaching. A series of investigations was devoted to the language of prayer with its various genres, beginning with that of vision, but also dealing with its capacity for making very different sorts of statements on God's relationship to man.[26] The principal objective of this intercultural effort was to improve our method and to reach a correct description of that special understanding between author and reader or listener—which was extremely important both at the time of the New Testament and today—with regard to our *way* of communicating. In other words, the aim is a better way of doing research and a more precise definition of literary and narrative genres.[27]

Particular Problems

In recent years, three types of problems have particularly concerned the study group in its interpretation of the Bible: cultural development during industrialization; education, i.e., the use of principles of modern pedagogy (psychology, sociology) in Bible instruction; and the use of exegesis in a global hermeneutic system ("scientific" exegesis and apostolate).

The first type of problem was dealt with using the model of Pauline theology and its reception. The situations in Japan and India were especially considered. How can the origin and growth of the primitive Church in the ancient metropolises of Ephesus or Corinth, as seen through the behavioral instructions found in the Pauline letters, be made fruitful for the present? What would be the value of a "letter of warning" (such as the Letter to the Galatians, which appears above all to constitute a scolding)?[28]

Specialists were invited to several seminars during which the group considered the second type of problem. In most industrial and economically developing countries, the Church is called upon to cooperate in education and formation. The wisdom and pedagogy of the Bible, as well as Jesus' activity as a teacher, offer many aids and stimuli for a correct response to this challenge.[29]

The third type of problem was tested in practice *in situ* during summer courses and then considered during seminars. It was possible to observe and discuss the topic "From Popular Religion to Modern Church" with Orthodox friends from the Balkans and Crete. Valuable help was also gained from the exchange of information and collaboration with the World Catholic Federation for the Biblical Apostolate. On the basis of exegesis of the gospels, an attempt was made to establish an image of Jesus in the perspective of the expectations and pastoral needs of Latin America.[30] The study group feels that the many efforts to find a suitable form for preaching and for the correct use of the Bible in Latin America are certain to be successful because so many zealous and experienced people are working on this problem and are in dialogue with one another, with the Christian population, and with those holding positions of responsibility. Proposals concerning principles and means for this biblical work, and involving further development of traditional methods in the context of a global hermeneutic system, were discussed over a period of several months by the members, and were presented at the First Latin-American Pastoral Biblical Conference in Bogotá in July 1985.[31]

As has been shown, this work is based on stimuli given by the Second Vatican Council. After twenty-five years, many forms of expression and questions may have changed, but the spirit that animated the Council moves forward, giving us a glimpse of the Church of the future that will proclaim Christ throughout the world, so as to bring about greater freedom, justice, and peace.

Translated from the German by Ronald Sway.

Notes

1. Cf. *L'Osservatore Romano* (26–27 December 1961).

2. We find in *Gaudium et spes* a clear awareness of this principle to the effect that the Church has indeed something to say to all people, with great modesty, yet without timidity: "Now that the Second Vatican Council has deeply studied the mystery of the Church, it resolutely addresses not only the sons of the Church and all who call upon the name of Christ, but the whole of humanity as well, and it longs to set forth the way it understands the presence and function of the Church in the world of today" (GS 2).

3. Cf. the research on over 160 definitions of "culture" and the consequent assessment in A.L. Kroeber and C. Kluckhon, *Culture: A Critical Review of Concepts and Definitions* (Cambridge, MA, 1952; reprint, New York, 1963).

4. C. Moeller, "Die Geschichte der Pastoralkonstitution," in *Das zweite Vatikanische Konzil, LThK*, 3 (1968), 242–279, here 247. Cf. also R. Tucci, "The Proper Development of Culture," in H. Vorgrimler (ed.), *Commentary on the Documents of Vatican II*, 5 (New York/

London, 1969), 247–287. These presentations, together with sources
and evaluations, seem to us to be essential contributions to an understanding of the history and significance of *Gaudium et spes*, particularly
because collaborators and observers are quoted who participated in the
whole drafting procedure.

5. Cf. F. Houtart, "Par delà le schéma XIII," 43ff., incorporated
into the "Ariccia Redaction" of the text, according to Moeller, "Die
Geschichte der Pastoralkonstitution," 261.

6. Lukas Vischer, *Überlegungen nach dem Vatikanischen Konzil,*
Polis 26 (Zürich, 1966), 58–73, and, on the two "Zürich texts," cf.
Moeller, "Die Geschichte der Pastoralkonstitution," 251ff., 255–260.

7. This is true for *Dei Verbum* and *Lumen gentium* inasmuch as in
these documents, the understanding of "revelation" and "Church" is
expressed in a new, more profound language than was the case for
earlier formations. The corresponding vision is also influenced *Unitatis
redintegratio, Gravissimum educationis, Nostra aetate, Dei Verbum, Apostolicam actuositatem, Dignitatis humanae,* and *Ad gentes.*

8. The memory of this is still very clear in the consciousness of
many Christians, even in countries where the Bible is now often read in
common. It is well known that the Bible in the vernacular could be
misused by heretics. This is why from the time of Paul IV (1559) until
Benedict XIV's Decree on the Index (1757), it was included in the list
of prohibited books that could not be read without the permission of the
bishop or the inquisitor. Considerable restrictions remained until the
time of the Second Vatican Council.

9. Concrete proof of this is the extraordinary increase in demand
for Bibles in local languages in non-European countries. This demand
is met, for example, by grants from Church aid organizations. The
World Catholic Federation for the Biblical Apostolate (WCFBA; in
Latin America: Federación Bíblica Católica para l'América Latina,
FEBICAM), based in Stuttgart, gives statistical information and offers
practical help for beginning and carrying on work on the Bible. By
way of literature and propaganda, pastoral work with the Bible has
without doubt prompted the greatest interest among the different sorts
of "basic communities." However, Bible work is in no way restricted
to these communities or to the Bible-reading circles of other groups.
On the contrary, in many countries, it has been integrated into the
regular teaching program, often in support of catechism, sometimes to
the extent that a special ecclesiastical organization, instituted by an
individual bishop or the bishops' conference of a region supports and
coordinates this work. Cf. the reports in *World Event* (of the
WCFBA), and regularly published in latter years in the journals
Concilium, Herder-Korrespondenz, Il Regno, etc., which deal with this
subject.

10. This kind of Bible reading has often been interpreted as the expression of a new understanding of the Church inasmuch as it can in fact lead to a more conscious understanding of membership of a community—as can other major new elements such as the basic communities. New models of the Church have often been described since the Council. A list of these with references to relevant authors can be found in C. Floristan, "Die dem pastoralen Handeln zugrundeliegenden Kirchenmodelle," *Concilium*, 20 (1984), 196, 499–504.

11. Expressly so in the Medellín Conference (1968), in the pastoral plans of the Brazilian Bishops' Conference since 1965, especially in 1985, and also in Africa and India.

12. We must return to the various theological interpretations of the individual themes and to the assessment of this breakthrough, of which there were perceptible tendencies even before the Council.

13. R. Tucci, "Einleitung und Kommentar zum II. Kapitel des II. Teils von *Gaudium et spes,*" in *Das Zweite Vatikanische Konzil, LThK*, 3, 447–485, esp. 453. In the remainder of our article, we frequently use this commentary, likewise B. Matteucci, "La promozione del progresso della cultura," in *La Costituzione Pastorale sulla Chiesa nel mondo contemporaneo* (Turin, 1966), 805–862.

14. Cf. Matteucci, "La promozione," 814.

15. If the text of the Letter to the Ephesians, which speaks of those "who once were far off" and who "have been brought near," of breaking down "the dividing wall" between "the two," and of a whole structure "that is joined together and grows into a holy temple in the Lord" (Eph. 2:11–22), is to be applied to a modern metropolis in industrial Japan, this is impossible without bearing in mind the cultural contrasts between missionaries coming from Europe and the Japanese people. Cf. K. Usami, *Somatic Comprehension of Unity: The Church in Ephesus*, Analecta Biblica 101 (Rome, 1983), 11–70; cf. the following note.

16. Usami, *Somatic Comprehension of Unity: The Church in Ephesus*, makes the attempt in the second and third chapters of his work to apply a "somatic" aspect that is, in the final analysis, nurtured in East Asian awareness, to the unity and structure of the Church as often described in western theology as the "mystical Body." Cf. also Z. Kiernikowski, *La crescita della communità—Corpo di Cristo. L'identitatà e il dinamismo della vita cristiana rispecchiate nella dinamica del testo della Lettera ai Colossei,* dissertation at the Pontifical Biblical Institute (Rome, 1981); P.M. Meagher, *"Faith active through Agape" (Gal. 5:6)—a Study of the Formation of a Christian Community of Agape According to the Letter to the Galatians,* dissertation at the Pontifical Biblical Institute (Rome, 1984).

17. Cf. A.A. Roest Crollius, "What is So New About Inculturation? A Concept and its Implications," *Gregorianum*, 59 (1978), 721–738, here 735; *id.*, "Inculturation and the Meaning of Culture," *Grego-*

rianum, 61 (1980), 253–373; T. Nkeramihigo, "A propos de l'inculturation du christianisme," *Telema*, 12 (October–December 1977), 19–26. In the first article mentioned, the author describes the development of the concept and refers to the Church documents that played an important role in this development.

18. Cf. G. Melischek, K.E. Rosengren, and J. Stappers (eds.), *Cultural Indicators: An International Symposium*, Stizungsbericht der österreichischen Akademie der Wissenschaften, Philosophisch-historische Klasse, 416 (Vienna, 1984).

19. Cf. the painstaking and extremely pertinent formulations of Article 56 in Chapter II of *Gaudium et spes.*

20. According to numerous participants in the Council and collaborators in the drafting of *Gaudium et spes*, the absence in the finally approved document of the concept of the person, and above all of the I–you relationship, which is so characteristic of the individual and which had formerly been developed in several of the earlier phases of Schema XIII, is really an accident. They attribute this absence to a lack of clarity in assigning Chapters I and II of the present document and an equal lack of clarity in assigning tasks to the various work groups and subcommissions. Cf. J. Ratzinger, "Kommentar zum I. Kapitel des I. Teils," in *Das Zweite Vatikanische Konzil, LThK*, 3 (1968), 313–354, here 325f.

21. GS 23–32. Semmelroth comments on this formula, especially in his commentary on number 25.

22. On the treatment of this document in the discussions in the Council Hall, cf. G. Caprile (ed.), *Il Concilio Vaticano II, Cronache del Concilio Vaticano II edite da "La Civiltà Cattolica,"* Vol. 1, "Primo periodo 1962–1963," 191–213 (several interventions by Cardinal K. Wojtyla); Vol. 2, 282ff.

23. It is, however, well known that it has been observed concerning this point that in the context of this formula, which cites the Encyclical *Miranda prorsus*, the text clearly and intentionally omits the point that Pius XII wished to emphasize, namely, that the right to information holds true within the Church as well. Cf. K.H. Schmidthüs, "Einleitung und Kommentar zu *Inter mirifica*," in *Das Zweite Vatikansiche Konzil, LThK*, 1 (1966), 112–135, here 120f.

24. Cf. A. Grillmeier on *De ecclesiae mysterio* and *De populo Dei*, i.e., on the titles of the first and second chapters of the Dogmatic Constitution on the Church, in *Das Zweite Vatikanische Konzil, LThK*, 1 (1966), 156ff., 176ff.; and G. Philips on the history of *Lumen gentium*, in *ibid.*, 139–155.

25. On the series of questions concerning Easter: K. Usami, "How are the Dead Raised? (1 Cor. 15:35–58)," *Biblica*, 57 (1976), 468–493; F. Lentzen-Deis, "Ostererfahrung und Auferstehungsglaube," in K.

Rahner and O. Semmelroth (eds.), *Theologische Akademie 7* (Frankfurt, 1970), 65–90; A. Büchele, *Der Tod Jesu im Lukasevangelium. Eine redaktionsgeschichtliche Untersuchung zu Lk 23,* Frankfurter Theologische Studien 26 (Frankfurt, 1978); H. Bloem, *Die Ostererzählung des Matthäus. Aufbau und Aussage von Mt 27,57—28, 20,* dissertation at the Pontifical Biblical Institute (Rome, 1979).

26. F. Lentzen-Deis, *Das Gebet Jesu* (Meitingen, 1976); L. Feld-kämper, *Der betende Jesus also Heilsmittler nach Lukas* (Bonn, 1978). For literary genres, cf. also note 27.

27. F. Lentzen-Deis, "Methodische Überlegungen zur Bestimmung literarischer Gattungen im Neuen Testament," *Biblica,* 62 (1981), 1–20; cf. *id., Die Taufe Jesu nach den Synoptikern. Literarkritische und gattungsgeschichtliche Untersuchungen,* Frankfurter Theologische Studien 4 (Frankfurt, 1970); J.P. Heil, *Jesus Walking on the Sea: Meaning and Gospel Functions of Matthew 14:23–33, Mark 6:45–52 and John 6:15b–21,* Analecta Biblica (Rome, 1981); E. Manicardi, *Il cammino di Gesù nel vangelo di Marco. Schema narrativo e tema cristologico,* Analecta Biblica (Rome, 1981); R. Infante, *L'Amico dello Sposo. Figura del minis-tero di Giovanni Battista nel vangelo di Giovanni* (Naples, 1984); R. Tosco, *Pietro e Paolo, ministri del giudizio di Dio. Studio del genere letterario e della funzione di Atti 5, 1–11 e 13, 4–12,* dissertation at the Pontifical Gregorian University (Rome, 1986).

28. Cf. notes 15 and 16.

29. Cf. E. Sanchez Roman, *Proyecto y educación en Mc 3, 13–19. Ensayo de Interpretación Inter-cultural del Proyecto de Jesús con los Doce,* dissertation at the Pontifical Gregorian University (Rome, 1968).

30. F. Lentzen-Deis, E. Sanchez Roman, J.I. Flores Gaytan, C.A. Mora Paz, and J.M. Portillo Sampedro, *Anunciar a Jesús. Ensayo de Método exegético* (Mexico, 1984). This book gives presentations on the method, a review of research, and exegetical examples. For Brazil, cf. W. Oliveira de Azevedo, *"Ele vos precede na Galiléia." Comunidade e Missão no Evangelho de Marcos,* dissertation at the Pontifical Gregorian University (Rome, 1985).

31. The talks given at this meeting and previously in Mexico are in press. A summary of the guiding principles mentioned is found in: *La Parabla Hoy* (Journal of the FEBICAM, Bogotá), 10 (1985), 83–88.

CHAPTER 58

The Contribution of the Council to Culture

Hervé Carrier, S.J.

Summary

This article consists of six sections: Vatican II as cultural event. Anthropological objectives. Theological-historical approach. Actors open to the plurality of cultures: (1) a new awareness of universality; (2) a new cultural and ecclesial perception. What the Council had to say about culture: (1) a modern definition of culture; (2) a call to cultural analysis; (3) the conciliar image of the world and the Church; (4) the encounter with the contemporary mentality. Evaluation and future prospects.

Vatican II as Cultural Event

Viewed in a sociological perspective, Vatican II can be seen as a cultural event of historic importance, and, in a certain sense, the Council as cultural event is as important as the statements found in its documents on culture. It can be said that after Vatican II, Catholics no longer saw the Church and the world in exactly the same way as they did before it. It is this collective cultural experience that must first be brought into focus if we are to evaluate the contribution of Vatican II to culture. Some original teaching on the relationship between the Church and the various cultures was of course set forth especially in *Gaudium et spes,* as also in other conciliar documents—and we shall stress the full significance of this—but it seems to us indispensable to understand in the first place the background and foundations of this teaching: in other words, the new attitude of mind, both theological and anthropological, that progressively grew within the Fathers of the Council as they investigated the meaning of the Church for contemporary men and women.

The cultural dimensions of the Council emerge clearly now that a certain period of time has passed and we can examine some of its characteristics in a clearer perspective: the originality of its declared objectives; the intellectual approach that gradually took shape at the Council; the quality and origins of the participants; and, above all, the theological-historical vision that bit by bit took on form and expression. Let us consider each of these aspects in turn, which will help us to throw light on the cultural significance of Vatican II.

Anthropological Objectives

The announcement of Vatican II by John XXIII already set the anthropological tone for the forthcoming Council, when he said that its perspective would be primarily pastoral, pointing out that this would require a new and courageous effort to understand and meet with the contemporary world. John XXIII noted the dramatic distance between Church and world. The aspect of the Pope's declarations that struck the Church and the media most immediately was his benevolent attitude toward the contemporary world. He said that he was dissociating himself from those who "in these modern times . . . can see nothing but prevarication and ruin," as if the situation of the world were constantly deteriorating. "We feel we must disagree with those prophets of gloom, who are always forecasting disaster, as though the end of the world were at hand." He certainly was not ignoring any of the great problems of the Church, its internal shortcomings, its difficulties, and the persecutions it suffered. However, he was casting a gaze over the present times that was made up primarily of comprehension and appreciation, for he knew that Divine Providence is always at work in the world, mysteriously laying the groundwork for a new order of human relations:

In the present order of things, Divine Providence is leading us to a new order of human relations which, by men's own efforts and even beyond their very expectations, are directed toward the fulfillment of God's superior and inscrutable designs. And everything, even human differences, leads to the greater good of the Church.

If the Church is to be understood by this new world, we must first of all discover and provide an intelligible guise for the full and unchanging teaching of the Church:

The substance of the ancient doctrine of the deposit of faith is one thing, and the way in which it is presented is another. And it is the latter that must be taken into great consideration with patience if necessary, everything being measured in the forms and proportions of a magisterium which is predominantly pastoral in character.

The seeds of the anthropological and pastoral intuition of the whole Council are found in these words, which also indicate an approach that is more "medicinal" than disciplinary. The Church certainly in no way condones error, and when necessary knows how to condemn it clearly. However, today it prefers the medicine of mercy to that of severity, seeking to win minds through the attraction of its teaching: "Nowadays, the Spouse of Christ prefers to make use of the medicine of mercy rather than that of severity. She considers that she meets the needs of the present day by demonstrating the validity of her teaching rather than by condemnations."[1] This means calling on Christians to become visible and credible witnesses within human society.

John XXIII also issued a courageous invitation to "separated Christians" in order to ensure a solid ecumenical participation in the work of the Council, and thus to involve all Christians in a shared discernment of their responsibilities toward a world that is challenging them dramatically.

The word aggiornamento (updating) has enjoyed a great success, and describes well the process John XXIII wanted for the Council. A twofold renewal is involved: in the first place, the Church purifies and redefines itself, and, on the other hand, it makes an effort to renew its understanding of the present world. This twofold theological and anthropological approach would become the main orientation and the source of inspiration for the whole Council. However, the Fathers of the Council only gradually became aware of this. Cardinal Montini's letter to the clergy of Milan in January 1963 bears witness to the questioning attitude and the spirit of research of the Fathers:

> At the Council the Church is seeking herself, trying with great trust and a great effort to define and understand herself better as she really is. After twenty centuries of history, the Church seems to be submerged by the civilization of the world, so that she appears to be in fact absent from the contemporary world. She is therefore feeling the need for recollection, self-purification, and self-renewal, in order to be able to set out again on her own path with great energy. . . . While she is thus working to define and identify herself, the Church is also examining the world, and trying to enter into contact with contemporary society. . . . And how is this contact to take place? It means reentering into dialogue with the world, discerning the needs of the society in which it acts, observing the shortcomings, the needs, the aspirations, the sufferings, the hopes that lie within men's hearts.[2]

This urgent, anxious questioning, so clearly in the style of the future Pope Paul VI, reveals the attitude of research that inspired the most aware participants in the Council.

Theological-Historical Approach

Two attitudes were visible from the outset: on the one hand, there were the supporters of a defense of the Church *ad intra* against a hostile world that the Holy See had condemned a number of times in important documents since the nineteenth century; and, on the other hand, there was a group that wanted to use a new perspective in analyzing the duties of the Church toward the world, which was to be seen, certainly in its moral failings and misery, but above all in its needs and aspiraitons, its anguish and hope. It would be an oversimplification to say that the Council was divided into conservatives and progressives. It was more a question of different emphases in conception as to the work of the Council, as based on two different types of intellectual attitude: on the one hand, the reflection on principles, which was more accustomed to deductive methods, and, on the other, the anthropological and pastoral approach. Roger Aubert has observed: "The great confrontation of the first session of the Council was not so much between conservatives and progressives, as between notionalists and existentialists."[3]

We should bear in mind that prior to the Council, the capacity for cultural analysis was almost wholly ignored in the theological formation usually provided at the time. For the most part, the word "culture" only had an intellectual or esthetic sense, with no anthropological implications. It is indicative that the word "culture" did not appear at all in certain work instruments familiar to theologians and philosophers, for example, the *Dictionnaire de Théologie Catholique* or the first editions of André Lalande's *Vocabulaire de la Philosophie*—no more than it did, for that matter, in the less recent editions of the great national encyclopedias. The majority of the Council Fathers did not yet view culture as an instrument for analyzing society, and it is hardly surprising that Vatican II should have been hesitant over accepting this point of view of anthropological analysis. It is, therefore, all the more praiseworthy that the Council should have come round to this idea in such a short time, thus, as we shall see in due course, updating its attitude to culture and cultures.

Some hesitation and stumbling was inevitable at the beginning of its work, so that the key theme of Vatican II, in the form of social and pastoral discernment, really only took shape toward the end of the first session, as John XXIII confided only a short time before his death. It was at this point that the influence of Cardinals such as Montini, Suenens, Lercaro, and König, and Bishops such as Wojtyla and Garrone, was felt, and that the Council decided to turn resolutely toward the world, with its anguish, its problems of hunger and poverty, and its hopes for peace and development. And by identifying itself, in the spirit of Christ, with this historical humanity, the Council came to a clear awareness of the challenge awaiting it, and thus gradually moved toward the famous Schema XIII, which would in due course, but only after some difficult debates, become one of the main texts of Vatican II: *Gaudium et spes*.[4]

The new Pope, Paul VI, set about interpreting the effort at clarification that was then being made, when he tried to define the orientation of the Council at the opening of the second session. He set the Council four objectives: (1) the Church must become aware of its identity, and provide itself with "a reflected definition"; (2) the Church is called to reform itself in an awakening and in a spiritual spring; (3) the Church must reconstitute the unity of Christians in an "ecumenicity that seeks to be total and universal"; (4) the Church must reach out to today's world, "throwing a bridge across to the contemporary world." Paul VI demonstrated a very fine analytical ability, giving an excellent description of what is at stake in this dialogue with the world, as seen in all its ambivalence with regard to the gospel. On the one hand the Church is called to withdraw spiritually into itself, but, on the other hand, this is in order to enable it to become more effective *ad extra* as a renewing leaven for the world:

> It is a very strange phenomenon: in seeking to give fresh force to its interior life in the spirit of the Lord, it separates and sets itself apart from the profane society in which it is immersed; at the same time, however, it acts as a life-giving leaven and an instrument of salvation for this world, by discovering and reinforcing its missionary vocation, in other words, its essential task of taking humanity, whatever its condition, as the impassioned object of its evangelizing mission.[5]

These are the elements of the reflection of the new Pope, and they would then find their full expression in his Encyclical *Ecclesiam suam*, which was promulgated during the Council (in 1964) and was devoted wholly to dialogue with the contemporary world.

Actors Who Were Open to the Plurality of Cultures

The discovery of the world in the diversity of mentalities and cultures would be greatly stimulated by the presence of bishops from every part of the world at the Council. It was the first time that a Council included a large number of bishops from the Third World, and the point of view of the churches of Asia, Africa, and Latin America had a considerable impact on bishops from European and North American countries. Apart from this, the representatives of eastern European countries threw a stark light on the present situation in the communist world.

A New Awareness of Universality

Even if the main actors at Vatican II seemed at first to be westerners and the antepreparatory texts tended to be their work, their way of thinking certainly did not dominate the debates, so that in the course of the Council, there was a decided maturing of minds and a new awareness of universality.

This fact has been of fundamental importance in the recent life of the Church and deserves in-depth study, which should be carried out jointly by theologians and sociologists. The truly international composition of the conciliar gathering has not yet, in our opinion, been examined in a proper perspective. In a stimulating talk given in the United States, Karl Rahner attempted a first analysis, showing, with considerable nuances, how the Church truly became aware of its universal character with Vatican II. The Council was a cultural event comparable with that experienced by the first Christians when they understood, after the Council of Jerusalem, that the gospel was to be announced to the Gentiles, which would mark the change from a "Jewish Christianity" to a "Gentile Christianity." Rahner states:

> First of all, I venture to assert that the difference between the historical situation of Judeo-Christianity and the situation into which Paul transplanted Christianity as in a radically new creation was not greater than the difference between European culture and the modern cultures of Asia and Africa as a whole to which Christianity has to be adapted, if it is really to become a world-Church it has begun to be.[6]

The Council became aware of the historical internationalization of the Church, and this awareness was then called on to develop, with all the ensuing consequences—but we shall only gradually be able to evaluate the importance of these. Although we are stressing this aspect of Vatican II here, it in fact requires a full in-depth study, similar to the one carried out by Alphonse Dupront for the Council of Trent. Dupront's sociohistorical analysis of the Council of Trent sought to define the cultural significance of this conciliar event through study of the composition of its members, its aims, its reflections, and the impact its course had on its own period. His analysis of "the mental and spiritual fact" of Trent is very stimulating and indicates some interesting lines of research for students of Vatican II, and it is only to be hoped that there will be a proliferation of similar studies on the most recent Council. [7]

Apart from the bishops themselves, there were other participants—the various experts, the representatives of religious and lay people, and the ecumenical observers—who made an active contribution to the particular configuration of Vatican II. Many of the experts were theologians who specialized in biblical, liturgical, and patristic renewal. There were also sociologists who were accustomed to carrying out their research within a pastoral perspective. These experts brought a rich experience of theological and historical investigation to the Council, drawn from reflection on biblical, liturgical and pastoral renewal, the exercise of the human sciences and religious sociology, and the practice of Catholic Action, with its method of "seeing, judging, and acting" that had over the past twenty years awakened Catholics to an awareness of cultural analysis in the service of evangelization.

Although the interdisciplinary reflection that was a feature of collaboration between the bishops and the experts was often improvised and confusing, after a good deal of patience and perseverance, it did bear its fruits, and its effects can be seen in all the great documents drawn up by the conciliar commissions. In these documents, the most traditional subjects, as well as the newer ones, are dealt with in a perspective that is both doctrinal and incarnated within time. An indication of this is found in the terminology used in the texts: the word "history" occurs sixty-three times; the word "culture" is used ninety-one times, and the word "cultural" thirty-four times; and the words "world," "society," "dialogue," "service," "novelty," "transformation," and "lay" are very frequent. The attention is decidedly on the present of the world and the Church. The terms *hodie* or *hodiernus* occur 145 times. Lexicographical studies have noted how different the terminology of Vatican II is from that of Vatican I, in which the word "culture," for example, occurs only once. [8]

The presence of observers from other Christian confessions represented another characteristic feature of the Council. We might say that they contributed their point of view, and lent their perspective to the whole gathering. Some of them who brought a certain amount of skepticism with them to Rome soon expressed their admiration, and also their confidence in ecumenical research and in the courageous openness of the Council to

the contemporary world. Statements to this effect were made by
the Secretary General of the World Council of Churches,
Visser't Hooft, and by the President of the World Methodist
Council, Rev. Corson, who observed that the Council was tack-
ling the urgent problems of the contemporary world: "I look to it
to tackle particularly problems such as that of the rights and
needs of the young nations, the missionary vocation of Christianity with regard to workers, religious freedom, and the responsibility of lay people."[9]

A New Cultural and Ecclesial Perception

This description of the intellectual and spiritual context enables us to understand the cultural experience lived through by
all those who took part in the Council. Together at the Council,
they experienced a deep immersion in the affairs of the Church
and the world, and they taught one another to use new eyes to
see humanity within history as it waits for Jesus Christ.

This collective sensitization paved the way for a deeper ecclesial awareness. Their dynamic understanding was expressed in
the concept of the people of God on the move through history—
an image of the pilgrim Church that is built up with time. This
concept is both biblical and historical, and provided the ecclesiology of Vatican II with its full existential and pastoral
breadth. Without in any way repudiating it, the Council went
beyond the concept of the Church as perfect society with its own
special rights, and clearly laid the stress on the Church as placed
within the human family as a leaven to serve humanity by evangelizing it. The history of salvation and earthly history must, therefore, be seen as a whole, inasmuch as they have the same
subject—man in his individual and collective aspects—and also
the same divine source. Faith allows us to see that "the earthly
and the heavenly city penetrate each other" (GS 40). *Gaudium et
spes* would echo the principle of *Lumen gentium* a number of
times: ". . . it is the same God who is at once savior and creator,
Lord of human history and of the history of salvation" (GS 41).

Theologians have emphasized the central importance of the
concept of the Church seen in its eschatological dynamism as
this is presented in *Lumen gentium*. With remarkable force and
strong hope, the whole of Chapter VII, "The Eschatological
Character of the Pilgrim Church," shows how the destiny of the

Church is bound up with the liberation of the whole of humanity. We find the following statement:

> . . . the pilgrim Church, in its sacraments and institutions, which belong to this present age, carries the mark of this world which will pass, and she herself takes her place among the creatures which groan and travail yet and await the revelation of the sons of God (cf. Rom. 8:19–22) (LG 48).

Even in the face of a sinful or hostile world, the Church does not set itself apart from men. Although it is, of course, distinct from the world, it will not allow itself to be separated from it, as Paul VI stated in *Ecclesiam suam*, and then repeated, in a formulation that conveys the full force of his conviction, at the opening of the third session, on 14 September 1964: "The Church is not in itself its own end, but wants to belong wholly to Christ, through Christ, in Christ, and wholly to men, among men, and for men."[10]

We can, therefore, say that the theological perspective of Vatican II cannot be separated from its cultural perception of the contemporary world. It is not possible to conceive of the Church outside living cultures, while, on the other hand, human cultures only find true salvation in Jesus Christ. This fact led a number of informed observers of the Council to state that the major document on the Church, *Lumen gentium*, only finds its full significance in the light of *Gaudium et spes*, on the Church in the contemporary world. Cardinal Garrone, who presided over the development of *Gaudium et spes*, recalled that it was Paul VI himself who wanted to make it a Constitution—a pastoral Constitution, maybe, but all the same, a true Constitution, as the Pope insisted to those who had doubts about the idea. Thus, Paul VI stepped in to see that the famous Schema XIII became a Constitution equal in dignity with the other conciliar Constitutions. Cardinal Garrone observes that in a certain sense, the whole of the Council rests on two main pillars: the first is represented by the Constitution on the Church, *Lumen gentium*, with the other two Constitutions—on revelation and the liturgy—that complement it; and the second corresponds to the Pastoral Constitution *Gaudium et spes*, which provides the link with the present situation of the world, and which "has the precise aim of adapting

Lumen gentium to things as they really are, . . . and to the overall problem of man within the world."[11]

No Council throughout history had placed humanity and the world at the Center of its debates in this way.[12] This is the "humanism" of Vatican II, of which Paul VI would speak in unforgettable tones at the close of the Council.

What the Council Had To Say About Culture

The foregoing description was indispensable if we are to assess the importance of the formal teachings of Vatican II on culture. It is maybe significant that the Constitution *Gaudium et spes* was only approved at the end of the Council. The Fathers needed first to have lived through this complex experience of discernment that we have just sketched out. This suggests that their lived experience and their formal teaching should definitely not be seen as isolated from one another. Let us begin with the statements about culture found in *Gaudium et spes* 53–62, after which we shall extend our observations to the other conciliar documents.

A Modern Definition of Culture

The remarkable thing about the definition of culture proposed by *Gaudium et spes* is its modern character, which is borrowed from the human sciences. The two dimensions of culture are found linked in perfect harmony. On the one hand, culture is seen as concerned with the progress of the individual, who develops all his or her potential through the application of intelligence and talents: this is culture as traditionally understood in the classical and humanistic sense. A second, more modern view of culture takes it as meaning the anthropological life experience and the typical mentality of each human group. This twofold dimension of culture as used in *Gaudium et spes* allows us to understand the relationship between the culture of the individual and the cultures of groups, between scholarly culture and living cultures, for it is humanity that is the subject and the beneficiary of all cultural progress.

Let us reread the definition proposed by *Gaudium et spes* 53, bearing in mind the whole cultural experience through which the conciliar gathering had just lived:

The word "culture" in the general sense refers to all those things which go to the refining and developing of man's diverse mental and physical endowments. He strives to subdue the earth by his knowledge and his labor; he humanizes social life both in the family and in the whole civic community through the improvement of customs and institutions; he expresses through his works the great spiritual experiences and aspirations of men throughout the ages; he communicates and preserves them to be an inspiration for the progress of many, even of all mankind.

Hence it follows that culture necessarily has historical and social overtones, and the word "culture" often carries with it sociological and ethnological connotations; in this sense one can speak about a plurality of cultures. For different styles of living and different scales of values originate in different ways of using things, of working and self-expression, of practicing religion and of behavior, of establishing laws and juridical institutions, of developing science and the arts and of cultivating beauty.

We are immediately struck by the fact that this text reveals a dynamic, historical, and concrete view of humanity in the process of building itself up. The text provides a reading key for contemporary history in the form of an anthropological reflection on the progress offered to humanity both individually and collectively. The Church thus provided itself with a modern analytical instrument in order to understand the world better and help it carry out its role in it. This represented a slow but decisive intellectual victory, for since Leo XIII, the Church had been more accustomed to speak of "civilization" and only slowly did it come to adopt the concept of anthropological culture. Even at the time of Pius XII, culture was still understood almost exclusively in the humanistic sense.

A Call to Cultural Analysis

Let us see the sense in which the cultural approach of Vatican II brought a new eye to bear on societies. We should remember that since the great social encyclicals of Leo XIII and Pius XI, and the famous Christmas addresses of Pius XII (not to mention his other writings), the Holy See had shown itself increasingly concerned with the "social question," and the problems of peace, work, capitalism and communism. Even so, the perspective was primarily ethical, so that the labor question, the abuses of capitalism, communist, or fascist regimes, and international conflicts were judged according to moral norms or as being in opposition to "Christian civilization."[13]

Vatican I had intended dealing with a certain number of "social questions," and some draft documents on such matters were indeed drawn up. However, the taking of Rome meant that the Council had to wind up its work prematurely, before it had had time to deal with these questions.[14]

All this reminds us that the Church already has a "social perception" of the modern world. However, the important point is that this social perspective still tended to take the form of moral judgment rather than sociological analysis. The originality of Vatican II would lie precisely in the fact that it took up the modern approach of anthropology, while it obviously in no way repudiated the traditional moral perspective.

The method of cultural analysis based on the human sciences made it easier to understand the collective behavior, thought patterns, dominant values, aspirations, and contradictions of our time. This anthropological approach would be seen at the Council not only as a necessary preliminary to any moral judgment on our times, but also as an indispensable prerequisite for the discovery of new cultures that are waiting for the gospel. The Church is becoming more methodically sensitive to the signs of the times, to significant developments, and to the values and countervalues that challenge the Christian conscience.

Although a number of Catholic scholars were, of course, already using the term "culture" in its more modern sense, the official documents hardly provided the faintest echo. Then, at Vatican II, the official Church updated its view of culture almost overnight. This represented an intellectual journey similar to that made by certain international organizations such as UNESCO or the Council of Europe, which have been trying for some time to move from the traditional concept of culture to one that encompasses the anthropological dimension of living societies as well as the sphere of literature, science, and the arts.[15]

The intention of Vatican II in providing itself with a tool for cultural analysis was that of laying stress on the close link between culture, evangelization, and the mission of the Church. Let us give some references from *Gaudium et spes* to start with, after which we can move on to a rapid survey of the other conciliar documents.

The Conciliar Image of the World and the Church

At the beginning of *Gaudium et spes* (Nos. 4–10), we find a cultural analysis of the contemporary world that even twenty years later seems to us remarkably acute. The contemporary world is described with its hopes and fears, and also the deep changes affecting it in the social, psychological, moral, and religious spheres. This world shows points of serious imbalance, and these, in contrast, point up the universal aspirations of the human race. The Church recognizes this contemporary situation and is thus particularly attentive to the underlying questions of men and women today. It sees the world from the point of view of the gospel, and is aware of the close bonds between culture and the message of salvation: "There are many links between the message of salvation and culture. In his self-revelation to his people culminating in the fullness of manifestation in his incarnate Son, God spoke according to the culture proper to each age" (GS 58). The Church also understands the extent to which cultures can influence religious life, and thus cultures can themselves become the privileged locus for evangelization:

> . . . the Church has existed through the centuries in varying circumstances and has utilized the resources of different cultures in its preaching to spread and explain the message of Christ, to examine and understand it more deeply, and to express it more perfectly in the liturgy and in various aspects of the life of the faithful (GS 58).

A central observation immediately leaps to the eye: culture is not dealt with in itself, in an abstract way; rather, the culture of contemporary man is always seen as the context for theological reflection and pastoral projection. This highlights one of the mainsprings of the Council, that is, the social and theological approach that underlay all its work. We would thus be unduly minimizing its contribution to culture if we considered only the passages of *Gaudium et spes* that deal specifically with the subject, thus seeing culture simply as one chapter among others. On the contrary, everything at the Council was concerned with culture, just as everything was concerned with theology. Contemporary and historical humanity is never absent from its concerns and reflections, and the analytical framework is always both ecclesial and cultural. And this is the perspective in which we must reread and interpret the main documents on bishops, priests, religious, lay people, liturgy, Christian unity, non-Christian religions, religious freedom, and the media. Let us take a few representative examples.

Bishops, priests, and those responsible for the pastoral ministry are warmly called on to use the modern tools of the human sciences, and especially of psychology and sociology, in order to throw light on the cultural circumstances in which they must proclaim the gospel (GS 62). Serious research in this field is strongly encouraged (GS 36).

Religious must seek the driving force of their original vocation and live out their charism in new cultural contexts (PC 3).

Lay people are to play a direct role in the affairs of the secular world, and in the fostering of cultures, so as to bear witness to their faith wherever human values are in question (AA 17).

In ecumenical dialogue, the cultural factors of disunion must be discovered, and from now on, all Christians must be encouraged to work together effectively in the social, economic, and cultural spheres (UR 12).

It is important to be able to discern the seeds of the Word hidden within the heart of non-Christian religions, and seek to integrate into an overall Christian approach all cultural values that are not in opposition to the Catholic faith (AG 11). It is also important that in-depth reflection should be carried out on this point in all the great sociocultural areas (AG 22).

The same approach should be applied to the adaptation of the liturgy to different cultures, while never losing sight of the norms of the universal Church in this regard. It is recommended that the gifts and characteristics of each culture should be carefully examined in order to see what can be assimilated into an authentically Christian liturgical practice (SC 27).

The media come in for special attention, since they have a considerable influence on culture and public morality (IM 12).

Faced with the formidable problem of modern atheism, the Church must reflect on the cultural conditions of belief and unbelief (GS 19–21).

The whole area of education is considered within a perspective of cultural development, with the aim of providing a well-rounded intellectual and spiritual formation for the young, making use of advances in psychology and teaching methods (GE 1).

Culture, understood in the sense of the life of the spirit, is a particularly characteristic dimension of this Council, and in a great variety of contexts, it deals with modern science, and also with its relationship to faith and human development, freedom in research, advances in teaching methods and the human sciences, the human and spiritual formation of priests, religious and lay people, the role of schools and universities, and artistic creation. The focus is always on the person in his or her personal and collective development—a statement that could be supported by citations from almost every document.

The Encounter with the Contemporary Mentality

In more general terms, we can see how attentive the Council was to the mentality of contemporary men and women, and how it sought to give full value to the typical cultural aspirations of our era, such as the desire for participation, the sense of corresponsibility, human solidarity, personal decision-making, interiorization, and religious freedom, as well as the responsibility of lay people, the role of women, the importance of the young, and the universal search for justice, peace, and development for all human beings. These social and pastoral interests can be seen in all the documents as a very practical concern in relation to evangelization. Let us take a look at some of the passages that are concerned especially with pastoral life.

Modern men and women are very conscious of their freedom and personal rights, and in addressing them, the Council emphasizes the free choice of the believer. The rule that religious adherence corresponds to a free commitment on the part of the individual is constantly recalled. This is one of the fundamental principles of the Declaration on Religious Freedom: ". . . the practice of religion of its very nature consists primarily of those voluntary and free internal acts by which a man directs himself to God. Acts of this kind cannot be commanded or forbidden by any merely human authority" (*DH* 3). This also applies to the Christian's act of faith: "The act of faith is of its very nature a free act. . . . The principle of religious liberty contributes in no small way to the development of a situation in which men can without hindrance be invited to the Christian faith, [and] embrace it of their own free will" (*DH* 10).

The critical spirit so typical of modern culture can undoubtedly represent a threat to a superficial faith, but equally it can purify the religious spirit.

> . . . a more critical ability to distinguish religion from a magical view of the world and from the superstitions which still circulate purifies religion and exacts day by day a more personal and explicit adherence to faith. As a result many persons are achieving a more vivid sense of God (*GS* 7).

Participation in the liturgy must be conscious and personal: "Mother Church earnestly desires that all the faithful should be led to that full, conscious, and active participation in liturgical celebrations which is demanded by the very nature of the liturgy," and liturgical reform must aim at this type of active and personal participation as a primary objective (*SC* 14).

The human sciences should be used so that pastoral action can be better adapted not only to the spiritual conditions, but also to the social, demographic, and economic circumstances of different peoples. A great contribution can be provided by "social and religious research conducted by institutes of pastoral sociology, the establishment of which is strongly recommended" (*CD* 16–17).

Lay people are encouraged to express their opinion freely within the Church and to play an active role in research, so that they can serve it better: "By reason of the knowledge, competence and pre-eminence which they have, the laity are empowered—indeed sometimes obliged—to manifest their opinions on those things which pertain to the good of the Church" (*LG* 37).

In more general terms, Catholics must make an effort to understand their historical period: ". . . the faithful ought to live in close conjunction with their contemporaries and try to get to know their ways of thinking and feeling, as they find them expressed in current culture" (*GS* 62). This is a necessary prerequisite for dialogue between the gospel and culture, which requires careful research:

> Let the faithful incorporate the findings of new sciences and teachings and the understanding of the most recent discoveries with Christian morality and thought, so that their practice of religion and their moral behavior may keep abreast of their acquaintance with science and of the relentless progress of technology: in this way they will succeed in evaluating and interpreting everything with an authentically Christian sense of values (GS 62).

We believe that this rapid overview shows one of the most original elements of this Council—in other words, its cultural, historical, and anthropological focus. In his closing speech, Paul VI made a point of stating with remarkable emphasis that this Council had been devoted above all to humanity: "All this doctrinal wealth has but one aim: that of serving man, and here we obviously mean all men, whatever their condition, their sufferings and their needs." When emphasizing "the human value of the Council," he appealed to the modern spirit for understanding, since our period judges everything on the basis of its utility to humanity. This cultural view of humanity is in no way abstract or anthropological, but pastoral: "Our humanism becomes Christianity." Through "the face of every man—especially when tears and sufferings have made it more transparent—we can and must recognize the face of Christ." The whole Council is summed up in this religious conclusion, he adds: "It is nothing other than a friendly and pressing appeal, urging humanity to rediscover God through the path of brotherly love."[16]

Evaluation and Future Prospects

With a view to providing a further projection of our analysis, we shall make three observations that will help to situate the contribution of the Council within a sociohistorical perspective.

1. The outstanding event that took place in the Second Vatican Council was that of making the whole Church aware of a modern approach to cultural changes as these are experienced by contemporary men and women. The Council Fathers became

acquainted with the different cultures, together with their amazing potential, and also their contradictions and conflicts, and
above all their deep-seated aspirations for peace, justice, and
brotherhood. This sensitization on both an intellectual and spiritual level is a gain from which the whole Church has benefitted
and which it can never again go back on. It is now an indispensable form of evangelical discernment in order to understand the
evolving societies of today in their unceasing shared quest for
justice and dignity. This attitude of mind and this attention to
different cultures represents a fundamental step forward taken by
Vatican II. It constitutes a true advance in the capacity for
discernment, which is undoubtedly far more important than the
concrete descriptions and historical reflections the Council has
left us as concerns present cultures. Indeed, the social analysis of
the Council Fathers can still be improved on, and now, twenty
years later, we can recognize its inevitable shortcomings as we are
struck by new cultural problems calling for the attention of the
Church today.

2. In the past twenty years, many cultural questions have
arisen about which it would obviously have been impossible for
Vatican II to have said much. The subsequent teaching of Paul
VI and John Paul II, and the reflections of the various synods and
ecclesial communities, would give these problems an important
place on their agendas.

As an example, we would mention the very contemporary
question of inculturation, which is at the center of lively debates
in the churches of Africa, Asia, and Latin America, but also in
the older churches. Vatican II was not unaware of the problems
underlying the question of inculturation, although it only considered the question in more general terms (cf. GS 58). Indeed, the
term "inculturation" was never even used by the Council, although it had been in current use among Catholics for at least
thirty years. [17] It was not until the 1977 synod that the word made
its appearance in an official text of the Church. [18]

We would also remember the whole debate aroused by the
evangelization of cultures, which the 1974 synod would in due
course describe as one of the priorities of the Church. Paul VI's
Apostolic Exhortation *Evangelii nuntiandi*, which followed this
synod in 1975—ten years after Vatican II—would provide what
has been called a true "charter" for the evangelization of cultures.
In this document, Paul VI was, of course, drawing inspiration

from Vatican II, but he greatly clarified its analysis, translating it into more practical lines of action.

Another contemporary concern is the question of the cultural policies pursued by modern governments in the name of a humanism that may be very praiseworthy in many cases, but that in others is in danger of becoming a form of ideological manipulation. There is a challenge here for Christians that was only considered indirectly by the Council (GS 59).

We should also mention the various questions linked to cultural development, cultural liberation, and cultural rights, all of which are major issues in social policies and action.

The Council was not able to foresee and deal with everything. However, if we reread its teachings in the perspective of present-day problems, we can find the main principles that can still provide us with useful guidelines in the search for solutions. In the first place, we can recognize an analytical approach that makes it possible to set about dealing with new problems with a modern sense of realism and in a spirit of objective research, which is a necessary precondition for any sure discernment.

3. While recognizing the original contribution of Vatican II to culture, we must in all honesty place its contribution within the context of a long historical tradition. We should remember, for instance, the work of Leo XIII, who was so concerned over the changes in Christian civilization at his time, and also that of Pius XI—the pontiff whose Encyclical *Divini illius Magistri* on education (1929) brought about the reform of Catholic universities and faculties. We should also think of Pius XII, whose exceptional mind did not ignore any of the more important human questions of his day. Even so, as we have already noted, until Vatican II, the official Church was more interested in speaking of civilization than of culture, and it was only at the Council that the language of anthropologists and cultural sociologists came to be definitively adopted.

Within this historical perspective, we must also note that the movement has continued apace since Vatican II. Research on new cultural problems has undeniably become both broader and deeper in the past twenty years.

The most noteworthy and promising recent development is the ability shown by the Church to translate the intuitions and declarations of the Council into terms of practical action. Paul VI and John Paul II have played an energetic role in this progress. For the sake of brevity, we shall confine ourselves to two particularly important points. Paul VI and John Paul II have in a sense dramatized what is at stake in the dialogue of the Church with present-day cultures, and have tried to make the involve-ment of Catholics in the service of cultures an active one.

For his part, Paul VI wanted the Synod on Evangelization in 1974 to study the thorny but pressing question of the evangeliza-tion of cultures, which he saw as the major drama of our age. Let us recall his words, which were so full of both concern and hope:

> The rift between the gospel and culture is undoubtedly an unhappy circumstance of our times just as it has been in other areas. Accordingly we must devote all our resources and all our efforts to the sedulous evangelization of human culture, or rather of the various human cultures.[19]

And it will be recalled that John Paul II took another step forward when, at the beginning of his pontificate, he proposed the creation of an office of the Holy See in Rome that was to deal with relations between the Church and the various cultures. After study and reflection, he therefore decided in 1982 to estab-lish the Pontifical Council for Culture, with the precise task of implementing the orientations of Vatican II and translating *Gaudium et spes* into a practical program for the whole Church. He was also aware of how much was at stake here. In the letter establishing the Pontifical Council for Culture, he stated: "Since the beginning of my pontificate, I have considered the Church's dialogue with the cultures of our time to be a vital area, one in which the destiny of the world at the end of this twentieth century is at stake." He went on to say that the mission of the new council would be that of implementing the cultural objec-tives of Vatican II: "For this reason, it seems to me opportune to found a special permanent body for the purpose of promoting the great objectives which the Second Vatican Ecumenical Council proposed regarding the relations between Church and culture."[20]

If we look at the tasks that John Paul II has assigned to this Council for Culture—and in a wider sense to the whole Church—we can gain an idea of the extent of the mission awaiting Catholics within the newly emerging cultures. All the various institutions and sectors of the Church are urged to cooperate in this mission:

the Roman curia, dioceses, Catholic organizations, religious, universities, and centers for research and cultural animation. Christians must give their attention to all the contemporary problems of culture: the progress of the intellectual disciplines and the arts, as well as the cultural policies of governments, the cultural conditions of the development of different peoples, and the activity of international organizations such as UNESCO, the Council of Europe, and the various bodies dealing with science, culture, and education. The whole Church must learn to recognize the new horizons of evangelization as represented by living cultures. It may be pointed out that this is an enormous task, but everything is basically encompassed in the fruitful approach inspired by Vatican II. In the words of John Paul II, "the Church will effectively consecrate itself, in the name of its specific mission, to the progress of culture and fruitful dialogue between cultures, as well as to their beneficial encounter with the Gospel."[21]

Translated from the French by Leslie Wearne.

Notes

1. John XXIII, Opening Speech to the Council (11 October 1962); English translation in W.M. Abbott (gen. ed.), *The Documents of Vatican II* (New York, 1966), 712–716.

2. G.B. Cardinal Montini, *Discorso al Clero 1957–1963* (Milan, 1963), 78–80; the emphasis is ours.

3. R. Aubert, "Attentes des Eglises et du monde au moment de l'election Paul VI," in *Ecclesiam Suam. Première Encyclique de Paul VI. Colloque International. Rome, 24–26 octobre 1980* (Brescia, 1982), 11–39, here 17.

4. See *ibid.*, 20.

5. Paul VI, Opening Speech to the Second Session of the Council (29 September 1963), in *Documenti: Il Concilio Vaticano II* (Rome, 1966), 1018.

6. K. Rahner, "Basic Theological Interpretation of the Second Vatican Council," *TI*, 20 (1981), 77–89, here 85–86.

7. A. Dupront, "Le Concile de Trent," in *Le Concile et les Conciles, Contribution à l'histoire de la vie conciliaire de l'Eglise* (Paris, 1960), 195–243.

8. See R. Aubert, M. Gueret, and P. Tombeur, *Concilium Vaticanum I. Concordances, Index, Listes de fréquence, Tables comparatives*

(Louvain, 1977), 202–240 (comparisons between the vocabulary of Vatican I and that of Vatican II).

9. Rev. Corson, quoted in Aubert, "Attentes des Eglises et du monde au moment de l'election de Paul VI," 39.

10. Paul VI, Opening Speech to the Third Session of the Council (14 September 1964), in *Documenti: Il Concilio Vaticano II*, 1037.

11. G.-M. Cardinal Garrone, *Cinquante ans de vie d'Église, la voix d'un grand témoin* (Paris, 1984), 27.

12. Dupront, "Le Concile de Trente," 242–243, observes, for example, the extent to which these questions were absent from the discussions of the Council of Trent, although the contemporary world was facing the universal conscience with serious problems: "Autre trait, plus brut, de l'univers temporel tridentin. Dans la montée envahissante du capitalisme moderne, face aux problèmes moraux posés par le commerce et le trafic de l'argent, pour lesquels le calvinisme, non sans tâtonnements, est en train de prendre position, le 'corpus' des décrets tridentins demeure silencieux. Convaincus que l'enseignement scholastique suffisait là-dessus, tout ce monde de prélats et de clercs de Trente,—la ville étant même parfois une ville d'étape, par où montait vers l'Empire le métal précieux des Indes—, est-il donc resté aveugle à son temps? L'histoire ne peut que poser la question, en una démarche d'éveil."

13. This is very marked, for example, in the two discourses of Pius XII concerning "Christian civilization"—on 1 September 1944 and on 20 February 1946.

14. The "social" schemata of Vatican I were well analyzed in the thesis published at the Gregorian University by Paolo Petruzzi, *Chiesa e società civile al concilio Vaticano I* (Rome, 1984).

15. It is interesting to note the parallels between the definition of culture found in *Gaudium et spes* 53 and that adopted by UNESCO in Mexico in 1983, at the World Conference on Cultural Policies. The UNESCO definition is found in *Mondiacult: Bilan d'une Conférence, Presence Catholique* (Paris, 1982), 3–4; the following English translation is found in *Church and Cultures*, 1 (1984), 13:

Culture may now be said to be the whole complex of distinctive, spiritual, material, intellectual and emotional features that characterize a society or social group. It includes not only the arts and letters, but also modes of life, the fundamental rights of the human being, value systems, traditions and beliefs; it is culture that gives man the ability to reflect upon himself. It is culture that makes us specifically human, rational beings, endowed with a critical judgment and a sense of moral commitment. It is through culture that we discern values and make choices. It is through culture that man expresses himself, becomes aware of himself, recognizes his incompleteness, questions his own achievements, seeks untiringly for new meanings and creates works through which he transcends his limitations.

16. Paul VI, Closing Speech to the Council (7 December 1965), in *Documenti: Il Concilio Vaticano II*, 1080.

17. See the testimony of P. Charles, in *Etudes Missiologiques* (Louvain, 1956), 137.

18. See the Message of the 1977 Synod to the People of God, in *L'Osservatore Romano* (English edition) (3 November 1977), 3.

19. Paul VI, Apostolic Exhortation *Evangelii nuntiandi* (1975), 20; English translation in A. Flannery (gen. ed.), *Vatican Council II: More Postconciliar Documents* (Grand Rapids, MI, 1982), 719.

20. John Paul II, Letter Instituting the Pontifical Council for Culture, in *AAS*, 74 (1983), 683–688; English translation in *L'Osservatore Romano* (English edition) (28 June 1982).

21. *Ibid.* See also H. Carrier, *Cultures: notre avenir* (Rome, 1985), Chapter VII ("Un Conseil du Saint-Siège pour la culture").

CHAPTER 59

From the Class War
to the Culture of Solidarity

A Fundamental Theme
of the Church's Social Teaching

Johannes Schasching, S.J.

Summary

The social teaching of the Church has often been criticized as being utopian. In other words, it is stated that its goals cannot be achieved in society as it is. This criticism has been made from the point of view of both individualistic and collectivistic ideologies and has been leveled mainly at the basic idea of the necessity and possibility of a social order based on solidarity. In this article, we shall outline three contemporary social problems—namely, the future of work; life and survival in keeping with human dignity; and responsibility for the Third World—and we shall show that only a "culture of solidarity" can adequately deal with these problems, which demand a solution.

In the First Part of the Pastoral Constitution *Gaudium et spes*, the Second Vatican Council gives a vivid description of the profound economic, social, political, and cultural changes affecting the world today. The Council then makes the following statement, which summarizes the goal and the fundamental direction of these changes:

Man as an individual and as a member of society craves a life that is full, autonomous, and worthy of his nature as a human being; he longs to harness for his own welfare the immense resources of the modern world. Among nations there is a growing movement to set up a worldwide community. (GS 9).

However, in order to avoid any possible misunderstanding, *Gaudium et spes* also states expressly that this fulfillment of man and the unity of nations cannot consist in the first place of economical and technical progress but of growth in inner unity and solidarity. Here the Second Vatican Council expresses what we might call one of the fundamental themes of the Church's social teaching, or what Pope John Paul II has described in the phrase, "from class war to a culture of solidarity."[1]

This fundamental thesis of the Church's social teaching soon came under attack. John Paul II's social Encyclical on human work (*Laborem exercens*) was followed by impassioned debates. Alongside numerous positive reactions there was also harsh criticism. The spokesman for one group expressed his point of view as follows:

The ethical goals set by the Pope, namely, the elimination of famine and suffering, a higher standard of living for the broad masses and social security for all, can only be achieved by the economic system criticized by the Pope as being "economistic." Therefore his criticisms remain unfounded until such time as he proposes another economic system that will better attain these goals.[2]

A second criticism came from the opposite camp:

John Paul II has completely misunderstood the meaning of the conflict, especially of the class war, for the progress of mankind. Therefore he cannot interpret history correctly, nor can he offer any useful help for forming the future.

However, in both these criticisms, we repeatedly find the word "Utopia." One spokesman put it this way: "Maybe we have witnessed the birth of what a future historian will call 'the Wojtylian Utopia.' "

The application of the expression "Wojtylian Utopia" was,

however, in no way restricted to this Encyclical Letter by John Paul II on human work, but was applied to the Church's social teaching in general. Thus, it seems necessary to come to grips with this fundamental theme, not in the form of an abstract discussion, but as applied to the society of today and of tomorrow and to its central problem areas.

The "Utopia" of the Church's Social Teaching

In simplified terms we might express this "Utopia" as follows: wherever people live they tend toward different forms of unity with each other, and they pursue various goals: in marriage and family life, in the home, at work, in different types of associations and in the state. However, something else can also easily be observed: these goals cannot be imposed from outside—e.g., love in marriage, affection within the family, roles in games, or fundamental rights of the state. They come from within, from the sense of individual communities.

Is the following point also obvious? The attainment of the various goals of human life in common does not come about automatically but requires conscious participation. Naturally, this conscious participation differs in degree according to the nature of the community, and there will be no fulfillment if individuals think only of themselves and exploit others. At a certain point, consideration for others and compromise is necessary. Naturally, this consideration has various degrees of intensity. It can lead to heroic selflessness in the relationship of a mother with her child and to steady comradeship in the work process. Yet, wherever people jointly pursue certain goals, we can normally presume a certain degree of solidarity. To repeat: this sense of solidarity can exist to very different degrees, and this is why we speak of "degrees of solidarity." Nonetheless, it is solidarity and therefore essentially different from external coercion or a blind mechanism.

Surely this is obvious? Evidently not, since it is this very point that comes under attack by critics. They argue that there are certain forms of human life in common that are indeed characterized by a high degree of solidarity: the family, friendship, neighborhoods. In these situations, responsible effort is meaningful and mutual solidarity may be experienced. It is also possible that at times, solidarity may be effectively expressed in public life: in the context of country farmers or artisans in a small town, for example. However, in industrial society, with its large companies, authoritarian organizations, and bureaucratic centers of power, other laws obtain—above all those of rationalization and specialization. Here the attainment of our goals no longer depends on personal behavior, but automatically demands effective mechanisms that are largely independent of the personal behavior of individuals.

Yet there are really only two of these laws: the iron law of the market that forces the individual to maximum productivity for which he or she is rewarded, or the mechanism of the totalitarian state that has absolute control over production and the distribution of goods and services, and therefore does not depend on the personal behavior of the individual in order to put its political goals into effect.

We can summarize these two positions as follows. Solidarity as a form of interpersonal behavior is essentially determined by the type of society one lives in. It has its usefulness and meaning even in industrial society—in the intimate areas of family, friendship, voluntary associations, etc. However, in the megastructures of industrial society—that is to say, in the area of production and distribution, where there are large companies, authoritarian organizations, and, above all, national and multinational structures—forces rule that have their own independent manner of functioning: market, competition, power, and domination.[3]

The Challenges Facing Us as We Reach the Year 2000

It is not possible to discuss all the questions that spontaneously arise here. Certain of these will be discussed in the third section of this essay. Here we are primarily concerned with another question: in the face of three contemporary worldwide problems, we wish to investigate whether they can be solved entirely, or for the most part, by social mechanisms or whether they require new forms of properly understood solidarity.

The Future of Work

Human work has always been a decisive factor in social change. John Paul II considers work to be the key to understanding the modern social question.[4] During the industrial revolution, it totally transformed the world of farmers and artisans. At the present time, we are witnessing a new phase in the scientific and technical revolution that will again engender profound social change.

An effect of this that can no longer be ignored is unemployment. Statistics show about 35 million unemployed in the western industrial countries, and over 12 million in the European community alone. In many countries, there are modest signs of an industrial boom to come, yet even a boom could hardly eliminate the basic problem. According to experts in West Germany, in order to achieve full employment, the annual growth rate would have to reach six percent, i.e., production would have to double in twelve to fourteen years. Yet, at the same time, this is declared to be neither possible nor desirable. Aside from the question of market outlets, there is the problem of the limits of natural resources and the environment.

However, it is clearly seen that unemployment represents the most expensive, socially harmful, and unjust form of reduction of working hours. Two million unemployed in West Germany cost 50 billion Deutschmarks per year in the form of payments by the Federal Department of Labor and in the form of reduced income for the state. To this, we must add a further 200 billion Deutschmarks lost in the social effects of unemployment. These effects, especially among young people, have been only partially studied and will be felt completely only after more time has elapsed. This problem has to be taken seriously, and we should not simply try to solve it by proposing ways of employing one's free time. What is at stake here is of major consequence, and it effects people at a stage in their lives for which it is subsequently very difficult to make up for what has been lost.

In our society, there is also talk of an increase in dissatisfaction in other areas of need. In other words, although industrial society has been successful to a considerable degree in satisfying the basic material needs of the masses and in creating a whole range of new material needs, at the same time, because of its specific nature, this same society creates a whole series of social problems and needs to which it is much less capable of responding: humane care for sick people, young people, and the aged; integration of the socially underprivileged; ways of spending integration of the socially underprivileged; ways of spending leisure time in keeping with human dignity; education; and ecology of the urban and natural environment.

These and many other social and sociopsychological areas of need are in no way problems of transition, but are already established elements of modern civilization, and are on the increase. And what is normally referred to as the quality of life is essentially dependent on our response to these problems.

The future of man's labor will be determined by various factors. A great deal of very sober consideration and realistic observation is necessary. A large number of laws will have to be passed, ranging from local agreements to international pacts. This will all happen, and it is utopian to imagine that such measures are not indispensable. Yet this is not all; nor is it even the most important factor. In West Germany, the task was recently formulated as follows: the crisis can only be overcome when all groups involved in the economic life of the nation make a concerted effort and agree on a pact of solidarity to overcome unemployment. In other words, the problems of distribution of work, unemployment among youth, and the satisfaction of other needs in the work market can no longer be solved automatically by the mechanisms now functioning, but a fundamental decision is needed based on the fact that the present crisis can only be overcome through solidarity on the part of all groups. This solidarity will demand consideration and sacrifice on the part of all—from the individual consumer to labor organizations, private entrepreneurs and their businesses, and the state.

If this basic decision is recognized and accepted in its essential terms, it does not mean that there will not still be conflicts. There will be need for clear legal provisions, and there will be risks because the future can never be totally planned in advance. However, solutions will be found that will give further help if they are sufficiently comprehensible and are accepted by the majority of those concerned. If this does not take place and we continue to rely on mechanisms and improvisation, the problems—especially those of a social nature—will intensify, with all the concomitant consequences.[5]

The Poverty of the Third World

The statistics concerning this poverty are so well known today that they need not be repeated. However, there is one fact, the consequences of which may not be fully known. In 1970, the population of the Third World amounted to seventy-four percent of the world population. In the year 2000, it will already amount to between eighty-one and eighty-four percent. Extremely worrying information is coming in from a number of Third World countries, especially in Africa, but also in Latin America. Of course, there are also encouraging successes, but instead of the hoped-for overall progress, development has been very uneven. Certain economic sectors have expanded excessively during periods of economic revival and speculation, whereas others have remained static or have degenerated. In a number of countries, self-sufficiency in basic foods has declined frighteningly, and there is an increase of total dependency on foreign countries. Five hundred and sixty million people are living in absolute poverty.

Of course, the problem of the Third World is extremely complex, and there is always the temptation to oversimplify the analysis and to propose radical solutions. Yet the problem looms today in all its harshness, especially if we look at it first of all not from its economic and political effects on industrial countries, but in terms of the human tragedy it represents. It is simply no longer acceptable in conscience that the world, in an age of human rights and precise information, should take for granted the fact that countless numbers of people die of hunger every day or must struggle for survival in conditions of extreme poverty.[6]

Here, too, the question immediately arises: Can the tragedy of the Third World be solved by economic and social means alone, or is not a new, worldwide effort of genuine solidarity needed as well? In any case, this is the express conviction inherent in the social teaching of the Church, above all in the Encyclical on the progress of peoples. We should not misunderstand the social teaching of the Church. It in no way says that measures adopted so far in favor of the Third World have not been undertaken in a spirit of solidarity. Nor does it say that the solution to the tragedy must be borne exclusively by the industrialized countries. The Church is very well aware of the fact that Third World countries must make decisions and take responsibility. It is of the opinion that in the long run, the problem of the Third World can only be solved by gradual incorporation of these countries into worldwide economic relations. It is for this very reason that in order to make this possible, the industrial nations must produce a new "pact of solidarity" that is not conditioned first and foremost by mechanisms and self-interest, but by a sense of responsibility for mankind.

The Question of Life and Survival

When in days gone by a peasant mismanaged his farm and deprived his heir of his inheritance, this was a local tragedy. Today, responsibility from one generation to another is essentially different. Given today's economic and technical means, the present generation is able to destroy the environment so thoroughly that future generations will have to bear the consequences. This devastation is in no way the result of a major rape of nature alone. It occurs through the invisible sum of small acts of egotism and irresponsible exploitation of natural resources. This is especially difficult to control when it serves to relaunch an economy and to ensure full employment.

During his visit to Austria, John Paul II stated clearly that the earth is not a reservoir that can be endlessly exploited. In this case, too, we are faced with the following question: Can responsibility for the future of our world from generation to generation be ensured by economic mechanisms, or is not behavior that very consciously expresses solidarity also necessary on the part of the present generation?[7]

Even more ominous is the question of survival. John Paul II is convinced that it is the most dangerous error of our time to believe that we have found in the mutual deterrent of atomic weapons the mechanism that will prevent war. Quite apart from the fact that constant rearmament involves the waste of vast intellectual and material resources that are urgently needed in order to overcome the tragedy of the Third World, it exposes us to an escalation of uncontrollable risks to such an extent that the likelihood of an atomic war is increasing. It is this very fear that gave rise to the massive movements for peace.

However, if the mechanism of deterrent rearmament is increasingly proving to be indefensible, what are the alternatives? There is no other way than that of mutual disarmament, which will be

possible only if the major powers go further along the path of
negotiation and mutual trust, overcome their desire to dominate
and are able to reach a minimum of solidarity that alone can
guarantee the survival of mankind.[8]

Paths Toward a Culture of Solidarity

How utopian is the basic idea of the Church's social teaching
in the face of the three major problems of contemporary mankind: the future of work, the tragedy of the Third World, and the
question of life and survival? One thing must be stated quite
clearly: the Church's social teaching would indeed be utopian if
it were to overlook two facts. The first is that solidarity alone is
not sufficient. On all levels of social life, other constructive
forces are necessary, especially in order to fulfill the major tasks
required of mankind. A high degree of objectivity and rationality
is necessary and, in certain areas, automation by mechanism. It
is clear that there will always be tensions and conflicts, but all of
this can certainly be made to harmonize with solidarity. Indeed,
we could go further and say that a certain amount of solidarity is
already at work in the sensible ordering and integration of all
these factors.

A second aspect must also not be overlooked. It would be
utopian to demand more than can be expected of human beings
by expecting the same degree of solidarity at every level of society. We have already referred to the existence of varying degrees
of solidarity. There is the kind of solidarity between friends and
members of a team that can lead one to go as far as to risk one's
own life, and there is the kind that we find difficult and that we
have to force ourselves to respect. There is also the kind that
finds its expression more in concessions and legal regulations
than in displays of affection. It is, nevertheless, genuine solidarity, since in the last analysis, it has its origins in mutual obligation and responsibility.

This leads automatically to the question of how in modern
society this attitude of mutual obligation and responsibility can
be developed—not just as the peculiarity of some individuals and
small groups but as the basic attitude of a nation. It is striking
that John Paul II often speaks in this context of a "culture of
solidarity." Culture is not the private property of a privileged

stratum, but the heritage of an entire nation. Furthermore, it is never taken from a single source, but from a multiplicity of riches: from the simplest folk song to the greatest opera, from a carved toy to a precious painting.

Likewise, the culture of solidarity is not derived from a single source. It requires a multiplicity of circumstances leading to practice and experience, which, over a lengthy process and in combination with each other, render possible the types of behavior and structures that comprise what is called the culture of solidarity. This is also part of the basic theme of the Church's social teaching.

One of these indispensable circumstances permitting practice and experience is, as ever, marriage and family. The very mention of these two concepts today produces an immediate reaction of skepticism. There is no doubt that the modern family has suffered greatly from a series of circumstances that have seriously diminished its role as a context for this practice and experience. Furthermore, it is not likely that the immediate future will bring about major changes in this respect. Nonetheless, it has been seen that despite its limits, the modern family represents an indispensable context for experiencing solidarity. Therefore, we can easily understand why all responsible forces—above all the Church's social teaching—set great store by the preservation and consolidation of the family.[9]

A second context for practice and experience of solidarity is the school and education. This area has increased in importance considerably over the last few centuries, precisely in relation to the change in the family. Of course, socially oriented education is not without its problems. It is all too susceptible to ideological abuse. Despite this, it is indispensable that future generations be introduced into and prepared for the social context that they will be called to determine. An essential component of this process is awareness of mutual responsibility and solidarity. It cannot be limited to theory. It is precisely during the formative years that social experience should have the corresponding practice. A broad field is opened up for pedagogical initiative.

A third context for practice and experience is the young generation itself. The period of the great youth movements, with their ability to create community, is long past. Youth today has other forms of encounter. In any case, they will determine the level of solidarity in tomorrow's world. At present, this generation is the victim of a lack of solidarity. They are relatively well informed (or at least the avant-garde is) about the mechanisms of organized society, and some of them reject this system in its totality, whereas others oppose it in a less aggressive way. This generation needs a credible experience of solidarity at various levels: at work, in career opportunities, in politics and government. The modern industrial society should offer tangible signs of solidarity, even if it runs the risk of not reaping the immediate profit that young people might be justified in expecting in other sectors. Here, too, a great deal is at stake.

A fourth context for experience and action is what is called the "intermediate social structures." This covers a multiplicity of social groups that cannot be defined precisely: local communities, professional associations, businesses, private interest groups, nonprofessional associations, leisure groups, cultural institutions, etc. This is the broad belt of social groups situated between the family and the state. On closer examination, it is surprising how many of these groups exist and how many ways the average person is integrated into them. Recently, John Paul II made the following remarkable statement:

> It is not possible to expect a fully developed attitude of solidarity from man with respect to the state and to the international community if this is not promoted and practiced on the level of intermediate social structures.

The Pope then continued as follows:

> The growth of this solidarity is substantially dependent on whether the intermediate social structures are successful in offering their members a real possibility of joint responsibility and participation, and whether they can keep themselves from becoming bureaucratic systems which increase man's social alienation and his demands on society.[10]

This puts it in a nutshell: behavior expressing solidarity in the average person bespeaks two convictions: that his or her behavior will actually have an effect on its object, and that the other will also behave toward him or her with solidarity. These conditions are best met in the intermediate social structures. It is well known that labor unions, cooperatives, and savings organizations were founded on the conviction that real hardship can be eliminated only by mutual solidarity.

Why do the intermediate social structures no longer have this power to bring about solidarity? It is interesting to note that John Paul II himself gives two reasons for this: first, it may be due to the fact that the state restricts and thus paralyzes them; second, the intermediate social structures themselves run the risk of "bureaucratic sclerosis," leaving too little space for their members to practice solidarity and to experience it. There is no doubt that we need to consider this question seriously, since these structures could produce substantial stimuli for recuperating a sense of solidarity.

A fifth context is what is known as the "political arena." We avoid the term "state" intentionally, although it obviously plays an important role. The "political culture" of a country is substantially responsible for making possible an awareness of solidarity or for engendering distrust, rejection, and a class mentality. This process is incipient in the very behavior and consciousness of the political parties and it expresses itself most—or least—credibly in its legislation, government, and justice. In the end, it has concrete repercussions on the personal behavior of those who receive political mandates. It would be impossible to discuss all the ramifications that are involved. However, there is no doubt that in this age of free information, the political arena—within its proper limitations—can be a major context for the practice and experiencing of solidarity. Or it can be decisive in making it decline.

The Pastoral Constitution *Gaudium et spes* formulates this task as follows:

> The growing complexity of modern situations makes it necessary for public authority to intervene more often in social, cultural, and economic matters in order to bring about more favorable conditions to enable citizens and groups to pursue freely and effectively the achievement of man's well-being in its totality (GS 75).

However, the Council also makes the following proviso:

> Governments should take care not to put obstacles in the way of family, cultural or social groups or of organizations and intermediate institutions, nor to hinder their lawful and con-

structive activity. . . . Citizens, on the other hand, either individually or in association, should take care not to vest too much power in the hands of public authority nor to make untimely and exaggerated demands for favors and subsidies, lessening in this way the responsible role of individuals, families and social groups (*ibid*).

Practice in solidarity has to take concrete form in a particular way as regards responsibility for developing countries, as we have already said. The Church's social teaching formulates this task in the following terms:

The solidarity which binds all men and makes them members of the same family imposes upon political communities enjoying abundance of material goods the obligation not to remain indifferent to those political communities whose citizens suffer from poverty, misery, and hunger, and who lack even the elementary rights of the human person (*Mater et magistra* 157).

A sixth area for the practice and experience of solidarity is the broad field of voluntary work. This may be off-putting to some, but it must be remembered that solidarity is to a very great extent an experience of good will and aid to our fellow man, and this can be done excellently through the many forms of voluntary service. Many of the social services provided by public authorities today were provided by voluntary associations in preindustrial society. Examples of this are service of the sick, orphans, and the destitute. Of course, the social network of modern society has its great advantages, but this same society engenders a whole series of new problems that can be dealt with only by the state—with great difficulty or failure, as we have already seen. So the demand for voluntary work becomes pressing once again.

Modern industrial society has a considerable reserve of voluntary workers at its disposal, and this can be of great significance for the development of a culture of solidarity. Through the reduction of work hours, early retirement, and a series of other factors, there is a large group of people looking for meaningful work. Some of them are certainly prepared to work without remuneration, while others could be given partial remuneration. These initiatives need in no way originate from the public authorities. Joint responsibility could well be borne by local groups and private organizations. We must bear in mind that a great deal is already being done along these lines—more than meets the public eye. However, the fundamental importance of voluntary work in a culture of solidarity should not be underestimated.

A seventh way of mediating solidarity is through all that which comes under the heading of social communication. As Vatican Council II puts it: "Public opinion exercises enormous influence nowadays over the lives, private or public, of all citizens, no matter what their walk in life" (IM 8). It is characteristic that the same Council, speaking of the formation of experts in modern means of communication, refers explicitly to the importance of the Church's social teaching, in other words, to the service of human society (cf. IM 15).

The freedom of the means of social communication from state control is a high value, which, however, also represents a great responsibility on the part of society. If public opinion is consciously or unconsciously saturated with negative events, it can be driven to adopt a basic attitude that is distant or even directly hostile to society. By publicizing events that are constructive for society, however, we can contribute to spreading and developing a basic attitude of solidarity.

An eighth context for practicing and experiencing solidarity is represented by the Church. The Second Vatican Council states expressly:

> Christ did not bequeath to the Church a mission in the political, economic, or social order: the purpose he assigned to it was a religious one. But this religious mission can be the source of commitment, direction and vigor to establish and consolidate the community of men according to the law of God (GS 42).

In this connection, we are naturally not considering the theological side of the question. However, from the sociological viewpoint alone, religion and the Church signify an indispensable contribution to the motivation and practice of solidarity.

In the deposit of faith, the Church possesses a large number of statements justifying solidarity between people. These are in no way marginal to its message, but belong to its very core. Hence, love for one's neighbor, readiness to help, and joint responsibility are in no way simply directives limited to the world; they are directly related to salvation. Naturally, it is essential that these statements be constantly incorporated into preaching—particularly now, when anonymity and alienation between human beings has made it extremely difficult to bring about authentic solidarity.

However, apart from the sociological sphere, the Church has other possibilities and tasks in this area inasmuch as the Church is not an abstract institution but lives in active local churches and parishes. It gathers people together for regular encounters in liturgical celebrations and bears shared responsibility for youth and families; it is concerned with social distress and the elimination of injustice. The life of the local churches depends substantially on their success in effecting joint participation and shared responsibility on the part of believing people. The significance of this solidarity is in no way restricted to the confines of the Church community, but is exceedingly fruitful for society as a whole.

How utopian is the Church's social teaching? How utopian is its basic principle of a "culture of solidarity" in the face of mankind's major tasks in the year 2000? Of course, it would be utopian to believe that the Church's social teaching alone can provide a tailor-made solution for all social problems. It cannot do so, and in many ways, it is looking for an answer, just as are a whole series of other social forces. However, it possesses a fundamental message that, if understood correctly and without prejudice, represents a substantial guide.

We wish to emphasize the fact that the society toward which we are moving has set enormous tasks for mankind in the areas of economics, politics, and interpersonal and international relations. No doubt the future will place at our disposal new scientific and technical knowledge that will be of substantial help in our response to these new tasks, but on its own, this will not be enough. As scientific and technical instruments proliferate, the question of criteria and norms becomes ever more urgent in order to regulate their use. The instruments themselves cannot provide these norms and goals, which must instead be sought from a higher consensus. And this consensus cannot be expected simply to appear ready-made before us, but is nothing other than the fruit of a culture of solidarity.

Translated from the German by Ronald Sway.

Notes

1. Address to the Catholic lawyers of Italy, *L'Osservatore Romano* (10 December 1983).

2. *Fortune Magazine* (2 November 1981).

3. Concerning the "autonomy of earthly affairs," cf. *Gaudium et spes* 36.

4. John Paul II, Encyclical *Laborem exercens* 3.

5. Oswald von Nell-Breuning, *Arbeit vor dem Kapital* (Vienna, 1983).

6. Paul VI, Encyclical *Populorum progressio* 30; English translation, Catholic Truth Society (London, 1967): "There are certainly situations whose injustice cries to heaven."

7. Petro C. Beltrão (ed.), *Ecologia e valori etico-religiosi* (Rome, 1985).

8. John XXIII, Encyclical *Pacem in terris* 126; English translation, Vatican Polyglot Press (Vatican City, 1963): "Men are becoming more and more convinced that disputes which arise between States should not be resolved by recourse to arms, but rather by negotiation."

9. The "Charter of the Rights of the Family" (1983) expressly calls the family a "community of love and solidarity."

10. Address to the Catholic lawyers of Italy, *L'Osservatore Romano* (10 December 1983).

CHAPTER 60

The Implications of the Teaching
of *Gaudium et spes* on Peace

Joseph Joblin, S.J.

Summary

The authors of *Gaudium et spes* wanted to reconsider war and peace in new terms. In their reflections, they did not make explicit use of the just war theory, but took a pastoral approach. There is still the question of whether they meant to break with the traditional approach seen in the interventions of the Church in the political sphere, which Paul VI and John Paul II would appear to have wanted to uphold in many cases. The present study shows that the interplay of pastoral and political concerns must be strengthened in the years to come, and also that the local churches must become involved in this movement.

———————
———————

Chapter V of Part Two of *Gaudium et spes,* on peace, is un-doubtedly the most frequently cited section of the Pastoral Constitution on the Church in the Modern World, since anybody who is concerned over the possibility of the atomic destruction of the world finds the statement there that "peace is possible"[1] if certain fundamental principles of morality are observed in international relations, and those who "call themselves Christians"[2] find guidelines as to how to act as servants of reconciliation in a dangerously divided world.

This concern to clarify the position of the individual person vis-à-vis violence led the authors of Chapter V to emphasize the responsibility of the individual and the various communities with regard to violence. In doing so, they left aside the political dimension that had for so long been one of the features of the action of the Church in the cause of peace.

Now that we are carrying out a first evaluation of the Council, it therefore seems helpful to consider the extent to which *Gaudium et spes* intended breaking with the past. In other words, did the Council's choice of a perspective based on its analysis of the "signs of the times" break with a tradition that admitted the existence and exercise of a political responsibility for peace, or did it, on the other hand, see it as still alive and relevant? And, in the latter case, how are these two lines to be harmonized?

This is the question the present article seeks to clarify, and to this end, we shall first of all recall how the Church has, historically speaking, been led to give a political dimension to its action for peace, and then go on to examine the position it may still be given today.

The Political Dimension of Peace

During the course of history, the Church has progressively come to recognize its political responsibility with regard to peace, and this responsibility took on clearer outlines in the last century in the context of the various forms of nationalism. The French Revolution made the political actors of the whole world realize the power they could obtain by mobilizing people in the service of a state ideology.[3] The triumphant liberalism of the nineteenth century had slipped from economics to politics, inasmuch as it had forced governments to place all their material and human resources at the service of the power of the state. This resulted in a growing rivalry between them for the monopoly of raw materials and markets. In the face of this situation, Pius IX understood that the Holy See and the papal states were in danger of being dragged into a new mechanism, in which each side would try to throw into the scales on its side all its moral and economic weight—and, prior to 1870, its military weight, too—to the detriment of the other, not for the sake of justice, but for simple material aims. Thus, we have the first declaration showing the completely new perception of the position of the papacy in international society: addressing the Consistory on 20 April 1849,

Pius IX noted that the Catholic world expected of the Roman
Pontiff "all the more rightly a shining justice and much more
serious reasons . . . to declare war" than was the case for
princes.[4] In this way, he was recognizing the special position of
the Pope as spiritual power in the modern world, together with
the specific responsibility this entailed. Even after the disappearance of the papal states, this view was supported even by non-
Catholic sovereigns. In 1897, Queen Wilhelmina of the Netherlands elicited a letter of support from Leo XIII for the Conference
of the Hague despite the position of Italy,[5] and in 1890, the
Emperor Wilhelm involved Leo XIII in the diplomatic Conference of Berlin on regulations as to working conditions.[6] These
two interventions indicated the special role that the Holy See
could play on the international scene in connection with two
types of humanitarian problems. The Holy See eventually saw its
competence in the field of humanitarian law explicitly recognized by the belligerents in 1914, when they agreed that the
Pope should act as go-between for the protection of refugees, the
supervision of the conditions of prisoners of war, and the exchange of sick prisoners, etc.[7]

However, the role of the Holy See was not limited to the relief
of unnecessary suffering during the First World War. It also had
political aims, and brought its influence to bear for the drawing
up of a fair peace between the parties. At the beginning, this
action brought the papacy indirectly into the diplomatic sphere,
inasmuch as the appeals of Benedict XV were addressed to the
consciences of peoples and of heads of state, especially Christian
ones, with a view to fostering within them the will to resist the
temptation to hatred, vengefulness, and the desire to dominate,
and also willingness to accept the idea of negotiating the end to a
pointless slaughter that was leading their countries to fall from
the high level of civilization they had previously reached into a
barbarism unacceptable to any responsible person.[8] The exercise
of this mission of peace made Benedict XV the actual artisan of
the policy sketched by Pius IX sixty years earlier, since he took
his equal responsibility to all people as the basis of his right to
call on each one to make a great effort at lucidity and courage.[9]

The call launched by Benedict XV to the warring parties on 1
August 1917 marked a new type of initiative of the Holy See on
the international stage. This initiative in favor of peace was
much more directly "political" than the previous ones, and this

can be seen in both its form and its content. In its form, inasmuch as it was communicated to the belligerent governments through diplomatic channels, and, where these did not exist, according to traditionally recognized procedures; thus, Great Britain acted as intermediary with France, which had broken off relations with the Holy See, and Prussia acted as intermediary with Bulgaria and Turkey. However, it was especially the content of the message that was new: apart from the normal reflections on the reasons why the belligerents of all sides should bring the conflict to an end, there were the personal suggestions of the Pope as to how the process of peace should be put into action together with the offer to assist in this, thus showing the Pope's intention of entering fully into the interplay between the political sides involved. In many cases of arbitration and conciliation in which the Holy See had been involved in the past, this had taken place on the invitation of the parties concerned to lend his good offices because of his moral authority and their trust in him. However, with the call of 1917, the papacy itself entered into the diplomatic arena, and thus reached what seems to be the high point in the exercise of a political responsibility for peace—although, however spectacular and exceptional it may have been in this form, it confirmed a type of presence that the Holy See has always maintained in the world, discreetly but with a certain permanence, through its diplomatic missions to the various states and international bodies.[10]

The Council and the Political Responsibility
of the Church for Peace

We say "political responsibility of the *Church*" and not only of the Holy See, for the question today is that of the part played by local churches in this type of presence of the Church in the world.

It must be admitted that these points were not really dealt with by those who drafted *Gaudium et spes*. If we take each of the two parts of Chapter V, we can see that the perspective adopted is that of the awakening of Christians to the exercise of their responsibility for peace. And this concern is not expressed only in the definition of peace. While the 1965 text (sometimes known as the "pink schema"), which was the basis for the final text, gave pride of place to peace as a result of the establishment of order (*tranquillitas ordinis*), only at the last moment did the subcommission entrusted with polishing the project change the perspective. Thus, it brought the bond between justice and peace to the forefront (whereas the notion of order is often associated with that of injustice in the modern world), and emphasized the responsibility of Christians to reform society "ceaselessly" in order to conform it ever more closely to the requirements of justice: "Peace is the work of justice."[11]

The basis of the whole doctrinal structure of Chapter V is the traditional statement that defensive war can still be seen as legitimate in certain circumstances. This in turn means the need to recognize the legitimacy of military service, but also that of respecting both nonviolence and conscientious objection, which are viewed as prophetic witnesses to how things should be. Nevertheless, not everything is permissible even in defensive war and preparations for it; hence, the twofold condemnation of the arms race and the indiscriminate use of modern arms against civilian populations. The second section, on the building of peace, then provides some general orientations: presuming that the international institutions are a prefiguration of the society to come, it supports them and takes them as the basis of its instructions, stating that their implementation will be translated into the participation of Christians in the life of these bodies, and the active presence of nongovernmental Catholic organizations in international life in order to represent Christian social thought on the international scene or help Christians to take part in development by offering them a structure for participation in political life.

The postconciliar period was marked by the efforts of Christian communities to assimilate these orientations. Basic groups such as bishops within their dioceses, or certain conferences of bishops, took the conciliar text as the basis for a full examination of conscience with regard to the attitude they should adopt, in the name of their lived faith, on the question of the defense policies of their governments. There was a real explosion of activity, leading to the spontaneous birth of many groups, especially in the Netherlands, Germany, England, the United States, and Canada,[12] and these groups made an effort to work out common approaches and also to collaborate with other peace movements. In the face of the monstrous development of the arms race, and also of the growing sophistication of weapons for mass destruction, they soon realized that the vital point was that of the immediate avoidance of the nuclear threat, and reflected on the duty of states even to unilateral disarmament.[13] It will be recalled that the most extreme pacifists in this movement adopted the slogan "Better red than dead!"

The pacifist movement in the Church gave rise to pastoral letters from various bishops, who thus contributed their points of view on the contemporary questions of defense to which many people—especially the young—give a high priority.[14] Their interventions can be seen within the pastoral perspective of helping Christians—and all those who share their concern to act morally for peace—in their decisions as citizens with regard to the policies of their government on peace or war. These letters can be seen as a sort of high-level, developed catechesis, explaining the teachings and helping to spread them. The perspective adopted is perfectly legitimate. However, certain people may wonder whether it has not broadened the very precise perspective adopted by the Council to the point of making us forget to some extent the political dimension the Church had hitherto given to its action for peace. Others will answer this concern precisely by stating that the intention of the Council was that of seeing the Church definitively give up its participation in international political life in order to play an essentially religious role. In other words, following the Council, can or should the Church, which is the people of God, still play a role in the political community of mankind?

The Church as the People of God
in the Service of Peace

It is not easy to give a definitive answer to the question thus raised of the permanence of a political role for the Church, since if such a role exists, it will be played along lines that depend to a large extent on the individual circumstances. A certain number of points can, however, be made.

1. The fact that the Church has exercised an influence in the political sphere even from prior to the age of Constantine and that its role has only grown over the centuries, makes it seem presumptuous for a believer to reject out of hand this manner of

serving the cause of peace among humanity. This view has long-established tenure in its favor, and those who challenge the legitimacy of this form of service should show its essential and fundamental incompatibility with the gospel.

2. This practice of the Church has taken on different forms, on the basis of prudent discernment of different circumstances.

3. The appeal of 1 August 1917 is a consequence of an initiative of the Holy See that had given it the position of a protagonist in a diplomatic game with new rules, which were just beginning to be seen. Thus, the war revealed the impass to which nationalist movements had led, and also the need for absolute sovereignty to submit to the requirements of the general good.

4. This new international attitude of the Holy See was adopted and even extended by the Popes following Benedict XV. Although the Second World War did not see any initiative as spectacular as the 1917 one, which provided the effective foundations for an immediate negotiation with a view to bringing the war to a close, the structures of relations between the Holy See, the various states, and the different international institutions continued to grow constantly stronger. More than 100 states now have diplomatic missions to the Holy See, and the Church is present—usually as an observer—at almost all worldwide or regional international organizations; it has also been a full member of the Helsinki proceedings from the very outset of their preparatory phase. The presence of the Holy See in these various bodies and meetings is in no way symbolic. The representatives of the Holy See are not afraid of entering into the thick of debates, and John Paul II has on a number of occasions directly and publicly addressed heads of state: on the eve of the Madrid Conference, which was to approve the implementation of the Helsinki Agreements,[15] and also to the heads of atomic powers on the disastrous consequences that any atomic conflict would be bound to have for all humanity.[16] These few examples go to show that neither Paul VI nor John Paul II has interpreted *Gaudium et spes* as indicating an end to the exercise of a responsibility of the Holy See within the international political community.

We must, therefore, accept that there are still two living traditions within the Church for the promotion of peace, one of which operates on the political level, and the other on the pastoral level. And nothing indicates that either of them is about to be eliminated. Is it, on the other hand, possible that they will grow closer together, thus augmenting the unified character of the action of the Church in the contemporary world?

It would seem at first glance that the answer to this question must be in the negative, in view of the fact that bishops have devoted all their efforts in the pastoral field to encouraging the individual action of Christians for peace, and have often criticized or expressed regret that the involvement of the ecclesiastical authorities on behalf of peace may have been overly political. Even so, three observations can be made that make it possible to forecast a renewal of the role of the Church in questions of peace on the international level—a renewal that is due specifically to the awakening of local Christian communities to an active responsibility in this area.

(a) To the extent that the educational action of local churches is successful, bishops will find themselves among the most authoritative interpreters of the new political force that Christian movements for peace will represent within a democratic society. In any case, are we not already seeing that bishops are being consulted—sometimes more publicly and sometimes more discreetly—by governments that want to understand their objections or preferences in matters of peace and war? The famous declaration made by Cardinal Krol in 1979 as President of the U.S. Conference of Catholic Bishops must surely be seen as an action of a local church on the national level with a view to pointing the policies of a government in a specific direction. From the point of view of the analysis carried out here, the condemnation of mass destruction and total war contributed nothing new to the debate on nuclear arms, since this has always been a feature of traditional Christian teaching. However, should the corollary added to this declaration—in other words, the urgent moral obligation to emerge from this situation—not be viewed as an entry into the active political sphere, inasmuch as it aims at legitimating deterrents for a certain time, and calls on people to negotiate in order to emerge from this situation as soon as possible?[17]

(b) It is known that while they were preparing their pastoral letter on peace, the American bishops sent their various drafts to many outstanding figures both in the United States and in other countries. A number of European bishops were most concerned when they read these drafts, since they felt that the actual circumstances of the populations entrusted to their own charge prevented them from adopting all the conclusions in the suggested pastoral letter of their transatlantic colleagues. In view of this concern, Monsignor Silvestrini, Secretary of the Council for the Church's Public Affairs, organized a meeting in Rome in order to reconcile the different points of view. Under the chairmanship of Cardinals Casaroli and Ratzinger, representatives of the bishops of the United States and of Europe met in the Vatican. This meeting clearly demonstrated the need to move beyond the previous style of action, in which moral judgments on individual wars was almost always linked to a national interpretation of the universal common good; such an attitude had to give way to the integration of these moral judgments into a broader view of the general good. Discussion between the various bishops concerned and the Holy See thus makes it possible for local churches to extend their responsibility to the whole world. The letters of the Bishops' Conferences of the Federal Republic of Germany, the United States, and France, which were published after the meeting, clearly echo these concerns.[18] The time has come to consider whether this collegial approach adopted by the bishops of different countries with a view to exercising their responsibility as regards peace has had any effect on the political level. It must surely have such an effect, inasmuch as their intention is that of awakening their populations to the real facts of defense in the present world and encouraging them to put pressure on their governments to bring their policies into line with the requirements of morality? And this is the sense in which the political powers have understood episcopal interventions, as a result of which they have opened up a dialogue with the bishops on these questions. The bishops' letters, of course, aim at the education of consciences, as the "pastoral" Council called on them to do. However, in proportion to the success of such education, the ecclesiastical authorities then see the role of the Church growing in the political sphere, as bound up with its mission of reconciliation and peace.

Some readers may find this conclusion paradoxical, and it is true that it runs counter to a broadly accepted view. We must, therefore, explain precisely what we mean.

Most of the episcopal declarations approved since the Council show the concern of the bishops to avoid the accusation of meddling in politics. They also hope to avoid being treated by certain sectors of the press as men of the Church dressed up as politicians, whose judgments on national defense depend on purely natural reason.[19] Such a view ignores the real significance of interventions of the Church in the political sphere: the Church enters the political sphere because of its moral mission and its task of reconciliation within a society that is universal and thus extends to all men and women. Now it cannot be denied the right, especially in this modern age, to fulfill this responsibility with impartiality and to make use of all the means that can be of assistance in its task. Thus, it stands even to simple reason that the international society of states cannot treat the Church as a simple social and political force belonging to the natural order. The moral guarantee it offers in proposing the best means of helping people to draw near to the common good means that governments must pay attention to what it says, and treat it as a sort of medication to help in its efforts.

Thus, we cannot see pastoral concerns and actions taken in the political sphere as distinct or contradictory: the latter are encompassed in the former, due to the very fact that their purpose is the establishment of good relations between people within the world.

(c) At the time of the Falklands War, the Argentinian and English bishops expressed their feeling of common responsibility for peace, and tried to act on this basis. On the request of the Pope, representatives of the bishops of the two countries met in Rome to concelebrate a Mass with John Paul II for peace. And instead of cancelling his visit to Great Britain, the Pope went there, and afterwards to Argentina.[20] These strictly religious manifestations may have seemed meaningless to public opinion, inasmuch as people have come to believe that the Church is an international force that must place itself at the service of reconciliation and peace. However, those familiar with the history of the recent international conflicts could not help noting the new nature of such a situation. The national churches in fact linked themselves closely to the national points of view during the various wars of the nineteenth century and the First World War, and even during the Second World War, identifying the cause of their particular country with a struggle of good against evil— which meant that they were unable to support the international role taken on by the Holy See in favor of peace.[21] However, this was not the case in 1982: instead of accusing each other of upholding a power that was acting in gross violation of international law and against the interests of the Church, they rallied round the Pope, in support of a higher interest, begging that violence should give way to negotiation. Even if no concrete results could be directly attributed to this action, this in no way disguises the evidence of a new approach of local churches in the cause of peace.

Conclusion: Complementarity of the Pastoral and Political Approaches

The pursuit of peace by political means can be defined as a conscious participation of an authority or a social movement in the relations between institutions according to the rules in force at this level, with a view to putting a stop to violence or preventing it from breaking out, by fostering mutual understanding between peoples.

Within the Church, only the Holy See has performed, and still performs, this type of intervention in the contemporary world. For this purpose, it has at its disposition a diplomatic service that enables it to be discreetly but permanently present with the various governments; and it also claims the right, as circumstances dictate, to submit proposals to the interested parties, especially in moments of crisis.

Experience has shown that public opinion plays a large role in the success of diplomatic initiatives, and it must thus make sure that those who govern it understand its views. If the allied and German governments did not consider accepting Benedict XV's call to put a halt to hostilities, this was because the political forces represented by these populations gave them to understand that they were in favor of the war.[22] The situation is the same today in the conflict between North and South, in which the defense of their acquired situation by the inhabitants of industrialized countries can only paralyze their governments in international negotiations. The fact that Catholic opinion is becoming aware of its universal responsibility for peace means that states may be led to hold dialogue with local churches (as they already do with the universal Church) on the policies to be followed in order to strengthen peace if nothing comes to halt the developments at present taking place.

Chapter V of *Gaudium et spes* must be read in this perspective, even if those who drafted it were not necessarily conscious of this. The pastoral point of view of this chapter cannot but lead to a development of the conscience of Catholics with regard to the conditions needed for building peace, affirming the overriding priority of human solidarity over national interests. Only more and more widespread acceptance of this rule of morality by public opinions, whether Christian or not, can offer a basis with a sufficiently universal character to engender trust—and, as we know, no disarmament undertaking and no deescalation in deterrents can be hoped for without such trust. This explains the notion of a "period of grace" expressed by Cardinal Krol in his deposition before the Congressional Commission in 1979: we cannot expect the rapid success of a simple negotiation on disarmament, but rather the slow and persevering creation of shared behavior and attitudes with a view to ensuring each and every person the satisfaction of his or her essential needs and the protection and fostering of his or her basic rights.

The reflections in the present article have had the aim of placing *Gaudium et spes* within an historical perspective that allows us to see the continuity and unity of the Church's action for peace. It has its roots in the Christian message of renewal and salvation in Jesus Christ, and its practical implementation is based on a reading of the signs of the times, and has no hesitation over entering into their rationale. The fact that today this rationale is opposed to distinguishing local individualism and calls on individuals and peoples to shake this off means that Christians must participate actively in this process within their local and national communities. And, rereading the text after twenty years, this seems to us to have been the precise attitude that *Gaudium et spes* wanted to foster.

Translated from the French by Leslie Wearne.

Notes

1. Message for World Day of Peace, 1 January 1973.
2. GS 88.
3. G. Mairet, "Peuple et nation," in F. Chatelet and G. Mairet, *Les idéologies. De Rousseau à Mao*, 3 (1981), 51–73, esp. 69: "La transformation radicale sur le plan de l'État introduite par la Révolution française consiste à transférer à la loi l'autorité détenue par le monarque." See also G. Mariet, "Liberté, égalité," in *ibid.*, 74–92.

4. Pius IX, *Allocution to the Consistory*, 20 April 1849.

5. "L'Église et la paix de Léon XIII à Jean XXIII," *L'Osservatore Romano* (French edition) (22 October 1965), 6; Y. de la Brière, "Benoît XV et le rôle international de la papauté," *Études*, 146 (1916), 145–161 and 312–339, esp. Ch. IV.

6. "Cronache," *Civiltà Cattolica*, 61/6 (1890), 234–236 and 367–368.

7. F. Ehrle, "Benedikt XV. im Weltkrieg, seine Friedensarbeit und Liebestätigkeit," *Stimmen der Zeit*, 91 (1916), 301–326; R. Leiber, "Die päpstliche Kriegsfürsorge," *Stimmen der Zeit*, 100 (1920), 197–208; J. Quirico, "L'oeuvre de Benoît XV en faveur des prisonniers de guerre," *Études*, 157 (1918), 5–20.

8. For example, to the Consistory, 6 December 1915.

9. P. Dudon, "Le Pape et la guerre," *Études*, 142 (1915), 289–311; de la Brière, "Benoît XV et le rôle international de la papauté," Ch. I; *id.*, "L'offre de médiation de Benoît XV," *Études*, 152 (1917), 641–659; *id.*, "L'encyclique *Pacem Dei*," *Études*, 164 (1920), 352–367; *id.*, "Le règne pontifical de Benoît XV," *Études*, 1970 (1922), 257–274; R. von Rostitz-Rieneck, "Der Papst in Feindesgewalt," *Stimmen der Zeit*, 89 (1915), 405–419; F. Ehrle, "Die päpstliche Friedensnote an die Häupter der kriegführenden Völker," *Stimmen der Zeit*, 94 (1917), 1–28; R. Leiber, "Die Unparteilichkeit Papst Benedickt XV. im Weltkriege," *Stimmen der Zeit*, 100 (1920), 81–99.

10. P. Blet, *Histoire de la représentation diplomatique du Saint-Siège à l'aube du XIXᵉ siècle*, Collectanea Archivi Vaticani 19 (Vatican City, 1982); R. Graham, *Vatican Diplomacy* (Princeton, 1959).

11. GS 78.

12. International Federation of Catholic Universities, *"The Peace Movements": Symposium organized by IFCU and the Club of Rome, Salzburg, February 1983* (Rome, 1984).

13. The question of unilateral disarmament has been popularized in Europe under pressure from the Dutch churches. Cf. Pax Christi, *Bulletin*, 5 (1981); British Council of Churches, *The Church and the Bomb* (London, 1982), 199 and esp. 133; G.F. Kennan, "Discours de réception du prix Einstein," *Disarmament (UN)*, 82 (1981); Hessische Stiftung Freidenskonfliktforschung (HSFK), "Freidensbewegung," *Suhrkamp* (1977), 226; *id.*, "Die neue Freidensbewegung," *Suhrkamp* (1982), 496 and esp. 284–309.

14. Pastoral Letter of the German Bishops, *Gerechtigkeit schafft Frieden* (Cologne, 1983); Pastoral Letter of the U.S. Bishops, "The Challenge of Peace: God's Promise and Our Response," *Origins*, 13/1 (May 1983), 1–32; Pastoral Letter of the French Bishops, "Gagner la paix," *Documentation catholique*, 11 (1983), 1093–1101.

15. Letter of John Paul II to Heads of State to present a memorandum on "Religious Freedom and the Helsinki Final Act."

16. Memorandum of the Pontifical Academy of Sciences to the Heads of Atomic States, 28 January 1984.

17. Cardinal Krol, "Declaration before American Congress in the Name of the National Conference of Catholic Bishops," in "In the Name of Peace; collective statements of the US Catholic Bishops on war and peace 1919–80," *NCCB*, 122 (1983), 73–74.

18. On the opening of the churches to a universal mentality, cf. J. Joblin, "La Iglesia y las nuevas perspectivas de la cuestion social," Editorial, *Razon y Fe*, 222 (1968), esp. 165ff.

19. *El Mercurio*, quoted in Robert A. Mitchell, *Latin American Bishops Speak: Human Rights, Needs and Power. An Analysis of Recent Statements by Latin American Conferences of Bishops* (*pro manuscripto*, 1977).

20. *Documentation Catholique* (1982), 672.

21. H.J. Benedikt, *Der neue Protestantismus. Motive und Formen den kirchlichen Kriegsopposition in den USA* (Cologne, 1971), 128; M. von Faulhaber, "Der Krieg im Licht des Evangelium," *Glaube und Leben*, 2 (1916), 48; Comité Catholique de Propagande Française à l'Étranger, *La guerre allemande et le catholicisme* (Paris, 1915); id., *L'Allemagne et les Alliés devant la conscience chrétienne* (Paris, 1915).

22. Leiber, "Die Friedenstätigkeit."

CHAPTER 61

Biomedical Progress
and its Demands on Moral Theology

Manuel Cuyás, S.J.

Summary

Biotechnology has given humanity the ability to change the very manner of existing and has opened up a new way of devising standards of conduct, including ethical principles, in an interdisciplinary and interconfessional dialogue. Under the title of bioethics, this new methodology involves the work of moralists, demanding that they pay more attention to the achievements of the experimental sciences and the they make a special effort to win acceptance by civil authorities of the values defended by the Catholic Church. It also presents new problems for moral theology, and obliges it to rethink its positions on many matters. As examples, this article discusses the ethical consequences of (a) the change in assumptions relative to *in vitro* fertilization, (b) the possibilities opened up by genetic engineering, and (c) the present distribution of available health resources.

In the sociocultural context of Vatican Council II, it was already evident that the Church had to remain alert to the progress being made in scientific studies, that it did not always have ready to hand the answers to possible questions, and that it was not possible to expect unanimity in the practical solutions adopted within a Christian outlook on life, even among persons motivated with equal sincerity (*Gaudium et spes* 43). The Council considered itself competent to illuminate the new questions in the light of ultimate and definitive truths concerning the origin and destiny of humanity, humanity's mission in the world, and the possibilities given to humanity through the mystery of Christ, acting throughout the course of history through the Church (GS 3, 29, etc. passim). It foresaw that progress in the biological, psychological, and social sciences would allow humanity not only to know itself better, but even to influence directly the life of societies through technical means (GS 5), since ". . . today . . . [humanity] has extended and continues to extend . . . [its] mastery over nearly all spheres of nature thanks to science and technology. Thanks above all to an increase in all kinds of interchange between nations the human family is gradually coming to recognize and constitute itself as one single community over the whole earth" (GS 33).

This dominion that humanity has been given over its manner of existing comes in great part as something new and unexpected. It is a result of knowledge achieved by the biological sciences, which is now able to change not only ways of being born and of dying through reproductive techniques and reanimation methods or inducement of lifeless narcosis, but also to interfere with personal judgment through neuropharmaceuticals and neurosurgery, and even, in the foreseeable future, to change hereditary biological endowments by cloning particular qualities. The fear that ill-considered application of such dangerous powers could irreparably prejudice the future of mankind deeply troubled R. Van Potter who, in 1971, in his work *Bioethics: Bridge to the Future*[1] sounded the alarm and pleaded for a common effort to get the ethical sensibilities of biologists raised to the level of their technical abilities. To this end, he created the neologism "bioethics," which quickly found a varied and even contradictory acceptance.

There was agreement, however, in recognizing that Van Potter's concern was justified. Under various names and organizational arrangements, institutes and committees were set up everywhere with the aim of giving ethical guidance to the developments opened up by biotechnology. Even while Van Potter was writing his book, philosopher Daniel Callahan and psychiatrist Willard Gayling were meeting periodically at Hastings on Hudson (New York) with a group of scientists expert in a variety of disciplines, and like them interested in the biological sciences, to approach, each from his own perspective, the new practical problems presented. Their aim was to find in their common effort the solution most respectful of the values at stake.

In 1971, André Hellegers founded the Joseph and Rose Kennedy Institute for the Study of Human Reproduction and Bioethics, which is independent but closely tied to Georgetown University (Washington), for the purpose of confronting in an interdisciplinary and interconfessional dialogue the ethical problems being raised by progress in biology, medicine, and related sciences, with particular emphasis on the repercussions they might have at the macroeconomic level (especially in the Third World) and on indices of demographic growth, stability, or decrease. The interconfessional aspect was institutionalized from the beginning by establishment of three chairs—Catholic, Protestant, and Jewish; the interdisciplinary, by granting scholarships and entrusting particular studies to specialists in different fields. As the fruit of its early efforts, we have available today the four magnificent volumes that comprise the *Encyclopedia of Bioethics*.[2]

The first center of a similar kind in Europe, the "Institut Borja de Bioètica" (1975), was founded by Francesc Abel in San Cugat del Vallès (Barcelona). When the Kennedy Institute for Bioethics was just beginning, he had worked with A. Hellegers, under whose direction he was writing his doctoral thesis in medicine, and it was logical that the new center should be erected on the pattern of that institution. Other like centers quickly followed, in Brussels at the New Louvain University (Belgium) and the Maastrich University (Holland). Contemporaneously on the world level, the International Study Group of Bioethics began work under the auspices of the International Federation of Catholic Universities (IFCU).

Up to the present, the most characteristic trait of the centers mentioned has been their interdisciplinary and interconfessional methodology. From a perspective both universal and attuned to the future, they are trying to find answers to new questions for reasons and with techniques that make them accessible, without neglecting the insights that can be furnished by the particular points of view of the religious bodies and the disciplines represented by those studying the problem. However, the nuance that at first made the goals of the Hastings Center more practical, the formulation of concrete solutions to problems presented, and

those of the Kennedy Institute more theoretical, the clear statement of difficulties and of values at risk so as to offer reference
points to be taken into account, gradually disappeared. The reason for this was that the latter institution found it necessary to
develop principles, and even standards, that would respond to
questions raised by the White House. This explains why it found
it necessary to ask whether the task it was performing differed
from what had always been the work of experts in ethics—to
formulate standards of conduct that guide conscience. Answering this in the negative, it decided to change its name to the
"Kennedy Institute of Ethics."

During this same period, ethics committees were being institutionalized in hospitals and higher-level health organizations or in
the service of national authorities (Presidents of the United
States and France, etc.). These committees included specialists
from various fields and representatives of end users whose goal
was to support or disapprove results or proposals submitted by
scientists. In nations that are already sensitized, it is now impossible to obtain government funds or even some private funds without the prior favorable opinion of these committees or institutions. Not even the pharmaceutical companies will provide funding without prior authorized ethical approval. It would be too
risky because of possible legal consequences.

During the early months of 1984, a meeting was held in Lyon
involving centers more or less alike, inasmuch as they were performing functions similar to those being conducted by the institutions already mentioned, and they founded the European Association of Ethics Centers. It was necessary to avoid the word
"bioethics," rejected by France and rarely used by German scientists.[3] In Italy, on the other hand, the term bioethics had been
given a particularly favorable welcome. Ideological prejudices
against proselytism, at times camouflaged under a professional
ethics pretext, and wariness about deontology, in the sense of the
interpretation of the rules of medical schools and societies that
are excessively concerned with the defense of privileges, had
kept the presence of a discipline charged with the scientific study
of the ethical imperatives of medical practice out of the university in an academic role. The term bioethics did not give rise to
these prejudices and has permitted the introduction of the topics
proper to the subject taught in other countries under the name of

ethics or deontology. To a greater or lesser degree, the topics and methods particular to bioethics as an independent field of study or as part of another subject have been introduced everywhere.[4]

Having reached this point in recent history, we must ask ourselves (1) whether biomedical progress justifies our having coined the new term bioethics, (2) whether it has modified the methods particular to moral theology, and (3) whether the content of the latter has been considerably widened.

Bioethics

My answer to the first question will be brief. Biotechnology raises problems too serious for wasting time on a question of name. The simple fact that the progress made in science and technology has extended the field of study proper to moral theology to new problems would not justify a change of name. Every branch of learning increases the content of its programs to the extent that knowledge progresses in the particular field. The formulation of the new term bioethics appears reasonable and useful because it calls the attention of the moralist to the fact that a new difficulty has been raised.

Up until a short time ago, to answer any question about the morality of a procedure, ethicians and moralists possessed a point of reference beyond dispute—if it humanizes, it is good; if it dehumanizes, it is bad. The control of biological techniques over humanity itself and the possibility of modifying its natural functions and its very manner of existence makes it difficult for the moralist today to be satisfied with the traditional ethical response and the verification of humanizing or dehumanizing effects in the present or in the short term. The scientist demands the suspension of ethical judgment as to his or present activity while he or she is achieving the ability to humanize more and better the person of the future. He or she cannot miss the train of progress, he or she says, and this demands verification of what is already technically possible. The destination of this train and the accidents that it may cause on its way concern him or her less. Faced with this formulation of the difficulty, the moralist cannot be satisfied with repeating answers developed from another perspective. He or she will continue to condemn all claims of justifying the means by the ends, but cannot fail to take into consideration at the same time the intention (destination of the train) and the possible new ethical evaluation of acting in different contexts. There are not a lot of actions immoral per se, independent of circumstances, at any time or place.

The Methods of Moral Theology

With regard to the impact of biotechnological progress on the methods particular to moral theology, we must begin by recognizing that scholars devoted to it have been obliged to perform consciously and under conditions they find new a task they had always discharged without giving it special attention—that of winning acceptance by national legislative authorities of the ethical principles of the Catholic Church.

The nation has the chief interest in the studies of its scientists which are an essential prerequisite for its future welfare. However, the consequences of biomedical techniques can affect, and indeed do affect, citizens both as individuals and as regards living conditions in general. The moral problem has acquired political dimensions. The social conscience shudders at the possible consequences of certain experiments, and the authorities find it necessary to create some legal standard that, while minimally limiting the scientist's freedom, provides maximum protection to the ethical values at risk. This is no easy task in a secular and pluralistic society whose citizens and associations consider themselves adult and possessed of the right to try to make their contested opinions prevail. In a democratic society, no political party, no ideology, and no religious idea has the right to impose its way of thinking on the government of the country. However, none of these groups can abdicate its own responsibility in the clash of opinions and interests that must allow the legislator to promulgate the norm that here and now best protects the values involved.[5] Moral philosophy is knowledge of the absolute. Politics is the art of the possible in the given circumstances.

The law should not prohibit everything that is ethically immoral. Its rightness depends solely on its promoting the common good, even if it has to tolerate for that purpose some unacceptable action.[6] The ethician who is called upon to participate in a committee whose business it is to draft a bill concerned with biomedical techniques in the circumstances of a

modern society must take into consideration the conditions that
this somewhat new task imposes upon him. As a practical matter, these amount to the following prerequisites for a real interdisciplinary and interconfessional dialogue, one proper to bioethics: (1) the humility necessary for learning from others to
consider aspects possibly not fully appreciated; (2) sincerity and
magnanimity in setting forth one's own convictions and in the
effort to ensure that the future law will respect the range of
one's values or those of the group; (3) reflection on one's own
arguments and an effort to appreciate those of others; and (4)
understanding regarding the legislator, whose decisions are limited by the technical and juridical solutions available and the
necessity of conjoining contrasting interests and opinions, as
well as by possible political considerations.

I would like to call attention particularly to one aspect of the
second condition mentioned that is neglected by some experts in
the course of their work, namely, that secular society does not
imply secularism and that respect for the opinion of others is
compatible with the express profession of one's own faith. Just as
interdisciplinary dialogue presupposes experts in the various
fields of study, so interconfessional dialogue requires that the
Catholic not fail to offer the light of revelation and of the magisterium. "For faith throws a new light on all things and makes
known the full ideal which God has set for man, thus guiding the
mind towards solutions that are fully human" (GS 11). It would
not be right to make a private matter of a light that can benefit
the whole world.

It is not the case that biotechnology has changed the methods
proper to moral theology. That will continue to be faithful to its
origins and to one or another of the already accredited systems.
The preference of an author for deontological or teleological
paradigms has never from the beginning been an obstacle to
taking the consequences of an action into account as regards the
former, or that the action be considered in itself as regards the
latter. Not even the kind of moral theology most attached to
deductive reasoning, one convinced that general principles must
find realization in the concrete instance, has failed to give special
attention to experience.

Biotechnology has only changed—albeit to a considerable
degree—the proportionate influence it has on one or another
paradigm and the weight ethical judgment gives to practical re-

sults. The work of the scientist having entered into the dynamism of natural laws (in the biological physiological sense of the term), it is required of the ethician that when he thinks about the natural law in the ethical sense, he take into account the consequences of his acting within a temporally and geographically broadened framework. Vatican II rightly emphasizes the power obtained over "practically all nature" in a society that "is gradually coming to recognize itself and to constitute itself as one single community over the whole earth" (GS 33). Furthermore, since what is involved are problems raised by progress in the experimental sciences, which are concerned primarily with the technical potential, the scientist's attention is centered on proven effects, and he or she has the right to see them taken seriously by whoever must judge his or her actions. The results obtained might falsify (in the epistemological sense given to the term in the thought of K.R. Popper and T.S. Kuhn)[7] the very theory or scientific truth that brought about the experiment, demanding that it be replaced by another greater or deeper truth leading to different conclusions.

Although the perception of values, leaving aside ethical considerations, does not depend directly on scientific-descriptive knowledge, a different exposition furnished by such knowledge or an enrichment through data provided by other specialists gives rise to a new synthetic appreciation of the goods involved, and this may modify a prior conclusive judgment of the ethician. Without discussing here whether universal ethical principles exist or not, I insist that there are not many countervalues capable of disqualifying an action under any hypothesis.

New Problems

Biotechnology has given moral theology new problems and forced it to rethink its responses to many others. As examples, I shall mention three here: (a) fecundation *in vitro* with transfer of the embryo (FIVET), (b) genetic engineering, and (c) just distribution of available health resources. The first changed presumptions, the second raises unbounded hopes and fears, and the third, although it has yet to motivate consciences, nevertheless already demands solutions because of new data. This is not the right place to study even one of these subjects in depth. I am bringing them up solely to illustrate the impact of biomedical progress on the field of moral theology. I shall deal with the first somewhat more at length, and with the other two, I shall merely indicate what the problems are.

The FIVET

When Pius XII utterly condemned extracorporeal fecundation—"as to *in vitro* artificial fecundation experiments," he said, "permit us to say only that is necessary to reject them as immoral and absolutely illicit"[8]—they were being performed for no other reason than to make progress in scientific knowledge of the phenomena that accompany, effect, or change penetration of the spermatozoa into the ovum, the fusion of pronuclei, and the early developments in the evolution of a new being. In these instances, the life of the new being was brought to an end because its deterioration due to unsuitable conditions made further study uninteresting. Experiments continued in this vein until 1970 when two things happened. The first was that in the United States, public opinion became alarmed by the lack of sensitivity shown by scientists about the possible consequences of their experiments, and it succeeded in having the government impose a moratorium or delay on *in vitro* experiments until rules could be devised that would make it possible to protect the rights involved. Because of this, England and Australia took over the leading positions in the mastery of these techniques. The second was that technical periodicals published the information that life begun *in vitro* had been brought as far as the state of being a blastocoele, and that work was being undertaken to remedy the sterility of a married couple through transfer of an embryo to a uterus hormonally readied for it.[9] This was at that time presented as a therapeutic activity, since the positive elements in the utopian definition promulgated by the World Health Organization (WHO) in 1946—namely, ". . . health in the state of complete physical, mental, and social well-being and not just the absence of pain or illness . . ."—had enriched the concept of medical duty, previously limited to assistential therapy (remedial) with elements of preventive therapy (protective) and even of political therapy (social reintegration of the person and correction of pathogenic situations, environments, or customs). The organicist concept of illness had been made obsolete. With the new techniques available, the gynecologist could not stand by unmoved by the anguish at first and the frustration later of a couple unable to have the child they desire as a biological outcome of their conjugal love because of the simple problem of the wife having blocked fallopian tubes.

In 1973, in Australia, an embryo in a very early stage was successfully transferred to the uterus and took hold, but it did not reach term, while in England a pregnancy was achieved but proved to be ectopic. In 1978, in England, the first birth of a human being, Leslie Brown, whose life began *in vitro*, took place. It is thought that luck was involved in this first success, since Robert Edward and Patrick Steptoe, who made the process feasible, were unable to fix the approximate time of emplantment and other decisive details in the scientific report issued in 1980. By 1981, the technique was well established, and from that time on the places where it was practiced multiplied and, where the necessary specialization existed, the percentage of success steadily increased.

The moral theologian takes into consideration this change in mentality as regards the therapeutic aspect and the assuredly laudable purpose now being pursued through extracorporeal fecundation. He keeps in mind the advice of Vatican Council II to the effect that ". . . when it is a question of harmonizing married love with the responsible transmission of human life, it is not enough to take only the good intention and the evaluation of motives into account; the objective criteria must be used, criteria drawn from the nature of the human person and human action, criteria which respect the total meaning of mutual self-giving and human procreation in the context of true love . . ." (GS 51). The moral theologian goes on rightly to ask whether what has just been called a "simple case" should continue to be condemned, namely, that which posits fecundation *in vitro* of a single ovum by semen of the husband and introduction of the embryo into the maternal uterus, there to continue its development until the moment of birth.

Opinions differ between those who perceive in this a kind of artificial insemination previously condemned by the magisterium[10] as unworthy of the human person, whose condition as subject requires that he or she be the fruit of interpersonal giving inherent in the irreplaceable conjugal act, and that he or she cannot have the character of being the object of a technical

process, and those of us who do not see in the FIVET more than
assistance to a purely biological process that follows upon the
intimate expression of love between husband and wife. Such
assistance would be of the *removens prohibens* kind, simply a
matter of getting around the obstacle that impedes the meeting
of the gametes in the physiologically natural place. The former
insists on the inseparability of the unitive and procreative factors
in sexual union and the necessity of the specific conjugal act as
origin of the child, while we deny that there is this asserted
unlinking of the two factors in the FIVET, which is wholly
directed toward overcoming, with technical assistance, an obstacle due to a biological anomaly impending continuity—including
physical continuity—between the interpersonal manifestation of
love and the subsequent physiological capacitation and meeting
of the gametes for fusion. Sexual union alone, we believe, should
be considered a human act with regard to the twofold objective
significance of the anatomical parts freely activated and converted into the act expressive of conjugal love.

The GIFT variant of the "simple case" appeared as a compromise solution to eliminate or diminish the repugnance felt by
some regarding the seeming production of human life that the
mechanical arrangement of the gametes *in vitro* implies. This
technique would help the natural process by introducing them
separately into the uterus and thus facilitate their combining
there or in the fallopian tubes. This is neither persuasive nor very
effective. In either case, no one can doubt that the new life
would owe its human existence to the reproductive capability
given by the Creator to the gametes when these unite under the
necessary conditions. Human intervention does not do more
than make possible the biological action of secondary causes.

In the foregoing, the case of the theoretical difficulty has been
set forth, as also the reasoning pro and con on the FIVET per se.
However, its practice, even not going beyond the "simple case,"
involves other ethical difficulties.

1. Physicians consider masturbation the only way to obtain
the husband's semen under satisfactory conditions. For some
moral theologians, this would already disqualify extracorporeal
fecundation. Others think that mechanical genital stimulation
when autoerotism and hedonism are absent cannot be considered
masturbatory in the ethical sense of the expression and that the

disapprovals that seem to include it did not take into consideration the objective change in meaning.

2. The "simple case" has a very low success rate with consequent interruption of the incipient life of zygotes that fail to become implanted in the uterus and of those which having become implanted spontaneously abort. These last alone are three times the number of those that occur as a result of "live" pregnancy. Although it seems certain that a very high number of lives begun normally are lost through natural causes, do persons have a right to bring them into being when they will be immediately subject to a risk of being lost that is equal to or perhaps much greater than normal? The free intervention of humanity confers an ethical dimension on biologically natural facts. No one may create difficulties not necessary for continuing human life. This is a new reason why some deny the ethical acceptability of the FIVET, while others think they can defend it. Taking a risk to save a life already existing is certainly not the same as taking a risk to begin one, but if it is moral to experiment, even without the consent of the one involved, when it is the last way to save that person's life, would it not be moral to make his or her existence possible? Those who favor the FIVET adduce in favor of its licitness in the absence of intention to do harm and the proportionality of the risk, given that this is the condition *sine qua non* for the coming of this new being into the world.

This last difficulty is in practice aggravated because in order to raise the percentage of pregnancies achieved through extracorporeal fecundation, the maturation of a number of ova is produced hormonally in a single cycle, three or four are fertilized, and these are introduced into the uterus. Experience has shown that this is the best number for assuring that at least one of them implants. The unintentional loss of a globally greater number of embryos seems to some ethicians a factor that may be disregarded on the supposition that the same opportunity for development is given to all, that the risk continues to be proportionate as a necessary condition for the life of each, and that the procedure remains justified because it saves the mother failed transfers and frustrated hopes with their accompanying psychological repercussions.

On 22 February 1987, the Congregation for the Doctrine of the Faith published its *Instruction Concerning the Respect Due to Human Life in its Beginnings and to the Dignity of Procreation*

(*Donum Vitae*) to reply to the chief questions raised by the new reproductive techniques. It did so "in light of previous teaching of the magisterium" (Preamble) and with the same framing of the problems. This made understanding of it difficult for those who had become accustomed to approaching them from new perspectives. It vigorously condemned, as was to be expected, any instrumentalization of human life already begun and the taking of disproportionate risks with it, but it did not take a stand on the difficulty we have just set forth (I). May one continue to believe that a justifiable risk is being taken with the life of embryos? The Instruction repeated, on the other hand, without leaving room for any distinctions, the rejection of all masturbation (II, 6), as also of artificial insemination and fecundation *in vitro*, even considered separately, as contrary to the human dignity of the new being and of the conception process itself (II, 5). The separation that the Instruction presupposes between the union of the husband and wife and the technically procured generation was judged as being wholly analogous to that of condemned contraceptive methods (II, 4). It left standing the acceptability of artificial insemination improperly so called, which had previously been found acceptable by Pius XII,[11] and any technical assistance that may be discovered that is limited to assisting the effectuation of the specifically matrimonial act or of favoring its fecundity. On the other hand, it rejected any method that takes the place of the proper intimate union of husband and wife (II, 7).

I must admit that I had paid less attention than I should have to the previous texts of the magisterium aimed at showing that the very dignity of the new being's origin and the respect due to his or her rights and to those of the parents, as well as the equality all possess, demand that conception be desired and obtained as the direct fruit of the specific act of conjugal love. I had interpreted the statements favoring this linkage between generation and intimate unitive act as either influenced by particular historical circumstances (contrary to what the document holds) or as declarations marginal to the objectives of the text, mere assertions of what existed and not of what ought to exist.

While we theologians are running the risk of making mistakes, with the good intention of opening a path into territory yet to be explored, and while we are discussing the least problematical of human reproductive techniques, scientific objectives and experiments seem to have passed from a therapeutic interest to a wild desire to perform feats further and further beyond what is known. From fecundation with one gamete derived from a source outside the marriage or stable cohabitation, there has followed fecundation with two extraneous gametes that are sometimes transferred to a womb merely loaned or rented to bring the pregnancy to term; the institutionalization of sperm and zygote banks, with attempts to obtain success in freezing and thawing ova; destruction of embryo "remainders" or "surpluses"; and the use of these for all kinds of experiments, such as attempts to fecundate human gametes with those of animals and vice versa, efforts made to gestate human life in animal uteruses, etc. To this could be added experiments made for the purpose of asexual reproduction—parthenogensis; production of gametes by taking advantage of the full potential of the cells prior to the first differentiation in them (it suffices to divide the embryo before it reaches the blastocyte phase), for cloning purposes; and creation of chimeras. Technical distortion leads to the idea that everything the imagination can conceive of as feasible must be accomplished, right up to the point of making technical progress the equivalent of human progress.

Aside from homologous artificial fecundation, the experts in human reproductive techniques have not dared to ask ethicians for more than a favorable judgment on fecundation with one gamete not belonging to husband or wife, under the guise of semiadoption, when one of the two spouses is infertile or the bearer of serious genetic flaws. They have succeeded only to the extent that some few see a certain possibility of a future basic revision of the unanimous judgment condemning it. A professor of moral theology could be satisfied with the global rejection of all these practices as contrary to the indispensable properties of marriage and the very dignity of human beings. The Instruction mentioned also does so very briefly (I, 6).

However, the civil authorities have been obliged to intervene, not only because the outraged sensibilities of its citizens demanded it, but also because the results of the experiments crossed over into public life and became entwined with personal rights, which they must safeguard. It is because of this problem that there has been a great increase in the number of consultative bodies and commissions established by various nations and the rapid production of ethicojuridical norms relative to specific problems concerning reproductive techniques. Ethicians have fre-

quently been called upon in the preparation of the documents
involved to contribute the specialized interdisciplinary and interconfessional work of the bioethician to which reference has
been made.

The United States has gone beyond many other nations regarding this concern. It is instructive to review the history of 45 CFR
46 (title 45 of the *Code of Federal Regulations,* Part 46), the
requirements of which must be fulfilled in order to receive any
federal government subsidy. The latest edition of this is due to
the President's Commission for the Study of Ethical Problems in
Medicine and Biomedical and Behavioral Research. First published in 1981, it was revised in March 1983 and again in March
1986.[12] The series of reports prepared by the Commission for
Legal Reform in Canada stand out because of the precision with
which they reflect the various opinions expressed in the preparatory study and the moderation with which they state the final
recommendation.[13]

The President of the French Republic also called on the
assistance of the *Comité Consultatif National d'Ethique pour les
Sciences de la Vie et de la Santé.* With close relationship to our
theme, it has already published its opinion on use of tissues of
dead human embryos or fetuses,[14] on artificial reproductive techniques,[15] and on prenatal or perinatal diagnostics.[16] The Council of Europe has for its promulgated recommendations on problems related to human genetics,[17] reproductive techniques, and
certain ways of proceeding with resulting embryos,[18] and concerning use of human embryos and fetuses.[19] These examples
are only a small sample of the proliferation of like documents
throughout the world. A select bibliography of what is available
at the *Institut Borja de Bioètica* (Sant Cugat del Vallès-Barce-
lona) was published in a special monograph issue of the periodical *Labor Hospitalaria.*[20]

The inclusion in the document of the Congregation for the
Doctrine of the Faith of a chapter (III) on "Moral and Civil Law"
was unusual. This chapter, dedicated to the governments of the
different nations for the purpose of calling to their attention the
values and moral obligations that civil legislation must respect
and approve with respect to the origins of human life and to
human life itself in its initial stages, is a clear indication of the
new task that biomedical progress imposes on the ethician. A
magisterial statement may be content with the proclamation of

ethical requirements, but the *Instruction* did not stop short of acknowledging that civil law "must at times tolerate, for the sake of public order, what it cannot prohibit without being the occasion of worse damage." In fact, to help attain the highest good now possible and to prepare for a better future calls for the virtue of prudence, and that calls for knowledge of present reality with its limited possibilities. This aspect of the task has also been neglected at times by the ethician, who is preoccupied exclusively with the orthodoxy of what he or she says when on a committee. As a member, he or she should keep it in mind if he or she does not want to sacrifice the good here and now attainable for the sake of a better law that cannot be approved.

I want to conclude this section with several lines from the document frequently referred to before that seem to support the work of the Catholic moral theologian facing the future: "The precise directives contained in this *Instruction* are not intended to be a brake on scholarly work but rather to give it renewed vigor on the path of irreplaceable fidelity to the doctrine of the Church" (Conclusion). The official Italian text says: *nella fedeltà irrinunciabile alla dottrina della Chiesa.* The Spanish version cannot be interpreted as a desire to block the way to a road already trodden upon.

Genetic Engineering

The purpose of this article makes it necessary to synthesize to the point of popularizing inexactness information about the discoveries that have made it possible. It consists fundamentally of the feasibility of transferring properties, functions, and even parts of the hereditary endowment of one living being to another, bringing about leaps in mutations that are not obtainable in agriculture and zoo technology. It entails a qualitative change in humanity's dominion over nature, including dominion over its own nature. What is newest is that such processes can be brought about under humanity's immediate control.[21]

Until very recent times, the gene, the transmitting agent of the different biological characteristics and functions, had not been identified. Even more recent is the development of methods that make it possible to isolate the genes (or groups of genes) that belong to one cell and to recombine them with those of another of the same or a different species.[22] Rapid progress in this direction was based on the discovery by Francis Compton Crick and James Dewey Watson of the unique live existing substance, deoxyribonucleic acid (DNA), constituted by four basic molecules (cytosine, guanine, thymine, and adenine) chained together in various combinations and configured in the manner of two threads helicoidally entwined, one facing the other, and having the ability of replicating or reproducing themselves. They made this public in 1953 in the periodical *Nature*. Every cell of anything living contains DNA. They differ from one another in accordance with the base factors and the various positions of DNA that are contained (function) in them. The gene is only a fragment of the chain, the producer, if it be active, of a particular enzyme. From 1970 on, scientists began to know more and more about "restriction enzymes." Each of these has the ability to detect in the DNA chain the portion in which the base elements are found arranged in the precise manner that constitutes a particular gene, and it cuts it exactly there. The existence of "plasmids" or loose fragments of DNA in a few cells, and their ability to introduce themselves into another cell, was already known. Genetic recombination consists schematically of the art of isolating a gene, or a particular group of genes, introducing it or them into a plasmid (some viruses are optimal vectors), and transferring this to another cell, where it wll be incorporated into the latter's DNA. If it succeeds in functioning there as in the original cell, we have hybridization with the desired characteristics.

Our ability to enter into the very nucleus of the cell to separate and recombine the chromosomes has so many similarities with the capacity to split the atom that it could not but awaken enormous suspicions and fears. Management of atomic energy began with a hecatomb and destroyed two cities (6 and 9 August 1945). Today, more than forty years later, "atoms for peace" and for prosperity continue to be the exception when compared with atoms for the arms that are deployed to deter the war with which they threaten us. Even their industrial use is not free from serious dangers, as the catastrophe of Chernobyl demonstrated with special eloquence.

The fear that the formation of new forms of life might occasion plagues difficult or impossible to stop had a greater effect on public opinion than hopes based on the fountains of riches and prosperity opened up to beneficial exploitation by the new possibilities. From the fear of possible epidemics caused by new microbial diseases resistant to any antibiotic, or producing toxins for which no antidote is known, attention quickly passed to concerns that the new forms of life induced in bacteria, plants, or animals might, even if they did not immediately harm man, damage other useful animals and cause eventual havoc in ecosystems with harmful and irreparable effects on the ecology of the environment. To complete this picture, the threat of biological warfare with devastating results was also brandished. The first two fears were based on natural happenings and mutations. The last adds to the calculation of unforseeable disasters the pernicious entrance of uncontrolled passions and of evil intent.

The first to give the alarm and to demand government regulation were scientists of the highest reputation and academic and ecclesiastical bodies of unquestioned prestige.[23] Experience has now shown that the dangers inherent in genetic recombination can be channeled within the limits of what is acceptable without turning to measures that are too restrictive and that might deprive society of immeasurable benefits.

The modification and the programming of biological characteristics in bacteria and other single-cell beings to give them a particular gene was quickly seen to be of great importance to business and industry. It made possible the production of organic molecules of incalculable value for health, such as insulin, albumin, interferon, growth hormones, etc., all of the highest purity and quality and produced in a short period at very reduced costs.

A short time later, the field of pluricellular organisms was entered into with considerable repercussions on agriculture and animal industry. Crops and livestock improved in quantity and quality. It was possible to incorporate in certain plants the properties of others that, on the one hand, made their cultivation more profitable (e.g., supply of fertilizers for their own vital synthesis), and, on the other, improved them in terms of nourishment of those who consume them (e.g., increase of protein). Biotechnology applied to cattle raising has also made it possible to increase meat production and to incorporate other useful characteristics into domestic animals.

Ethical thinking could not help but notice that certain genetic mutations take place spontaneously in nature, although in infinitesimal quantities: the influenza virus, for example, changes its structure and qualities every year, making it difficult to prepare a satisfactory vaccine for the next epidemic. Humanity has had

recourse from ancient times to the multiplicating action of micro-
organisms (bacteria or fungi) to season bread, cheese, beer, etc. by
means of yeasts and fermenting agents.[24] But it is not because of
this that genetic recombination is ethical. Nature, as a physical or
biological category, is not a criterion of morality. An ethical judgment, positive or negative, depends solely on whether the particular way of proceeding benefits or damages human beings as such.[25]
It is clear that, in general, the dangers of biotechnology, however
great they may be, are commensurable with those of other human
activities that are sources of good and evil. Ethics does not need to
forge principles of a new stamp for rash personal action in this
field. The same applies to dangers, since they can be caused by
human folly or perversity, even in the case of possible biological
warfare.

In matters of morality, the greater the good or evil involved,
the more urgent is the prudence required. To paralyze genetic
research in lower beings would involve giving up a good part of
humanity's dominion over them and possible enormous benefits.
To let it go ahead without foreseeing the possible damages might
lead to disasters of incalculable magnitude.

From the very beginning, the application of genetic research
to humanity raised every greater hopes and very serious concerns.
In 1953, the same year in which the scientific world came to
know the structure of DNA, there took place in Rome the First
International Symposium on Genetic Medicine. In his discourse
to the participants, Pope Pius XII, after stating that "practical
genetics has in no way limited its role to that of passive specta-
tor," because "the fundamental tendency of genetics and of eugenics is to influence the transmission of hereditary factors to
advance what is good and eliminate what is harmful," and that
"this tendency is irreproachable from the moral point of view,"[26]
concluded his moral comment with these words:

> The practical objectives that make genetics moral are noble
> and worthy of recognition and encouragement. What is asked
> of it is only that in considering the means to be used in
> achieving its objectives, it always keep in mind the fundamen-
> tal difference between the vegetable and animal world on the
> one side and man on the other. Among the former it can fully
> use means for improving species and breeds. In the human
> world, on the contrary, it finds itself dealing always with per-

sonal beings whose rights are untouchable, with individuals who are themselves subject to inflexible moral laws when they exercise their capacity for bringing new life into being. Thus the Creator himself has established barriers in the moral field that no human power is competent to eliminate.[27]

The Creator (for those who do not believe in chance and evolution) has granted humanity dominion over all that surrounds it and responsible control over its own life.[28] Genetic recombination has not only put into humanity's hands new ways of affecting the health or illness of the individual and his or her descendants, but also—through alteration of the basic structures of his or her existence as it is programmed in the genes—of determining to a great extent his or her physiological and psychic constitution, and of attacking his or her identity and even the very existence of the human species by changing the biological information common to all the individuals belonging to it. In lower beings, we can alter even the species, but where the human person is concerned, his or her individuality must be respected, because each individual has an inalienable destiny of his or her own. Man is "the only creature on earth that God has wanted for his own sake" (GS 24). The relationship between biological integrity and personal or specific identity is very deep. Technology and science make progress possible, but they do not guarantee it. They widen the field of human responsibility, but it is up to human responsibility, through ethical study, to decide from a viewpoint beyond acquired knowledge what the truly humanizing use of the new capabilities is and to promote it.

On the one hand, a person must be treated always as an individual possessed of self-determination in the free choice of his or her acts (rights of the person). On the other hand, he or she feels obliged, and is obliged, to act in accordance with his or her rational nature and to grow toward a more perfect realization of his or her own being (fundamental moral imperative).[29] Recourse to genetic recombination in a person for the purpose of curing or preventing illnesses, as also for bringing out particular qualities or even to improve the biological inheritance of future generations, must always respect the identity of the individual and of the species, the equal dignity of everyone, and each one's access to his or her maximum personal realization.

Genetic Recombination for Therapeutic Goals. Physicians naturally put their greatest hopes regarding genetic recombination in therapeutic objectives. If the harmless *Escherichia coli* cloned with the human insulin gene so improved the condition of diabetics by producing this hormone—which is so important in the treatment of illness—in a purified state and in industrial quantities, how much better would not the remedy be if it were possible not just to treat the symptoms but to eliminate the very cause of the trouble by genetic, and inheritable, cure of the patient.[30]

The experts quickly became aware that they would have to begin with some kind of somatic therapy. This would transform the host cell or tissue, leaving the hereditary properties of the individual intact. Only later would it be possible to make the leap to germinal therapy, which requires dealing with early embryos or gametes intended for reproduction. The gene introduced and its function would be transmitted to future generations. In this way, there would be progress from a remedial genetic therapy to one which would be preventive, as occurred in traditional medicine, and even eugenics could be considered relative to at least strengthening qualities proper to human beings. Each of these possible actions is subject to particular difficulties from the scientific and technical point of view and requires ethical study alert to the peculiarities of the case.

We have learned not to consider anything imagined in science fiction as impossible, but we must admit that we are still far from being able to actualize in man the ideas presented. Even limiting ourselves to somatic therapy, there remain at least the four following difficulties. (1) The human cells active in replication (necessary condition for integration of exogenous DNA) and capable of being extracted, cultivated, and manipulated *in vitro*, and reimplanted, are few. (2) Given genes that function *in vitro* usually lose activity *in vivo*. (3) Ninety percent of genetic information remains inactive in man, and known techniques do not make it possible to determine the location of the chromosome where the cloned gene would be inserted nor its effects on the rest. By inserting it, we might activate some of the others, cancel out the activity of those that are functioning, or induce other disasters. (4) How to assure control of the guest material by the receptor is not known. Without such control, the insulin gene would bring on fatal hyperglycemia.

To overcome the first difficulty, there are advantages in intervening in the early stages of the embryo. Ethically, it ought to be a case of a true therapeutic experience with strict adherence to all the required conditions. John Paul II presupposed this when, in 1982, he expressed his gratification because "the research of modern biology makes it possible to hope that the transfer and mutation of genes may improve the condition of those affected by chromosomal illnesses, and thus the smallest and weakest of human beings may be cured during their intrauterine life or in the period immediately following birth."[31]

Germinal genetic recombination involves transmission to descendants and, therefore, demands even more the fulfillment of required conditions. The consent of those affected is certainly lacking, but it may be supposed that it would be less respectful of their dignity to let them transmit a genetic illness when it is remediable. It would thus be possible to check progressive deterioration of the human species due in part to the fact that medical progress is preventing the natural extinction of certain defects by permitting those affected to live to the age of fecundity.

Recommendation No. 934 of the Parliamentary Assembly of Europe, voted in January 1982, asked the twenty-one member nations to safeguard a presumed right of their citizens to receive "their genetic inheritance not artificially manipulated." None of the governments concerned has followed the recommendation. Is genetic inheritance so sacred that we cannot touch it even to improve it? Let us not forget that its deterioration comes spontaneously from damage caused to health by progenitors and from chance defective combinations. Should human reason not make right what irrational nature has made defective? "A strictly therapeutic intervention which has the curing of various illnesses as its objective, such as those which are caused by chromosome deficiencies, will in principle be considered desirable, provided that it tends toward the true promotion of man's personal welfare without attacking his integrity or worsening his condition. Such an intervention is indeed within the logic of the Christian moral tradition."[32]

To consider the difficulties that genetic engineering would involve regarding perfective objectives would lengthen this article excessively without adding much to the informative ends that are its purpose. Let it suffice to comment that no ideal human genotype exists. No one is authorized to establish what qualities should prevail in the "perfect" person. Intelligence is not more noble than love or freedom, nor is artistic sensibility or affection less human than rationality. Experience teaches, furthermore, that generalized preferences change with the times and that it is commonly the followers of reductionist ideologues who have always busied themselves with correcting the scale of values in effect. No one knows what kind of predominance in faculties will, in general, be in the interests of social life. Interfering with genetic inheritance involves a new kind of hereditary existence, the continuation of which could not be interrupted immediately whenever desired. What right would we have to determine the biological conditions of people of the future?

On the other hand it would not be licit to improve the individual qualities of some at the expense of full realization of the potential of others, and there is no doubt that a collective situation of privilege leads to arrogance, forcing others down to an inferior level, with clear lack of equity and even of justice. Gene manipulation might bring about the generation of slaves biochemically conditioned for a certain kind of work and incapable of anything else. The "brave new world" of Aldous Huxley could become reality in the hands of whoever might have adequate laboratories and the biological techniques. This would mean a society petrified in an arbitrary hierarchization, one that would be oppressive and inhuman. The inferior persons would be deprived of the inalienable right one has to make more of himself or herself and to improve, and this under any hypothesis would be morally unacceptable.

Just Distribution of Available Resources

Progress in biostatistics and epidemiology now makes it possible not only to detect a progressive movement toward a steadily increasing average age throughout the world and differences between one population and another, but also to measure the disproportionate presence of an illness in a particular ethnic group or nation and the corrective efficacy of economic investment, depending on whether it is directed toward making individuals well (assistential therapy) or toward controlling the problem and eliminating its causes (preventive and political therapy).[33]

When on 12 September 1978, the Conference on Basic Health Assistance meeting in Alma Ata (Kazakhstan, USSR) issued its impressive Declaration, it was more than thirty years after the constitution of the World Health Organization proclaimed in its article 25 that "enjoying the greatest state of health of which one is capable constitutes one of the fundamental rights of all men, without regard to their religion, race or political opinion. The health of all peoples is a condition for peace in the world." After adopting this principle (1) as its own, the conference declared unacceptable, from the political, social, and economic points of view, the flagrant inequalities that exist regarding the health conditions of populations, both among developed nations and developing nations, as well as within particular countries (2). Whether this constitutes, as was declared, a "source of common concern to all countries" (ibid.) may be questioned. It is certain that it ought to be, and that such an objective demands contributions from the social and economic fields, as well as from the monetary area (1), a spirit of solidarity (8), and a more thorough and efficient use of world resources (9). "One of the chief social objectives of governments, international bodies and the entire world community in the next 10 years must be to obtain for all the populations of the world between now and the year 2000 a level of health which will permit them to live a socially and economically productive existence" (5). With the slogan "Health for all in the year 2000," it has been possible to sensitize the various social groups to support medical services everywhere that are close to the population and efficient, so that they can stimulate collective and individual collaboration on the part of peoples and "to take on the principal health problems of the community, providing the information, prevention, care, and rehabilitation services necessary to resolve them" (6, 2). The decade mentioned in No. 5 is about to end. Advanced medical techniques that require great investments for special assistance to benefit a very few have progressed in a spectacular manner during this period. However, care of the newborn has not improved enough to reach a drastic diminution of infant mortality,[34] and the principal problems continue to be unremedied, those that rob years from lives and diminish the welfare of huge multitudes because of lack of health education, adequate supplies of potable water, vaccines against the major infectious diseases, and distribution of the most ordinary medicines. The resources needed for this would be insignificant in terms of national and international budgets, and the results would be surprising even in the short term. It is not strange that a reasonable distribution of available health resources should have been, from the beginning, a constant concern of bioethics. With their disposition toward interdisciplinary dialogue, ethicians involved in it have been able to contribute principles for resolving questions involving conflicting interests.

The old treatises on medical ethics were concerned with justice only with regard to the interpersonal relationship between physician and patient. What is demanded now is a preferential concern for macroeconomic problems. The change is due to the fact that we have the means to predict the outcome of one or another investment and that the institutionalization of medical services—with a growing assumption of them by the State—converts health into a public interest matter and presents problems in a social-justice perspective. This new focus responds perfectly to the preeminence of the common good proclaimed by Vatican II in the chapter of *Gaudium et spes* dedicated to the community of men (No. 26) and the role that it assigns to it in the life of the political community (No. 74). What we have to say about the distribution of resources at the national level should also be applied on a world scale, but we know what difficulties this involves and how little influence the documents of the Holy See calling for greater justice in international relations have had in the communications media. It suffices to recall what little attention was given to the Encyclical *Populorum progressio* on the obligation to promote the development of peoples[35] and to the document of the Justice and Peace Commission on the grave problem of international indebtedness.[36] The neglect of this last is especially surprising on the part of the media, which gave a considerable welcome to other pronouncements of that same commission. There is no doubt that there is a need to arouse a greater sense of solidaristic responsibility in the world community.

It is taken for granted today that every citizen has the right to have the State take care, in one way or another, of his substantial needs regarding health. A first difficulty arises from the fact that the utopian definition of health to which we made reference does not contain limiting features and may furnish grounds for unlimited demands regarding the prolongation of life or the quality of life. It is necessary to confine expectations to real necessities with due regard for the available resources, which are never abundant.

As in the just distribution of national income to the first

fundamental principle, "to each one according to his or her needs," there must be joined a second, "to each one according to his or her contribution," in order that there may be sufficient wealth to distribute, so in the furnishing of health services, the utilitarian concept that aims at the end, "the best health for the greatest number" (social health), must be complemented by the demands of distributive justice, which is more concerned with the means (the health of individuals according to their needs).

Health and life are goods that cannot be valued in merely economic terms. A simple cost-benefit analysis would let the newborn child with grave defects and the elderly ill die, because they require large investments with few results in terms of the global percentage that establishes the health status of the collectivity. Even without leaving the social area, it would be impossible to calculate the symbolic value that saving just one life has, to the benefit also of those who dedicate their efforts to it and of the entire public as well, which sees the virtues most necessary for living peacefully together encouraged.

The problems related to the distribution of resources may be reduced to three headings, the contents of which are interrelated: (1) conflicts between health care and other social goods (national budget), (2) conflicts between remedial care and preventive care (health budget), and (3) selection of beneficiaries, when it is not possible to care for all those in need of care.[37]

1. It has not been possible in the past nor will it be possible in the future to establish a universally valid percentage of what should be apportioned to health as opposed to culture, defense, communications, etc. Medical, economic, legal, social, political, and ethical factors converge in this difficulty. It would be irresponsible to hand over study of the problem and its solutions for the benefit of the most influential ideology or political party. Only prior interdisciplinary and interconfessional dialogue can bring to light the values in play and ensure a solution that is in the interests of the common good. It is well to remember that health progress in the developed nations is due more to the increase in the standard of living than to scientific and technical progress in medicine.[38]

2. No one doubts the great importance in the short and medium term of good medical training and of resources dedicated to research, but conflict in this area usually revolves around remedial and preventive measures. The latter (vaccines, environ-

ment, life-style) have shown themselves to be more efficacious than the former in raising the average health level of a population. However, data furnished by biostatistics and medical sociology show that about ninety percent of resources available for health are spent in general on care, five percent on ecology (since concern for the environment took on political dimensions), and only the remainder on improving such efficient factors as the biological and life-style elements. The disproportion is justified by the symbolic value of care for a present need and a proven result, by the duty of compensating for inequalities produced in health as a result of the social situation or kind of work (when the latter is damaging, it has rarely been freely chosen), and because the State cannot limit freedom for the sake of a healthier life-style (without tobacco consumption, without the risks due to faster traffic, etc.) unless protection of the rights of others with evident benefit demands it.

The obligation to give equal treatment in equal conditions admittedly does not prevent leaving isolated cases without curative assistance when they would involve great expense and few benefits. J.F. Childress comments very wisely that it would not be just to do so with respect to illnesses that strike only particular social groups. That would in fact involve class or ethnic discrimination. When AIDS affected only one African nation (infected by a virus coming from certain monkeys), the western nations ignored the battle and the studies that might have been able to anticipate by more than twenty years the hurried research now being performed.

3. The problem of the physician or of the hospital in selecting the patients to be given urgent care, when the means for giving it to all in need of it are lacking, has not found a solution that is just in every respect. We must be satisfied with furnishing rational criteria that preserve a certain degree of equality. The only reference points that are exclusively medical are reduced by Engelhard-Rie to these three: probability of success, the predictable quality of life, and the length of such life, all of which must be evaluated in the light of the necessary costs. To the extent that the latter increase and the weight of the factors mentioned decreases in the ill person, there is less reason to select him or her as compared with others whose qualifications in this respect are increasing.[39] It is not the case that the criterion is 100 percent objective. The prospects for success also depend on the willing-

ness of the ill person to cooperate, understood as a desire to live
and a psychological capacity for self-control and perseverance.
Statistics and percentages are of no value in weighing this aspect
of the clinical situation. In any event, the selection guide proposed is medically valid and reasonable. There is no guarantee,
however, that it would be welcomed by those affected.

In a pluralistic society having various measures of values, a
criterion based on a presumed social desire to furnish more medical care to those who have contributed more or will contribute
more to the welfare of all, taking into account age and civic
functions exercised or to be exercised, etc., becomes more difficult to accept, however much utility might be served by thus
selecting. This is so because life is important to all men in the
same way. No consideration is strong enough to weaken the
strength of this argument on the side of equality. Engelhard
proposes that provision of health services by society have a limit
equal for all, and he supports the idea that it is in society's
interest to subsidize more sophisticated services.

The only preference generally accepted regards helping first,
in circumstances equal for all, the one whose qualities would be
here and now beneficial for the rest—the physician in an emergency within his field, the seaman able to guide a lifeboat to port
in a shipwreck, etc. To see themselves subject to some other
value judgment on the part of the physician would weaken the
patients' trust in him.

On the basis of this last argument, various authors maintain
that the simple order of request for services or of arrival at facilities is the only criterion of selection that is both objective and
acceptable to those not selected.[40] Every other criterion in this
view is discriminatory and a violation of equality of opportunity,
which is demanded as a fundamental value of society. However,
a criterion so fortuitous and depersonalized, so far by its very
nature from rational thought, has not failed to cause a certain
repugnance. Mere chance would be decisive. However, not following this criterion has brought penal consequences to one
hospital that, rather than leave persons in serious condition to
their fate, admitted more sick persons to an intensive care unit
than were allowable, considering the continuous care, frequent
necessary actions, and immediate use of scarce technologies that
are characteristic of this kind of service.

One of those who arrived first having died, a very doubtful

verdict obliged the hospital to "indemnify" the family. On the other hand, ethics has always demanded that the physician not fail to furnish whatever care is possible to a person in need of urgent attention.

I have mentioned this case only to show that when selection of those to be benefitted is required even at the microeconomic level, biotechnical progress presents conflicts of interest that are impossible to resolve without prior interdisciplinary study. It is understandable that the hospital should ask the law for a decision as to how to act in similar cases. It would feel safer. However, would the hospital remain faithful to the objectives that were the reasons for building it? Would not concern for the welfare of the hospital change the means into the end? The temptation to do this is evident in too many instances at the service level, and even more at the national and international levels.

Equality of opportunity in health care is a goal that still seems far off, because it means abandoning privileged positions and because the possible solutions involve various fields of knowledge—economic, juridical, political, medical, and ethical. A wider and more efficacious sensitization is needed regarding the existing disparities concerning health and life expectations. We can have no doubt that progress realized in the fields of biostatistics and epidemiology are of concern to the ethician, obliging him or her to enlarge the area of his or her ethical study and to question the effectiveness of his or her activity on the world scale.

Translated from the Spanish by Edward Hughes.

Notes

1. Renselaer Van Potter, *Bridge to the Future*, Prentice-Hall Biological Science Series, Carl P. Swanson (ed.) (Englewood Cliffs, NJ, 1971).

2. Warren T. Reich (ed.), *Encyclopedia of Bioethics* (New York, 1978).

3. Klaus Demmer, "Das Bioethische Gespräch. Initiativen Katholischer Universitäten," *Herder Korrespondenz*, 40 (1986), 489–493.

4. Frencesc Abel, "Bioética: un nuevo concepto y una nueva responsabilidad," *Labor Hospitalaria*, 36 (1985), 101–111; "Ciencia y ética en tensión y diálogo. Bioética nueva disciplina y nuevos prob-

lemas," *I Jornadas sobre Progreso Científico y Etica*, Consejo Superior de Investigaciones Científicas, Delegación de Cataluña (in press).

5. Manuel Cuyás, "La Iglesia ante una ley civil sobre el aborto," *Razón y Fe*, 198 (1978), 175–185.

6. Congregation for the Doctrine of the Faith, *Instruction on Respect for Nascent Human Life. Response to Certain Current Questions* (22 February 1987), 3.

7. Karl Raimund Popper, *La lógica de la investigación científica* (Madrid, 1962); Thomas S. Kuhn, *La estructura de las revoluciones científicas*, Fondo de Cultura económica, 213 (Mexico, 1971).

8. Pius XII, *Discourse to the Universal Congress on Fecundity and Sterility*, meeting in Naples, 19 May 1956 (*AAS*, 48 [1956], 467–474, cited on 471).

9. This possibility was suggested in an unsigned editorial in the *New England Journal of Medicine* in 1937, but the necessary techniques were lacking. I take the information from Adriano Bompiani, "Problemi biologici e clinici aperti dall'ingegneria genetica, dall'inseminazione artificiale e dalla fecondazione in vitro con embryo transfer nella specie umana," in *Manipolazione genetiche e diritto*, Quaderni di "Iustitia," 34 (Rome, 1977), 35–88. I am quoting from pp. 68–70.

10. Pius XII, *Discourse to the Fourth International Congress of Catholic Physicians*, 29 September 1949 (*AAS*, 41 [1949], 560–561); *Discourse to the Italian Catholic Union of Midwives*, 29 October 1951 (*AAS*, 43 [1951], 850); Pius XII, *Discourse to the Universal Congress on Fecundity and Sterility*, meeting in Naples, 19 May 1956 (*AAS*, 48 [1956], 470–471); *Discourse to the 7th Congress of the International Hematology Society*, 12 September 1948 (*AAS*, 50 [1958], 733).

11. Pius XII, *Discourse to the Fourth International Congress of Catholic Physicians*, 29 September 1949 (*AAS*, 41 [1949], 560).

12. Francesc Abel presents the historic circumstance of the document in the introduction to Chapter 5 of *Códigos deontológicos y normativas ético-jurídicas recientes*, monographic issue of *Labor Hospitalaria*, 18 (1986), 233–235.

13. Commission de réforme du droit du Canada, *20 Rapport— L'euthanesie, l'aide au suicide et l'interruption du traitement* (Ottawa, 1983). I cite report No. 20 as an example. The title itself indicates the difficulty involved in distinguishing the various problems implicit in a possible law regulating this question.

14. *Avis sur les prélévements de tissus d'embryons ou de foetus humains morts à des fins thérapeutiques, diagnostiques et scientifiques* (22 May 1984).

15. *Avis sur les problèmes nés des techniques de reproduction artificielle* (23 October 1984).

16. *Avis sur les problèmes posés par le diagnostic prénatal et périnatal* (13 May 1985).

17. Working Party of the Ad Hoc Committee of Experts on Ethical and Legal Problems Relating to Human Genetics (Strasbourg, 9–12 October 1984).

18. Ad Hoc Committee of Experts on Progress in the Biomedical Sciences (CAHBI), *Provisional Principles on the Techniques of Human Artificial Procreation and Certain Procedures Carried out on Embryos in Connection with Those Techniques* (Strasbourg, 5 March 1986). This was complemented by the report on discussion and comment on these "provisional principles" (Trieste, 23–24 June 1986).

19. Conseil de l'Europe, *Utilisation d'Embryons et Foetus Humains à des fins diagnostiques, thérapeutiques, scientifiques, industrielles et commercielles* (24 September 1986).

20. "Códigos deontólogicos y normativas ético-jurídicas recientes," in *Labor Hospitalaria*, 18 (1986), 197–274; bibliography on 272–274.

21. Luis J. Archer, *Temas biológicos e problemas humanos* (Lisbon, 1981), 9–32.

22. Ver Juan-Ramón Lacadena, *Genética,* (Madrid, 1981); Jean Marie Moretti and Olivier de Dinechin, *Le défi génétique* (Paris, 1982).

23. M. Singer and D. Soll, Letter to the Presidents of the National Academy of Sciences and the National Institute of Medicine in the name of the participants in the Gordon Conference on Nucleic Acids (1973), *Science,* 181 (1973), 1114; P. Berg and other members of the Committee on Recombinant DNA Molecules of the National Academy of Sciences, *Science,* 185 (1974), 303; Dr. C. Randall, Secretary General of the National Council of Churches; Rabbi B. Mandelbaum, Secretary General of the Synagogue Council of America; Bishop Thomas Kelly, Secretary General of the United States Catholic Conference, Letter to the President of the Commission for Study of Ethical Problems in Medicine and Biomedical and Behavioral Research, 20 June 1980, *Splicing Life,* U.S. Government Printing Office (Washington, DC, 1984), 95–96.

24. Franz Böckle, *Die Herausforderung des Christen durch die Biotechnik,* Zentralkomitee der deutscher Katholiken (Versammlung, 23–24 November 1984), 6, 7.

25. Alfons Auer, "Gentechnologie—eine Herausforderung an die Ethik," *Theologische Quartalschrift,* 162 (1982), 261–262. "The mere establishment of the fact that genetic manipulation occasions a profound change in nature does not constitute any argument against it," Johannes Reither, "Gen-Technologie und Moral. Brauchen wir eine Gen-Ethik?" *Stimmen der Zeit,* 200 (1982), 570–571.

26. Pius XII, *Discourse to the Participants in the First International*

Symposium on Medical Genetics, 7 September 1953 (*AAS,* 45 [1953], 596–607, cited on p. 605).

27. *Ibid.,* cited on p. 605.

28. Gen. 9:5–7.

29. Pius XII, see note 27.

30. Hans Jonas, "Ethics and Biogenetic Art," *Social Research,* 52 (1985), 491–504, cited on pp. 501–502.

31. John Paul II, *Discourse to a Group of Research Biologists,* 23 October 1982 (*AAS,* 75 [1983], 35–39, cited on p. 38).

32. John Paul II, *Discourse to Members of the 35th Assembly of the World Health Organization,* 29 October 1983 (*AAS,* 79 [1984], 389–395, cited on pp. 392–393).

33. André Hellegers exaggerates the changes that have taken place in medical matters, adding to the progress made in the special fields mentioned those that have been realized in bacteriology and virology, in psychosomatics and genetics. See "Distribution of Health Resources," *Concilium,* 11/110 (1975), 523–532.

34. In one of the most recent reports on the health situation in the world, the World Health Organization noted that in the poorest countries, infant mortality is twenty times greater than in the western nations, and it characterized this situation as unpardonable in light of the knowledge and resources now available.

35. Paul VI, *Populorum progressio,* 26 March 1967 (*AAS,* 59 [1967], 257–299).

36. Comisión Pontifica "Iustitia et pax," *Al servizio della comunità umana: un approccio etico al debito internazionale,* 27 December 1986, *L'Osservatore Romano,* 28 January 1987, attached document.

37. James F. Childress, *Priorities in Biomedical Ethics* (Philadelphia, 1981), 75–97.

38. Carlo M. Martini, "Tecnologie biomediche e giustizia sociale," *Nuovi saggi di medicina e scienze umane* (Milan, 1985), 403–413.

39. H. Tristan Engelhard, Jr., and Michael A. Rie, "Intensive Care Units, Scarce Resources, and Conflicting Principles of Justice," *Journal of the American Medical Association,* 255 (1986), 1159–1164.

40. Paul Ramsey, *The Patient as Person* (New Haven, 1970), 256–259.

CHAPTER 62

Vatican II and Communications

Avery Dulles, S.J.

Summary

The theology of communication is intimately connected with ecclesiology: to every model of ecclesiology, there corresponds a type of communication. This principle is confirmed in the texts produced by the Council, which reflect the ecclesiological perspectives of the bishops and theologians. This article describes the five ecclessiological models with the implications they demand in the concept and usage of the media. The second part evaluates the Decree *Inter mirifica* in the light of conciliar and postconciliar texts. It concludes with reflections on the position of a Church that wants to be present to the world of our time with its new techniques of communication and at the same time faithful to the message of Christ.

Communications might be described as the way in that people are brought to share certain ideas, feelings, attitudes, or styles of action through contact with others. It does not necessarily signify the transfer of articulated thoughts from a teacher to a learner, though this is one prominent form of communication. It can equally well take place through a kind of catalytic action in which ideas or attitudes come to birth through social encounters. More particularly, religious knowledge and attitudes are not passed on like a baton. They are often "maieutically" induced by processes that activate the religious propensities of the "recipients."

The theology of communications is the study of how God brings about the convictions and commitments connected with religious faith. Faith normally requires for its proper development a community of believers who support one another's investigations and commitments. The theology of communications is, therefore, closely connected with ecclesiology.

The Catholic Church has always looked upon Jesus Christ as the supreme self-communication of God. Lateran Council IV (1215) gathered up the sense of many New Testament passages when it declared that Jesus Christ as the Incarnate Word manifested the way of life with special clarity (*viam vitae manifestius demonstravit*, DS 801). The Council of Trent (1546) spoke of the gospel as the source of all saving truth and moral discipline (*fontem omnis et salutaris veritatis et morum disciplinae*, DS 1501). The same council solemnly taught that the gospel is transmitted through Scripture and apostolic Traditions. Vatican Council I (1870) repeated in substance the teaching of Trent on Scripture and Tradition, but made significant advances by its pronouncements on revelation, faith, and the magisterium. Not only did Vatican I detail the ways in which revelation is communicated to the faithful in the Church, it also spoke eloquently of the Catholic Church as a sign raised up among the nations, inviting them to come to faith and at the same time confirming the faith of its own members (DS 3013–3014).

When Vatican II addressed the question of how religious knowledge is communicated, therefore, it was able to follow in the footsteps of several earlier councils. In many of its assertions, Vatican II simply paraphrased what has been taught in previous centuries, and in all its pronouncements sought to avoid contradicting what had been previously taught. It would be a mistake, therefore, to read Vatican II in a vacuum or to emphasize its innovations as though all its significant teachings were fresh departures.

One would search in vain in the documents of Vatican II for a single theology of communications. The authors of the sixteen documents, each of which was produced by teams of bishops and theologians, and amended many times, represented a variety of theological perspectives. It is convenient to distinguish five major outlooks that are reflected here and there in the council documents.[1]

Five Models of Communication

The first ecclesiology, which I call hierarchical or institutional, is that of the Scholasticism that had been dominant in the seminary manuals for some decades before the Council. This approach, as compared with medieval Scholasticism, is rather narrowly concerned with the authority of office and the obligatory character of official doctrine. It tends to view communications, in the theological sense, as a descending process beginning from God and passing through the papal and episcopal hierarchy to the other members of the Church. Scripture and Tradition are depicted as sources entrusted to the hierarchical magisterium, which is charged to safeguard and interpret the deposit of faith, especially by the issuance of binding decrees. While little is said about the mode of communication, the assumption seems to be that the teaching of the Church is contained in clear, concise statements that have been issued by legitimate authority in proper form, and that it is widely available, at least to the clergy, in printed texts.

This point of view, classically set forth by Pius XII in *Humani generis* (1950), was reflected in many of the preparatory documents for Vatican II, and continued to be defended by the so-called conservative minority throughout the Council. This outlook asserted itself particularly in Chapter III of the Constitution on the Church, *Gaudium et spes.* In his official *relatio* for the 1964 revision of Chapter III, Archbishop Pietro Parente told the council Fathers:

> The structure of the Church is such, already in the ontological order, that the different elements are inseparably united according to a hierarchical subordination, which is that of the faithful to the priests and to the bishops, that of the bishops to the pope, and that of the pope to Christ. No life and no power can be thought of as existing in this organism which does not derive from Christ, the invisible head, so as to pass through Peter and the bishops to the faithful.[2]

The theory of communications implied in the hierarchical model appears most clearly in Article 25 of the Constitution—a favorite text of institutionally minded theologians who appeal to Vatican II. This text states the conditions under which the extraordinary and the ordinary magisterium can teach infallibly, and it goes on the assert, in terms reminiscent of *Humani generis,* the obligation of the faithful to assent to the authentic but non-infallible doctrine of the hierarchical magisterium.

As Antonio Acerbi remarks, the doctrine of the magisterium in Chapter III of the Constitution on the Church gives the impression that all teaching and ministry originate from above, through the action of the Pope and the bishops. The description of the teaching office in this chapter

> presents the episcopal magisterium as though the bishops in their teaching role were in no way related as listeners to the faithful people. A minimalistic standpoint remains operative in this section: i.e., the principle of the authentic magisterium and the conditions of validity of its exercise are asserted without attention to the ramifications of such an act in the totality of the Church's faith and the concrete mode of application of the principle (which would place the episcopal magisterium more explicitly in relation to the faith of the community).[3]

A second ecclesiology present in the documents of Vatican II is what I like to call the herald model. It came into twentieth-century Catholic theology from Protestant biblical theology and Karl Barth's theology of the word. This model, operative in the Dogmatic Constitution on Divine Revelation, *Dei Verbum,* and in many parts of the Decree on Missionary Activity, *Ad gentes,* has left traces on Article 17 of the Constitution on the Church. According to this article, "the Church has received from the apostles as a task to be discharged even to the ends of the earth [the] solemn mandate of Christ to proclaim the saving truth." Hence, the Church continues unceasingly to send heralds to proclaim the gospel and thereby prepare hearers to receive and profess the faith. Christ is dynamically present in his word when the Scriptures are read in the Church and when the biblical message is proclaimed (cf. SC 7).

The first and second models share in common the idea that religious communication takes place primarily through the written and proclaimed word and that the proper response to the word is one of submission and faith. The word, moreover, is entrusted to heralds or teachers who are commissioned to disseminate and defend it. Within this larger agreement, five points of difference may be noted.

1. The first model is concerned with relationships within the Church between those who administer the Word and those to whom they minister. The second model looks upon the ministry of the Word as a ministry of the Church on behalf of outsiders.

2. The first model makes a sharp distinction between the hierarchy as authoritative teachers (*ecclesia docens*) and the rest of the faithful as learners (*ecclesia discens*). In the second model, this distinction is less important. Since the whole Church is missionary by its very nature (AG 2), all baptized believers are bearers of the message. The obligation of spreading the faith weighs indeed most heavily on bishops as successors of the apostles (AG 5), but no disciple of Christ is exempt from this responsibility (LG 17). The laity, as sharers in Christ's prophetic office, have the right and duty to collaborate in the task of evangelization (LG 34; AA 2; AG 41).

3. The content of the Church's authoritative teaching according to the first model is the doctrine of faith and morals contained explicitly or implicitly in the deposit of faith, including whatever is needed to explain or defend the faith. The content of missionary proclamation is the good news of salvation through the death and resurrection of Christ. The gospel can be summarized in a variety of ways, of which the following, from the Decree on Missionary Activity, may serve as a sample: "It is sufficient [for conversion] that a man realize that he has been snatched away from sin and led into the mystery of the love of God, who has called him to enter into a personal relationship with him in Christ" (AG 13).

4. The hierarchical model, as it has functioned in modern times, presupposes that the official teaching is available in written texts that are accessible to the faithful everywhere, or at least to the pastors. Thus, it is tied to communication through print. The kerygmatic model, which has been revived in the twentieth century, harks back to an age in which oral culture was dominant. The gospel message is summarized in brief creedal or confessional formulas that can easily be memorized.

5. The two modes of communication call for different responses. The response to authoritative hierarchical teaching varies according to the nature of the doctrine and the manner of its proposal. It may call for an assent of divine and Catholic faith, or

for ecclesiastical faith, or for a lesser degree of assent called "religious submission of mind" (*obsequium animi religiosum*). The response to missionary proclamation, on the other hand, is a free act of conversion to the Lord, elicited under the influence of the Holy Spirit, who opens human hearts to the message of salvation (*AG* 13, with reference to Acts 16:14). The fundamental act of Christian faith, by which one entrusts one's whole self to the God who reveals and promises, is more fully analyzed in the Constitution on Divine Revelation (*DV* 5). In summary, one may say that the response to hierarchical doctrine is a submission of the intellect to an authority that commands respect; the response to kerygmatic preaching is an existential adherence of the whole person to the tidings of salvation.

A third ecclesiological model in Vatican II is the sacramental, which predominates in the first chapter of the Constitution on the Church and in the Constitution on the Liturgy, *Sacrosanctum concilium*. According to this model, religious communication occurs not only through words, but equally through persons and events (*DV* 2). Christ himself is seen as the supreme revelatory symbol, the living image who renders God in some way visible. Christ communicates not only by what he says, but even more by what he is and does. The pattern of his life, and especially of his death and resurrection, manifest God's being and intentions on our behalf (*DV* 4).

In many of the council documents, the Church is described as a kind of sign or sacrament in which Christ is not only signified, but continues to be present and active for the salvation of the world. In this perspective, a merely verbal proclamation, while not inappropriate, would be insufficient. The oral witness of the word would lack substance and credibility unless it were backed up by the witness of personal life. Each Christian community, according to the Decree on Missionary Activity, must become a sign of Christ's presence in the world (*AG* 15).

The Vatican I doctrine of the Church as a "sign for the nations" is thus taken up in a new and more dynamic context. The Church is obliged to become in historical tangibility what in principle it already is by its very existence—a sign and instrument of Christ's living presence (*LG* 1, 48). To the extent that believers fail to live up to their calling "they must be said to conceal rather than reveal the authentic face of Christ" (*GS* 19; cf. *UR* 4).

The Constitution on the Liturgy, drawing on the achievements of the liturgical movement in the decades preceding the
Council, emphasized the communicative aspect of worship. "The
liturgy is thus the outstanding means by which the faithful can
express in their lives and manifest to others the mystery of Christ
and the real nature of the true Church. . . . Day by day the
liturgy builds up those within the Church into the Lord's holy
temple. . . . To outsiders the liturgy thereby reveals the Church
as a sign raised up above the nations (cf. Is. 11:12; SC 2).

The sacramental mode of communication, while it has analo-
gies with symbolic communication as we know it in ordinary
human experience, has certain distinctively theological qualities. The sacred signs produce their saving effect thanks to the
power of Christ at work in them. He is present when the gospel is
proclaimed, when the Scriptures are read, when the congregation prays and sings, and when the sacramental rites are performed (SC 7). The liturgy has a transforming impact only on
rightly disposed believers, who allow themselves to be taken up
into the mystery of the living Christ. The liturgy is not simply an
act of the officiating clergy, but that of all the members of the
assembly according to their distinct roles (SC 14).

A fourth ecclesiological model, implying yet another theology of communication, is that of the Church as community or
communion. The Church in this model is viewed as a fellowship of life, charity, and truth (LG 9) animated by the Holy
Spirit. For the clearest expression of this model, one may study
Chapter II of the Constitution on the Church, entitled "The
People of God." Here the Church is said to be composed of
many types of persons, having their own distinct abilities and
charisms, working together to build up the whole Body in love
(LG 12). Although not much is said here about communications, it is implied that all play an active role and have the
obligation both to contribute their insights and to be receptive
to the insights of others. By their mutual union, they anticipate
the solidarity of the heavenly city, and thereby bear witness to
the hope that is in them (LG 10).

The communion model of ecclesiology, when applied to communication within the Catholic Church, favors common witness
and dialogue. In its Decree on Ecumenism, *Unitatis redintegratio*,
Vatican II extended the communion model to relationships between separated churches and ecclesial communities. By virtue

of their incorporation in Christ through faith and baptism, as well as other ecclesial elements, Christians of different ecclesiastical allegiances enjoy a real, though imperfect, communion with one another (*UR* 3). From this, it follows that members of these separated bodies may appropriately bear common witness to those central beliefs that they hold in common (*UR* 11–12) and engage in respectful dialogue about points that still cause difficulty between them. In such dialogue, they may be able to profit from one another's insights and broaden the areas of agreement, thus intensifying their mutual communion. The Decree on Ecumenism, strongly recommending these methods of communication, ushered in a whole new era in the relations between the Catholic Church and the other Christian communities. Although a long road still lies ahead, the progress of the past twenty years has been astonishing.

It might seem that the four models already examined would exhaust the ecclesiologies of Vatican II, but there is, in my opinion, yet a fifth. In some passages of the Pastoral Constitution on the Church in the Modern World, and more rarely in other documents, one finds evidences of what I would call a secular-dialogic theology. In this approach, the non-Christian world is seen not simply as raw material for the Church to convert to its own purposes, nor as a mere object of missionary zeal, but as a realm in which the creative and redemptive will of God is mysteriously at work. On this premise, the kind of dialogue that we have examined under the heading of communion ecclesiology can be extended to non-Christian religions and even to secular ideologies. In such dialogue, the Church can hope to gain as well as to give, to learn as well as to teach. There is also the possibility of joint witness with non-Christians for authentic human and religious values.

This fifth theological perspective appears already in the opening paragraphs of the Pastoral Constitution *Gaudium et spes*. Christians are here described as inextricably involved with the rest of humanity in the process of world history, which at the present time is bringing the whole human family into a common stream. Rapid worldwide communication, according to this document, is having an unsettling effect on previously isolated cultural groups, especially in the traditional societies (*GS* 6). The advent of the new mass culture, disseminated by new media of communication, is fraught with possibilities of disorientation and social conflict or, alternatively, of a universal human solidarity (GS 53–55). Christians should enter responsibly into this process, casting their influence on the side of justice, peace, and unity.

In order to be of service to humanity, the Church finds it necessary to interpret the signs of the times—a term by which the Council evidently means "authentic signs of God's presence and purpose in the happenings, needs, and desires in which this People has a part along with other men of our age" (GS 11). The discernment of these signs is described as the task of the whole People of God, pastors and faithful together (GS 44). In discussing this process, the Pastoral Constitution makes it clear that the laity are not to be passively dependent on the hierarchy:

> Let the layman not imagine that his pastors are always such experts that to every problem that arises, however complicated, they can readily give him a concrete solution, or even that such is their mission. Rather, enlightened by Christian wisdom and giving close attention to the teaching authority of the Church, let the layman take on his own distinctive role (GS 43).

In the later sections of the same document, the freedom of the laity to express their views on matters in which they are competent is strongly asserted (GS 62). Secular-dialogic theology, therefore, has repercussions on the kind of dialogue that takes place within the Church.

At a number of points, the Pastoral Constitution alludes to the intrinsic value of human institutions that have grown up without help from the Church. Renouncing any attitude of haughty superiority, the Council professes "great respect" for "all the true, good, and just elements found in the very wide variety of institutions which the human race has established for itself and constantly continues to establish" (GS 42). This respect includes the readiness of the Church to benefit from these advances. "The Church herself knows how richly she has profited from the history and development of humanity" (GS 44). The experience of history and the development of science and culture have opened roads to truth and disclosed new depths in the nature of the human person (*ibid.*). As an example, the Pastoral Constitution might have referred to the doctrine of religious freedom set forth in the Declaration on Religious Freedom, *Dignitatis humanae.* In its first sentence, this Declaration professes to be responding to the sense of the dignity of the human person that has been imposing itself on the contemporary consciousness of humanity. To keep abreast of this unfolding consciousness can, therefore, be important for the development of Catholic doctrine.

The two-way exchange that is appropriate to this model is not limited to interlocutors who are formally religious. Based on the common experience of individuals in community, such dialogue can extend to secular ideologies, not excluding atheism (GS 21). But this theological model also provides an excellent foundation for interreligious dialogue. According to the Declaration on the Relation of the Church to Nonchristian Religions, *Nostra aetate,* these religions "often reflect a ray of that Truth which enlightens all men" (NA 2). The Pastoral Constitution uses in this context the language of revelation. "All believers of whatever religion," it states, "have always heard [God's] revealing voice in the discourse of creatures" (GS 36). Revelation, as seen in this theology, does not begin with Scripture and Tradition, or even with Jesus Christ, but with the Word in whom all things have been created. Grace is presumed to be operative in the whole of human history. The Church, though it is privileged to know God's supreme self-disclosure in his Incarnate Son, can continually deepen its grasp of the divine by dialogue with other religious traditions and by interpreting the signs of the times.

Implications for the Use of the Media

I have left for the concluding portion of this article the application of the general principles of communication to the several media. I shall draw upon explicit references to the media in the documents of Vatican II and also upon certain postconciliar documents that have sought to apply the principles of Vatican II to the situation of the Church today. As an organizing principle for this section, I shall follow the five models previously explained. Depending upon one's preferred model of ecclesiology, the relation of the Church to the media is variously conceived.

In the institutional model, the Church is viewed as the authoritative teacher of faith and morals. In the documents of

Vatican II that favor this model, little attention is directed to the media as means whereby the hierarchy communicates sound doctrine to the faithful. The assumption seems to be that the traditional channels—such as papal encyclicals, decrees of Roman Congregations, pastoral letters, catechetical instruction, seminary training, and sermons—retain their previous value.

The principal Vatican II document concerning communications is the Decree on the Means of Social Communication, *Inter mirifica.* Prepared in advance of the first session, this document was debated in the fall of 1962 and approved, with minor changes, in the fall of 1963. Although it accurately summarizes some important principles from earlier papal teaching, this Decree fails to incorporate the more characteristic themes of Vatican II, such as ecumenism, personal freedom, and dialogue.

In *Inter mirifica,* the institutional model of the Church as authoritative teacher seems to be taken for granted. The instruments of social communication are described as tools at the disposal of human beings, to be used for achieving the supreme goal of all creation, which is the praise of God and the salvation of souls. The Church has the tasks of instructing humanity in the worthy use of the media and of utilizing them to bring people to salvation through faith in Christ (*IM* 3). These two tasks are more fully expounded in the doctrinal and pastoral sections of the Decree.

The doctrinal section is preponderantly taken up with the demands of the moral order, including the requirements of truth, justice, and charity, which are in no case to be violated. The communications industry is exhorted to avoid the temptation to exploit the baser desires of its audiences for the sake of monetary gain (*IM* 9). Civil authorities are said to have the duty to intervene where necessary to protect the common good (*IM* 12).

In the pastoral section of the Decree, both clergy and laity are exhorted to apply themselves energetically to the use of the media in the apostolate. A number of general directives are given regarding Catholic education, the Catholic press, and the establishment of offices of social communications at the diocesan, national, and universal levels of Church governance (*IM* 19–21). Provision is made for the annual observance of World Communications Day (*IM* 18), and for the issuance of a pastoral instruction on communications to be drawn up after the Council under the supervision of the proposed office for the media of social communication to be set up at the Holy See (*IM* 23).

More or less in line with the Decree on the Means of Social Communication are the passing references to communication in the Declaration on Christian Education, *Gravissium educationis*, which favors the penetration of the educational media with a more Catholic spirit (*GE* 4), and in the Decree on the Ministry and Life of Priests, *Presbyterorum ordinis*, which suggests that the new media might be advantageously used to promote vocations to the priesthood (*PO* 2).

The institutional approach to communications in these three documents may be seen as basically sound as far as it goes, but hardly as adequate for the total communications situation of the Church in the present day. This approach fails to take into account the characteristics of dialogue that were sensitively analyzed in Paul VI's Encyclical *Ecclesiam suam* (1964). It also overlooks the radical impact of the new media on communication within the Church itself, the importance of two-way communication within and beyond the Church, and the need of the pilgrim Church to learn from other religions and from secular movements and agencies.

As understood in the second model, to which we now turn, the prime task of the Church is evangelization. Several documents of Vatican II in which this ecclesiology is prominent allude in passing to the potential of the mass media for transmitting the Christian message. In the Decree on the Missionary Activity of the Church, *Ad gentes*, and in the Decree on the Apostolate of the Laity, *Apostolicam actuositatem*, the value of the media for communicating awareness about the work and situation of the missions is mentioned as a resource for engendering a livelier missionary spirit among the Catholic faithful (*AG* 36; *AG* 10). The Decree on the Pastoral Office of Bishops in the Church, *Christus Dominus*, which strongly accents the role of the bishop as minister of the word, declares that the various media of communication should be employed for the proclamation of the gospel (*CD* 13). This statement, taken in context, appears to refer both to preaching and to doctrinal instruction.

The teaching of Vatican II on these points was further developed by the Synod of Bishops in 1974 and by the Apostolic Exhortation of Paul VI, *On Evangelization in the Modern World*, issued in 1975 as a reflection on the Synod. The Pope here proposes a rather complex concept of evangelization, going beyond the limits of the kerygmatic model and including seven

elements: "the renewal of humanity, witness, explicit proclamation, inner adherence, entry into the community, acceptance of
signs, apostolic initiative" (*EN* 24). The proclaimed message, he
points out, does not reach its full development until it is listened
to, accepted, and assimilated through adherence to the ecclesial
community, through sacramental worship, and through a committed Christian life. The mass media may and should be used for
a kind of "first proclamation" (*EN* 45), sometimes called "preevangelization" (51), as well as for catechesis and the further
deepening of the faith (45), but to obtain fully personal adherence and commitment, it is important for broadcasts to be followed up by personal instruction and direction as well as by
active participation in the Church's life (23, 46).

Citing the observations of Paul VI in *Evangelii nuntiandi*, the
Latin American bishops, at their Third General Conference
(Puebla, 1979), advocated greater use of the Media of Group
Communications as a supplement to the mass media:

> Without neglecting the necessary and urgent presence of the
> mass-oriented media, it is urgent that we intensify our use of
> the Media of Group Communication. Besides being less costly
> and easier to handle, they offer the possibility of dialogue and
> they are more suited to a person-to-person type of evangeliza-
> tion that will evoke a truly personal adhesion and commit-
> ment (*EN* 45–46).[4]

Passages such as these help to distinguish the Catholic concept
of evangelization, which includes personal transformation and
the regeneration of society, from the narrower concept of evangelization as mere call to put one's trust in Christ as Savior, which
is current in certain Protestant "evangelistic" circles. The two
concepts of evangelization have different implications with regard to the media to be used.

The third model, which regards the Church as a sacramental
embodiment of redemption, particularly stresses the liturgy as the
place where the Church as sign comes to fullest visibility. The
documents of Vatican II that propose this understanding of the
Church, such as the Constitution on the Sacred Liturgy and the
Dogmatic Constitution on the Church, reflect an awareness that
sacraments are sacred actions performed in a worshiping community and calling for full and active participation. No sacrament

achieves its transformative impact when taken simply as a spectacle. The Council does not exclude the broadcasting of ecclesial events, and even of the liturgy, but recommends this with suitable reserve: The broadcasting and televising of sacred rites must be done with discretion and dignity, under the guidance and guarantee of a suitable person appointed for this office by the bishops. This is especially important when the service in question is the Mass (SC 20).

The Council was apparently conscious of the risk that in seeking to create a media event, broadcasters might obscure or distort the proper nature of the liturgy. As Karl Rahner had noted in an essay first published in 1953,[5] certain rites of the Church can appear ridiculous when projected indiscriminately to unbelievers and persons of no religious background, especially if these spectators are merely curious and lacking in religious sincerity. With respect to television, Rahner argues for the maintenance of something like the ancient *disciplina arcani*. In this connection, it may be of interest to note that the new Rites for the Christian Initiation of Adults, approved by the Holy See in 1972, provide for the dismissal of catechumens from the liturgy after the service of the Word and before the Eucharist proper. These points should be taken into consideration and weighed against the obvious pastoral advantages of having the Mass broadcast on the occasion of papal journeys, for example, or for the benefit of the aged and the infirm.

As the Latin American bishops noted at their Medellín Conference (1968), recent technological developments raise in new form the question of the spiritual efficacy of visual and musical presentations in comparison with the preached and written word. They wrote:

The spoken word is the normal vehicle of faith: *fides ex auditu* (Rom. 10:17). In our times the "word" also becomes image, colors, and sounds, acquiring varied forms from the diverse media of social communication. The media of social communication, thus understood, are a *must* for the Church to realize her evangelical mission in our contemporary world.[6]

Since the early centuries, the Catholic Church, like the Eastern Orthodox, has constantly defended the use and veneration of images against Iconoclasts of many types. The Fourth Council of

Constantinople, in A.D. 870, made a bold comparison between holy images and the Holy Scriptures:

> We prescribe that the sacred image of Our Lord Jesus Christ should be venerated with the same honor as the books of the holy Gospels. For just as we are all brought to salvation through the letters of Scripture, so by the action of the colors in images all—learned as well as ignorant—equally find profit in what is within reach of all. For painting proclaims and presents in colors the same Scripture (*graphē*) that the word sets forth in letters (DS 653–654).

Important differences exist, of course, between the cult of holy icons in eastern Christianity and the use of film and television in the contemporary West. But both raise similar questions regarding the apostolate. Modern communications technology offers instruments of tremendous spiritual power that the Catholic Church has scarcely begun to utilize. As I said on a previous occasion:

> Catholicism, as a highly sacramental religion, has an extraordinarily rich heritage on which to draw. It has a splendid variety of liturgical forms, a magnificent musical heritage, and impressive patrimony of religious art and architecture, a long and dramatic history, and a worldwide presence bringing it into contact with diverse races, cultures, and religions. All these features provide precious resources from which to construct vivid, appealing religious programs.[7]

It would not normally be appropriate to issue a direct call for Christian faith in film and television broadcasts directed to general audiences. But such broadcasts could well serve to break down hostile prejudices, to build up a more favorable image, and to arouse interest on the part of the uncommitted, while at the same time confirming the faith and energizing the commitment of those who already believe. Although such presentations do not fit easily in the category of evangelization characteristic of our second model, they can, in terms of our third model, contribute in important ways to the apostolate.

The fourth ecclesiological model, which depicts the Church as a community of free exchange and dialogue, is best suited to spontaneous and informal styles of communication such as talk shows and interviews. The passages of Vatican II favoring this model of the Church emphasize free expression and mutual listening, but make no reference to the modern media of communication. The communications aspect of this model is explored more amply in the Pastoral Instruction on Communications, *Communio et progressio,* issued by the Pontifical Commission for the Means of Social Communication in 1971, in conformity with the directive of Vatican II's *Inter mirifica* mentioned before. Several brief quotations may serve to indicate the general tenor of this Instruction:

> Those who exercise authority in the Church will take care to ensure that there is a responsible exchange of freely held and expressed opinion among the People of God (116).
>
> The free dialogue within the Church does no injury to her unity and solidarity. It nurtures concord and the meeting of minds by permitting the free play of the variations of public opinion (117).
>
> The normal flow of life and smooth functioning of government within the Church require a steady two-way flow of information between the ecclesiastical authorities at all levels and the faithful as individuals and organized groups (120).

Also emphasized in this Instruction are the freedom of the Catholic faithful to publish their opinions (118) and the responsibility of the Catholic press to give a true and honest picture of the Church (123). The means of social communication are recommended as an aid to fostering dialogue within the Church (125).

The United States bishops, in their bicentennial hearings (1975–1976), in the consultations for their pastoral on moral values and for the National Catechetical Directory, and in their recent collective pastoral letters on peace and on the economy, have adopted the dialogic mode of communication recommended in Vatican II's Pastoral Constitution and in *Communio et progressio.* In so doing, they have provoked some criticism from theologians favoring a more hierarchical, authoritarian model. Archbishop Rembert Weakland, taking note of this criticism, has correctly identified the root of the problem:

> Underneath this criticism is a definite concept of ecclesiology. Its proponents see a strongly hierarchical model of

the Church, where the faithful are taught by the bishops, who are in possession of the gifts of the Spirit needed for such authoritative teaching. The model adopted by the U.S. Conference believes that the Holy Spirit resides in all members of the Church and that the hierarchy must listen to what the Spirit is saying to the whole Church. This does not deny the teaching role of the hierarchy, but enhances it. It does not weaken the magisterium, but ultimately strengthens it. Discernment, not just innovation or self-reliance, becomes a part of the teaching process.[8]

This model of communication has greatly helped to overcome the excesses of clericalism, juridicism, and authoritarianism that became characteristic of Roman Catholicism after the Reformation, and especially in the nineteenth century. But we should be on guard against a naïve overconfidence in the community model sometimes displayed in the decade of enthusiasm that followed Vatican II. An undirected spontaneous dialogue on the part of Church members who have not been thoroughly socialized into the Christian tradition and the Catholic way of life is not necessarily conducive to deeper wisdom and broader consensus. On the contrary, such dialogue may polarize the Church, arouse unrealistic expectations, and provoke angry recriminations. These untoward results are intensified when the electronic media purport to give candid portrayals of the present ferment in the Church. Because the media have an inbuilt bias toward conflict and contradiction, popular broadcasts of interviews and panel discussions frequently impair the Church's image as a sign of unity and reconciliation. Catholics engaged in the apostolate of the media should seek ways of countering these negative effects.

The fifth ecclesiological model, as mentioned before, makes its appearance in certain sections of the Pastoral Constitution on the Church in the Modern World, *Gaudium et spes*. It depicts Christians as participating in "the joys and the hopes, the griefs and the anxieties" of the whole human race (GS 1) and as being in a position to assist the entire human family by "simultaneously manifesting and exercising the mystery of God's love for man" (GS 45). In order to serve more effectively, the Church must "scrutinize the signs of the times" (GS 4) and profit from the achievements and gifts of those who are not its own members.

In greater detail than any of the council documents, the Pastoral Instruction of 1971 spells out the implications of this fifth model for communications. The contemporary world is described as "a great round table" (19) in which a worldwide community of cooperation and fellowship is being forged (73). By participating in this universal dialogue, the various religions can move toward a common brotherhood under God (98). Through the media, Christians are better able to perceive the qualities of the emerging world society and to address its needs and questions in an effective manner (97). Educators seeking to be of service can utilize the new media for instructing those who lack knowledge in modern methods of agriculture, medicine, hygiene, and community development, as well as for combating illiteracy (20, 48). But training and self-discipline are demanded so that the potential benefits of the new media may be realized and the dangers of blind passion, escapism, and exploitation are avoided (21–23).

The Medellín Conference of the Latin American bishops included in its Conclusions a chapter on the mass media, in which the secular dialogic point of view predominates. The media are valued for their capacity to awaken the consciousness of the masses, to promote people's aspirations for a better life, and to manifest the urgency of radical social change (16:2). For reasons given by Vatican II, the Church must participate in this process:

The involvement of Christians in today's world obliges them to work in the media of social communication external to the Church in keeping with the spirit of dialogue and service which marks the Constitution *Gaudium et spes*. The Catholic professional, called to be the leaven in the dough, will better perform his mission if he integrates himself in these media in order to broaden the contacts between the Church and the world, and at the same time contribute to the transformation of the latter.[9]

The type of polycentric encounter among diverse human groups characteristic of the fifth model can greatly help the Church to escape from the cultural isolation and the dogmatic narrowness by which it has at times been afflicted. But these benefits must not blind us to certain concomitant dangers. By exposing the audience to a selected variety of images, problems, programs, and interpretations, communications technology could foment clashes of opinion or could subtly insinuate a hierarchy of values quite alien to the gospel. The connatural tendency of the press and the electronic media to emphasize conflict, change, and novelty could lead to spiritual agitation and undermine the kind of firm and lasting commitment required by Christian faith. Ideally, the faith of Catholics should be nurtured in a relatively stable and propitious environment of trust and discipleship, in which the riches of the tradition can be gradually appropriated. But for persons who do not have an opportunity for such formation in discipleship, the Church must seek to offer simple and attractive presentations of the core of Catholic Christianity. The ideas and attitudes of the multitudes are today influenced far more by emotionally charged images than by precise and laborious arguments. For this reason, the Church is compelled to enter into the arena of secular-dialogic communications and to develop communicators skilled in the use of the electronic media.

The pastoral leadership of the Church and the theological disciplines have much to learn from communications technology. The effectiveness of the apostolate in every age has depended on the Church's ability to make use of the dominant forms of communication. In the words of Paul VI, "The Church would feel guilty before the Lord if she did not utilize these powerful means of communication that human skill is daily rendering more perfect" (*EN* 45). Doctrinal or practical decisions that rested on faulty communications, or were incapable of being successfully communicated, would be pastorally unwise. Yet the criterion of successful communication should not be elevated to the status of an absolute. Not everything that is congenial to the mass media is consonant with the gospel of Christ. Sometimes God is more effectively sought in privacy and silence than in the blare of publicity.

In the perspectives of theology, therefore, communications, like every other human reality, has to be interpreted and evaluated in the light of the gospel. Concern with the techniques of communication must always be subordinated to the primacy of the Christian message. Vatican II, while it had little to say directly about the media of communication, provided a theological vision that we shall do well to ponder. The various ecclesiological models implicit in the council documents are very helpful for identifying and appraising the numerous styles of communication that are available to the Church in our day. They suggest that the Church should use a large variety of media and methods in its encounter with the different publics that make up its own membership and that of the surrounding world.

Notes

1. In what follows, I rely on the schematization in Avery Dulles, *Models of the Church* (Garden City, NY, 1974). For the purposes of this presentation, I have inverted the order of Models 2 and 4.

2. AS, III/2, 210. Cf. Antonio Acerbi, *Due Ecclesiologie: Ecclesiologia giuridica ed ecclesiologia di comunione nella "Lumen gentium"* (Bologna, 1975), 523.

3. Acerbi, *Due Ecclesiologie,* 524–525.

4. *The Puebla Conclusions* (Washington, DC, 1979), No. 1090, p. 172.

5. Karl Rahner, "The Mass and Television," in his *Mission and Grace,* Vol. 1 (London, 1963), 255–275.

6. Second General Conference of Latin American Bishops, *The Church in the Present-Day Transformation of Latin America in the Light of the Council.* Part II. *Conclusions* (Bogota, 1970), 16:7, p. 239.

7. Avery Dulles, "Mass Evangelization through Social Media," testimony for U.S. Catholic Conference Hearing on Communications, 8 March 1979, in *Catholic Mind,* 78/1344 (June 1980), 43–49, quotation from pp. 46–47.

8. R.G. Weakland, "Where Does the Economics Pastoral Stand?" *Origins,* 13/46 (26 April 1984), 758–759.

9. *The Church in the Present-Day Transformation,* 16/12, 239–240.

CHAPTER 63

The Decree on the Means
of Social Communication
Success or Failure of the Council?

André Ruszkowski, S.J.

Summary

In its first part, this article shows how the conciliar Decree *Inter mirifica* established social communications among the major concerns of the Church, and also consolidated the basic structures needed for action that has been bearing its fruits in every continent for twenty years now. In the second part, it gives the reasons for hoping in a progressive development, especially thanks to the efforts at training and research being undertaken on every level.

Introduction

After a quarter of a century, the memory of certain incidents from Vatican II is fading. How many people today remember the ferment that shook not only the tiers of seats in the Council Hall established in St. Peter's, but also the surroundings of the basilica and the various corners of Rome where information and discussion centers had been set up for people from every continent? The commotion was caused by the text put to the vote at the second session (in 1963), which then became the Decree on the Means of Social Communication, *Inter mirifica*. No means were spared in the attempt to prevent its approval! There were articles in the press, radio commentaries broadcast to every part of the world, and even pamphlets distributed to the public and to the Council Fathers on their way to the basilica. Although the pro-testers were not able to prevent the vast majority from voting in favor of the proposed text, they did manage to stir up a minority larger than that for any other conciliar document to cast *non placet* votes. The final result was 1960 votes for and 164 against, and the Decree was therefore promulgated on 4 December 1963.[1] However, this did not halt its critics. On the contrary: certain commentaries gave the impression that the Council had just committed some unpardonable gaffe. Twenty-five years later, it is easier to discuss it all more calmly.

There were two possible attitudes for those who hoped that the highest authority of the Church would speak out on social communications.

The general public, including believers concerned over the role of the media in their lives, would have appreciated some solid doctrinal teaching on a question that was still relatively new. On the other hand, there were those, still few in number, who were already involved in various practical efforts at ensuring a Christian presence in the new world of the mass media, and who hoped for something other than simple doctrinal statements. For them, the main point was to gain recognition for social communications as one of the major concerns of the Church. This would lead to an indispensable institutionalization within the Church, which would then provide more official backing for what had until that point been the spontaneous and unorganized efforts of the pio-neers already involved in all sorts of projects throughout the world. From the point of view of the latter group, the Council offered a unique opportunity to demonstrate the interest of the Church in social communications and its determination to pro-vide itself with the structures indispensable for any effective action in this field—action that also presupposes the establishment of a doctrinal basis. We should not forget that many international-level communications experts agree that the theory of communica-tions is only in its very early stages, and we should, therefore, not be surprised that at the time of the Council, the bishops did not yet have at their command the elements necessary to produce such a doctrinal statement. This is why they gave up the original idea of a the doctrinal Constitution that had been drafted by the preparatory commissions, and adopted the formula of a short Decree that was predominantly pastoral in approach.

Although the result was a disappointment for those who would have liked some in-depth doctrinal statements, it fulfilled the expectations of those among us who had been involved in the efforts that were already being made, and who saw the Decree as recognition of our efforts and the most authoritative encouragement to continue them within an institutional framework approved by the Council.

The word "institution" tends to be unfashionable at the moment. Everybody will agree that an institution is not a final end in itself, and that it becomes pointless when it seeks to exist for itself alone, forgetting the true reasons for its existence. However, it is totally unrealistic to imagine that it is possible to provide an effective presence in the social sphere without a minimum of organization, and thus of institutional order. Certain opponents of the Church as institution would also do well to consider whether they could have acquired the skills needed in order to challenge it, and also the framework that makes such opposition possible, were it not for the institution of the Church itself, with its schools, seminaries, universities, and publications.

The Decree *Inter mirifica* institutionalizes social communications in the Church, and, in so doing, it provides a solid foundation for all future development. The first part of this study will try to show the way in which this is done. After this, we must move on to consider whether, despite their initial disappointment, even those among media specialists, and also the general public who had hoped to find deeper and fuller orientations in a conciliar document, should not in fact see some reasons in it for hope.

This twofold approach will fulfill its aim if it enables us to make a fairer evaluation of what is not only one of the most criticized documents of the Council, but is also one of the least known and understood.

Toward an Appreciation of
the Importance of *Inter mirifica*

For all of us who were already involved in one way or another in the preconciliar period in what aimed at being Christian action in connection with the main "instruments" of social communication—press, cinema, radio, and television—a new era opened on 4 December 1963 with the proclamation of the conciliar Decree *Inter mirifica*. Some people who were especially aware of what they saw as the weaknesses of the document perhaps did not understand this fact well enough. However, it is to be hoped that now, a quarter of a century later, they too can recognize its importance.

There are three factors that indicate the full measure of this importance: (1) thanks to the Decree, social communications were solemnly established as one of the major concerns of the Church, so that they would henceforth be allotted a proper place on its "agenda"; (2) together with the other conciliar documents and the Pastoral Instruction *Communio et progressio* that followed them, the Decree defined the institutional framework for the action of the Church on different levels within the sphere of social communications, which was thus accorded recognition; (3) the experience of twenty-five years has demonstrated not only that the framework is still valid, but also that it has already begun to bear increasingly promising fruit. Let us now take a closer look at these three factors.

Social Communications: A Major Concern for the Church

Beginning with its first article, the conciliar Decree stresses the acceptance by the Church, among the marvellous technical inventions (*inter mirifica*), of everything that encourages man's intellectual and spiritual life and opens up new paths for communication. The second article states that in view of the importance of this question, the Council has found it necessary to define its principles in this connection, following the positions previously taken up in the teaching of the Pope and bishops.

Cardinal André-Marie Deskur, who was one of those chiefly responsible for the drafting of the Decree (he was at that time Secretary of the Pontifical Commission for Social Communications) emphasizes the consequences of the conciliar text for the Church. In his report to the 1983 Synod of Bishops, he specifically stated:

Moreover, it was necessary to take into consideration a perspective that seems to be becoming constantly more firmly established in the sphere of the pastoral ministry of social communications: the need for the Church to play an active part in communications activities.

The Church must therefore follow more faithfully the guidelines of *Inter mirifica* and *Communio et progressio*, and thus bring a more practical pastoral approach to its specific task of transmitting the message of salvation, by observing the rules of communications.[2]

It would be difficult to express better the conviction that with its authority, the Council "legitimized" the efforts of those pioneers who had for years been hoping to see social communications recognized as a special sphere for pastoral work.

However, the Decree does not confine itself to a general statement on the place of communications in the concerns of the Church, but also formulates a number of essential points of its doctrine (Chapter I, Nos. 3–12) and of its action (Chapter II, Nos. 13–21).

And among the points of doctrine, how can we avoid special mention of the now famous Article 5 on the right to information? The text has the following to say concerning the controversial issues of the use of the media:

The first of these issues is information, or the search for news and its publications. Because of the progress of modern society and the increasing interdependence of its members on one another, it is obvious that information is very useful, and, for the most part, essential. If news of facts and happenings is communicated publicly and without delay, every individual will have permanent access to sufficient information and thus will be enabled to contribute effectively to the common good. Further, all of them will more easily be able to contribute in unison to the prosperity and the progress of society as a whole.

There exists therefore in human society a right to information on the subjects that are of concern to men either as individuals or as members of society, according to each man's circumstances. The proper exercise of this right demands that the content of the communication be true and—within the limits set by justice and charity—complete. Further, it should be communicated honestly and properly. This means that in the gathering and in the publication of news the moral law and the legiti-

mate rights and dignity of man should be upheld. All knowledge is not profitable, but on the other hand "love builds" (1
Cor. 8:1).

The journalists who spoke out against this text, in place of which
they would have preferred to see an exaltation of the "freedom of
information" reserved to themselves and their publications, were
reluctant to recognize the value of a solemn declaration of the
fundamental right of each individual and each society to receive
the information it needs in order to survive and develop. This
declaration was made in terms that were more precise and more
juridical even than those used by the United Nations in its draft
declaration on the Freedom of Information in 1948. As Father
Jacques Cousineau, S.J., rightly remarked, "It is thus the Church,
thanks to Vatican II, that has been the first international organization to speak out authoritatively on one of the vital and most
burning problems of our contemporary society."

Other points of doctrine, both of a moral (Nos. 4–7) and
social order (Nos. 8–12), are outlined in the Decree in the hope
of further development, either within the framework of the prom-
ised Pastoral Instruction, or in various contributions of the magisterium. The fact that the accent is placed on the moral aspect
is explained by the need to define the attitude of the Church as a
society with regard to the use of the media.

Instead of launching into a polemical refutation of the other
accusations or criticisms made against this part of the Decree at
that time, let us instead consider its contribution on the level of
practical organization and action.

Guidelines for Action

(a) *Encouragement to Catholic undertakings in the fields of the
press, cinema, radio and television (No. 14).* The pioneers of such
enterprises would no longer be seen as freelance operators who
have to fend for themselves. So long as they are serious about
their tasks, and competent, they have the right to the support of
the Christian community, including the Church authorities.

(b) *Encouragement of a "full overall training" in order to "acquire
the competence needed to use these media for the apostolate," through
the provision of sufficient schools, institutes or faculties (No. 15).*
The period of self-taught experts who thought they could do

everything is over. The Church accepts that it has a responsibility for the formation of experts in social communications.

(c) *Encouragement "in Catholic schools at all levels, in seminaries
and lay apostolate associations" for the acquisition of "instruction and
practical experience tailored not merely to the character of each medium but the needs of each group" in order to become discerning and
informed "recipients"* (No. 16). The way is thus opened toward a
fundamental orientation of modern pastoral work: that of offering contemporary men and women the enormous service of preparation and training for personal growth in a society dominated by
the media.

(d) *Encouragement of financial contributions to help pastoral work
in the communications field. This is one of the reasons for the annual
organization of a World Communications Day* (Nos. 17 and 18).
There must be at least a minimum of financial resources if this
work is to be carried out properly.

(e) *The establishment by the Church of an operational structure on
the various levels of its hierarchy: a pontifical commission* (No. 19),
national offices (No. 21), *diocesan activities and projects* (Art. 20),
and international organizations recognized by the Holy See (No. 22).
Within this structure, projects that already exist will be reorga-
nized, and new offices will be set up. A process is set in motion
that will entail coordination of the expansion of what can be
considered the "clerical bureaucracy" (in the hierarchical chain
of Pope–bishop–parish priest), and also the support and encouragement of projects originating with the various people involved
(priests, male and female religious, and lay people). The problem
is particularly clear with regard to national offices, since in many
countries, these were set up on the spontaneous initiative of the
lay people and priests concerned. The conciliar Decree provides
these offices with a more official status, which had long been
hoped for, and which we happily noted in an article in *La Rivista
del Cinematografo.*[3] Even so, certain problems arose in cases
where the bishops of a given country preferred to organize their
own secretariat for social communications alongside the national
office already in existence. The situation varies considerably
from one continent to another or even one country to another,
and it would seem that it will continue to evolve for some time to
come. It depends among other things on the more general question of the place of lay people in the Church—which was of
course the subject of the recent Synod of Bishops.

The situation seems simpler on the international level, where the Holy See retains its full authority with regard to the ecclesial structure, through the Pontifical Commission for Social Communications, while the ICO/SCs (International Catholic Organizations for Social Communications) envisaged in number 22, which coordinate the action of the national offices on this level, must be "approved" or "recognized" by the Holy See and are dependent (*pendent*) on it. It is interesting to observe that although number 178 of the Pastoral Instruction *Communio et progressio* again uses the term "approval" for the three ICO/SCs— UCIP (the International Union of the Catholic Press), OCIC (the International Catholic Organization of the Cinema and Audiovisuals), and UNDA (the International Catholic Organization for Radio and Television)—it no longer speaks of their "dependency" on the Holy See.

When evaluating the contribution of Vatican II in the sphere of social communications, we must remember that other documents produced later than *Inter mirifica* also contribute important elements in this connection, so that they too had to be taken into considration by *Communio et progressio*, which lists them in its Article 2. Thus, we have the Constitution on the Church in the Modern World, the Decree on Ecumenism, the Declaration on Religious Freedom, the Decree on the Missionary Activity of the Church, and the Decree on the Pastoral Office of Bishops in the Church.

When the Pontifical Commission for Social Communications came to work on the text of the Pastoral Instruction, it therefore had at its disposition the whole *corpus* of conciliar documents, and did not have to confine itself only to *Inter mirifica*. In his well-documented article on the tenth anniversary of *Communio et progressio*,[4] Father Enrico Baragli, S.J., criticizes the fact that those responsible for the document introduced three subjects that were not found in the Decree *Inter mirifica*: a theology of the mass media, and the questions of information and public opinion *within the Church*. In order to judge the validity of this criticism, we must consider whether the conciliar documents taken as a whole would justify the inclusion of these questions, since it would be surprising if the Pastoral Instruction were to contradict the documents of the Council simply out of fidelity to a text that was approved at a relatively early stage of the conciliar work.

Despite all their shortcomings, it is the conciliar documents as a whole—with *Inter mirifica* in first place—and *Communio et progressio,* which, in the words of Paul VI as cited by Baragli, provide "an irreplaceable guide for anyone who works in this sector of the apostolate."

The Decree Has Borne Fruit

The documents must be judged by their fruits. Now, without falling prey to a simplistic and excessive triumphalism, and while recognizing the problems, setbacks, and weaknesses, it must be admitted that by giving social communications a status in the life of the Church, the Decree *Inter mirifica* opened up a period of increasingly satisfactory initiatives and fulfillment on every level.

(a) *As regards the pontifical commission,* a number of things should be noted:

(i) Paul VI's Motu proprio *In fructibus multis* of 11 April 1964 provides the Pontifical Commission for the Means of Social Communication with its definitive status.

(ii) The Pastoral Instruction *Communio et progressio* appeared on 23 May 1971, after seven years of work, the ins and outs of which have been described by E. Baragli in his monumental work[5] and summarized by J. Cousineau.[6]

(iii) The twentieth annual World Day of Social Communications was celebrated in 1986, with the theme of the role of the media in the Christian formation of public opinion. The themes in previous years had considered social communications in relation to the progress of peoples, the family, youth, human unity, the proclamation of the truth, the promotion of spiritual values, evangelization in the contemporary world, reconciliation, fundamental human rights and duties, publicity, the recipients of messages, the protection and development of childhood within the family and within society, family duties, responsible human freedom, the aged, the promotion of peace, the encounter between faith and culture, the Christian promotion of youth, and the promotion of justice and peace. And the theme chosen by the Pope for the 1988 celebration is "Communication: A Bond of Solidarity and Brotherhood among Neighbors and Nations."

Each of these world days has been the occasion for various papal messages and numerous studies and articles, which means that there is now a good quantity of doctrinal material available to encourage in-depth research.

(iv) The pontifical commission has become the mainspring in a movement toward regionalization on the level of episcopal conferences. While Bishop Deskur was President, regional meetings were held in Latin America, Africa, and Asia, and the movement is continuing under the presidency of Archbishop John P. Foley, with the bishops of Europe, North America, Oceania, and Australia organizing their own regional episcopal commissions for social communications.

(b) *As regards regional episcopal commissions,* activities are developing from year to year. At the plenary session of the pontifical commission held in Rome from 25 to 28 February 1986, activity reports were presented for the regions of Africa, Latin America and North America, Asia, and Europe and Oceania.

(i) *The example of CELAM.* In Latin America, the Department of Social Communications of CELAM (the Episcopal Conference of Latin America) played a decisive role in paving the way for the deliberations of the Third General Assembly of CELAM held at Puebla from 28 January to 13 February 1979. This represented the concretization of a process that was set in motion at the First Assembly, which was held in Rio de Janeiro in 1955, and that continued through numerous specialized meetings and the first inter-American meeting of the Pontifical Commission for Social Communications, which was held in Quito in 1972 and which already had the benefit of "Document 16" produced by the Second Assembly of CELAM (held at Medellín, Colombia, in 1968).

The stages of this evolution are described in Benito Spolentini's book *Communicación e Iglesia Latinoamericana.* [7]

Thanks to all this preparation, the Puebla meeting was able to adopt wide-ranging pastoral orientations, even though it preferred to leave aside the chapter of the preliminary document entitled "Theologico-Pastoral Reflection." [8]

As Monsignor Luciano Metzinger, who was at the time Director of the Social Communications Department of CELAM, emphasizes in an article on "Puebla and Social Communications," [9] the final Puebla Document marked a fundamental development with regard to this question, particularly in the following text: "Evangelization, the proclamation of the Kingdom, is communication. Hence social communication must be taken into account in every aspect of the transmission of the Good News" (No. 1063).

According to Monsignor Metzinger, this text places social communications at the very center of the life and activities of the Church, since it is involved in every aspect of evangelization.[10] The Puebla Document draws on *Communio et progressio* and *Evangelii nuntiandi*, recognizing communication as a vital social act that is born with man and that has been strengthened in modern times by powerful technological resources (No. 1064).

There is, therefore, a need to "integrate communication into the overall pastoral effort" (No. 1080), or, in other words, to make sure it is present in every area of pastoral activity. The first criterion suggested by Puebla goes hand in hand with another: that of "giving priority to training both the public in general and pastoral agents at every level in social communication" (No. 1081). Unfortunately, the framework of the present study does not permit us to enter into details on the recommendations contained in the Puebla Document. These recommendations provided the inspiration for further action on the part of the Department of Social Communications of CELAM and can help bishops from other continents to plan their own activity. In 1985, the Department of Social Communications of CELAM was able to list the following activities:

1. cooperation with the national offices in the region;
2. meetings with Catholic organizations for social communications;
3. a seminar on liturgy on the radio and television;
4. publication in Portuguese of the work *Towards a Theology of Communications in Latin America* (published in Spanish in 1984);
5. a dictionary of communications terms for the use of pastoral workers, and of ecclesiastical terms for the use of communications workers, published in 1986;
6. recognition of training programs for seminarians and religious;
7. publication of the previously mentioned book of B. Spolentini;
8. a Latin-American meeting at Caracas to revise the communications manual to be published shortly by the Department of Social Communications;
9. a seminar held at Quito on "The Church and the New Technologies," organized under the auspices of the Department of

Social Communications by the International Catholic Organizations for Social Communications and with the financial assistance of UNESCO;

10. a practical guide for the general public is now being prepared by the Department of Social Communications whose aim is to help develop the critical sense of media recipients, so as to foster a more active attitude toward the media;

11. a meeting in Bogota from 21 to 25 April 1986 to decide on the methodology to be used for a series of courses to be held throughout the continent, aimed at bishops, priests, male and female religious, and lay people.

(ii) *The Panafrican Episcopal Committee for Social Communications continues to take on a clearer structure.* This body has its headquarters in Nairobi, Kenya, and held its sixth meeting at Lomé, Togo, from 1 to 3 May 1985.

Among the topics on its agenda, there were two of particular importance: training and structure. An attempt is being made to establish a number of training centers in Africa because of the advantages of training carried out within the local cultural framework rather than in other continents. Such training should assist in the recruitment of staff for the committee's structures, since it is often difficult to find regional coordinators.

The interest of the committee in the growing role of video in Africa should also be noted.

(iii) The Office of Social Communications of the Federation of the Asian Bishops' Conferences works particularly closely with the Asian branches of the international Catholic organizations for social communications, OCIC-Asia and UNDA-Asia. Catholic periodicals have organized three regional CPAs (Catholic Press Associations), which were admitted to the UCIP as such at the congress held in Vienna in 1977. It is estimated that there are about 500 Catholic publications in Asia.

For lack of space, we can list only the most outstanding examples of the radio and television activities coordinated by the Asian Bishops' Office.

(1) *In eastern Asia.* In Japan, there are daily Catholic programs on between twenty-three and thirty-two radio stations.

In Korea, radio programs are produced and broadcast on nine stations.

In Taiwan, the Kuang Chi program service offers training, and produces 100 radio programs per week, and daily television programs on three national channels, as well as video- and audiotapes in Mandarin and Taiwanese.

(2) *In southeast Asia.* In the Philippines, the Church has twenty radio stations, one television station, five production centers, and nine school and training centers. Special mention should be made of Radio Veritas with its overseas programs in thirteen languages.

In Thailand, the national office produces 104 religious radio programs weekly for the Bangkok stations, and 520 religious news bulletins for regional stations. Television programs are also produced for religious feast days.

In Indonesia, seven radio stations under Church auspices are in daily operation, and production and training activity are also carried out.

(3) *In southern Asia.* In India, the government operates a radio and television broadcasting monopology. Even so, Catholics have twenty-five production centers for audio- and videotapes for home and local use, ten radio production centers, and five TV production centers, as well as seventeen training centers.

Then, in the press field, we would note the existence of two agencies: UCA News (Union of Catholic Asian News) in Hongkong, and SAR News (South Asian Religious News Service) in New Delhi.

(iv) *CEBM organizes activities in Europe.* At their 1982 meeting, the Council of European Episcopal Conferences decided to set up a Committee of European Bishops responsible for the Media (CEBM), composed of six bishops (one for each of the six language areas), a representative of the Secretariat of CEEC, six experts (one from each of the six regions), and three European representatives of the ICO/SCs (UNDA, OCIC, UCIP).

The CECB has already held three meetings—in Madrid from 1 to 3 July 1984, in Munich from 4 to 7 July 1985, and in Dublin from 5 to 9 November 1986. The following topics have already been discussed by the CEBM:

1. relations between episcopal conferences and those working in the communications field;
2. the possibility of using the latest computer and data-bank techniques in ecclesiastical structures;
3. Christian formation of communications experts and workers;

4. possible collaboration between European countries for the exchange of information, programs, and concerns;
5. the possibilities of helping our fellow Christians in eastern Europe;
6. the exchange of videocassettes, and the possible setting up of a tape library together with a list of the material available;
7. possibilities and problems in connection with the development of satellite broadcasting, including direct satellite broadcasting;
8. the need for communications training for seminarians, male and female religious, and priests.

The Dublin meeting was of special importance (each country was represented by three delegates, including at least one bishop), and was concerned particularly with the following subjects:

1. difficulties in producing religious programs for radio, television, and video, and how to foster European cooperation;
2. the need to organize the exchange of videocassettes and to develop strong European cooperation with a view to the production and utilization of suitable programs;
3. the problems of a religious presence through satellite broadcasting, bearing in mind the laws of different countries on author's copyrights, legislation on the media and their control, and also labor and union questions;
4. the use of computers and data banks in our churches;
5. the possibility of improving the present situation as regards the internal and external communications of our churches, by using both the classical types of communication and also new techniques;
6. the involvement of the Church in private radio stations.

At the end of their meeting, the CEBM appointed a permanent office, to be situated in Brussels, to carry on the work begun at the conference.

(v) *North American joint meeting.* The Communications Commissions of the Conferences of Catholic Bishops of Canada and the United States met together in Montreal from 13 to 15 September 1985 for a joint session in the presence of Archbishop John P. Foley, President of the Pontifical Commission for Social Communications. The three resolutions approved concern the following priorities:

1. the improvement of broadcasting systems: the two episcopal commissions must undertake a joint study on the advisability and practical implications (financial, cultural, and technological) of the participation of Catholic Canada in the Catholic Network of American Telecommunications; the study must also assess the availability of productions and norms for their exchange;

2. education for the media, and the encouragement of quality productions: the staff of the commissions will undertake a study of the resources available in the two countries for education for the media;

3. the training of Catholic communications experts: one of the major concerns of the Catholic conferences of the two countries should be the setting up of professional training facilities for their clerical and lay communications personnel; such training must stress the professional nature of relations with the secular media and also the need to take into account the religious, culutural and educational levels of the various milieu with which the Church wants to communicate.

(vi) *Oceania is also working.* In the absence of any closer structuring, Australia and New Zealand must be discussed separately.

In February 1985, a conference entitled "Towards a New Vision" was organized by the Australian Episcopal Committee for Social Communications, at which about 100 participants studied such themes as "Changing Models in Communications. Implications for Society and for the Church" and "A Communications Model for the Contemporary Church." It was decided that in each state or territory, an association of Catholic media workers should be formed in order to improve the coordination of their work and formulate strategies for the future.

A national survey was held, and it is expected that the bishops' conference will issue a major declaration in the near future regarding the Australian Church and social communications. Australian activities include special projects, the satellite question, computers, and World Communications Day.

In New Zealand, the bishops have followed training courses for relations with the media. The national Catholic office for communications places *Media Matters,* a program for the critical appreciation of the media, at the disposal of families and parishes, and an internal newsletter entitled *In Touch* maintains contact between the office and the parishes. Five video presentations on the sacraments have been produced. Oral archives are being organized containing narratives recounted by "elders." The director of the office has brought audiovisual material back from Africa on the famine in Ethiopia and the Sudan in order to encourage action on behalf of these countries. And there is an ecumenical initiative in the form of a three-day session organized by the Committee of the Churches on Radio Braodcasting with the professional help of Radio New Zealand, in order to train new assistants.

This rapid overview of the activities of the regional commissions has been made possible by the documentation kindly placed at our disposition by the Pontifical Commission, and our sole aim was that of showing the extent to which the conciliar Decree *Inter mirifica* has managed to set in motion a whole process involving the hierarchical Church in the field of social communications. However, it should be borne in mind that it is only an overview, and makes no claims at all to being an exhaustive report on these activities.

(c) *As regards the religious orders.* The inspiration provided by the Decree and by the postconciliar documents, especially *Communio et progressio,* has also been felt among religious orders and institutes.

While not forgetting that many of the pioneers of Catholic involvement in the media long before the Second Vatican Council belonged to religious orders, it must be recognized that the general attitude of these orders, and especially that of their superiors, tended to be one of great reserve and suspicion toward their activities. Such activity was decidedly not encouraged by superiors: at best, it might be tolerated, but it certainly was not on any list of priorities. The case of Father Alberione and the Society of St. Paul is an exception that confirms the rule. The Dominicans, with their pioneers in Catholic radio, together with the Jesuits, who were moving from books to reviews, and then on again to radio and cinema, and others who gradually joined in this movement, found the conciliar position a powerful argument to "convert" their superiors and confrères to the fact that a good proportion of the human and material resources of their communities should be redirected toward communications.

Indeed, Article 177 of *Communio et progressio* expressly states: "Religious orders and congregations will give thought to the many pressing tasks of the Church in the field of social communications and consider what they themselves can do to fulfill them under their constitutions." Thus, when I was carrying out a personal survey in 1983, I discovered that in 1975 there were already 560 Jesuits actively involved in 597 institutions for social communications. In 1982, 475 Dominicans were working in the four sectors of relations, training, consciousness-raising, and research. In 1979, the Divine Word Missionaries published a preliminary list of 255 of their memebers who were active in 161 institutions. And we could continue with the Franciscans, the Oblates of Mary Immaculate, the Salesians, the White Fathers, the Maryknoll Fathers, and the Society of the Foreign Missions—not to mention the orders of female religious. Many of these orders have set up special offices for social communications, for example, the Jesuit office, Jescom. And in order to ensure better coordination between religious generalates, Multimedia International was founded in 1970, with the aim of "helping male and female religious to know and utilize the media in their apostolate." During its first ten years (1970–1980), Multimedia worked to spread awareness of the importance of the media among superiors of the various institutes. Now that this has been achieved to a great extent, the present aim is that of satisfying needs that have so far not been fulfilled within the institutional framework.

It would be difficult to exaggerate the importance of the mobilization of the human and material resources at the disposal of religious institutes in favor of social communications. However, it is to be hoped that it will be possible to avoid any squandering of these resources through a lack of sufficient coordination with the various pastoral projects planned under the auspices of national and international espicopal commissions, or indeed those of local bishops. And this is not to mention how useful it would be to have more effective integration of the activities of male and female religious with those of the priests and lay people working in the International Catholic Organizations for Social Communications and their national offices.

The programs for media formation produced by certain orders, for example the Jesuits and the Divine Word Missionaries, are of special value.

(d) *The international Catholic organizations for social communications.* Despite their recognition by a number of papal documents and the now traditional practice of the Holy See (which is best illustrated by the numerous messages of the Pope to different con-

gresses and conferences), the status of the three ICO/SCs—
UCIP, UNDA, and OCIC, respectively, for press, radio and television, and cinema—was not very clearly defined in the Vatican.

Their heads, therefore, welcomed the general text of the Decree *Inter mirifica,* which stated in Article 22:

> The influence of the means of social communication extends
> beyond national frontiers, making individuals citizens of the
> world, as it were. National projects should, consequently, co-
> operate with each other at international level. The offices
> mentioned in par. 21 should each collaborate closely with its
> corresponding international organization. These international
> organizations are approved by the Holy See alone and are
> responsible to it.

And Article 178 of *Communio et progressio* clarifies the question
of which organizations are intended, and on their behalf calls for
collaboration not only from the national offices, but also from
the central offices of religious institutes:

> The national offices (cf. par. 169 . . .) and the corresponding
> central offices of the religious congregations will cooperate with
> the international organizations for the press (UCIP), for mo-
> tion pictures (OCIC), and for radio and television (UNDA).
> This will be done in accord with the statutes of these interna-
> tional organizations as approved by the Holy See.

Thus, the place of the three ICO/SCs within the institutional
framework of the Church was recognized, so that their activity
could now develop on a solid basis.

(e) *National Episcopal Commissions, and National Offices.* Let
us merely remember what has already been noted with regard to
the dispositions of *Inter mirifica*—which were then taken up in
greater detail by *Communio et progressio*—as concerns the special
episcopal commissions and the national offices. The present development of these bodies represents one of the most important
fruits of Vatican II, and more especially of the two documents in
question.

It therefore seems possible to conclude this first part of our study
by recognizing that the Decree *Inter mirifica,* which was harshly
criticized at the time of its promulgation, in fact has the threefold

merit of having placed social communications on the list of the Church's priorities for the years to come, laid the institutional foundations for ecclesial action in this sphere, and borne tangible fruits during the twenty-five years since its approval.

We now have to consider, if only briefly, whether even the critics can now find reasons for hope.

Reasons for Hope

We could suggest many reasons to be hopeful over the future of social communications in the life of the Church. The Decree *Inter mirifica* and the Pastoral Instruction *Communio et progressio* opened up a path that can know no turning back.

Rather than lingering further over the many initiatives already taking place at all levels (parish, diocesan, national, regional, international, and worldwide), we feel it is preferable to draw particular attention to the promise contained in the recognition of four factors by the conciliar and postconciliar documents. Although this recognition is not a total guarantee, it provides at least the justifiable expectation of a positive development. The four factors are as follows: (1) the value of the profession of communicator; (2) the role of the "recipients" of the media; (3) the need for appropriate formation for both communicators and recipients; (4) the need for scientific research on the phenomenon of communication. We can find specific orientations on each of these points in the conciliar texts.

The Value of the Profession of Communicator

In its eleventh article, *Inter mirifica* already stresses the important role played in society by journalists, writers, actors, designers, editors, publishers, producers, program planners, distributors, exhibitors, sellers, critics, and all the others who in any way "are involved in the making and transmission of communications." This importance entails a corresponding and specific moral responsibility because of the power they have to orient humanity toward good or evil.

Communio et progressio provides numerous practical instances of the importance thus attributed to the profession of communicator, first of all by highlighting the spheres in which communicators exercise their activity.

The *press,* of its power and nature, is of towering importance . . . and has a deep influence (No. 136).

The *cinema* is a part of contemporary life. It exerts a strong influence on education, knowledge, culture and leisure. The artist finds in film a very effective means for expressing his interpretation of life and one that well suits his times (No. 142).

Radio and *television* have given society new patterns of communication. They have changed ways of life (No. 148).

The *theater* is one of the most ancient and lively forms of human expression and communication. . . . Today, it commands a large audience, not only of those who go to plays, but also of those who follow drama on radio and television (No. 158).

The authors of *Communio et progressio* state that "the communications media can be seen as powerful instruments for [human] progress" (No. 21). They recognize that communicators have "a most important part" to play in forming public opinion, gathering up different views and transmitting them (No. 27). They also state that "those whose job it is to give news have a most difficult and responsible role to play" (No. 36).

In connection with artistic creators, they quote a passage from Paul VI's address to the producers of social communications media on 6 April 1967:

It is a fact that when you writers and artists are able to reveal in the human condition, however lowly or sad it may be, a spark of goodness, at that very instant a glow of beauty pervades your whole work. We are not asking of you that you should play the part of moralists. We are only asking you to have confidence in your mysterious power of opening up the glorious regions of light that lie behind the mystery of man's life (No. 55).

Still according to *Communio et progressio,* "communicators breathe life into the dialogue that happens within the family of man" (No. 73).

The text quotes Paul VI again (allocution to the Officers of the Catholic Association of Italian Journalists, on 24 January 1969), in order to say that journalists

> . . . are obliged to pay continual attention to and carry on an uninterrupted observation of the world: "You must continually stand at the window, open to the world; you are obliged to study the facts, the events, the opinions, the current interests, the thought of the surrounding environment" (No. 75).

The role of critics is considered irreplaceable "in getting communicators to maintain the highest standards of integrity and service and continually to make progress" (No. 78).

In encouraging "those who have the means" to contribute financially to the creation and running of communications, it also calls on them to respect "the proper liberty of the communicators, the artists or what we have called the recipients" (No. 80).

Following the line of the Instruction of the World Council of Churches (Uppsala, 1968, p. 381), *Communio et progressio* recommends paying attention to dramatists and journalists who devote "all the force of their genius and . . . all the depth of their talent" to describing "in significant terms the frequent alienation of man from God" while "asserting human liberty" (No. 36).

As regards Christian experts and specialists, it is recognized that "the excellence which they bring to their professional duty is itself a powerful testimony to Christianity" (No. 103), and that Catholic communicators "have the right to expect" from the Church "the kind of spiritual help that meets the special needs of their important but difficult role" (No. 104).

The concern of the Church to collaborate is clearly stated in number 105 of *Communio et progressio:*

> Fully aware of the importance of their profession and of the special difficulties it involves, the Church is very willing to undertake a dialogue with all communicators of every religious persuasion. She would do this so that she may contribute to a common effort to solve the problems inherent in their task and do what is best for the benefit of man [for the common good].

It would be difficult to be more positive.

The Role of Recipients

The importance of "recipients" is highlighted by *Inter mirifica* in its Article 9, which speaks of their obligations. The document emphasizes the free choice made by recipients (readers, viewers, listeners) among the various communications offered by the media. Such a choice involves a moral responsibility and entails the obligation to keep abreast of the various programs offered.

In the section devoted to the right to receive and provide information, *Communio et progressio* calls on recipients to show understanding toward the conditions in which information professionals work, but it also reminds them that they have "the right and the duty" to demand a "rapid and clear correction" of any false or distorted news, "to protest whenever omissions or distortions occur, . . . [and] to protest whenever events have been reported out of context or in a biased manner" (No. 41).

A wider knowledge of this recommendation would certainly have a beneficial influence on the workings of both the written and spoken news services. Speaking of the possibilities of enriching contemporary culture offered by the media, *Communio et progressio* encourages recipients to add "the exercise of personal reflection and an exchange of views with others" as a condition for using the media "to deepen and refine their cultural life" (No. 50).

In other words, recipients are called on not to remain passive, but to become active. And this is the crux of a whole orientation. However, the clearest formulation is found in number 81, which states in unequivocal terms:

> The recipients can do more to improve the quality of the media than is generally realized; so their responsibility to do this is all the greater. Whether or not the media can set up an authentic dialogue with society depends very largely upon these recipients. If they do not insist on expressing their views, if they are content with a merely passive role, all the efforts of the communicators to establish an uninhibited dialogue will be useless.

If recipients remain passive, they lose their capacity to influence the media, and they will have only themselves to blame for the dubious quality of the programs they are then offered. If they become active, they can improve this quality.

The Ever-Present Need for Training

The Council repeatedly stresses the need for training, both for professional workers in the communications field and also for simple recipients. It notes that people cannot simply become either professionals or recipients without any basic preparation, and that it is necessary to study seriously in order to use the media properly, whether to communicate a message or to receive it. Vatican II calls us all to closely study the media and the problems of social communication as essential elements in our human and Christian existence.

Inter mirifica devotes its number 15 to the training of communications professionals, and number 16 to that of recipients.

With regard to the professionals, the text states specifically that it is necessary to train competent priests, religious, and lay people who will be capable of using the media for the purposes of the apostolate. The stress is placed on lay people, for whom schools, faculties, and colleges must be provided in increasing numbers, where journalists, the producers of films and radio and television programs, and others can receive a complete training, imbued with the Christian spirit and the social teaching of the Church. Nor should the training of actors and literary, cinema, radio, and television critics be forgotten.

With regard to the recipients—or "utilizers"—who belong to all cultural levels and groups, the document states that they need a special theoretical and practical training suited to their level, so that they know how to use the media. Initiatives with this aim, particularly with reference to the young, should therefore be encouraged in increasing numbers in Catholic schools at all levels, and in seminaries and lay apostolic associations.

The Decree even expresses the hope that when pupils are taught their catechism, they should also be taught the elements of Christian doctrine and morality with regard to communications. The Instruction then provides many practical details on teaching and training.

Thus, number 15 states that "communicators"—in other words, the various producers and others who use the media—

have a moral obligation to acquire competence and proper training. The same article also states:

> "Recipients" are those who . . . read, listen to or view the various media. Everything possible should be done to enable these to know about the media, so they will be able to interpret this message accurately, to reap their benefit in full and play their part in the life of society.

In Chapter II, which is devoted to "The Best Conditions for the Proper Working of the Media of Social Communication," a special section (Nos. 64–72) discusses training. It starts with the following statement: "A training that grounds a man in the basic principles governing the working of the media in human society . . . is nowadays clearly necessary for all" (No. 64).

Such a training "should include a practical consideration of the special nature of each medium and of its status in the local community and how it can best be utilized. And this should be done with special reference to man and society."

Very precise guidelines are then given for the training of recipients (Nos. 65–70) and then that of the communications professionals (Nos. 71–72). Speaking about the latter, the Instruction states that it is necessary "to found faculties of social communication in institutions of higher learning, and these with authority to confer degrees" (No. 71). It observes that "professional skill is not enough: human qualities are needed, and first among these is the spirit of openness, self-giving and dialogue" (No. 72).

With regard to Catholics (bishops, priests, religious, and lay people) who are called upon to express themselves in the media in the name of the Church, the Instruction emphasizes that an in-depth knowledge of these media is an obligation, and that the training required in order to use them should be ensured by specialized national commissions or organizations (No. 106). The same concern over the need for training in keeping with Christian principles is expressed with regard to Catholic recipients: "Catholic schools and organizations cannot ignore the urgent duty they have in this field" (No. 107). According to the same article, it is necessary "to teach young people not only to be good Christians when they are recipients but also to be active in using all the aids to communication that lie within the media," so as to become true citizens of this era of social communications that is just now beginning.

A completely new departure is the recommendation to parents, educators, priests, and Catholic organizations to "encourage young people with the right qualities to take up a career in social communication" (No. 109). Had this line been followed from 1920 onward, the best journalists, film makers, and radio and television producers in the world would not have been recruited outside the Church, but within it.

In order to be able to take part in this effort at education, and even to collaborate on productions, bishops, priests, and religious must "of their own accord keep in touch with the latest developments in communications so as to be well informed themselves. Otherwise they will lack the familiarity with the media which their actual use requires" (No. 110).

The Instruction lays particular stress on the training of seminarians, who must "know how the media work upon the fabric of society and the technique of their use," since "this knowledge should be an integral part of their ordinary education. Indeed, without this knowledge an effective apostolate is impossible in a society which is increasingly conditioned by the media" (No. 111, which also refers to the *Basic Plan for Priestly Formation*, or *Ratio Fundamentalis*, produced by the Sacred Congregation for Catholic Education in 1970).[11]

In laying down these guidelines, the Council opened up a promising perspective for a Christian presence in the media. However, it must be admitted that these exhortations have unfortunately received very little practical follow-up, and that the hoped for and necessary training is only just beginning in a very modest and tentative way—and often, the impression is, without any true conviction or commitment on the part of the superiors responsible.

This in no way reduces the value of the conciliar documents, and cannot crush the hope that in time—and it is to be hoped a relatively *short* time—and under the pressure of events, decisions will be taken to put effective training programs into operation. The fact that a number of religious families are giving this matter serious consideration is an encouraging sign.

As far as the training of future priests is concerned, we would note the presentation by the Sacred Congregation for Catholic Education, on 19 March 1986, of a *Guide to the Training of Future*

Priests concerning the Instruments of Social Communication. Apart from the twenty-eight articles of the document itself, there are two appendices containing all the references in previous documents and a list of subjects to be considered. This document represents the application of the principles previously stated in the *Basic Plan for Priestly Formation* of 19 March 1985 (which is a revised version of the 1970 document mentioned before), especially in numbers 68 and 69.

Indispensable Research

It is simple logic that if communications professionals and recipients are to receive an adequate training, knowledge of the subject to be taught is needed. And this obviously entails research, a research that must be as serious and scientific as possible, just as is the case in other areas of knowledge.

The phenomenon of social or mass communication, the modern media, and what some authors refer to as "mass culture" is a new one. "Scientific" research in this field has been carried out for less than one century, and nobody would seriously try to claim that we yet have a solidly established *theory of communications*— although there is no shortage of *theories*. However, there is a real intellectual leaven at work among the many individual experts and researchers, and in the centers that are springing up all over the world. Christians have greater need of this research than others, because communications challenge them on more fronts, corresponding to the richer dimensions they recognize the human being as having.

The Second Vatican Council also had something to say in this connection: we have only to recall numbers 13 and 15 of *Inter mirifica*, cited before, which advocate a training program that cannot be put into operation without previous research; and *Communio et progressio* also refers to this point many times. Thus, number 99 of the Instruction recommends "cooperation in research in the media, especially in professional training and education . . . [in order to] help towards the fair and equal advancement of all peoples." Similarly, but referring mainly to theologians, number 108 makes the following recommendations:

The whole question of social communications deserves attention from theologians particularly in the areas of moral and pastoral theology. Religious education, too, ought to include instruction on the modern media and their principal implications. This will be more readily achieved when theologians have studied the suggestions in the First Part of this Instruction and enriched them with their research and insight.

Without research, it would be impossible to follow up the recommendation that

> . . . priests and religious [should] understand how public opinion and popular attitudes come into being so that they can suit both the situation and the people of their time. They can find the media of great help in their effort to announce the Word of God to modern men (No. 111).

This is reflected in the earnestness of the exhortation contained in number 113:

> Catholic universities and educational institutions should be more assiduous in the promotion of scientific studies and research on social communications. They will try to collate all the findings of research, themselves play a part in this research, and make all of it available to the service of Christian education.

We could discuss the implications of this recommendation at length, together with the unfortunate lack of enthusiasm the majority of Catholic universities throughout the world have shown in following it up. The few exceptions deserve all the more admiration, and it is to be hoped that their example will spread like an oil spill, since the future of the Christian presence in the world depends to a large extent on this area.

In this context, it is impossible to avoid mention of the efforts of the Society of Jesus, which ensures the running of the Centre for the Study of Communication and Culture, founded in London in 1977. For the years 1985–1987, the activities of this center included research and publications in five sectors: (a) religious communication in contemporary cultures; (b) the Church and new communications technologies; (c) communication and education; (d) the use of participatory minimedia and "alternative" media; and (e) the philosophies and politics of communications.

The center publishes the results of its work in the form of individual studies, and also in the journal *Communication Research Trends*. Special mention should be made of the efforts of the center in the direction of very open cooperation with other specialized bodies, both official and private, in every part of the world, but particularly in the developing countries. Thanks to these contacts, the influence of the center is being felt further and further afield, and it is able to offer considerable services to Christians involved in the communications sector.

Catholic researchers also have a quarterly journal entitled *Communicatio Socialis*, which is published in West Germany and deserves wider distribution.

An example of a serious, in-depth approach to the problems of social communication can be found in the recent publication of the Evangelical Church of Gemany on new information and communication techniques.[12]

We cannot sidestep the fact that our Church has lagged behind in this field of research on social communications, when we read the statement of Bishop Vilnet, President of the Bishops of France, in the special issue (April–May 1986) of *Spirit:* "We are devitalized in the intellectual sphere, and far from the level of presence we should have."[13] The efforts of those who have had the courage to set to work are thus all the more admirable. Such people are now to be found in all sorts of places, grouped around universities and training centers. Thanks to them we can face the future more confidently.

A "Communicating" Papacy

Among our reasons for hope, there is one that does not flow directly from the conciliar documents on communications, although it would maybe not have become so broadly effective if Vatican II had not incorporated the phenomenon of the media into the life of the Church.

We are, of course, referring to the papacy of John Paul II, the spreading influence of which shows the extent to which the message he seeks to proclaim personally throughout the world during his journeys is amplified and echoed by the mass media, especially television. This has led to a previously unheard-of effective capacity to communicate, which is the constant amazement of the experts. It is no longer possible to count the number of analyses devoted to the repercussions of these journeys.

In the conclusion of this article on the Pope's visit to Quebec, a Professor of Communications at Laval University, Michel de Repentigny, writes:

> The media have done better: they have simultaneously shown the Pope to the people, held up a mirror to themselves, and broadcast to their readers and viewers the touching images of their own participation in the Pope's visit.[14]

The bimonthly Italian journal *Mass Media* devoted its January–February 1986 issue to "The Pope Who Travels." Among other articles, we find the observation of Professor Abraham Moles of Strasbourg that the Pope "can proclaim the Good News he represents in an extraordinarily striking way, and much faster than the best press agencies." And Derrick de Kerckhove, who was Marshall MacLuhan's assistant for many years, sees the televised image of the Pope as "an electronic symbol of humanity and one of the most important images of the twentieth century."

In the Venezuelan journal *Communicación* (issues 49–50, 1985), Jesús Maria Aguirre opens a study on the Pope and the media with a critical analysis of the coverage of the papal visit to Venezuela. Among the positive elements, he notes the importance of the "national mission" carried out in preparation for the visit:

> This religious and civic action has earned the Catholic Church the respect not only of a government controlled by the party least associated with religion, but also that of the whole population, whose Catholic self-image was thus strengthened, even in the presence of partisan differences.

While rejoicing over the improvement in the communication policies of the Venezuelan church and deploring the efforts at manipulation by certain interested circles, the author observes that no event in the modern history of Venezuela had monopolized the daily press to such an extent.

Here we see the culmination of a phenomenon that had already begun with John XXIII, and to which Jules Gritti devoted his book *Le Pape à la Une* in 1980.

When we mention this in the context of Vatican II, we are obviously not claiming that the Pope's personal capacity for communication is a result of the Council. Rather, we want to show the extent to which the present system of social communications affects the apostolic mission of proclaiming the Good News to all nations.

At its General Assembly in February 1986, the Pontifical Commission for the Means of Social Communication made the wise move of setting in train a study of prospects for the year 2000, for we can expect that technological progress will mean that by then the successors of Peter and the Apostles will be able to send their voice and their image literally to all the peoples of the earth and to each individual inhabitant. Will they be prepared for this new Pentecost? It would surely be tempting the Holy Spirit to depend solely on him in order to learn to speak this universal language. It is thus to be hoped that in the face of future prospects, the College of Bishops will as a whole devote the best of its attention and resources to preparing the Church for the challenge awaiting it if it wants to proclaim the Word in a world that is very much shaped by social communications.

When Vatican II recognized the problem and laid the foundations for appropriate action by the Church, it indicated the path to be followed.

Conclusion

In the first part of this study, we showed why the pioneers of what was then called the "apostolate of the media" should have been pleased with the approval of the Decree *Inter mirifica*, together with the further enrichment found in other conciliar documents and the Pastoral Instruction *Communio et progressio*.

In the second part, we stressed the reasons for hope that Vatican II will provide inspiration for all those who raise questions concerning the role of social communications in the life of the Church and of our contemporaries.

Some people may object that our point of view is excessively optimistic, and even shows a quasitriumphalistic naïveté. We should, therefore, like to say that we did not feel it was very constructive to look back simply in order to list all the criticisms that can be made of the conciliar documents. We preferred to look to the future, and thus to highlight everything in these documents that can provide orientations for positive action, and everything that challenges the Church on its various levels and calls it to action. If we do have regrets, it is not so much because of inadequacies in the conciliar and postconciliar documents, but, rather, because of the shortcomings that have prevented their recommendations from being more widely implemented.

Here again, however, we find the main reason for hope in the humility that has enabled people to recognize the need to study, and that is already beginning to bear fruit in the field of training and scientific research. There is a dynamics at work here that can be looked to for as yet unimagined fruit.

Specialists in the field increasingly stress the vital function of communications. Thus, we have Budd and Ruben, for instance, who see the communications environment as being as fearsome and fraught with pitfalls for modern man as the physical environment was for primitive man; or, again, there is the psychiatrist Watzlawik who states simply that it is impossible *not* to communicate. The work of such people is enough to convince us of the extent to which communications have become a fundamental element in our lives both as individuals and as society.

We would hope that our response to the orientations found in the documents of the Council can give them life, so that "social communications may be present in all the aspects of the transmission of the Good News." This would represent the fulfillment of the wish expressed by John Paul II to the members of the Pontifical Commission for the Means of Social Communication. [15]

Translated from the French by Leslie Wearne and Lloyd Baugh, S.J.

Notes

1. *"Inter mirifica,"* AAS, 56 (1964), 145–157.
2. Session of 20 October 1983.
3. 7 (1964), 313–315.
4. *Lateranum*, 2 (1982), 424–425.
5. E. Baragli, *Comunicazione, comunione e Chiesa* (Rome, 1973), 1447 pages.
6. J. Cousineau, *Eglise et Mass media* (Montreal, 1973), 28–31.
7. Ediciones Paulinas: OCIC-AL; UNDA-AL; UCLAP; WACC (Buenos Aires, 1985), 232 pages.
8. Cf. *ibid.*, 192.

9. *Medellín*, 26 (June 1981), 234–242.

10. *Ibid.*, 235.

11. *AAS*, 62 (1970), 321–384, esp. Nos. 4 and 68.

12. *Die neuen Informations-und-Kommunikations-Techniken. Chancen. Gefahren. Aufgaben verantwortlicher Gestaltaung. Herausgegeben vom Kirchenamt im Auftrage der Evangelischer Kirche in Deutschland* (Gutersloher, 1985), 126 pages.

13. Cited by *Le Monde* (22 May 1986).

14. M. de Repentigny, "La visite du Pape à Québec," *Communication Information*, 7/2.

15. 27 February 1986: "The Church thus has a ministry to communication and a ministry of communication. Within the Church, this twofold ministry can foster that communion in Christ emphasized by the recent Synod of Bishops. In the world at large, this ministry can foster that community of concern so essential to the articulation of a sound public philosophy and to the achievement of true peace. It can promote the recognition of the rights and responsibilities of every person as a child of God—God who has communicated to us life itself and his saving message through the Word made flesh, our Lord and Savior Jesus Christ."

CHAPTER 64

Mass Media and Culture in Contemporary Catholicism
The Significance of Vatican II*

Robert White, S.J.

Summary

The Decree on the Means of Social Communication, *Inter mirifica*, exhorted the Church to recognize the profound influence of the public mass media in our societies and urged Catholics to use the new media in the mission of the Church. In fact, the new world of mass popular media has not become part of the culture of contemporary Catholicism. There is still a great ambivalence toward the popular media in Catholic culture and generally catholic film and broadcast procedures do not have a very significant presence in the public media. However, there is a new pattern of communication emerging in the Church and there is a new type of media humanism growing in Catholic culture. Ironically, this has been influenced more by the major Council documents such as the Dogmatic Constitution on the Church (*Lumen gentium*) and the Pastoral Constitution on the Church in the Modern World (*Gaudium et spes*) than by *Inter mirifica*.

---

*This article has drawn heavily on a previous article by the author, "The New Communication Emerging in the Church," *The Way Supplement*, 57 (Autumn 1986), dealing with *Communication, Media and Spirituality*. The author wishes to thank the editors of *The Way* for permission to use sections of that previous publication in the present article.

Introduction

The article of Prof. Ruszkowski (Chapter 63) has outlined very well the progress of Catholic communication apostolates since Vatican Council II. With the Decree *Inter mirifica,* the Catholic Church, for the first time in a major conciliar meeting, officially recognized the profound influence of the mass media in our societies and the importance of using the media in the mission of the Church. *Inter mirifica* and, subsequently, *Communio et progressio* (the Pastoral Instruction that defined specific applications of the norms of *Inter mirifica*) at least put communications on the agenda of things to be done by the Church.

The progress is especially notable in terms of a new organizational structure such as the offices of communication in the Vatican, at the level of episcopal conferences, and at the local diocesan level. Church personnel and some lay professionals are now better organized for concerted action in associations such as UNDA (for broadcasting), OCIC (for cinema), and UCIP (for press). There are far more systematic efforts in training pastoral personnel in the use of the media. Increasingly, the pastoral work of the Church uses media, especially at the level of group communication and in local broadcasting.

One must ask, howver, whether *Inter mirifica* and *Communio et progressio* have been a catalyst for change and *aggiornamento* similar to decrees such as the *Constitution on the Sacred Liturgy, Ecumenism, Religious Freedom* and *The Laity,* or the Constitutions that have touched on the conception and structure of the Church?

One might argue that, from an a priori perspective, the Decree on the Means of Social Communication (*Inter mirifica*) should have been such a catalyst. Christianity is preeminently a religion of communication, placing central emphasis on a divine self-communication, the incarnation, and a Church that is continually communicating itself in different cultures. The Church has the mandate to proclaim the Word of God and to form ecclesial communities that are constituted by shared communication among members. Written scriptures and the intergenerational communication of tradition are central to Catholic life. The vitality of the Church has depended very much on adapting the gospel witness to the forms of communication of a particular era. In the past, Catholicism has been relatively quick to incorporate new forms of communication, for example, the use of visual

media in icons and architecture or popular drama and the quick
adoption of print media in the early Renaissance. Most important, *these media became an integral part of Catholic culture and
spirituality.*

There is quite widespread agreement, however, that *Inter
mirifica* and related pastoral instructions on communications
have not have the same significance for the *aggiornamento* of the
Church as most of the other Decrees and Constitutions of the
Council.[1] One must ask why?

The present article explores three questions or theses regarding this:

1. Essentially, *Inter mirifica* exhorted the Church to recognize the
   profound influence of the public mass media in our societies
   and urged Catholics to use the new media (meaning especially
   cinema and broadcasting) to proclaim the gospel. In fact, the
   new world of mass media has *not* become an integral part of
   the *culture* of contemporary Catholicism. Bishops, pastors,
   and other religious leaders rarely see communication through
   the new electronic media as central to pastoral practice. Pastors generally do not have a sense of the impact of the popular
   media in the daily lives of the faithful, and there is little
   encouragement to use newer forms of mass media as part of
   their spiritual development. Media apostolates are rarely an
   integral part of planning in a diocese, parish, or religious
   congregation, but depend on the sporadic initiative of individuals who remain marginal to other pastoral activities. The
   communication education of priests and other pastoral ministers in seminaries or in other theological and pastoral institutes is still inadequate or nonexistent; there is even evidence
   that the quality of homiletics or other communication training has actually *declined* since Vatican II.

   The first part of this article examines what it might mean if
   the Catholic Church were to become fully inculturated into
   the new world of popular mass media.

2. There has been a profound ambivalence in Catholic culture
   regarding the propular mass media. Catholics see that somehow the media are most influential, but at the same time, they
   dismiss the media as, at best, trivial or, more often, as corrupt-
   ing. Neither *Inter mirifica* nor *Communio et progressio* have
   been the catalysts that bring Catholicism to confront the roots

of its ambivalence toward the media. In spite of much more organization, more specialized training, and more Church-sponsored media production facilities, these efforts have not brought about a more significant presence of the Church's gospel message in the *public* media.

3. The major argument of this article is more hopeful. There is, in fact, a new pattern of communication emerging in the Church that is establishing a more effective communicative relationship of the Church to the larger society and adapting the internal communication of the Church to contemporary culture. This new pattern of communication is, at least indirectly, a response to the new world of pluralist, secular mass media.

Ironically, the major catalysts for the new style of communications in the Church have not been the documents dealing directly with the media, but the Pastoral Constitution on the Church in the Modern World (*Gaudium et spes*), the Dogmatic Constitution on the Church (*Lumen gentium*), the Decrees on religious freedom, on the liturgy, and other Decrees that have influenced the development of new theological orientations and a new structure of the Church. These movements in the Church emphasize more a new pattern of "communication" rather than specifically "media," but, indirectly, there is arising a new and more positive attitude toward the world of the popular mass media.

"The New World of Popular Mass Media" as an Integral Part of the Culture of Contemporary Catholicism

What Is Meant by "Popular Mass Media"?

Many observers point to the creation of the cheap, daily press—the "penny newspaper"—in the 1830s (and in the new cities of the United States) as the beginning of the institution of the mass media.[2] The roots may be as old as the invention of the printing press, but prior to the 1830s, newspapers were more specialized commercial gazettes or the partisan instruments of political parties. Even with subsidies from sponsoring political groups, the small circulation made them relatively expensive. The penny newspaper aimed at mass circulation by using the "impartial" subsidy of advertising and reducing the cost to the buying power of the poor. As new communication technologies were introduced, the same principles of mass marketing were applied to recorded sound, film, radio and television. Gradually, the major characteristics of the *institution* of popular media took shape:

(a) The mass media avoided alienating potential users by remaining at least ostensibly apolitical and aconfessional, thereby becoming a neutral and "secular" forum for all ideas. Newspapers, especially, aimed to present "objective facts," allowing readers of all persuasions to make their private decisions on the basis of the facts and their personal interests. On the liberal and democratic principle that more information means more equitable and more legitimate public decisions, the media took every newsworthy event to be made public, investigated, explained, analyzed, debated, and decided upon before the whole nation. The media defended the legitimacy of their own privileged freedom by presenting themselves as the defenders of the public interest and as the critics of those who abused power and aristocratic position. In this "marketplace of ideas," what the majority would "buy" gained the stamp of truth and moral approval. News, the ebb and flow of public opinion, and fashion began to crowd out other forms of traditional authority as the basis of forming personal and public value commitments. If any religious group or other movement wished to "sell" their ideas, they had to learn how to dramatize their meaning and message on the stage of the free, neutral mass media without appearing to be crude manipulative propaganda.

(b) In order to reach a mass public, the new media left behind the learned and didactic style and adapted to the newspaper or other format the enjoyable, easily understood popular forms of oral and face-to-face *entertainment*. People have always entertained themselves by exchanging town gossip about sensational crimes, disasters, the spectacular activities of the wealthy and aristocratic, major public debates, and the battles of war. This became the "news" of the popular press. All genres of story telling—from heroic adventures to ghost stories—became newspaper short stories, serialized novels, or the drama of film, radio and television. Similarly, sports, humor, advice on folk medicine, and other forms of entertainment were adapted to media formats.

Industrialization brought a sharp demarcation of life into periods of highly mobilized work and leisure periods in evenings, weekends, or holidays. Leisure is the time when one could do what one likes and think one's own thoughts. With increasing standards of living, there has been greater emphasis on consumption and leisure as the more fully human, free, and subjectively expressive area of life. Since the mass media became defined as entertainment and a major leisure-time activity, they have provided a time when people could leave behind work and pragmatic concerns, allow their imaginations to roam free, reflect on alternative worlds presented by the media, and search for their own personal meaning of life. The vivid combination of music, dramatic dialogue, and visual images in cinema, television, and rock music have attuned imaginations to the subjectively expressive, the ecstatic, and the exotic experience.[3]

The mass media—even news—are essentially a story-telling and narrative discourse built around the classical structure of folk tale and myth. The media sweep up new information and organize it within the frame of a suspenseful plot, clearly delineated heroes and villains, and hopeful outcomes.[4] People come to the media with worries, questions, and confusion in the back of their minds; the media present ordered formats of meaning that leave us reassured about the ultimate orderly meaning of the world about us. Popular moralistic and religious symbolism and popular conceptions of the meaning of life have always been profoundly influenced by folk tale and myth. Today, the popular religious imagination draws much of its symbolism from the mass media.

(c) Every society finds a way to repeat and reaffirm its mythical conceptions of history that give the society a collective sense of destiny, and today we do this largely through the mass media. But the media can fill newspaper and broadcasting space and hold audiences only if they present continually new information, new songs, new jokes, and a new twist on old plots. Thus, we are bombarded with new scientific information and with new world views of foreign cultures or our own exotic subcultures. The traditional wisdom is constantly being questioned and lifetime beliefs and commitments become increasingly difficult in the face of so many alternative meanings of life.

Catholicism has traditionally relied on the local community and the extended family to be the carriers of its cultural values and to be the locus of socialization. These social units are much less significant in a mass-mediated culture, and the Church is faced with looking for new forms of community in which personal commitment to Christian values can develop and the individual can sort out the variety of values and world views that are continually being presented.

To summarize, the mass media have become the forum in which virtually the whole society participates in the creation of a common culture. Simply to read a newspaper, go to the cinema, or view television is a form of deciding what kind of culture we want. The media are the arena of public debate in which we explore new values, new world views, and new cultural myths.

Catholic Culture and a Public Media Culture

When we speak of the "culture" of Catholicism, we refer to the values and ways of perceiving the world that influence a particular way of participating in the larger culture of the society. As a subculture, Catholicism is a way of life, a set of traditional folkways in families and nations, and a procedure for taking collective decisions as a church. Catholicism is a complex of symbols, folk tales, and rituals as well as a formal theology. At the core of this Catholic culture is a personal and collective sense of relatedness to ultimate Mystery that is rooted in human existence. This sense of call and response to God gives meaning to every facet of human activity and to every dimension of human culture. Most of the great religious symbols of Christianity, including the symbol of the cross itself, have quite secular origins and are given a fuller religious meaning by their integration into the Christian view of history as a history of salvation.

It is at this point of informing the broader culture with religious meaning that media—whether this may be story telling around the hearth or the experience of television—become important for a religious culture. The media in this broad sense become the space and forum in which we create and recreate a culture; the media are also the point of interaction between our religious sense and the creation of culture. If Catholicism is not sure how to enter into the media culture of a particular era, it becomes difficult for Catholicism to integrate its culture with the broader process of cultural development. In the end, the Catholic culture also loses its vitality and meaning for people.

Although the opening of Catholic culture to a particular media culture may be considered that of a much broader enculturation, certain aspects of Catholic culture become particularly crucial for this opening.

Most basic is a theology of contemporary communication. That is, theological discussion has articulated the relationship of the fundamental elements of a theological tradition with the characteristics and conditions of communication in contemporary cultural contexts. One might point to the debates in early Christianity regarding the role of iconic representation as the development of a theology of communication that was to have immense consequences for Catholic culture up to our own times. The evolution of such a theology of communication makes it *logical* and *imperative* to use certain forms of communication and media as a means of revealing the loving presence of God in the world and communicating the gospel.

A theology of communication not only points up the importance of *using* the media, but also articulates a theological tradition with the typical forms of discourse and symbolic language that are inherent in the institutional organization of media. If the popular mass media are a public and pluralistic marketplace of ideas and are defined as essentially a narrative story-telling discourse to be used as entertainment in leisure time, then a theology of communication will highlight those aspects of Catholic theological tradition that relate to this.

As we noted before, the media are a public and collective meeting point to celebrate, create, question, and transform a culture. A theology of communication will articulate a theological tradition with the dominant organization of symbols in the contemporary public culture.

A second aspect of the opening of Catholic culture to a media culture is a widespread understanding of how the use of these media is a sacramental or quasisacramental means of grace and an important context for growth in spiritual union with God. A coherent tradition of spirituality grows up around the symbols and typical forms of discourse associated with these media. In cultures dominated by oral communication, the origins and development of faith come from "hearing" the Word of God. In cultures resting more on literate media, countless conversions are

attributed to the occasion of reading. These forms of communication thus become a necessary part of pastoral practice, the characteristic style of pastoral communication in the Church, and the
meeting point for the formation of ecclesial communities.

A third aspect, closely associated with the quasisacramental
conception of media, is the development of new styles and strategies of popular religious communication. These strategies of pastoral communication draw on the popular media and characteristic discourses of these media. Recent historical studies have
shown that the great revitalization of Catholicism in the nineteenth century was based very largely on the development of the
popular religious communication style of the parish missions.[5]
The theological content and rhethorical form of the parish mission had a profound influence on the beliefs and practices of
Catholicism right up to Vatican Countil II.

Fourth, pastoral leadership looks for a structure of the institutional church and forms of local Christian community that will
be consonant with the new styles and strategies of popular religious communication. The new form of human interaction in
Christian communities permits the use of emerging styles of pastoral communication and extends these styles to modes of liturgical
worship, catechetical instruction, governance, decision taking,
and ways of bringing together the different charisms into a solid
mutually supportive union.

Fifth, the Church will find ways of forming its pastoral leadership in the new styles and discourses of religious communication as
well as the use of new media. The communication education of
pastoral personnel will be fully integrated with theological formation. Indeed, as a new theology of communication emerges,
linked with every dimension of a theological tradition, this theology becomes the foundation for a new media consciousness in
pastoral leadership.

Finally, media of all kinds carry with them financial costs and
the need for an administrative organization. The opening of
Catholicism to a new media culture brings a commitment to
finding the necessary financing or reorganization of priorities in
the use of existing resources. If the Church sees a particular form
of communication as important in a given cultural context, then
motivating the faithful to support this communication—whether
this be building cathedrals or establishing television stations—
becomes central in Catholic culture.

How Evangelical Churches Became Churches of the Electronic Media

Perhaps the best way to illustrate what it might mean for the new world of popular media to become an integral part of a religious culture is a comparison with the role of the media in another Christian tradition: evangelical and fundamentalist protestantism. The tradition of Catholicism with its institutional, sacramental, and communitarian emphasis is quite different from the theological and pastoral tradition of the evangelical churches. Catholicism would almost certainly find a different form of expression in the mass media. Many religious leaders of the more institutional churches are highly critical of the intense prosyletization, the neglect of local Christian community, and apparently naïve acceptance of questionable mass media "selling" formats.[6] But no churches have shown greater zeal in the use of media—a zeal that is encouraged in *Inter mirifica*—than the evangelical churches. In many countries, such as the United States, the evangelical churches have become by far the dominant religious presence in the mass media, and the world of mass media has become an integral part of the faith of members of the evangelical and fundamentalist churches.

The evangelical churches moved to use radio for preaching almost immediately upon its inception in the 1920s, and this tradition of media ministry has grown steadily since then. Underlying this attraction to the media is a theology that places central emphasis on preaching as a means of grace and conversion. Evangelicals measure the vitality of their churches very largely in terms of the number of conversions of non-Christians and the unchurched. As Avery Dulles points out, the theology of revelation of the evangelicals—identifying the literal propositions of the Bible with the Word of God and endowing this Word with an inherent power of God's grace—provides a strong motivation to multiply the Word through the pulpit of the microphone and the television camera.[7] Evangelists are unequivocal in their view that the mass media are a providential means of bringing about the conversion of the world.

The media ministry of the evangelicals, however, is only a logical outcome of a long tradition of openness to the world of popular mass media. William G. McLoughlin points out that the religious "revival" as a strategy of mass religious communication took shape in that period of American history of the 1830s and 1840s just when the institution of popular media was beginning to develop. Revivalists such as Charles Grandison Finney borrowed the sensationalist communication techniques of populist politicians, the new penny newspapers, and the incipient art of advertising to draw mass audiences.[8] They quickly adopted the popular language and forms of discourse of the common man just as the popular press had done. Finney argued, " 'New measures are necessary from time to time to awaken attention and bring the gospel to bear upon the public mind.' Better a full church with undignified preaching than an empty one with it. 'The results justify my methods.' (Finney) said frankly."[9] The tent revival developed all of the showmanship of the popular media that had roots in the nineteenth-century vaudeville circuit and traveling circus: ingenious methods of advertising to draw audiences; colorful, imaginative preaching; dramatic personal testimony of conversion and quick resolution of physical or personal ills; a clear, simple biblical message with few complicated theological or moral distinctions.

All this was "made for television" or other audio-visual media, and the format moved directly from the revivalist tent into the television studio. Later television evangelists have unhesitatingly—too uncritically in the view of many—accepted the commercial media with all of its conditions as a God-given instrument. They have quickly adopted many of the formats of radio and television: serial drama, the talk show, bright images of success, sophisticated techniques of persuasion, and elaborate marketing research to pinpoint audience interests.[10] The focus is not theological argument, but the vivid symbols of everyday human problems. Televangelists have ingeniously overcome the impersonal distance of the big media through large-scale letter correspondence, facilities for audience phone-in (a technique shared by radio disc jockey programs), and distribution of cheap follow-up reading materials.

The culture of the evangelical churches has always been attuned to many aspects of popular culture. One example of this in the United States is the development of gospel music that has continually adapted the rhythms and forms of American popular music. Today, gospel music is an immensely popular variation on country and western and rock music. Gospel singers are counted among the top performing artists of popular music and many pop music stars such as Bob Dylan cross back and forth between religious and secular pop music.[11]

The televangelists have by far the largest audiences among religious broadcasters, and the majority of these are members of the evangelical churches—people who have had the initial experience of "born-again Christians." That so many evangelical Christians follow these religious broadcasts closely is not surprising, since this is encouraged in the evangelical churches as an integral part of the devotional life of the faithful.

Although leaders in media ministries claim that their objective is to build up local Christian congregations; in fact, evangelical theology has a much more fluid and noninstitutionalized conception of ecclesial organization. This model of church is more consonant with the kind of electronic parachurch that the evangelical and fundamentalist media ministry seems to encourage.[12] It also seems to be consonant with the much more fluid, individualistic, and noninstitutional culture of today.[13]

The formation of pastoral leadership in the evangelical churches places central emphasis on communication education, and the biographies of great evangelists such as Billy Graham indicate that seminary training was very largely a matter of continual and direct practice of preaching.

One of the striking characteristics of the television evangelists is the ability to generate large amounts of funding to cover the extremely costly purchase of television time and to produce television programming. In the United States, the 1985 annual donation figures for Pat Robertson's Christian Broadcasting Network were $233 million; Jim Bakker's PTL Network, $100 million; Jerry Falwell's Old Time Gospel Hour, $100 million; Oral Roberts, $120 million; and Jimmy Swaggart, believed to be $140 million.[14] Early traveling revivalists had little direct institutional church support, and they had to learn to finance themselves by appeals for large numbers of small donations from their momentary audiences of working-class people. Just as the Catholic Church has motivated its members to support a costly parochial school system that is believed to be an important means of communication in Catholic culture, so also the evangelicals have encouraged support of media ministry as central in their tradition.

In brief, every facet of the culture of this Christian tradition has become closely linked with the popular mass media—the theology, the devotional life of the faith, the preparation of pastoral personnel, the forms of ecclesial organization, and the administrative-financial support of the church.

This is not to argue that the Catholic Church should imitate the styles of media ministry of the evangelical and fundamentalist churches. Some Catholic broadcasters in the United States and elsewhere have borrowed much from the approaches of the "prime-time preachers," but this is often looked upon with unease by many Catholic leaders in media apostolates. One can point to regions of the Church, such as Latin America, where the Church has developed very successfully a wide-scale use of radio. The Catholic Church in Latin America now has more than 350 radio stations and the model of "popular radio" there is an extension of the revitalization of the Church expressing well the new theology, the forms of ecclesial organization, and popular religiosity characteristic of Latin America. As we note later, the Latin-American church is perhaps one example where the new world of popular media has become, to a degree, an integral part of Catholic culture. But this has not happened at a general level in the Catholic Church.

One cannot argue that the Second Vatican Council has not had a profound influence on Catholic culture over the last twenty years, because one can point to such an influence from other documents of the Council. Another way of understanding why *Inter mirifica* has not been a catalyst leading to an opening of Catholic culture to a media world is to examine briefly the historical conditions that caused other Decrees to have a much greater influence.

The Second Vatican Council and Cultural Change in the Church

When a particular Decree of Vatican Council II has had greater significance in the culture of the Church, the action of the Council has usually only served as the legitimating and affirming catalyst in a much larger process. Generally, there have been a number of important conditions.

One such condition influencing more rapid cultural change is the experience of considerable cultural conflict among a broad cross section of Catholics because of a given theological or pastoral posture of the Church. For example, the official pre-Vatican

II position of the Church regarding religious freedom in a pluralistic democratic society was presenting difficulties for the participation of Catholics in the public life of countries where a liberal democratic tradition held sway. There was already a fairly widespread consensus in the Church that a new practical formulation was needed that would articulate Catholic theological and pastoral practice with the realities of modern sociopolitical life.

Another condition is a body of historical, theological, and cultural research that had developed a new theological and pastoral formulation and that could show that the new formulation is consonant with the historical roots of Catholicism. Such research shows clearly that the existing doctrinal teaching and pastoral practice of the Church is related to today's pastoral problems and to unnecessary cultural conflicts experienced by Catholics. This research has already progressed considerably toward a theology that articulates the doctrinal and theological tradition with new cultural institutions.

A third condition is the widespread popularization of a new theological and pastoral formulation as an attractive and needed innovation. This popularization is generally carried out in Catholic journals of opinion and in the reading materials of pastoral leadership (younger clergy and religious, seminarians, the educated laity, etc.), so that a favorable public opinion is beginning to be formed. Especially important is the presence of innovative leadership among the faculties of seminaries and the formation of a new generation of clergy in the new thinking regarding liturgy, ecumenism, new forms of ecclesial structure, etc.

A fourth condition is the existence of pastoral experiments with the approbation of ecclesiastical authorities, showing that new proposals are both practical and beneficial.

One could enumerate other similar conditions for the catalytic influence on the Second Vatican Council on Catholic culture, but it is sufficient to indicate that these conditions were not present in the case of *Inter mirifica* and even for *Communio et progressio*. At the time of the formulation of *Inter mirifica*, there was considerable disagreement regarding how the Church should approach the question of communication and the public media.[15] The kind of groundwork described before had not been done, and, one must admit, is still only in its beginning stages. One of the reasons that the Catholic Church has had such a difficult time coming to a consensus regarding the media is deep ambivalence in Catholic culture regarding the new world of popular mass media.

Catholic Ambivalence and Unease
Regarding the Popular Media

There has been a long-standing distrust and negative attitude toward the popular media from the inception of the popular press in the early nineteenth century. The unfortunate statement of the Encyclical *Mirari Vos*, published by Pope Gregory XVI on 15 August 1832, on the press reflecting liberal and anticlerical movements is an exaggeration, but not untypical of a widespread feeling:

> Here belongs that vile and never sufficiently execrated and detestable freedom of the press for the diffusion of all sorts of writings: a freedom which, with so much insistence, they dare to demand and promote. We are horrified, venerable brothers, contemplating what monstrosities of doctrine, or better, what monstrosities of error are everywhere disseminated in a great multitude of books, pamphlets, written documents—small certainly in their size but enormous in their malice—from which goes out over the face of the earth that curse which we lament.[16]

The freedom of the media as a public forum not controlled by any major institution, the light entertainment style, and the continual novelty—essential characteristics of the new popular media noted before—all conflicted with the culture of Catholicism.

Throughout the nineteenth and well into the present century, a heavy cloud of censorship and moral rating systems were thrown over film and other forms of mass entertainment. Priests, religious, and especially seminarians were discouraged from having too much exposure to or dealing with the world of popular media. The media were treated in a purely moralistic fashion and there was little appreciation of the cultural creativity in the popular arts. There was also little ability to think in terms of the conditions of entertaining large audiences. In general, it was felt that the popular media were trivial, degrading, and of relatively little importance for the development of the religious imagination and religious idealism. Catholic culture placed a high value on a romantic classical high culture, but did little to cultivate an appreciation of contemporary artistic effort that reflected current cultural exploration.

Some have also argued that Catholic culture is very much centered on the print medium and that this has been an obstacle to developing talent able to communicate easily in the visual media of film, television, and videocassettes. This thought appeals to the theory of McLuhan that literacy and print media have cultivated a linear and abstract style of thinking, whereas the electronic media cultivate an aural-oral-visual sense and a greater balance of imagination and emotion.[17] This argument may be valid, but a more direct influence was the rationalism of neoscholastic theology and the emphasis on an abstract and metaphysical mode of explanation for much of the Catholic belief system.

Neoscholastic theologies of revelation tended to identify the word of God with the clear, concise, logically defined dogmatic propositions of the Church. In an attempt to meet the arguments of nineteenth-century rationalism that the teachings of the Church were based on imaginative projections and subjective emotional feelings, neoscholastic theology excluded as an adequate religious language the symbolic and connotative forms of religious expression. The language of religious faith that was inculcated at all levels of education—from the catechism to seminary instruction—was highly abstract. This created a barrier to accepting the novel, film, and the more popular arts of television and popular music as a substantive or appropriate form of religious communication. These might be illustrative, but religious faith meant an understanding and acceptance of truth at a more abstract and intellectual level.

The exhortation to use the mass media in *Inter mirifica* appeared just at the time that a strong personalistic emphasis was entering the stream of Catholic culture in the 1960s. Catholicism discovered depth psychology and personality development, which emphasized a type of nondirective therapeutic counseling or small-group discussion. Catholic culture was reacting vigorously to forms of clerical and authoritarian communication that had characterized the Church especially during the nineteenth and early twentieth centuries. The spirit of the Second Vatican Council was interpreted by many as a move away from this kind of communicative structure in the Church. The popular religious

communication that had depended so heavily on moralistic exhortation in parish missions, preached retreats, and catechetical
instruction in Catholic schools tended to be questioned by many
Catholics. An expressive, nondirective, and participatory form
of small-group communication was generally judged to be more
appropriate for the development of the faith. In many parts of
the world, there was a strong move toward a basic Christian
community form of ecclesial organization and toward more participatory decision making in the Church. All this deflected
attention and interest in the use of the mass media in the
Catholic Church. Over the past thirty years, there has been
increasing interest in the audio-visual media as a new "language"
of religious communication, but there has been far more reflection and creative experimentation on audio-visual media for
small-group communication.

Coupled with this emphasis on interpersonal and small-group
communication is a pervading attitude of distrust of the mass
media as an appropriate context for religious communication.
The public media are seen as manipulative and depersonalizing
or as causing harmful effects such as imitative violence. In this
view, the mass media induce a passive conformity to materialistic
essentially anti-Christian values. The decline of the public service concept of broadcasting, especially in the commercial media, and the submission of even noncommercial broadcasting
systems to audience ratings has been interpreted as creating a less
favorable atmosphere for religious programs or programs carrying
Christian values.

In some parts of the world, especially in Latin America, there
is the view that the commercial mass media are instruments of
the capitalistic financial and managerial classes with programming criteria dominated by multinational advertising revenue
and the interests of privileged elites. In some Third World countries, the public media are directly controlled by governments
and are virtually the mouthpiece of the dominant political interests. A strong commitment to social justice is an integral part of
Catholic culture in many of these regions. Catholic program
producers have experience of media gatekeepers, rejecting program proposals that voice an authentic and prophetic gospel
message. Many feel that to gain access to the media, one must
submit to the essentially commercial secularizing conditions of
the mass media. Groups such as UNDA and OCIC have tried to

counter these tendencies by offering prizes to good programming and have a general policy of support for higher-quality public-service broadcasting. But there is a widespread attitude that gaining favorable access to the public media or influencing the direction of public-media policy is a losing battle and that it may be better to allocate limited resources to group communication or types of narrow casting that are directed to Catholic or ecumenical audiences.

A further factor in the ambivalence of Catholic culture toward the world of popular mass media is the emphasis on liturgical worship, local parish community, and the sacramental priesthood as the channel of divine grace and the locus of faith development. Seeking mass conversion by multiplying the Word of God has never occupied the same level of importance as in the evangelical protestant tradition. Many Catholic leaders have rejected the forms of evangelical and fundamentalist media ministry as the very antithesis of what Catholicism should be doing. Since the Second Vatican Council, Catholics have been preoccupied with making the liturgical renewal function as a form of communication or with introducing more participation of the laity at the parish level—again a new form of communication in the Catholic Church. The very success of the other major decrees of the Council in fomenting movements in the Church has been an influence countering the exhortation of *Inter mirifica* to use the public media.

Finally, over the last 150 years, the Catholic Church has adopted a strategy of communication based largely on parish organization and a parochial school system. Generally, Catholics feel that this more direct and directed form of communication is a more effective means of evangelization and religious socialization than the media. This has involved an enormous investment of money and trained personnel. To redirect some of these resources to costly media apostolates might require abandoning previous commitments. This kind of decision is especially painful in view of the fact that the Church has developed its institutional organization around schools and a certain type of parish organization. Church leaders feel that at least they know how to administer schools effectively and can motivate the faithful to support these schools. Launching into large-scale media apostolates about which the Church is uncertain is a step into unknown territory.

Access to Public Media for Religious Programs

In spite of the exhortation of *Inter mirifica* to use the public media, there is evidence that in many parts of the world, the Church may have less significant presence in the media for explictly religious programs than at the time of the Second Vatican Council.

At the inception of radio broadcasting in the 1920s and 1930s, there was a prevailing view that broadcasting was a public trust and should be regulated according to norms of public service. There was sufficient support for defining religious programming as part of this public service. Christianity was considered a central part of the cultural heritage of Europe and the extensions of European culture in other parts of the world. Broadcasting systems not only offered programming time at no cost, but encouraged Christians to contribute because of the legitimacy this gave to a new medium.

Many radio broadcasting systems were quite willing to allow the Churches to supply religious speakers, but they wanted to control the quality. They also wanted to establish norms of access to prevent domination by religious groups that were considered fringe sects and did not represent the central religious interests and tastes of the public. This led to the establishment of religious broadcast departments in national and commercial broadcasting organizations, which might have representatives of the major religious denominations on the staff, but which kept the control within the organization. Most broadcasting systems kept the influence of the churches to an external advisory board.

In the early years of broadcasting, the Catholic Church, along with other major faiths, were often allowed to present, within the framework of public-service broadcasting, a fairly integral Catholic message. The only problem of the Church was to supply qualified speakers or other forms of programming. However, there was a continual problem of presenting religious programming that was ostensibly religious but acceptable to a pluralistic society of many different beliefs and an increasingly number of nonbelievers. Increasingly over the years, religious programming departments preferred to produce their own programs, maintaining a balance of neutrality in the highly sensitive area of religious beliefs. Often, this has meant that religious programs are treated as a type of sociocultural documentary of broad interest to the public or as part of a public debate on religiophilosophical issues. If the Church is an attractive cultural object according to the values and interests of the public at the time, it will very likely be presented attractively. But the Church usually has little control over programming except to encourage public protest over some gross misrepresentation.

A further problem is the increasing privatization of the mass media and the growth of a policy of commercial broadcasters selling time to whatever religious group can pay the competitive price. This has meant that religious groups such as the evangelical fundamentalists, which are skilled at raising funds to purchase broadcasting time, have far more access to the media than the Catholic Church.

The conditions of public broadcasting vary greatly from country to country, and in some countries, the Church has more satisfactory access to the media than in others. But, in general, the increasing difficulty of gaining access—especially an access that would permit an explicit Christian message—has added to the ambivalence toward the media in Catholic culture.

The New Pattern of Communication
Emerging in the Church

In spite of the ambivalence of Catholicism regarding the popular media, and the problems of gaining access to the media, there are hopeful signs that the culture of Catholicism is adapting its communication to the new world of popular mass media. It is also defining its contribution to media reforms that will make the media more truly a public service.

As was noted in the introduction, the major impetus to the new styles of communication in the Church are coming not so much from *Inter mirifica*, but from the central documents such as the Pastoral Constitution on the Church in the Modern World (*Gaudium et spes*), which have been the leitmotiv of the Council and a major factor in the new self-definition of the Church today.

First of all, there is greater realization that the mass media are an autonomous public forum in a pluralistic society and that these media cannot and should not be the instrument of any particular institution no matter how important the values of these institutions. Although the Church has a right to make its cultural significance present in the media, the most important presence may not be its own productions, but the way the Church projects its symbolic cultural meaning within the public forum. The corporate actions and way of life of Catholics are symbols that dramatize on the public stage the values of Catholics in ways that dogmatic propositions can never completely capture. This acceptance and respect for the autonomy of the pluralistic public media is bringing about a new communicative relationship of the Church to modern society that is the defining matrix for all of the Church's communication.

Second, there is developing a new theological method and a new theological language more attuned to the contemporary culture. Theologians today are realizing that contemporary poetry, art, novels, drama, and the popular arts of film and television are an important source for the religious imagination and the source of faith symbols for today.

Third, a new pattern of internal communication based on small-group communication is emerging. The small-group and basic Christian communities provide a more expressive and participatory context for personal religious development and corporate witness of faith. The small Christian community becomes the free cultural space for interpreting the meaning of mass media and for defining the values that Catholics wish to express in the mass media.

Fourth, there is greater realization that the new communication technologies are not simply neutral and value-free instruments for a good cause, but come to us wrapped in an institutional organization that may or may not be consonant with Christian values. The new physical capacity for storing, transmitting, or displaying information may be providential, but the institutional organization of this is a product of human society that needs to be continually questioned and evaluated. As Catholics have worked with the media, they have found ways to transform these institutional packages so that they reflect gospel values. In this way, Catholics have developed new models of radio, television, and group communication that are considered important contributions to public-communications policy.

The Relationship of the Church with the Larger Society

In the nineteenth century, the Church developed a relationship with modern culture that created a parallel Catholic subculture. The Church fostered a separate structure of schools, labor unions, political parties, youth movements, and other occupational and age organizations. The Church presented itself as a more perfect subsociety, upholding traditional order, preserving the timeless wisdom of the past, and maintaining the institutions of family and community. Catholic social teaching provided harmonious, certain answers to all human and social problems in contrast to endless interest-group debate and revolutionary agitation. The waves of prestigious converts confirmed a theology of culture that viewed Catholic culture as the reflection of the supernatural in history and the secular as the reflection of unredeemed nature. The communicative relationship of the Church with the larger society was based on the symbolism of the Church as a perfect and holy subculture within a corrupt secular society.

In the period after World War II, new theologies of culture saw God's redeeming action not as something above the secular process of historical evolution, but working through the process of secular development. The Second Vatican Council encouraged a new communicative relationship with society: the fullest involvement of Christians in the human and social development of society. The Church accepted the fact of a pluralist society and proposed that Catholics join forces with other religious and secular groups in the difficult public search and struggle for a more just and human order for all people, Catholics and non-Catholics alike. The Church accepted the fact of a mass-mediated culture and sought to build a communication of symbolic gospel witness through a free, public, secular mass communications that the Church itself does not control. Instead of a sectarian and triumphalist image, the Church entered the public debate making the paradox of its powerlessness, simplicity, and commitment to the poor the basis of socioethical witness in an affluent and consumer-oriented society.

This communication is anchored in a type of faith reflection that takes as its starting point not just Catholic tradition, but a prayerful analysis of God's redeeming action revealed in the contemporary efforts to build a more human and just order in society. The christian community attempts to identify those symbols and actions that seem close to the way Christ would act in this situation. These actions are often assumed with full consciousness of their potential symbolic and dramatic significance in a mass-mediated culture, but in a culture accustomed to the technique of propaganda, advertising, and public relations, the paradox of the gospel is most often revealed in the symbols of utterly selfless and disinterested love such as a Mother Teresa or an Archbishop Romero.

The most important presence of the Church in the media is not necessarily the media that the Church itself produces, but the role that religious faith and Catholicism are given in the folk tale narrative discourse of mass media that reproduce the myths and values of the culture.

Today, the major pastoral statements of the Church such as the documents of Medellín and Puebla in Latin America or the statements of the bishops in the United States on peace and the economy attempt to offer socioethical leadership not simply by building up the institutional structure of the Church, but by working to realize the highest sociocultural-political ideals of the country or region. The preparation of these statements often invites the whole Christian community to articulate its integration of faith and life, and the deliberations are often carried out in the full glare of the mass media.

New Theologies of Communication

At the heart of the neoscholastic theological synthesis in the nineteenth century was the model of Church as the authoritative teacher established by Christ to communicate the divine truths entrusted to it in apostolic times. The divine knowledge is made known by means of words and intelligible concepts—not, for example, an imaginative and emotional experience—and this knowledge is summarized in clear and concise written formulas in the Bible or in the teaching of the Church. These propositions were considered to be above history and cultural contexts and to be universally and univocally applicable as a guide to faith and morals in all cultural and historical contexts.

As Avery Dulles points out, the neoscholastic theology of revelation was a powerful base for an aggressive preaching of the Word of God.[18] The acceptance of the propositional formulas was a clear indicator of the uniqueness and superiority of Catholicism in all cultural contexts. Evangelization and conversion were simplified because people knew exactly what to believe. With the certitude that the formulas of doctrine are of divine origin and necessary for salvation, the Church had strong motivation to proclaim, teach, and use the media as instruments and to send missionaries to all parts of the world.

The conception of the Church as authoritative teacher fitted well the rhetorical and didactive views of communication and the definition of the media as the sacred trust of an elite to inform, teach, and instill good tastes of entertainment. Popular views attributed to the media an almost unlimited power to change attitudes, and the Church, too, saw the media as a powerful means of proselytization.

The reasons for a shift from the neoscholastic theologies of communication are complex, but central to the process were the biblical and historical studies that argued that the exact written formulas of doctrine were not in themselves identical with divine knowledge, but also reflected the literary genres, historical circumstances, and cultural context of the time. Although the insistence on the clear, concise, and conceptual nature of doctrine may have responded to the rationalism of the nineteenth century, it became clear that the communicative discourse of the Bible and religion in general rests more on the connotative and evocative power of imagery, symbols, parable, and myth. The assent of faith is rarely a purely intellectual process or a simple acceptance of authoritative teaching on the basis of supernatural signs. Underlying the inspiration of faith is an intuitive and imaginative convergence of meaning that is motivated by religious symbols and that organizes the meaning of individual lives and whole cultures around ultimate meaning and mystery.

More recent theologies of revelation suggest that the most characteristic and appropriate expression of religious experience is symbolic language.[19] The multifaceted and connotative nature of symbols brings together in a unified pattern of meaning a wide range of human knowledge and experience: analytic science and philosophy, the literary imagination, the subconscious and everyday common-sense solutions. Symbolism is also an intentional language that holds out an ideal to be attained and a gradual search for ultimate, all-econcompassing meaning. The emphasis on the symbolic and imaginative dimension in religious discourse points up the importance of mythic conceptions of history, narrative, parable, paradox, and ritual for the organization of meaning in the assent of faith. This has brought out the importance for religious communication of symbolism in liturgical worship, in religious art, and in music. It also became apparent that many of the symbols of the religious imagination have their origin in contemporary poetry, novels, film, and in more popular arts such as television.[20] This builds a bridge between theology and mass-mediated culture.

Recent theological developments have also encouraged more attention to local popular cultures and popular religiosity as the source of the symbolism of the religious imagination. Homiletics and catechetics has gradually begun to shift from instruction and exhortation regarding the doctrinal and moralistic formulas of Church teaching to reflection on the meaning of the biblical passages in one's daily life. This, combined with group-discussion methods such as the "see, judge, and act" approach of Catholic Action, encouraged Catholics to take as the starting point not the received theology, but their sociocultural context and to ask how a group could give witness to the gospel and reproduce the actions of Christ in this context.

These groups tended to develop their own theological analysis of the evil inherent in their context, the theological explanation of the apostolic actions of the group, and the conceptions of their action in terms of biblical symbols such as the Kingdom of God or the primitive community of Christians. Pastors and theologians working with these groups began to articulate and systematize these local theologies, and their experience convinced them that this was a more appropriate theological method because it linked faith and life.

This greater respect for popular culture and popular religiosity as a source of the religious imagination has been another factor leading the Church toward greater attention to the popular media as also a source of the religious imagination. The new theological methods described before are proving to be the basis of the new theologies of communication and of a mass-mediated culture in the Church.

Associated with these new theologies of communication are new conceptions of priestly identity and priestly formation. If the preparation of priests in the past meant providing a fund of sound doctrine with which to give more formal guidance to people already filled with a Catholic culture, today priestly formation must cultivate a greater sensitivity to the religious symbolism that is emerging from the religious experience of Catholics. The identity of the priest centers around the spiritual art of fashioning new metaphors of faith that are both faithful to divine revelation and practically meaningful for this group of Christians. The priest does this by simultaneous attention to God's Word and our human experience, and by the continuing effort to put into new words what both teach us.[21] The priest, in the context of the Christian community, is called upon to be the first link in forming a new communicative language of faith.

New Styles of Popular Religious Communication in the Church

If the most characteristic form of religious communication in the pre-Vatican II Church was popular preaching in the parish mission, preached retreats, etc., today it is a participatory and expressive style of communication in smaller groups. Just as the parish mission was the basis of a great revitalization of the faith in the nineteenth century,[22] so this new form of communication is often the basis of religious renewal.

In some parts of the world, this is demonstrated in the spread of prayer groups, the charismatic renewal, Bible-discussion groups, different kinds of marriage or youth encounter groups, and various types of basic Christian communities. In all of these more recent forms of religious communication, there are a number of common elements: an open and intimate expression of personal religious experience and of affective prayer; an accepting, healing, and integrating response from other members of the group; a nondirective and "animator" style of group leadership; a more informal paraliturgical or sacramental celebration, intending truly to "celebrate" the sense of unity found in each other; and an attempt to link the expression of faith and biblical reflection to actions of service in the community or family.

In some cases, this style of religious communication has been strongly influenced by Freire's dialogical and "consciousness-raising" form of group discussion. In this, participants are encouraged to become aware of their unthinking dependency on the cultural environment and to see themselves as active partipants in the creation of culture and history. "Group media" such as audio-visuals, which reflect the cultural environment or introduce a theme, are often used as the "text" around which the discussion of the sociocultural environment is developed. In contexts of great social inequalities, the aim is awareness of the imposition of cultural patterns by powerful elites. Since the media are perceived as having such an important role in the creation of culture, participants are encouraged to be active in gaining access to the media or in creating their own "popular media." In more affluent societies, where many people are heavy users of television, "media education"—raising consciousness of the influence of advertising and the media in general on cultural and religious values—is increasingly important.

Many of the more traditional forms of pastoral communication have been influenced by this more participatory, dialogical, and expressive style. The Sunday liturgies encourage participation and even dialogue. Instead of preached retreats, we have one-to-one guided retreats or group retreats with dialogue. Catechetics, too, use largely discussion-group methods and employ media as a basis for reflection rather than an aid to the traditional, directive, and teacher-centered methods.

One of the most effective Catholic uses of media is the "popular radio" model in Latin America and in the Philippines. This model of radio has incorporated many of the aspects of a more participatory and dialogical communication. Many of these radio stations have gained large audiences in a largely Catholic population by becoming the "voice of the voiceless" and encouraging many kinds of direct participation. Different groups in the audience—labor unions, peasant organizations, youth groups, lay leaders of basic Christian communities—are given regular radio time and are encouraged to produce their own programs. Many stations use neighborhood reporters who supply "alternative" information regarding injustices and problems of the poor that would not ordinarily be broadcast through more official or commercial channels.

Associated with this new pattern of religious communication is a new structure of ecclesial organization that permits and encourages this style of communication. This is found, for example, in the increased role of episcopal collegiality, the importance of regional or national episcopal conferences, collective pastoral planning among clergy and lay leaders, parish councils, a more participatory liturgy and consultations with the clergy and laity in the preparation of pastoral policy statements. This changing pattern of communication is also related to the way different classical models and symbolic images of Church, such as mystical union or sacramental sign, are expressed in ecclesiology and in the practice of the Church.

Transforming the Media in the Image of the Gospel

An important trend in Catholic thinking regarding communications is an increasing questioning of what might be called the "instrumentalist" notion of media. There are minor differences of interpretation of this, but, in general, the instrumentalist view tends to stress use of the media without questioning the implications of its institutional organization. It tends to see the media as simply a channel—a big microphone—through which to pass the content of the gospel message. This perspective approaches media technology as a neutral instrument that must be used for the goals of Christianity.

The desire to turn the media toward idealistic purposes is nothing but laudable, but the instrumentalist view forgets that technology never comes as a perfectly neutral package. It usually brings with it a typical social pattern of communication, for example, very vertical and authoritarian or more interactive and stimulating questions. Particular media already have a "language" with its typical ways of conveying meaning through long-established symbols and audio or video artistic constructions. Media have typical genres of programming and they are directed to particular groups of people with particular needs. Also associated are characteristic social contexts of its use—at home with peers or family members, in a classroom or discussion group. Frequently, the hardware and the software are designed for marketing with all this in mind. Furthermore, media owners expect that anyone who wants to use "their" media will understand this and be ready to accept the editing of gatekeepers. To get on the air, it has to be "good" radio or "good" television according to these norms of good.

The fallacy of the instrumentalist view is that it tends to accept this package either without questioning or thinking that the disadvantages are outweighed by the possibility of using the institutional structure of mass media to reach a mass audience. In fact, the institutional package implies a long series of value choices.

The criticism of instrumentalism is not a rejection of communication with the mass media or a preference for small media. The small audio-visual media or practically any other pattern of communication is subject to the same problems. Rather, it is a strong encouragement to examine every dimension of the institutional package and to see how and to what extent the "technology" must be adapted so that it expresses Christian values. In this case, the medium and its institutional organization may be a message so loud that the content is never heard. It is clear that the gospel is never expressed simply in its idea content. It involves the whole institutional complex that constitutes a particular medium. The adaptation might lie in the decision to serve a particular audience that is characteristically neglected. It might call for locating the medium within a new communication pattern and finding ways to make local media truly interactive and accessible.

In this view, the Christian not only seeks to send a message, but to establish a pattern of communication in which the free and creative expression of the person is recognized, respected, and invited. It is a recognition that every person is an active participant in building a culture. This means encouraging broad access to channels of communication and taking part in the organization of a communication system, whether this be as small as the family circle or as large as a national broadcasting network. It means a special effort to open up the possibilities of active communication to the less powerful, the poor, and those who are at the margin of society.

The new approach to media that seeks not just to use the media for the institutional purposes of the Church, but to transform the media for the good of the whole society is most evident where the Church has developed the new communicative relationship with the larger society described before. The effort to transform the media is part of a broader commitment to build a more just and human society. In Latin America, for example, Christians working in radio started with a traditional instrumentalist version of radio and gradually, with the background of a liberation theology, transformed it into a more participatory communication, the voice of the voiceless. Likewise, they took audio-visual teaching aids and gradually transformed this into media for a liberating group communication. In Latin America, Christians have been leaders in the movement for a New World Information and Communication Order that seeks a more democratic organization of the public media. In other parts of the world, Christians have been active in developing public-access cable channels, community radio, and in protecting the rights of media consumers.

Conclusions: A New Media Humanism
Emerging in Catholic Culture

As one looks back over twenty or thirty years of the collective reflection and experience of the media in the Church, it becomes evident that the ambivalence of Catholicism regarding the new world of popular mass media can be interpreted in various ways. One interpretation is that the Church has feared the popular media as a threat and as a challenge to the rigidities of its past institutional investments. Another interpretation is that collectively the Church has wanted to take a longer and more profound look at this phenomenon in order to understand and appreciate its full significance for human development and faith development. Whatever the interpretation, it is clear that there is growing within Catholic culture a kind of media humanism enlightened by the gospel.

Gradually, the Church is rejecting an instrumentalist view that appreciates the media largely for its powerful persuasive—even manipulative—effects. The ideal of a participatory and dialogical communication in which love and the respect for human freedom and creativity is the guiding principle is becoming more clearing defined. This ideal is tending to inform all conceptions of communication whether direct or mediated. The ideal also stresses the active and intelligent use of the media and a democratic governance of the media that guarantees a just public service. There is an appreciation of the contemporary media as a context for developing a balance of the affective, imaginative, and interpretative dimensions of the human personality. The media are seen as a forum for cultural creativity and as a democratic expression of popular culture, departing from earlier elitist conceptions of media and society.

The seeds have been sown. It is likely that this ideal of a media humanism will grow and flower within Catholic culture. The new world of popular mass media is, in fact, becoming an integral part of Catholic culture, but the meaning of media is being

reinterpreted in terms of the Catholic humanistic tradition, social philosophy and the best of Catholic theology. One sees in
the Catholic media humanism the great influence of the Second
Vatican Council, especially the Pastoral Constitution on the
Church in the Modern World (*Gaudium et spes*). In this sense,
the Second Vatican Council has been of great significance for
opening the culture of contemporary Catholicism to the new
world of the popular mass media.

Notes

1. John Orme Mills, "*Inter mirifica:* Twenty Years After," manu-
script submitted to *Rassegna di Teologia* (August 1984).

2. Jeremy Tunstall, *The Media Are American* (New York, 1977),
24–28.

3. Bernice Martin, *A Sociology of Contemporary Cultural Change*
(Oxford, 1981).

4. Roger Silverstone, *The Message of Television: Myth and Narrative
in Contemporary Culture* (London, 1981).

5. Jay P. Dolan. *Catholic Revivalism: The American Experience
1830–1900* (Notre Dame, IN, 1978); Jonathan Sperber, *Popular Catholicism in Nineteenth-Century Germany* (Princeton, NJ, 1984).

6. Virginia Stem Owen, *The Total Image: Or Selling Jesus in the
Modern Age* (Grand Rapids, MI, 1980); Peter Horsfield, *Religious Television: The American Experience* (New York, 1984).

7. Avery Dulles, *Models of Revelation* (New York, 1983), 47.

8. William G. McLoughlin, *Revivals, Awakenings and Reform* (Chicago, 1978), 126–128.

9. *Ibid.*, 126.

10. Horsfield, *Religious Television.*

11. Susan Klingel, "He Touched Me: The Paradox of Contemporary Christian Music—Religious Ministry or Big Business." Paper presented at the 72 Annual Meeting of the Speech Communication Association, Chicago, 16 November 1986.

12. Stewart M. Hoover, *The 700 Club as Religion and as Television:
A Study of Reasons and Effects.* Unpublished doctoral dissertation, University of Pennsylvania, 1985.

13. Robert N. Bellah, Richard Madsen, William M. Sullivan, Ann
Swidler, and M. Steven Tipton, *Habits of the Heart: Individualism and
Commitment in American Life* (Berkeley, 1985).

14. "Donations to Religious Causes Rise Twice as Fast as Inflation,"
Religious Broadcasting (September 1986), 10.

15. Emil Santos, "Toward a Theology of Pastoral Communication,

Part II, Chapter II, A Brief History of *Inter mirifica.*" Unpublished doctoral thesis, Rome, 1986.

16. Cited by Benito Spoletini, *Communicación social e Iglesia,* Ediciones Paulinas, 13.

17. Pierre Babin and Marshall McLuhan, *Autre Homme Autre Chretien a L'age electronique* (Lyon, 1977).

18. Dulles, *Models of Revelation,* 48–49.

19. *Ibid.*

20. John Shea, *Stories of Faith* (Chicago, 1980), 45.

21. Robert J. Leavitt, "Priesthood and Seminary," *Seminaries in Dialogue* (Washington, DC, 1983), 17.

22. Dolan, *Catholic Revivalism:* Sperber, *Popular Catholicism in Nineteenth-Century Germany.*

Bibliography

This bibliography contains the books and articles published on the Second Vatican Council by the contributors to Volume Three.

Jean Beyer, S.J.
"De statu vitae professione consiliorum evangelicorum consecratae," *Periodica*, 55 (1966), 3–48.
"Decretum 'Perfectae Caritatis' Concilii Vaticani II," *Periodica*, 55 (1966), 430–498, 653–693; 56 (1967), 3–60, 331–356, 519–533; 57 (1968), 80–130, 373–434.
"Storia del Decreto 'Perfectae Caritatis,' " in *Vocazione e missione degli Istituti Secolari* (Milan, 1967), 51–78.
De vita per consilia evangelica consecrata (Rome, 1969).
"De consilio presbyterali adnotationes," *Periodica*, 60 (1971), 29–101.
"Le Conseil presbytéral," *L'Année Canonique*, 15 (1971), 83–95.
"Responsiones: I—De interpretando articulo nono Decreti 'Perfectae Caritatis,' " *Periodica*, 60 (1971), 487–494.
"Il guisto pluralismo degli Istituti secolari," *Vita Consacrata*, 8 (1972), 314–320.
"Come interpretare il n. 9 del Decreto 'Perfectae Caritatis,' " *Vita Consacrata*, 8 (1972), 532–539.
"*Laïcat ou Peuple de Dieu,*" in *La Chiesa dopo il Concilio II* (Milan, 1972), 233–247.
"Una nuova disciplina della vita consacrata," in *Problemi e prospettive di diritto canonico* (Brescia, 1977), 147–164.
"Église universelle et Églises particulières," in *Investigationes theologico-canonicae* (Rome, 1978), 57–73.
"Hierarchica communio: una chiave dell'ecclesiologia della 'Lumen Gentium,' " *La Civiltà Cattolica*, 132/2 (1981), 460–473.

"Chiesa universale e chiese particulari," *Vita Consacrata*, 18 (1982), 74–87.

Dal Concilio al Codice (Bologna, 1984).

"Studium Codicis, Schola Concilii," *Seminarium*, 23 (1983), 455–471.

Du Concile au Code de Droit canonique. La mise en application de Vatican II (Paris/Bruges, 1985).

"Principe de subsidiarité ou 'juste autonomie' dans l'Églis," *Nouvelle Revue Théologique*, 108 (1986), 801–822.

"La vie religieuse au Concile Vatican II," *Nouvelle Revue Théologique*, 109 (1987).

Mariasusai Dhavamony, S.J.

"The Religious Quest of Hinduism," in *L'Église et les Religions*, Studia Missionalia 15 (Rome, 1966), 65–82.

"La Chiesa e l'induismo," *Via, Verità e Vita*, 17 (1969), 42–51.

Evangelization, Dialogue and Development. Selected Papers of the International Theological Conference at Nagpur, Documenta Missionalia 5, ed. (Rome, 1972).

Evangelization, Documenta Missionalia 9, ed. (Rome, 1975).

Evangelization and Interreligious Dialogue, ibid., 245–272.

"Méthode et moyens d'évangelisation," in *Élements de théologie missionnaire* (Rome, 1978), 64–74.

"Proclamation and Communion," *Omnis Terra*, 110 (1980), 281–296.

Jacques Dupuis, S.J.

"The Christocentrism of Vatican II," *The Clergy Monthly*, 31 (1967), 361–370; 32 (1968), 245–257.

Jesus Christ and His Spirit (Bangalore, India, 1977).

Ivan Fuček, S.J.

"Duhovne vježbe u pokoncilskom strujanju" [De Exercitiis ignatianis in luce Vaticani II], *Bogoslovska Smotra*, 39 (1969), 101–126.

"Odsutna dimenzija koncilski obnove" [De oratione, dimensione adhuc absente Vaticani II], *Obnovljeni Život*, 26 (1971), 325–338.

"Lik redovničkog poglavara" [Superior religiosus in 'Perfectae Caritatis'], in *Poglavar—lik i uloga* (Zagreb, 1973), 5–17.

"Poziv u Kristu—Nove antropološke postavke moralne teologije" [Vocatio in Christo, sec. 'Optatam Totius,' n. 16], *Bogoslovni Vestnik*, 33 (1973), 166–183.

"Jedinstvo duhovnog života svećeničkog pripravnika" [De integratione vitae spiritualis clerici, sec. 'Optatam Totius' et 'Ratio Fundamentalis'], *Vjesnik Djakovacke Biskupije*, 1 (1974), 8–10.

"Prezbiteri i vjernici" [Relationes praesbyteros inter et laicos: "Praesbyterorum Ordinis," n. 9], *Obnovljeni Život*, 29 (1974), 28–42.

"Od tolerancije do vjerske slobode" [A tollerantia ad libertatem religiosam in 'Dignitatis Humanae'], *Obnovljeni Život*, 30 (1975), 207–222.

"Krist—konkretna norma morala" [Christus-norma moralitatis concreta, sec. 'Optatam Totius,' n. 16], *Obnovljeni Život*, 31 (1976), 421–436.

"Teološki naglasci novog Reda pokore" [Aspectus theologici novi 'Ordo paenitentiae' ut exsecutio 'Lumen Gentium,' n. 11], *Bogoslovska Smotra*, 46 (1976), 71–90.

"Savjest u nauci drugog vatikanskog sabora" [Conscientia moralis in doctrina Vaticani II, 'Gaudium et Spes,' n. 16], *Bogoslovska Smotra*, 47 (1977), 101–211.

"Nužnost krštenja za spasenje" [Necessitas baptismi ad salutem, sec. Vaticanum II], *Bogoslovska Smotra*, 48 (1978), 56–77.

"Ljubav i radjanje—odgovorno roditeljstvo" [De amore et procreatione iuxta Vaticanum II, 'Gaudium et Spes,' nn. 47–52], *Bogoslovska Smotra*, 49 (1979), 79–94.

"Moralno-religiozni razvoj djeteta" [De formatione morali-religiosa infantium, iuxta 'Gravissimum Educationis'], *Obnovljeni Život*, 34 (1979), 504–529.

"Briga za čovjeka u Crkvi danas" [Homo-sollicitudo Ecclesiae in Vaticano II et litt. enc. 'Redemptor Hominis'], *Bogoslovska Smotra*, 50 (1980), 142–167.

"Trajna teološka formacija u tijelu Crkve" [De permanente formatione theologica, iuxta optata Vaticani II], *Obnovljeni Život*, 36 (1981), 506–513.

"Perspektive bračne ljubavi nakon Koncila" [Amor coniugalis in documentis Ecclesiae explicativis 'Gaudium et Spes,' nn. 47–52], *Obnovljeni Život*, 37 (1982), 17–38.

"Moderne teškoće u slavljenju Gospodjnjeg Dana kroza svjetlo novoga Crkvenog Zakonika" [Dies dominica—difficultates celebrationis sec. mentem 'Sacrosanctum Concilium,' n. 106 et CIC 1983, cc. 1246–1248], *Obnovljeni Život*, 39 (1984), 346–359.

"Suvremeni ateizam-izazov kršcanima" [De habitudine christianorum ad atheismum, 'Gaudium et Spes,' nn. 19–21], *Obnovljeni Život*, 39 (1984), 37–47.

"Prenositi ili prijeciti zivot?" [De modo transmittendi vitam humanam, iuxta mentem 'Gaudium et Spes,' nn. 47–51; 'Humanae Vitae,' nn. 9–14; 'Familiaris Consortio,' nn. 28–35], *Obnovljeni Život*, 40 (1985), 5–30.

René Latourelle, S.J.

"La Révélation et sa transmission selon la Constitution 'Dei Verbum,' " *Gregorianum*, 47 (1966), 5–40.

"Le Christ, Signe de la Révélation selon la Constitution 'Dei Verbum,' " *Gregorianum*, 47 (1966), 685–709.

"La Rivelazione," in *Commento alla Costituzione dogmatica sulla divina Rivelazione* (Milan, 1966), 68–90.

"La testimonianza della vita, segno di salvezza," in *Laici sulle vie del Concilio* (Assisi, 1966), 377–395.

"La Constitution sur la Révélation: points d'émergence," *Relations* (1966), 99–101.

"Vatican II et les signes de la Révélation," *Gregorianum* 49 (1968), 225–252.

"Il Vaticano II e il tema della Rivelazione," in *Mysterium salutis* II/1 (Brescia, 1969²), 238–255.

"Rivelazione," in *Dizionario del Concilio Ecumenico Vaticano secondo* (Rome, 1969), 1729–1745.

"Le Christ, signe de la Révélation, selon la Constitution 'Dei Verbum,' " *Sélection-Recueil-Théologie du Vatican, II* (1969), 7–18.

"Vatican II et le témoignage des chrétiens," in *Le témoignage des chrétiens* (Tournai/Montreal, 1971), 28–44.

"La Costituzione dogmatica sulla divina Rivelazione. Commento," in C.M. Martini and L. Pacomio (eds.), *I libri di Dio* (Rome, 1975), 242–269.

"La teologia dei segni," *L'Osservatore Romano* (14 October 1982), 5.

"La novità del Concilio Vaticano II nella vita della Chiesa," in R. Fisichella (ed.), *Giovani e Concilio* (Milan, 1983), 35–54.

"Das II. Vaticanum. Eine Herausforderung an die Fundamentaltheologie," in E. Klinger and K. Wittstadt (eds.), *Glaube im Prozess. Christsein nach dem II. Vatikanum. Für Karl Rahner* (Freiburg im Breisgau, 1984), 597–614.

Johannes B. Lotz, S.J.

"Zum ökuminischen Ertrag der Zweiten Konzilsperiode," in J. Neumann (ed.), *Auf Hoffnungen. Eine Sammlung ökumenischen Gedanken* (Meitingen, 1964), 79–108.

Emilio Rasco, S.J.

"La Bibbia come fondamento," *Adista Dossier*, 11 (1985), 19–20.

Ary A. Roest Crollius, S.J.

"Vaticano II e le religioni non cristiane," *Rassegna di Teologia*, 8 (1967), 65–75.

Manuel Ruiz Jurado, S.J.

"Los signos de los tiempos," *Manresa*, 40 (1968), 5–18.

André Ruszkowski, S.J.

"Il decreto conciliare e gli uffici nazionali," *La Rivista del Cinematografo,* 7 (1984), 313–315.

Communication sociale et pensée sociale, Cahiers d'Études et de Recherches 9 (Montreal, 1970).

"Vatican II et les communications sociales," in *Le Concile revisité* (Montreal, 1986), 235–253.

Contents
of All Three Volumes

Volume One

Volume Two

PART IV

Liturgy and Sacraments

PART VI

The View of Humanity

Volume Three

PART VII

The Consecrated Life

PART IX

Questions of Theological Formation

PART X

New Prospects